Sixth Edition

Behavior Management

POSITIVE APPLICATIONS FOR TEACHERS

Thomas J. Zirpoli

McDaniel College

PEARSON

Boston   Columbus   Indianapolis   New York   San Francisco   Upper Saddle River
Amsterdam   Cape Town   Dubai   London   Madrid   Milan   Munich   Paris   Montreal   Toronto
Delhi   Mexico City   Sao Paulo   Sydney   Hong Kong   Seoul   Singapore   Taipei   Tokyo

Vice President and Editor in Chief: Jeffery W. Johnston
Executive Editor: Ann Castel Davis
Editorial Assistant: Penny Burleson
Vice President, Director of Marketing: Margaret Waples
Senior Managing Editor: Pamela D. Bennett
Production Editor: Sheryl Glicker Langner
Project Manager: Susan Hannahs
Photo Coordinator: Lori Whitley

Senior Art Director: Jayne Conte
Cover Designer: Suzanne Behnke
Cover Art: Diana Ong/SuperStock
Full-Service Project Management: Nitin Agarwal/ Aptara®, Inc.
Composition: Aptara®, Inc.
Text and Cover Printer/Bindery: RRDonnelley/Harrisonburg
Text Font: Garamond

Credits and acknowledgments borrowed from other sources and reproduced, with permission, in this textbook appear on the appropriate page within the text.

Photo Credits: pp. 2, 68, 99, 230, 357, Anne Vega/Merrill; p. 4, Copyright WHO; p. 8, National Library of Medicine; p. 32, Stan Wakefield/PH College; pp. 36, 116, 140, 185, 218, 277, 326, 329, 352, Anthony Magnacca/Merrill; p. 54, www.comstock.com; p. 65, Julie Peters/Merrill; pp. 86, 256, Scott Cunningham/Merrill; pp. 104, 111, Chris Rupp; p. 122, Liz Moore/Merrill; p. 158, Patrick White/Merrill; p. 166, Hope Madden/Merrill; p. 180, Pearson Learning Photo Studio; p. 206, BananaStock/Thinkstock; p. 213, Jack Hollingsworth/Photodisc/Thinkstock; p. 235, Laura Bolesta/Merrill; p. 263, Jupiterimages/Creatas Images/Thinkstock; p. 288, Ken Karp/PH Photo; p. 294, Larry Hamill/Merrill; p. 340, Karen Mancinelli/Pearson Learning Photo Studio; p. 372, Katelyn Metzger/Merrill; p. 386, Pixland/Thinkstock; p. 403, Valerie Schultz/Merrill and p. 413, Frank Siteman.

Many of the designations by manufacturers and seller to distinguish their products are claimed as trademarks. Where those designations appear in this book, and the publisher was aware of a trademark claim, the designations have been printed in initial caps or all caps.

Library of Congress Cataloging-in-Publication Data
Zirpoli, Thomas J.
 Behavior management: positive applications for teachers / Thomas J. Zirpoli. —6th ed.
  p. cm.
 Includes bibliographical references and index.
 ISBN-13: 978-0-13-706320-8 (alk. paper)
 ISBN-10: 0-13-706320-2 (alk. paper)
 1. Behavior modification—United States. 2. Children—United States—Conduct of life. 3. Behavioral assessment of children—United States. 4. Classroom management—United States. I. Title.
 LB1060.2.Z57 2012
 370.15'28—dc22

                                                                                    2010034573

10 9 8 7 6 5 4

www.pearsonhighered.com

ISBN 10:   0-13-706320-2
ISBN 13: 978-0-13-706320-8

Dedicated in memory of my father, Thomas James Zirpoli, who taught his children and grandchildren the value of doing well in school and continuing their education.

PREFACE

This text acknowledges the comments and suggestions of many reviewers and users for updating and improving the previous edition. The text continues to provide readers with both a technical and functional understanding of applied behavior analysis, as well as a discussion of the everyday applications of behavior management in classrooms and other educational settings. We try to communicate this information in language that is understandable to professionals and paraprofessionals. As with the fifth edition, readers will observe several major differences in this text compared with other behavior management or applied behavior management texts. These differences are based on specific values regarding the management of behavior and the recognition of current trends in society.

NEW TO THIS EDITION

In this edition, a greater emphasis has been placed on schoolwide and individual strategies for positive behavior supports as well as response to intervention strategies. Chapter 2, "Legal Considerations for Schools," has been updated with the newest amendments to special-education law. Chapter 8, "Formal Behavioral Assessment," has been updated with the latest revisions to standardized assessments. Chapter 10 provides a greater focus on positive behavioral supports and reinforcement strategies. Chapters 12 and 13 are new and provide strategies for schoolwide and individual positive behavior supports. All 14 chapters have been updated with the latest research and publications.

This text recognizes the growing preschool field, as well as the expansion of day care and other services provided for infants, toddlers, and preschoolers. Although the basic principles of behavior management apply for all children, preschool teachers and day care workers must understand that infants and young children have unique characteristics that demand special consideration. The growth of early childhood programs requires that we address this population directly, and so we acknowledge the special issues of early childhood behavior in Chapter 4.

Adolescent issues are also a significant and growing concern to many educators. The number of adolescents referred to out-of-home treatment facilities is at an all-time high. Clearly, this population requires special attention in the field of behavior management, and we address these special issues directly in a new Chapter 5.

A person's behavior is influenced by his or her ethnic background, gender, language, and culture. In a much improved and updated Chapter 3, we urge all educators to learn about and become sensitive to their own worldview and the worldview of their students, as well as the individual differences of their students and how these characteristics may influence a student's behavior. The danger of stereotyping is always possible while writing about diversity. We have tried to avoid this trap, recognizing the uniqueness of all individuals, while at the same time acknowledging the influence of traditions and customs of those who share a common ethnic and cultural background.

Finally, we recognize that the best and most effective behavior management strategy is the teaching and reinforcement of appropriate behaviors. This belief is integrated throughout the text.

This text includes the basic mechanics of applied behavior analysis. In many areas, however, the text breaks from the traditional applied behavior analysis texts and includes current topics and issues in behavior management, as well as special populations (e.g., diversity, early childhood, and adolescent issues). We hope our readers will find these additional chapters useful and informative. We also hope that our readers will share their thoughts with us on how this sixth edition may be improved. We welcome and look forward to your comments. Please e-mail the author at tzirpoli@mcdaniel.edu with your comments and suggestions.

AUDIENCE

This text is designed for use in both undergraduate and graduate behavior management, classroom management, or applied behavior management courses. The text is appropriate for the preservice and inservice training of regular and special educators; preschool, elementary, and secondary educators; educational administrators; counselors; psychologists; and social workers.

ACKNOWLEDGMENTS

First, thank you to the individuals who made significant and important contributions to this project: Joel Macht, Davidson College, who contributed Chapter 9; Mitchell Yell, University of South Carolina, who contributed Chapters 2 and 11; Stephanie D. Madsen, McDaniel College, for Chapter 5; Daria Buese, McDaniel College, for Chapter 6; Victoria Russell, Towson University for Chapter 8; and Julia L. Orza and Janet G. Medina, McDaniel College, who contributed Chapter 3.

Second, thank you to the administration and faculty at McDaniel College who supported my scholarship so that I could complete this project.

Third, thank you to the reviewers of the manuscript for their timely and helpful reviews: Candace Baker, Texas A & M International University; Michal C. Clark, California State University, Bakersfield; Dana L. Harader, Texas A & M University, Commerce; Donna Kearns, University of Central Oklahoma; Michael R. Mayton, Tennessee Technological University; and Rex Schmid, University of West Florida.

Finally, I appreciate the advice, assistance, and support from the helpful professionals at Pearson Education, especially Ann Davis, Sheryl Langner, Penny Burleson, Michelle Livingston, and Nitin Agarwal who are always there when I need their help.

Thomas J. Zirpoli

BRIEF CONTENTS

CONTENTS

FOUNDATIONS FOR UNDERSTANDING AND MANAGING BEHAVIOR

CHAPTER 1

Basic Concepts of Behavior and Behavior Management

Thomas J. Zirpoli

Why do people behave the way they do? It was probably first a practical question: How could a person anticipate and hence prepare for what another person would do? Later it would become practical in another sense: How would another person be induced to behave in a given way? Eventually it became a matter of understanding and explaining behavior. It could always be reduced to a question about causes.

—SKINNER (1974, P. 10)

Understanding why individuals behave the way they do and how behavior may be taught, changed, or modified is the primary concern of this text. In this chapter, historical foundations, basic concepts, assumptions, as well as common misconceptions of behavior and behavior management are addressed.

HISTORICAL FOUNDATIONS TO UNDERSTANDING BEHAVIOR AND BEHAVIOR ANALYSIS

There are many schools of thought regarding behavior and behavior management. Most of these theories have evolved over time, each building on the research of previous scholars and practitioners. *Classical conditioning, operant conditioning,* and *social learning* are the "general theoretical positions . . . that form the basis of contemporary behavior modification approaches" (Morris, 1985, p. 4). These concepts, in addition to *behavior therapy* and *applied behavior analysis,* are the foundation of behavior management strategies employed in schools and classrooms today, and they are the focus of this introductory chapter.

Classical Conditioning

Classical conditioning (also called *Pavlovian conditioning*) refers to the relationship between *stimuli* and *respondent behavior* responses.

Stimulus refers to any "condition, event, or change in the physical world" (Cooper, Heron, & Heward, 1987, p. 18). Stimuli include light, noise, touch, temperature, taste, smells, textures, and so on, that evoke/elicit responses or respondent behavior.

Stimuli may be unconditioned or conditioned. An *unconditioned stimulus* (UCS) is naturally stimulating or unlearned. Examples include food and sex. A person does not have to learn that food and sex are reinforcing. A *conditioned stimulus* (CS), however, is one that has been learned or conditioned. For example, a child may learn to fear anyone wearing white clothing after spending months in a hospital that included painful treatments by medical personnel dressed in white.

Respondent behaviors are usually not controlled by the individual and are frequently referred to as involuntary, reflex behaviors or unconditioned responses. An unconditioned stimulus usually produces an unconditioned response. For example, a bright light (unconditioned stimulus) will probably produce unconditioned responses such as closing the eyelids, covering the eyes, and turning away. These respondent behaviors are not learned; they occur automatically as a result of the stimulus (light).

IVAN P. PAVLOV: THE FATHER OF CLASSICAL CONDITIONING   Ivan P. Pavlov (1849–1936), a Russian physiologist and 1904 Nobel Prize winner, is commonly referred to as the father of classical conditioning. During his research on animal digestion, Pavlov studied how different foods placed in the digestive system elicited unconditioned reflexes such as the production of gastric secretions and saliva. More significantly, Pavlov discovered that these responses could be stimulated when certain stimuli associated with the presentation of food were also present in the environment. For example, Pavlov observed that his dogs began to produce saliva when his assistant merely opened the cage door at mealtime.

Ivan Petrovich Pavlov (1849–1936)

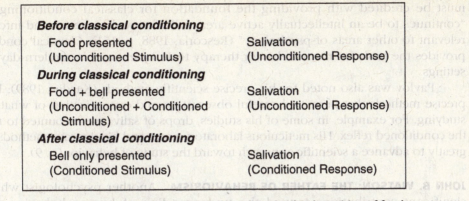

Before classical conditioning

| Food presented | Salivation |
| (Unconditioned Stimulus) | (Unconditioned Response) |

During classical conditioning

Food + bell presented	Salivation
(Unconditioned + Conditioned	(Unconditioned Response)
Stimulus)	

After classical conditioning

| Bell only presented | Salivation |
| (Conditioned Stimulus) | (Conditioned Response) |

FIGURE 1.1   Model of Pavlov's classical conditioning by the pairing of food and a bell to elicit a conditioned salivation response in a dog

In 1927, Pavlov conducted his now famous study demonstrating that he could condition a dog to produce saliva (an unconditioned response) following the ringing of a bell. In his study, Pavlov paired the presentation of food (an unconditioned stimulus) with the ringing of a bell (a neutral stimulus to the dog). Over time, Pavlov found that merely ringing the bell, even in the absence of food, caused the dog to salivate. The ringing of the bell had become a learned or *conditioned stimulus* producing a learned or *conditioned response* (salivation). Pavlov went on to discover that the bell could lose its ability to elicit the production of saliva if it were repeatedly rung without the presentation of food. The dog learned that the bell was no longer associated with food and thus no longer acted as a conditioned stimulus for salivation. A model of Pavlov's classical conditioning of a salivation response in his dog is provided in Figure 1.1.

Pavlovian conditioning has expanded significantly since the days of Pavlov. Rescorla (1988) describes the modern understanding of classical conditioning this way:

> Pavlovian conditioning is not a stupid process by which the organism willy-nilly forms associations between any two stimuli that happen to co-occur. Rather, the organism is better seen as an information seeker using logical and perceptual relations among events, along with its own preconceptions, to form a sophisticated representation of its world. (p. 154)

Rescorla and others have expanded the traditional understanding of classical conditioning. Balsam and Tomie (1985) note that learning must be understood beyond the identification of conditioned and unconditioned stimuli. The properties of the stimuli and the context in which these stimuli are presented not only become part of the stimulus (called a *stimulus package*) but play a role in the type of response forms that follow. A conditioned stimulus presented in one environment may elicit a different response in a second environment. For example, how a child responds to another child's provocation within the classroom environment may be very different from how the child would respond to the same stimulus within the child's neighborhood.

Indeed, behavior is far more complex than a simple understanding of the pairing of stimuli and associated responses; many other variables are involved. Pavlov, however, must be credited with providing the foundation for classical conditioning, which "continues to be an intellectually active area, full of new discoveries and information relevant to other areas of psychology" (Rescorla, 1988, p. 151). Classical conditioning provides the basis for many behavior therapy techniques used in modern-day clinical settings.

Pavlov was also noted for his precise scientific methods (Kazdin, 1989): He used precise methods that permitted careful observation and quantification of what he was studying. For example, in some of his studies, drops of saliva were counted to measure the conditioned reflex. His meticulous laboratory notes and his rigorous methods helped greatly to advance a scientific approach toward the study of behavior (p. 9).

JOHN B. WATSON: THE FATHER OF BEHAVIORISM   Another psychologist who made significant contributions toward the understanding of human behavior and the advancement of the scientific method for psychological research was John B. Watson (1878–1958). Influenced by the work of Pavlov, Watson led the way in the study of behavior on the American front. He called himself a *behaviorist* (Watson, 1919) and advocated a different psychological approach to understanding behavior, which he referred to as *behaviorism* (Watson, 1925). Learning, according to Watson, could explain most behaviors.

Like Pavlov, Watson conducted experiments using the principles of classical conditioning. In a famous study with an 11-month-old baby named Albert, Watson and Rayner (1920) paired a startling loud noise with the touching of a white rat. While Albert was playing with the rat, the noise was sounded each time he touched the rat. After only seven pairings, Albert, who was startled by the loud noise (unconditioned stimulus), was conditioned also to fear the white rat (a previously neutral stimulus). Even without the loud noise, Albert cried when he was presented with the white rat. The rat had become a conditioned stimulus that elicited the conditioned response of fear.

Watson urged the psychological establishment to study observable or overt behavior rather than mental phenomena that could not be directly observed (e.g., emotions, feelings, thoughts, instinct). In his *Psychology from the Standpoint of a Behaviorist,* Watson (1924) criticized psychologists for their use of subjective and unproven interventions and the lack of a scientific methodology as modeled by Pavlov. Although, by his own admission, he went "beyond my facts" (p. 104) and extended his research findings on conditioning and learning to explain all behavior, he nevertheless set the stage for a new psychology.

Operant Conditioning

An *operant* is a behavior or response that is controlled or at least influenced by events within the environment (Skinner, 1974). For example, as a result of environmental influences (a teacher's request), students learn to talk quietly when visiting their school library. It is important to differentiate operant behavior from the previously described respondent behaviors, such as blinking in response to a bright light, which are involuntary or reflexive.

Operant conditioning refers to the relationship between overt events in the environment and changes in specific target behaviors. These events are classified as either antecedents or consequences.

WHAT HAPPENS PRIOR TO THE BEHAVIOR?   *Antecedents* are events in the environment that precede a target behavior or operant. For example, when John hits Mike after Mike takes a toy from John, the antecedent for hitting is the action of Mike taking a toy away from John. An observant teacher could easily identify the antecedent to John's hitting. However, the relationship between an antecedent and a behavior may not be so obvious. For example, when a child comes to school hungry and attends poorly to the teacher, hunger is an indirect antecedent to the poor attention. Unless a teacher were told that the child was hungry, he or she may not be able to identify hunger as the antecedent to the child's poor attention in the classroom.

WHAT HAPPENS AFTER THE BEHAVIOR?   A *consequence* refers to events in the environment that occur *after* a target behavior or response. For example, when a teacher pays attention to a child for disruptive classroom behavior (i.e., talking out, making noise), the attention serves as a consequence for the disruptive behavior. According to Donnellan, LaVigna, Negri-Shoultz, and Fassbender (1988), "A consequence is defined as an environmental stimulus or event that contingently follows the occurrence of a particular response and, as a result of that contingent relationship, strengthens or weakens the future occurrence of that response" (p. 20).

In operant conditioning, the consequence is identified as *reinforcing* if the preceding behavior increases or is maintained at a current rate, duration, or intensity. The consequence is identified as a *punisher* if the preceding behavior decreases in rate, duration, or intensity. This relationship among antecedents, behaviors, and consequences serves as the foundation for operant conditioning as well as for most applications employed in applied behavior analysis. According to behaviorists, when this relationship is understood, the manipulation of antecedents and consequences may be used to teach new skills and modify current behaviors.

EDWARD L. THORNDIKE: THE LAWS OF BEHAVIOR   Operant conditioning has its roots in animal research. Edward L. Thorndike (1874–1949) was one of the first researchers to apply basic operant conditioning principles and study the relationship between animal behavior (responses) and environmental conditions, especially the relationship between behavior and consequences. In his *law of effect,* Thorndike (1905) talked about the relationship between acts that produced "satisfaction" and the likelihood of those acts (behavior) to recur (p. 203). In his *law of exercise,* Thorndike (1911) outlined how behaviors became associated with specific situations. The study of these associations between responses and consequences and between responses and situations is sometimes referred to as *associationism.* Thorndike's work provided a solid foundation for future research on positive reinforcement (*law of effect*) and stimulus control (*law of exercise*).

Thorndike (1911) demonstrated that the provision of reinforcement as a consequence increased the rate of learning. In his famous cat experiments, Thorndike used food to reinforce cats when they learned how to remove a barrier and escape from a box. After repeated trials, he noted the time it took the cat to escape from the box to get to the food decreased.

BURRUS FREDERIC SKINNER: THE FATHER OF OPERANT CONDITIONING   Thorndike's research on reinforcement influenced the work of B. F. Skinner (1904–1990), whose name

B. F. Skinner (1904–1990)

has become synonymous with operant conditioning and behavior modification. Skinner (1938) also conducted many of his early studies using laboratory animals such as rats and pigeons. He expanded on Thorndike's research on the relationships between various consequences and behavior. Skinner also helped clarify the differences between operant conditioning and Pavlov's classical conditioning (Kazdin, 1989): "The consequences which shape and maintain the behavior called an operant... have become part of the history of the organism. To alter a probability is not to elicit a response, as in a reflex" (Skinner, 1974, pp. 57–58).

Skinner (1974) described the concept of operant conditioning and the relationship between behavior and consequences as "simple enough":

> When a bit of behavior has the kind of consequence called reinforcing, it is more likely to occur again. A positive reinforcer strengthens any behavior that produces it: a glass of water is positively reinforcing when we are thirsty, and if we draw and drink a glass of water, we are more likely to do so again on similar occasions. (p. 51)

Skinner is also noted for expanding his laboratory research to the promotion of operant conditioning as a method for improving societal conditions. His book *Walden Two* (1948) outlines how these principles could be used to develop a utopian society. His next book, *Science and Human Behavior* (1953), promotes the application of operant conditioning in education, government, law, and religion.

Skinner (1953) stated that behaviorists needed to be more concerned with the *description* of behavior and the antecedents and consequences related to behavior than with the explanation of behavior. He also emphasized the importance of the current situation regarding a specific behavior rather than the long-term history of the behavior problem. For example, Skinner was more interested in teaching a child to sit in his seat within a classroom environment (by reinforcing the child for sitting) than trying to explain or understand *why* the child frequently ran around the classroom.

Skinner did not totally reject the philosophy of cognitive psychology or, as he called it, "the world within the skin" (1974, p. 24). He did, however, seem to grow wary of the minimal progress made in understanding behavior under the traditional principles of cognitive psychology: "Behaviorism, on the other hand, has moved forward" (1974, p. 36). Operant conditioning clearly emphasizes the study of observable, overt behaviors that can be measured and studied by methods of direct observation.

The Behavioral Versus Psychoanalytic Approach

The work of Pavlov, Watson, Thorndike, and Skinner represented a major shift from the work of Sigmund Freud (1856–1939) and others who promoted a more traditional *psychoanalytic approach*. Whereas the behavioral approach focuses on overt behaviors and environmental events related to those behaviors, the psychoanalytic approach focuses on psychological forces such as drives, impulses, needs, motives, conflicts, and personality traits existing within the individual. Whereas the behavioral approach views inappropriate behavior as conditioned or learned, the psychoanalytic approach views inappropriate behavior primarily as the result of some maladaptive psychological process or some underlying defect in the child's personality.

Dissatisfaction with the psychoanalytic approach has revolved around several issues. First, assessment procedures commonly used in the psychoanalytic approach remove the child from the situation in which inappropriate behaviors occur. The psychiatrist or psychologist preparing the assessment may never observe the child within the environment (home or classroom) where the problem behaviors occur. Direct observations are usually limited to behaviors observed within the professional's office where, according to Brown (1990), 85% of children with challenging behaviors behaved appropriately.

Second, the identification of underlying psychological causes of behavior yields little information that can be used in the development of an intervention plan, especially for classroom teachers. In fact, there is usually limited communication between therapists and teachers.

Third, the generalization of therapy or treatment (e.g., psychotherapy or psychoanalysis) effects to functional environments such as the home or classroom is challenging, and there are many barriers to demonstrating research effects from therapy room to classroom (Mufson, Pollack, Olfson, Weissman, & Hoagwood, 2004). Table 1.1 provides an outline of differences between the psychoanalytic and behavioral approaches.

Social Learning Theory

The student of social learning theory strives to understand how behavior is influenced by classical and operant conditioning principles, along with the influences of the child's social environment and cognitive development. Human behavior, according to social learning theory, is much too complex to understand without this integrated approach.

ALBERT BANDURA: THE FATHER OF SOCIAL LEARNING THEORY Albert Bandura, a Canadian psychologist who received his Ph.D. training at the University of Iowa in 1952, studied aggression in adolescents and found behaviorism too simplistic (Boeree, 1998) to

TABLE 1.1 Behavioral Versus Psychoanalytic Approach

Variable	Psychoanalytic Approach	Behavioral Approach
Behavioral focus	Covert behaviors such as drives, impulses, and motives	Overt behaviors such as walking and talking
Cause of inappropriate	Maladaptive psychological process or underlying defect	Conditioned or learned behavior in personality
Assessment approach	Conducted by psychiatrists or psychologists outside the environment where the behavior occurs; limited direct observation	Direct observation of the student's behavior within the natural environment (e.g., home or classroom)
Concern for environmental variables	Low	High
Concern for psychological variables	High	Low
Empirical support	Low	High
Classroom applications	Low	High

explain the behavior he observed. He proposed that a child's behavior, environment, and cognitive processes "operated as interlocking determinants of each other" (Bandura, 1977, p. 9).

Bandura (1977) stressed that "personal and environmental factors do not function as independent determinants, rather they determine each other . . . in a reciprocal fashion" (p. 9). He refers to this integrated approach as a process of *reciprocal determinism.*

Bandura studied the importance of *observational learning* or *modeling* on the acquisition of behavior. According to Bandura (1977), an individual observes a behavior, cognitively retains the information observed, and performs the modeled behavior. He labeled these three steps attention, retention, and reproduction and added that reinforcement and motivational processes regulate the reproduction of behavior.

Bandura (1969) is most famous for his research on how children model aggressive behavior. He once testified to Congress that exposure to TV violence has four effects on children: First, TV violence teaches children how to be aggressive. Second, TV violence glamorizes violence. Third, frequent exposure to TV violence desensitizes children to cruelty and the effects violence has on others. Lastly, TV violence provides our children with a false reality of the world (Van De Velde, 2002).

In a text titled *Self-Efficacy: The Exercise of Control,* Bandura (1997) published a scholarly review of his own research on social learning theory, as well as the work of his students and colleagues. He defines *self-efficacy as* "people's beliefs about their capabilities to produce designated levels of performance that exercise influence over events that affect their lives. Self-efficacy beliefs determine how people feel, think, motivate themselves and behave" (Bandura, 1994, p. 71). People who have a strong sense of efficacy "look at challenges to be mastered rather than threats to be avoided" (p. 71). They bounce back after failure and increase their efforts in the face of failure. People with a weak sense of efficacy avoid challenges out of fear of failure. They dwell on their weaknesses and failures. A student's self-efficacy influences how a student approaches classroom tasks and assignments, and ultimately, the student's behavior. A history of success develops a strong self-efficacy; a history of failure develops a weak self-efficacy. Teachers can promote stronger self-efficacy in students by establishing classroom situations for students to be successful and then reinforcing that success.

Behavior Therapy

Rimm and Masters (1974) state that while behavior modification and *behavior therapy* share many of the same principles, behavior modification stresses operant conditioning, and behavior therapy stresses classical conditioning. Some say that behavior therapy is a practical application of classical conditioning. Also, whereas behavior modification and operant conditioning have been used primarily with overt behaviors that are observable and measurable, such as aggression and tantrums, behavior therapy and classical conditioning have been used primarily with covert behaviors, such as fears.

Several treatment strategies are frequently associated with behavior therapy. Three of them—systematic desensitization, modeling, and biofeedback—are discussed next.

SYSTEMATIC DESENSITIZATION   Joseph Wolpe, a South African medical doctor, first developed *systematic desensitization* as a form of classical conditioning to reduce anxiety in cats. Building on Pavlov's research, Wolpe (1958) demonstrated that the strength of anxiety-producing stimuli could be reduced when paired with non-anxiety-producing stimuli. First, Wolpe exposed cats to only a small amount of the anxiety-producing stimuli. He then exposed the cats to positive stimuli such as food. Eating food and engaging in other positive behaviors in the presence of small amounts of the anxiety-producing stimuli reduced the anxiety response. Over time, Wolpe slowly increased the amount of anxiety-producing stimuli paired with the competing positive stimuli (eating food) until the anxiety response was eliminated.

Systematic desensitization has been used to reduce childhood phobias (King, Heyne, Gullone, & Molloy, 2001), speech anxiety (Ayres & Hopf, 2000), claustrophobia (Bernstein, 1999), and high school students' math anxiety (Zyl & Lohr, 1994).

MODELING   *Modeling* refers to the observation and learning of new behaviors from others. Within a therapeutic application, modeling may involve a child who is afraid of dogs watching other children play with dogs. This type of modeling application has been successfully used to "treat" other fears (e.g., snakes, heights, water) (Bandura, 1971).

BIOFEEDBACK   *Biofeedback* involves providing an individual with immediate information (visual and/or auditory) about a physiological process (e.g., heart rate, pulse rate, blood pressure, skin temperature) and the use of operant conditioning (reinforcement and/or punishment) to modify the physiological process. The goal of biofeedback is to teach individuals how to control or manipulate involuntary physiological processes.

Biofeedback has been used with adults to treat a variety of conditions, including panic disorder (Meuret, Wilhelm & Roth, 2001), poor health (Russoniello & Estes, 2001), sexual dysfunction (Araoz, 2001), and incontinence (Folkerts, 2001). With children, biofeedback has been used in the treatment of headaches and seizures (Womack, Smith, & Chen, 1988), incontinence (Duckro, Purcell, Gregory, & Schultz, 1985; Killam, Jeffries, & Varni, 1985), constipation and encopresis (Lampe, Steffen, & Banez, 2001), pain (Allen & Shriver, 1998), anxiety (Wenck & Leu, 1996), and poor academic performance (Robbins, 2000).

Applied Behavior Analysis

The term *applied behavior analysis* refers to the direct application of behavior change principles in nonlaboratory, everyday situations and settings "to produce socially significant changes in behavior" (Horner, 1991, p. 607). Kazdin (1989) defines applied behavior analysis as an "extension of operant conditioning principles and methods of studying human behavior to clinical and socially important human behaviors" (p. 23). Using behavioral principles to improve on-task behaviors—number of math problems completed and following directions, for example—would be considered an applied use of behavior modification.

The use of operant or behavioral principles and techniques in applied settings began in the late 1950s and early 1960s (Kauffman, 1989). Early research using behavior modification strategies with people in applied settings employed persons living in institutional settings. This research included people with severe developmental and emotional disabilities.

IVAR LOVASS: THE FATHER OF APPLIED BEHAVIOR ANALYSIS   Ivar Lovass was born in 1927 near Oslo, Norway. In 1952, he began working on his doctorate degree in psychology at the University of Washington. During his studies, Lovass worked as a psychiatric aide at a private hospital in Seattle that included children with autism.

In 1961, he became an assistant professor at UCLA and continues his work there as director of the Lovass Institute for Early Intervention. In 1961, most researchers believed that children developed autism because their mothers did not show them enough affection. They were called "refrigerator moms." Treatment included giving these children lots of love and affection. But Lovass observed that just loving the children did not change their behavior, and he was frustrated that researchers did not have data to support their treatment theories.

Lovass began to experiment with operant conditioning and Skinner's use of rewards and punishments with his students with autism. Because these methods were used successfully to change the behavior of animals in the laboratory, Lovass wondered whether they could be employed with his students.

Lovass started by teaching his students to point to their body parts (nose, ears, mouth). When they responded correctly, he would give them an M&M (reinforcement). If they responded incorrectly, he would yell, "No!" (punishment).

Over time, Lovass was able to teach his students with autism many skills. But his methods were controversial, especially his use of "aversive" punishments that included yelling, slapping, and even electric shocks. After a lot of negative publicity and the introduction of human rights protections for the disabled, Lovass stopped using aversives. But the damage was already done; many people had developed negative, and frequently false, perceptions about using operant conditioning, or *behavior modification*, as was the common term.

As time passed, and as the successful use of behavior change strategies were documented, behavior modification techniques started to be used with people who had mild disabilities and with many nondisabled populations.

In the first issue of the *Journal of Applied Behavior Analysis* (founded by Montrose Wolf in 1968), Baer, Wolf, and Risley (1968) outlined several basic elements of applied behavior analysis that are still applicable today.

- While both applied and basic research ask "what controls the behavior under study," applied research looks beyond variables that are convenient for study or important to theory (p. 91).
- Behaviors should be observed and studied within their natural environments (the real world) rather than in the laboratory.
- Applied research is interested in observable behaviors, not what an individual can be made to say or feel (p. 93).
- The real-world application of applied behavior analysis may not allow precise laboratory measurements, but "reliable quantification of behavior can be achieved" (p. 93).
- Behaviors and techniques used to modify behavior should be "completely identified and described" so that a "trained reader could replicate that procedure" and produce the same results (p. 95).
- A behavioral technique should be judged as having an application for society (applied) when it produces a behavior change that has "practical value" (p. 96).
- The generality or durability of behavioral change over time is an important concern that should "be programmed, rather than expected or lamented" (p. 97).

In a second review of the important elements of applied behavior analyses, Baer et al. (1987) restate that applied behavior analysis ought to be *applied, behavioral, analytic, technological, conceptual, effective,* and capable of appropriate *generalized outcomes* (p. 313). These qualities are consistent with the dimensions of applied behavioral analysis outlined previously and listed by the same authors some 20 years earlier (Baer et al., 1968). According to the authors, these dimensions "remain functional" (p. 314).

Table 1.2 summarizes the general theoretical streams of behavior management that have been outlined in this chapter. Table 1.3 presents an overview of historical researchers discussed in this chapter and their important contributions to the understanding of behavior.

TABLE 1.2   General Theoretical Streams of Behavior Management

Theoretical Stream	Focus of Research
Classical conditioning	The relationship between stimuli and reflex response (conditioned and unconditioned)
Operant conditioning	The relationship between overt events in the environment (antecedents and consequences) and changes in behavior
Social learning or cognitive theory	The relationship among behavior and student's social and cognitive development; integrates classical and operant learning principles
Behavior theory	The practical application of classical conditioning primarily with covert behaviors and mental illness
Applied behavior analysis	The practical application of operant conditioning in nonlaboratory, everyday situations and settings

TABLE 1.3   **Historical Figures in Behavioral Research and Important Contributions**

Researcher	Important Contributions
I. Pavlov (1849–1936)	A Russian physiologist and Nobel Prize winner. Considered to be the father of classical conditioning. Conducted research on animal digestion and unconditional reflexes. Conditioned a dog to produce saliva in response to a bell by pairing the bell with the presentation of food. Promoted the use of precise scientific methods.
J. B. Watson (1878–1958)	The father of behaviorism. Wrote *Psychology from the Standpoint of a Behaviorist* in 1919 and *Behaviorism* in 1925. Noted for his research in classical conditioning of fear responses. Urged the psychological establishment to study overt behavior rather than mental phenomena that could not be directly observed.
E. L. Thorndike (1874–1949)	Applied operant conditioning to the study of animal behavior and studied the relationship between behavior and environmental consequences. Outlined his research on positive reinforcement and stimulus control in *Law of Effect* (1905) and *Law of Exercise* (1911).
B. F. Skinner (1904–1990)	Considered to be the father of operant conditioning. Noted for his study of rat and pigeon behavior in his "Skinner Box." Expanded on Thorndike's research on the relationship between behavior and consequences. Promoted the use of operant conditioning as a method of improving social conditions in *Walden Two* (1948) and *Science and Human Behavior* (1953). Emphasized the study of observable, overt behaviors that could be measured.
J. Wolpe (1915–1997)	A South African medical doctor noted for his research in classical conditioning and behavior therapy. Developed an anxiety reduction treatment called *systematic desensitization* still used today to reduce anxieties and phobias.
A. Bandura (1925–)	The father of social learning theory. Noted for his research on the use of modeling to teach behavior. Promoted an integrated approach in which personal and environmental factors operate as interlocking determinants of each other. Warned of the social influences of mass media on behavior.
L. Lovass (1927–2010)	The father of applied behavior analysis. One of the first researchers to apply the principles of operant conditioning, especially reinforcement and punishment, to children in applied settings. He is especially noted for his work with children with autism.

BASIC CONCEPTS OF BEHAVIOR AND BEHAVIOR MANAGEMENT

When behaviorists talk about behavior and the management of behavior, they employ their own language and terminology. Understanding these basic concepts of behavior is critical to understanding the foundations of behavior management techniques.

Behavior

Behavior may refer to both *covert* responses (e.g., feelings and emotions) and *overt* responses (e.g., tantrums and aggression) (Rimm & Masters, 1974). Behaviorists are largely concerned with overt responses or behaviors that are observable and measurable. These are the behaviors that teachers and parents are able to observe and change. Baer et al. (1968) state that something must be observable and quantifiable to qualify as a behavior.

A behavior is considered *observable* when it can be seen and *measurable* when it can be counted in terms of frequency and/or duration. These two criteria must be met in order to make the direct observation of behavior meaningful and reliable.

Behaviors may be in the form of unconditioned reflexes (eye blinks) or purposeful intent (giving someone a kiss). Some behaviors are conditioned or learned (avoiding a hot stove), and some are simply the result of modeling (a young girl acting like her older sister). Behaviors may be as simple as body movements (touching) or very complex, involving the integration of many behaviors (telling a story). Our everyday lives are filled with many examples of behaviors that can be observed, measured, studied, and modified in some way.

Responses

A *response* is a behavior that is observable and measurable. Individuals are constantly responding as they move around and complete daily tasks. Many of these behaviors or responses are under stimulus control—for example, getting up in the morning in response to the alarm clock, following a schedule throughout the day, responding to others in a manner consistent with a previous history of knowing that person, and so on. Many behaviors are in response to new stimuli that are added to the environment, such as a new student walking into the classroom or a sudden change in the schedule. Many behaviors are in response to internal feelings, such as being hungry and getting something to eat or feeling tired and taking a nap.

Response generalization refers to changes in behaviors other than the behavior(s) targeted for change or modification. For example, if a teacher turns the classroom lights on and off to get the students to look at her and pay attention, and the students *also* put their hands on their desk and sit up straight, these additional behaviors represent a response generalization from the target behaviors (looking at the teacher and paying attention).

Stimuli

Stimuli are events or activities within the environment that are capable of forming a relationship with behavior as either an antecedent or a consequence. In keeping with our previous example, when the teacher turns the classroom lights on and off, she wants this to become an antecedent stimulus for the students to look at the her and pay attention. A pat on the back by a teacher is a stimulus that could be provided as a reinforcing consequence following a child's outstanding performance.

A stimulus may become a *discriminative stimulus* for a specific behavior when it is repeatedly associated with that behavior. Again, turning the lights on and off may become a discriminative stimulus for looking at the teacher and paying attention (behavior). A bell in school may serve as a stimulus for students to change classes. Although the sound of a bell does not naturally elicit students to change classes, it may become a conditioned or learned stimulus after it is consistently used to signal students to change classes. When the relationship between the discriminative stimulus and behavior is firmly established, then the behavior is considered to be under stimulus control.

Stimulus generalization refers to the performance of a behavior following a stimulus (prompt or cue) not presented during the initial stimulus–response training. For example, if the teacher merely reached for the light switch and the children responded as they were taught to respond (looking and paying attention) to the lights being turned on and off, we would say that stimulus generalization had occurred from one stimulus (turning the lights on and off) to another stimulus (reaching for the light switch).

Antecedents

Antecedents are stimuli that occur prior to behaviors. In a classroom setting, antecedents are abundant and include the classroom curriculum, the classroom setting, the behavior of other students, and the teacher's behavior, to name a few.

The study of behavior antecedents provides us with the opportunity to change behavior before it occurs. Clearly, certain environmental conditions are likely to elicit behaviors in individuals that may be avoided or prevented by means of simple environmental modifications. By making these changes, the antecedents to certain behaviors are removed, and the likelihood of observing certain behaviors is decreased or eliminated. For example, placing children within an environment containing few rules and little supervision is likely to promote the occurrence of many inappropriate behaviors.

When monitoring the antecedents to a target behavior, a long list of interrelated stimuli may be observed. For example, in Classroom Connection 1.1, antecedents related to the behavior of Jill's running out of the classroom may include the onset of the reading lesson, the behavior of another child in her reading group, her general seating arrangement, or a combination of all these factors.

CLASSROOM CONNECTION 1.1
Example of Classroom Antecedents and Consequences Related to Running-Away Behavior

Jennifer, an elementary schoolteacher, had a student, Jill, in her first-grade class who frequently ran out of the classroom and onto the playground. Unfortunately, Jennifer's classroom, located on the first floor, had a direct-access door to the playground. Although Jennifer tried to keep the door locked, Jill had learned how to unlock the door and run onto the playground before anyone could stop her. Jennifer noticed that this behavior usually occurred shortly after the children were directed into their reading groups. Although Jill was progressing well with her reading, Jennifer also noticed that Jill did not get along well with the other members of her group.

Jennifer could not leave her students unsupervised. Thus, while monitoring Jill from the classroom window, she would call her principal, report that Jill had run onto the playground (again), and ask the principal to bring Jill back to the classroom. At this point the principal would go to the playground, bring Jill back into the school's main office, and talk to Jill about the dangers of running away from her classroom. The principal was a gentle man and was greatly admired by all the students in the school. After talking with Jill for about 5 minutes, the principal would provide her with a drink of juice and return her to Jennifer's classroom. Upon returning to the classroom, Jennifer would thank the principal and direct Jill to rejoin her reading group.

General Reflection for Classroom Connection 1.1:

What were the antecedents and consequences of Jill's running-away behavior? Who provided the consequences for her behavior? In your opinion, were these consequences primarily reinforcing or punishing? Do you think Jill will want to run away again? What advice would you provide Jennifer, the classroom teacher, and the school principal?

Consequences

Consequences are events or changes in the environment following a target behavior. Cooper et al. (1987) outline several forms of consequences. In the first form, a consequence is represented by the *addition* of a new stimulus to the environment. For example, a child's asking for a snack in an appropriate polite manner (target behavior) may be followed by attention from the teacher and a snack (new stimulus). In Classroom Connection 1.1, Jill was presented with the principal's attention and a drink of juice (reinforcing consequences) after running away from her classroom (target behavior or behavior targeted for change).

In the second form, a consequence is represented by the *removal* of a stimulus already present within the environment. For example, when a child is behaving in an inappropriate manner, a teacher may decide to ignore the child (remove attention) until the maladaptive behavior is terminated.

A consequence may also be represented by a *change* in current environmental stimuli following a target behavior. While attention to a behavior may be added or terminated as outlined earlier, the level of attention may be modified or changed as a consequence of a child's behavior. For example, a teacher's changing facial expression while listening to a child's story represents an ever changing consequence for the child's ongoing behavior.

In addition to the form a consequence may take, a second and very important element of consequences is the effect of the consequence on the preceding target behavior. The question of "effect" refers to how the consequence influences or changes the target behavior. For example, the probability of the target behavior occurring again may be increased or decreased, or the actual rate of occurrence may increase or decrease as a result of the consequence. Other possible behavioral changes may include an increase or decrease in duration and intensity. All of these behavioral changes are related to the consequence(s) that followed the behavior. Thus, a reciprocal relationship between behavior and consequence is established. Each has an influence on the other, and each can be manipulated in an effort to modify the other.

Reinforcement

Reinforcement, discussed in greater detail in Chapter 10, is a type of stimulus that serves as a consequence for a response or behavior. However, by definition, a stimulus may not be considered a reinforcer unless it affects the preceding behavior in one of the ways outlined in the following list. Used appropriately, reinforcement has several potential effects on the response it follows. For example:

- Reinforcement may *maintain* the current rate, duration, or intensity of a response.
- Reinforcement may *raise the probability* that a new response will occur again.
- Reinforcement may *increase* the future rate, duration, or intensity of a response.
- Reinforcement may *strengthen* a response that is weak and inconsistent.

Because of these properties, behaviorists believe that reinforcement provides the key to understanding the etiology and management of behavior. Reinforcement is a powerful tool used to teach new behaviors and change current behaviors; it is the foundation of Skinner's operant conditioning. It is the treatment of choice for today's contemporary application of behavior modification and, specifically, applied behavior analysis.

An important property of reinforcement that teachers must understand is that the effects of reinforcement do not differentiate between appropriate and inappropriate behaviors. Reinforcement is under the control of the user who may, even unknowingly, apply it following any behavior, appropriate or inappropriate. Reinforcement may be, and frequently is, used to maintain or increase inappropriate as well as appropriate behaviors. The most common example of this is the child who has temper tantrums that are reinforced when teachers or parents give in to the child's demands.

A primary objective of this text is to provide a greater understanding of how reinforcement may be used to increase appropriate behaviors and how the removal of reinforcement may be used to decrease inappropriate behaviors.

Punishment

Punishment (discussed in greater detail in Chapter 12), like reinforcement, is also a type of stimulus that may serve as a consequence for behavior. By definition, a stimulus may be classified as a punisher only if the preceding response/behavior changes in one of the following ways:

- The probability of a new behavior occurring again is decreased.
- The future rate, duration, and/or intensity of a current behavior is decreased or eliminated.
- Other dimensions of the behavior are weakened.

Like reinforcement, punishment does not differentiate between appropriate and inappropriate behaviors. Unknowingly, teachers may punish appropriate behaviors, as well as behaviors perceived to be inappropriate. For example, when we become angry with young children for asking too many questions, we may be punishing age-appropriate behavior. Moreover, punishment procedures tend to have many undesirable side effects.

Prompts and Cues

Although some consider *cues* to involve verbal guidance and *prompts* to involve physical guidance, in this text we use the terms synonymously and use the term *prompt* to describe both terms. Prompts are antecedent stimuli that supplement discriminative stimuli in order to produce a specific target behavior. Donnellan et al. (1988) define a prompt as "the assistance provided to the learner after the presentation of the instructional stimulus, but before the response. This procedure is used to assure a correct response" (p. 53). For example, a teacher may supplement ringing a bell (a discriminative stimulus for starting an activity) with the verbal prompt "Children, what are you supposed to do when you hear the bell?"

The use of prompts to supplement a discriminative stimulus is usually a temporary instructional aid and should be systematically phased out as soon as possible. In the previous example, the teacher does not want to use the additional verbal prompt for the whole school year. The goal is for students to respond to the discriminative stimulus (ringing the bell) without additional prompts. This is accomplished when the teacher slowly phases out the use of prompts and reinforces students for responding to the discriminative stimulus. Several different types of prompts are briefly described and discussed in the following sections.

CLASSROOM CONNECTION 1.2
Setting Up Natural Prompts in the Classroom Routine

Susan, an eighth-grade teacher, does not want to spend each morning instructing her homeroom students how to walk into her classroom, get their materials ready for their first class, sit down and listen to the morning announcements, wait for the bell, and, after the bell rings, leave her room in an orderly fashion for their first class. While verbal cues and prompts would work, she knows that she would end up having to yell over all the noise. Besides, she wants her students to follow the natural prompts of the homeroom routine without her daily guidance and verbal directions.

On the first day of school, Susan provides a verbal and visual overview of the homeroom routine. After the students walk into her room, she instructs them to look at the homeroom routine she outlined on the board as follows:

- Walk into the classroom and directly to your desk.
- Prepare your materials for your first class.
- Remain seated and wait for the morning announcements.
- Listen to the announcements (no talking at this time).
- Remain in your seat while waiting for the first bell to ring.
- Raise your hand and wait to be recognized before asking questions.

- After the first bell rings, walk to the door and directly to your first class.

Susan reviews the routine by reading each line and asking the students if they have any questions. For the first week of classes, she keeps the outline on the board and asks the students to "Remember the routine we talked about on the first day." She verbally reinforces the students when they follow the routine and corrects them when they do not. After the first week, Susan no longer needs to verbally prompt the students. Instead, she can focus on individual students who are slow to learn the routine and need individual guidance, reinforcement, and consequences as they learn the natural prompts of the homeroom classroom.

General Reflection for Classroom Connection 1.2:

What do you think of Susan's morning routine, and how would that routine be modified for younger students who do not change classrooms and for older high school students? What kind of reinforcement and consequences would be appropriate for Susan to use with her homeroom group when they follow or don't follow the morning routine? What would you recommend for younger and older students?

NATURAL PROMPTS   A *natural prompt* is an environmental stimulus that naturally occurs prior to target behaviors. Natural prompts are always preferable; unnatural or artificial prompts should be replaced with natural prompts whenever possible. For example, in Classroom Connection 1.2, the start of morning announcements becomes a natural prompt for the students to sit down, be quiet, and listen to the announcements. Susan can teach her students to exhibit these target behaviors without telling them (a verbal prompt) each and every day. Initially, a verbal prompt may be necessary ("The announcements are starting, so you must sit down, be quiet, and listen to the announcements"). When the target behavior is reinforced ("Thank you for sitting down, being quiet, and listening to the announcements!") as the artificial verbal prompt is phased out over time, the natural prompt (the start of the announcements) will soon serve as the discriminative stimulus for the target behavior.

Figure 1.2 provides a list of target behaviors and the natural prompts frequently associated with each. The less dependent the children are on artificial prompts, especially

Target Behaviors	Natural Environmental Prompts
Getting up in the morning	Alarm clock
Going to school on time	Clock or watch
Being quiet and listening	Teacher or someone else beginning to talk
Changing classes	School bell
	Classroom clock
Being loud and playful	Entering the gym or playground
Raising your hand	When you need help
	When you have a question
	When you know the answer to a teacher's question

FIGURE 1.2   Target behaviors and natural prompts

verbal prompts, and the more they are reinforced for responding appropriately to natural prompts, the easier behavior management becomes for teachers.

VERBAL PROMPTS   Verbal prompts are the most common type of prompt used with children and include the following (Cuvo & Davis, 1980):

- Giving directions or instructions regarding a whole target behavior. This may serve as the stimulus for the expected appropriate behaviors ("Class, it's time for lunch").
- Specific prompts concerning expected behaviors within a task ("Line up by the door" or "Go to the bathroom and wash your hands"). These provide additional verbal prompts (instructional prompts) for the specific behaviors included within the whole target behavior—going to lunch.
- Asking questions ("What should you do now?").

In the following example, a verbal direction serves as the stimulus for a student's behavior:

- **Behavior:** Going to the lunchroom for lunch.
- **Discriminative stimulus:** A specific time, such as 12 noon, or a verbal stimulus such as "Class, it is time for lunch."
- **Additional instructional verbal prompts:**
  1. "Line up by the door."
  2. "Walk to the bathroom and wash your hands."
  3. "Walk to the cafeteria."

Initially, a teacher may have to use the discriminative stimulus and additional instructional verbal prompts when teaching the child what is expected when the discriminative stimulus is given. Over time, the teacher should phase out the use of the additional verbal prompts and allow each step in the sequence of going to the cafeteria for lunch to act as the natural prompt for the next behavior. Thus, *lining up by the door at 12 noon* serves as a natural prompt for *walking to the bathroom to wash hands*, and so on.

When gestural, modeling, and physical prompts are necessary, teachers are encouraged to pair these prompts with verbal prompts. As the more intrusive prompts are relinquished, the verbal prompt serves as the discriminative stimulus for the appropriate behavior. Over time, even the verbal prompt may be phased out as still more natural prompts (environmental conditions, time of day, etc.) serve as the discriminative stimulus for the appropriate student behavior.

The effectiveness of verbal prompts alone, and verbal prompts used in combination with other prompts, has been studied with a variety of populations, including high-risk college students (Hodges, 2001), high school students (Houghton, 1993), and even elderly nursing home patients with dementia (Coyne & Hoskins, 1997).

GESTURAL PROMPTS   A *gestural prompt* refers to a simple gesture, usually a pointing prompt, that visually directs an individual in a particular direction. For example, in addition to the verbal prompt "Line up by the door," a teacher may also point in the direction of the door. In this case, the gestural prompt (pointing) is paired with the verbal prompt ("Line up by the door"). Over time, the gestural and verbal prompts should be phased out, and the students should receive reinforcement for completing the target behavior following the discriminative stimulus "Class, it's time for lunch."

MODELING PROMPTS   *Modeling prompts* "consist of demonstrating part or all of the desired behavior to the student who imitates or repeats the action immediately" (Snell & Zirpoli, 1987, p. 126). As with gestural prompts, modeling should be paired with an appropriate verbal prompt or verbal discriminative stimulus that the child will be expected to respond to after the modeling prompt is phased out. For example, when instructing a group of students on expected behavior during story time, the teacher may model where and how the children should sit quietly with their hands to themselves without disturbing others. Then, following the verbal discriminative stimulus "Children, it is time to read a story," the teacher may ask the children to imitate or practice this behavior while a story is being read to them. Appropriate behaviors are then reinforced ("Mario, I like the way you are listening!"). Sometimes the teacher may ask another student to model a particular behavior for the other students. Regardless of who is providing the model, Bandura (1971) recommends that

- the children's attention should be gained prior to the presentation of the model,
- the children readily imitate the model, and
- the modeled behavior be kept short and simple, especially for young children.

Kazdin (1989, p. 21) states that the imitation of a model by an observer is more likely when

- the model (child) is similar to the observer,
- the model is more prestigious than the observer, and
- several models perform the same behavior.

PHYSICAL PROMPTS   A *physical prompt* consists of physically guiding a child in the performance of a target behavior. Obviously, physical prompts are the most intrusive prompt form and are recommended only as a last resort. They should be phased out as soon as possible since they are very unnatural and, when used to modify a student's behavior, may promote hostility and defensiveness.

BASIC ASSUMPTIONS ABOUT BEHAVIOR AND BEHAVIOR MANAGEMENT

Beyond the basic concepts of behavior management discussed so far, some basic assumptions about behavior also guide a behaviorist's thinking. These assumptions about behavior and how behavior is changed provide a foundation for understanding why a person behaves the way he or she does and how the person's behavior may be modified.

For example, it is important to note that effective practices in behavior management place a primary emphasis on overt behaviors and current influences (antecedents and consequences) within the environment that are observed to be related to those behaviors. In other words, although most behaviorists do not deny the possible relationship between a student's challenging behaviors and real psychological, physiological, or other emotional disturbances, they are more interested in assessing a person's overt behaviors within a specific environment than a person's mind. They are aware that a classroom teacher can be taught to modify classroom antecedents and consequences more easily than the thoughts within a student's mind, if at all.

And while most behaviorists do not disregard the influences of heredity, nor are they insensitive to a child's developmental stage when evaluating a behavior problem, they understand that behavior is learned and that students must be taught appropriate social skills if they are to be successful adults in a social world.

A more complete outline of the basic assumptions of behavior and behavior management appears in the following sections. While most behaviorists believe that at least some of the following assumptions have exceptions, these assumptions do represent the philosophical foundations of current behavior management strategies.

Assumption 1: Most Behaviors Are Learned

Behaviorists believe that the majority of behaviors observed in children are learned. That is, children tend to exhibit behaviors that are reinforced and avoid behaviors that have not been previously reinforced or have been punished. Behaviorists believe that there is no difference between appropriate and inappropriate behaviors—both are learned in the same manner. The goal of behavior management is to provide learning experiences for individuals that promote appropriate, prosocial behaviors.

Assumption 2: Most Behaviors Are Stimulus-Specific

Behaviorists believe that individuals behave differently within different environments. That is, the behavior a child shows within a particular situation indicates only how the child typically behaves in that specific situation. This is because each environment contains its own set of antecedents (e.g., people, tasks, expectations) and consequences (reinforcers and punishers) for behavior. In addition, individuals have different histories of reinforcement and punishment within different environments.

For example, a child may have learned that within one environment (the home), tantrums are reinforced. In another environment (the school), however, tantrums are not reinforced. As a result, the child's rate of tantrums is likely to be different in the home (frequent tantrum behaviors) compared with the school (little or no tantrum behaviors).

Assumption 3: Most Behaviors Can Be Taught, Modified, and Changed

Because most behaviors are learned, teachers can teach new behaviors and change or modify current behaviors. Behaviorists are quick to point to the many research studies that document the efficacy of behavioral techniques and the lack of evidence supporting the traditional psychoanalytic approach. Since the behavioral approach is effective in teaching new behaviors and modifying current behaviors, it serves as a functional approach for teachers in everyday situations.

Assumption 4: Behavior Change Goals Should Be Specific and Clearly Defined

Effective behavior management strategies are based on planned and systematic approaches. Behavior change goals are stated in specific terms, and they are clearly observable and measurable. Behaviorists talk about reducing *specific* behaviors such as "talking when the teacher is talking," "hitting others," and "getting out of seat." The strategies used in the behavioral approach are also very specific and must be applied systematically. Objectives, methods, reinforcement strategies, intervention strategies, and so on, are outlined in writing so that everyone who has contact with the student can apply the program consistently.

Assumption 5: Behavior Change Programs Should Be Individualized

Behaviorists believe that individuals function differently within different environments in which there are different antecedents and consequences. Each of us has developed many different associations among many different behaviors, antecedents, and consequences. Also, individuals respond differently to different types of environmental stimuli and responses. For example, what one student finds reinforcing, another may find punishing. Thus, behavior change programs must be individualized for each child and the child's environment. The idea of using a single behavior management strategy for all students within a school or even a classroom is not congruent with the basic assumptions of behaviorism and effective behavior management.

Assumption 6: Behavior Change Programs Should Focus on the Here and Now

Unlike the psychoanalytic approach, in which a considerable amount of time and effort is invested by delving into an individual's past experiences, the behaviorist is not overly concerned with past events. Instead, the behaviorist concentrates on current events within an individual's environment in order to identify the influences on the person's current behavior. The behaviorist looks at what is going on in the classroom environment and sees little benefit from identifying and discussing underlying causes of childhood fears, anxieties, relationships with others, and so on; these approaches have no role in changing current behaviors.

Assumption 7: Behavior Change Programs Should Focus on the Child's Environment

While the psychoanalytic approach concentrates primarily on the individual and looks for an explanation of problem behaviors within the individual, the behaviorist concentrates on the individual's environment and looks for an explanation of problem behaviors within that environment. Behaviorists are interested in environmental, situational, and social determinants of behavior. While the psychoanalytic approach views inappropriate behavior mainly as the result of a flawed personality and other internal attributes, the behavioral approach considers antecedents and consequences as the most significant factors related to appropriate and inappropriate behavior. It is not necessary for the child to have "insight" as to why he or she is behaving in a certain way for that behavior to be changed.

Assumption 8: Behavior Change Programs Should Focus on Reinforcement Strategies and Other Positive Behavior Supports

As stated in Assumption 7 above, the behaviorist concentrates on the individual's environment and looks for an explanation of problem behaviors within that environment. To that end, the behaviorist also assumes that the development and use of reinforcement strategies (see Chapter 10) and other positive behavior supports (see Chapters 12 and 13) not only increase targeted and other appropriate social behavior, but decrease the frequency of inappropriate behaviors.

In addition to the basic concepts and assumptions of behavior and behavior management, behaviorists have had to defend themselves against many misconceptions about their field and the application of their research to the typical classroom teacher. In the next section, the myths and misconceptions about behavior and behavior management arel be discussed in light of the basic concepts and assumptions of behavior just discussed.

MYTHS AND MISCONCEPTIONS ABOUT BEHAVIOR AND BEHAVIOR MANAGEMENT

Myths and misconceptions associated with behavior management procedures have led to public and professional hostility toward behavioral principles, behavior modification in general (Martin & Pear, 2007), and the use of behavioral procedures in the classroom (see Akin-Little, Little, & Gresham, 2004). These misconceptions have developed over the long history of behavior management as the term *behavior modification* and the techniques associated with the term have been abused and misused. The association of behavior modification with nonbehavioral methods such as drug therapy, electroconvulsive therapy, psychosurgery, and sterilization provides an example of common errors made among the uninformed. According to Kazdin (1978):

> It cannot be overemphasized that these techniques are not a part of behavior modification. They are not derived from psychological research nor do they depend upon reversible alterations of social and environmental conditions to change behavior. (p. 341)

Although many of these medical interventions do change or modify behavior and thus may be confused with behavior modification, "clear differences exist between medical and behavioral interventions" (Kazdin, 1978, p. 341). Unfortunately, many educators do not understand these differences.

The perception of punishment as the primary strategy of behaviorists, especially during the early years of application by Lovass, has also led to negative reactions, even among professionals. Alberto and Troutman (1995) go so far as to discourage teachers from using the term *behavior modification* when communicating with others about behavior management techniques:

> We simply suggest that teachers avoid using the term with uninformed or mis-informed people. In many cases, other professionals, including administrative staff and fellow teachers, may be as confused as parents and school board members. . . . It may be as necessary to educate these fellow professionals as it is to teach children. (p. 43)

Some suggest replacing the terminology used in behavior modification with more humanizing language (Saunders & Reppucci, 1978; Wilson & Evans, 1978). Kazdin and Cole (1981) found that individuals labeled identical intervention procedures as less acceptable when they were described in behavioral terms (reinforcement, punishment, contingencies) versus humanistic terms (personal growth and development).

In an interview with Coleman (1987), B. F. Skinner talked about the decline of behaviorism, blaming it on the association between behaviorism and punishment. Skinner was an opponent of punishing methods such as spanking and other aversive techniques used to control behavior. On numerous occasions before his death in 1990, Skinner encouraged caregivers to use positive behavior management approaches and to avoid the use of aversive interventions. Changing the negative image of many effective behavior management techniques will require a significant amount of education for professionals and the general public. An attempt to outline additional behavior management concerns and a brief discussion of each are provided next.

Myth 1: Changing Another Person's Behavior Is Coercive

For some, trying to change another person's behavior is a violation of that person's freedom and other rights. For example, in Classroom Connection 1.3, Randy's teacher does not believe that it is coercive to mandate that he wear a coat before going outside. To her, teaching Randy to wear a coat in the winter is both educational and a health-related concern.

To further address this issue, we must first consider what our responsibilities are regarding the children placed in our care. Do teachers have a responsibility to prepare students for their place within society, to teach them the social skills necessary to survive in the world, and to teach behaviors that will allow them to interact effectively and communicate with others within the home, school, workplace, and general community? Most teachers (and parents) would respond yes. The question then is not whether it is coercive to change a child's behavior; we do this daily in our homes and schools. Rather, the significant questions are *who* decides whether a child's behavior should be changed, w*hat* behaviors should be changed, and w*hich* techniques should be used to change the behavior (Gelfand & Hartmann, 1984).

Myth 2: The Use of Reinforcement to Change Behavior Is a Form of Bribery

Some teachers believe that reinforcing students for appropriate behavior is simply a form of bribery used to get them to behave appropriately. In a worst-case situation, the students may even turn the tables and try to bribe the teacher (e.g., "I'll behave if you give me a cookie"). Kazdin (1975) states that people who confuse reinforcement with bribery

CLASSROOM CONNECTION 1.3
Using Natural Consequences to Teach Compliance

Jill is a kindergarten teacher who teaches a group of 5- and 6-year-olds within an inclusive program. Included in her group of 16 students are 3 students with a variety of disabilities. One of these students, Randy, has several labels including learning disabled and ADHD. Noncompliance is his primary challenging behavior.

One winter day, Jill asked her students to put on their coats as she prepared them for a visit to the playground. "I don't want to put on my coat," yelled Randy. "You don't have to put on your coat, Randy," responded his teacher. "But only children who have their coats on may go outside to play. Mary [the teacher's aide] will stay inside with the children who don't want to put on their coats and go outside to play." Jill then gathered up the children who had put on their coats and took them to the playground. Randy immediately had a temper tantrum and started to yell and scream. Both Jill and Mary ignored Randy's behavior.

When Randy's mother came to pick him up from school, Jill told her what happened. "We can never get

Randy to wear a coat," said his mother. "So we just let Randy decide if he needs to wear one or not." "Not in this classroom," Jill responded. "Our rule is that all the children must wear a coat before going outside in the cold. Those who don't follow the rule will stay inside."

The next day when Jill announced that it was time to go outside and everyone should put on their coats, Randy quickly put on his coat and joined his classmates on the playground. From that point on, Randy was seldom noncompliant about putting on his coat. Interestingly, his mom continued to complain about Randy's inappropriate behavior, especially his temper tantrums, at home.

General Reflection on Classroom Connection 1.3:

Why do you think that Randy no longer has temper tantrums in Jill's classroom, but his mom continues to have problems with Randy's behavior at home? Similarly, how and why do some students behave differently for different teachers within the same school?

---

do not understand the definition and intent of each. He describes the difference between bribery and reinforcement this way:

> Bribery refers to the illicit use of rewards, gifts, or favors to pervert judgment or corrupt the conduct of someone. With bribery, reward is used for the purpose of changing behavior, but the behavior is corrupt, illegal, or immoral in some way. With reinforcement, as typically employed, events are delivered for behaviors [that] are generally agreed upon to benefit the client, society, or both. (p. 50)

Clearly, there are significant differences between bribery and giving students attention for appropriate behaviors. Moreover, if students do not get our attention following appropriate behavior, they will try to get our attention by acting inappropriately. In Classroom Connection 1.3, Randy's behavior was met with both punishing and reinforcing consequences. When he was noncompliant, he was not allowed to go outside with the other children and, thus, his behavior was punished. When he did wear his coat, he was allowed to go outside and, thus, his behavior was reinforced. Many teachers use consequences in this manner every day but will state that they do not believe in using reinforcement or other principles of behavior management.

Myth 3: Students Will Learn to Behave Appropriately Only for Reinforcement

The fear that using reinforcement will lead to manipulation by students is generally unsupported (Kazdin, 1975). Manipulative behavior, however, can be promoted in students. For example, if a teacher provides a reinforcer to a student for terminating disruptive behavior, the child is likely (a) to be disruptive more frequently and (b) to demand a reinforcer before terminating future disruptive behavior. However, if the teacher provides reinforcement to the student following a specific period of time during which disruptive behavior is not observed, the student is less likely to engage in disruptive behavior. In the first case, the student learned that *disruptive behavior* was reinforced. In the second case, the student learned that the *absence of disruptive behavior* was reinforced.

Myth 4: Students Should "Work" for Intrinsic Reinforcers

Although "doing the right thing" for its intrinsic value is certainly an admirable situation, extrinsic reinforcers are a part of everyday life. People who say that extrinsic reinforcement is inappropriate appear to have higher expectations for children than adults. How many adults would continue going to work without an occasional paycheck? How many adults appreciate a pat on the back for a job well done? How many adults work harder at activities they find reinforcing? The behaviorist applies these simple principles to the management of behavior. As previously stated, extrinsic reinforcers are a part of everyday life, and teachers should learn how to use these natural reinforcers to teach new skills and promote appropriate behaviors. As children grow older and become more mature, we hope that they will learn the value of intrinsic reinforcement.

Myth 5: All Students Should Be Treated in the Same Way

The issue here is whether one student should be singled out for a behavior program in which the student will receive a special reinforcer for learning a new behavior. For example, if John, 1 of 25 children in a classroom, frequently gets out of his seat, is it fair to reinforce him for staying in his seat? What about the other students who already stay in their seats and do not need a special program? These questions focus on the issue of fairness; teachers do not want their students to think that one child is receiving special attention. In fact, research shows that caregivers *do* interact differently with individual children (Bell & Harper, 1977; Zirpoli, 1990). All children have individual needs that call for individual attention. Some students need more individual attention than others. The idea of treating everyone the same is incongruent with effective educational practice.

Regarding our previous example, John's teacher has a professional responsibility to identify John's needs and to use the best method for him and his behavior. If reinforcement of in-seat behavior will increase John's in-seat behavior, then John has the right to receive the most effective intervention. Although the other children who already have appropriate in-seat behavior do not need a systematic reinforcement program, good educational practice tells us that they should also receive attention for their appropriate behavior in order to maintain that behavior. The level of attention for in-seat behavior may vary because John's needs are different from his classmates'. However, the other students are unlikely to have a problem with this difference; children are very sensitive to other children who have special needs. Research has shown that children recognize and accept these differences, frequently better than adults (Casey-Black & Knoblock, 1989; Melloy, 1990).

Summary

Classical conditioning refers to the relationship between various environmental stimuli and reflex responses. Classical conditioning was initially promoted by Pavlov, who demonstrated that he could condition a response (salivation) in a dog at the sound of a bell (conditioned stimulus). Today, our understanding of learning has expanded beyond the simple relationship of conditioned and unconditioned stimuli. However, the work of Pavlov, Watson (1919), and others has provided a firm foundation for many current intervention strategies.

Operant conditioning describes the relationship between environmental events and behavior. Antecedent events occur prior to the target behavior. Consequent events occur after a target behavior. A consequent event is considered a reinforcer if the preceding behavior increases or is maintained. A consequent event is defined as a punisher if the preceding behavior decreases in rate, duration, or intensity. Operant conditioning has its roots in the animal research conducted by Thorndike (1905, 1911) and Skinner (1938, 1953). Thorndike demonstrated the relationship between reinforcement and rates of learning. Skinner, whose name is synonymous with operant conditioning and behavior modification, helped clarify the differences between operant conditioning and classical conditioning. He encouraged researchers to study observable behavior and promoted the use of valid and reliable scientific methods of behavioral research.

The primary differences between the behavioral and psychoanalytic approaches include the focus on overt rather than covert behaviors, a different understanding of inappropriate behavior, a different approach to assessment, and a different understanding of the importance of environmental and psychological influences on behavior. The behavioral approach provides teachers and parents with direct applications for classroom and home settings.

Social learning theory expands the behavioral model and stresses the interdependence and integration of internal variables (thoughts and feelings) with environmental factors. The role of modeling, for example, was researched by Bandura (1977) as a significant learning tool.

Behavior therapy is considered a modern, practical application of classical conditioning involving several treatment strategies. These strategies include systematic desensitization, flooding, aversion therapy, covert conditioning, modeling, and biofeedback. Wolpe (1958) used systematic desensitization as an anxiety-reducing procedure.

Applied behavior analysis expanded laboratory principles of operant conditioning to everyday situations and settings. Baer et al. (1968, 1987) state that applied behavior analysis ought to be applied, behavioral, analytic, technological, conceptual, effective, and capable of generalized outcomes.

The basic concepts of behavior management include behavior, responses, stimuli, antecedents, consequences, reinforcement, punishment, and prompts and cues. Prompts may be natural, verbal, gestural, modeling, or physical. Behaviorists believe that most behaviors are learned, behaviors are stimulus-specific, and behaviors can be taught and modified. Behavioral interventions focus on individualized programming, interventions for the here and now, and goals that are specific and clearly defined.

Many myths and misconceptions exist concerning behavior management techniques. These have developed over a long history of abusive interventions with a focus on punishment. The perception of punishment as the primary strategy of behavior management has led to negative reactions, even among professionals. Others believe that changing another person's behavior is coercive, the use of reinforcement is a form of bribery, and children should work for intrinsic, not extrinsic, reinforcers. Current behavioral interventions, however, stress the reinforcement of appropriate behavior and focus less on the modification of inappropriate behavior directly.

Discussion Questions

1. What are the differences between classical and operant conditioning? Provide examples of each as observed in everyday situations.
2. Describe the primary differences between the psychoanalytic and behavioral approaches to understanding behavior.
3. Discuss and give examples of how some of the treatment strategies in behavior therapy are related to classical conditioning.
4. Discuss the treatment strategies frequently associated with behavior therapy. Could any of the treatment strategies be applied to the classroom setting and, if so, how?

5. Discuss the relationship among antecedents, behavior, and consequences in operant conditioning. Give examples of this relationship as observed in everyday experiences.
6. List and give examples of the different types of prompts and cues that may be used as antecedent stimuli to teach new behaviors.
7. Discuss the basic *concepts* of behavior and behavior management.
8. What is behaviorism? Discuss the basic *assumptions* of behavior and behavior management.

References

Akin-Little, K. A., Little, S. G., & Gresham, F. M. (2004). Current perspectives on school-based behavioral interventions: Introduction to the miniseries. *School Psychology Review, 33*(3), 323–325.

Alberto, P. A., & Troutman, A. C. (1995). *Applied behavior analyses for teachers*. Upper Saddle River, NJ: Merrill/Pearson Education.

Allen, K. D., & Shriver, M. D. (1998). Role of parent-mediated pain management strategies in biofeedback treatment of childhood migraine. *Behavior Therapy, 29*(3), 477–491.

Araoz, D. (2001). Sexual hypnotherapy for couples and family counselors. *Family Journal, 9*(1), 75–82.

Ayres, J., & Hopf, T. (2000). Are reductions in CA an experimental artifact? *Communication Quarterly, 48*(1), 19–27.

Baer, D. M., Wolf, M. M., & Risley, T. R. (1968). Some current dimensions of applied behavior analysis. *Journal of Applied Behavior Analysis, 1,* 91–97.

Baer, D. M., Wolf, M. M., & Risley, T. R. (1987). Some still-current dimensions of applied behavior analysis. *Journal of Applied Behavior Analysis, 20,* 313–327.

Balsam, P. D., & Tomie, A. (1985). *Context and learning*. Hillsdale, NJ: Erlbaum.

Bandura, A. (1969). *Principles of behavior modification*. New York: Holt, Rinehart, & Winston.

Bandura, A. (1971). Psychotherapy based upon modeling principles. In A. E. Bergin & S. L. Garfield (Eds.), *Handbook of psychotherapy and behavior*

change: An empirical analysis (pp. 653–708). New York: Wiley.

Bandura, A. (1977). *Social learning theory*. Upper Saddle River, NJ: Prentice Hall.

Bandura, A. (1994). *Self-efficacy*. In V. S. Ramachaudran (Ed.), Encyclopedia of human behavior (Vol. 4, pp. 71–81). New York: Academic Press.

Bandura, A. (1997). *Self-efficacy: The exercise of control*. New York: Freeman.

Bell, R. Q., & Harper, L. V. (1977). *Child effects on adults*. Hillsdale, NJ: Erlbaum.

Bernstein, S. (1999). A time-saving technique for the treatment of simple phobia. *American Journal of Psychotherapy, 53*(4), 501–513.

Boeree, G. C. (1998). *Albert Bandura*. Available from http://www.ship.edu/∼cgboeree/bandura.html

Brown, I. D. (1990, April). *Attention deficit-hyperactivity disorder and self-control training*. Paper presented at the 68th Annual Convention of the Council for Exceptional Children, Toronto.

Casey-Black, J., & Knoblock, P. (1989). Integrating students with challenging behaviors. In R. Gaylord-Ross (Ed.), *Integration strategies for students with handicaps* (pp. 129–148). Baltimore: Brookes.

Coleman, D. (1987, August 16). B. F. Skinner. *New York Times*.

Cooper, J. O., Heron, T. E., & Heward, W. L. (1987). *Applied behavior analysis*. Upper Saddle River, NJ: Merrill/Pearson Education.

Coyne, M. L., & Hoskins, L. (1997). Improving eating behaviors in dementia using behavioral strategies. *Clinical Nursing Research, 6*(3), 275–291.

Cuvo, A. J., & Davis, P. K. (1980). Teaching community living skills to mentally retarded persons: An examination of discriminative stimuli. *Gedrag, 8,* 14–33.

Donnellan, A. M., LaVigna, G. W., Negri-Shoultz, N. N., & Fassbender, L. L. (1988). *Progress without punishment: Effective approaches for learners with behavior problems.* New York: Teachers College Press.

Duckro, P. N., Purcell, M., Gregory, J., & Schultz, K. (1985). Biofeedback for the treatment of anal incontinence in a child with ureterosigmoidostomy. *Biofeedback and Self-Regulation, 10,* 325–334.

Folkerts, D. (2001). Nonsurgical options for treating incontinence. *Nursing Home Long Term Care Management, 50*(5), 40–42.

Gelfand, D. M., & Hartmann, D. P. (1984). *Child behavior analysis and therapy.* New York: Pergamon.

Hodges, R. (2001). Encouraging high-risk student participation in tutoring and supplemental instruction. *Journal of Developmental Education, 24*(3), 2–8.

Horner, R. H. (1991). The future of applied behavior analysis for people with severe disabilities. In L. H. Meyer, C. A. Peck, & L. Brown (Eds.), *Critical issues in the lives of people with severe disabilities* (pp. 607–612). Baltimore: Brookes.

Houghton, S. (1993). Using verbal and visual prompts to control littering in high schools. *Educational Studies, 19*(4), 247–255.

Kauffman, J. M. (1989). *Characteristics of behavior disorders of children and youth.* Upper Saddle River, NJ: Merrill/Pearson Education.

Kazdin, A. E. (1975). *Behavior modification in applied settings.* Homewood, IL: Dorsey.

Kazdin, A. E. (1978). *History of behavior modification.* Baltimore: University Park Press.

Kazdin, A. E. (1989). *Behavior modification in applied settings.* Pacific Grove, CA: Brooks/Cole.

Kazdin, A. E., & Cole, P. M. (1981). Attitudes and labeling biases toward behavior modification: The effects of labels, content, and jargon. *Behavior Therapy, 12,* 56–68.

Killam, P. E., Jeffries, J. S., & Varni, J. W. (1985). Urodynamic biofeedback treatment of urinary incontinence in children with myelomeningocele. *Biofeedback and Self-Regulation, 10,* 161–172.

King, N. J., Heyne, D., Gullone, E., & Molloy, G. N. (2001). Usefulness of emotive imagery in the treatment of childhood phobias. *Counselling Psychology Quarterly, 14*(2), 95–102.

Lampe, J. B., Steffen, R. M., & Banez, G. A. (2001). Empirically supported treatments in pediatric psychology: Constipation and encopresis. *Clinical Pediatrics, 40*(8), 471–473.

Martin, G., & Pear, J. (2007). *Behavior modification: What it is and how to do it.* Upper Saddle River, NJ: Pearson/Prentice Hall.

Melloy, K. J. (1990). *Attitudes and behavior of non-disabled elementary-aged children toward their peers with disabilities in integrated settings: An examination of the effects of treatment on quality of attitude, social status and critical social skills.* Unpublished doctoral dissertation, University of Iowa, Ames.

Meuret, A. E., Wilhelm, F. H., & Roth, W. T. (2001). Respiratory biofeedback: Assisted therapy in panic disorder. *Behavior Modification, 25*(4), 584–606.

Morris, R. J. (1985). *Behavior modification with exceptional children.* Glenview, IL: Scott, Foresman.

Mufson, L. H., Pollack, Olfson, M., Weissman, M. M., & Hoagwood, K. (2004). Effectiveness research: Interpersonal psychotherapy for depressed adolescents from the lab to school-based health clinics. *Behavioral Science, 7*(4), 251–261.

Rescorla, R. A. (1988). Pavlovian conditioning: It's not what you think it is. *American Psychologist, 43,* 151–160.

Rimm, D. C., & Masters, J. C. (1974). *Behavior therapy: Techniques and empirical findings.* New York: Academic Press.

Robbins, J. (2000, September 26). Some see hope in biofeedback for attention disorder. *New York Times,* p. F7.

Russoniello, C. V., & Estes, C. A. (2001). Biofeedback: Helping people control their health. *Parks and Recreation, 36*(12), 24–30.

Saunders, J. T., & Reppucci, N. D. (1978). The social identity of behavior modification. In M. Hersen, R. Eisler, & P. Miller (Eds.), *Progress in behavior modification* (Vol. 6). New York: Academic Press.

Skinner, B. F. (1938). *The behavior of organisms: An experimental analysis.* New York: Appleton-Century.

Skinner, B. F. (1948). *Walden two.* New York: Macmillan.

Skinner, B. F. (1953). *Science and human behavior.* New York: Macmillan.

Skinner, B. F. (1974). *About behaviorism*. New York: Knopf.

Snell, M. E., & Zirpoli, T. J. (1987). Intervention strategies. In M. E. Snell (Ed.), *Systematic instruction of persons with handicaps* (pp. 110–149). Upper Saddle River, NJ: Merrill/Pearson Education.

Thorndike, E. L. (1905). *The elements of psychology*. New York: Seiler.

Thorndike, E. L. (1911). *Animal intelligence: Experimental studies*. New York: Macmillan.

Van De Velde, C. (2002, January 16). The power of social modeling: The effects of television violence. Bing Distinguished Lecture Series, Bing School, Stanford, CA.

Watson, J. B. (1919). *Psychology from the standpoint of a behaviorist*. Philadelphia: Lippincott.

Watson, J. B. (1924). *Psychology from the standpoint of a behaviorist* (2nd ed.). Philadelphia: Lippincott.

Watson, J. B. (1925). *Behaviorism*. New York: Norton.

Watson, J. B., & Rayner, R. (1920). Conditioned emotional reactions. *Journal of Experimental Psychology, 3*, 1–4.

Wenck, L. S., & Leu, P. W. (1996). Anxiety in children: Treatment with biofeedback training. *Journal of Clinical Psychology, 52*(4), 469–474.

Wilson, G. T., & Evans, I. M. (1978). The therapist–client relationship in behavior therapy. In A. S. Gurman & A. M. Razin (Eds.), *The therapist's contribution to effective psychotherapy: An empirical approach*. New York: Pergamon.

Wolpe, J. (1958). *Psychotherapy by reciprocal inhibition*. Stanford, CA: Stanford University Press.

Womack, W. M., Smith, M. S., & Chen, A. C. N. (1988). Behavioral management of childhood headache: A pilot study and case history report. *Pain, 2*, 279–283.

Zirpoli, T. J. (1990). Physical abuse: Are children with disabilities at greater risk? *Intervention in School and Clinic, 26*, 6–11.

Zyl, T. V., & Lohr, J. W. (1994). An audiotaped program for reduction of high school students' math anxiety. *School Science & Mathematics, 94*(6), 310–314.

Legal Considerations for Schools

Mitchell L. Yell
University of South Carolina

> *Discipline and order is essential (in our schools) if the educational function is to be performed.*
>
> —JUSTICE BYRON R. WHITE, *GOSS V. LOPEZ* (1975, P. 584)

Administrators and teachers have been challenged by student discipline problems since the beginning of public education in the United States. In fact, one of the earliest education textbooks published discussed classroom management and teachers' problems in disciplining students (Bagley, 1907). Recently, efforts to address the problem of student discipline have taken on a greater sense of urgency because of the increases in aggressive and violent behavior in our nation's schools.

Opinion polls of the general public as well as professional educators indicate that both groups believe that student behavior problems are the major issue facing our schools (Harris, 1996; Rose & Gallup, 1998). These polls indicate that the public and teachers believe that schools are no longer able to effectively discipline students and that we are losing control of our schools.

Courts have recognized the crucial role of schools in maintaining a safe and orderly educational environment and have granted great latitude to teachers to exercise this control through the use of discipline. However, they have also recognized that students, while at school, have rights that must be respected. Such rights include the right to (a) reasonable expectations of privacy, (b) due process procedures, and (c) free expression. School officials and teachers, therefore, must balance these students' rights with the need to maintain safety and order in the school environment.

The purpose of this chapter is to examine teachers' rights and responsibilities with respect to disciplining students in public schools. First, I examine the basis of a teacher's authority over student behavior. Next, I provide a brief overview of the rights of students in public schools when they are disciplined. In this section, I will address disciplining students with disabilities separately from disciplining students without disabilities. This is because there is very little federal law regarding disciplining nondisabled students, whereas federal law specifically addresses the discipline of students with disabilities in the *Individuals with Disabilities Education Act* (IDEA). In fact, students with disabilities must have proactive behavior programming included in their individual education program (IEP). A brief discussion of schoolwide discipline follows. The chapter concludes with recommendations for teachers and school officials to follow when disciplining students.

TEACHERS' DUTY TO ENFORCE DISCIPLINE

The courts recognize the importance of giving teachers and school administrators authority over student behavior. This authority originates from the English common law concept of *in loco parentis* (i.e., in place of the parent). According to this concept, parents grant school personnel a measure of control over their children when they place their children in school (Yell, 2006). The principal and the teacher have the authority not only to teach, therefore, but also to guide, correct, and discipline their students. Clearly, such control is necessary to accomplish the mission of schools. In loco parentis does not mean that the teacher has the same control over a child when at school as a parent would when the child was at home. It does mean that school officials and teachers, acting with knowledge of appropriate laws and regulations, have a duty to maintain an orderly and effective learning environment through reasonable and prudent control of students. Although the concept does not have the importance it once did, it is, nonetheless, an active legal concept that helps to define the school–student relationship. Thus, with respect to the use of disciplinary procedures, in loco parentis implies that teachers have a duty to see that school order is maintained by requiring students to obey reasonable rules and commands, respect the rights of others, and behave in an orderly and safe manner when at school. This means that students should clearly know which behaviors are acceptable and which are prohibited. If students violate reasonable school rules, by behaving in ways that are prohibited, they should be held accountable. Moreover, student accountability to rules usually implies that violators will be subject to disciplinary sanctions or consequences.

All students, with and without disabilities, have rights in disciplinary matters based on the due process clause of the Fifth and Fourteenth Amendments to the U.S. Constitution. Both the Fifth and Fourteenth Amendments prohibit states from depriving any person of life, liberty, or property without due process of law. This means that prior to taking an action that may lead to such a deprivation, individuals have the right to, at a minimum, be notified of the charges against them and be able to attend a hearing in which they can tell their version of the facts. The next section addresses the rights of students in situations involving disciplinary actions by school officials.

STUDENTS' DUE PROCESS PROTECTIONS

The Supreme Court in *Goss v. Lopez* (1975; hereafter *Goss*) held that students have constitutional protection in the form of due process rights when school officials use disciplinary procedures such as suspension. The due process protections afforded students, however, are limited by the state's interest in maintaining order and discipline in the schools. The courts, therefore, have had to strike a balance between student rights and the legitimate needs and interests of the schools.

The two general areas of due process rights afforded students are procedural and substantive. In terms of discipline, *procedural due process* involves the fairness of methods and procedures used by the schools; *substantive due process* refers to the protection of student rights from violation by school officials and involves the reasonableness of the disciplinary processes (Valente & Valente, 2005). School authorities, however, are vested with broad authority for establishing rules and procedures to maintain order and discipline. Unless students can show that they are deprived of a liberty or property interest, there is no student right to due process. According to a federal district court in Tennessee, "teachers should be free to impose minor forms of classroom discipline, such as admonishing students, requiring special assignments, restricting activities, and denying certain privileges, without being subjected to strictures of due process" (*Dickens v. Johnson Board of Education*, 1987, p. 157).

Procedural Due Process: The Right to Fair Procedures

The Supreme Court has stated that

> it is doubtful that any child may reasonably be expected to succeed in life if he is denied the opportunity of an education. Such an opportunity, where a state has undertaken to provide it, is a right that must be made available to all on equal terms. (*Brown v. Board of Education*, 1954, p. 493)

The importance of education to a student's future certainly requires that disciplinary actions that result in the student being deprived of an education (e.g., suspension, expulsion) be subjected to the standards of due process. The purpose of due process procedures is to ensure that official decisions are made in a fair manner. Due process procedures in school settings do not require the full range of protections that a person would get in a formal court trial (e.g., representation by counsel, cross-examination of witnesses). They do, however, include the basic protections such as notice and hearing.

The U.S. Supreme Court in *Goss* outlined the due process protections that must be extended to all students. This case involved nine high school students who had been suspended from school without a hearing. The students filed a lawsuit claiming that they had been denied due process of law under the Fourteenth Amendment. The Supreme Court agreed, ruling that the students had the right to at least minimal due process protections in cases of suspension. It stated, "Having chosen to extend the right to an education . . . [the state] may not withdraw the right on grounds of misconduct absent fundamentally fair procedures to determine whether the misconduct had occurred (p. 574).

The Court noted that schools have broad authority to prescribe and enforce standards of behavior. However, in its decision, the Supreme Court held that students are entitled to public education as a property interest, which is protected by the Fourteenth Amendment. Because education is protected, it may not be taken away without adhering to the due process procedures required by the Constitution. The school's lawyers had argued that a 10-day suspension was only a minor and temporary interference with the student's education; the high court disagreed, stating that a 10-day suspension was a serious event in the life of the suspended child. When school officials impose 10-day suspensions, therefore, they must grant the suspended student the fundamental requisite of due process of law, the opportunity to be heard.

The opportunity to be heard, when applied to the school setting, involves the right to notice and hearing. The right to notice and hearing requires that students are presented with the charges against them and have an opportunity to state their case (Yudof, Kirp, & Levin, 1992). These protections will not shield students from properly imposed suspensions, but they will protect them from an unfair or mistaken suspension. The Court in

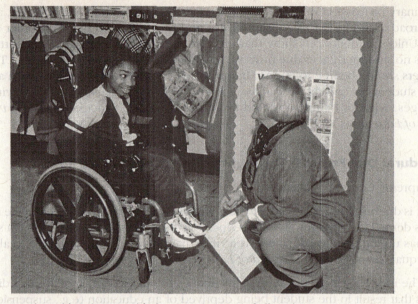

Legal considerations provide for the education of all students

Goss recognized the necessity of order and discipline and the need for immediate and effective action, stating that suspension is a "necessary tool to maintain order [and] a valuable educational device" (p. 572). The prospect of imposing lengthy and cumbersome hearing requirements on every suspension case was a concern to the Court. However, the majority believed that school officials should not have the power to act unilaterally, free of notice and hearing requirements. The Court held that when students are suspended for a period of 10 days or less, therefore, the school must give them oral or written notice of the charges, an explanation of the reasons for the suspension, and an opportunity to present their side of the story.

The notice and hearing requirement does not mean that a formal notice to a student and a meeting must always precede suspension. It is permissible to have a reasonable delay between the time the notice is given and the student's hearing. For example, if the behavior poses a threat to other students or the academic process, a student can be immediately removed from school. The notice and hearing should then follow within 24 to 72 hours. A teacher or an administrator who is disciplining the student could also informally discuss the misconduct with the student immediately after the behavior occurred. This would give the student notice and an opportunity to explain his or her version of the facts before the teacher or administrator carried out the disciplinary sanction. In this case, the notice and hearing would precede the discipline.

It is important to remember that the basic due process protections outlined by the Supreme Court in *Goss* apply only to short suspensions of under 10 school days. According to the Court, longer suspensions, or expulsions, require more extensive and formal notices and hearings. Disciplinary procedures such as time-out, detention, response cost, and overcorrection do not require that due process procedures be extended to students. It is a reasonable assumption that when using in-school suspension, the notice and hearing procedures should be followed. Table 2.1 lists the due process protections

TABLE 2.1 Students' Due Process Protections

Short-Term Suspension (may be a formal or informal meeting)

- Written or oral notice of charges
- Opportunity to respond to charges

Long-Term Suspension and Expulsion (must be a formal meeting)

- Written notice specifying charges
- Notice of evidence, witnesses, and substance of testimony
- Hearing (advance notice of time, place, and procedures)
- Right to confront witnesses and present their own witnesses
- Right to a written or taped record of the proceedings
- Right of appeal
  - Brief in-school sanctions do not require a due process hearing
  - Dangerous students may be immediately removed

Source: The Law and Special Education, by M. L. Yell (Upper Saddle River, NJ: Merrill/Pearson Education, 2006).

that teachers and administrators must follow when using short-term suspensions and expulsions. These procedures apply to all students, disabled and nondisabled alike.

Substantive Due Process: The Right to Reasonableness

The courts have tended to give great authority to teachers and school officials to write rules that govern student behavior in school. Additionally, courts have granted school officials the authority to develop and impose consequences on students who break their rules. This power has a limit, however. These rules and consequences must not violate students' constitutional principles, as discussed earlier (e.g., privacy, due process, expression). Generally, rules and consequences will not violate students' constitutional rights when they are reasonable. Reasonable rules and consequences have a carefully considered rationale and a school-related purpose. Schools may not prohibit or punish behavior that has no adverse effect on the school environment. Furthermore, schools cannot use disciplinary penalties or restraints that are unnecessary or excessive to achieve safety and order in school. In other words, reasonable rules and consequences are rational and fair, and they are not excessive for a school environment.

Rules must be sufficiently clear and specific to allow students to distinguish permissible from prohibited behavior. School rules that are too vague or general may result in the violation of students' rights because students will not have a clear understanding of them. Appropriate school rules are specific and definitive. They provide students with information regarding behavioral expectations.

A federal district court in Indiana addressed the issue of the reasonableness of a school's use of discipline in *Cole v. Greenfield-Central Community Schools* (1986). The plaintiff, Christopher Bruce Cole, was diagnosed as emotionally disturbed under Indiana state law and exhibited management and adjustment problems. The school had attempted, and documented, numerous positive behavioral procedures that it had used to improve Christopher's behavior. When these procedures failed, school officials decided to use behavior reduction strategies. The student's teacher began to use time-out, response cost, and corporal punishment. The plaintiff sued the school, contending that in using these procedures, the school had violated his civil rights.

The court recognized that Christopher, although he had a disability covered by the IDEA, was not immune from the school's disciplinary procedures. The court held that the validity of the plaintiff's claim, therefore, rested on the "reasonableness" of the disciplinary procedures used by the school in attempting to manage Christopher's behavior. The court analyzed four elements to determine whether the rules and consequences were reasonable: (a) Did the teacher have the authority under state and local laws to discipline the student? (b) Was the rule violated within the scope of the educational function? (c) Was the rule violator the one who was disciplined? and (d) Was the discipline in proportion to the gravity of the offense? Finding that all four elements of reasonableness were satisfied, the court held for the school district.

Summary of Due Process Protections and Discipline

All students in public schools, with and without disabilities, have constitutional rights. However, students in public schools do not possess the same rights as people do in the community setting. This is because educators must maintain a safe and orderly environment. To maintain such an environment, school officials and teachers need to impose rules of conduct on their students. Moreover, if students break these rules, teachers may apply consequences in the form of disciplinary sanctions on the students.

Teachers and school officials must adhere to two fundamental prerequisites in developing rules and imposing disciplinary procedures. First, the rules must be clear to all students and their parents. Furthermore, the rules must have a school-based rationale. Similarly, disciplinary procedures that will serve as consequences for rule violation must be clearly stated and understood by all students and their parents. Consequences must be applied on a fair and consistent basis. Furthermore, if the disciplinary sanctions involve suspension, students must be given notice of the offenses they committed and have an opportunity to tell their side of the story.

Many states have laws regarding disciplinary procedures that may be used with students. Teachers need to be aware of their state laws and regulations. Very few federal laws affect discipline of nondisabled students in public schools. This is not the case with students who are disabled, however. The next section is an examination of the federal law that addresses the discipline of students in special education. It is extremely important that teachers and school officials understand their rights and responsibilities in this area.

Also following are a discussion of the disciplinary requirements of the IDEA 1997, a brief review of the provisions of the federal law that directly address discipline, and recommendations for teachers and administrators to follow when disciplining students with disabilities.

DISCIPLINING STUDENTS WITH DISABILITIES

Since the passage of the Education of All Handicapped Children Act in 1975, disciplining students with disabilities has been a very controversial and confusing issue. This law, renamed the IDEA in 1990, created a detailed set of rules and guidelines to ensure the appropriate education of students who were eligible for special education programs.

However, it contained no specific federal requirements regarding discipline. Administrators and teachers, therefore, have had little guidance with respect to their rights and responsibilities when having to discipline students with disabilities.

Because of this lack of federal guidance, the discipline of students with disabilities has been governed by the rulings in numerous court cases that examined this issue, including the U.S. Supreme Court. The rulings in these cases have resulted in the formation of a body of case law that has brought some clarity to this issue. Generally, this case law indicated that disciplinary actions against students with disabilities were subject to different rules and limitations than the same disciplinary procedures used with students who were not disabled (Katsiyannis & Maag, 1998; Yell, 2006).

One area of difference was that the courts viewed suspensions and expulsions of students with disabilities as changes in placement, even in instances of dangerous behavior, if these suspensions exceeded 10 days. Because such procedures were changes in placement, they had to be conducted in accordance through the IEP procedures of the law (Mead, 1998). Courts also created a rule that became known as the *manifestation determination*. Prior to considering expulsion, a group of persons knowledgeable about the student and the student's disability had to determine whether the student's misbehavior was related to his or her disability. If no relationship was found, a student could be expelled. However, courts differed in their rulings regarding the provision of educational services following an expulsion. These rulings provide some guidance regarding discipline; however, many believed a federal standard was needed.

In hearings that preceded the reauthorization of the IDEA, Congress heard testimony regarding the difficulties educators faced when having to use disciplinary sanctions with students in special education. Seeking to strike a balance between educators' duty to maintain safe classrooms and schools and special education students' right to receive a free appropriate public education, Congress included provisions regarding discipline in the IDEA Amendments of 1997 (hereafter IDEA 1997). The disciplinary provisions clarified a number of the issues previously considered by the courts. In 2004, President George W. Bush signed into law the *Individuals with Disabilities Education Improvement Act* (hereafter IDEA 2004), which reauthorized and amended the IDEA, including altering some of the discipline provisions of IDEA 1997.

Disciplinary Provisions of IDEA 1997 and 2004

Prior to discussing the IDEA 1997 and the IDEA 2004, it is important that we understand two major points regarding the discipline sections of the law. First, the IDEA 1997 emphasizes the use of positive behavior programming for students with disabilities to increase the likelihood of success in school and in postschool life. Congress was clearly concerned about preserving safety and order in the school environment, yet it also stressed including this proactive behavioral programming in students' IEPs. The purpose of proactive programming is to teach appropriate behaviors rather than merely eliminate inappropriate behaviors. Second, school officials may discipline a student with disabilities in the same manner as they discipline students without disabilities, with a few notable exceptions. For example, procedures such as verbal reprimands, warnings, contingent observation, exclusionary time-out, response cost, detention, in-school suspension, and the temporary delay or withdrawal of goods, services, or activities (e.g., recess, lunch) are permitted as long as these procedures do not interfere significantly with the student's IEP goals and are not applied in a discriminatory manner (Yell, 2006). The disciplinary provisions of the IDEA 1997 and the IDEA 2004 only address suspensions and expulsions in excess of 10 school days. The remainder of this section addresses specific issues in more detail.

Suspensions and Expulsions

SHORT-TERM SUSPENSIONS   The IDEA authorizes school officials to suspend students with disabilities to the extent that suspensions are used with students without disabilities. There is no specific amount of time that school officials must adhere to in suspending students with disabilities. However, when a student is suspended for more than 10 school days, educational services must be provided.

A comment to the regulations further clarifies this issue (*IDEA Regulations*, 1997). The comment provides the example of a student with disabilities who is suspended for two 5-day suspensions in the fall term. If that student is then suspended for a third time in the spring term, educational services must be provided from the first day of the third suspension. Therefore, school officials may implement additional short-term suspensions for separate incidents of misconduct, as long as the school provides educational services. If a student is suspended for fewer than 10 school days, a school district is not required to continue educational services (*OSEP Discipline Guidance*, 1997).

Schools should use out-of-school suspensions judiciously. Martin (1999) contends that the frequency and amount of short-term removals, if they are excessive, may indicate a defective IEP. He argues that the greater the number of short-term disciplinary removals, the greater the likelihood that a hearing officer will find that the behavior portion of the IEP is inappropriate and a deprivation of the student's right to a free appropriate public education.

SERIAL SUSPENSIONS   When using suspension, school officials may not remove a student for a series of short-term suspensions if these suspensions constitute a pattern of exclusion. Such a pattern constitutes a unilateral change of placement and is illegal under the IDEA 1997. However, not all suspensions in excess of 10 days would constitute a change in placement. The law and regulations are not clear regarding when suspensions in excess of 10 days become a change in placement. To determine whether a series of suspensions constitute such a change, school officials must evaluate the circumstances surrounding the suspension. As noted in Classroom Connection 2.1, the team should consider factors such as length of each removal, the total amount of time that the student is removed, and the proximity of the removals to one another (*IDEA Regulations*, §300.520, Note 1). Thus, determination of when a series of suspensions become a change in placement can only be decided on a case-by-case basis. The IEP team, therefore, is the most qualified team to conduct this inquiry.

LONG-TERM SUSPENSIONS AND EXPULSIONS   School officials may unilaterally place a student with disabilities in an appropriate interim alternative educational setting for up to 45 calendar days if the student (a) carries or possesses a weapon to or at school, on school premises, or at a school function (a *weapon* is defined as a "weapon, device, instrument, material, or substance . . . that is used for, or is readily capable of, causing death or serious bodily injury"; 20 U.S.C. §615[k][10][D]); (b) knowingly possesses, uses, or sells illegal drugs or sells a controlled substance at school or a school function (a *controlled substance* refers to a legally prescribed medication, such as Ritalin, that is illegally sold by a student); or (c) inflicts serious bodily injury on another person while at school, on school premises, or at

CLASSROOM CONNECTION 2.1
Keeping Records of Student Suspensions

Teachers of students with disabilities should keep thorough records of the number of days in which their students have been suspended out of school. Although keeping suspension records may seem like an administrative duty, principals are often unaware of their responsibilities when they suspend students with disabilities. When administrators do not adhere to the procedural requirements of the IDEA when suspending students from school, they may inadvertently violate the law. By keeping suspension records the teacher can keep track of his or her students and ensure that such violations do not occur (e.g., inform the principal that a violation will occur if a student is suspended for 10 consecutive days).

Additionally, when a student's out-of-school suspension approaches 10 cumulative days, the teacher can convene the student's IEP team to (a) conduct a functional behavioral assessment if needed, (b) develop or revise a behavior intervention plan, (c) determine

whether a student's placement has been changed by the out-of-school suspensions, (d) determine educational services that will be provided to the student when suspensions exceed 11 days, and (e) conduct a manifestation determination. The records that a student's teachers keep should include the following information:

- Name of the student
- Conduct that led to the suspension
- Days of removal, including the date in which the students was removed and returned
- Running total of days removed

General Reflection for Classroom Connection 2.1:

What are the requirements of the IDEA with respect to suspending students with disabilities from school? Why is it important that teachers keep records when their students are suspended from school? What information should you keep in these records?

a school function (*serious bodily injury* involves a substantial risk of death, extreme physical pain, protracted and obvious disfigurement, or protracted loss or impairment of the function of a bodily member, organ, or mental facility; 20 U.S.C. §1415[k][7][D]).

Until the passage of the IDEA 1997, school districts had to seek a temporary restraining order from a court to remove a student with disabilities who presented a danger to him- or herself or others. The IDEA now authorizes school officials to seek temporary removal of a dangerous student by requesting that a hearing officer order the student removed to an interim alternative educational setting for 45 days (IDEA 20 U.S.C. §1415[k][2]). Therefore, if school officials believe that a student may present a danger to self or others and seek to have the student removed from school, they must convince a hearing officer that (a) should the student remain in the current placement, he or she is substantially likely to injure him- or herself or others; (b) the school district has attempted to minimize the risk of harm; (c) the student's current IEP and placement were appropriate; and (d) the school's interim alternative educational setting is appropriate. The hearing officer may then change the student's placement to the interim alternative educational setting for up to 45 days. During this time, the IEP team should meet to determine what actions will be taken regarding the situation (e.g., change placement, rewrite the IEP, move to expel the student).

The Manifestation Determination

The IDEA 1997 first clarified a procedure long required by the courts, referred to as the manifestation determination. A *manifestation determination* is a review of the relationship between a student's disability and misconduct. It must be conducted when school

TABLE 2.2 The Manifestation Determination

1. Was the conduct in question the direct result of a school's failure to implement a student's IEP?

If the answer is yes, the behavior is considered a manifestation of the disability, and the determination ends. If the answer is no, the team must answer the final question.

2. Was the conduct in question caused by, or did it have a direct and substantial relationship to, a student's disability?

If the answer is no, then there is no manifestation between the disability and the misconduct, and the student may be disciplined in the same manner as would a child without disabilities. If the answer is yes, the behavior is considered a manifestation of the disability, and the determination ends.

officials seek a change of placement, including suspension or expulsion in excess of 10 school days. In situations in which a student has been suspended in excess of 10 days, the review should take place no later than 10 days following the disciplinary action. The IDEA 2004 changed and simplified the procedures required in a manifestation determination.

The manifestation determination must be conducted by a student's IEP team, his or her parents, and other qualified personnel. When conducting the review, the IEP team must consider all relevant information regarding the misbehavior, including evaluation and diagnostic results, observations, and the student's IEP and placement. The team's task is then to determine whether the misconduct was caused by or had a direct and substantial relationship to a student's disability. The specific questions the team must answer are depicted in Table 2.2.

If the team determines there is no relationship between the misconduct and disability, the same disciplinary procedures as would be used with students who are not disabled may be imposed on a student with disabilities, including long-term suspension and expulsion. Educational services, however, must be continued. The student's parents may request an expedited due process hearing if they disagree with the results of the manifestation determination. The student's placement during the hearing will be in the interim alternative educational setting. If, however, the team determines that a relationship did exist, the student may not be suspended or expelled. Change of placement procedures, however, may still be initiated using the IEP process.

The Interim Alternative Educational Setting

When a student is suspended in excess of 10 cumulative days in a school year or expelled, the school district must continue to provide a free appropriate public education. That is, educational services must continue in an interim alternative educational setting (IAES; IDEA, 20 U.S.C. §1415[k][3]). As noted in Classroom Connection 2.2, the IEP team determines the IAES. Although the IAES is usually not in the current educational setting, the student must be able to continue to participate in the general education curriculum and continue to receive the services and modifications listed in the IEP. In this placement, students must continue to work toward the IEP's goals and objectives, including those that address the behavior problems that led to the placement.

Using homebound instruction or tutoring as an IAES is not specifically prohibited by the IDEA; nevertheless, homebound placements are problematic. School districts must

CLASSROOM CONNECTION 2.2
Determining Educational Services When a Student Is Placed in an IAES

When a principal places a student with disabilities in an IAES for an offense as described in the text, the student's IEP must convene to plan his or her instructional services. Because the student must continue to work on his or her goals, the team must ensure that the IEP is implemented in the IAES. Additionally, any related services (e.g., speech therapy, physical therapy), supplementary aids, or program modifications that the student receives through the IEP must also be provided in the new setting. The IDEA also requires that the student continue to be involved in the general curriculum, although in a different setting. Thus,

the student should continue to receive the school district's general curriculum that he or she received in the previous setting (e.g., social studies, science). During the time that the student is in the IAES, the IEP team should meet to determine whether the IEP should be changed.

General Reflection for Classroom Connection 2.2:

When can a principal unilaterally place a student with disabilities in an IAES? What are the requirements of an IAES? During the time when a student is in an IAES, what should the school district be doing?

continue to provide the special education and related services listed in a student's IEP while he or she is in the IAES. This would include access to all special education and related services as well as access to the general education curriculum. Clearly, providing these services in a homebound setting would be difficult. Furthermore, a comment in the proposed regulations suggests that a homebound placement will usually be appropriate only for a limited number of students, such as those who are medically fragile and not able to participate in a school setting (*IDEA Regulations*, §300.551, Note 1). In answer to a series of questions regarding discipline, the Office of Special Education and Rehabilitative Services (OSERS) noted that in most circumstances homebound instruction is inappropriate as a disciplinary measure; however, appropriateness would have to be determined on a case-by-case basis (*Department of Education Answers Questions*, 1997).

Proactively Addressing Behavior Problems of Students with Disabilities

The IDEA 1997 and the IDEA 2004 require that if a student with disabilities has behavior problems (regardless of the student's disability category) that impede his or her learning or the learning of others, the team that writes the IEP shall consider strategies to address these problems (IDEA, 20 U.S.C. §1414 [d][3][B][I]). This includes (a) conducting an assessment of the problem behavior; (b) writing measurable annual goals and benchmarks or short-term objectives to address the problem behaviors; and (c) providing the appropriate special education and related services, including supplementary aids and services, that are required to allow the student to meet the goals and objectives. For such students, a proactive behavioral intervention plan (BIP) may be developed and included with the IEP.

The purpose of the BIP is to address the behavior problems through the consideration of strategies, including positive behavioral interventions, strategies, and supports to ameliorate the problems. This plan is clearly more than a management plan delineating disciplinary procedures to be used with a student. The BIP should be based on a functional behavioral assessment and developed with the intent of positively intervening to ameliorate the problem behavior and of teaching appropriate behavior (*Senate Report*, 1997). When a student is suspended for more than 10 school days or when a manifestation determination is conducted, a functional assessment of behavior must be conducted, and the BIP must be revised or developed if it does not exist.

Neither the IDEA 1997 nor the IDEA 2004 delineate the components of a functional behavioral assessment (FBA) beyond stating that when conducting an FBA following a 10-day suspension or 45-day removal, the assessment team must address the behavior that led to the removal. Failure to comply with the FBA requirement has led to hearing officers overturning school districts' disciplinary actions because they violated IDEA 1997 (*Board of Education of the Akron Central School District*, 1998).

Summary of Disciplining Students with Disabilities

The disciplinary provisions of the IDEA 1997 and IDEA 2004 have been the subject of much controversy. While some have argued that the law makes the task of schools more difficult in disciplining students with disabilities, others assert that it merely codifies much of the existing case law (*Understanding Discipline*, 1997). It is certain, however, that these provisions will lead to increased litigation. Until the courts begin to clarify some of the ambiguities and gaps within the law, the discipline of students with disabilities will remain unclear. Administrators and teachers should consult state laws and regulations prior to developing discipline policies. States will be required to bring their statutes and regulations into compliance with the IDEA amendments, but they may be more prescriptive than the federal law. In such cases, educators must adhere to the laws and guidelines of their states.

Both the IDEA 1997 and the IDEA 2004 are consistent in that they emphasize *proactive, positive behavioral supports and interventions* for students experiencing behavioral challenges. This textbook describes the procedures that teachers should use to effect behavior change. Educators must understand that the intent of law is to address and ameliorate behavior that impedes student learning and teach socially appropriate replacement behaviors.

SCHOOLWIDE DISCIPLINE

One approach to reducing discipline problems in school is to adopt schoolwide discipline plans that focus on teaching appropriate behavior while preventing misbehavior from occurring. These efforts are aimed at the prevention of both disruptive (e.g., noncompliance) and violent behavior (e.g., physical assault) through using schoolwide discipline programs rather than through merely focusing on reacting to discipline problems after they have occurred (Horner, Sugai, & Horner, 2000; Walker & Epstein, 2001). *Schoolwide discipline programs* refer to strategies that schools develop both to prevent and to respond to problem behavior. Such programs have been shown to have great promise as an effective way to define, teach, and support appropriate behaviors and address disruptive behavior in the schools.

One such effort was the U.S. Department of Education's publication *Early Warning, Timely Response: A Guide to Safe Schools* (Dwyer, Osher, & Warger, 1998). In late 1998, every school administrator in the United States received a copy of this report. The purpose of the guide was to help school districts develop comprehensive violence prevention plans. The guide summarized the research on violence prevention, interventions, and crisis response in schools. According to the guide, well-functioning schools had a strong focus on learning and achievement, safety, and socially appropriate behaviors (Dwyer et al., 1998). Additionally, Horner and others (2000) noted that if schools are to be safe, effective environments, proactive behavior support must become a priority.

Although no one model of schoolwide discipline is used in schools, three basic practices are often followed in effective disciplinary systems (Horner et al., 2000; Walker, Colvin, & Ramsey, 1995). First, schools with effective policies invest in preventing problem behavior by defining, teaching, and supporting student behavior. This means that school personnel develop important expectations or rules about student behavior and clearly communicate these expectations to students. Moreover, school officials recognize students who adhere to these expectations and respond effectively when students do not. Second, effective schoolwide discipline systems have rapid, effective support systems for identifying and addressing needs of students who are at risk of developing problem behavior. According to Lewis and Sugai (1999), these procedures often involve increased adult monitoring and group behavior support. Third, schools using effective discipline systems have support for high-intensity problem behavior. Such systems focus on a small number of students who display high rates of disruptive behavior and include specialized individual behavior programs (e.g., FBAs and BIPs).

Developing Schoolwide Discipline Policies

According to Sugai, Sprague, Horner, and Walker (2000), from 85% to 90% of students begin school having already learned the social skills necessary to be an effective learner. That is, they (a) pay attention, (b) are actively engaged in learning, and (c) follow school rules and procedures. The most important part of any schoolwide discipline procedure is to ensure that these skills become a part of the school's culture (Horner et al., 2000). One way for schools to ensure that such behaviors become ingrained in a school's culture is through the development and systematic use of universal interventions. The key idea behind universal interventions is reducing the number of new cases of problem behavior. Sugai and others (2000) refer to *universal interventions* as systemic interventions in which school personnel develop a system of rules and consequences that focus on improving the overall level of appropriate behavior of most students in a school. The most important components of universal interventions are that (a) behavioral expectations in the form of rules are defined and taught to all students and (b) inappropriate behaviors are corrected through the systematic application of consequences.

Rules and Consequences

When developing universal interventions, schools must define, teach, and support expected student behaviors. To maintain discipline and to operate efficiently and effectively, schools must have rules that regulate student conduct. This means that students should clearly know which behaviors are acceptable and which behaviors are prohibited. Schools recognize and reinforce students who follow the rules regarding acceptable behaviors. Additionally, if students violate reasonable school rules by behaving in ways that are prohibited, they should be held accountable.

Student accountability to rules implies that violators will be subject to disciplinary sanctions or consequences. School officials have long known that students are more likely to conduct themselves appropriately when they understand (a) the types of behavior that are expected of them when they are in school, (b) the consequences of engaging in behaviors that meet these expectations, and (c) the consequences of engaging in prohibited behavior. A number of courts have addressed the issue of schoolwide discipline policies, tending to give great authority to teachers and school officials to write rules that govern student behavior when they are in school (Yell, Katsiyannis, Bradley, & Rozalski, 2000).

When developing school policies regulating student conduct, rules and consequences should have a carefully considered rationale and a school-related purpose. This means that rules should be clear enough to allow students to distinguish permissible from prohibited behavior. Appropriate school rules are specific and definitive. School rules that are too vague or general may result in the violation of students' rights because students will not have a clear understanding of them. In fact, if a court finds that a school rule is so vague that students may not understand what behavior is prohibited, it is likely that that rule would be legally invalid (Gorn, 1999). Thus, teachers and administrators must take care that their school rules are sufficiently clear and are communicated to students. Furthermore, rules must be school related; in other words, school officials may not prohibit or punish conduct that is not related to their school's educational purposes.

As previously noted, an important legal requirement for developing schoolwide discipline policies is that rules and consequences must be reasonable. From a legal perspective, this means that the rules should be rational and fair. Rules that are vague and consequences that are excessive and unsuitable to the particular circumstances may be legally invalid. Additionally, disciplinary procedures that are harsh or excessive are also likely to be ruled legally invalid if they are challenged in court. This means that school officials must use reasonable means to achieve compliance with a school's rules. Reasonable rules and consequences are rational and fair and not excessive or unsuitable to the educational setting.

When schools focus on improving the overall level of appropriate behavior by developing schoolwide rules and consequences, they can expect that problem behavior will be prevented in 80% to 90% of all students (Sugai et al., 2000). However, 10% to 20% of students will not respond to such interventions. For these students, more intensive interventions are required.

Programming for Students with Serious Behavior Problems

Lewis and Sugai (1999) found that the level and intensity of interventions must be increased for students at risk for developing serious problem behavior (5% to 15% of the student population) and for students who already have chronic and intense problem behavior (1% to 7% of the student population). Unfortunately, for many students who may fall into these categories, there are no legal guidelines to guide school districts in developing these more intensive and individualized interventions for problem behavior. Although federal laws and programs fund the development of violence prevention programs in schools (e.g., the Safe and Drug Free Schools and Communities Act of 1994), unless students have a disability, laws address only reactive and exclusionary practices (e.g., zero tolerance policies, searches of students and their property; for a review of these laws, see Yell & Rozalski, 2000). For students with disabilities, however, the IDEA is very specific and exact when directing schools to address problem behavior (see the previous discussion on students with disabilities).

IMPLICATIONS FOR TEACHERS AND ADMINISTRATORS

Maintaining a safe and orderly education environment is one of the most important duties teachers face. Certainly it is one of the most difficult. If our schools are to be places where students can learn, we have to adopt rules to indicate which behaviors will be rewarded and which behaviors will not be tolerated. When we have to use disciplinary procedures, it is important that we understand our rights and responsibilities as well as those of our students. Those who teach students in special education face an even more complex situation when applying disciplinary procedures. It is also important that school officials fashion school district policies and procedures that comport with the law. Following are suggested guidelines that will help to ensure that administrators and teachers meet federal, state, and court requirements when using discipline with public school students.

Develop School District Disciplinary Policies and Procedures

School district administrators should develop written policies and procedures for teaching appropriate behavior and disciplining students when they violate school rules. These policies and procedures must ensure that schools maintain safe and orderly environments while continuing to provide students with an appropriate public education. These policies should include rules of student conduct and disciplinary sanctions when those rules are broken. Developing the policies with the participation of administrators, teachers, parents, and students will help to ensure that they are reasonable and related to a legitimate educational function. Teachers, administrators, staff, and parents should have access to and understand information in the school district's discipline policy. Methods to ensure parental access include mailing discipline policy brochures to district parents and having teachers explain the procedures in parent–teacher conferences. It is important that policies and procedures apply equally to all students and that they be administered fairly and consistently.

When a student is in special education, the teacher should inform the parents of the district policies and procedures. Furthermore, the district's discipline policies should be appended to the IEP. This will ensure that they are discussed and understood by all parties. If there are any changes to this policy (e.g., teachers use in-school suspension instead of out-of-school suspension), the changes should be noted in the IEP.

Proactively Address Problem Behavior

We must remember that the purpose of discipline is to teach. As educators, our goal should not be solely the elimination of problem behavior. Rather, it should be the elimination of problem behavior and the teaching of positive prosocial behaviors. Positive behavioral programming (e.g., conflict-resolution training, anger control training) should be an important part of our school district practices.

In the case of students with disabilities who have a history of misbehavior, the problem behavior must be addressed in their IEPs. The IDEA requires that "in the case of a child whose behavior impedes his or her learning or that of others (the IEP team must) consider, where appropriate, strategies, including positive behavioral interventions, strategies, and supports to address that behavior." In an OSEP memorandum (*OSEP Discipline Guidance*, 1997), Judith Huemann, the assistant secretary of the OSERS in the Department of Education, states that as part of the IEP process, teams have a responsibility to consider a child's behavior. Additionally, she writes that school districts should take prompt steps to address misconduct *when it first appears*. She suggests that when a student exhibits problem behavior, the IEP team should conduct a functional behavioral assessment and determine the needed programming to properly address the behavior. This requirement applies to all students in special education, regardless of their disability category. Additionally, because these elements will be discussed at an IEP meeting, the plan would have an increased probability of success because of parental support and participation. The plan is also less likely to be legally challenged (Hartwig & Ruesch, 2000). Clearly, positive behavior intervention should be used. If behavior reduction strategies are part of the student's program, they should also be included in the IEP.

Provide Training in Behavioral Interventions to Teachers

Teachers must be trained in the use of positive behavioral programming (e.g., developing rules and consequences reinforcing appropriate behavior) and consequences when students violate rules (e.g., time-out, response cost). Additionally, special education teachers should receive intensive training in (a) conducting functional behavioral assessments, (b) writing behavioral goals and objectives, and (c) developing behavioral intervention plans. Such training should include the appropriate use of disciplinary procedures as well as legal ramifications of these procedures. A policy letter from the Department of Education notes the importance of training teachers and staff in the effective use of behavior management strategies, indicating that the appropriate use of these strategies is essential to ensure the success of interventions to ameliorate problem behavior (*OSEP Discipline Guidance*, 1997).

According to Drasgow and Yell (2002), appropriate training is especially important for school personnel who conduct FBAs and develop BIPs because failure of IEP teams to translate the law's requirements to students' educational programs will likely result in inappropriate IEPs and thus the denial of a free appropriate public education (FAPE). The denial of an FAPE may, in turn, lead to due process hearings, litigation, and application of the law's sanctions against the offending school districts. Preservice and inservice educational opportunities should be provided, therefore, to ensure that members of IEP teams thoroughly understand their responsibilities under the IDEA 1997 and have the skills to carry them out. Public schools must ensure that personnel involved in implementing FBAs and BIPs have the necessary training and expertise. Public schools will be well served if this technology is implemented in a proactive manner to address serious and chronic maladaptive behaviors.

Document Disciplinary Actions

When using disciplinary procedures with students with and without disabilities, teachers must keep thorough written records of all disciplinary actions taken. An examination of court cases and administrative rulings in disciplinary matters indicates that in many instances, decisions turned on the quality of the school's records (Yell, 2006). That is, when a school district is sued over a particular disciplinary incident, the court will examine the school's rules and consequences to determine whether they are fair and reasonable. Often they will also examine the records that were kept, if any, on the particular behavior incident. Records on emergency disciplinary actions are also important. Such records should contain an adequate description of the incident, disciplinary action taken, and the signatures of witnesses present.

Evaluate the Effectiveness of Interventions

Finally, it is crucial that school officials and teachers evaluate the effectiveness of the schoolwide policies and procedures and individual students' discipline plans. If schoolwide discipline plans, classroom rules and consequences, and individualized student programs are to be effective, school personnel should develop and implement a set of procedures for monitoring program effectiveness (Drasgow & Yell, 2002). The collection of meaningful data will allow school officials and teachers to determine the efficacy of the schoolwide policies and to maintain effective components of the program while eliminating the ineffective components.

There are a number of reasons for collecting data on an ongoing basis. To make decisions about whether an intervention is reducing target behaviors in the school or in a student, teachers need data collected during the course of the intervention. If formative data are not collected, school officials and teachers will not know with certainty whether the procedures they use are actually achieving the desired results (Yell & Shriner, 1998).

Teachers and administrators are accountable to supervisors, parents, and communities; data collection is useful for informing these groups. From a legal standpoint, it is imperative that school officials and teachers collect such data. Courts do not readily accept anecdotal information but certainly would view data-based decisions much more favorably (Yell & Drasgow, 2001).

Summary

School districts, administrators, and teachers have legal rights and responsibilities to ensure a safe and orderly environment for their students where students can receive a meaningful education. To do this, educational personnel need to develop schoolwide discipline plans and behavior support programs that define, teach, and reinforce appropriate behaviors while discouraging and reducing inappropriate behaviors. Schoolwide discipline programs eschew the traditional discipline methods of reducing inappropriate behaviors through punishment and exclusion, and instead focus on a positive, proactive, problem-solving model for promoting appropriate behavior and discouraging inappropriate behavior. For students with the most serious problem behavior, the IDEA requires adoption of a similar problem-solving approach using FBAs and BIPs to address these students' problems.

Schoolwide discipline plans that are properly developed and implemented will result in safe and orderly schools where teachers can teach and students can learn. Such programs should begin with positive educational programming that does not rely on punitive reductive procedures to change behavior, but rather develops skill-based programming and discipline systems designed to improve the education of their students.

Discussion Questions

1. The Individuals with Disabilities Education Act Amendments of 1997 and the Individuals with Disabilities Education Improvement Act of 2004 (IDEA) require school-based teams to use positive behavior interventions and supports, and to move away from reliance on punishment when address-ing problem behavior. What are positive behavior interventions and supports, and why does the law encourage their use?

2. What are the due process protections for students? How can schools ensure that due process protections are available to all students?

3. What does the IDEA require when using short-term suspensions with students who are receiving special education services?

4. What discipline procedures can schools use for students receiving special education services? Specifically, what action can a school take when a

student receiving special education services brings a weapon to school?

5. What is an interim alternative educational setting? What must schools do to ensure that these settings are appropriate?

6. What is a manifestation determination?

References

Bagley, W. C. (1907). *Classroom management*. Norwood, MA: Macmillan.

Board of Education of the Akron Central School District, 28 IDELR 909 (SEA NY 1998).

Brown v. Board of Education, 347 U.S. 483 (1954).

Cole v. Greenfield-Central Community Schools, 657 F. Supp. 56 (S.D. Ind. 1986).

Department of Education answers question on regulations. (1997, November 21). *The Special Educator, 1*.

Dickens v. Johnson Board of Education, 661 F. Supp. 155 (ER.D. TN 1987).

Drasgow, E., & Yell, M. L. (2002). School-wide behavior support: Legal implications. *Child and Family Behavior Therapy, 24*, 129–145.

Dwyer, K. P., Osher, D., & Warger, W. (1998). *Early warning, timely response: A guide to safe schools*. Washington, DC: U.S. Department of Education.

Gorn, D. (1999). *What do I do when. . . : The answer book on discipline*. Horsham, PA: LRP.

Goss v. Lopez, 419 U.S. 565 (1975).

Harris, L. (1996). *Violence in America's public schools: A survey of the American teacher*. New York: Metropolitan Life Insurance Company.

Hartwig, E. P., & Ruesch, G. M. (2000). Disciplining students in special education. *Journal of Special Education, 33*, 240–247.

Horner, R. H., Sugai, G., & Horner, H. F. (2000). A school-wide approach to student discipline. *The School Administrator, 24*, 20–23.

Individuals with Disabilities Education Act, 20 U.S.C. §1401-1485.

Individuals with Disabilities Education Act Regulations. Available from http://www.ed.sc. edu/spedlaw/lawpage.htm.

Katsiyannis, A., & Maag, J. (1998). Disciplining students with disabilities. *Behavioral Disorders, 23*, 276–289.

Lewis, T. J., & Sugai, G. (1999). Effective behavior support: A systems approach to proactive school-wide management. *Focus on Exceptional Children, 31*(6), 1–24.

Martin, J. L. (1999, May). *Current legal issues in discipline of disabled students under IDEA: A section by section comment on §1415(k), discipline regulations, and initial case law*. Paper presented at the Annual Conference on Special Education Law, San Francisco.

Mead, J. F. (1998). Expressions of congressional intent: Examining the 1997 amendments to the IDEA. *Education Law Report, 127*, 511–531.

OSEP Discipline Guidance, 26 IDELR 923 (OSEP 1997).

Rose, L. C., & Gallup, A. M. (1998). The 30th annual Phi Delta Kappa/Gallup poll of the public's attitudes toward the public schools. *Phi Delta Kappan, 80*, 41–56.

Senate report of the Individuals with Disabilities Act Amendments of 1997. Available from wais. access.gpo.gov.

Sugai, G., Sprague, J. R., Horner, R. H., & Walker, H. M. (2000). Preventing school violence: The use of office discipline referrals to assess and monitor school-wide discipline interventions. *Journals of Emotional and Behavioral Disorders, 8*(2), 94–102.

Understanding discipline under the new IDEA. (1997, July). Special issue. *The Special Educator, 1*.

Valente, W. D., & Valente, C. M. (2005). *Law in the schools* (6th ed.). Upper Saddle River, NJ: Merrill/Prentice Hall.

Walker, H. M., Colvin, G., & Ramsey, E. (1995). *Antisocial behavior in school: Strategies and best practices*. Pacific Grove, CA: Brooks/Cole.

Walker, H. M., & Epstein, M. H. (2001). *Making schools safer and violence free: Critical issues, solutions, and recommended practices*. Austin, TX: Pro-Ed.

Yell, M. L. (2006). *The law and special education* (2nd ed.). Upper Saddle River, NJ: Merrill/Pearson Education.

Yell, M. L., & Drasgow, E. (2001). Litigating a free appropriate public education: The Lovaas hearings and cases. *Journal of Special Education, 33,* 205–214.

Yell, M. L., Katsiyannis, A., Bradley, R., & Rozalski, M. (2000). Ensuring compliance with the disciplinary provisions of IDEA 1997: Challenges and opportunities. *Journal of Special Education Leadership, 13,* 3–18.

Yell, M. L., & Rozalski, M. E. (2000). Searching for safe schools: Legal issues in the prevention of school violence. In H. M. Walker & M. H. Epstein (Eds.), *Making schools safer and violence free: Critical issues, solutions, and recommended practices.* Austin, TX: Pro-Ed.

Yell, M. L., & Shriner, J. G. (1998). The discipline of students with disabilities. *Education and Treatment of Children, 19*(3), 282–298.

Yudof, M. G., Kirp, D. L., & Levin, B. (1992). *Education policy and the law* (3rd ed.). St. Paul, MN: West.

PART
Two

UNDERSTANDING YOUR STUDENTS

Diversity in the Classroom

CHAPTER 3

Julia L. Orza and Janet Medina

What is normal and acceptable in a child's culture may be regarded as abnormal or unacceptable in school and may result in conflict, mislabeling, or punishment. Along with objective recording of behaviors, a child's social and cultural background should be taken into account when assessing performance.

—HEWARD (2006, P. 115)

There is always the danger of stereotyping when discussing different cultures, and we certainly try to avoid that in this chapter. Each one of us is a unique individual with a unique self-identity shaped by our experiences, values, attitudes, the people we encounter, and the communities that socialize us. As stated by Banks and Banks (1989, p. 13):

> Although membership in a gender, racial, ethnic, social class, or religious group can provide us with important clues about individuals' behavior, it cannot enable us to predict behavior. Knowing one's group affiliation can enable us to state that a certain type of behavior is probable.

So while we will try to avoid stereotyping, we believe that cultural influences on behavior have largely been ignored in the field of behavior management and must be specifically addressed. According to the Bureau (2009b), 15.8% of the U.S. population is Hispanic, 12.9% African American, 4.8% Asian/Native Hawaiian/Other Pacific Islander, and 1% American Indian/Alaska Native. The census also reports an additional 1.7% of the population as "Two or more races." As outlined in Table 3.1, minorities currently make up 44.1% of students in U.S. elementary and secondary schools (National Center for Educational Statistics, 2009) for the 2007–2008 school year. And as shown in Table 3.2, the number of nonwhites is projected to increase to 55.8% of the U.S. population by the year 2050.

The number of foreign-born citizens in the United States doubled from 1970 (5%) to 1996 (10%) (Bruce, 1997). In 1998 alone, 660,477 immigrants from 208 countries around the world were granted permanent resident status in the United States. Twenty percent of them came from Mexico.

TABLE 3.1 Percent of United States Elementary and Secondary Schools Nonwhite Population, 2007–2008

Black/African American	Hispanic	American Indian/ Alaska Native	Asian/Pacific Islander	Total
17.0	21.1	1.2	4.8	44.1

Source: National Center for Educational Statistics (2009).

TABLE 3.2 Percent of United States Nonwhite Population, 1999, and Projected Population for 2010 and 2050

	Black	Hispanic	American Indian & Alaska Native	Asian	Total (of any race)
1999	12.8	11.9	0.88	4.08	29.6
2010	12.86	16.03	1.03	4.65	34.57
2050	12.97	30.25	1.24	7.84	52.30
Projected increase	1.4	154.0	41.0	92.0	76.7

Source: U.S. Census Bureau (2008).

By 2008, 12.5 percent of the U.S. population was foreign born (Migration Policy Institute, 2008). In many cities more than half the population is foreign born. As a result, many school systems (e.g., New York, Chicago, Los Angeles) must accommodate over 100 languages or dialects.

In 2000, the top four languages, other than English, spoken by individuals over 5 years old at home in the United States were Spanish, Chinese, French, and German (U.S. Census Bureau, 2001). Between 1990 and 2000, the number of Spanish and Chinese speakers over 5 years old in the United States had each increased by about 60 percent (Shin & Bruno, 2003).

In 2000, it was reported that only 25% of non-English speakers over 5 years old spoke English very well (Shin & Bruno, 2003), and over eight million school-age children in the United States live in homes where English is not spoken (U.S. Census Bureau, 2001). While this diversity is not a new experience for the United States (the number of foreign-born citizens from 1910 to 1940 ranged from 10% to 15% of the population), it brings unique needs to America's public schools, along with many opportunities.

Several myths and overgeneralizations are associated with individual cultures and races. These myths, along with a lack of appreciation for, and celebration of, different cultural norms, contribute to a frequent misunderstanding and misinterpretation of student behavior. Often a student who has been reared in a strong cultural environment becomes frustrated when teachers and peers consider him or her backward or slow for following the behavioral traditions of his or her culture—the only behavior the student knows. An examination of individuals within the context of their own cultural background, conducted from a descriptive rather than ethnocentric point of view, is essential for understanding behavior (Hale-Benson, 1987).

Part of the evolution of multicultural thinking and appreciation in the American classroom includes a switch from advocating the 19th-century Americanization model (merging all students into one "American" ideal) and the "melting pot" ideology developed in the early 1900s (which asserts that all immigrants should give up their culture and assimilate into the "better" American culture), to the more recent "salad bowl" analogy, with "various groups maintaining their distinctive identities while contributing to the quality of the whole society" (Tiedt & Tiedt, 2005, p. 4). Both students and educators need to recognize and value individual differences and acknowledge diverse cultural roots as strengths (Tiedt & Tiedt, 2005). To assist teachers in this task, Web sites that access knowledge bases for various ethnic, racial, gender, language, and other cultural identities are included at the end of this chapter (see Table 3.5 later).

An additional focus of this chapter is on the cultural background and biases of teachers. Often overlooked in the training to become a diversity-sensitive educator is the need on the part of the teacher to examine the effects of his or her own cultural identity, bias, and stereotyping on student behavior. Lacking awareness of our own values, background, and cultural influences makes it difficult to recognize and value another's unique perspective. As stated by Grossman (1995), teachers do not have to be prejudiced to use biased behavior management techniques:

> Even well meaning teachers can misperceive and misunderstand students' behaviors when they interpret them from their own perspective. They can perceive behavior problems that do not exist, not notice problems that do exist, misunderstand the causes of students' behaviors, and use inappropriate techniques to deal with students' behavior problems. (p. 358)

All students need to be connected to family, cultural values, and belief systems. Showing respect for these values and beliefs is a way of showing respect for individual students, their families, and their cultures.

DIVERSE LEARNERS

In this chapter we discuss diversity in terms of not only race and ethnicity but additional sources of cultural identity that can affect a student's behavior, including religion, sexual orientation, health, language, ability/disability, and gender (Cushner, McClelland, & Safford, 2003). Teachers are encouraged to expand their knowledge of these categories and become aware of their own values and biases related to them.

Teachers will also see a diversity of learners (e.g., exceptional and disabled) and learning styles within their classroom. For example, during the 2006 school year, the U.S. Department of Education (2009a) reported that 17.6% of students ages 6–21 who were served under the IDEA 2004 spent more than 60% of their time in a regular school in an inclusion program. Almost 24% will spend 21%–60% of their time in a regular school environment. Table 3.3 outlines the four major disability categories that apply to most students receiving special education services.

In addition, there have been long-standing accusations of an overrepresentation of bilingual and minority students in special education. In some cases, presumably due to inappropriate assessment, neglect, or fear of litigation, there has also been an underrepresentation of bilingual and minority students in special education in some areas (Baca & Cervantes, 2004; Collier, 2009; Gonzalez, Yawkey, & Minaya-Rowe, 2006; Hallahan & Kauffman, 2006; Hoover, Klingner, Patton, & Baca, 2008). Table 3.4 provides a breakdown of the percent of students receiving services under the IDEA by race/ethnicity and

TABLE 3.3 Prevalence Rate of Students Receiving Special Education Services by Disability Category in 2007

Category	Percent of All Students Ages 6–21
Learning disability	3.89
Speech or language impairments	1.72
Mental retardation	0.74
Emotional disturbances	0.67
All other disabilities	1.94

Source: U.S. Office of Special Education Programs (http://www.ideadata.org/PartBTrendDataFiles.asp, 2007).

TABLE 3.4 Percent of Students Receiving Special Education Services by Race/Ethnicity and Disability Category, Ages 6–21, 2007

	Percent of Race/Ethnicity				
Category	American Indian/Alaska Native	Asian/ Pacific Islander	Black (Not Hispanic)	Hispanic	White (Not Hispanic)
Learning disability	1.75	1.74	20.67	22.17	53.67
Speech or language impairments	1.38	3.29	15.42	18.33	61.58
Mental retardation	1.32	2.21	31.92	15.05	49.50
Emotional disturbances	1.61	1.15	28.92	11.56	56.76
Estimated resident population	0.96	4.22	15.07	18.88	60.87

Source: U.S. Office of Special Education Programs (http://www.ideadata.org/PartBTrendDataFiles.asp, 2007).

disability category out of all students ages 6–21 served under the IDEA. The final row contains the percent of estimated residential population in 2004 for ages 6–21 by race/ethnicity (http://www.IDEAdata.org, 2004).

DEFINITION OF TERMS

Language is always changing. It responds to social, economic, and political events and is therefore an important barometer and descriptor of a society at any given time. Language also becomes obsolete; it could not be otherwise because it is a reflection of societal changes. (Nieto, 2004, p. 23)

Nieto's (2004) quote is important to keep in mind as we attempt to offer definitions of terms related to multicultural education and diverse learners. The reader can find many variations and alternatives to the concepts defined here, especially between the various disciplines. We have chosen the broadest representations of terms most commonly discussed in education.

Culture

Culture is an umbrella term that "denotes a complex integrated system of values, beliefs, and behaviors common to a large group of people. A culture may include shared history and folklore, ideas about right and wrong, and specific communication styles" (Tiedt & Tiedt, 2005, p. 11), and it also includes the ways in which we use and react to our physical environment, symbols, economy, education, information and technology, and sociological and psychological climates. Okun, Fried, and Okun (1999) offer a useful and more complete description of the concept, including common ideas about culture, worldviews, and high- and low-context cultures.

Ethnicity

Ethnicity is "a group classification in which members believe that they share a common origin and a unique social and cultural heritage such as language or religious belief" (Gladding, 2001, p. 45). This term originates from the Greek *ethnos*, which means "nation."

Race

Race, often misused as synonymous with *ethnicity* or *nationality*, is "an anthropological concept that classifies people according to their physiological characteristics" (Gladding, 2001, p. 100), such as skin color and facial characteristics. There is much debate in the education literature about how effective knowing one's race is for cultural understanding and about whether race is merely a political classification. Hodgkinson (2000/2001) reports that racial categories in the U.S. Census have no scientific validity and that there is significant disagreement over which racial terms are appropriate terms to use (e.g., *African American* vs. *Black*, and *American Indian* vs. *Native American*). It is important to remember that both race and ethnicity are social constructs, created by a society, affected by a society, and judged by a society. Behavior is learned within the framework of a particular ethnic group or culture and usually taught within a family structure.

The following terms describe additional multicultural principles of behavior:

- *Accommodations:* This term refers to adaptations to learning, instruction, or assessment made by teachers for students with disabilities or English language learners (ELLs) to enhance learning and opportunities for academic success. Many accommodations used for students with disabilities or ELLs positively affect learning for all students (Vaughn, Bos, & Schumm, 2003).
- *Acculturation:* This term describes "the ways people learn the customs, beliefs, behaviors, and traditions of a culture; or the degree to which individuals from minority cultures identify with or conform to the attitudes, lifestyles, and values of the majority culture" (Gladding, 2001, p. 2).
- *Assimilation:* This is "an approach to acculturation that seeks to merge small ethnically and linguistically diverse communities into a single dominant national institutional structure and culture" (Garcia, 2002, p. 415).
- *Assistive technology:* As defined by the Individuals with Disabilities Education Improvement Act, or the IDEA 2004 (PL 108–446), the term *assistive technology*

means any item, piece of equipment, or product system, whether acquired commercially or off the shelf, modified, or customized, that is used to increase, maintain, or improve functional capabilities of individuals with disabilities. The term does not include a medical device that is surgically implanted or the replacement of such device (IDEA 2004, 602[1]).

- **Bias:**   "This is a personal preference which prevents one from making fair judgments or assessments" (Schwartz, Conley, & Eaton, 1997, p. 36).
- **Bigotry:**   "This is a stubborn intolerance of any race, nationality, or creed that differs from one's own" (Schwartz et al., 1997, p. 36).
- **Bilingual special education:**   This term refers to educational programming and assessment designed to address the specific and complex needs of culturally and linguistically diverse students with exceptionalities (CLDE). Currently, there are no consistent models from state to state regarding either certification or education of CLDE students (Baca & Cervantes, 2004).
- **Culture of poverty:**   A social theory (originally termed subculture of poverty by Oscar Lewis in 1996) explaining the cycle of poverty. Based on the concept that the poor have a unique value system, the theory suggests the poor remain in poverty because of their adaptations to the burdens of poverty (Wikipedia, 2010).
- **Cultural conflict:**   This term refers to differences between a child's culture and the culture of the child's immediate community (e.g., neighborhood and school setting).
- **Cultural pluralism:**   This term describes "the existence within a society of a number of varied groups with distinct values and lifestyles. Also known as *cultural diversity*" (Gladding, 2001, p. 34).
- **Cultural relativity:**   This is "the idea that any behavior must be judged first in relation to the context of the culture in which it occurs" (Randall-David, 1989, p. 2).
- **Enculturation:**   This is "the process by which a person acquires the native culture" (Collier, 2004, p. 14).
- **English language learner (ELL):**   ELL is the term used to describe an individual who speaks one or more languages other than English as the first language and who either lacks or is in the early stages of developing proficiency in English (Center for Research on Education, Diversity & Excellence, n.d.).
- **Ethnocentrism:**   "This is the belief that one's cultural ways are not only valid and superior to other people's, but also universally applicable in evaluating and judging human behavior" (Schwartz et al., 1997, p. 22).
- **Exceptional learners:**   In terms of education, exceptional learners are individuals who require and benefit from special education and related services in order to enhance their potential for academic success (Hallahan & Kauffman, 2006).
- **Multicultural education:**   This type of education entails "a curriculum whose content educates students on the contribution of more than one culture" (Garcia, 2002, p. 417).
- **Racism:**   Racism is "prejudice displayed in blatant or subtle ways due to recognized or perceived differences in the physical and psychological backgrounds of people. It is a form of projection usually displayed out of fear or ignorance" (Gladding, 2001, p. 100).
- **Stereotype:**   This is "a concept or representation of a category of persons that can be inaccurate in terms of how it exaggerates real differences and the perception of those differences" (Okun et al., 1999, p. 2).

WORLDVIEW

Worldview describes how a person perceives his or her relationship to the world. A person's worldview influences communication, individual goals, belief systems, problem solving, decision making, socialization, conflict resolution, and behavior (Ibrahim & Kahn, 1984; Sundberg, 1981). Worldviews of teachers and students interact in the classroom and affect the behaviors of both. An effective classroom manager, however, understands his or her own worldview and tries to understand the worldviews of his or her students.

Without consideration of a student's worldview, teachers could misapply both cultural knowledge and techniques, leading to ethical violations and misunderstandings. Since within-group variation is much greater than between-group variation, worldview helps a teacher go beyond applying only general culture information (representative of an entire race, religion, nationality, etc.) to interpret student behavior. Ibrahim (1991) explains: "General information provides an important background but does not provide all the answers" (p. 14). Ibrahim's theory, based on an earlier philosophical and existential framework (see Kluckhohn, 1951), "is a cognitive-values perspective that uses worldview and cultural identity as mediational forces in an individual's life" (p. 15).

Ibrahim and Kahn (1987) developed the Scale to Assess World View (SAWV) to help identify a person's worldview and to use as an evaluation instrument in communication and development. Although it is not necessary for teachers to administer this instrument to their students or themselves, a general understanding of the categories within the scale will greatly assist teachers in understanding and interpreting their own worldview and that of their students. This information, along with culture-specific knowledge, will increase the chances of accurate and unbiased interpretation of behavior.

The Five Categories of Worldview

The five categories of worldview, with the possible range of assumptions along a continuum in each, are as follows:

• *Nature:* This category examines our "people versus nature" orientation, including whether we believe people subjugate and control nature, live in harmony with nature, or accept the power and control of nature over people. People who believe that they have the power to act on and change their environment, have choices about what to do and how to behave, and feel control in their lives are at one end of the continuum. People who feel oppressed in or by their environment, lack power to make decisions or create change, and believe that "whatever happens will happen" are at the other end of the continuum of this category. Questions for this category include these: How do we survive and react to our environment? Does this individual believe in living in harmony with nature? Is nature accepted as all-powerful and controlling? For example, Native Americans often orient more toward the nature end of the continuum, and they have a great respect for the power of nature, the seasons, and feeling controlled by those forces. Two sample items from the SAWV that pertain to this category are "The natural world is such a beautiful place it is a shame to destroy it with buildings, highways, and dams" and "I believe life is easier in the city where one has access to all modern amenities" (Ibrahim & Kahn, 1984). Therefore, students who grow up in families distrustful or fearful of technology may not adjust well to a classroom or teacher that depends heavily on technology and does not respect more traditional and less modern ways of seeking knowledge and information.

• *Time orientation:*   This category examines our temporal focus, including whether we value and function according to the past, present, or future. Strict adherence to time schedules plays a large role in the school system, so it is easy to understand how a student who comes into conflict with the rules about class and assignment schedules, curricular deadlines, and so on, will struggle. Time can be viewed in many ways, and people value their use of time in a variety of ways. The U.S. culture tends to value the future and emphasize things like planning ahead, setting goals, and "moving on." Also, the school system typically promotes following "the plan," and promptness and being on time are very important. A teacher who understands that someone with a different worldview may interpret time very differently can help open lines of communication to help the student adjust to school culture and expectations without disrespecting the child's own family, values, and culture. Trying to convince a student of the value of studying for the upcoming test next week may be difficult when that student is very concerned about having any friends to sit with at the next lunch period! Keep in mind that some students may be raised in environments where a different set of values related to time exists. For instance, some cultures believe that while promptness is a goal, personal commitments are more important, and plans should be flexible, subject to change, and not interfere with those personal relationships. Therefore, restricting parents or guardians to come to school for an appointment at a specific time, and for only a certain time span, may send a message of disrespect to a family believing that their child is more important than a time schedule.

Related to this category is the concept of multitasking versus completing one task at a time. Different cultures can place importance on one or the other and have difficulty adjusting to the opposite style. Students who lack the organizational skills or access to role models for juggling many things at once can become easily frustrated. Also consider the values promoted in many of our time-related expressions—"Tomorrow is another day," "This too will pass," and "The early bird gets the worm," along with popular views that time can be wasted and time is money—and we begin to see how examining our own assumptions about time, as well as our students', can help us manage the classroom better.

Questions to ponder for this category include these: Is the person concerned with the past, present, or future? Is life viewed as finite or eternal (people who believe they have only their time on earth may behave differently than someone who believes in an afterlife)? Does the person have a monochronic or polychronic sense of time? For example, many Latin Americans consider being late as a sign of respect, and African Americans are generalized to be polychronic. Two sample items from the SAWV that pertain to this category are "Nowadays, a person has to live pretty much for today and let tomorrow take care of itself," and "We need to model our lives after our parents and ancestors and focus on our glorious past."

• *Activity orientation:*   This category examines our preferred modality of human activity, including being, being-in-becoming, and doing. Another way to think about this category is in terms of how one creates change or acts on the environment—Is it through behavior (action oriented), cognitions (detached-meditative), or affect (expressive-emotional)? For example, a teacher may be trained (and thus more comfortable) to focus on the cognitive realm and to explore the thought processes behind solving problems or making decisions, yet a child may be learning at home that one's "gut" reaction and intuition should guide him or her. Adolescents experiencing the many hormonal changes in their body may be prone to emotional outbursts, and young children may be behaviorally spontaneously acting out until some of the processes for waiting and postponing gratification set in. For example, Asian Americans are often characterized as in control of undesirable emotions and displaying an outward calmness (Uba, 1994). Questions for this category include the following: Is the student a thinker, a doer, or a feeler? What mechanism does the person use to act and change? For example, women are generalized as primarily expressive-emotional and men are action oriented, so the manner in which each gender handles collaborative group work may be different. Women may wish to focus on the process of developing the relationships in the group in order to complete a task, but men may avoid that and work directly toward task completion. Two sample items from the SAWV that pertain to this category are "Contemplation is the highest form of human activity," and "I believe that feelings and human relationships are the most important things in life."

• *Human relationships:*   Examines our "relational orientation" or how we function in social relationships, including linear-hierarchical, collateral-mutual, and individualistic. There is quite a bit of research that delineates the idea that while individualism has been assumed to be the norm in the United States, the influence and importance of collectivism is increasing and should be respected (Ady, 1998; McCarthy, 2005). Collectivism encourages the subordination of individual goals to the goals of the larger group or organization. An individualist may favor autonomy and independence, while a collectivist may favor collaboration and interdependence. Relationships in collectivistic cultures tend to be stable, while relationships in individualistic cultures are more temporary (McCarthy, 2005). The U.S. culture symbolizes a highly individualistic culture that encourages striving for personal achievement, pursuing social freedom, and taking personal responsibility. Other cultures may be founded upon social commitment and harmony and respect for authority. Based on these differences, it is easy to imagine that a conflict may arise in a situation at school with a student raised in a family that values supporting the family system above all else and sacrificing individual competition for the good of the family success. South Asian Americans are described as viewing community as an extended family, and one has responsibilities to this community, which influences how self-respect and self-control are mediated for each person (Ibrahim, Ohnishi, & Sandhu, 1997). Collectivist cultures tend to seek advice, help, or take orders only from in-groups so the school would have to become part of that student's cultural in-group in order to connect with the child and family.

This category also concerns itself with issues related to decision making, power and authority, helping practices, roles and responsibilities, and social relationships versus social isolation. Questions for this category include these: Does this individual value a variety of social relationships or seek social isolation? Are relationships drawn in terms of lines of authority, rights and rank, subordinate-superior, or hierarchy? How does this student accept authority and from whom? Is collectivism valued over individualism? For example, the African American culture is often characterized by collectivism, while Anglo Americans are said to identify more with individualism and autonomy. Two sample items from the SAWV that pertain to this category are "No weakness or difficulty can hold us back if we have enough will power," and "Women who want to remove the word *obey* from the marriage service do not understand what it means to be a wife."

• *Human nature:*   This category examines our view of "humankind," including good, bad, or immutable (a combination of good and bad). A person who believes that all human beings have the potential for good is at the opposite end of the continuum compared to someone who believes that most people are born with the propensity to do bad things. A child experiencing trauma or raised under conditions of severe poverty or oppression may learn to distrust the world and feel unsafe around people. Someone sent early and consistent messages that the world is a bad place and systems are unfair can develop a negative outlook on the world. Questions for this category include these: How does the person feel about him- or herself? How does the person feel about others? Are people viewed as basically evil, neutral, good, or some combination? For example, a troubled, at-risk youth who has not met with academic or social success in school may see everything in his or her world (e.g., school and parents) as "bad." The youth believes that the system and related authority are holding him or her back and she or he is powerless in that system. Two sample items from the SAWV that pertain to this category are "Most people would stop and help a person whose car is disabled," and "Although people are intrinsically good, they have developed institutions which force them to act in opposition to their basic nature."

A student's worldview may be in conflict with the expectations and values of the school system, as described here. Ibrahim (1991) explains that knowledge of the worldview construct can assist in a better understanding of the acculturation level and specific concerns of the student and can increase trust, empathy, rapport, and communication related to modes of student behavior. When considered along with things like a student's sociopolitical history, affiliation groups, and personal experiences, comprehension of worldview aids a teacher in interpreting and ameliorating behavior.

The following sections include further discussion and examples of behaviors related to the values, worldviews, and socialization of various racial and ethnic groups, each gender, people of different sexual orientations, and people with disabilities.

CULTURAL INFLUENCES ON BEHAVIOR

Gay (2000) states that "teaching is a contextual and situational process. As such, it is most effective when ecological factors are included in its implementation" (p. 21). Low social status, racism, oppression, less respect, and less power and influence on historical and societal levels can certainly make an impact on minority cultures. Most literature suggests that effective teaching of students from minority cultures should involve recognition of and attention to these issues and the role these constructs play in the lives of the students (Gopaul-McNicol & Thomas-Presswood, 1998; Ladson-Billings, 2000; Nieto, 2000; Schwartz, 2001). Understanding the variety of issues and values associated with groups can aid in better classroom management. An important point to keep in mind is that while it may be convenient to compute lists and guidelines for interacting with and understanding groups of people, this does create an almost homogenized viewpoint of communities that can be misleading. For example, the term *Asian American* could incorporate upward of 29 different subgroups, each with their own language, religion, and principles (Diller & Moule, 2005). Similarly, not all students with disabilities have the same characteristics and needs (Heward, 2006).

Collectivism Versus Individualism

A reference to *individual behavior* involves activities and events designed to emphasize self. The term *collateral behavior* is used to describe actions dedicated to advancing the endurance and improvement of the community (Diller & Moule, 2005). Formal school systems often promote individualism and autonomy and even assess and evaluate students individually. However, there are students from cultures that place more emphasis on the collective (participation as part of a tribe or community). Values such as independence, uniqueness, and individual goal orientation may be restrained in favor of family care and honor, group solidarity, and social harmony. For example, African American children are often raised to believe in the collective view of success and to be concerned with the African American community (including church, clubs, neighborhood, etc.) as a

An African American child learns at an early age that behavioral expectations of the predominantly White school community may vary significantly from those of his or her neighborhood community.

whole. Relationships are viewed in terms of loyalty to the kin, community, and strong interdependence. In terms of worldview, African Americans are considered to engage in relationships that are collateral-mutual and emphasize cooperation, kinship, rituals, and standards and that operate from "closed" social systems (Okun et al., 1999). Because of historical, socio-economic, and marital factors, African American familial structures and interactions include immediate and extended relatives, as well as neighbors, friends, godparents, step relatives, and so forth. A student's "family" may include many different people and roles beyond the transitional "blood relative" definition.

The majority of critiques and discussions of African Americans have generally portrayed their families as disorganized, matriarchal, and single-family directed. Ladson-Billings (2000) discovered that literature searches with the descriptor "Black education" directed one to see "culturally deprived" and "culturally disadvantaged." This view has resulted in a deficiency model for studying the culture and behavior of African Americans that devalues the culture in the classroom. Any explanation of behavior, however, must consider the environmental context and larger social systems, and goals or outcomes for students should take into account the emphasis of individualism or collectivism in a student's culture.

Individuals with disabilities may face academic and social obstacles in education that can be confusing and isolating. For a long time, students with disabilities depended on others (teachers, parents, siblings, friends, administrators, etc.) to make all personal and educational decisions for them. An important skill that all students can benefit from is acquiring and exercising self-determination—essentially, making decisions about and increasing the level of control in their own lives (Hallahan & Kauffman, 2006; Heward, 2006). Self-advocacy allows students with disabilities to be more confident about identifying learning strengths and needs, long- and short-term goals, and values and interests in order to advocate for themselves with others, such as teachers, parents, and other students (Vaughn, Bos, & Schumm, 2003).

Asian students and their families place greater importance on a collective and group experience with a focus on interdependence (Diller & Moule, 2005). Additionally, students who transition from school in Japan, for example, may be used to a more rigorous, less individualized education that may entail academic and physical education courses that include both Western and Japanese curriculum. Japanese students are among the few internationally that must take entrance exams to attend high school, and they may attend "cramming school" after school and/or during the summer to prepare (Santrock, 2007).

Perhaps the individuals who have received the least amount of attention in terms of research are individuals who come from multiethnic/multicultural and multilingual families. The combination may arise from the intermarriage of parents from two different cultures and/or races or through the adoption of a child from a different race and/or culture than the parents. The 2000 census was the first to ask about multiracial backgrounds; therefore, less information is available for this population, though it is apparently increasing. Students from these families may face confusion or isolation in coming to some self-identification, as well as acceptance or rejection from peers. Some may opt to "pass" as White in order to avoid anticipated stereotyping, discrimination, or explanation (Diller & Moule, 2005; Nieto, 2004; Wardle & Cruz-Janzen, 2004).

Verbal and Nonverbal Communication

Language switching and language mixing may be common in households with different generations and different levels of acculturation. The majority of first-generation Hispanics/Latinos speak Spanish. According to the U.S. Census Bureau (2009a), 78% of Hispanics 5 years and older speak Spanish at home. While there are increasing numbers of Hispanic children only speaking English at home, the Pew Hispanic Center (2006) found that 52% of foreign-born Hispanics say they speak only Spanish at home. Children are often asked to translate for parents in a school setting, even though this may violate family rules of authority and respect. Teachers should be aware of the pressure on the child and embarrassment on the part of the parent. When one is accustomed to holding conversations in his or her native language, the communication will be much more animated. Mexican Americans are very visual and prefer to use more of the senses while communicating. A sensual conversational style is intimate and carries more emotion so that conversation is lively when spoken within the native language and familiar vocabulary. Speaking Spanish is also an expression of pride in one's culture and self. In Spanish or in English, conversations may be animated when expressing emotional events or feelings in a trusting situation.

For many cultures, open participation is the rule for joining a group discussion. One does not need to wait patiently for a timely pause in order to enter the conversation. For example, interruptions in Hispanic/Latino culture are not considered rude. These conversational expectations are direct opposites to mainstream politeness, along with Asian and Native American modes of "correct" behaviors. For Hispanics/Latinos, these cultural expectations are meant to bring people together and encourage them to participate in conversations and interactions with one another. Contrast this with cultural expectations of Native American culture. Typically, Native Americans must feel they can succeed at a task before they will initiate it. This view is different from the European American "try and try again until you succeed" virtue. For example, before participating in a new game, Native American students may spend a significant amount of time just watching and learning how to play. They may not participate in the activity unless they believe they can succeed.

Educators are encouraged to allow for longer waiting periods when questioning Native American students. Hilberg and Tharp (2002) found that American Indian and Alaska Native students tend towards a global, or holistic style of organization, a visual style of mentally representing information, and a preference for a more reflective style in processing information. Also, public displays of affection are a rarity for traditional Native Americans. In school, however, a gentle touch or a pat of encouragement on the student's shoulder is acceptable. Hugging is also acceptable for young students.

In research, evaluating differences in verbal and nonverbal communication styles between males and females, girls were found to be more adept at communicating in large groups; while there were no significant differences in peer communication, girls spoke more frequently with adults; boys were apt to use more self-assertive speech, especially when speaking to strangers; and girls seemed more comfortable using language to connect to others (Santrock, 2007).

Respectful Behavior

Cultures vary in what is defined as acceptable and respectful behavior, and this can conflict with the expectations for behavior in a school or individual classroom. Considering the behaviors of all the Native American people and nations across America would be unmanageable because there are so many different nations or tribes, with their own languages, dialects, and customs. The U.S. government formally recognizes 542 different Indian tribes. Currently, the four biggest tribes are the Cherokee, Navajo, Latin American Indian, and Choctaw. Thus, not all Native Americans share the same culture, look the same, or have the same behavioral traits. Native Americans are conservatives, liberals, urban, rural, traditional, contemporary, etc; and they raise their children accordingly. However, the following generalizations about this culture provide examples of behaviors and values that may impact a classroom.

Although similarities are found in the outward submission conveyed to authority, such as church figures, business leaders, and elderly family members, Native Americans view "respectful behavior" differently than non–Native Americans. For Native Americans, demonstrating respect of elders, with their more powerful spirits and a wealth of knowledge obtained through longevity, is based on religious and cultural values. Respect is an integral part of the Native American culture and transfers into all aspects of life. Respect for others has a significant effect on individual behavior and on social mores within the Native American culture.

One of the most unique expressions of respect is that of "noninterference." This belief includes a tolerance for others that allows family and friends to make their own mistakes and live their own lives without interference. Respect has precedence over all aspects of the Native American student and the family's behavior, underlying the thoughts and actions observed by teachers. Although each Native American nation has its own customs, this powerful value is the foundation of most Native American cultures.

Related to something as simple as eye contact, Native American children may look away from an adult or hold their heads down during initial interactions with adults. Traditional children will not raise their heads to their teachers because the teacher is an adult who should be respected. Also, adults may gaze away from the person with whom they are speaking as a sign of respect and religious custom. Maintaining eye contact for Native Americans may be considered an act of disrespect, hostility, or rudeness (LaFromboise, 1982).

Traditionally, and in some homes today, Native American children learn not to argue with or criticize parents or offer views different from parents' views in their presence. For many children, this respect carries into all adult relationships, especially relationships with figures of authority and elders. In this framework of relationships, traditional Native Americans perform in American society in a nonassertive or passive manner. Native Americans may walk away from a potential problem whenever they feel uncomfortable. For example, one may walk away from a situation that has the potential for aggressive behavior. Also, although they may have strong feelings and emotions about an issue, they may refrain from expressing these feelings in order to keep the human relationships respectful. Opinions and feelings are sometimes better expressed to other perceptive people with the use of body language and other subtle gestures and movements (LaFromboise, 1982).

Observing and listening are essential skills in the Native American culture. Traditionally, children observed their elders working or attending other "adult" activities and meetings. Today, Native Americans will frequently bring children along rather than leaving children to the care of relatives or enlisting the services of a baby-sitter. Community events are usually planned with the whole family in mind (Light & Martin, 1985).

Traditionally, Native American children were taught to value stillness and quiet in preparation for learning. Family elders had a certain "look" for children that reminded them their behavior at that moment was not appropriate and they must remain still and quiet, observing and listening. Although some of this attitude has changed, listening still is an important characteristic of Native American people. For example, when involved in a conversation, a Native American may sit with his eyes closed and simply listen and think about what others have to say. This behavior should not be considered a sign of rudeness or inattention.

Child Rearing and Discipline Practices

A significant challenge facing teachers is that of socialization of students through classroom management. It is crucial that teachers keep in mind the balance of key relationships

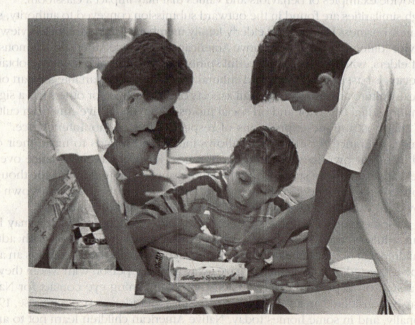

Hispanic/Latino children may prefer working more in cooperative groups than on independent assignments.

between a teacher's approach to classroom discipline and the family's child-rearing practices coupled with the teacher's awareness and understanding of cultural variations in the family's reactions to classroom discipline (Hallahan & Kauffman, 2006). It is important to try to avoid an ethnocentric view of right and wrong regarding child-rearing practices of culturally and linguistically diverse students, though teachers may be faced with conflicting ethical issues of potential neglect or abuse that may not be easy to disregard.

In the United States, where the individual is the most basic social unit, individual rights and responsibilities are emphasized. Accordingly, American parents train their children to stand up for their own rights and the rights of others, to be autonomous, and to become independent of them. However, types of social structure differ between cultures, such as Confucian and American cultures, in which the methods of discipline used in each culture are correspondingly different. In contrast, in Korea and other East Asian countries where the family is the basic social unit, the individual is primarily part of the family. Accordingly, Asian parents teach their children not to think for themselves but to think of themselves as part of the group. They put greater emphasis on teaching their children to be loyal to their group—whether family or nation—than on individual rights or responsibilities. The concept of "our" rather than "my" is emphasized. For example, Asian children say "our mother" or "our family" instead of "my mother" or "my family." In school and at home, the student is exhorted to obey authority and to conform to group norms and be like everyone else (Zhang & Carrasquillo, 1995). The value of uniformity and conformity is strongly instilled in children from an early age.

Some Asian parents often use commands, exhortation, fear-inspiring tactics, or, as the last resort, physical punishment. During the preschool years, Asian mothers tend to be excessively indulgent and often do not discipline their children. They may believe that the child is too young to know better and that discipline is more appropriate for older children. Instead, mothers may try to pacify their children with candy or toys or scare tactics as a primary method of behavioral control (Prendergast, 1985; Walker, 1987). As a result, some of these young students may have some problems adapting to the guidelines and structure of the educational setting.

Franklin (1992) identifies several child-rearing practices common among African American families that may influence student behavior in the classroom. For example, African American children learn how to be assertive at a young age; take on significant family responsibilities at an early age; experience "high-energy, fast-paced home environments, where there is simultaneous variable stimulation (e.g., television and music playing simultaneously)" (p. 118); and are socialized about racism and poverty at an early age.

Acculturation and Enculturation

At age 5 or 6, children are learning how to make sense of their world from a culture-specific perspective. Through enculturation, children learn and attain their native culture (Collier, 2004). At a time when African American children are learning who they are, where they are, and how they fit into the world, they are introduced to formal schooling, which promotes acculturation. Many of these youngsters quickly become aware of hostility toward their race at an early age. To succeed in school, some students develop a minimal connection to their own culture or become creative in their efforts to fit in with their peers while meeting the demands of school and home. A child who wants to fit in with his or her peers, practice the cultural family values, and obey school rules can often juggle many roles in order to acculturate and enculturate.

Students who do not develop a strong connection with their school community may find it easier to drop out—intellectually, emotionally, and physically. For many African Americans, the knowledge learned in school has no direct relationship to their own real world and culture if the school system values concepts more in line with traditional Western, White, middle- and upper-class culture. Frequently, knowledge learned through their cultural environment is not valued by the school. For example, many educators are critical of native dialects and want all students to learn Standard English. As stated by Erickson (1972), "Until recently a major function of the public school was the Americanization of immigrants. Rigid adherence to Standard English in the classroom was one of the school's defensive responses to its inundation by culturally different immigrant children" (p. 19). It is important to understand that additional dialects and communication forms exist (e.g., Ebonics, also called Black English or African American Language, is common among urban and working-class African Americans) and may be an important part of the student's cultural identity.

Relationships

Family relationships, birth order, and duties can often have an all-encompassing importance. In many cultures, the status of the older sibling, for example, depends on his or her ability to care for the smaller children. Likewise, the well-being of younger siblings depends on the help given by older siblings. The rearing of girls is different from the rearing of boys. All of this can impact a child's behavior in school.

Many Southeast Asian refugee adolescents face a multitude of issues related to acculturation: the overall U.S. culture, the culture of Southeast Asia, the culture of being a refugee, the adolescent culture of the United States, and the adolescent culture of being a refugee. Faced with these difficult decisions of honoring the old culture and adopting the new culture, they may create a *third culture* incorporating all of the aforementioned elements (Rice & Dolgin, 2002).

Standards for social behavior between the sexes are probably most contrasting in Confucian and American cultures. In Confucian tradition, boys and girls are brought up in strict separation from an early age. This custom is deeply rooted in the Confucian teachings, starting with the Confucian dictum of the five cardinal relationships mentioned earlier. It is further reinforced by the Confucian precept that boys and girls must not sit together after the age of 7. Although today there are some signs that this custom is changing in some urban segments of the country, the Confucian teaching on male-female relationships still has a formidable hold on the mind and manner of Asian people and virtually dominates the social fabric of their lives. Traditionally and at the present time, the separation between boys and girls in Asian countries is strictly enforced in elementary school. In the lower grades, boys and girls may share the same classroom, but the boys are seated on one side of the classroom and girls on the other. Some teachers may even try to make a boy sit with a girl as punishment. Needless to say, the enforcement of strict division between the sexes or the mixing of the sexes in the classroom can influence interactions and relationships, depending upon the acculturation level of the child and the family situation, as demonstrated in Classroom Connection 3.1.

Most Mexican American students and family members are accustomed to sharing and helping one another. Teachers report that their students are frequently busy helping each other instead of listening to the teacher. Many Mexican American children would probably be comfortable in a cooperative and dependent environment (i.e., cooperative

CLASSROOM CONNECTION 3.1
A New Student in School

Mercedes Tamayo is a new student who arrived in the United States just 4 months ago. She has been placed in Kim's fifth-grade classroom because, although she is 12 years old, she is physically very small compared to her age peers. Her mother is living in Quito, Ecuador (her home country), with her younger sister and, so far, has not been able to get a visa to travel to the United States. Mercedes arrived in the United States with her father, aunt, and younger brother. She is the oldest child. They all now live with her grandmother and grandfather in your school district. The grandparents speak Quechua, a little Spanish, and no English. The father and aunt speak Quechua, Spanish, and very little English. Mercedes and her brother speak Spanish as their primary language, a little Quechua, and very little conversational English, though they are catching on quickly.

Mercedes has demonstrated a great deal of reluctance to read in class, especially aloud. In Ecuador, she made it only to the third grade, missed a year of class due to some local unrest, and was retained for a year. Her father has hinted that perhaps Mercedes was

in some kind of special class in Quito, but cannot explain it well. Kim is also noticing that she tends to want to sit alone, not participate in activities with the other students, and cries whenever she is called on to answer a question in class. Mercedes has not made any new friends in the fifth grade, and she is responsible for walking her younger brother, who is in kindergarten, home from school every day.

Reflection for Classroom Connection 3.1:

Mercedes Tamayo is experiencing a number of difficult adjustments in her life. How do you think her separation from her mother may be affecting her behavior? In addition, children who are going through the process of acculturation may exhibit behaviors such as increased anxiety and difficulty in maintaining attention in class. In addition to the obvious language assistance she needs, what would you recommend to her teacher, Kim, to decrease her anxiety in class, increase her classroom interaction, and help her build relationships and friendships with peers?

learning, sharing tasks, peer teaching). Traditional Mexican American children may perform poorly in situations that emphasize or require individual competition and individual achievement. Thus, teachers are recommended to use more group discussions, group projects, and group reinforcement when possible with these students.

Adolescents who are culturally and linguistically diverse may come from families that employ dating and relationship practices that differ from their European American counterparts. For example, while dating is often discouraged, Mexican American adolescent males may be expected to seek out sexual experiences with promiscuous girls and prostitutes, yet their families may use a matchmaker to arrange for a marriage with a suitable girl (Rice & Dolgin, 2002).

RECOMMENDATIONS FOR SCHOOLS AND TEACHERS

Some teachers believe that it is inappropriate to change their behavior or make other accommodations for students from different cultures. They think that all students should be treated in the same way. Part of this attitude may stem from a reliance on the 19th-century "culture neutral" model of schooling that was designed to create one system that merged all students regardless of cultural origins (the melting pot theory mentioned earlier). However, Ladson-Billings (2000) explains the shortfalls of thinking that "equality means sameness" and warns us about the dangers of applying the same remedy to all situations and contexts (p. 208). "If teachers expect all individuals to behave the same way or interpret everyone's behavior from a single culturally determined point of view, they may fail to respond to the unique needs of many of their ethnic minority students" (Grossman, 1995, pp. 122–123).

For example, Okun, Fried, and Okun (1999) identify nine common identities of Hispanics/Latinos: interdependence, conformity, avoidance of interpersonal conflict, strong loyalty and attachment, clearly defined gender roles, obedience to authority, flexible attitudes toward time, support to extended family, and collective identity. They also identify eight commonly agreed-on identities of Asian Americans: precedence of group interests over individual interests, harmonious relationships, importance of fulfilling obligations, respect for elders, control of undesirable emotions, outward calmness, avoidance of confrontation, and high value on education. And they identify 12 commonly agreed-on identities of Native Americans: privacy, present-time orientation, harmony with nature, generosity, cooperation, interrelatedness of all life, belief in a Supreme Creator, power of the spoken word, support of families, shared child rearing to establish bases of collective responsibility, more visual than auditory, and importance of silence (pp. 263–264).

When considering any culture, Altarriba and Bauer (1998) recommend attention to issues surrounding a child's migration and place of residence, socioeconomics, value orientations (including worldview), family characteristics and values, and language.

Teachers must be familiar with the traditional values and belief systems so that they appreciate the various effects they may have on children's behaviors. How much each individual adheres to these values and behaviors will be the mystery discovered in the classroom. The following categories, with specific applications to various cultures, are just a few of the areas that teachers can focus on to determine how to best respond to each student.

Deal with Feelings of Alienation

Teachers need to understand that some groups often report higher levels of alienation and isolation in their relationship with public schools. This alienation should be examined in light of the school's culture and the parents' perception of that culture, along with an understanding of the parents' previous experiences within the school system. The U.S. Department of Education (2009b) reports that African American students are suspended much more often than Whites. This disciplinary discrepancy can contribute to increased mistrust and alienation among students and parents. Similarly, students who are being raised by same-sex parents may internalize the stigma or bias that is portrayed by socialization agents such as media or religion and isolate themselves from the school events.

Value Extended Family

From the previous information about collectivism and social relationships, it is clear that family can be defined many ways. In a study of teenage parents and their families, Tatum, Moseley, Boyd-Franklin, and Herzog (1995) stress the importance of the "extended family" in the lives of African American students. Tatum et al. describe this extended family as a "complex extended family" or "a closely knit network of households that might include a mother, father, children, grandmother, grandfather, aunts, uncles, and cousins" (p. 19). The extended family may also include many nonblood "relatives," such as "boyfriends, neighbors, friends, godparents, and, in some cases, members of the church family, such as a minister, brothers and sisters in the church" (p. 19). The authors state that it is a serious error for those working with African American students not to learn about the significant others in the student's life because all of these extended family members often play significant roles in "parenting" the student. Tatum et al. also stress that child care frequently takes on an "intergenerational theme" across parents and grandparents. So while teachers may assume that important notes should be mailed "home" to a student's parents, the student may be temporarily staying with grandparents. Teachers are encouraged to view the bonds of the extended family and the adaptability of family roles as strengths of the African American family that provide important coping skills, caretaking, and socialization functions (Gopaul-McNicol & Thomas-Presswood, 1998).

Facilitate Positive Parent–School Relationship

Teachers often contact family members only when one of their children is in trouble. Since the teachers become associated with predominantly negative information about their children, the teacher–parent relationship becomes strained. As a result, parent–teacher interactions may become dominated by confrontation rather than mutual respect. This situation frequently occurs when teachers are working with parents of students who have behavioral problems. But teachers can learn how to balance comments about a child's inappropriate behavior with positive remarks that will communicate to the parent that the teacher also recognizes the good things about their child.

A consistent pattern of discrimination is also established by administrators who make changes in school assignments, policy, or instructional methods without first consulting people, including people of color, from the larger school community. One way to alleviate some of these concerns is to have an active and effective parent–community involvement advisory board for each school that looks at the whole or general needs of the school rather than isolated parts (Banks & Banks, 1989).

Due to disparities in economic conditions, African Americans and their children are sometimes treated as clients, not as consumers, by school personnel. Educators often attribute poor academic performance of African Americans to a lack of parental interest, when in fact education is a strong value in the African American culture. Banks (2004) found that African American parents may not want to be passive participants, and their children passive recipients, in the education process. As with other parents, however, many African American parents feel that they lack the personal knowledge or confidence to confront school officials about their concerns.

Maintain High Expectations

Grossman (1995) found that teachers tended to have lower expectations for poor, African American students and "tend to evaluate them lower than objective evidence warrants, praise and call on them less often, criticize them more often, and use harsher and more punitive disciplinary techniques with them" (p. 357). Schwartz (2001) claims, "School practices may fail to account for the knowledge, cognitive abilities, culture, and values of African American students. The reasons for differential treatment of students of color and White students are many and complex, but the result is often the same: African American students may feel encouraged to act out" (paragraph 3). McCadden (1998) found that teachers try to control Black males more than Whites and that White males are excused for their bad behavior more often than Black males.

The following list, adapted from Randall-David (1989) and Berry and Asamen (1989), outlines some behaviors frequently associated with the African American culture and misinterpreted by teachers:

- Look away while listening
- Stand close to others when talking
- Are reluctant to talk about family problems and personal relationships

- Are concerned with present more than future goals
- Embrace cultural norms if they are living in low socioeconomic conditions but not if they live in middle- or upper-class conditions
- Believe that most individuals within the White culture do not understand or want to understand their culture
- Express their emotions more intensely than other students

Schwartz (2001) recommends that teachers enforce fair and culturally sensitive classroom rules, model knowledge of and respect for diverse cultures, contextualize misbehavior by eliciting reasons and various perspectives before disciplining students, and customize punishments based on promoting responsibility and positive change rather than humiliation and retribution.

Recommendations to teachers and other professionals for success when working with Hispanic/Latino Americans include establishing personal rapport, working in groups, and having group discussions. Once trust has been established, tasks can be divided into smaller units. At first, the student must understand the group goal; then he or she can be asked to perform something individually. It is important to define the totality and ensure that each task is well defined and understood before proceeding with smaller units in the lesson. Unfortunately, some teachers may view this group-dependent behavior as immature instead of culturally based (Grossman, 1995). Grossman recommends that teachers understand the importance of sharing among Hispanic/Latino students. Teachers should know that Hispanic/Latino students are more likely to share their materials and personal belongings and expect others to want to do the same. They may feel rejected or confused when peers talk in terms of what is "mine" versus "yours."

Randall-David (1989, pp. 55–59) lists the following behaviors associated with the Hispanic/Latino culture:

- Touching people with whom they are speaking; may engage in introductory embrace, kissing on the cheek, or slapping on the back
- Standing close to people with whom they are speaking
- Interpreting prolonged eye contact as disrespectful
- Keeping family or personal information from strangers
- Having a high regard for family and extended family
- Treating their elders with respect
- Helping other family members and friends with child care
- Expressing emotions strongly
- Having traditionally prescribed sex roles for males and females
- Consulting parents on important issues

Not surprisingly, teachers frequently describe the behavior of Asian children as respectful and obedient, as well as highly motivated to learn. However, because many Asian students may not be as assertive as other students, some teachers may perceive them as unmotivated or unresponsive (Grossman, 1995).

As with other minority groups, conflicts emerge between the values Asian children learn at school and those taught at home. For example, in traditional Indochinese homes, the children are taught to respect older people and to be quiet, polite, modest, and humble. The conflicting behavioral expectations of the home and school sometimes confuse the students and put them in a position of forced choice, which often results in conflict at home and in the school (Zhang & Carrasquillo, 1995). For example, one teacher reported that it took an entire year to convince an Asian student that it was appropriate and important for him to participate in class discussion, ask the teacher questions, and express his own opinion of subjects. Indeed, for some Asian students, asking questions in the classroom is considered an insult to the teacher (Grossman, 1995).

Schwartz (1996) recommends the following to facilitate parental involvement of Asian parents:

- Explain that parent involvement is a tradition in American education.
- Encourage involvement without increasing family tension by respecting tradition that demands that the young obey the elderly.
- Offer a family English literacy project to help parents understand how teaching and learning takes place in the United States and to bridge the generational gaps within families.
- Make it clear that a child's psychological or academic problems are not a source of shame and that cooperation between family and the professionals can solve them.

Teachers should take extra precautions with their language when communicating with Asian parents about their children. Remember that what you say about their children may be perceived as a remark about the whole family. In addition, Asian parents may not understand such concepts as learning or behavior disabilities. Schwartz (1996) also reminds us to understand the following points:

- Asian students and parents may regard eye-to-eye contact between strangers as shameful.
- Some Asians' smiles or laugher may express confusion and embarrassment, not pleasure.
- Asian culture may consider emotional restraint, formality, and politeness as essential for appropriate social behavior.
- Some Asians may view time as flexible and may not show up for meetings on time.
- When a teacher reprimands a student, the student may believe that he or she is bringing shame to the family.

INTEGRATING A MULTICULTURAL APPROACH IN THE CLASSROOM

Appropriate behavior is frequently associated with children feeling positive about themselves and others. "If children are to feel good about themselves and develop a positive self-esteem, they must receive positive messages from teachers and children around them" (Zirpoli, 1995, p. 253). These positive messages must also reinforce the child's culture, including the child's language, customs, family traditions, and behaviors related to the child's culture. As demonstrated in Classroom Connection 3.2, experience with one culture may or may not prepare a teacher to work with students from other cultures.

Schwartz et al. (1997) state:

> As a teacher, you will be challenged to create harmony from many different voices as you teach respect for diversity while stressing our common human attributes. You will have the task of examining your own attitudes and prejudices as well as those of your students as you cultivate fair and objective attitudes. (p. 29)

While many educators state that they strive to recognize individual differences in students and that they respect these differences, research may indicate otherwise.

CLASSROOM CONNECTION 3.2
A New Teaching Experience

Beth Blue grew up in an urban environment in New York City. Though she had traveled extensively around the United States and Canada, as well as had made a brief trip to the West Indies and another to Europe, she has lived in the New York metropolitan area for most of her life. Beth is a math teacher and really feels that she has developed strategies that make learning math fun for all students; and having taught in such an urban area, she feels that she has encountered every type of student possible in every plausible teaching situation.

After a number of years teaching in the New York area, Beth decided that she wanted a change in her life and responded to an advertisement for a middle school math teacher at a school on the Navajo Reservation in New Mexico. She flies out to Farmington, New Mexico, for an interview at the school and is in awe of the strange but beautiful scenery. Even though the interview process takes place over a short span of a few hours, the interview goes well, Beth is offered the job, and she immediately accepts. With no preparation for the new environment, Beth packs her bags and plans to move into a hotel in Farmington while she looks for an apartment. She cannot believe her luck when, upon her arrival, she finds out that an apartment is available near the school. Desperate to secure a place to live, she arranges to take the apartment, sight unseen. On her way to the apartment, she stops by the real estate office to pick up the key. When she arrives at the apartment building, she notices that all the names on the mailboxes

are names she has never seen before, like Begay and Yazzie. Then when she approaches the door to the apartment she notices vestiges of nail holes on the door jam—as though something had been nailed to the outside of the door. Undaunted and exhausted, she settles in and gets a good night's sleep.

On her first day of teaching, Beth encounters a number of new and disturbing events. The classroom is empty, and there are no textbooks. The bell rings, and no students appear. Soon after, students begin to dribble in, until after about a half hour they are all assembled, and she feels she can begin. Beth charged in with her usual enthusiasm, only to find that students will not raise their hands to be called on, look down when asked to respond, and almost always responded in Navajo. In addition, the students were not able to sit quietly at their desks while she lectured, and their performance on written tests was very weak. When she would point at a child to get their attention, she could hear small gasps, and the child would look away or down.

Reflection for Classroom Connection 3.2:

Beth Blue made some assumptions based on her experiences teaching students in a large urban area. Even though she undoubtedly worked with students from underrepresented backgrounds, she probably has not had the unique experience of working with Native American students, particularly on a reservation. What cultural behaviors is she dealing with, and what would you recommend to help her be successful in her new environment?

"Research indicates that teachers and administrators often have low expectations for language minority students, low income students, and students of color" (Banks, 2004, p. 17), and most educational practitioners have gone through training programs that require only one course in multicultural education (Gopaul-McNicol & Thomas-Presswood, 1998). "More disturbing, a substantial number of teacher education students do not believe that low-income and minority learners are capable of learning high-level concepts in the subjects they are preparing to teach" (Cushner et al., 2003, p. 13).

Cushner et al. (2003) describe the disturbing discrepancy between the makeup of the average student population (over one-third of them are students of color and bilingual) and the teachers (most of the country's teachers are European American, White females), claiming that many students lack role models of their own background as well as teachers with experience with people from other cultures. Half of the country's states do not offer professional credentialing for teachers of culturally diverse students, although "in states that are greatly affected by growing numbers of language minority students, concern for professional teaching standards is developing, but the progress has been uneven" (Garcia, 2002, p. 288). To face the challenges of the culturally diverse classroom, educators must evaluate the effectiveness of the learning environment (including classrooms, activities, and curriculum) for all learners.

Garcia (2002, p. 121) offers, in addition to schoolwide practices, a list of teacher practices, including high expectations of diverse students, treatment of diversity as an asset to the classroom, ongoing professional development on issues of cultural and linguistic diversity and practices that are most effective, and curriculum development that addresses cultural and linguistic diversity.

Banks (2004, p. 18) describes the eight characteristics of the multicultural school:

- The teachers and school administrators have high expectations for all students and positive attitudes toward them. They also respond to them in positive and caring ways.
- The formalized curriculum reflects the experiences, cultures, and perspectives of a range of cultural and ethnic groups as well as of both genders.
- The teaching styles used by the teachers match the learning, cultural, and motivational styles of the students.
- The teachers and administrators show respect for the students' first languages and dialects.
- The instructional materials used in the school show events, situations, and concepts from the perspectives of a range of cultural, ethnic, and racial groups.
- The assessment and testing procedures used in the school are culturally sensitive and result in students of color being represented proportionately in classes for the gifted and talented.
- The school culture and the hidden curriculum reflect cultural and ethnic diversity.
- The school counselors have high expectations for students from different racial, ethnic, and language groups and help these students to set and realize positive career goals.

Celebrate Diversity

Teachers and staff can do many things to recognize and celebrate their students' cultures, making them feel positive not only about themselves but also about the differences observed in others. These methods may be incorporated into the daily activities and materials of the educational setting. Derman-Sparks (1990) and Derman-Sparks, Gutierrez, and Phillips (1993) make these recommendations for teachers:

- Create an environment that celebrates diversity. For example, make wall collages showing young children from many racial and ethnic groups participating in common activities.
- Play music and sing songs from different ethnic groups and in different languages.
- Provide activities to help young students explore their own skin color by having children draw pictures of themselves. Have skin-colored crayons available.
- Provide learning materials, especially books that reflect diverse images of students. These materials should be sensitive to gender roles, students from different racial and cultural backgrounds, students with different abilities and disabilities, and students who come from a variety of family compositions. (Tiedt and Tiedt [2005] offer a list of age-appropriate multicultural fiction and nonfiction titles.)
- Teachers and staff should model their own value of regard for diversity. For example, teachers and staff should talk positively about each student's culture.

- Communicate to the students that teasing or rejecting another student based on the child's culture or identity is not acceptable behavior.
- Provide opportunities for students to interact with others who are racially or culturally different. For example, invite parents of African American children into the classroom to talk about and help celebrate Martin Luther King Day.
- Invite role models into the classroom to talk about their profession (doctors, nurses, firepersons, etc.) who also represent diversity among the community.
- Listen to and answer students' questions about themselves and others. Look for "teachable moments."
- Teach students how to recognize stereotypes of different groups in what they read and see on TV or in the movies. Discuss how these stereotypes may make some people feel about themselves and others.
- Invite students to talk about family traditions, special foods, and customs.

Tiedt and Tiedt (2005) present practical examples of infusing multicultural concepts across the curriculum, including art, language arts, mathematics, music, physical education, science and technology, and social studies lesson plans. Clark (2004) also offers a simple guide to motivate and inspire any type of child in the classroom, by reminding us about the power of basic concepts like enthusiasm, appreciation, compassion, and humor.

EXPLORING YOUR CULTURAL IDENTITY AND THAT OF YOUR SCHOOL COMMUNITY

> I have a responsibility to myself to study and understand the lenses through which I see and experience the people and happenings around me. Only when I have a sense for how my own perceptions are developed in relation to my life experiences can I truly understand the world around me and effectively navigate my relationships with colleagues and my students. (Gorski, 2001, p. 10)

In addition to increasing one's multicultural knowledge base and incorporating it into the classroom, it is essential that every educator explore his or her own cultural identity and become aware of any values or bias that may interfere with validating diversity, interpreting behaviors accurately, and providing a multicultural education. Merely celebrating alternative holidays or including diverse activities in lesson plans does not constitute diversity-sensitive classroom management. Teachers need to make a real and honest connection with students to communicate that they understand and value each student's culture. In order to have this connection and relationship, teachers also need to understand their own culture and its influence on everyone's behavior.

A growing body of literature related to education focuses on the "Whiteness" and homogeneity of our teachers. For example, 85% of U.S. schoolteachers are White and 82% of them are female (National Center for Education Information, 2005). The emphasis is on improving teacher education programs by including a focus on the trainee's cultural identities and privilege, becoming multilingual, identifying and challenging bias and racism, providing community-based multicultural immersion experiences, increasing course work in multiculturalism, and increasing the minority role models in schools and training programs (Ladson-Billings, 2000; Nieto, 2000; Sleeter, 2001). The next section offers Internet addresses that access a large body of literature on activities and exercises that teachers can do to increase awareness of their own cultural identity and bias.

Internet Resources

Technology and computer use is rapidly increasing across the educational scene, for training, teaching, communication, and so forth. According to Internet World Stats (2010), Americans comprise the largest group of Internet users, with more than 77% of Americans currently having access to the Internet. Benefits of the Internet include expanding our informational knowledge base, increasing our access to diverse voices and cultures, increasing our interaction with people across borders and boundaries, and supplementing traditional materials with access to larger databases, collections, artifacts, other classrooms, and archives. One of the challenges of using the Internet in the classroom is ensuring that it is consistent with principles of multicultural education. There exist disparities in Internet use between groups of people: Those of higher socioeconomic background (89%) and better educated (88%) are more likely to have access to the Internet. Only about 38% of individuals with disabilities use the Internet. In looking at ethnicity, Hispanics (59%) tend to use the Internet more than African Americans (43%), but not as much as Whites (67%) (Benschop, 2004; Gorski, 2005; Horrigan & Rainie, 2005).

Teachers should be aware of the plethora of resources on the Internet, not only to aid them in their classroom but also to help them learn more about their students' cultures and learning styles, as well as their own culture and learning styles. Students can use the Internet to better understand experiences and worldviews of people different from themselves, thus minimizing miscommunication and misunderstandings in the classroom. Table 3.5 includes a sample list of the hundreds of Web sites that can help the teacher in this process. See Gorski (2005) for an excellent source on Web sites for classroom use, such as lesson plan banks and exchanges and interactive pen pal sites. But for all the advances in technology available to aid students with learning and social challenges in the classroom, the power of parental support, as demonstrated in Classroom Connection 3.3, cannot be overemphasized.

TABLE 3.5 Multicultural Education Websites

Name	URL	Description
Active Learning Practices for Schools	http://learnweb.harvard.edu/alps	This site offers a learning community of educators working toward the improvement of education. Hosted by the Harvard Graduate School of Education, this site offers educators tools for reflecting on their teaching practice and connects them to others doing the same thing.
CAST (Center for Applied Special Technology)	http://www.cast.org	A not-for-profit organization that uses technology to expand educational opportunities for all people, especially those with disabilities, through Universal Design for Learning and by focusing the development of learning models, approaches, and tools that are usable by a wide range of learners.
Center for Multilingual, Multicultural Research	http://www.usc.edu/dept/education/CMMR	Located at the University of Southern California, this center serves as a starting point for teachers who want information about bilingual, multicultural, and cross-cultural education.
Closing the Gap	http://www.closingthegap.com	Through their newspaper, resource directory, annual conference, and Web site, Closing the Gap provides practical up-to-date information on assistive technology products, procedures, and best practices.

(Continued)

TABLE 3.5 *Continued*

Name	URL	Description
Council for Exceptional Children (CEC)	http://www.cec.sped.org/	The CEC is the leading professional organization for educators in the field of special education. This Web site provides information related to resources, advocacy, legal issues, and collaboration with other professionals.
CrossCultural Developmental Education Services (CCDES)	http://www.crosscultured.com	CCDES delivers technical assistance, professional workshops, and college courses to assist individuals and school districts to navigate No Child Left Behind with a focus on English Language Learner (ELL) and special education issues, as well as an emphasis on parent education and empowerment.
International Education & Resource Network	http://www.iearn.org	The International Education and Resource Network (iEarn) connects young people around the world for collaborative projects related to social and global issues. There is also a section for teachers.
Kathy Schrock's Guide for Educators	http://school.discovery.com/schrockguide	This is a categorized list of sites useful for enhancing curriculum and professional growth. It is updated often to include the best sites for teaching and learning.
Learning Disabilities On Line	http://www.ldonline.org	This is the leading Web site on learning disabilities for parents and teachers of students with learning disabilities sponsored by WETA (public radio and television).
Multicultural Education and the Internet	http://www.mhhe.com/socscience/education/multi_new	This site is hosted by McGraw-Hill's Higher Education Division and is tied directly to Paul Gorski's book, *Multicultural Education and the Internet* (2nd ed.). This site offers referenced Web links to each chapter, multicultural superlinks, links to promising practices, access to intercultural activities, and a link to the Multicultural Pavilion.
Multicultural Pavilion	http://www.edchange.org/multicultural	This site provides resources for educators to explore and discuss multicultural education, facilitates opportunities to work toward self-awareness and development, and provides a forum for dialogue on multicultural issues (MCP is the listserv).
National Association for Bilingual Education	http://www.nabe.org	NABE promotes educational excellence and equity for English language learners and represents the professional educators who serve them. NABE encourages enhancing native language fluency and literacy in conjunction with English language literacy development.
National Association for Multicultural Education	http://nameorg.org	NAME is a clearinghouse and professional organization dedicated to enhancing multicultural education at all levels of education.
Teachers of English to Speakers of Other Languages (TESOL)	http://www.tesol.org	TESOL promotes English language proficiency for students who are English speakers of other languages (ESOL).
Teaching Tolerance	http://www.teachingtolerance.org	Sponsored by the Southern Poverty Law Center, this Web site and organization provides a wealth of material related to diversity and education.

CLASSROOM CONNECTION 3.3
Learning and Social Challenges in the Classroom

Dwayne Simons is a 10th-grade student at Plamely Park High School. He was diagnosed with a learning disability when he was 10 years old in the 4th grade and has received support services in the general classroom since then. Dwayne's IEP indicates that he will be fully included in general education with his nondisabled peers. His primary academic difficulties center on poor reading and writing skills, though he enjoys mathematics and has a voracious appetite for history, especially medieval history. In addition, Dwayne plays lacrosse on the high school team. Dwayne's parents have only attended one IEP meeting in the past 6 years, though they have been invited repeatedly, and they have deferred decisions about Dwayne's education to the IEP team. They have never attended a Back-to-School evening or a parent–teacher conference, but they do come intermittently to his lacrosse games.

Dwayne's parents have not attended school beyond high school; in fact, his father dropped out of school when he was 16 and in the 10th grade, and his mother only finished 9th grade and left school when she became pregnant at age 14. Dwayne's father has made it very clear that he does not value education. At the one IEP meeting he attended, he commented that he only read at a fifth grade reading level and could not understand why the school thought Dwayne should do any better.

Dwayne has always been reluctant to read aloud in class in front of his peers, does not offer to participate willingly in class, and often talks to himself and others around him, even when he is supposed to be listening. Additionally, Dwayne seems to have difficulty catching on to subtle nuances, has difficulty understanding more abstract jokes, and cannot accurately read body language. Last week, in a heated discussion with his reading teacher, she turned to leave, thinking she had signaled that the conversation was ended, and he followed her, still talking to her back. Unable to deflect him, she dove into the women's restroom, assuming he would stop. Instead, without looking where he was going, he followed her.

Recently, Dwayne's teachers noticed that his level of self-esteem and motivation has dropped significantly. Dwayne has begun to demonstrate signs of learned helplessness—the feeling that no matter what he does, he will fail, so there is no reason for him to try. Consequently, while Dwayne had managed to maintain B's and C's in his academic classes, his grades are now reflecting more C's, D's, and an F. In addition, he has missed several lacrosse practices and performed poorly in the past few games—a concern that the lacrosse coach has brought to the assistant principal. The special education teacher has sent a note home to his parents, but there has been no response, and a subsequent call to his parents has not been answered.

Reflection for Classroom Connection 3.3:

Dwayne appears to be struggling with several issues, academic and social. What steps would you recommend, on both fronts, to support Dwayne in schools? What, if anything, can be done to help Dwayne's family see the importance of their participation and support? Lastly, what can teachers do to cue and prompt Dwayne to recognize and display appropriate social behavior?

Summary

Before we can begin to understand a child's behavior, we must first have at least a basic understanding of the child's cultural identity, including race and ethnicity. Otherwise, our behavioral expectations will be invalid, and we will be guilty of ethnocentrism and enculturation. We believe, however, that, in addition to the challenges, educators should consider the many educational opportunities of working with an increasingly diverse population of students. The first step, however, is for educators to learn about their students' cultures and the cultural influences on their behavior. A second, but just as important, step is for educators to have a clear sense of their own worldview and cultural identity.

Worldview, or how a person perceives his or her relationship to the world, is an important concept to understand and apply to self, students, and community. Exploring one's own worldview and how it may differ from a student's worldview can help bridge communication gaps and decrease misinterpretation of behaviors.

Recognizing ecological and sociopolitical factors related to cultural identity that influence behavior can also help educators with classroom management. Things like collectivism, nonverbal communication, discipline practices, and enculturation levels influence behavior in the classroom.

Racial and ethnic minorities make up over 37% of elementary and secondary students in the United States, and 29.6% of the overall U.S. population. They include students from diverse cultural backgrounds such as African Americans, Native Americans, Asian Americans, Hispanic/Latino Americans, and many others. African Americans are the largest minority group in the United States. They represent about 12.8% of the current U.S. population and, by the year 2050, will represent 14.4% of the population. Although their educational status has improved significantly, African Americans are still disproportionately represented in programs for students with special academic and behavioral needs. They are still more likely than White children to be behind a grade level in school and drop out of school. Nearly one of every two African American children lives in poverty, and they are less likely than White children to have the benefits of a college education.

The Hispanic/Latino American population grew faster than any other racial or ethnic group from 1980 to 2000. Thirty million Hispanic/Latino Americans now comprise 12.5% of the U.S. population. Hispanic/Latino Americans include Dominicans, Cubans, Puerto Ricans, Central and South Americans, and Mexican Americans. Mexican Americans account for the largest percentage of Hispanic/Latino Americans.

The primary influences on Hispanic/Latino behaviors include the Hispanic/Latino family, the Spanish language, and religion/spirituality. Family relationships and duties have an all-encompassing importance. Hispanics/Latinos are noted for their festivals and celebrations, usually centered around family, church, or community. Touching and hugging are common during interactions, as are sharing and helping others within the community. Thus, Hispanic/Latino children are usually comfortable within cooperative learning environments and may perform less favorably in situations demanding individual competition.

The Asian American population is one of the fastest-growing ethnic groups in the United States. Asian Americans, 10 million strong, make up 4% of the U.S. population. Asian Americans include the Chinese, Filipinos, Japanese, Koreans, and many other ethnic groups. Although it is true that many Asian Americans are model students and almost 30% of Asians arrive in the United States with 4 years of college education, these facts often obscure the immense diversity within Asian American communities and the many existing challenges for Asian American students.

Asian Americans are also a very diverse group. For the Chinese, Japanese, and Koreans, however, Confucianism serves as the foundation for most social and cultural issues. According to Confucian society, the worth of a person is primarily determined by sex, age, and social status, not by the intrinsic value of life or self.

The Native American population is a small but growing population. They make up 0.94% of the total U.S. population and about 1% of the public school population. The Native American population consists of over 500 different nations or tribes, languages, dialects, and customs. Many Native Americans do not share the same culture and certainly not the same behavioral traits. There are, however, some cultural influences on Native Americans of which educators should be aware.

Discussion Questions

1. Discuss the concept of worldview and how it may contribute to better understanding of classroom behavior. Give examples for some of the cultural identities discussed in this chapter.

2. Frequently, the social skills learned by children within the home environment conflict with behavioral expectations within the school environment. Offer some examples of these conflicts and how

they may be resolved in ways that are sensitive to cultural differences.

3. What are some ways in which classroom teachers can better understand and clarify their own cultural identity and behavior?

4. Pick two or three Web sites mentioned in this chapter and explore the resources offered. Compare the usefulness of each for your own classroom.

5. What are some ways in which a classroom teacher can make the educational environment more inviting to students from different cultural backgrounds? How may these changes influence the behavior of some students and their relationship with others?

References

Ady, J. C. (1998). Negotiating across cultural boundaries: Implications of individualism-collectivism and cases for application. In T. M. Singelis (Ed.), *Teaching about culture, ethnicity, and diversity* (pp. 111–120). Thousand Oaks, CA: Sage.

Altarriba, J., & Bauer, L. M. (1998). Counseling the Hispanic client: Cuban Americans, Mexican Americans, and Puerto Ricans. *Journal of Counseling & Development, 76,* 389–395.

Baca, L. M., & Cervantes, H. T. (2004). *The bilingual special education interface* (4th ed.). Upper Saddle River, NJ: Merrill/Pearson Education.

Banks, J. (2004). *An introduction to multicultural education.* Needham Heights, MA: Allyn & Bacon.

Banks, J., & Banks, C. M. (1989). *Multicultural education: Issues and perspectives.* Boston: Allyn & Bacon.

Benschop, A. (2004). *Internet users: Demography and geography of the Internet.* Retrieved from http://www2.fmg.uva.nl/sociosite/websoc/demography.

Berry, G. L., & Asamen, J. K. (1989). *Black students: Psychosocial issues and academic achievement.* New York: Sage.

Bruce, R. A. (1997). *Managing change in the coming millennium.* Louisville, KY: University of Louisville.

Center for Research on Education, Diversity, and Excellence. (n.d.). Retrieved January 16, 2006, from www.crede.org.

Clark, R. (2004). *The excellent 11: Qualities teachers and parents use to motivate, inspire, and educate children.* New York: Hyperion.

Collier, C. (2004). *Separating difference from disability* (3rd ed.). Ferndale, WA: CrossCultural Developmental Education Services.

Collier, C. (2009). *Separating difference from disability* (4th ed.). Ferndale, WA: CrossCultural Developmental Education Services.

Cushner, K., McClelland, A., & Safford, P. (2003). *Human diversity in education: An integrative approach.* New York: McGraw-Hill.

Derman-Sparks, L. (1990). Understanding diversity. *Scholastic Pre-K Today, 5,* 44–53.

Derman-Sparks, L., Gutierrez, M., & Phillips, C. B. (1993) *Teaching young children to resist bias: What parents can do.* Washington, DC: National Association for the Education of Young Children.

Diller, J. V., & Moule, J. (2005). Cultural competence: A primer for educators. Belmont, CA: Thomson/Wadsworth.

Erickson, F. D. (1972). "F'get you Honky!": A new look at Black dialect and the school. In A. L. Smith (Ed.), *Language, communication, and rhetoric in Black America* (pp. 18–27). New York: Harper & Row.

Franklin, M. E. (1992). Culturally sensitive instructional practices for African-American learners with disabilities. *Exceptional Children, 59,* 115–122.

Garcia, E. (2002). *Student cultural diversity: Understanding and meeting the challenge.* Boston: Houghton Mifflin.

Gay, G. (2000). *Culturally responsive teaching: Theory, research, and practice.* New York: Teachers College Press.

Gladding, S. (2001). *The counseling dictionary.* Upper Saddle River, NJ: Merrill/Pearson Education.

Gonzalez, V., Yawkey, T., & Minaya-Rowe, L. (2006). *English-as-a-second-language (ESL) teaching and learning.* Boston: Pearson.

Gopaul-McNicol, S., & Thomas-Presswood, T. (1998). *Working with linguistically and culturally different children: Innovative clinical and educational approaches.* Needham Heights, MA: Allyn & Bacon.

Gorski, P. (2005). *Multicultural education and the Internet* (2nd ed.). New York: McGraw-Hill.

Gorski, P. C. (2001). *Multicultural education and the Internet: Intersections and integrations*. New York: McGraw-Hill.

Grossman, H. (1995). *Special education in a diverse society*. Boston, MA: Allyn & Bacon.

Hale-Benson, J. (1987). Self-esteem of Black middle-class women who choose to work inside or outside the home. *Journal of Multicultural Counseling and Development, 15*, 71–80.

Hallahan, D. P., & Kauffman, J. M. (2006). *Exceptional learners: Introduction to special education* (10th ed.). Boston: Allyn & Bacon.

Heward, W. (2006). *Exceptional children: An introduction to special education* (8th ed.). Upper Saddle River, NJ: Merrill/Pearson Education.

Hilberg, R.S., & Tharp, R.G. (2002). Theoretical perspectives, research findings and classroom implications of the learning styles of Native American and Alaska Native students. ERIC Digest EDO RC-02-3. ERIC Clearinghouse on Rural Education and Small Schools, Charleston, WV: AEL.

Hodgkinson, H. (2000/2001). Educational demographics: What teachers should know. *Educational Leadership, 58*, 6–11.

Hoover, J. J., Klingner, J., Patton, J., & Baca, L. (2008). *Methods for teaching culturally and linguistically diverse exceptional learners*. Upper Saddle River, NJ: Pearson Education.

Horrigan, J. B., & Rainie, L. (2005). *Internet: The mainstreaming of online life*. Retrieved from the Pew Internet and American Life Project, http://www.pewinternet.org/pdfs/Internet_Status_2005.pdf.

Ibrahim, F. A. (1991). Contribution of cultural worldview to generic counseling and development. *Journal of Counseling & Development, 70*, 13–19.

Ibrahim, F. A., & Kahn, H. (1984). *Scale to assess worldviews*. Unpublished manuscript, University of Connecticut at Storrs.

Ibrahim, F.A., & Kahn, H. (1987). Assessment of world views. *Psychological Reports, 60*(1), 163–176.

Ibrahim, F. A., Ohnishi, H., & Sandhu (1997). Asian-American identity development: South Asian Americans. *Journal of Multicultural Counseling and Development, 25*, 34–50.

Internet World Stats. (2010). *Internet Coaching Library*. Bogota, Colombia: Author. Kluckhohn, C. (1951). Values and value orientations in the theory of action. In T. Parsons & F. A. Shields (Eds.), *Toward a general theory of action* (pp. 388–433). Cambridge, MA: Harvard University Press.

Ladson-Billings, G. (2000). Fighting for our lives: Preparing teachers to teach African American students. *Journal of Teacher Education, 51*, 206–214.

LaFromboise, T. (1982). *Assertion training with Native Americans: Cultural/behavioral issues for trainers*. ERIC Clearinghouse on Rural Education and Small Schools.

Light, H., & Martin, R. (1985). Guidance of American-Indian baseline essays. Their heritage and some contemporary views. *Journal of American Indian Education, 25*, 42–46.

McCadden, B. M. (1998). Why is Michael always getting timed out? Race, class, and disciplining other people's children. In R. E. Butchart & B. McEwan (Eds.), *Classroom discipline in American schools: Problems and possibilities for democratic education* (pp. 109–134). Albany: State University of New York Press. (ED423584).

McCarthy, J. (2005). Individualism and collectivism: What do they have to do with counseling? *Journal of Multicultural Counseling and Development, 33*, 108–117.

Migration Policy Institute. (2008). *American Community Survey*. Washington, DC: Author.

National Center for Educational Statistics. (2009. *Mini digest of educational statistics*. Washington, DC: Author.

National Center for Education Information. (2005). *Profile of teachers in the U.S.* Washington, DC: Author.

Nieto, S. (2000). Placing equity front and center: Some thoughts on transforming teacher education for a new century. *Journal of Teacher Education, 51*, 180–187.

Nieto, S. (2004). *Affirming diversity: The sociopolitical context of multicultural education* (4th ed.). Boston: Allyn & Bacon.

Okun, B. F., Fried, J., & Okun, M. L. (1999). *Understanding diversity: A learning-as-practice primer*. Pacific Grove, CA: Brooks/Cole.

Pew Hispanic Center. (2006). *Foreign-born Hispanics speaking Spanish at home*. Washington, DC: Author.

Prendergast, N. (1985). *A Vietnamese refugee family in the United States from 1975–1985: A case study of education and culture*. Doctoral dissertation, Loyola University, Chicago. University Microfilms International, Ann Arbor, MI.

Randall-David, E. (1989). *Strategies for working with culturally diverse communities and clients*. Rockville, MD: Association for the Care of Children's Health.

Rice, F. P., & Dolgin, K. G. (2002). *The adolescent: Development, relationships, and culture*. Boston: Allyn & Bacon.

Santrock, J. W. (2007). *Adolescence* (11th ed.). Boston: McGraw-Hill.

Schwartz, S. E., Conley, C. A., & Eaton, L. K. (1997). *Diverse learners in the classroom*. New York: McGraw-Hill.

Schwartz, W. (1996). *A guide to communicating with Asian American families*. New York: ERIC Clearinghouse on Urban Education.

Schwartz, W. (2001). *School practices for equitable discipline of African American students*. New York: ERIC Clearinghouse on Urban Education (ED455343).

Shin, H. B., & Bruno, R. (2003). *Language use and speaking ability: 2000*. Census 2000 Brief. Retrieved from http://www.census.gov/prod/2003pubs/c2kbr-29.pdf.

Sleeter, C. E. (2001). Preparing teachers for culturally diverse schools: Research and the overwhelming presence of Whiteness. *Journal of Teacher Education, 52*, 94–106.

Sundberg, N. D. (1981). Cross-cultural counseling and psychotherapy: A research overview. In A. J. Marsella & P. B. Pederson (Eds.), *Cross-cultural counseling and psychotherapy* (pp. 28–62). New York: Pergamon.

Tatum, J., Moseley, S., Boyd-Franklin, N., & Herzog, E. P. (1995, February/March). A home-based, family systems approach to the treatment of African-American teenage parents and their families. *Zero to Three*, 18–25.

Tiedt, P. L., & Tiedt, I. M. (2005). *Multicultural teaching: A handbook of activities, information, and resources* (7th ed.). Needham Heights, MA: Allyn & Bacon.

Uba, I. (1994). *Asian Americans: Personality patterns, identity, and mental health*. New York: Guilford Press.

U.S. Census Bureau. (2001). *Languages spoken in America*. Washington, DC: Author.

U.S. Census Bureau. (2008). *Percent of U.S. Non-White Population*. Washington, DC: Author. U.S. Census Bureau. (2009). *American Community Survey*. Washington, DC: Author.

U.S. Department of Education. (2009a). *American Recovery and Reinvestment Act of 2009: IDEA Recovery Funds for Services to Children and Youths with Disabilities*. Washington, DC: Author.

U.S. Department of Education. (2009b). *School Characteristics and Climate: Student Suspensions and Expulsions*. Washington, DC: Author

Vaughn, S., Bos, C. S., & Schumm, J. S. (2003). *Teaching exceptional, diverse, and at-risk students in the general education classroom* (3rd ed.). Boston: Allyn & Bacon.

Walker, W. D. (1987). *The other side of the Asian academic success myth: The Hmong story*. Qualifying paper, Harvard Graduate School of Education, Boston.

Wardle, F., & Cruz-Janzen, M. I. (2004). *Meeting the needs of multiethnic and multiracial children in schools*. Boston: Allyn & Bacon.

Wikipedia, the free encyclopedia. Retrieved August 17, 2010, from http://en.wikipedia.org/wiki/culture_of_poverty.

Zhang, S. Y., & Carrasquillo, A. L. (1995). Chinese parents' influence on academic performance. *New York State Association for Bilingual Education Journal, 10*, 46–53.

Zirpoli, T. J. (1995). *Understanding and affecting the behavior of young children*. Upper Saddle River, NJ: Merrill/Pearson Education.

Issues in Early Childhood Behavior

Thomas Zirpoli

High quality childcare and early education are critical to the success of two national priorities: Helping families work and ensuring that every child enters school ready to succeed.

—CHILDREN'S DEFENSE FUND (2005)

The importance of understanding and effectively managing the behavior of young children cannot be overemphasized for four primary reasons. First, many caregivers (in this chapter the term *caregiver* will be used to describe parents, early educators, preschool teachers, aides, and other adults who care for young children) report that behavior management is their biggest challenge when working with young children. Yet, many early childhood caregivers receive little or no behavior management education during their preservice training.

Second, appropriate social behaviors are positively correlated with academic performance. Children who have learned how to sit quietly and listen when a story is being read are likely to sit and listen to a story read by educators within a preschool setting. Children who stay on task, listen to their teachers, and follow classroom rules are more likely to be liked by both adults and peers, and succeed in the classroom. Indeed, researchers have identified significant relationships between children's individual characteristics and how adults evaluate children's intelligence, personality, and other attributes (Kilgore, Snyder, & Lentz, 2000).

Third, caregivers should have a good understanding of young children's behavior because of the significant role they play in the development of those behaviors. Young children learn appropriate and inappropriate social skills from many sources. But, for many children, the educational setting provides the only structured setting in which prosocial behaviors are modeled and reinforced. Thus, the caregiver's role in the educational setting may take on additional significance for many children. Also, many early childhood programs are becoming less center based and more home based. Caregivers must be able to model and teach effective behavior management skills to the families they visit and serve.

Lastly, the best time to teach appropriate social behaviors effectively and prevent the development of inappropriate behaviors is when children are young (Dunlap, Strain, Fox et al., 2006).

During these critical years of early development, children establish behavioral patterns while they learn the response value of appropriate and inappropriate behaviors. For example, children who learn at a young age that tantrum behaviors "work" are likely to use them throughout childhood and into adolescence. Thus, it is important to teach children when they are young which behaviors are considered appropriate and which are not, and that appropriate behaviors are reinforced and inappropriate behaviors are not.

EARLY DEVELOPMENT OF BEHAVIOR: THE FIRST TWO YEARS

The Newborn

Newborns are totally dependent on others. For the most part, their behavior is directly related to their physical condition and environment. Newborns cry when they need to be changed, when they are hungry, or when they are in some sort of discomfort. They do not cry to manipulate their parents into giving them excessive attention. In other words, you cannot spoil a newborn. The newborn needs lots of caregiver attention, warmth, and love. He or she will develop a sense of security knowing that there are caregivers willing and able to care for his or her basic needs.

The Infant

Ainsworth (1979) and Bowlby (1982) completed the first extensive studies of attachment in infants. Ainsworth found that mothers of securely attached infants were more responsive to their infants' basic needs and that the infants were more cooperative and less aggressive in their interaction with their mothers than "anxiously attached" infants.

Between the 3rd and 6th months, infants begin to develop an understanding of the relationship between their behavior and responses from others (Ensher & Clark, 1986). About this time, infants may begin to use a variety of behaviors, including crying, simply to seek the attention of others, especially significant others such as parents. At this time, caregivers may begin to regulate their response to these behaviors so that appropriate behaviors are reinforced and inappropriate behaviors are not.

At about 6 months of age, children may exhibit several inconvenient or even irritating behaviors that represent a passage through normal cognitive and motor stages of development. For example, the child may enjoy dropping things from the high chair and looking to see where the object goes. With this simple behavior, the child begins to learn about cause and effect and object permanence. Thus, a 6-month-old child should not be punished for these learning behaviors.

A significant milestone for the 7- to 8-month-old infant is the development of anxiety toward strangers. During this time, the infant demonstrates a strong attachment to the primary caregiver, usually the mother. Parents frequently feel the need to apologize for their child's crying and clinging during separation. Caregivers should be assured that the child is developing normally and understand that, especially during this period, the child needs reassurance and comfort. By the time the infant approaches 18 months, he or she will be able to cope with separation from the primary caregiver. Attachment to many others is evident in their ease at being with other familiar caregivers.

At 6 to 8 months, children want to crawl around and explore (learn). Caregivers should provide safe places for the child to explore rather than confine the child to a playpen or crib for long periods. At 9 to 12 months, the child will be cruising furniture and, by 12 to 18 months, walking. Again, providing a safe environment allows children to explore and develop new cognitive and motor skills.

Feeding time for infants and young children is likely to be challenging for caregivers. At 6 months of age, infants may push the spoon away from the feeder to show that they are finished. Nine-month-olds begin to feed themselves crackers and toast. By 15 months, finger feeding is typical. Being able to use a cup without spilling may be seen by 18 months. The point is that learning to eat and drink is part of normal development, and opportunities for self-feeding should be allowed. Young children are not neat eaters, but rather than punishing them for their messes and spills, caregivers should make cleanup easier by pouring only small amounts of liquids into cups, putting drop cloths under high chairs, and using appropriate child-sized utensils. If children start to throw food or drop it on the floor, remove the food for a short time (2 to 3 minutes) and say, "No throwing food on the floor." Children will soon get the message that this is unacceptable behavior.

The 1-Year-Old

By the end of the 1st year, children begin to show interest in other children. They frequently enjoy being around other children and playing beside them. Expecting a 1-year-old to play with other children, however, is unrealistic. They delight in exploring other children, which may take the form of hair pulling, poking (particularly around the face), and grabbing toys. Putting objects in their mouth is still a primary means of exploration for the 1-year-old—and that may include biting other children. Although these actions may appear to be aggressive, they are simply children's way of exploring their environment.

Language development is a critical component of early development. By the end of the 1st year, the child typically speaks one-word utterances (which consist primarily of nouns) and can name familiar objects such as "bottle," "cup," "milk," "ball," and "mommy." By the second birthday, children are usually capable of speaking two-word utterances such as "mommy go," "kitty run," "bite finger," and "dolly hat." Parents frequently understand the language of their young children even when no one else can. For example, a child who points to the refrigerator and says "milk" is understood by the parent to mean, "Mommy, I'm thirsty. Could you please give me a glass of milk?" Unfortunately, because of limited language development, children are often unable to communicate their wants and needs to caregivers.

Young children who are tired, unhappy, wet, or in need of a hug may become frustrated and express themselves through crying, tantrums, or other means that caregivers judge inappropriate. But caregivers must understand that children may not possess the words to express themselves. Caregivers are usually on the right track to comfort distressed toddlers and try to read the body language that may be saying "I'm tired" or "I'm wet." Providing basic needs such as warmth, food, sleep, and physical contact should be the first intervention when comforting young children.

The 2-Year-Old

By the time children reach their second birthday, they should be on the way to developing an awareness of some basic behaviors considered appropriate and inappropriate. Behavior rules may apply to the home, car, preschool, grocery store, and so on. The toddler learns these rules when caregivers verbally repeat the rules and praise compliance. On the other hand, toddlers learn not to follow rules if they do not clearly understand them and when caregivers are inconsistent with enforcement. For example, young children learn that they must always sit in the car seat when traveling by hearing about the importance of the car seat, consistently using the car seat, and never, under any circumstances, traveling in the car without using the car seat (regardless of crying or other tantrum behaviors).

Young children are quick to learn their limits and their ability to amend the limits established by early educators. It is up to caregivers to set clear limits and be consistent in enforcing them. Children develop an understanding of the word *no* by their first birthday. Caregivers should avoid saying "no" when they do not really mean it. Children quickly learn that the word *no* may have a different meaning for some caregivers. For example, a child may learn that for some caregivers, *no* means "maybe." Around these caregivers, children are likely to be noncompliant and exhibit other challenging behaviors.

As outlined in Table 4.1, during the first 2 years of life, children progress rapidly in many areas. By the end of the 2nd year, the child is beginning to develop a sense of self; however, young children continue to need structure in their environments as much as they need room and freedom to explore. Some early educators believe the two are incompatible; they are not. In fact, young children who feel secure within a structured environment will feel free to explore and take risks within the boundaries established by loving caregivers.

Table 4.1 provides an overview of some of the important behavioral milestones in young children.

TABLE 4.1 Important Behavioral/Social Milestones in Young Children

Behavior	Age of Onset Range (months)
Responds positively to feeding and comforting	B–1
Looks at another face momentarily	B–1
Shows social smile	0.6–3
Quiets with sucking	0.6–3
Shows distress and excitement	0.6–3
Discriminates mother	1–5
Responds with vocal sounds when talked to	1–6
Laughs	3–5
Shows awareness of strange situation	3–6
Discriminates strangers	3–6
Shows interest in mirror image	5–7
Laughs at games (peek-a-boo)	5–7
Cooperates in games	5–12
Resists having a toy taken away	5–12
Plays pat-a-cake	5–12

Behavior	Age of Onset Range (months)
Imitates facial expressions	7–9
Shows stranger anxiety	8–10
Tugs at adult to get attention	8–12
Offers toy to adult	12–16
Demonstrates affection toward others	12–17
Enjoys playing with other children	12–17
Engages in tantrums	12–18
Demonstrates mastery pleasure	12–24
Enjoys listening to simple stories	18–23
Responds to adult praise and rewards	18–23
Follows directions related to daily routines	18–23
Expresses ownership or possession	18–23
Shows jealousy toward others	18–24
Enjoys rough-and-tumble play	18–24
Wants to help with simple jobs	18–24
Develops a sense of self-importance	18–24
Engages in parallel play	18–24
Begins to share toys	20–26
Attempts to comfort others in distress	22–24
Initiates own play activities	24–36
Participates in group play	24–36
Shares property with others	24–36
Engages in dramatic play	24–30
Relates experiences	24–36
Demonstrates parallel and role play	28–32
Helps at little household tasks	36–48
"Performs" for others	36–48
Group play takes place of parallel play	42–50
Shows affection and hostility with peers	46–50
Has many fantasy fears	46–50
Plays cooperatively with other children	48–60
Plays competitive exercise games	48–60
Calls attention to own performance	54–62
Relates fanciful stories	54–62
Shows many real fears	58–62
Increases in organized play with rules	68–76

Sources: Bayley Scales of Infant Development, by N. Bayley, 1993, San Antonio, TX: Psychological Corporation; *Battelle Developmental Inventory,* by J. Newborg, J. R. Stock, & L. Wnek, 1988, Allen, TX: DLM; *Child Development Inventory,* by H. Ireton, 1992, Minneapolis: Behavior Science Systems; *HELP Checklist: Ages Birth to Three Years,* by S. Furuno, K. A. O'Reilly, C. M. Hosaka, T. T. Inatsuka, T. L. Allman, & B. Zeisloft, Palo Alto, CA: VORT; *Vineland Adaptive Behavior Scales II,* by S. Sparrow, D. Balla, & D. Cicchetti, 2005, Circle Pines, MN: American Guidance Service.

ENVIRONMENTAL INFLUENCES ON YOUNG CHILDREN'S BEHAVIOR

More than 24 million children in the United States are age 5 and below (U.S. Census Bureau, 2000). And for all those children, no variable regarding their well-being and overall social behavior is more important than the environment in which they develop and grow.

All children misbehave at times—this, of course, is normal. A caregiver's response to inappropriate behaviors, however, will frequently determine the future course for both the misbehavior and the child. When a caregiver provides attention to a child during a temper tantrum, for example, the child is likely to exhibit tantrum behavior in the future as a means of getting adult attention and having demands met. In fact, the frequency and intensity of tantrums will increase over time as the child learns how to use tantrums to manipulate adult behavior. On the other hand, when a caregiver refuses to give in to a child's demands during and immediately following a temper tantrum, the child is unlikely to demonstrate tantrum behavior in the future. Thus, the relationship is clear between the rate of children's misbehavior and the response they receive from significant caregivers in their environment.

When children misbehave, parents and caregivers frequently focus on assessing and identifying what may be wrong with the *child,* what treatment or intervention might be best for the *child,* and so on. This focus-on-the-child approach, while appropriate for children with specific emotional disorders, fails to recognize the significant role of the child's *environment* and the people in that environment in shaping the child's behavior. In our fast-paced, busy world, parents seem to have less time to devote to the needs of their children than in previous times. Frequently, both teachers and parents look for quick and easy answers to questions regarding children's inappropriate behavior. We believe that the blame-the-victim syndrome places too great an emphasis on how to "fix" children; instead, we need greater emphasis on improving the quality of children's environments.

Young children are exposed to a variety of environmental variables that place them at risk for antisocial behavior. Understanding these variables will help caregivers understand the influences affecting children and their behavior. Specific factors that place children at risk are discussed next.

Poverty

Poverty will be discussed first because it has the most significant impact on children's overall well-being, academic success, and social behavior. Unfortunately, children suffer the highest poverty rates of any age group in America (Lynch, 2004). In 1974, children replaced the elderly as the poorest subgroup of our nation's population. By 1980, the rate of poverty among children was six times that of the elderly (Schorr & Schorr, 1989). Today, 18% American children live in poverty (Annie E. Casey Foundation, 2009).

A family's income plays a significant role in the type of basic care a child receives. For example, children in low-income families have less access (44%) to important early intervention programs than children from higher-income families (65%) (Children's Defense Fund, 2003). Yet, they are the chidren who need early intervention the most!

According to a study by the Illinois State Board of Education (2001), poverty is the single greatest predictor of academic and social failure in U.S. schools. An analysis of state data in Illinois and Kentucky found that income level alone accounted for 71% of the variance in standardized achievement scores. It may surprise some educators to note that additional variables such as English proficiency, student race, class size, and several teacher-related variables accounted for only an additional 7% to the predictability of student performance. And, as Kauffman (2001) points out, academic failure in school is directly related to challenging classroom behavior.

Children raised within impoverished environments are at risk for challenging behavior problems because they are frequently living in neighborhoods where there are limited positive role models for appropriate social behaviors. Frequently, the only adults children see who are making a "decent" living are making it in illegal activities. These children are more likely to be exposed to community violence, and this exposure is positively related to teachers' ratings of children's aggression within the classroom (Farver, Xu, Eppe, Fernandez, & Schwartz, 2005). "As neighborhood conditions worsened, the positive relationship between emotional support and mothers' nurturant parenting was weakened" (Ceballo & McLoyd, 2002, p. 160). As outlined by Walker and Sprague (1999), poverty sets the foundation for a variety of negative outcomes including school failure, delinquency, and violence.

Persistent Parental Unemployment

Poverty among children is directly related to adult unemployment. Indeed, over 24 million American children in 2007 had no parent in their household who worked a full-time job, year-round (Annie E. Casey Foundation, 2009).

The Annie E. Casey Foundation (2005, p. 6) lists several "obstacles that impede parents from steady employment" and thus keep their children in poverty. These include

- an inability to secure affordable and accessible child care,
- low parental literacy levels,
- limited transportation options that make if difficult for parents to commute to available jobs,
- disincentives that strip government benefits from families when they become employed and earn wages,
- parental substance abuse,
- domestic violence,
- a parental history of incarceration preventing them from securing a job, and
- a parental history of mental health disabilities—especially depression.

Single-Parent Families

Second only to poverty, "children in single-parent families are at increased risk for academic failure; increased likelihood of dropping out of high school or becoming a teen parent; and increased levels of depression, stress, anxiety, and aggression" (Annie E. Casey Foundation, 2005, p. 52). Thirty-two percent of American children live in single-parent households (Annie E. Casey Foundation, 2009).

Single-parent homes are not just made up of unmarried mothers. Single fathers make up almost one in five single parents living with their children (U.S. Census Bureau, 2005). Research suggests that boys are less aggressive when a strong father or dominant male is in the home (Vaden-Kiernan, Ialongo, Pearson, & Kellam, 1995). But other factors such as the strength and consistency of parenting provided by the remaining adult, and a variety of other environmental and economic factors, can significantly lower the risk.

In addition, an increasing number of fathers (3.6 million in 2003) are staying home with the kids while Mom goes to work (U.S. Census Bureau, 2005). This is a 54% increase from 1986, and it reflects a new generation of dads who, unlike many of their fathers, believe it is important to play a primary role in the parenting of their children. Thus, teachers are seeing more and more dads at school and parent–teacher conferences.

Regardless of who is providing the parenting, strong parenting and a supportive environment, including the support offered by a child's school, is the key to positive academic and social outcomes for children.

Babies Born Premature and/or Dysmature

A full-term pregnancy is between 37 and 41 weeks. Babies born 37 weeks or less after conception are considered preterm or premature. Those born between 35 and 37 weeks generally do well. Those born before 32 weeks are at risk for a variety of medical and developmental disabilities (Brown, 2004). According to Brown (2004), about 12% of all live births in the United States were born preterm in 2003 and represented a 13% increase from 1993. An additional variable for the increase in preterm births, according to Brown, was the increasing age of new mothers and the increased use of in vitro fertilization.

Also, 8.3 percent of all live births in the United States in 2006 were dysmature or low birth weight babies (less than 2,500 grams or 5.5 pounds; Annie E. Casey Foundation, 2009). Infants born premature and/or dysmature are likely to be especially challenging for parents because of frequent crying and poor sleeping patterns, and being difficult to feed and, in general, to comfort. Crying behavior may be constant and irritating due to the high-pitched nature of the premature child's cry. It is no wonder that these infants are at high risk for maltreatment by caregivers, especially inexperienced, young parents.

Early childhood teachers need to understand that challenging behaviors associated with prematurity and dysmaturity will decrease as the infant develops beyond the normal 9th month of gestation. Patience, support from others, and a sense of humor will get most caregivers through this difficult time. The behavior of most children born prematurely will be consistent with their peers before their second birthday.

Fetal Alcohol Syndrome

First introduced in 1973 by Kenneth Jones and David Smith at the School of Medicine, University of Washington, the term *fetal alcohol syndrome* (FAS) refers to the consumption of too much alcohol by the mother during pregnancy. It is one of the leading preventable causes of disabilities in young children (Fritz, 2000). May and Gossage (2005) estimate a prevalence rate of FAS of 5 to 20 cases per 10,000 births in the United States during the 1980s and 1990s. According to Chavez, Cordero, & Becerra (1989), incidences of FAS per 10,000 total births for different ethnic groups were as follows: Asians, 0.3; Hispanics, 0.8; whites, 0.9; blacks, 6.0; and Native Americans, 29.9.

The long-term detrimental consequences on these children may include permanent neurobehavioral and affective disorders and many other developmental disabilities (Randall, 2001). Fritz (2000) lists the following problems associated with children exposed to excessive alcohol in utero:

- Central nervous system abnormalities
- Impaired motor skills

- Behavior and cognitive abnormalities
- Various physical problems, including heart abnormalities, scoliosis, and hearing impairments

Schonfeld, Mattson, Lang, Delis, and Riley (2001) documented significant deficits in verbal and nonverbal fluency among children with heavy prenatal alcohol exposure.

Lead Poisoning

Although the Center for Disease Control and Prevention (2002) reports that lead in the U.S. population has decreased by 68% between 1991 and 2002, lead poisoning is still "the most common environmental health problem affecting children in the United States" (Enders, Montgomery, & Welch, 2002, p. 20). Lead is a neurotoxic substance that is absorbed through the lungs and stomach. Lead poisoning is the accumulation of too much lead in the body after repeated exposure.

The most common sources of lead poisoning today include lead-based paint found in older homes; lead-laden dust and soil found around old buildings; and lead-based materials such as old plumbing systems, which affect water supplies (Enders et al., 2002). Interestingly, children absorb about half the lead they ingest, while adults absorb only 10%. In addition to their greater absorption rate, young children are at greatest risk from lead poisoning "because of the impact on (their) developing central nervous system" (Enders et al., 2002, p. 20). Children who have elevated lead levels demonstrate a variety of problems, including developmental disabilities and behavioral difficulties.

Child Maltreatment

Child maltreatment, a generic term, may be used to describe physical abuse (20% of child maltreatment), sexual abuse (10%), neglect (60%), and emotional or psychological abuse (5%) (National Association of Counsel for Children (2005). More than 3 million cases of child maltreatment are reported in the United States each year. This figure compares to 1 million cases reported in 1980 (National Clearinghouse on Child Abuse and Neglect Information, 2004).

Clearly, child maltreatment is the ultimate example of a dysfunctional interaction between caregivers and the children in their care. The study of child maltreatment allows researchers to understand the many and interacting variables associated with caregiver–child relationships and interaction patterns. These variables include social and cultural factors, environmental factors, characteristics of the caregiver (parent or early educator), and characteristics of the child or victim (see Zirpoli, 1990, for a complete review of each of these factors).

In addition to the societal consequences of child maltreatment, for the abused child there are physical, psychological, and behavioral consequences. Examples of these consequences, provided by the U.S. Department of Health and Human Services (2008), are given in Table 4.2.

BREAKING THE CYCLE OF CHILD MALTREATMENT   Given the variables associated with child maltreatment, how can teachers and other caregivers help break the cycle? Some solutions require significant changes in national priorities and attitudes. Early educators, however, are in the best position to advocate for these changes.

TABLE 4.2 Selective Outcomes of Child Maltreatment

- Physical consequences range from minor bruises or cuts to broken bones, hemorrhage, or even death. More than 25% of maltreated children placed in foster care for longer than 12 months had recurring health concerns.

- Psychological consequences include both short-term feelings of isolation and fear, and long-term mental health issues such as low self-esteem, depression, and difficulties with relationships. Maltreated children score lower than their nonabused peers on measures of cognition, language development, and overall academic achievement.

- Behavioral consequences of maltreatment are evident throughout the life span. Young victims of abuse are twice as likely to be diagnosed with behavioral disorders. Maltreated children are 25% more likely during their adolescent years to experience delinquency, teen pregnancy, and drug use, and are 11 times more likely to be arrested for criminal behavior. As adults, maltreated children are almost three times more likely than their nonabused peers to be arrested for criminal behavior, including violent crimes. Interestingly, about one-third of abused children will grow up to become abusive adults.

First, we must put an end to the widespread tolerance of physical punishment of children. As professional educators, we can start in our own educational settings. Second, we must advocate a highest-priority status for children and the issues related to their protection and enrichment (physical, mental, and emotional). This stance means full funding for Head Start; the Women, Infants, and Children (WIC) program; and other effective programs that serve impoverished children. Third, we must ensure that all caregivers, regardless of background or income, have the appropriate, necessary community support to provide their children with a protecting, healthy, and enriching environment. Such support means that appropriate prenatal care for *all* women, appropriate medical care for *all* children, and quality early educational settings for *all* children are available, regardless of family income or ability to pay. These are sound investments for the future of our nation's children and for the future of our nation.

THE NEED FOR EARLY INTERVENTION

With 64% of mothers with children under the age of 6 and 77% of mothers with children ages 6 to 17 in the workforce (U.S. Department of Labor, 2004), a majority of children (80%) are receiving at least part-time child care. The proportion of single mothers with jobs has increased from about 58% in 1993 to about 70% in 2003 (Children's Defense Fund, 2005).

About 61% of children birth to age 6, 47% of children in kindergarden through 3rd grade, and 53% of children in fourth through eighth grade spend at least part of their day in an out-of-home child-care setting or early education program (Federal Interagency Forum on Child and Family Statistics, 2009) The most common form of out-of-home child care in 2005 was center-based (24%), followed by care by relatives and care by nonrelatives (Federal Interagency Forum on Child and Family Statistics, 2009). The increase in maternal employment, single-parent families, and families with two working parents are the primary reasons for the greater demand for early childhood programs. For many children, these programs provide early, quality intervention with many beneficial outcomes—for example, the opportunity to develop appropriate social skills necessary for success in school.

Although more children are attending preschool than ever before, the number of children entering kindergarten or first grade without basic readiness skills is also increasing. These readiness skills include basic social behaviors such as listening, compliance, following directions, and staying-in-seat and on-task behaviors. The increasing number of children with behavior problems reported by teachers may be attributed to both the growing number of children living in impoverished environments and without strong parenting at home. These children, along with a growing number of homeless children, represent a new population of preschoolers and young elementary school children with challenging behaviors.

Children considered at risk because of prematurity, low birth weight, alcohol and drug effects, and general poverty are best served early in life. The earlier intervention begins, the better the short- and long-term outcomes for children and their families. Early childhood intervention programs such as Head Start, the Abecedarian Project in North Carolina, and the Chicago Child–Parent Center Program have had and continue to have dramatic effects on the lives of children considered at risk for developmental problems and antisocial behaviors (see Bracey, 2003, for an overview of these programs and others). Unfortunately, due to a lack of full federal funding, many eligible children are unable to participate in Head Start programs.

THE EFFICACY OF EARLY INTERVENTION

According to Bracey (2003, p. 32), the "best known and longest term" study on the efficacy of early intervention is the Perry Preschool Project initiated in 1962 when 58 African Americans were randomly assigned to preschool and 65 to a control group. Students in both groups were then given the same sequence of assessments and interviews over many years. At age 19, the preschool students had higher high school graduation rates and were less likely to need special education services. They also scored higher on standardized assessments. At age 27, 71% of the preschool group completed high school compared with 54% of the control group, 42% of the preschool group had incomes over $2,000 per month compared to only 6% of the control group, and 36% of the preschool students owned homes compared with only 13% of the control group. In addition, the preschool students had more stable marriages, fewer out-of-wedlock births, and fewer arrests.

Campbell, Ramey, Pungello, Sparling, and Miller-Johnson (2002) conducted long-term follow-up studies on 57 children in the Abecedarian Early Childhood Project at the University of North Carolina, Chapel Hill. At age 21, those children who participated in the project through age 5 scored higher on IQ, reading, and math tests; were more likely to graduate from a 4-year college; delayed parenting; and were more likely to be successfully employed. Regarding behavior, the Abecedarian children were less likely to smoke and use illegal drugs, but no less likely to use alcohol.

In more recent studies of the long-term effects of Early Head Start, Love, Kisker, Ross, Raikes, Constantine, Boller et al. (2005) found that providing services to low-income families with infants and toddlers has multiple outcomes for parents and children. They found that when families participated in the Early Head Start program: (a) children were more engaged with parents, (b) children had fewer negative interactions in play situations, (c) children were less aggressive, (d) parents were more emotionally support-ive of their children, and (e) parents provided more language development than parents and children in control groups.

Variables Associated with Effective Early Intervention

Quality early childhood programs have several major components. First, the earlier services are provided, the better the outcome for child and family. Beard and Sugai (2004) studied the effectiveness of First Steps to Success, an early intervention program involving a partnership between parents and teachers of elementary school children at risk for antisocial behavior. They found that "if interventions are implemented in the early elementary years, the likelihood of preventing future antisocial behavior is improved" (p. 396).

Second, effective programs have a low caregiver-to-child ratio, with no more than sixteen to twenty 3- to 5-year-olds for every two adults (National Association for the Education of Young Children, 1997).

Third, programs that involved parents and combined center-based and home-based services and supports provided the best results for parents and children (Love et. al., 2005). Professional caregivers must work with parents as *partners* in their children's de-velopment, and effective programs provide services, especially training, to the parents in addition to the children (Beard & Sugai, 2004; Hancock, Kaiser, & Delaney, 2002).

POSITIVE BEHAVIORAL SUPPORTS FOR YOUNG CHILDREN

Establishing a Caring and Loving Environment

Children need to know that they are loved and accepted. Even very young children de-velop an understanding about how caregivers feel about them. They listen to what care-givers say to them and to others about them, and they observe how caregivers behave. Children who feel secure in their environment and in their relationships with caregivers are less likely to misbehave as a way of getting inappropriate attention.

When a child misbehaves, caregivers are likely to focus on the child and the child's behavior in an effort to stop the inappropriate behavior and prevent its recurrence. It may be difficult for the caregiver to understand how the environment may be a contributing factor to the misbehavior. Environmental variables that may contribute to the misbehavior include the following:

- The behavior of the caregiver (e.g., is misbehavior reinforced?)
- The behavior of others in the environment (e.g., how do peers respond to the child's behavior?)
- Factors relating to the environment in which the child exhibits the behavior (e.g., physical environment, classroom curriculum, cognitive and social demands)

We will look at three suggestions as to how caregivers can demonstrate to young children that they are loved, liked, and accepted.

TELL STUDENTS YOU LIKE THEM A caregiver cannot assume that children know some-one likes them—you must tell them! Caregivers should get into the daily habit of telling children they are liked, especially after appropriate behavior. Some caregivers may have

Most of all, children need to know that they are loved by the significant adults in their lives.

a very difficult time saying "I like you" or expressing positive feelings to the children placed in their care. If expressing feelings in this way becomes part of the daily routine, however, caregivers will find it becomes easier to do so. Children should leave their educational setting saying, "My teacher really likes me!"

Families who communicate their feelings about each other when children are young will have an easier time expressing feelings when the children become adolescents. Thus, efforts to communicate affection when children are young provide an investment for future parent–child communication patterns.

Educators can help children establish healthy attitudes about expressing their feelings in the classroom. Talking about feelings and giving children opportunities to talk about how they feel teach children that their feelings are real and part of being a person. They also give educators a chance to teach children how to identify, be sensitive to, and respect the feelings of others. These lessons will help provide a solid foundation for the development of appropriate social skills.

SET ASIDE INDIVIDUAL TIME   Set aside some special time, if only a few minutes per day, with each child. Use this time to talk and listen to the child and to let that child know how important he or she is. These private conversations also give children a chance to express any feelings, concerns, or reactions to the day's events. Moreover, regardless of how difficult the day has been for both of you, this special time provides an opportunity for at least one positive caregiver–child interaction.

Many children do not have a significant adult in their lives outside the school environment. They may live in a single-parent household with a parent who is busy and preoccupied with trying to support the family. We all know how important it is for children to have one special adult to talk to, share their feelings, and provide positive feedback and support. Often that adult is a teacher or counselor from the child's school. Educators need to be aware of these social needs and willing to give some time (even a few minutes each day) to show a student that someone cares.

GIVE CHILDREN AFFECTION   With all the attention to and appropriate concern about the sexual abuse of children, some caregivers are hesitant to touch, hug, or otherwise express affection toward the children in their care. Some schools have even told educators not to touch their students. This reaction is very unfortunate. Children need affection to develop normally and to be emotionally happy and secure. Children in today's society spend more and more time out of their homes and away from loving parents. Thus, the affection of other caregivers becomes even more crucial, especially for infants and young children. Schools are encouraged to develop policies that also outline acceptable touching (e.g., pats on the shoulders, handshakes).

BUILDING SELF-ESTEEM IN YOUNG CHILDREN   Children who have healthy self-esteem are usually happy children who feel good about themselves and others. Happy, self-assured children are likely to interact positively with caregivers and other children. In addition to its social and behavioral benefits, healthy self-esteem is positively related to academic achievement.

Demonstrating to children that they are loved, liked, and accepted is the first step to building their self-esteem. We can now look at some specific suggestions for increasing children's self-esteem.

ALLOW AND ENABLE CHILDREN TO BE COMPETENT   Hendrick (1990) states that "the purpose of early education is to foster competence in young children" (p. 4). *Competence* is the self-assured feeling that one is capable of doing something "all by myself." Teachers and parents alike can help children participate in competence-building activities by allowing them to do things for themselves. Caregivers who provide opportunities for children to wash dishes after snacks or meals at low sinks or who give preschoolers jobs (e.g., feeding the family dog, being the leader at school) are providing children with opportunities to feel competent.

TELL CHILDREN ABOUT THE GOOD THINGS THEY DO   Too often caregivers focus on children's *inappropriate* behaviors instead of *appropriate* behaviors. When this happens, children are taught to associate caregiver attention with inappropriate behaviors. As a result, inappropriate behaviors increase. Unfortunately, it seems easier to focus on inappropriate behaviors than appropriate behaviors. Caregivers must make every effort to give greater attention to the appropriate things children do. This can be accomplished by telling children, "You're such a good worker" or "I like the way you played with John," or "I like the way you solved that problem with Mary." Make it a point to attend to the good things children are doing. Teach the children that there is an association between caregiver attention and *appropriate* behavior.

SPEAK TO CHILDREN APPROPRIATELY   Many caregivers do not understand how their own behaviors teach appropriate and inappropriate behaviors to children. Caregivers influence children's learning every time they interact with them. Two things are important to keep in mind when speaking to children. First, *what* you say is important. Sarcastic, negative statements promote feelings of worthlessness. If a child does something inappropriate and you must say something, talk about the *behavior,* not the child. Although their behaviors may sometimes be bad, *children* are never bad. To maintain a child's dignity and self-worth, describe what the child did that you dislike, but do not criticize the child as a person. Inappropriate statements from a significant caregiver may severely damage a child's self-esteem.

Second, *how* you speak to children is very important. Some caregivers believe that the louder they shout, the more effective they will be in changing children's behaviors. However, talking to children firmly, but calmly, is more effective in both the short- and long-term. In addition, when caregivers stop shouting, the environment becomes a calmer place for children to learn and develop. Children exhibit less inappropriate behavior within calm, positive environments where they are getting lots of attention for appropriate behaviors (Hetherington & Martin, 1986).

TEACH CHILDREN THAT MISTAKES ARE NORMAL   Everybody makes mistakes. When children make mistakes, tell them that everyone errs and that no one is perfect. Caregivers have opportunities to model appropriate ways to deal with mistakes whenever they commit an error—for example, by saying, "I was wrong and I am sorry." Children who observe this behavior are more likely to say "I was wrong" or "I am sorry" when they make mistakes because they will feel confident that it is alright to make errors. Also, children will not be afraid to try new things when they are not worried about making mistakes.

Teaching young children that it is normal to make mistakes and to talk about them will help them confront and talk about mistakes as adolescents and adults. Being able to say "I was wrong and I am sorry" will serve as a functional behavior throughout the child's life and across all social settings.

ALLOW CHILDREN TO HAVE LIMITED CHOICES   Children will learn how to make good choices if they are allowed to practice making choices from an early age. Some choices young children can make include selecting books or stories to read before bedtime, choosing juice to drink during snack time, deciding what clothes to wear, and so on. As demonstrated in Classroom Connection 4.1, giving children limited choices is an excellent way to reduce power struggles. Caregivers frequently feel that, to be in control of children's behavior, they must resort to giving directives. Sometimes, directives are appropriate; however, young children who are struggling to develop their independence may respond negatively to a lack of choices, leading to a cycle of caregiver-versus-child battles. Of course, caregivers should limit the range of choices. For example, when we say that children may decide what to drink, the caregiver first limits the choice ("Do you want orange juice or apple juice?"). In this way, mature adults remain in control while providing opportunities for children to make safe choices.

Everyday events provide opportunities to discuss choices. For example, when children fight over a toy, caregivers can use the event to help children think about alternative behaviors and choose appropriate behaviors on their own. Asking questions about their behaviors (e.g., "Can you think of another way of telling her that you want to play with that toy?") and giving them an opportunity to explore alternatives and consider the consequences of their behaviors ("How do you think he would feel about that?") are other ways to teach children how to make choices about their behaviors.

CLASSROOM CONNECTION 4.1
Fighting Over Toys

Kelly has been a preschool teacher for 3 years. She has learned that fighting over toys is usually the result of a lack of desirable toys within the preschool environment, a crowded room, and/or a disorganized room. In Kelly's program, she limits the number of children in each play zone. This is done in several ways. For example, she places only four chairs around the blocks table. The play dough table has three chairs, three rolling pins, and three cutters. Kelly's book center has five carpet squares for children to sit on while reading. The children in her class know that if the chairs or carpet squares are taken, they must move to another play area. Also, the children are encouraged to move from one play center to another.

Kelly sets up her play areas differently each day to allow her to introduce a variety of play materials. She places herself and her assistants throughout the room to allow adequate supervision. With this arrangement, Kelly's preschoolers have opportunities to play with many different toys and materials that are desirable.

Still, fights over toys may occur. Kelly encourages the children to ask for toys when another child has something they want. She also teaches them the concept of trading one toy for another. If a child is still aggressive, however, Kelly removes the child from the play area for a specific time period (a few minutes) and remembers to reinforce the child when he or she is observed playing appropriately. Most important, Kelly remembers to verbally reinforce all the children when they are playing appropriately. In Kelly's class, you will frequently hear her say, "I like the way you guys are sharing with your friends!"

General Reflection on Classroom Connection 4.1:

What do you think of Kelly's strategy of having a limited number of chairs or carpet squares at each play station within her preschool? Do you think she should have specific time limitations for children at each play station? Kelly has a lot of toys that she rotates in and out of storage. Should some toys (e.g., Legos) always be available? Which ones?

Hendrick (1990) notes that children who are allowed to make choices are more creative. She says that "for an experience to be creative for children, it must be generated from within them, not be an experience 'laid on' from outside" (p. 250). For example, rather than providing children with coloring books during art activities in a classroom, the teacher could provide collage materials for children to create their own original artwork. Sometimes, caregiver-directed activities provide limited opportunities for problem solving. Indeed, children who are given choices may have an advantage when it comes to solving problems related to their social behavior. For example, the child who divides and shares blocks with a friend is able to plan a solution to the problem (i.e., both children wanting to play with blocks), rather than acting on the immediate impulse to be possessive.

LET CHILDREN KNOW YOU VALUE THEIR OPINIONS   When children are reinforced for expressing their own opinions, they learn the value of their personhood, in addition to the value of their feelings, beliefs, and opinions. Children can be encouraged to develop their own feelings and ideas and to express their own opinion when caregivers ask, "What do you think?" or "How do you feel about that?" These kinds of queries let children know that they (and their feelings) are important, too. In addition, this is a great way to teach and practice how to interact and converse appropriately with adults and other children.

VARIABLES ASSOCIATED WITH APPROPRIATE BEHAVIOR IN YOUNG CHILDREN

Several variables are associated with appropriate behavior in young children, including the level of adult supervision, consistency of consequences, readiness for academic achievement, and environmental considerations. The absence of these variables has been found to place children at risk for antisocial behaviors.

Supervision

The strongest predictor of appropriate behavior in children is the quantity and quality of caregiver supervision (Kauffman, 2001; Lewis, Colvin, & Sugai, 2000). When caregivers monitor children's behavior—where the children play and with whom their children play—they are showing children that they care about their well-being, that there are specific physical and behavioral boundaries, and that there are caregivers who will monitor their safety.

Caregivers must strive for a healthy balance between restrictiveness and permissiveness. When caregivers are overly restrictive, children tend to be submissive, dependent, and unable to take risks. When caregivers are overly permissive, children tend to be noncompliant, delinquent, and careless. A lack of caregiver supervision is also related to children's association with property destruction (e.g., breaking toys) and student misbehavior during school transition periods (Colvin, Sugai, Good, & Lee, 1997). Hetherington and Martin (1986) state that children will have positive outcomes when parental discipline is firm and consistent, yet loving and responsive.

Consistency

Perhaps the most significant variable in managing young children's behavior is consistency. "Consistency helps make an environment predictable" (Bailey & Wolery, 1984, p. 242). Consistency builds understanding and trust between caregivers and children. Children learn what to expect and what is acceptable and unacceptable behavior when caregivers are consistent in what they say and how they respond. Children learn the likely consequences for their behaviors when caregivers consistently follow through.

In the absence of consistency, children are likely to be rebellious when caregivers finally do try to respond to inappropriate behaviors. Children tend to be noncompliant with caregivers who are inconsistent because they have learned that the caregiver doesn't always mean what they say or say what they mean. Caregivers who are inconsistent when disciplining children tend to be harsh and hostile because they are frustrated by their children's lack of compliance. In fact, they have taught their children not to listen to them by not following through in a consistent manner. This inconsistent and hostile relationship is associated with children's aggressive, noncompliant, and delinquent behavior.

Readiness Skills

When young children enter school, at either the preschool or kindergarten level, educators have certain expectations about their skills and behavior. Unfortunately, many young children do not have the skills or behaviors to meet even minimal teacher expectations. The potential outcome for these children includes social and academic failure, poor relationships with educators and peers, and the risk of falling further and further behind the norm throughout their school years.

Parents and early childhood caregivers can improve the chances of success for young children entering school by teaching them basic readiness skills, including appropriate

- social interactions with caregivers (listening, compliance, following directions);
- social interactions with peers (sharing, playing, turn taking); and
- environmental behaviors (use of toys and other materials, in-seat behavior, attention to environmental cues).

Caregivers teach these skills through verbal instructions and practice. We have already provided the example of children who have been read to from an early age; they are likely to sit and listen when caregivers read a story within an educational setting. Sitting and listening are not just behaviors; they are skills that children must learn to succeed in school. Children who learn to share and cooperate from an early age are likely to get along with their peers in later years. Children who learn to take care of their toys and not to be destructive are likely to generalize these skills and behaviors to the school environment. These children will be ready to learn and ready to expand their social relationships with new caregivers and peers.

Environmental Considerations

Both teachers and parents alike need to realize the importance of environmental influences on young children's behavior. The purpose of considering these influences is to establish an environment that serves to *prevent* inappropriate behaviors in preschoolers (McEvoy, Fox, & Rosenberg, 1991; Nordquist & Twardosz, 1990). Of course, prevention is the best form of intervention. While structuring the physical environment, one should keep in mind that the preschool child is struggling to become independent yet still requires caregivers' close support and guidance. Although the preschool setting is the most typical educational environment outside the home, the passage of Public Law 99-457 in 1989 has promoted the provision of early childhood services within the context of the family. Thus, many early childhood intervention programs are home based.

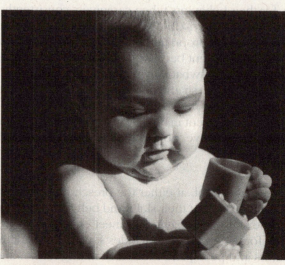

The behaviors of young children are shaped by a variety of internal and environmental influences.

THE EDUCATIONAL SETTING FOR YOUNG CHILDREN

Rimm-Kaufman, LaParo, Downer, and Pianta (2005) studied setting and quality variables in the classrooms of 250 kindergarten students and found that "children's on-task and off-task behavior and aggression toward peers varied as a function of the teachers' choice of classroom setting" (p. 377). Several variables related to the environment influence behavior within educational settings: social density, the physical layout, appropriate use of materials, effective scheduling, transitions, and staffing qualifications and ratios (Zirpoli, 1995).

Social Density

Social density refers to the number of children within the educational setting. Crowded settings are associated with less caregiver availability and responsiveness (Dunst, McWilliam, & Holbert, 1986), less positive social interaction among children (Evans, 2001; Legendre, 2003), less cooperation with peers (Rimm-Kaufman et al., 2005), and higher stress levels in children (Legrendre, 2003). While most states have minimum space requirements for early childhood settings, these requirements provide only minimum standards, not recommended or state-of-the-art standards.

Throughout the day, many children feel overwhelmed by high levels of activity, noise, or ongoing contact with other children and caregivers. Providing safe, cozy areas for time alone is encouraged. Beanbag chairs, rocking chairs, cushioned areas with tape recorders and earphones, book nooks, and lofts can provide a great escape for young children. Sand and water tables are frequently effective for calming an overstimulated child. The soothing, tactile sensation of warm water on the hands is a great stress reducer for many children.

Physical Layout

The physical layout should be safe, alleviating too many restrictions set by the teacher. It should be divided into activity areas or learning centers, which include areas for art, dramatic play, science, language arts, sand and water play, music, manipulatives, and other games. Also, preschool programs must have areas for nap time, toileting, and eating, and space for children's personal belongings.

The physical layout should include separate active and quiet activity spaces, which will prevent play from one area affecting activities in other areas. At the same time, quiet activities should be in close proximity of other quiet activities. Quiet activity areas provide a place where children can retreat or pull themselves together when feeling overwhelmed from too much activity or involvement with many others. These include spots for reading, listening to tapes, and enjoying art activities.

By separating and defining play spaces, caregivers can eliminate many inappropriate behaviors. Tables, shelving, room dividers, and other furniture can create physical boundaries as the simplest way of defining separate activity areas. Importantly, caregivers should avoid large, open spaces that invite children to run around within the classroom. These activities, of course, should be promoted in more appropriate settings such as the gym or playground.

Caregivers should also limit the number of children per activity area to decrease the incidence of children fighting over space, toys, or other materials (Zirpoli, 1995). The following methods can help limit the number of children per activity area:

- *Chairs:* Place a specific number of chairs at an activity table that corresponds to the number of children allowed at that table at a time.

- **Tickets:**   Use tickets to limit the number of children allowed to enter an activity area. For example, four tickets could be placed in slots at the bottom of the ladder of a loft. If a ticket is available at the bottom of the stairs, the child may enter the loft. The child must take the ticket at the bottom of the ladder, take it to the top of the ladder, and place the ticket in the appropriate slot provided before entering the loft. When the child leaves the loft, the child returns the ticket in the original slot at the bottom of the ladder, indicating to other children that they may enter the loft.

- **Carpet Squares:**   The number of carpet squares may correspond to the number of children allowed to play in a specific activity area. For example, a block area designed for two children would have only two carpet squares on the floor within this play space. When both carpet squares are occupied, other children understand that they must select another activity.

- **Pictures:**   Pictures of children playing paired with a corresponding number of children who may enter an area can be laminated and placed on the wall or table near an activity. For example, a playhouse door may have a picture of two children playing alongside the number "2," indicating that a maximum of two children are allowed in the playhouse at a time.

- **Small Rugs:**   A bucket of small rugs may be used to define individual work and play spaces. A child may roll out a rug on the floor where she intends to play with a toy or other material. Other children understand that when a child is on one of these rugs, she wishes to be alone. When the individual play is finished, the child returns the materials to the appropriate place and the rug to the bucket. This is a great way to give children permission to play alone while a variety of group activities are available throughout the classroom (Zirpoli, 1995, p. 130).

Appropriate Use of Materials

The appropriate use of materials within the preschool environment means providing opportunities for children to explore the environment independently with challenging yet age-appropriate materials. Young preschoolers are usually just beginning to share toys at playtime. Caregivers who expect children to share toys without guidance have unrealistic expectations. Children in a preschool class typically sit alongside one another but play by themselves. The teacher can facilitate the children's learning to respect others and their playthings.

Many schools use small carpet squares or rugs on which children sit and place their play materials (Bailey & Wolery, 1984). The children are taught that they must wait for materials to be placed back on the shelf or ask permission to play with materials. Children are more likely to ask or allow other children to share playthings on "their" rug if they are not forced to share and if they are given time when they may play with the materials alone. With limited and preferred items, caregivers may use timers. Children are usually compliant in turning over playthings to others when their time is up as long as the same rule applies to the other children as well.

Specific materials may be selected to promote desired behaviors. For example, playing with play dough or fingerpaint and listening to story tapes or quiet music are calming activities. Calming activities may be used prior to circle or story time to encourage appropriate behavior.

Effective Scheduling

One cannot discuss environmental factors in the classroom without addressing the issue of scheduling. Young children are likely to be more comfortable in the preschool classroom if they know what to expect. By following routines, children learn to expect snacks, free time, group times, stories, outdoor play, lunch, nap time, and so on. McEvoy et al. (1991) recommend that the preschool schedule "be divided into short time segments, depending on the length of the child's attention span and the nature of the activity" (p. 21). Schedules should follow the child's natural rhythm. Active play and group times should occur when children are well rested and fed. Passive and quiet activities, such as story time, should be used when children are tired or as a means of entertaining children during transition times (e.g., waiting for parents to pick up the child from school).

In the typical preschool classroom, a great portion of the child's day is spent waiting for an activity to begin, waiting for an activity to end, waiting in line to go to the bathroom, and waiting for others to settle down quietly for group times. These frequent transitions are one of the high-risk periods for behavior problems. Young children have great difficulty sitting quietly and waiting for long durations. Finding ways to reduce transition periods can significantly lessen behavioral problems in the classroom.

Rather than insisting that children be seated quietly before beginning group activities such as story times, teachers should instruct children to join the group for story time and begin reading when most are seated. Beginning a group activity with familiar songs or active finger plays will entice most children. When young children demonstrate a lack of interest in an activity, the teacher should be flexible and change the activity. McEvoy and Brady (1988) suggest that children rotate through activities independently rather than as a group. McWilliam, Trivette, and Dunst (1985) note a positive relationship between the level of a child's engagement with the environment and the efficacy of early intervention, including appropriate behavior. Small-group, child-directed activities rather than large-group, teacher-directed activities generally are recommended when trying to reduce the amount of transition time and to prevent disruptive behavior during the transition.

Transitions

Transition periods can be a source of problem behaviors. Hurrying children during transition times is likely to cause some behavior problems, so planning and giving children warnings will be helpful. For example, when moving children from one situation (e.g., a play activity) to another (getting ready for lunch), scheduling time for putting toys away and washing hands will save caregivers the need to rush the children and will be a warning to children that they are about to move to a different activity. Caregivers must be sensitive to the needs of children who, based on their developmental age, will need varying degrees of time to move from one activity to another. As Classroom Connection 4.2 shows, allowing for some transition time and advance preparation will decrease the challenges.

Staffing Qualifications and Ratios

Early childhood caregivers must be knowledgeable about young children's physical, cognitive, and social-behavioral development. They must understand the difference between inappropriate and age-appropriate behaviors. Most important, they must be knowledgeable about responding to children's behaviors. Teachers' expectations for young children

CLASSROOM CONNECTION 4.2
Making Transitions Fun with Young Children

Susan is a preschool teacher who knows that transition periods are difficult for young preschoolers. Thus, she tries to prepare her students in advance of any transition. For example, when it is getting close to the time when the children must clean up after a play period, she shows them that she is setting the timer and tells them, "When the bell rings in 5 minutes, it will be cleanup time."

When the timer bell rings, Susan uses a song to indicate that it is cleanup time. Like most young children, her children love to sing. By singing through the transition time, Susan gives the children something to do while they put their materials away. She frequently includes the children's names in the songs. For example, "I like the way that Julia is cleaning, and I like the way that Josh is putting his toys away" are made part of the song. Susan tries to ignore the children who are not following the directions, and, by including them in the song, she gives the children who are following directions lots of attention.

Susan also plays games with students to make transitions fun. For example, after a storytelling period about a caterpillar turning into a butterfly, she has the children pretend that they are caterpillars who are asleep in their cocoons waiting to become butterflies and fly away. She then tells the students that when she touches them on their shoulders, they become butterflies and they can fly away to the snack table—the next activity. One by one, she touches each student, and they fly away to the next activity.

General Reflection on Classroom Connection 4.2:

Susan certainly knows how to have fun with her students! How much of a factor do you believe a teacher's personality has in managing a classroom full of preschoolers? And when children are having fun, what effect do you think that has on their compliance and general interaction with other students? Can we teach teachers to have fun?

are often too high. For example, teaching readiness skills, such as sitting and listening, are frequently overdone during the traditional "circle time" or group activities.

Classrooms should be active places where young minds can explore and young bodies can exercise. Group times should be fun but optional. If activities are inviting and stimulating, young children will readily join in song or story time. In many settings, however, there is considerable variance in children's developmental levels. Hence, not all children will be able to sit or be interested in the same materials. Small groups, whenever possible, are recommended. Reading times should not only be shared during large group times but also incorporated throughout the day on a one-to-one basis.

As with space density discussed earlier, minimum standards for child–caregiver ratios do not match state-of-the-art standards. They are what they are called: minimum standards. In many states, these standards are, at best, inappropriate. Table 4.3 outlines the National Association for the Education of Young Children (2005) recommended child–caregiver ratios per age and group size.

Supervision is one of the most important variables related to appropriate and inappropriate behavior in young children. The quantity and quality of staff supervision is a variable that may be manipulated to prevent inappropriate behaviors. In comparisons of one-to-one and zone staffing patterns, the zone arrangement was found to be superior in early studies by Dunst et al. (1986). When using zone staffing for supervision,

> caregivers are assigned activities or areas within the environment to supervise. Children are free to move to different activities within the classroom rather than wait for other children to finish activities. In the zone method, it is advisable to space staff throughout the classroom unless a group activity is scheduled. (Zirpoli, 1995, p. 148)

TABLE 4.3 Recommended Child–Caregiver Ratio per Children's Age and Group Size

Children	Age Range	Group Size	Ratio
Infants	Up to 15 months	6	1:3
Infants	Up to 15 months	8	1:4
Toddlers	12–28 months	6	1:3
Toddlers	12–28 months	8–12	1:4
Toddlers	21–36 months	8	1:4
Toddlers	21–36 months	10	1:5
Toddlers	21–36 months	12	1:6
Preschoolers	30–48 months	12	1:6
Preschoolers	30–48 months	14	1:7
Preschoolers	30–48 months	16	1:8
Preschoolers	30–48 months	18	1:9
Preschoolers	48 months +	16	1:8
Preschoolers	48 months +	18	1:9
Preschoolers	48 months +	20	1:10
Preschoolers	60 months +	16	1:8
Preschoolers	60 months +	18	1:8
Preschoolers	60 months +	20	1:9
Kindergarten	60 months +	20	1:10
Kindergarten	60 months +	22	1:11
Kindergarten	60 months +	24	1:12

Source: Information from The National Association for the Education of Young Children (2005).

Other recommendations for setting up the preschool environment to promote appropriate behavior and prevent inappropriate behavior are provided in Classroom Connection 4.3.

In summary, environmental modifications suggested for the prevention of inappropriate behaviors include these:

- Allow adequate room for children to move within activity areas and from one area to the next. Children should not feel that they have to fight for their physical space.
- Employ rules that will reduce fighting over materials.
- Reduce transition or waiting times for activities—plan for transition.
- Keep children busy—busy children have little time for inappropriate behaviors.
- Provide a predictable and consistent environment through effective scheduling.
- Engage children in interesting activities at their developmental levels.
- Reinforce appropriate behaviors.
- Maintain a safe environment for children. Such a setting reduces the frequency of having to say, "No," "Don't touch that," "Stay away from there," and so on.
- Allow children to rotate through activities independently rather than as a group.
- Promote competence, confidence, and independence.
- Give children simple, age-appropriate responsibilities.
- Use daily rituals and routines to help make the home setting predictable and comforting.

CLASSROOM CONNECTION 4.3
Organization for the Preschool Environment

Lisa is a preschool teacher, and with school about to begin in a couple of weeks, organizing her classroom is her top priority. Lisa wants to arrange her classroom setting so that it is inviting and supportive. Most important, she wants to arrange the classroom setting so that the room encourages appropriate behavior.

She starts by putting compatible interest centers near each other. For example, she makes sure that the block area is not next to the quiet book/music area. Next, she makes sure that each area is well defined, as it is important that her children know where the art area begins and ends. Lisa decides to use small room dividers, carpet squares, and tape on the floor to designate her areas. Her children will have these cues to assist them in remembering to keep the crayons, blocks, and other materials in their assigned area.

Finally, Lisa sets up the room so that she can easily scan the room and see all of the children at all times. This is important to her because she wants to be able to intervene immediately in situations where she is needed.

After her room is set up, Lisa makes a schedule of activities. The schedule is important to her for two reasons. First, it will help her structure the day, as much as possible, for the children. Second, it will help her and her aides know where they should be and when. Free-play activities are the primary activity on her schedule. In addition, small- and large-group activities are also scheduled.

Lisa will allow her children to move through activities individually. For example, during a small-group activity such as pasting or coloring, some children will finish before other children, and she believes that they should be allowed to leave an activity as they finish. In addition, during free play she will encourage her children to practice skills that were introduced to them during the small- and large-group activities.

Next, Lisa orders materials to support her scheduled activities. She tries to select many materials that are prosocial or that require children to play cooperatively. For example, she orders lots of puzzles and building blocks. Lisa plans to rotate the toys in her classroom to keep them fresh and interesting. Thus, only some of the toys will be out on the shelves at the same time. Finally, she will place some very desirable materials on a shelf out of the children's reach. She knows that while the children will be able to see the toys, they will have to ask us for the toy or find a friend with whom to share a toy. This is one of her strategies to encourage language and social skills development.

Lastly, Lisa will assign her staff to certain areas of the classroom rather than assigning children to staff. By using a "zone" coverage strategy, Lisa and her staff will be able to work with an individual child when he or she enters a certain area of the classroom. In this way, Lisa and her aides will be able to work with all the children.

Lisa knows that not all of her children's inappropriate behaviors will disappear in a well-organized classroom. However, she is determined to eliminate many problems related to classroom disorganization. She will do everything she can to reduce or eliminate waiting time or downtime. She plans to be ready for her children when an activity begins. In addition, while her free-play setting may look like "free choice" to the children, Lisa will set up each area to help children practice important skills. For Lisa, having an organized classroom environment helps her and her staff work more effectively with all the children, regardless of their behavioral needs.

General Refection on Classroom Connection 4.3:

What other classroom organizational strategies can you recommend for the preschool teacher?

- Allow children to have special things they do not have to share. Encourage—do not force—children to share.

CAREGIVER–PARENT RELATIONSHIPS

The role of professional caregivers in facilitating positive and effective parent–child interactions cannot be overstated. When teachers and others make positive comments to parents regarding their children, parents tend to feel good about their child and to interact with him or her more frequently and positively. On the other hand, when teachers make many negative comments to parents about a child, parents tend to feel negatively about their child and interact with him or her less frequently and positively (Bell & Harper, 1977; Zirpoli & Bell, 1987).

Unfortunately, some teachers tend to regard parents and parental involvement in mainly negative terms. Instead of viewing parents as partners in the challenge of educating children, some teachers tend to perceive parents as an obstacle to their work (Williams & Chavkin, 1985). Other teachers complain that because they have so many students, they just don't have the time to work with parents. For example, the Michigan Education Association (2005) reports that the average teacher in Michigan teaches 105 students and has regular communication with only 16% of parents.

Teachers must understand, however, that there are significant gains to be had from encouraging parental involvement and helping them develop positive parent–child interactions. Indeed, training parents how to communicate, interact with, and manage the behavior of their preschool children has a positive influence on parent–child interactions in the home, which in turn, produces healthier outcomes for young children (Campbell, 1995; Delaney & Kaiser, 2001; Hancock et al., 2002). And, as parents became more interested and involved in their children's school and achievement, their children's attitudes and achievement also improved (Sattes, 1985).

Parents tend to reduce contact with teachers who always have "bad" news about their child's current performance or behavior. For example, parents may stop attending teacher–parent conferences if they consistently hear only negative news about their child. A good rule of thumb for teachers is to balance negative statements to parents with at least an equal number of positive statements. For example, when talking to parents about their child's inappropriate behavior, mention situations during which the child's behavior was appropriate. Try to make parents feel good about their children. Be supportive. Parenting is a difficult job even with well-behaved children. Parenting a child who has

Children need strong parents to guide their social development.

challenging behaviors may be all that a parent can handle. Adding to the parents' already stressful feelings and anxiety about the child's behavior will not be helpful.

When parents do not maintain contact with teachers or are not supportive, teachers should take the initiative to contact parents. These initiatives may go unrewarded, and parents may continue to be unresponsive; nonetheless, it is still the teacher's professional responsibility to maintain regular, positive contact with the students' home environments. Although teachers may not realize or perceive any significant outcomes from these efforts, they must understand the potential positive influence these efforts have on parent–child relationships.

Summary

With more and more young children attending some form of day care service, preschool, or early childhood intervention program, an understanding of some special behavioral considerations for newborns, infants, and young children is necessary. In addition, a new and growing problem with premature infants and infants born addicted to drugs (and related behaviors) is emerging. Research has demonstrated the effectiveness of early intervention in helping children develop academic readiness and appropriate social skills. Effective early intervention programs are integrated, comprehensive, normalized, adaptable, family referenced, and outcome based.

For the most part, the behavior of newborns is directly related to their physical situation and environment. Their cry is their primary means of communication to significant others. As infants develop, their understanding of the relationship between their behavior and the behavior of others increases. By their second birthday, young children are developing an awareness of appropriate versus inappropriate behavior. Much of their behavior is shaped by how well caregivers establish limits and guidelines.

Premature and dysmature infants may be especially challenging for caregivers. Drugs, alcohol, and lead also place children at risk for developmental and behavioral problems. Poverty is, perhaps, the greatest handicap facing children in the United States. Indeed, 18% of all American children live in poverty.

Child maltreatment, a significant problem in the United States, is influenced by four primary variables: social-cultural influences, environmental conditions, caregiver characteristics, and child characteristics. Breaking the cycle of child maltreatment involves terminating the widespread acceptance of physical punishment and making children's needs a national priority through the provision of early intervention to all at-risk children and families.

Appropriate caregiving for young children includes the establishment of a caring and loving environment as they develop. This atmosphere is accomplished by letting children know they are valued, by setting aside individual time, and by giving young children affection. Self-esteem may be developed in children by allowing and enabling children to be competent, telling children about the good things they do, speaking to children appropriately, teaching children it is all right to make mistakes, allowing children to make choices, letting children know their opinions are valued, and teaching children to respect individual differences.

Variables associated with appropriate behavior in young children include providing appropriate supervision, establishing a consistent and predictable environment, and teaching readiness skills for academic success. A greater emphasis must be placed on the prevention of inappropriate behaviors through a sensitivity to children's developmental stages, environmental considerations, and special attention to daily routines and children's physical needs.

Teachers are encouraged to facilitate parent–child–teacher relationships by making frequent contacts with parents and having positive comments to share about their children. Negative statements to parents about their children should always be balanced with positive comments to make parents feel good about their children and reinforce parent–teacher contacts.

Discussion Questions

1. Describe some of the social problems placing newborns and young children at greater risk than ever before.
2. Discuss the effectiveness of early intervention and the long-term benefits, especially with regard to costs.
3. What factors are related to child maltreatment?
4. List and discuss the elements of effective care giving for young children.
5. Discuss some of the variables of classroom environments and associated influences on young children's behavior. With these variables in mind, design a preschool classroom setting.
6. Discuss the components of a preschool schedule that facilitate appropriate behavior. With these variables in mind, develop a preschool schedule for 4-year-olds.
7. How may teachers and parents facilitate effective parent–child–teacher relationships? Discuss the importance of effective parent–child–teacher relationships.

References

Ainsworth, M. D. S. (1979). Attachment as related to mother-infant interaction. In J. S. Rosenblatt, R. A. Hinde, C. Beer, & M. C. Busnel (Eds.), *Advances in the study of behavior* (Vol. 9, pp. 1–51). New York: Academic Press.

Annie E. Casey Foundation. (2005). *Kids count data book*. Baltimore: Author.

Annie E. Casey Foundation. (2009). *Kids count data book*. Baltimore: Author.

Bailey, D. B., & Wolery, M. (1984). *Teaching infants and preschoolers with handicaps*. Upper Saddle River, NJ: Merrill/Pearson Education.

Beard, K. Y., & Sugai, G. (2004). First step to success: An early intervention for elementary children at risk for antisocial behavior. *Behavioral Disorders, 29*(4), 396–409.

Bell, R. Q., & Harper, L. V. (1977). *Child effects on adults*. Hillsdale, NJ: Erlbaum.

Bowlby, J. (1982). *Attachment*. New York: Basic Books.

Bracey, G. W. (2003). Investing in preschool. *American School Board Journal, 190*(1), 32–35.

Brown, A. (2004). *Baby 411: Clear answers and smart advice for your baby's first year*. Boulder, CO: Windsor Peak Press.

Campbell, F. A., Ramey, C. T., Pungello, E. P., Sparling, J., & Miller-Johnson, S. (2002). Early childhood education: Young adult outcomes from the Abecedarian Project. *Applied Developmental Science, 6,* 42–57.

Campbell, S. B. (1995). Behavior problems in preschool children: A review of recent research. *Journal of Child Psychology and Psychiatry, 36,* 113–149.

Ceballo, R., & McLoyd, V. C. (2002). Social support and parenting in poor, dangerous neighborhoods. *Child Development, 73*(4), 1310–1321.

Center for Disease Control and Prevention. (2002). Lead report. Atlanta, GA: Author.

Chavez, G. F., Cordero, J. F., & Becerra, J. E. (1989). Leading major congenital malformations among minority groups in the United States, 1981–1986. *Journal of the American Medical Association, 261*(2), 205–209.

Children's Defense Fund. (2003). *Pre-kindergarten initiatives: Efforts to help children enter school ready to succeed*. Washington, DC: Author.

Children's Defense Fund. (2005). *Child-care basics*. Washington, DC: Author.

Colvin, G., Sugai, G., Good, R. H., III, & Lee, Y. (1997). Using active supervision and precorrection to improve transition behaviors in an elementary school. *School Psychology Quarterly, 12,* 344–363.

Delaney, E. M., & Kaiser, A. P. (2001). The effects of teaching parents blended communication and behavior support strategies. *Behavioral Disorders, 26*(2), 93–116.

Dunlap, G., Strain, P. S., Fox, L., Carta, J. J., Conroy, M., Smith, B. J., Kern, L., Hemmeter, M. L., Timm, M. A., McCart, A., Sailor, W., Markey, U., Markey, D. J., Lardieri, S., & Sowell, C. (2006). Prevention and intervention with young children's challenging behavior: Perspectives regarding current knowledge. *Behavior Disorders, 32*(1), 29-45.

Dunst, C. J., McWilliam, R. A., & Holbert, K. (1986). Assessment of preschool classroom environments. *Diagnostique, 11,* 212–232.

Enders, J., Montgomery, J., & Welch, P. (2002). Lead poison prevention. *Journal of Environmental Health, 64*(6), 20–26.

Ensher, G. L., & Clark, D. A. (1986). *Newborns at risk.* Rockville, MD: Aspen.

Evans, G. W. (2001). Environmental stress and health. In A. Baum, T. Revenson, & J. Singer (Eds.), *Handbooks of health* (Vol. 4, pp. 365–385). Hillsdale, NJ: Erlbaum.

Farver, J. M., Xu, Y., Eppe, S., Fernandez, A., & Schwartz, D. (2005). Community violence, family conflict, and preschoolers' socioemotional functioning. *Developmental Psychology, 41*(1), 160–170.

Federal Interagency Forum on Child and Family Statistics. (2009). *American's children: Key national indicators of well-being.* Washington, DC: U.S. Government Printing Office.

Fritz, G. K. (2000). Keep your eye on fetal alcohol syndrome. *Child and Adolescent Behavior Letter.* Providence, RI: Brown University.

Hancock, T. B., Kaiser, A. P., & Delaney, E. M. (2002). Teaching parents of preschoolers at high risk: Strategies to support language and positive behavior. *Topics in Early Childhood Education, 22*(4), 191–212.

Hendrick, J. (1990). *Total learning: Developmental curriculum for the young child.* Upper Saddle River, NJ: Merrill/Pearson Education.

Hetherington, E. M., & Martin, B. (1986). Family factors and psychopathology in children. In H. C. Quay & J. S. Werry (Eds.), *Psychopathological disorders of childhood.* New York: Wiley.

Illinois State Board of Education. (2001). *Predicting the school percentage of ISAT scores that are below state standards.* Washington, DC: U.S. Department of Education.

Kauffman, J. M. (2001). *Characteristics of behavior disorders of children and youth* (7th ed.). Upper Saddle River, NJ: Merrill/Pearson Education.

Kilgore, K., Snyder, J., & Lentz, C. (2000). The contribution of parental discipline, parental monitoring, and school risk to early-onset conduct. *Developmental Psychology, 36*(6), 835–845.

Legendre, A. (2003). Environmental features influencing toddlers bioemotional reactions in day care centers. *Environmental and Behavior, 35,* 523–549.

Lewis, T. J., Colvin, G., & Sugai, G. (2000). The effects of precorrection and active supervision on the recess behavior of elementary students. *Education and Treatment of Children, 23*(2), 109–121.

Love, J. M., Kisker, E. E., Ross, C., Raikes, H., Constantine, J, Boller, K., et. al. (2005). The effectiveness of Early Head Start for 3-year-old children and their parents: Lessons for policy and programs. *Developmental Psychology, 41,* 885–901.

Lynch, R. (2004). *Exceptional returns: Economic, fiscal, and social benefits of investment in early childhood development.* Washington, DC: Economic Policy Institute.

May, P. A., & Gossage, J. P. (2005). *Estimating the prevalence of fetal alcohol syndrome: A summary.* Washington, DC: National Institute on Alcohol Abuse and Alcoholism.

McEvoy, M. A., & Brady, M. P. (1988). Contingent access to play materials as an academic motivator for autistic and behavior disordered children. *Education and Treatment of Children, 11,* 5–18.

McEvoy, M. A., Fox, J. J., & Rosenberg, M. S. (1991). Organizing preschool environments: Suggestions for enhancing the development/learning of preschool children with handicaps. *Topics in Early Childhood Special Education, 11,* 18–28.

McWilliam, R. A., Trivette, C. M., & Dunst, C. J. (1985). Behavior engagement as a measure of the efficacy of early intervention. *Analysis and Intervention in Developmental Disabilities, 5,* 59–71.

Michigan Education Association. (2005). *MEA Voice Today.* East Lansing, MI: Author.

National Association for the Education of Young Children. (1997). *Standards.* Washington, DC: Author.

National Association for the Education of Young Children. (2005). *Standards*. Washington, DC: Author.

National Association of Counsel for Children. (2005). *Child maltreatment report*. Denver, CO: Author.

National Clearinghouse on Child Abuse and Neglect Information. (2004). *Preventing child abuse and neglect report*. Washington, DC: Author.

Nordquist, V. M., & Twardosz, S. (1990). Preventing behavior problems in early childhood special education classrooms through environmental organization. *Education and Treatment of Children, 13,* 274–287.

Randall, C. L. (2001). Alcohol and pregnancy: Highlights from three decades of research. *Journal of Studies on Alcohol, 62*(5), 554–562.

Rimm-Kaufman, S. E., LaParo, K. M., Downer, J. T., & Pianta, R. C. (2005). The contribution of classroom setting and quality of instruction to children's behavior in kindergarten classrooms. *Elementary School Journal, 105*(4), 377–394.

Sattes, B. (1985). *Parent involvement: A review of the literature*. Charleston, WV: Appalachia Educational Laboratory.

Schonfeld, A., Mattson, S., Lang, A. R., Delis, D. C., & Riley, E. P. (2001). Verbal and nonverbal fluency in children with heavy prenatal alcohol exposure. *Journal of Studies on Alcohol, 62*(2), 239–247.

Schorr, L. B., & Schorr, D. (1989). *Within our reach: Breaking the cycle of disadvantage*. New York: Anchor Books.

U.S. Census Bureau. (2000). *Current Population Survey, March 1999*. Washington, DC: Author.

U.S. Census Bureau. (2005). *Father's day*. Washington, DC: Author.

U.S. Department of Health and Human Services. (2008). *Long term consequences of child abuse and neglect*. Washington, DC: Author.

U.S. Department of Labor. (2004). *Employment characteristics of families in 2001*. Washington, DC: Author.

Vaden-Kiernan, N., Ialongo, S., Pearson, J., & Kellam, S. (1995). Household family structure and children's aggressive behavior: A longitudinal study of urban elementary school children. *Journal of Abnormal Child Psychology, 23,* 553–568.

Walker, H. M., & Sprague, J. R. (1999). The path to school failure, delinquency, and violence: Causal factors and some potential solutions. *Intervention in School and Clinic, 35,* 67–73.

Williams, D., & Chavkin, N. (1985). *Guidelines and strategies to train teachers for parent involvement*. Austin, TX: Southwestern Educational Development Laboratory.

Zirpoli, S. B. (1995). Designing environments for optimal behavior. In T. J. Zirpoli (Ed.), *Understanding and affecting the behavior of young children* (pp. 122–151). Upper Saddle River, NJ: Merrill/Pearson Education.

Zirpoli, T. J. (1990). Physical abuse: Are children with disabilities at greater risk? *Intervention in School and Clinic, 26,* 6–11.

Zirpoli, T. J., & Bell, R. Q. (1987). Unresponsiveness in children with severe disabilities: Potential effects on parent–child interactions. *Exceptional Child, 34,* 31–40.

Issues in Adolescent Behavior

Stephanie D. Madsen
McDaniel College

> *The solution of adult problems tomorrow depends in large measure upon the way our children grow up today. There is no greater insight into the future than recognizing that, when we save children, we save ourselves.*
>
> —MARGARET MEAD (N.D.)

When teachers tell people that they work with adolescents, others sometimes comment on their bravery. While it can be rewarding to work with teens, it is also true that the normal and striking developments that happen during adolescence (typically defined as ages 12–18) can create challenges. Adolescents change rapidly in terms of physical, cognitive, social, and emotional development. They often demand greater freedom and responsibility, but demonstrate poor decision-making skills. Having a solid understanding adolescent development can be helpful in designing plans to modify adolescent behavior. The purpose of this chapter is to (a) introduce you to the key developmental changes of adolescence by emphasizing the resulting changes in adolescents' behavior, (b) explore factors associated with adolescents' optimal development, (c) review successful approaches to behavior modification with adolescents, and (d) highlight issues particular to interventions with adolescent populations.

UNDERSTANDING THE CHANGING BEHAVIOR OF ADOLESCENTS

People develop throughout their entire lives, but the changes that take place during the second decade of life are truly striking. Physical, cognitive, and social changes happen at the same time that adolescents are experiencing changes in their environments (such as transitioning to a new school). In understanding adolescent behavior, it is helpful to note how adolescents advance in each of these areas, as well as areas where they still have some growing to do.

Physical Changes

The physical changes the body goes through in adolescence are the most rapid it has seen since infancy. The major physical changes, and some of the ways they affect behavior, are outlined here.

PUBERTY The most obvious physical change during adolescence is puberty. Puberty marks the onset of the capability of reproduction. In the United States, the average age for girls to begin menstruating is 12.5 years, with European American girls typically starting a bit later than African American girls (Brooks-Gunn & Reiter, 1990). Most girls (95% of the population) enter puberty between the ages of 9 and 16. Boys lag behind girls by a few years; boys' average age for reaching sexual maturity is 14 years. Most boys (95% of the population) enter puberty between the ages of 10 and 19 (Brooks-Gunn & Reiter, 1990).

Others' reaction to pubertal changes can affect adolescents' behaviors. Once a child looks physically mature, he or she may be assumed to have greater mental and emotional maturity too, regardless of whether or not this is true. The timing of puberty—whether one matures early, late, or on time with respect to peers—plays an important role in determining whether pubertal changes are a positive or negative force in adolescents' lives. For boys, maturing early has some social benefits. Early-maturing boys are perceived as adult-like and may be given more leadership roles. Boys gain muscle in puberty and their peers value the resulting increased strength and speed in sports. Still, research has demonstrated some psychological costs for early-maturing boys including depression, anxiety, and feelings of hostility (Ge, Conger, & Elder, 2001). Girls experience early maturation in a more uniformly negative way. These girls often report feeling awkward around their peers, tend to hang out with an older crowd, begin dating earlier than their peers, and may be pressured into sexual experiences before they are ready (Stattin & Magnusson, 1990). Maturing late may actually be advantageous for girls in terms of protecting them from negative body image issues associated with the naturally occurring weight gain of puberty. Boys who mature later than their peers might find that situation to be personally challenging, but research has not revealed any long-term negative effects.

Historically speaking, the average age for reaching puberty is decreasing. This secular trend may be due to better nutrition, sanitation, and control of infectious disease. Although the average age for girls to begin menstruating is unlikely to dip far below 12 years, a significant minority of girls may show one or more signs of puberty by age 7 (Kaplowitz, 2004). Therefore, the effects of puberty may begin well before adolescence, often to the surprise of parents, teachers, peers, and the child herself.

BRAIN DEVELOPMENT The brain reaches 95% of its adult volume by age 5 or so, but it continues to develop substantially in adolescence and even into young adulthood. Some changes that happen during this period make the brain more efficient:

- Unnecessary connections among brain cells are eliminated.
- The formation of myelin sheaths around nerve fibers is completed, allowing messages to travel faster in the brain.
- Brain functions become more localized on either the right or the left hemisphere of the cerebral cortex.
- The corpus callosum (i.e., the cable of nerves connecting the brain's hemispheres) thickens.

These changes are reflected in adolescents' greater memory and problem-solving abilities. But as the brain's efficiency increases, it loses the ability to easily take on new functions. The brain does not recover from trauma as easily, and if certain experiences have not happened before adolescence, the skills associated with them may be more difficult to acquire. For example, although most secondary language instruction happens during adolescence, our brains would actually be more receptive to learning this material earlier in life.

Changes in levels of some neurotransmitters (e.g., dopamine and serotonin) in the brain's limbic system impact the way that adolescents respond to and interpret emotional events (Spear, 2000). These changes make adolescents more emotional, more responsive to stress, and less responsive to rewards. As a result, adolescents frequently report feeling bored (in fact, this is the most common emotion reported in school) and they are more likely to seek out novelty and take risks.

Dramatic changes in this area of the brain may account for striking changes in adolescents' behaviors (Spear, 2000). One of the last parts of the brain to finish developing is the prefrontal cortex, or the area at the front of the brain responsible for planning and anticipating the consequences of our actions. Because adolescents are still developing these neurological capabilities, they may have trouble thinking of the long-term impact of their risky behavior on their own. To compensate for the underdevelopment of the prefrontal cortex, the adolescent brain relies heavily on the emotional center of the brain, the amygdala, resulting in a tendency to react on instinct and behave impulsively (Spear, 2000).

CHANGES IN MOODS   Adolescents are known for rapid mood swings and general moodiness. Hormones are partially responsible for these emotional changes, especially among younger adolescents. Early in the pubertal process, when the hormonal system is being turned on, hormones fluctuate rapidly and result in fluctuating moods. As a result, boys tend to become more irritable, aggressive, and impulsive in early adolescence, whereas girls tend to react with more depressed moods.

Beyond early adolescence the direct link between hormones and moods is relatively weak. Stressful changes in adolescents' environments may be just as important as biological factors in influencing their moods. Using a method known as the *experience sampling method*, researchers outfitted adolescents with beepers in order to track the effect of environmental factors on moods. Adolescents carried the beepers with them everywhere they went for a week. The adolescents were beeped at random times. When they were beeped, adolescents recorded where they were, what they were doing, whom they were with, and whether their mood was positive or negative. The researchers found that adolescents experienced emotional extremes (both positive and negative) more often than adults. However, changes in moods were linked to what the adolescent was doing rather than biological changes (Larson, Csikszentmihalyi, & Graef, 1980). So a teen might be bored while in class, happy to see his girlfriend at lunch, and stressed while going over errors from last weekend's game with his coach. Since adolescents change contexts and activities quite frequently, their moods change more often than those of adults or children.

SLEEP REQUIREMENTS   Researchers have also suggested that adolescents' moodiness might be due to their failure to get enough sleep. Most adolescents (and many adults) operate in a state of sleep deprivation (Maas, 2002)—a fact that is especially troubling given the importance of sleep in periods of rapid brain maturation (Dahl, 1999). Adolescents' preference for staying up late and then sleeping in are actually tied to biological changes. When allowed to determine their sleep schedules, most adolescents stay up until 1 A.M. and sleep until 10 A.M.; getting a full 9 hours of sleep. But school schedules often force adolescents to adhere to sleep schedules better suited to children or adults, leaving adolescents sleepy during school hours (Carskadon, Wolfson, Acebo et al., 1998). Girls tend to get less sleep than boys. Why? They wake up earlier so that they will have more time to groom (Fredriksen, Rhodes, Reddy, & Way, 2004). Sleep loss has been associated with increases in depression and decreases in self-esteem across adolescence. As a group, adolescents are sleepiest between 8 A.M. and 9 A.M. and most alert after 3 P.M., posing obvious challenges to those trying to maintain their attention during class!

Cognitive Changes

Middle schools and high schools offer many subjects not available to elementary school students. Adolescents can now take classes in areas such as higher-level math (e.g., algebra, calculus), foreign languages, sciences, and civics. Each of these subjects takes advantage of advances in adolescents' expanding cognitive abilities. Compared to students in elementary schools, adolescents have a greater capacity to think systematically, use memorization and attention abilities, and consider abstract concepts.

HYPOTHETICO-DEDUCTIVE REASONING   The scientific method involves developing a series of hypotheses or predictions and then testing them in an orderly fashion by isolating relevant variables and excluding irrelevant ones. In his classic pendulum problem, Jean Piaget gave children strings of different lengths and objects of different weights and asked them to determine the factor that influences the speed of the pendulum (Piaget & Inhelder, 1969). Children usually failed this test because they randomly tested different combinations and ended their testing before they had exhausted all possibilities. Adolescents were able to systematically test the different factors and determine that only the length of the string makes a difference. Considered a hallmark of adolescent cognitive development, this ability to reason systematically is referred to as *hypothetico-deductive reasoning.* Older adolescents are better at consistently using formal reasoning, whereas younger adolescents appear to use this ability in some situations but not others. The use of formal reasoning does not appear to be universally present in all cultures. Instead it is heavily tied to participation in a schooling system that promotes this type of thinking.

Adolescents' advances in reasoning abilities can also pose new challenges to teachers. Adolescents are now capable of developing more sophisticated arguments promoting their preferences. The standard adult response of "because" or other weak arguments are no longer likely to be left unchallenged. But adolescents' cognitive reasoning skills can be useful in solving social problems. For example, if a teacher asks his or her class to help determine a consequence for failing to complete an assignment, adolescents are likely to weigh all aspects of the situation and consider multiple perspectives before arriving at a conclusion.

ABSTRACT THINKING   Younger children find it easiest to reason about the concrete world (i.e., the things that they can see and touch), while adolescents are able to reason about abstract concepts or ideas (e.g., justice, peace, the environment). This ability creates a more complex world for adolescents to think about. For example, consider two siblings, Amanda (age 9) and Eleanor (age 17), both of whom just completed science units on the problem of pollution. The units left both of them concerned and anxious to do their part to help the environment. Amanda, focusing on the concrete world, convinces her friends to help her clean up the neighborhood park. Eleanor has the advanced cognitive capabilities to consider the long-term implications of pollution, the moral obligations of corporations with poor environmental practices, and the difficulties associated with seemingly simple, obvious solutions such as outlawing all industry. After careful thought, Eleanor organizes her friends to help out with the political campaign of a local candidate who supports industry reform. Both Amanda and Eleanor are reasoning about the environment, but Eleanor is able to conceptualize the problem in a more abstract way and deal with the issues on a deeper level.

SOCIAL COGNITIVE BELIEFS   Cognitive developments intersect with social ones, altering ways that adolescents think about themselves and those around them. Adolescents sometimes feel as though they are the focus of everyone's attention, creating an *imaginary audience* that is watching them and taking note of their every behavior (Elkind & Bowen, 1979). Though adolescents are attuned to peers' behaviors, they often take their concern about others' attentions to an unjustified extreme. For example, a teen who spilled her lunch in the cafeteria might think it reasonable to ask to transfer to a new school since "everyone" saw it. Adolescents spend more time alone than they did in childhood (Larson, Richards, Moneta, & Holmbeck, 1996), perhaps reflecting the tremendous energy required to act in an environment of perceived constant surveillance.

The *personal fable* refers to adolescents' beliefs that their experiences, thoughts, and feelings are totally unique. This is reflected in adolescents' feelings that they are invulnerable, resulting in actions that seem foolish to adults (e.g., fast driving, excessive drinking). The personal fable stems, in part, from adolescents' relative unfamiliarity with their changing world and their changing selves. For example, when an adolescent first falls in love, this feeling might be stronger than any he or she has ever experienced before. Given this overwhelming feeling, the adolescent might feel it is reasonable to conclude that there has never been a love like this before and that risky behaviors (for example, unprotected sex) are warranted by the situation. Feelings of uniqueness and invulnerability might lead the adolescent to believe he or she is immune from unwanted outcomes such as pregnancy or disease. The personal fable diminishes as the adolescent builds up more experiences and learns from the experiences of those around him or her.

Social Changes

IDENTITY   When asked to describe themselves, very young children tend to mention their possessions ("I have a red tricycle") or their appearances ("I am tall"). By elementary school, children include social group membership ("I am a Boy Scout"), relationships ("I am Malika's friend"), and some psychological traits ("I am nice") in their definitions (Livesley & Bromley, 1973). By adolescence, descriptions become more complex. Adolescents not only realize that who they are might change with different settings or relationships ("I am shy at school but outgoing with my friends"), but also can imagine who they might be ("I am going to become a better athlete by practicing harder"). Compared to children in middle childhood, adolescents view themselves in terms of what makes them different or unique from their peers, showing that they value their individuality. Adolescents also are capable of reflecting on and evaluating themselves, which leads them to believe that they should be able to make their own decisions and create their own set of values.

Adolescents who are supported by significant adults in their lives have a better chance for coping with the daily challenges.

These changes in thinking about the self are tied to the broader issue of developing an identity, which involves the integration of all the different aspects of the self. Adolescents form their identities by trying on different ideas, appearances, behaviors, and relationships. Adults may sometimes be frustrated by an adolescent who wants to attend a service from a different religion, dress in a nontraditional way, or hang out with a different set of friends. Although adolescents still need adult guidance, exploration of different possibilities of the self is considered essential for forming a healthy identity. Once an identity is established, it can be used to guide the individual's future actions.

AUTONOMY   At one time psychologists believed that adolescents needed to deindividuate from adults and to completely separate from adult values to be emotionally healthy. Now they realize that a more appropriate goal is for adolescents to become autonomous, gaining ownership over their thoughts and behaviors, but to remain emotionally connected to others (Ryan & Lynch, 1989). Still, adults and adolescents must negotiate the timing and extent of this independence.

In his expectancy-violation-realignment model, Collins (1990) suggests that the handing over of authority from adults to adolescents is a gradual process. Both adults and adolescents carry expectancies about how the other should behave (e.g., an expectation that the adolescent will adhere to a curfew). Times of rapid change, such as adolescence, lead to violations of expectations (e.g., curfew is broken), resulting in conflict. To maintain the relationship (and any hope of influencing the adolescent in the future), the adult and adolescent need to resolve their conflict and realign their behavior (e.g., adolescent resolves never to break curfew again) or, more commonly, their expectations (e.g., a new rule is created, stating that the adolescent must phone for a curfew extension). In this way, the relationship is maintained, and more and more control is gradually relinquished to the adolescent.

What do teens and adults argue about? Most conflicts are about rather mundane issues such as hairstyle, clothing, and curfew. But issues of autonomy, or who should control the teen's thoughts and behaviors, are at the heart of these arguments (Steinberg, 1990). In a study of autonomy, Smetana (1988) asked adolescents in the 6th, 8th, and 10th grades and their parents to think about 24 hypothetical situations and to decide whether the adolescent or the parent should be in control of the issue. Some of these issues concerned friendship (e.g., when to see friends, who your friends are), personal matters (e.g., watching television, choosing clothes), and prudential matters (e.g., smoking, eating junk food, drinking), while others concerned moral issues (e.g., taking someone else's money). Not surprisingly, parents and adolescents each believed that *they* should retain control of most of the issues, but adolescents tended to view the issues as a matter of personal choice. However, both parents and adolescents agreed that parents should retain jurisdiction when the issue was a moral one. So, although adolescents striving for autonomy create conflict within their family, most adolescents retain the values of their family and wish to maintain those relationships (Collins, 1997). In fact, very few adolescents (about 3% of girls and 5%–9% of boys) reject their parents outright (Rutter et al., 1976). Instead, parents remain important figures in adolescents' lives and are valued for the aid and advice they provide (Furman & Buhrmester, 1992).

Adolescents' desire for autonomy extends beyond the reach of the family and into the classroom. Classroom Connection 5.1 illustrates how one teacher made use of adolescents' desire for autonomy as a positive source of change.

CLASSROOM CONNECTION 5.1
Using Rewards That Are Developmentally Salient to Adolescents

Ms. Degnan teaches seventh grade language arts. Her classes run smoothly, for the most part, and she is able to get through her lessons as planned. However, she finds that the students in her 8th hour section just cannot seem to get things together to finish their work on time. This class spends more time chatting and moves slower compared to the other sections.

Ms. Degnan wants to bring this section up to speed. She considers how a behavioral approach might make use of the developmental issues already at play in adolescents' lives. She knows that adolescence is a time of striving for greater autonomy; being granted a little autonomy in the classroom might be a strong motivating factor for these students. She also knows that her students are just learning to use their increased metacognitive skills; they can set longer-term goals and plan for how to manage their time to meet these goals.

Using this information, Ms. Degnan announces to her 8th hour that she is going to start posting each day's "agenda" on the board. Students can see exactly what they need to accomplish each day. Agenda items that are not completed will be assigned as homework. She tells them that they will be responsible for keeping the class on schedule, granting them greater autonomy

in the process. The class also discusses time management issues.

Under this new system, students encourage each other to complete their tasks on time. Ms. Degnan is careful to post agendas that are manageable so that the class will be negatively reinforced (i.e., by receiving no homework) for staying on task. Occasionally, Ms. Degnan will post an entire week's agenda on the board. If students finish all of the items on Tuesday's agenda, she asks if they would like to get started on Wednesday's agenda. At the end of the week, if the class has met its posted agenda, students are allowed to have a bit of free time or to do something else that they enjoy as a reward. By giving the students greater responsibility and by making use of their growing cognitive abilities, Ms. Degnan is able to get her class back on track.

General Reflection for Classroom Connection 5.1:

What are some other rewards that might be especially motivating to adolescents given their recent developmental changes? How might you use these rewards in a classroom setting to decrease inappropriate classroom behaviors?

PEER RELATIONS   In the second decade of life adolescents begin to spend more time with their friends than they do with their families (Larson et al., 1996). Friendships are a source of mutual understanding, intimacy, and commitment.

Although friendships can be positive forces in adolescents' lives, peer pressure can also be a concern. Research shows that conformity to peers peaks in early to mid-adolescence and is greatly diminished by late adolescence (Berndt, 1979). In all stages of adolescence, *who* the adolescent's friends are is important (Hartup & Stevens, 1997). Adolescents who have delinquent friends are much more likely to participate in delinquent acts. It seems that delinquent adolescents not only select each other as friends but also "train" each other in how to behave delinquently; one of the best predictors of stopping antisocial behavior is parting with friends who also engage in this behavior (Dishion, Andrews, & Crosby, 1995). Alternatively, having a group of friends who value academics may lead an adolescent to improve his or her academic performance. Classroom Connection 5.2 gives an example of how one creative middle school teacher used peer influence to get her class to complete their math homework assignments.

Romantic peer relationships become important in adolescence. Most adolescents report having been in a romantic relationship in the past 18 months (Carver, Joyner, & Udry, 2003). These relationships tend to be brief, lasting an average of 4 months at age 15 (Feiring, 1996). Adolescents with boyfriends or girlfriends typically have more extreme mood swings, reporting higher highs and lower lows than their single friends (Larson, Clore, & Wood, 1999).

Contextual Changes

In addition to all of the changes occurring within the adolescent, adolescents' environments are also changing in important ways. Consider these examples of contextual changes and how they might influence adolescent behavior:

- *School transition:*   Middle school and high school offer far less structure and support compared to elementary school.
- *Changing legal status:*   Adolescents are granted adult status in some arenas (e.g., driving, voting) but not others (e.g., drinking alcohol).
- *Entry into employment:*   Almost all adolescents are employed at some point while attending high school, exposing them to a context with greater responsibilities and possibly more mature peers.
- *Broader sociocultural factors:*   Assumptions fueled by stereotypes affect how the public responds to adolescent behaviors.

Cumulative Effect of Changes

Clearly adolescence is marked by change. Simmons and her colleagues (1979) studied the cumulative effect of multiple changes in adolescence. They followed 800 young people at the transition from elementary school to junior high school and found that girls who began menstruating, started dating, and changed schools during the same year experience the greatest declines in self-esteem across the transition to junior high. It appears that the *number* of stressful events going on in adolescents' lives may be more important than any one specific stressful event. Other researchers have supported this idea that we should be

CLASSROOM CONNECTION 5.2
Helping Students Establish Good Homework Habits

Mrs. Hadden teaches 7th grade math. Her students were on-task during classroom hours, but when it came to homework few students arrived to class with it completed. It had gotten so that on any given day only 10 students in a class of 25 had completed their homework problems. Mrs. Hadden had explained how important the daily homework problems were for practicing the concepts they learned in class. She explained that by doing the homework, students would perform better on tests, but her explanations seemed to fall on deaf ears. She realized that her students needed to experience this connection between their behaviors and their academic success firsthand.

Mrs. Hadden knew that early adolescents were especially prone to peer influence, and she decided to use this fact in a positive way while designing her behavioral plan. She also knew that if she wanted to see success, it would work best to gradually shape her students' behaviors rather than begin with long-term expectations that her students would feel were out of reach.

With these facts in mind, Mrs. Hadden told her students that if every student brought in his or her completed homework, she would drop three problems from the next day's homework assignment. Although this meant having her students potentially do fewer homework problems, she felt that they would still be getting enough daily practice and that this trade-off was worth it to get every student into the daily homework habit. Her students were excited by this challenge. On the first few days they got close, but one or two students failed to complete their homework. Mrs. Hadden simply let the class know that they hadn't met their goal, without naming which students were to blame. But the "guilty" students invariably confessed and their peers encouraged them to get their homework done, even calling them or helping them if they got stuck on tough problems. This positive peer pressure did the trick, and soon her entire class brought in their completed homework problems on a regular basis.

Once they had three weeks of success with this new arrangement, Mrs. Hadden announced a new challenge: if everyone did their homework for the whole week, she wouldn't assign any homework on Fridays. This would leave their weekends free of math homework—a reward they were willing to work hard for. When, after a few weeks, they were successful with this new arrangement, she issued yet another challenge: if everyone completed their homework for an entire month, she would reward them with a free period where they could go outside. Her students, now well into the habit of daily homework, met this final challenge with little difficulty.

After the first month when everyone had been reliably completing homework assignments, Mrs. Hadden gave a math test. After returning the test to her students, she asked for a show of hands from the students who had achieved a higher test score on this test compared to the last one. Almost every hand in the class went up. Those students who had performed poorly in the past (not coincidentally, many of the same students who had failed to complete homework assignments in the past) were especially likely to have seen improvement. She used this opportunity to help them see the connection between homework practice and achievement. Although she had often made this point to her students before, this time they had experienced the rewards firsthand and finally got the point.

General Reflection for Classroom Connection 5.2:

If Mrs. Hadden's goal was really to get her students to complete their homework for months at a time, why didn't she just challenge them to complete their homework for an entire month in the first place? Why was it important to start with smaller challenges? Mrs. Hadden decided to make a short-term trade-off by letting her students do fewer homework problems to get them in the habit of practicing math concepts on a daily basis. Do you think this trade-off was worth it? Why were peers more successful in influencing other students to complete their homework than their teacher had been? Do you think that this approach would have been as successful with a third-grade classroom? Why or why not?

most concerned about adolescents who are experiencing multiple changes at once, and we should be especially concerned about adolescents who lack the resources to deal with all of these changes simultaneously.

PREDICTING POSITIVE OUTCOMES FOR ADOLESCENTS

What do we know about factors in adolescents' lives that promote optimal behavioral outcomes? Although high self-esteem, feeling accepted, and participating in extracurricular activities are commonly assumed to help these factors, in fact they do *not* predict fewer problem behaviors in adolescence (Gottfredson, 2001). Instead, research shows that a variety of both internal and external assets relate to positive outcomes; they protect adolescents from high-risk behaviors, enhance the likelihood of engaging in positive behaviors, and promote resilience in the face of adversity. The more protective factors an adolescent has working in his or her favor, the more likely he or she is to avoid problem behaviors. Adolescents without the benefit of these protective factors are not doomed to poor outcomes, but they may face greater challenges.

Internal Assets

Some of the most important assets for youth are the ones they carry within themselves. Four key internal assets identified by the Minneapolis Search Institute include:

- a commitment to lifelong learning and education,
- positive values that guide future choices,
- social competences to build relationships and make wise decisions, and
- positive identity in the form of a strong sense of self-worth (Benson, Scales, Leffert, & Roehlkepartain, 1999).

Where do such internal assets come from? When families, schools, media, religious institutions, and neighborhoods work together, youth have the greatest chance of benefiting from these supportive features.

External Assets

The remaining assets may be considered external since they reside outside the adolescent. These external assets offer adolescents feelings of support, empowerment, boundaries, and high expectations.

SUPPORTIVE RELATIONSHIPS   Peers and friends provide important sources of self-validation, cooperation, mutual respect, and security (Newcomb & Bagwell, 1996). These relationships are especially important in adolescents' lives because they represent voluntary relationships where members are on equal levels in terms of cognitive development and social power. This context is ideal for providing mutual support and for developing important conflict-resolution skills within a safe environment.

Parents can also be developmental assets for adolescents. Extensive research has shown that authoritative parenting, or parenting that combines warmth with structure and rules, is related to the best outcomes for adolescents (Steinberg, 2001). Adolescents with authoritative parents are less likely to engage in problem behavior, including drug and alcohol use, and delinquency. These adolescents also enjoy better mental health, including higher self-esteem and lower rates of anxiety and depression. They also teach higher levels of school achievement than adolescents whose parents who do not use this combination of warmth and structure.

Although middle school and high school students generally view teachers with greater mistrust and find fewer opportunities to establish relationships with teachers than they did as elementary school students (Eccles et al., 1993), teachers remain important influences in adolescents' lives. Support from teachers is different from both parent and peer support in that it relates to interest in attending class, pursuing academic goals, and adhering to rules and norms (Wentzel, 1998). Adolescents who perceive their teachers as supportive are more likely to behave prosocially and to engage in behaviors that promote their learning (Wentzel & Battle, 2001).

Other adults in adolescents' lives may also act as developmental assets. Grandparents, mentors, coaches, and neighbors can all provide guidance for adolescents. Such guidance is especially important in the absence of a strong parent-adolescent relationship.

BALANCING SCHOOL AND WORK ROLES Given that most American adolescents are employed at some point during high school, how might work experiences in adolescence contribute to positive outcomes? Adolescent's perceptions of the effects of their employment are overwhelmingly positive (Mortimer, Harley, & Aronson, 1999). Adolescents cite gains in responsibility, money management, and acquiring social skills as key benefits.

Hours worked per week does not have a significant effect on time spent doing homework (Mortimer et al., 1999), in large part because working adolescents spend significantly less time watching television. Adolescents appear to benefit most from employment that is limited to part-time work. Minor delinquency is greater for adolescents who work long hours or who do not work at all than it is for adolescents occupied by part-time work (Wofford, 1988). Similarly, working excessive hours limits educational attainment, while part-time work encourages adolescents to balance their roles as students and employees (Mortimer et al., 1999).

Beyond the number of hours worked, it is important that the level of the job be appropriate to the adolescent's capabilities. Adolescents who work in highly stressful jobs are more likely to experience depression (Shanahan, Finch, Mortimer, & Ryu, 1991), whereas those working in jobs with high autonomy and clearly defined roles experience gains in self-esteem (Barling, Rogers, & Kelloway, 1995).

COMMUNITY FACTORS One often overlooked but important developmental asset for adolescents is the value that communities place on youth. Unfortunately, just one in five adolescents feels that his or her community values youth (Benson et al., 1999). Sixty percent of adolescents feel that they are part of caring neighborhoods, only 25% feel that their schools provide a caring environment, and adolescent reports of perceived caring decline from middle to high school. These factors may be particularly important because they represent the influence of relationships beyond the immediate family. Such relationships are important for building self-esteem, transmitting cultural customs, developing social competencies, and, perhaps most critically, compensating for negative family relationships.

Avoiding Developmental Deficits

In a study of 99,462 6th- through 12th-grade youth, the Minneapolis Search Institute uncovered five key correlates of poor outcomes for adolescents:

- Being home alone
- Attending parties where there is drinking
- Being a victim of violence
- Overexposure to television
- Experiencing physical abuse

Although these factors do not necessarily cause poor developmental outcomes, engaging in or experiencing these behaviors corresponds with other high-risk behaviors such as drinking, gambling, using drugs, and perpetrating acts of violence. On average, an adolescent will experience approximately two of these five deficits (Benson et al., 1999). Measures that help adolescents to avoid these deficits (e.g., greater parental monitoring of activities, youth centers providing structured after-school activities, violence prevention programs) are likely to promote positive developmental outcomes for adolescents.

BEHAVIORAL INTERVENTIONS FOR ADOLESCENT POPULATIONS

Society has a critical interest in socializing our children to become effective citizens and socially competent individuals. Part of this process involves equipping students with the social skills they will need to avoid problematic behavior and to promote positive social relationships both in and out of school. The school setting is seen as an optimal arena for teaching these skills for two main reasons. First, school is compulsory, thus making it possible to reach most of the youth population at once. Ninety-six percent of youth ages 15–17 attend high school, and 85% stay through graduation (U.S. Census Bureau, 2010a, 2010b). Second, interventions conducted in the school setting reach children during their formative years and optimally can teach appropriate behaviors before inappropriate ones are learned.

Although schools have been interested in shaping their students for a long time, the contributions of the behavioral approach are relatively recent. Earlier approaches were not always very effective. In the 1950s and 1960s, schools often relied on scare tactics to prevent adolescents' problem behaviors (e.g., showing films of gory accidents to convince adolescents to drive responsibly). Alternatively, schools sometimes taught students about the underlying causes of problem behaviors (e.g., informing adolescents that they are more susceptible to peer pressure, and so need to take care to avoid peers' negative influence). However, neither of these approaches have been shown to be effective (Forman & Neal, 1987). In the mid- to late 1970s, the humanistic approach was popular. This approach focused on raising students' self-esteem and teaching stress management. But these efforts may have been misguided since even adolescents who engage in delinquent behavior usually report high self-esteem. In the 1980s, programs drew from social influence models and taught students to "just say no" to avoid peer influence. Like their earlier counterparts, these programs were not highly effective in helping adolescents to avoid problem behaviors (Herrmann & McWhirter, 1997). Behavior modification–based programs have had greater success in teaching and maintaining critical social skills. However, such programs need to be implemented with care when working with adolescent populations.

Behavioral interventions differ based on the desired outcome. Some programs help adolescents select behaviors that will not disrupt the classroom or contribute to a negative school climate. Other modification programs focus on reducing common risky behaviors (e.g., unprotected sex, drugs, gambling, violence, and tobacco use) by (a) improving adolescents' resistance and refusal skills or (b) bolstering their social skills.

Positive Behavioral Interventions and Supports

Positive Behavior Interventions and Supports (PBIS) programs have become increasingly popular in recent years and are now used in over 7500 schools to help reduce students' disruptive behaviors (Bradshaw, Koth, Thornton, & Leaf, 2009). Disruptive behaviors such as being off task, failing to follow instructions, or being disrespectful eat away at instructional time and create a stressful environment for teachers and students. Advocates of PBIS programs emphasize that behavioral expectations need to be taught in the same way that any other core curriculum subject is taught (Positive Behavioral Interventions & Supports, 2010). By teaching behavioral expectations, these programs take an approach that is positive and proactive, rather than negative and reactive (Taylor-Greene & Kartub, 2000). So, instead of punitively reacting to students' disruptive behaviors by writing referrals or taking a stance of zero tolerance, schools using PBIS teach students appropriate behavior and reinforce them when they make appropriate choices. If a student persists in making disruptive choices, teachers follow a clear continuum of consequences.

PBIS can be implemented at the schoolwide level, or it can be targeted at students who are at risk for problem behaviors. When instituted as a schoolwide primary prevention program, teams of representatives from the school first attend special training sessions on PBIS. These teams typically include some teachers, school administrators, and a school psychologist or counselor. The team then develops a set of 3–5 behavioral expectations that are stated positively and are easy to remember (e.g., "Be Safe, Be Responsible, Be Respectful"). An important point is that these expectations tell students what to do, rather than what *not* to do. Why is this so important? Because it is more effective to reinforce wanted behavior than it is to punish unwanted behavior. The team then works to spell out exactly what the behavioral expectations mean for the classroom and for nonclassroom areas such as the cafeteria, the bus, or the gym. For example, "Be Responsible" may include doing your own work in class, taking care of waste and recycling at lunch, using appropriate language on the bus, and sharing equipment at the gym. Note, again, that these expectations are stated in terms of what to do, rather than what not to do (e.g., don't cheat, don't litter, don't swear, and don't hog the equipment). The team will come up with approximately three positively stated examples for each setting.

Upon returning to the home school, the team trains their colleagues in the program. At the start of the school year, these behavioral expectations are actively taught, just as any other important lesson plan would be. The school uses a "gotcha" program to "catch" students making appropriate choices that align with the behavioral expectations. These students are given some sort of card or note that typically states what behavioral expectation was being followed and what the setting was. Copies of this card are sent home and to the main office, where weekly drawings might be held to reward students meeting behavioral expectations. Alternatively, cards might be used in a token economy in which students could redeem them for rewards. In either scenario, the rewards used must be ones that students find highly desirable.

As part of PBIS, the school must also lay out a very clear continuum of consequences for failing to meet behavioral expectations. For example, students might first get a warning, then lose a privilege, and then, if the offense is severe, be referred to the main office. It is important that there be consistency in terms of what consequences accompany each behavior. In that way, students who chose disruptive behaviors are aware of what consequence they are, in effect, choosing. Such consistency also helps with another important aspect of PBIS—assessment.

Schools using PBIS actively collect data as a part of this program so that they can assess the effectiveness of their program. They track the number of office referrals, what kinds of behavioral expectations are violated, and the settings in which these violations happen. They also collect surveys from staff and students regarding the program. These data not only provide information about the effectiveness of the program, but also help inform decisions about how to strengthen the program. For example, if violations more frequently occur in the hallways between classes, changes to the rules, routines, or the environment might be instituted.

PBIS programs in middle and high schools can be very effective in promoting a positive school environment. These programs not only reduce discipline referrals, but they increase academic and social success by creating learning environments that are safe and productive (McIntosh, Chard, Boland, & Horner, 2006). Classroom Connection 5.3 provides an example of how a team of middle school teachers adapted a PBIS program to promote positive behaviors among the students they shared.

Resistance and Refusal Skills

Interventions focused on resistance and refusal skills (RRSs) are concerned with helping students avoid problem behavior. RRS programs typically follow a common protocol. First, students identify types of social pressure. For example, students might discuss situations where they feel tempted to drink. Second, a variety of effective resistance and refusal techniques are demonstrated using videotaped vignettes or live skits. Third, students rehearse refusal through role-play with other students or the instructor (Rohrbach, Graham, Hansen, Flay, & Johnson, 1987).

One example of a typical RRS program is the Say It Straight program, which is aimed at preventing adolescents' alcohol and drug use (Englander-Golden, Elconin, & Miller, 1985). This program asks students to role-play situations where they encounter friends pressuring them to use drugs. These role-plays are videotaped as adolescents replay the scenario several times, practicing a variety of different communication styles. For example, an adolescent might behave passively in the first scene, aggressively in the second, and assertively in the third. A group of the "actor's" peers watch the videotape and offer feedback about the messages (verbal and nonverbal) after each interaction. Once the most effective approach is determined, the adolescent repeats the role-play by practicing that approach.

Of course, having the skills to resist does not automatically mean that the adolescent will be able to resist when faced with a real-life situation (Hovell et al., 2001). Acquiring these skills is merely the first step. The true measure of the effectiveness of an intervention program is the extent of change in adolescents' behaviors.

The most effective school-based RRS programs are those that are highly comprehensive in addressing all possible factors that contribute to the adolescents' risky behaviors

CLASSROOM CONNECTION 5.3
Behaviors Others Admire: Adapting PBIS to a Smaller Scale

Mrs. Howard is the team leader at her middle school, coordinating the efforts of teachers in science, social studies, language arts, and math. Her team was frustrated that they often lost valuable class time due to students' simple disrespect and thoughtlessness. This created a negative learning environment for teachers and students alike. The team was familiar with behavioral approaches and wanted to reward students' good choices, rather than always punishing their poor choices. Their school did not yet have a schoolwide PBIS program, and so they decided to adapt elements of PBIS to create a gradewide program.

To do this, her team of teachers decided that they wanted more of their students to exhibit Behaviors Others Admire and dubbed their idea the "BOA" program. They explained to their students that they could earn "BOA" cards by displaying admirable behaviors such as staying on task in class, helping others, and returning forms or signed report cards the very next day. Because this team of teachers worked closely together, they made sure that the positive behavioral expectations were consistent for these students, whether they were in science class or social studies. When a student earned a BOA card, his or her name and the reason for earning the BOA was put on the card. Every Friday the team held a drawing, and the winner received a small prize such as a movie pass.

In addition, students could work to achieve eligibility for end-of-the-quarter team activities such as an hour of kickball, an ice cream party, or a movie. Students were highly motivated to take part in these events—they did *not* want to miss an activity that all of

their friends got to attend. To be eligible to take part, students had to earn at least 10 BOAs, turn in all assignments, carry a quiet reading book with them at all times, and have no office referrals. The team tracked these important data to help them improve their program. Over time they noted improvements in students' behaviors; at the end of the quarter about 90% of students were able to take part in the team activity. Still, the team did notice that the program seemed more effective at the beginning of each quarter and lost some steam as the quarter drew to a close.

Seeing the success of this innovative team, Mrs. Howard's middle school eventually implemented a schoolwide PBIS program. Many of the PBIS program's specific behavioral expectations, such asthat students be respectful, responsible, and safe, were already a part of the BOA program. The school benefited from the team's experience since they were able to offer insights regarding the effectiveness of a program of positive expectations.

General Reflection for Classroom Connection 5.3:

Mrs. Howard's team worked together to create a common set of expectations for these students, regardless of which class they were in. Why was this an important element of the program? Why not let each individual teacher decide which behaviors would receive BOAs in his or her classroom? Mrs. Howard's team noticed that their program was most effective at the beginning of the quarter and that students seemed less motivated as the quarter wore on. Why might this be? What could her team try in order to keep students motivated throughout the quarter?

(Farmer, Farmer, & Gut, 1999). For example, teachers' behaviors might be examined to ensure that discipline strategies are not unintentionally negatively reinforcing students' unwanted behaviors; perhaps sending an adolescent out of the room allows him to get out of a tedious class session and so is reinforcing for that adolescent. The students' social goals should be considered; perhaps the use of RRS interferes with the support adolescents receive from their friends—being refused by one's friends could leave a teen in a lonely situation. Finally, the social roles of peer groups at a school might be evaluated; perhaps targeting the values and behaviors of a particular clique is necessary to influence the majority of students. It is not enough to focus solely on the behavior without considering multiple influencing factors.

Social Skills Training

Social skills training (SST) programs take the view that adolescent problem behaviors are actually a result of social skills deficits. The logical way to address problem behaviors, then, is to provide training in the relevant social skills. In particular, SST programs target decision-making skills, assertiveness skills, building relationships, and effective conflict resolution.

As with RRS programs, SST is often done in groups of peers. Adolescents are asked first to identify or define their goal. For example, a shy adolescent might set a goal of joining a group of students for lunch. Second, adolescents are asked to generate alternative solutions for reaching this goal. The student might just sit down with a group, try to set up a lunch meeting in advance with an existing group, or ask a few students to join her. Third, each of the alternatives is evaluated. Younger adolescents' limitations in abstract thought can sometimes hinder their progress in this step without outside guidance (Halford, 1989). Finally, a plan for implementation is generated and the adolescent decides what action to take (D'Zurilla & Goldfried, 1971).

In recent years SST programs have gone beyond the basic provision of skills to promote (a) generalization of these skills to situations outside the training setting and (b) maintenance of these skills over time (Christopher, Nangle, & Hansen, 1993). In addition, most SST programs do not stop at one skill but hope to provide adolescents with a broad repertoire of skills on which they might draw.

One example of a SST program that embodies these goals is the Social-Competence Promotion Program for Young Adolescents (Weissberg, Barton, & Shriver, 1997). This 45-session comprehensive program enhances adolescents' cognitive, emotional, and behavioral skills so that they can effectively address social tasks. In the first phase of the program, students are taught to use a problem-solving process, much like the one just outlined. In the second phase, students are exposed to information specifically targeting substance use. For example, students are given accurate information about consequences of substance use, learn about social and media influences on substance use, and discuss ways to involve students and the larger community in prevention efforts. In the third and final phase, students learn about human growth and development, AIDS prevention, and teen pregnancy. Students are encouraged to apply problem-solving skills to situations involving social relationships and sexuality. Teachers are asked to model problem-solving skills spontaneously as opportunities arise in the classroom, increasing the likelihood that adolescents will transfer these skills to situations outside the intervention effort.

ISSUES PARTICULAR TO BEHAVIORAL INTERVENTIONS WITH ADOLESCENTS

Is It Ever Too Late to Intervene?

In 1997, the White House held a conference to discuss ways to intervene in children's lives between the ages of 0 and 3 in the hopes that early intervention would effect long-lasting change. Programs like Head Start aim to set children on a good developmental pathway even before they enter school. At the same time, a push for more adolescents to be tried as adults in our court systems suggests that society holds little hope for rehabilitating youth within the juvenile system (Steinberg & Scott, 2003). Given these trends of focusing on interventions early in life, is it possible that it is too late to really change students' behaviors by the time they reach adolescence?

Fortunately the answer is no. Behavior is modifiable at any point, though the techniques that worked with younger children may not always be optimal for adolescent populations. It is especially important to continue intervention programs into middle school and high school since that is when students are at a greater risk for problem behaviors, and the negative consequences of poor decisions become more serious. For example, adolescents need to be provided with the skills to resist drugs and alcohol and to practice safe sex. Although younger children might be instructed in conflict-resolution skills, adolescents' greater propensity for violence and increased susceptibility to peer influence creates a new urgency for these skills.

Who Should Lead the Intervention—Teachers or Peers?

Most interventions are led in groups, but they vary in terms of whether teachers or peers lead the sessions. Who is most effective with adolescent populations—teachers or peers? The answer depends on the intervention's goals. If the goal of the intervention is to change students' behaviors when interacting with teachers, it is best to have teachers lead the training. For example, Pentz (1980) found that teachers, parents, and peers were all effective at increasing students' self-reported and observed assertiveness. However, teacher-led groups were most effective in producing assertiveness when students were actually interacting with teachers in real-life situations. If the goal of the intervention is to alter students' interactions with peers, it is important to include peers in the intervention. Although teachers are viewed as more credible sources of factual information than peers, peers have greater social credibility among students. Peers also provide more opportunities for rehearsing new skills in training sessions, and they can model appropriate behavior outside of the training sessions (Perry & Murray, 1989).

The use of peers in behavioral interventions is becoming more widespread. The chief advantage appears to be in facilitating the training and in helping students to generalize their skills to the situations beyond the training sessions. But three caveats should be kept in mind. First, there is little research available on how the training experience affects the peer-trainers themselves. Second, it may be more difficult to honor students' rights to confidentiality when peers are involved in the training. Third, while peers can be effective models and teachers, not all peers are equally suited for this task.

Could Interventions Ever Have Unintended Harmful Effects?

Educators begin interventions with the intention of improving adolescents' lives. But in some cases behavioral interventions do more harm than good. Unintended, harmful outcomes, known as *iatrogenic effects*, happen when control groups (who received no intervention) function better than groups who took part in the intervention. When and how do iatrogenic effects occur in interventions serving adolescent populations?

Despite the best of intentions, simply beginning an intensive intervention effort can unintentionally lead to increases in problem behavior in some cases. Imagine that a high school decided to stage an all-out attack on underage drinking. The school hosted special assemblies, lined the halls with posters about underage drinking, and included special units in classes on resisting drinking. In the face of such an intensive intervention, students might come to the (mistaken) conclusion that underage drinking is extremely prevalent at their school. Why else make such an issue of it? Students who believe that most of their peers drink are more likely to start drinking too. And so in the end the intervention could increase the very behavior the educators had hoped to decrease.

Less intensive interventions that rely on a purely educational approach (in the absence of skills training) have proved harmful in some cases as well. For example, educational programs aimed at reducing substance use help adolescents become familiar with drugs or alcohol, but do not provide resources on how to avoid these substances. The end result can be *increased* substance use among intervention participants (Arnold & Hughes, 1999).

Programs that focus purely on resistance skills (e.g., Just Say No) can backfire too. These programs may sensitize students to difficulties of saying no to friends—something they may not have worried about before. The best approach for avoiding these types of iatrogenic effects is to combine education about the true incidence of problem behaviors (e.g., how many students drink at a given school) with resistance skills (e.g., rehearsing how a student might turn down a drink without alienating his or her friends) (Donaldson, Graham, Piccinin, & Hansen, 1995).

Grouping deviant peers together in interventions has been flagged as another potential problem in behavioral interventions (Arnold & Hughes, 1999; Dishion, McCord, & Poulin, 1999). Adolescents who engage in antisocial behavior such as lying, cheating, or stealing may already be highly susceptible to peer influence. Providing these youth with ready access to other antisocial adolescents encourages friendships. These friends then "train" each other in deviant behavior (Dishion, Andrews, and Crosby, 1995). One possible solution is to include diverse groups of adolescents in intervention efforts, rather than just including those with problem behaviors. This approach encourages more diverse friendships that can continue after the intervention ends.

The only way to truly know if an intervention is causing more harm than good is to study a control group. This group of students should be identical to those receiving the intervention in every way except that they do not take part in the intervention. Unfortunately, many researchers and program developers fail to include a control group in their studies of interventions. The validity of claims made about such interventions is questionable, even if it appears that the intervention was beneficial at first glance. It is possible that the intervention had no effect and that the adolescents' problem behaviors simply decreased with time or due to a change in environment unrelated to the intervention. In the worst case, it is possible that an intervention actually *increased* problem behaviors by unintentionally reinforcing the very behaviors it was intended to decrease. Without a control group to compare the intervention group to, it is simply impossible to know for certain.

How Can We Conduct Interventions and Cover Required Course Material?

Behavioral interventions were once relegated to clinicians who worked with only the most troubled adolescents. Today we realize that all adolescents can benefit from instruction in social skills and in selecting behaviors appropriate for academic success, and so these types of interventions are commonly conducted within our schools. But schools are also responsible for preparing students to meet high school graduation requirements. How can schools take time away from their academic agendas to help students succeed in the social realm? Perhaps because of the pressure to meet educational testing standards, schools are less likely to adopt and maintain special programs that are separate from regular subject matter such English or social studies or do not increase achievement.

Although such approaches are rare, Stevahn and her colleagues offer one promising way of accomplishing both academic and social behavior goals (Stevahn et al., 1997). In their study, one group of 9th-grade students received more than 9 hours of training in conflict-resolution skills that was integrated into the study of literature. Students were asked to identify the conflicts in their readings (e.g., the conflict between the Capulets and the Montagues in Shakespeare's play *Romeo and Juliet*), write about the conflict, write a script for what each character would say using the newly learned negotiation procedure to reduce conflict, and act out their script in a role-play. The control group spent the same amount of time studying the identical literature, but without conflict-resolution training. At the end of the study, the first group not only showed better knowledge of and willingness to use the conflict-resolution procedure, but also demonstrated a greater command of the literature compared to the control group. This finding is particularly impressive since the control group devoted their entire study time to learning the literature, rather than dividing their time between conflict-resolution skills and studying the literature. This type of intervention encourages deeper processing of course material, which leads to greater success in recalling that information later (Craik & Tulving, 1975). Given the importance of both academic and behavioral agendas to the well-being of adolescents, more programs that successfully integrate behavioral interventions into course curriculums need to be developed.

Summary

Adolescents' changing behavior reflects rapid biological, cognitive, social, and contextual developments to which they must adapt. It is both highly challenging and rewarding to work with adolescents.

Youth in adolescence are at a higher risk of engaging in problem behavior than they are as children or adults. Adolescents who encounter many changes at once, who experience developmental deficits, and who lack developmental assets may be at the greatest risk for problem behavior.

Behavioral interventions for adolescents typically try to reduce risky behaviors by teaching resistance and refusal skills, or by bolstering adolescents' social skills. These programs assume that problem behaviors reflect a skills deficit and that providing adolescents with the appropriate skills will allow adolescents to avoid risky behavior.

It is not too late to expect change in adolescence. Teachers or peers may effectively lead interventions, though the most effective leader will be the one who most closely reflects the situation in which the adolescent will find him- or herself. Interventions should include control groups to protect against unwanted harmful effects of the intervention. Interventions that successfully incorporate course material are more likely to be adopted by schools.

Discussion Questions

1. Think about an adolescent you know who engages in a lot of risky behavior, and one who engages in relatively little risky behavior. What is the balance of developmental assets and risk factors like for each adolescent?
2. What are some typical adolescent behaviors that are frustrating to adults but actually may be a natural outgrowth of the physical, cognitive, and social transitions of this developmental period?
3. In the section on parent–adolescent relations and autonomy, Collins's (1990) expectancy-violation-realignment model is described. Although this model was intended to describe change in parent–adolescent relations, do you think that it might

apply to changing teacher–student relations across adolescence as well? How so? Give an example.

4. A school principal has asked you to design an intervention/prevention program aimed at reducing school violence. What features would you most want the program to have? What aspects would you be careful to avoid in designing your program?

References

Arnold, M. E., & Hughes, J. N. (1999). First do no harm: Adverse effects of grouping deviant youth for skills training. *Journal of School Psychology, 37,* 99–115.

Barling, J., Rogers, K. A., & Kelloway, E. K. (1995). Some effects of teenagers' part-time employment: The quantity and quality of work makes the difference. *Journal of Organizational Behavior, 16,* 143–154.

Benson, P. L., Scales, P. C., Leffert, N., & Roehlkepartain, E. C. (1999). *A fragile foundation: The state of developmental assets among American youth.* Minneapolis, MN: Search Institute.

Berndt, T. J. (1979). Developmental changes in conformity to peers and parents. *Developmental Psychology, 15,* 608–616.

Bradshaw, C. P., Koth, C. W., Thornton, L. A., & Leaf, P. J. (2009). Altering school climate through school-wide positive behavioral interventions and supports: Findings from a group-randomized effectiveness trial. *Prevention Science, 10,* 100–115.

Brooks-Gunn, J., & Reiter, E. O. (1990). The role of pubertal processes. In S. Feldman & G. Elliot (Eds.), *At the threshold: The developing adolescent* (pp. 16–53). Cambridge, MA: Harvard University Press.

Carskadon, M. A., Wolfson, A. R., Acebo, C., Tzischinsky, O., & Seifer, R. (1998). Adolescent sleep patterns, circadian timing, and sleepiness at a transition to early school days. *Sleep, 21,* 871–881.

Carver, K., Joyner, K., & Udry, J. R. (2003). National estimates of adolescent romantic relationships. In P. Florsheim (Ed.), *Adolescent romantic relation and sexual behavior: Theory research and practical implications* (pp. 23–56). Mahwah, NJ: Lawrence Erlbaum.

Christopher, J. S., Nangle, D. W., & Hansen, D. J. (1993). Social-skills interventions with adolescents: Current issues and procedures. *Behavior Modification, 17,* 314–338.

Collins, W. A. (1990). Parent–child relationships in the transition to adolescence: Continuity and change in interaction, affect, and cognition. In R. Montemayor & G. R. Adams (Eds.), *From childhood to adolescence: A transitional period?* Advances in Adolescent Development: An annual book series, Vol. 2. (pp. 85–106). Thousand Oaks, CA: Sage.

Collins, W. A. (1997). Relationships and development during adolescence: Interpersonal adaptation to individual change. *Personal Relationships, 4,* 1–14.

Craik, F. I. M., & Tulving, E. (1975). Depth of processing and retention of words in episodic memory. *Journal of Experimental Psychology, 104,* 268–294.

Dahl, R. E. (1999). The consequences of insufficient sleep for adolescents: Links between sleep and emotional regulation. *Phi Delta Kappan,* 354–359.

Dishion, T. J., Andrews, D. W., & Crosby, L. (1995). Antisocial boys and their friends in early adolescence: Relationship characteristics, quality, and interactional process. *Child Development, 66,* 139–151.

Dishion, T. J., McCord, J., & Poulin, F. (1999). When interventions harm: Peer groups and problem behavior. *American Psychologist, 54,* 755–764.

Donaldson, S. I., Graham, J. W., Piccinin, A. M., & Hansen, W. B. (1995). Resistance-skills training and onset of alcohol use: Evidence for beneficial and potentially harmful effects in public schools and in private catholic schools. *Health Psychology, 14,* 291–300.

D'Zurilla, T. J., & Goldfried, M. R. (1971). Problem solving and behavior modification. *Journal of Abnormal Psychology, 78,* 107–126.

Eccles, J. S., Midgley, C., Wigfield, A., Buchanan, C. M., Reuman, D., Flanagan, C., & MacIver, D. (1993). The impact of stage-environment fit on young adolescents' experiences in schools and in families. *American Psychologist, 48,* 90–101.

Elkind, D., & Bowen, R. (1979). Imaginary audience behavior in children and adolescents. *Developmental Psychology, 15,* 38–44.

Englander-Golden, P., Elconin, J., & Miller, K. J. (1985). Say It Straight: Adolescent substance abuse prevention training. *Academic Psychology Bulletin, 7,* 65–79.

Farmer, T. W., Farmer, E. M. Z., & Gut, D. M. (1999). Implications of social development research for school-based interventions for aggressive youth with EBD. *Journal of Emotional & Behavioral Disorders, 7,* 130–136.

Feiring, C. (1996). Concepts of romance in 15-year-old adolescents. *Journal of Research on Adolescence, 6,* 181–200.

Forman, S. G., & Neal, J. A. (1987). School-based substance abuse prevention programs. *Special Services in the Schools, 3,* 89–103.

Fredriksen, K., Rhodes, J., Reddy, R., & Way, N. (2004). Sleepless in Chicago: Tracking the effects of adolescent sleep loss during the middle school years. *Child Development, 75,* 84–95.

Furman, W., & Buhrmester, D. (1992). Age and sex differences in perceptions of networks of personal relationships. *Child Development, 63,* 103–115.

Ge, X., Conger, R. D., & Elder, G. H. (2001). The relation between puberty and psychological distress in adolescent boys. *Journal of Research on Adolescence, 11,* 49–70.

Gottfredson, D. C. (2001). *Schools and delinquency.* New York: Cambridge University Press.

Halford, G. S. (1989). Reflections on 25 years of Piagetian cognitive developmental psychology: 1963–1988. *Human Development, 32,* 325–357.

Hartup, W. W., & Stevens, N. (1997). Friendships and adaptation in the life course. *Psychological Bulletin, 121,* 355–370.

Herrmann, D. S., & McWhirter, J. J. (1997). Refusal and resistance skills for children and adolescents: A selected review. *Journal of Counseling & Development, 75,* 177–187.

Hovell, M. F., Blumberg, E. J., Liles, S., Powell, L., & Morrison, T. C. (2001). Training AIDS and anger prevention social skills in at-risk adolescents. *Journal of Counselling and Development, 79,* 347–355.

Kaplowitz, P. (2004). *Early puberty in girls: The essential guide to coping with this common problem.* New York: Ballantine Books.

Larson, R., Csikszentmihalyi, M., & Graef, R. (1980). Mood variability and the psychosocial adjustment of adolescents. *Journal of Youth and Adolescence, 9,* 469–490.

Larson, R. W., Clore, G. L., & Wood, G. A. (1999). The emotions of romantic relationships: Do they wreak havoc on adolescents? In W. Furman, B. B. Brown, & C. Feiring (Eds.), *The development of romantic relationships in adolescence* (pp. 19–49). New York: Cambridge University Press.

Larson, R. W., Richards, M. H., Moneta, G., & Holmbeck, G. (1996). Changes in adolescents' daily interactions with their families from ages 10 to 18: Disengagement and transformation. *Developmental Psychology, 32,* 744–754.

Livesley, W. J., & Bromley, D. B. (1973). *Person perception in childhood and adolescence.* Hoboken, NJ: Wiley.

Maas, J. (2002). *What you should know about sleep.* Paper presented at the 24th Annual National Institute on the Teaching of Psychology, St. Petersburg, FL.

McIntosh, K., Chard, D., Boland, J., & Horner, R. H. (2006). A demonstration of combined efforts in school-wide academic and behavioral systems and incidence of reading and behavior challenges in early elementary grades. *Journal of Positive Behavior Interventions, 8,* 146–154.

Mead, M. (n.d.). Quotation retrieved December 21, 2005, from http://www.brainyquote.com/quotes/quotes/m/margaretme133350.html.

Mortimer, J. T., Harley, C., & Aronson, P. J. (1999). How do prior experiences in the workplace set the stage for transitions to adulthood? In A. Booth, A. C. Crouter, & M. J. Shanahan (Eds.), *Transitions to adulthood in a changing economy: No work, no family, no future?* (pp. 131–159) Westport, CT: Praeger.

Newcomb, A. F., & Bagwell, C. L. (1996). The developmental significance of children's friendships. In W. M. Bukowski, A. F. Newcomb, & W. W. Hartup (Eds.), *The company they keep: Friendship in childhood and adolescence.* New York: Cambridge University Press.

Positive Behavioral Interventions & Supports. (2010). Retrieved April 3, 2010 from www.pbis.org.

Pentz, M. A. (1980). Assertion training and trainer effects on unassertive and aggressive adolescents. *Journal of Counseling Psychology, 27,* 76–83.

Perry, C., & Murray, D. (1989). Prevention of alcohol use and abuse in adolescence: Teacher- vs. peer-led intervention. *Crisis, 10,* 52–61.

Piaget, J., & Inhelder, B. (1969). *The psychology of the child.* New York: Basic Books.

Rohrbach, L. A., Graham, J. W., Hansen, W. B., Flay, B. R., & Johnson, C. A. (1987). Evaluation of resistance skills training using multitrait-multimethod role play skill assessment. *Health Education Research, 2,* 401–407.

Rutter, M., Graham, P., Chadwick, O., & Yule, W. (1976). Adolescent turmoil: Fact or fiction? *Journal of Child Psychology and Psychiatry, 17,* 35–56.

Ryan, R. M., & Lynch, J. H. (1989). Emotional autonomy versus detachment: Revisiting the vicissitudes of adolescence and young adulthood. *Child Development, 60,* 340–356.

Shanahan, M. J., Finch, M. D., Mortimer, J. T., & Ryu, S. (1991). Adolescent work experiences and depressive affect. *Social Psychology Quarterly, 54,* 299–317.

Simmons R., Blyth, D., Van Cleave, E., & Bush, D. (1979). Entry into adolescence: The impact of school structure, puberty, and early dating on self-esteem. *American Sociological Review, 44,* 948–967.

Smetana, J. G. (1988). Adolescents' and parents' conceptions of parental authority. *Child Development, 59,* 321–335.

Spear, L. P. (2000). Neurobehavioral changes in adolescence. *Current Directions in Psychological Science, 9,* 111–114.

Stattin, H. & Magnusson, D. (1990). *Pubertal maturation in female development.* Hillsdale, NJ: Erlbaum.

Steinberg, L. (1990). Autonomy, conflict, and harmony in the family relationship. In S. Feldman & G. Elliot (Eds.), *At the threshold: The developing adolescent* (pp. 255–276). Cambridge, MA: Harvard University Press.

Steinberg, L. (2001). We know some things: Parent–adolescent relationships in retrospect and prospect. *Journal of Research on Adolescence, 11,* 1–19.

Steinberg, L., & Scott, E. S. (2003). Less guilty by reason of adolescence: Developmental immaturity, diminished responsibility, and the juvenile death penalty. *American Psychologist, 58,* 1009–1018.

Stevahn, L., Johnson, D. W., Johnson, R. T., Green, K., & Laginski, A. M. (1997) Effects on high school students of conflict resolution training integrated into English literature. *Journal of Social Psychology, 137,* 302–315.

Taylor-Greene, S. J., & Kartub, D. T. (2000). Durable implementation of school-wide behavior support. *Journal of Positive Behavior Interventions, 2,* 233–235.

U.S. Census Bureau. (2010a). *School enrollment: 2006–2008.* Retrieved March 26, 2010, from http://factfinder.census.gov.

U.S. Census Bureau. (2010b). *Educational attainment: 2006–2008.* Retrieved March 26, 2010, from http://factfinder.census.gov.

Weissberg, R. P., Barton, H. A., & Shriver, T. P. (1997). The social competence promotion program for young adolescents. In G. W. Albee & T. P. Gullotta (Eds.), *Primary prevention works* (pp. 268–290). Thousand Oaks, CA: Sage.

Wentzel, K. R. (1998). Social support and adjustment in middle school: The role of parents, teachers, and peers. *Journal of Educational Psychology, 90,* 202–209.

Wentzel, K. R., & Battle, A. A. (2001). Social relationships and school adjustment. In T. Urdan & F. Pajares (Eds.), *Adolescence and education: General issues in the education of adolescence* (pp. 93–118). Greenwich, CT: Information Age Publishing.

Wofford, S. (1988). *A preliminary analysis of the relationship between employment and delinquency/crime for adolescents and youth adults.* National Youth Survey No. 50. Boulder: Institute of Behavioral Science, University of Colorado.

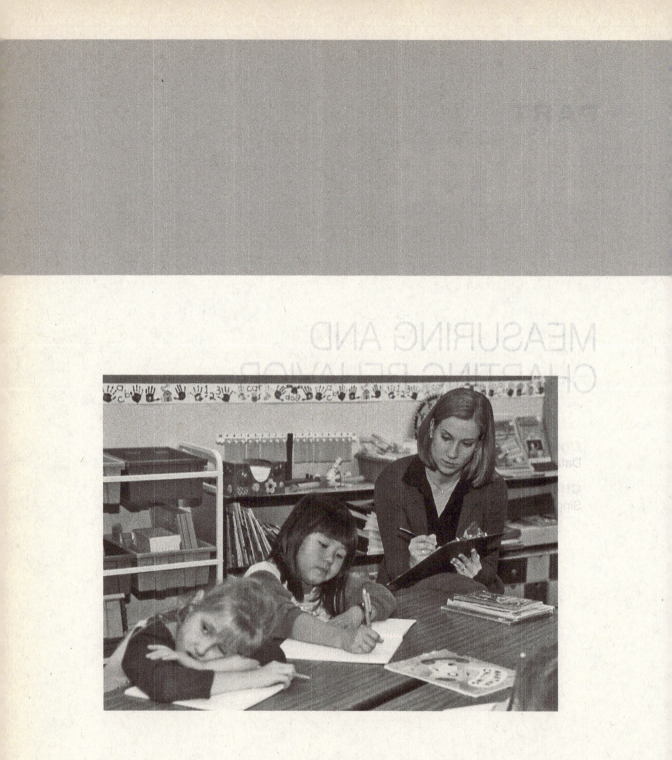

CHAPTER 6

Data Collection Techniques

Thomas Zirpoli and Daria Buese
McDaniel College

> *There is a need for intervention and measurement methods that are practical and which allow for the documentation of empirically and socially valid outcomes. Teachers require measurement systems that are useful in formative program evaluation; competent instructional decision making is ongoing and does not occur only upon completing of a program.*
>
> —MEYER AND JANNEY (1989, P. 269)

The primary goal of this chapter is to provide teachers with an understanding of the importance of direct behavioral observation, the measurement of behavior, and the documentation of these observations and measurements. In addition, by the end of this chapter, teachers will have the technical skills to complete these important tasks.

TARGET BEHAVIORS

A *target behavior* is the behavior targeted for observation, measurement, and assessment and/or modification. The target behavior is identified by teachers as the behavior needing to be learned, increased, or decreased. Frequently, teachers are faced with several students who may have many challenging behaviors and training needs. In such situations, teachers are encouraged to prioritize behaviors according to their severity and need for remediation. Several questions have been recommended to assist in identifying and prioritizing target behaviors that need to be modified or eliminated (Barlow & Hersen, 1984; Kazdin, 1982):

- Is the behavior dangerous to the student or to others in the student's environment?
- Is the behavior interfering with the student's academic performance or placement?
- Is the behavior interfering with the student's social integration or causing the student to be socially isolated from peers?

- Is the behavior interfering with effective parental interactions (e.g., bonding or communication)?
- Is a change in the target behavior likely to produce positive outcomes for the student in the areas of academic performance and social acceptance?

Once target behaviors are identified, they must be clearly defined so that they can be objectively observed and measured. This, perhaps, is the most critical step in assuring accurate, reliable observations and measurements of target behaviors.

Defining Target Behaviors

Target behaviors must be defined precisely so that there will be a minimum amount of variation from one observer to the next in the interpretation of the behavior. Precisely defined behaviors are stated in terms that are observable and measurable. *Observable* means that you can see the behavior occur. *Measurable* means that you can quantify the frequency, duration, or other dimensions of the behavior (dimensions of behavior are discussed later in this chapter). For example, increasing John's "appropriate" behavior and/or decreasing John's "inappropriate" behavior are not target behaviors that are stated in observable and measurable terms; the behaviors are not directly observable since the observer does not have a precise behavior to observe.

A target behavior defined as "increasing John's attendance in English class" is precise and may be easily observed and measured. Few individuals would have trouble understanding what to count when measuring the frequency of John's English class attendance. The following lists provide additional examples of observable and nonobservable target behaviors:

Examples of Observable Target Behaviors

Chris will *complete his assignments* during math class.

Adam will *use his fork* to pick up food during mealtime.

Julia will *talk to other children* on the playground.

John will *ask for a break* when he is angry.

Tommy will *complete all school assignments* before going home.

Jeremy will *share his toys* with other children during free play.

Jill will *practice the piano* 1 hour per day.

Jason will *say "Thank you"* when given gifts for his birthday.

Mike will *say "Excuse me"* before interrupting others at home.

Justen will *look both ways* before crossing the street.

Melissa will *wait for her turn* during group work at school.

Examples of Nonobservable Target Behaviors

Chris will *be a good boy* during math class.

Adam will *be polite* during mealtime.

Julia will *be cooperative* on the playground.

John will *think* before he acts when he is angry.

Tommy will *remember* to do his schoolwork.

Jeremy will *be nice* to the other children during free play.

Jill will *apply herself* during piano practice.

Jason will *understand* the importance of saying "thank you."

Mike will *demonstrate appropriate manners* with others.

Justen will *be careful* when crossing the street.

Melissa will *get along* with others during group work.

Notice that in most cases, the target behavior is presented in positive terms. Teachers should try to state target behaviors in terms of how children should behave instead of how they should not behave. This will help teachers focus on positive student behaviors instead of unacceptable or disruptive behaviors.

Target behaviors should be defined as precisely as possible to ensure that the behavior is understood and rated consistently (Chafouleas et al., 2007). Hawkins and Dobes (1977) state that definitions of target behaviors should be *objective, clear,* and *complete*. A target behavior is *objective* when the observer can see the behavior or when the behavior is overt. Covert feelings or states are not objective. For example, "hitting other children" is overt and can be observed and measured. "Feeling angry" at other children is a state that is difficult to define, observe, and accurately measure. A target behavior is *clearly* defined when the definition is "unambiguous, easily understood, and readily paraphrased" (Barlow & Hersen, 1984, p. 111). For example, stating that a student "will behave" during group activities is not a clearly defined target behavior. Stating that the student "will stay seated" or "will keep her hands on the desk" is clear and unambiguous. A *complete* definition "includes the boundaries of the behavior, so that an observer can discriminate it from other, related behaviors" (Barlow & Hersen, 1984, p. 111). In the previous example, the target behavior "will behave" does not discriminate one behavior (e.g., "staying in seat") from other behaviors that could also be the intended behavior to be observed under the definition of "will behave" (e.g., "keeping hands on desk"). After a target behavior is identified and defined, teachers must establish a behavioral objective.

Establishing Behavioral Objectives

A *behavioral objective* describes an anticipated behavior, new or modified from current behavior, subsequent to the completed behavior change program. As demonstrated in the first of the following examples, a behavioral objective includes several basic elements: the desired *terminal behavior* (in-seat behavior), the *conditions* under which the behavior is to occur (during each 45-minute math class), a level of performance or *behavioral criteria* (45 consecutive minutes), and a specified number of *consecutive observations* (three math classes) during which the behavioral criteria must be exhibited. The terminal behavior is what the student's behavior will look like after the behavior change program is completed. If the target behavior is the behavior you wish to teach or modify, the terminal behavior defines the student's behavior when the behavioral objective has been achieved. For example, a student may have a problem staying in his seat during math class. "Staying in seat" or "getting out of seat" is the target behavior. "Staying in seat for the entire 45-minute math class" may be the terminal behavior you wish to observe at the end of your behavior change program. An appropriate behavioral objective may be stated as follows:

> *Tom will stay in his seat during each 45-minute math class, unless he has permission from the teacher to leave his seat, for three consecutive math classes.*

Behavioral criteria may be stated in many ways depending on the behavior and environmental expectations. In the preceding example, the behavioral objective for Tom's in-seat behavior was stated in terms of *what* behavior will be exhibited (staying in his seat), *when* the behavior will be exhibited (during each 45-minute math class), and for *how many* (three consecutive) math classes the behavior must be exhibited. Criteria may also be stated in the form of a percentage when a certain percentage of correct or appropriate responses is desired. For example:

> *Tom will comply with teacher requests with a 90% compliance rate over four consecutive days, or Tom will complete 80% of his class assignments for five consecutive school days.*

During the behavior change program, a student's behavior may be evaluated on the basis of the behavioral criteria outlined in the behavioral objective. The criteria outlined in behavioral objectives should reflect realistic expectations based on current performance (determined by a review of baseline data), academic necessity, and social norms.

Before teachers can develop behavioral objectives, baseline observations and data collection must be completed (as described later in this chapter). Baseline observations not only provide information about current performance levels from which behavioral objectives are developed, but also help determine whether the target behavior is as problematic as perceived. With this information, teachers can establish objectives that are challenging yet realistic. Table 6.1 provides a review of these terms and their definitions.

TABLE 6.1 Definitions for Writing Behavioral Objectives and Examples

Term	Definition	Example
Target behavior	The behavior you want to teach or modify. When teaching a new behavior, the target and terminal behavior may be the same.	Temper tantrums at the grocery store or asking "please" when making a request.
Terminal behavior	The desired behavior.	The absence of temper tantrums.
Behavioral criteria	A desired performance level of the terminal behavior. When the child reaches this performance level, the program is complete.	Zero tantrums for five consecutive shopping trips to the grocery store.
Behavioral objective	A statement including the terminal behavior and the behavioral criteria.	John will have zero tantrums for five consecutive shopping trips to the store.

Naturalistic Observation

The purpose of naturalistic observation is to observe and record behavioral patterns across natural settings and situations, to measure the dimensions of specific target behaviors, and to identify the variables associated with specific target behaviors. All of this information will be useful to help understand the function of a particular target behavior. In addition, once you begin a behavior change plan, observational data provide information on the effectiveness of behavior interventions and necessary modifications to ongoing programming.

Green (1990) recommends that observers record occurrences of the target behavior under different conditions and pay particular attention to

- the time of day;
- factors in the physical environment such as space, noise, temperature, light, and materials;
- behaviors of others before and after occurrences of the problem behavior (see next section on ABC analysis);
- task demands;
- the student's communication skills; and
- conditions under which the disruptive behavior *does not* occur.

These factors will help teachers understand when a target behavior occurs and under what conditions. In addition, a functional analysis must include the systematic presentation of different antecedents and consequences to verify the purpose of the target behavior. This procedure is outlined in the next section on ABC analysis.

Anecdotal Observation: The ABC Analysis

A good start to identify or confirm the purpose of a target behavior is to observe and record the antecedents and consequences of the behavior. This can best be done through an ABC analysis:

A = Antecedent

B = Behavior

C = Consequence

Sometimes referred to as an *anecdotal observation*, an *ABC analysis* was first described by Bijou, Peterson, and Ault (1968). During an anecdotal observation, the observer records everything noticed about an individual's behavior. For example, if an anecdotal observation was completed for Josh during a 15-minute free-time period, the observer would record Josh's behaviors, who he played with, what he played with, and what he said. The product of this anecdotal observation would probably include a narrative describing Jason's behavior during the 15-minute observation period. From this information, specific target behaviors may be identified for modification. It is important to note that ABC recording presents an *objective* description of actual behavior, not interpretations of that behavior. For example, "Josh hit Mike," not "Josh was angry."

In addition to behavioral observation and data collection, an anecdotal record includes an analysis of antecedent and consequent events occurring within the observed environment. As Lennox and Miltenberger (1989) state, understanding behavior is incomplete without understanding the "events surrounding the target behavior and, subsequently,

Child's name: Michael	Observer: Ms. Garris
Environment: Playground	Date: 11/6/10
Observation start time: 12:30 pm	Stop: 12:45 pm

Antecedent Events	Observed Behavior	Consequent Events
12:36: Students are running around in a circle.	Michael pushed Tim from behind.	Tim turned around and yelled at Michael to "Stop!"
12:42: Students are standing in a circle and talking.	Michael told Tim, "You're a nerd," and hit him on the head.	Tim said nothing and did nothing. Michael laughed.
12:45: Bell rings for kids to return to classroom. Kids begin to run toward building.	Michael hit Tim on the back as the two were running toward the building.	Tim continued to run toward the building. Did not give Michael a response. Michael laughed.

FIGURE 6.1   Example of a record form for an ABC analysis

[determining] the extent to which specific events may be related to the occurrence of the behavior" (p. 306). The focus of an ABC analysis is on "external events that appear to influence the behavior" (Snell & Grigg, 1987, p. 78) and "is one of the few assessment methods that provide a clear avenue for identifying variables outside of the child that may be important in developing hypotheses about possible interventions" (Merrell, 2001, p. 16).

To complete an ABC analysis or anecdotal record of the antecedents, behaviors, and consequences within a student's environment, practitioners should prepare an observation form that will facilitate record keeping during the observation period. This form may be a simple sheet of paper divided into three sections: antecedent events, observed behaviors, and consequent events. An example of an anecdotal observation form, suitable for an ABC analysis, is provided in Figure 6.1.

As a direct observational tool that "provides information about what is really happening in the student's environment," the ABC analyis is an important tool when completing a functional behavioral assessment (discussed in Chapter 9) (Robinson & Smith, 2005, p. 2). An ABC analysis provides teachers with the following information:

- *A descriptive record of a student's behavior during a specific observational period.* The observational period could coincide with activities or settings in which the person's behavior has been especially problematic.
- *A descriptive record of the student's environment.* This would include the significant people in the student's environment and their interactions with those significant others, and the activities occurring within the student's environment.
- *Information about antecedent events occurring before the student's behavior.* This information will help teachers identify events that may set the stage for specific

behaviors. For example, what are the adult or peer behaviors (requests, demands, proximity) that occur prior to the student's behavior?

- *Information about consequent events occurring after the student's behavior.* This information will help teachers identify events that may maintain, reinforce, or punish specific behavior. For example, what comments do others make following the student's behavior, or how do other students respond after the student's behavior?

The preceding information will help teachers identify disruptive behaviors, events that are maintaining the disruptive behavior, alternative social skills that need to be learned, and environmental conditions that need modification to meet the needs of the student.

Assessment Interviews

In addition to a structured observation as described in the ABC analysis, Umbreit and Blair (1997, p. 77) developed an assessment interview. They used the assessment interview to identify "the conditions under which a target behavior is likely and unlikely to occur" from the perspective of teachers, parents, or other significant others who spend a significant amount of time with the student and have the opportunity to observe patterns related to the target behavior. These interviews with significant others can help identify:

- when and how often the behavior occurs;
- how long the behavior has been occurring;
- the behavior reduction procedures the staff has previously used;
- whether other behaviors signal or occur along with the target behavior; and
- whether the target behavior's occurrence is related to skill deficits, allergies, medication, hunger or thirst, or other discomfort.

DIMENSIONS OF BEHAVIOR

After a target behavior has been identified and defined and behavioral criteria have been established, two additional questions remain (Tawney & Gast, 1984, p. 112): What are the dimensions or "characteristics" of the student's behavior that should be observed and measured, and how will the dimensions of the target behavior be measured? This section addresses the first question by defining and discussing the five primary dimensions of behavior: frequency, duration, rate, latency, and intensity.

Frequency

Frequency or *number* refers to a simple count of the number of times a behavior occurs during a specific time period. If one frequency count is to be compared with a second, the observation period must be constant across both. For example, if you observe Chris having 5 tantrums on day 1 and 10 tantrums on day 2, the duration of the observation periods across the two days must be the same for the two frequency counts in order to be directly comparable. In other words, you cannot assume that Chris had more tantrums on the 2nd day since the increase may be due to a longer observation period. Because teachers do not always have a constant observation period from day to day, frequency counts alone are not recommended.

When a constant observation period can be established, frequency counts are best used when the target behavior has clear starting and stopping points (Foster, Bell-Dolan, & Burge, 1988). For example, counting the number of times one student *hits* another student is easily done. However, counting the number of times a student *talks* to another student may be more complicated since clear starting and stopping points between *talks* may be blurred.

Kazdin (1989) recommends that frequency only be used when each occurrence of the target behavior "takes a relatively constant amount of time each time it is performed" (p. 58). Using our previous example, each *hit* probably takes the same time to perform, while each *talk* may not. A student could talk for 1 second to one student ("Hi!") or have a 5-minute conversation with a second student. A simple frequency count (two) would not discriminate the two *talking* behaviors as different. For behaviors that may vary in duration, teachers are encouraged to measure frequency and duration.

Another caution regarding the use of frequency counts alone is knowing the number of response opportunities. For example, if a teacher reports that a student completed five assignments during math class, this information is incomplete without knowing the total number of assignments requested. Knowing that the student completed 5 of 5 or 5 of 10 assignments communicates a more complete picture of the student's performance than the frequency count alone. A second example involves the measurement of compliance. If a teacher reports a frequency count of eight compliances during a school day, without reporting the total number of opportunities to be compliant, the information is incomplete and not very useful. A frequency count of 8 compliances of 10 opportunities represents a different level of performance than 8 compliances of 20 requests.

Duration

Duration data are recommended when teachers are concerned about how long a behavior continues once started or the amount of time consumed when a behavior is performed. Duration is a necessary dimension to measure when teachers want to increase or decrease the amount of time a student performs a behavior or participates in an activity. In addition to how often some behaviors occur, the duration of behaviors such as crying, throwing temper tantrums, listening, or working on a task is a significant dimension that should be measured. For example, if a student has a 60-minute temper tantrum one day and a 5-minute tantrum the next, information that the student had one tantrum each day (frequency) does not provide a complete picture of the student's behavior. In this example, the duration of tantrum behavior has significantly decreased from the 1st to the 2nd day. This change in behavior would not have been noted if the duration of the behavior was not measured.

There are two types of duration: *total duration* (Tawney & Gast, 1984) and *response duration* (Kazdin, 1989). *Total duration* refers to the total amount of time a student performs a target behavior during an observation period. For example, if a student had two tantrums during a 1-hour observation period and each tantrum lasted 5 minutes, the total duration was 10 minutes. Teachers would be interested in measuring total duration if they were trying to increase or decrease the total amount of time a student was engaged in an activity or behavior within a specific time period or activity. For example, a teacher may wish to increase a student's total time on task in a reading class. Total duration may be used to estimate the percentage of total observation time in which a student is engaged in a behavior (Kazdin, 1989). For example, if a student worked on task for a total duration of 30 minutes during a 45-minute class period, it may be stated that the student was on task for 66.6% of the class period.

$$(30/45 = 0.666 \times 100 = 66.6\%)$$

Response duration refers to the amount of time a student performs each individual target behavior. In the earlier example, the response duration for the first and second tantrum was 5 minutes. Teachers would be interested in measuring response duration if they were trying to increase or decrease the amount of time a student exhibits a specific behavior. Referring back to our temper tantrum example, it is helpful to know the duration of each individual tantrum, not total duration, when trying to decrease tantrum behavior. In addition, the use of response duration allows teachers to estimate a median response duration per behavior occurrence.

Rate

Rate refers to the frequency of a target behavior divided by the number of minutes or hours of observation time. This will yield a rate-per-minute or rate-per-hour measurement:

frequency of behavior/observation time = rate

For example, if John is noncompliant 10 times during a 5-hour observation period, John's hourly rate of noncompliance is 2. This was calculated by dividing the frequency (10) of noncompliance by the number (5) of observation hours (10/5 = 2).

frequency of noncompliance/total observation hours = rate per hour of noncompliance

Rate is often stated in terms of minutes. For example, if a teacher observes Julia kicking her desk six times during a 30-minute social studies class, then Julia's kicking rate per minute is 0.20. This was calculated by dividing the frequency (6) of kicking by the number (30) of observation minutes (6/30 = 0.20).

frequency of kicking/total observation minutes = rate per minute

Rates are useful when the observation periods are not constant and vary in duration. The measurement of the rate allows teachers to compare the frequency of behavior across observation periods even if the duration of the observation period varies from day to day. For example, if Julia kicks her desk 12 times during another 1-hour observation period, her minute rate of kicking is 0.20 (12/60 = 0.20). The minute rate (0.20) from the first observation period may be compared with the rate (0.20) from the second observation period since the difference in the duration of the observation period was accounted for during the rate calculation. In this case, a summary of Julia's performance for the 2 days may conclude that the rate of her kicking was constant (0.20 per minute). On the other hand, if the teacher reported frequency alone (6 kicks on day 1 and 12 kicks on day 2), an observer might incorrectly conclude that Julia's kicking behavior doubled on the 2nd day.

Teachers are recommended to use rate when reporting the number of times a behavior occurred unless the observation periods are constant. However, given the busy schedules of classrooms and homes, observation periods are unlikely to be constant, and teachers should plan on using rates when reporting behavioral data.

Latency

Latency refers to the amount of time it takes for a student to begin a behavior once he or she has received a direction or an instruction to complete a task or modify a behavior. Latency is most useful when teachers are concerned about students' compliance or behaviors related to following directions. For example, when a teacher asks a student to help pick up toys after a free-time activity, latency is recorded by keeping track of the number of minutes or seconds between the initial request and the point when the student actually starts to pick up the toys. When teachers are working with children who tend to be noncompliant, the objective is to reduce the latency period to an acceptable level (5–10 seconds). This goal is accomplished by reinforcing children when they show improvement in decreasing their latency period and when they respond appropriately within an acceptable period of time.

Sometimes teachers want to increase latency periods. A common example is the student who responds incorrectly to a teacher's directions because he or she begins an activity before the teacher provides all the instructions. Children who are too quick to answer a teacher's question, without allowing some time to think about the question, may commit many errors because of short latencies. When this is a problem, teachers may want to require a certain latency period (thinking time) before children are allowed to volunteer an answer.

Intensity or Magnitude

Intensity refers to the force or strength of a behavior. Intensity of behavior is a useful measurement with behaviors such as acts of aggression, temper tantrums, verbal responses, or other noises and body movements. For example, since the variability in crying behavior is considerable, teachers working with a student who cries when he or she is brought to day care each morning may be interested in measuring intensity, in addition to the frequency and duration of crying. A student who cries for 5 minutes once each morning may seem, with just frequency and duration measures, to be making poor progress adjusting to day care. However, the intensity measurement may record a significant change in the student's crying behavior from "loud screaming" to "mild whining."

Intensity measures are either estimates based on a predetermined qualitative scale or, for a more objective measure, an automated apparatus used to measure a behavior's intensity. For example, Greene, Bailey, and Barber (1981) have used an automated apparatus to measure noise levels during a program to decrease disruptive behavior on school buses. In most cases, however, teachers do not have access to such automatic equipment; moreover, qualitative estimates of intensity will probably serve the needs of most teachers and parents. When an objective method of measuring the intensity of a target behavior is not possible, such as Josh's hitting behavior in Classroom Connection 6.1, the following are some example scales that may be used, depending on the behavior:

- Very strong, strong, weak, very weak
- Mild, moderate, severe, very severe
- Very loud, loud, quiet, very quiet
- Very fast, fast, slow, very slow

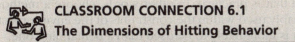

CLASSROOM CONNECTION 6.1
The Dimensions of Hitting Behavior

Jennifer is a counselor at an elementary school and received a request for assistance from the kindergarten teacher, Judy, about a boy named Josh who was hitting other students. School had just started, and Judy wanted to eliminate Josh's aggressive behavior as soon as possible. But Jennifer insisted that Judy first collect some baseline data and complete an ABC analysis as part of a functional behavioral assessment of Josh's hitting behavior. Judy agreed to complete a frequency count of Josh's hitting behavior for one full week, or 5 days of school. During the 5-day baseline period, Judy recorded the following number of hits by Josh per day: 5, 2, 8, 6, and 5. She also rated the

intensity of each hit using the following descriptors: "moderate," "hard," and "very hard." She completed an ABC analysis of each hit in an effort to determine the environmental influences and function of his behavior.

General Reflection for Classroom Connection 6.1:

In looking at Judy's data, what is the daily rate of Josh's hitting behavior? Why didn't Judy document duration data? What other descriptors could she have used to measure the intensity of Josh's hitting? If you were Jennifer, how would you instruct Judy to respond to Josh's hitting behavior during the 5-day baseline period?

It must be stressed, however, that these "ratings" provide subjective measurements of behavior. When these are used, precise criteria should be established per rating, and independent observers should complete reliability checks.

MEASUREMENT OF BEHAVIOR

Unfortunately, many teachers consider data collection as too demanding and don't see the benefits of behavioral observation, measurement, and documentation. Thus, it is important that we demonstrate to teachers that data collection and documentation, even data graphing, may be completed without significant sacrifices of time from the typical classroom routine.

Wacker (1989) provides two primary reasons why teachers should measure behavior: to document what occurred and to identify the variables responsible for the occurrence. "Measurement, in short, provides us with guidance regarding what we should do next" (p. 254). In addition, a systematic process of behavioral measurement can

- help teachers identify learning and behavior problems;
- provide information concerning program effectiveness;
- identify the need for program modifications; and
- facilitate communication with parents, administrators, other teachers, and support personnel.

Tawney and Gast (1984, p. 84) provide several guidelines for measuring and evaluating behavior:

- Define the target behavior in measurable and observable terms.
- Collect sufficient data to provide the information necessary to make programming decisions. It is not necessary to collect data constantly on all behaviors.
- Become familiar with data collection alternatives so intelligent decisions can be made regarding the most effective measurement method per student and behavior.

- Select a data collection method that is practical. In other words, choose a method that can be consistently and reliably used within the constraints of the environment. A simple data collection system is more likely to be used than a demanding one.
- Integrate data collection into the daily routine. Again, data collection should not take an extraordinary effort on the part of teachers.
- Review and evaluate the data regularly, and use the data to make programming decisions.

The primary purpose of data collection is to provide teachers with objective information with which to make informed programming decisions. It is disturbing to observe teachers collect data only to fulfill an organizational requirement, place the data in a file, and never use the data for program evaluation.

Several types of data collection methods or observational recording systems are used to monitor behavior. An understanding of these different methods will allow teachers to select the simplest and most informative data collection procedure. A description of the primary types of behavioral observation and measurement methods is outlined in the next sections.

Frequency Recording/Event Recording

When observing for an individual target behavior, an easy method of measuring the target behavior is simply to count the behavior every time it occurs during a specific time period. This method of data collection is called *frequency recording* or *event recording*. The result of a frequency recording is a frequency count or rate of occurrence per observation period. For example, a teacher may use event recording to count how many times a student hits other students during a 30-minute recess. Koorland, Monda, and Vail (1988) make the following recommendations concerning event recording:

- Event recording should be used only when the target behavior is "discrete, uniform in duration, brief, and repeatable" (p. 59).
- The observation periods per day may be fixed or variable. Thus, teachers may decide to count a target behavior once per day, twice per day, or whatever schedule is convenient with the teacher's schedule.
- The duration of each observation period may vary. When the observation period is constant, a frequency count may be reported per observation. When the observation periods vary, however, the rate of the behavior must be determined by dividing each number of occurrences per observation period with the number of minutes per observation period.

Figure 6.2 illustrates an event-recording data form used to count hitting behavior. Data collected include the number of times hitting was observed, the length of the observation periods in minutes, and the rate of hitting per minute. Note that the observation periods vary in length, and the rate per minute is calculated for each observation so that the data are comparable. The rate of the target behavior, per minute, may also be charted on a graph as demonstrated in Figure 6.2.

Duration Recording

Recording the duration of a behavior is important when teachers are concerned with the amount of time a student engages in a target behavior. Teachers may record duration along with frequency by making a note of the time the target behavior begins and ends.

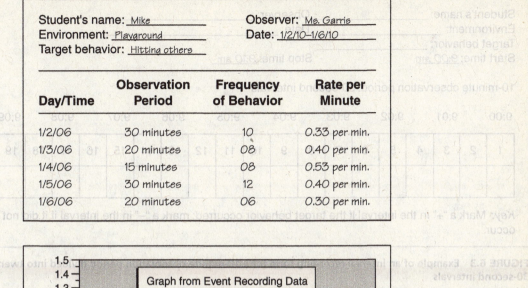

Day/Time	Observation Period	Frequency of Behavior	Rate per Minute
1/2/06	30 minutes	10	0.33 per min.
1/3/06	20 minutes	08	0.40 per min.
1/4/06	15 minutes	08	0.53 per min.
1/5/06	30 minutes	12	0.40 per min.
1/6/06	20 minutes	06	0.30 per min.

Student's name: Mike
Environment: Playground
Target behavior: Hitting others
Observer: Ms. Garris
Date: 1/2/10–1/6/10

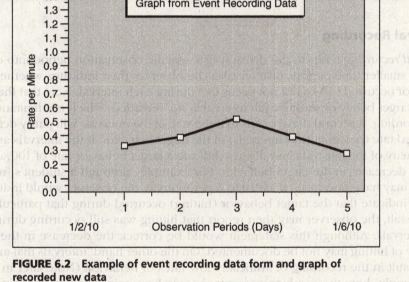

FIGURE 6.2 Example of event recording data form and graph of recorded new data

A duration can then be calculated. For example, if a student begins to tantrum in the morning at 10:15 and ends at 10:25, the duration of the tantrum is 10 minutes.

Duration may be recorded in two ways. First, teachers may be interested in the *average duration* of a behavior over a specific period of time. For example, if a student had three tantrums during one class period lasting 10, 5, and 3 minutes each, the average duration is 6 minutes.

$$10 + 5 + 3 = 18/3 = 6$$

Second, teachers may also be interested in the *total duration* of the target behavior. Using our same example, the total duration of tantrum behavior is 18 minutes.

Student's name: _____ Observer: _____
Environment: _____ Date: _____
Target behavior: _____
Start time: _9:00 am_   Stop time: _9:10 am_

10-minute observation period: 30-second intervals

| 9:00 | 9:01 | 9:02 | 9:03 | 9:04 | 9:05 | 9:06 | 9:07 | 9:08 | 9:09 |

1	2	3	4	5	6	7	8	9	10	11	12	13	14	15	16	17	18	19	20

Key: Mark a "+" in the interval if the target behavior occurred; mark a "−" in the interval if it did not occur.

FIGURE 6.3 Example of an interval recording form for a 10-minute observation period divided into twenty 30-second intervals

Interval Recording

Interval recording refers to the division of a specific observation period into equal intervals of smaller time periods or intervals. The observer then indicates whether the target behavior occurred (+) or did not occur (−) during each interval. Note that the frequency of the target behavior during each interval is *not* recorded, which is a limitation of interval recording. A second drawback is that the size of the intervals will partly determine the recorded rate (percentage of intervals) of the target behavior. If the intervals are too long, a summary of the intervals may always indicate a target behavior rate of 100%, regardless of real decreases in the target behavior. For example, although a student's frequency of hitting may have decreased from 10 to 5 per interval, the observer would indicate only a "+" to indicate that the target behavior (hitting) occurred during that particular interval. As a result, the observer may then report that hitting was still occurring during 100% of the intervals. Although this statement would be correct, the decrease in the actual frequency of hitting may not be documented. On the other hand, intervals that are too short may result in the recording of artificially low rates of behavior. (Note later in Figure 6.3, for example, how the resulting percentages may be manipulated by changing the duration of the intervals.)

The size of each interval within the total observation period may range from 5 to 30 seconds. Trudel and Cote (1996) used 6-second intervals to observe and record the behavior of ice hockey coaches during games. Because they were observing 16 different categories of coach behaviors and 8 categories describing to whom their behavior was directed, Trudel and Cote decided to use a 6-second interval to "decrease the possibility of occurrence of too many behaviors within a given interval" (p. 50).

Kazdin (1989) recommends 10- to 15-second intervals; Cooper, Heron, and Heward (2007) suggest 6- to 15-second intervals; and Alberto and Troutman (2009) state that the intervals should not be longer than 30 seconds. Repp, Nieminen, Olinger, and Brusca (1988) have found that shorter intervals produced more accurate data than longer intervals.

Student's name: _Chris_   Observer: _Ms. Hawkins_

Environment: _Science_   Date: _3/2/10_

Target behavior: _On Task_

Start time: _9:00 am_   Stop time: _9:10 am_

10-minute observation period: 30-second intervals

9:00		9:01		9:02		9:03		9:04		9:05		9:06		9:07		9:08		9:09	
1	2	3	4	5	6	7	8	9	10	11	12	13	14	15	16	17	18	19	20
−	+	+	+	−	+	+	−	+	+	+	−	−	+	+	+	+	−	+	+

Key: + = The behavior occurred during the interval.

       − = The behavior did not occur during the interval.

Summary of Interval Recording Observation

Total number of intervals	20
Intervals target behavior occurred	14
Percentage of intervals behavior occurred	70%
Intervals target behavior did not occur	6
Percentage of intervals behavior did not occur	30%

FIGURE 6.4 **Sample data for an interval recording form for a 10-minute observation period divided into twenty 30-second intervals**

The total observation period for interval recording may range from 10 to 60 minutes, depending on the teacher's schedule. An example of an interval recording form is provided in Figure 6.3.

A 10-minute observation period is divided into 30-second intervals. Since there are twenty 30-second intervals during a 10-minute observation period, the 10-minute observation period is divided into 20 intervals. Thus, the total number of intervals depends on the total observation time and the length of the intervals.

Once the length of the total observation period and the size of the intervals have been decided, the next step is to observe the student and indicate whether the target behavior occurred during each interval. It does not make a difference how many times the target behavior occurred during each interval. During the observation period, a "+" is recorded if the behavior occurred at any time during each interval and a "−" if it did not (see Figure 6.4). At the end of the interval, teachers may calculate the percentage of intervals in which the target behavior occurred and did not occur. This is calculated by dividing the number of intervals with a "+" by the total number of intervals. In our hypothetical data provided in Figure 6.4, the target behavior was observed in 14 of the 20 intervals. By dividing 14 by 20, we find that the target behavior occurred during 70% of the total intervals.

The two primary methods of interval recording are partial-interval recording and whole-interval recording. *Partial-interval recording* requires the observer to record whether the behavior occurred at any time during the interval. The frequency or duration

Students' names: _Mellisa, Jill & Julia_

Target behavior: _Talking_

Environment: _____ Date: _____

Start time:_____ Stop time: _____

5-minute observation period: 30-second intervals

Name		1		2		3		4		5
Mellisa										
Jill										
Julia										

Key: Next to the appropriate child's name, mark a "+" in the interval if the target behavior was observed; mark a "−" in the interval if the target behavior did not occur.

FIGURE 6.5 **Interval recording form for a 5-minute observation period divided into ten 30-second intervals for three students**

of the behavior within the interval is not monitored. *Whole-interval recording,* however, requires the observer to record the occurrence of the behavior only if the behavior was present throughout the entire interval. Thus, the duration of the behavior is monitored.

The decision to use partial- or whole-interval recording depends primarily on the observed behavior. The partial-interval approach is preferred for behaviors that are short in duration (hitting and touching), while the whole-interval approach is appropriate for behaviors that occur for an extended duration (off task and talking). Repp et al. (1988) note that, in comparison with continuous measurement, partial-interval recording tends to overestimate the continuous measures, while whole-interval recording tends to underestimate.

Teachers may use interval recording to monitor the behavior of several students or behaviors at the same time. However, teachers should not try to monitor more than three children or behaviors during a single observation period. Figure 6.5 shows a sample recording form used to monitor talking behavior among three children during a 3-minute observation period divided into ten 30-second intervals. A similar form could also be used to observe three different behaviors for one student.

Time Sampling

Time sampling, sometimes referred to as *momentary time sampling,* refers to another common method of behavior measurement. Like interval recording, time sampling requires the observer to divide the total observation period into smaller time intervals. However, unlike interval recording in which the observer records whether the behavior occurred at *any* time during the interval, time sampling requires the observer to record whether the behavior was observed at the *end* of the interval. For example, if an observer were monitoring Julia's on-task-behavior, the observer would look at Julia at the end of

Student's name: _____   Observer: _____
Environment: _____   Date: _____
Target behavior: _____
Start time: _9:00 am_   Stop time: _9:10 am_

60-minute observation period: 5-minute intervals

9:00   9:15   9:30   9:45   10:00

1	2	3	4	5	6	7	8	9	10	11	12

Key: Mark a "+" in the interval if the target behavior was observed at the end of the observation period; mark a "−" in the interval if the target behavior was not observed.

FIGURE 6.6   Time sampling form for a 60-minute observation period divided into twelve 5-minute intervals

each interval and record a "+" if she was on task at that *moment* or a "−" if she was not on task. Time sampling is most appropriately used when monitoring behaviors that have some duration. For example on-task/off-task, in-seat/out-of-seat, and talking are examples of behaviors that may be monitored with time sampling.

The total length of observation for time sampling may be significantly longer than interval recording since the observer is actually required to look at the student only at the end of each interval. In addition, while the intervals in interval recording are usually seconds long, the intervals in time sampling are usually minutes long. For example, a 60-minute observation period may be divided into twelve 5-minute intervals. Like interval recording, the observer records the percentage of intervals for which the target behavior was recorded (number of "+" notes divided by the total number of intervals). A recording form for such an observation is provided in Figure 6.6.

Two concerns arise with regard to time sampling. First, as the length of the intervals increases, the amount of observed or sampled behavior decreases. As the amount of observed behavior decreases, the collected data are less likely to be consistent with the actual occurrence of the target behavior. Thus, it is recommended that interval periods for time sampling not exceed 5 minutes. Second, if the student knows that a teacher is monitoring his or her behavior and that the teacher is looking at the student only at the end of a specific time interval, the student may modify his or her behavior so that the target behavior is not observed at the end of the interval. If this is a problem or a potential concern, teachers have three options: (a) keep the interval length a secret, (b) use interval recording instead of time sampling, or (c) vary the length of the interval. While varying the length of the intervals, teachers maintain an average interval period (e.g., 5 minutes), while the actual intervals may range, for example, from 2 to 8 minutes.

Murphy and Harrop (1994) completed a comparison of momentary time sampling (MTS) and partial-interval recording (PIR) using 60 college students' observations of two

10-minute videotaped sequences. They found that MTS yielded less error into observers' recordings than PIR and that observers showed some preference for MTS.

As with interval recording, time sampling allows observers to calculate the percentage of total intervals the behavior was observed and not observed. For example, if the behavior was observed at the end of 6 of 12 intervals, we would report that the behavior was observed during 50% of the total intervals.

ACCURACY OF BEHAVIORAL OBSERVATION AND MEASURES

Repp et al. (1988, p. 29) outline several factors that may "potentially affect the accuracy of data collected during direct observations": reactivity; observer drift; the recording procedure; location of the observation; observer expectancy; and characteristics of subjects, observers, and settings. Personal values and biases are additional sources of observer error. Each of these is described in the following sections.

Reactivity

Reactivity refers to changes in a student's behavior as a result of being observed. For example, when children know that a teacher is counting how often they get out of their seats, the children may increase or decrease the target behavior in response to this knowledge. The exact effect on a student's behavior depends on the student, the behavior, the observer, and many other situational variables. Since the observer cannot be sure whether his or her presence will have an impact on the student's behavior, sometimes unobtrusive observations (i.e., when the student is unaware that his or her behavior is being observed) are preferable. For example, unobtrusive observations are recommended when baseline data, discussed later in this chapter, are collected.

Direct observation is a necessary and significant element of behavioral assessment.

Observer Drift

Observer drift refers to a gradual shift by the observer of his or her understanding of the target behavior being observed and measured. For example, a teacher counting the frequency of a student getting out of his or her seat may have a different definition of the target behavior at the end of the observational period than the original definition used at the beginning of the observational period. In this case, differences observed and recorded in the student's behavior from one day to the next may have more to do with observer drift than actual changes in the student's behavior.

To control for observer drift, the target behavior should be defined in very specific terms that will remain clear throughout the duration of a program. Moreover, teachers should define the topography (what the behavior looks like) of the target behavior prior to any observation. Thus, when out-of-seat behavior is being observed, teachers should define what "out-of-seat" means—what is counted and what is not counted as an out-of-seat behavior. For example, a good description of out-of-seat behavior may state "Paul will be considered to be 'out of seat' when his buttocks are at least 12 inches from his chair." This clearly defines out-of-seat behavior such that teachers know when to count the target behavior as occurring. Observer drift is more common when target behaviors are vaguely defined.

The Recording Procedure

The *recording procedure* refers to the procedure selected to measure the dimensions of a behavior (e.g., frequency, duration). The primary methods of measuring behavior include event recording, interval recording, and time sampling. As we have discussed, some procedures produce a more accurate picture of the behavior than others depending on the dimensions of the behavior to be measured.

Location of the Observation

At the beginning of this chapter, we discussed the importance of direct observation within natural settings. That is, if a student is exhibiting an unacceptable behavior within a classroom setting, it is important that the student's behavior be observed and measured within the classroom. Direct observations in natural settings provide a more accurate picture of the student's typical behavior within functional environments. Observations within natural environments also allow the observer to monitor teacher behavior, peer behavior, and other environmental influences related to the unacceptable behavior. These same considerations hold true for unacceptable behavior exhibited in other environments.

Observer Expectancy

Observer expectancy refers to the expectations teachers have about the children they observe. For example, when a teacher hears "things" from other teachers about a student's behavior, the teacher develops certain expectations about the student's behavior. These expectations may bias a teacher's observation of the student.

Teachers' expectations may also affect how children behave. Observer expectations are less likely to influence observational data when target behaviors are clearly defined.

Also, the periodic use of independent observers for reliability checks will help monitor these influences on teacher observations.

Characteristics of Subjects, Observers, and Settings

Characteristics of subjects, observers, and settings refer to variables such as gender differences, the complexity of the behavior being observed, and familiarity with the setting and children being observed. Studies suggest that gender differences of both the student and the observer may influence the data collected during direct observation (Repp et al., 1988). Using both male and female observers to observe and measure children's behaviors is an excellent solution to gender influences. However, given the overwhelming proportion of female teachers in our schools, this may not be practical within school environments.

Regarding the setting, research has shown that "familiarity with the setting may make observation easier and thereby increase observer accuracy" (Repp et al., 1988, p. 32). This is certainly a positive finding for classroom teachers and parents who are interested in observing and measuring behaviors within their own school or home setting.

Personal Values and Bias

Personal values refer to social, cultural, or religious values that affect a teacher's perception of children's behavior. For example, different personal values regarding behavior will affect a teacher's definition of "appropriate" and "inappropriate" behavior. Observer *bias* refers to beliefs or emotional feelings about individual children. For example, among teachers, teachers may report different observations than parents who were asked to observe for the same behavior. Whether a teacher likes a student, how the student looks, and the culture and gender of the student are other variables that may bias the teacher's perceptions and observations (Bell & Harper, 1977; Grossman, 1995; Repp et al., 1988; Zirpoli & Bell, 1987).

Many variables may provide a threat to the accuracy of data collected during direct observation. However, these threats are easily overcome. First, teachers should become aware of the potential threats given their specific situation and available resources. Second, as previously stated, the target behavior must be stated in observable and measurable terms. This is the most important variable regarding the accurate measurement of behavior. A clear, concise definition of the target behavior will help eliminate misunderstandings of exactly what behaviors are and are not included in the target behavior. Third, teachers may want to practice using their data collection method and correct any "bugs" before a full-scale implementation. Fourth, reliability data should be completed periodically to check for the reliability of data across teachers. Checking reliability is discussed later. Repp et al. (1988, p. 33) outline five additional recommendations to improve the accuracy of data collected during direct observations:

- *Train observers well regarding the definition and measurement of the target behavior.*   This point is especially important for teachers within educational environments where many teachers may be involved in collecting data.
- *Use an adaptation period for both teachers and children.*   This approach is necessary only when the teacher is a stranger to the student and reactivity becomes a potential problem. It is not an issue for parents or teachers who are collecting data within their own classrooms.

- *Observe unobtrusively.*   Try to integrate data collection into the teaching routine.
- *Use permanent products (e.g., videotapes, audiocassettes).*   This is not always possible or practical when teaching or caring for children in the home. However, at times a teacher may need to document a student's behavior on film in order to show others and receive suggestions and other assistance.
- *Observe frequently and systematically.*   Obviously, a longer period of observation is likely to document a more accurate "picture" of a student's typical behavior than a shorter period. However, a systematic approach to data collection need not take a significant amount of a teacher's time.

Data Collection Aids

Teachers do not have to purchase sophisticated and expensive recording devices when collecting data. For example, teachers may use a simple wrist counter or golf counter to record frequency during event recording. Also, teachers may use a wristwatch with a second hand or a stopwatch to monitor duration. Descriptions of other less technical, homemade aids or techniques follow.

POCKET COUNTING   *Pocket counting* is the transfer of pennies or other small objects from one pocket to another each time a target behavior is observed. At the end of the observation period, the teacher simply counts the number of pennies in the receiving pocket to measure the frequency of the target behavior. The frequency count can then be recorded on the appropriate data collection form.

THE EMPTY JAR   Teachers may drop pennies or other small objects into a jar each time a target behavior occurs. At the end of the observation period, the teacher simply counts the number of objects in the jar to measure the frequency of the target behavior. We observed one teacher drop paper strips into jars placed on the students' desks each time appropriate behavior was observed. At the end of the day the student with the most paper strips was provided with a special reinforcer. The paper strips also provided the teacher with a frequency count of appropriate behaviors exhibited per student or small groups of students.

MASKING TAPE ON THE WRIST   Another teacher told us about placing masking tape on her wrist. A few select names and target behaviors were written on the tape, and the teacher recorded slash marks next to the appropriate behavior. At the end of class, the teacher counted the slash marks, which served as a frequency count per target behavior. Of course, a clipboard with a data collection form would serve the same purpose. Teachers could tape a watch or stopwatch to the clipboard in order to measure both frequency and duration. However, some teachers may consider a clipboard obtrusive and difficult to carry while teaching or completing other teacher responsibilities.

These recording tools ease the task of data collection in addition to facilitating accuracy and reliability. Teachers should use their imagination and creativity when planning data collection methods and procedures. The most effective methods achieve the following aims:

- To make data collection easier than if no tools were used
- Not to interfere with teaching or other teacher duties
- To be simple to use
- To ensure accurate monitoring of the target behavior

RELIABILITY OF OBSERVATIONS

When measuring a target behavior, *reliability* refers primarily to the accuracy of data collected across observers. This kind of reliability is most commonly called *interrater reliability;* other terms include *interobserver reliability* and *interobserver agreement* (see, e.g., Hintze, 2005). For example, when observing a student's out-of-seat behavior, two observers are said to have perfect (100%) interrater reliability when both observe and record the student getting out of the seat the same number of times. However, if one teacher observes 5 occurrences of the behavior while a second teacher observes 10, the interrater reliability between the two observers is only 50% (5/10 = 0.5 ∞ 100 = 50%). Another kind of reliability, *intraobserver reliability,* provides independent confirmation that the data collected by one observer are accurate (Hintze, 2005).

Kazdin (1989) cites three primary reasons why reliability is important. First, the assessment of an individual's behavior should be a function of the individual's true behavior, not a function of inconsistent data collection. If teachers are going to use direct observation to evaluate the effectiveness of an intervention program, the data collected must be reliable. Second, monitoring reliability identifies and minimizes the possible biases of individual observers. Having a second observer periodically monitor the same target behavior provides a check and balance on the first observer's observation and recorded data. Last, reliability provides evidence regarding how well the target behavior is defined. High reliability scores reflect a well-defined target behavior. Low reliability scores may reflect a target behavior that is not clearly identified and defined, which may result in an inconsistent application of the intervention plan. Inconsistency is the primary deficiency of many behavior management programs.

Teachers will obtain satisfactory reliability measures when target behaviors are clearly defined and all observers are adequately trained. Observer training should include an overview of the program, the topography of the target behavior(s) to be observed, and the measurement techniques to be employed during observation.

Reliability measures greater than 70% to 80% are usually considered adequate. Of course, the closer the reliability is to 100%, the better. When reliability is lower than 70%, serious questions should be raised regarding the accuracy of the collected data.

Reliability of Frequency Counts

If a frequency count or event recording procedure is employed, interrater reliability may be calculated by dividing the lower frequency by the higher frequency. Referring back to the previous example, one observer recorded 5 out-of-seat behaviors; the second observer, 10. The lower frequency (5) is then divided by the higher frequency (10), which equals 0.5. This quotient (0.5) is then multiplied by 100, and an interrater reliability of 50% is calculated as demonstrated here:

$$5 = \text{Frequency recorded by first observer}$$
$$10 = \text{Frequency recorded by second observer}$$
$$\text{Reliability} = 5/10 = 0.5 \text{ ∞ } 100 = 50\%$$

Reliability of Duration and Latency Measures

A similar procedure is used to calculate interrater reliability when two observers are measuring the duration or latency of a target behavior. These measures involve a measurement of time instead of frequency. To find the reliability between the two time periods, the shorter duration/latency observed is divided by the longer duration/latency observed. For example, if one observer records that a student was on task for 10 minutes and a second observer records that the same student was on task for 15 minutes, their interrater reliability would equal 66.6%, or 67%, as demonstrated here:

$$10 \text{ minutes} = \text{Duration observed by first observer}$$
$$15 \text{ minutes} = \text{Duration observed by second observer}$$
$$\text{Reliability} = 10/15 = 0.666 \infty 100 = \text{Approximately } 67\%$$

Reliability for Interval Recording and Time Sampling

To calculate interrater reliability for interval and time sampling procedures, a slightly more complex method is required. As previously outlined, both interval recording and time sampling involve dividing an observation period into smaller intervals of time. Two concerns arise regarding the reliability of data collected using these two procedures. First, observers want to know whether the *number* of intervals of target behavior recorded across the two observers is reliable. We will call this *frequency reliability,* which is calculated in the same manner as event recording reliability. Thus, if one teacher observes the behavior in 7 intervals and the second teacher observes the behavior in 12 intervals, their frequency reliability is calculated as follows:

$$7/12 = 0.58 \infty 100 = 58\%$$

The second reliability concern during interval recording or time sampling may be referred to as *agreement reliability*. This measure is more important than frequency reliability because it communicates a more accurate picture of the interrater reliability between two observers. In looking at Figure 6.7, note that both teachers recorded that the student was on task 5 of the 10 intervals. Thus, their frequency reliability is 100% (5/5 = 1 ∞ 100 = 100%). Also note, however, that both observers *agree* on when the student was on task (interval 7) and when the student was not on task (interval 3) only in 2 of the 10 intervals. That is, during interval 7 both observers marked a "+," indicating that they observed the student to be on task, and during interval 3 both observers marked a "−," indicating that they did not observe on-task behavior. Interestingly, although they both recorded that the student was on task 5 of the 10 intervals and received a 100% frequency reliability, the observers hardly agree at all!

To calculate the agreement reliability for interval recording and time sampling, the following formula is recommended:

$$\text{Agreements/Total intervals} \infty 100 = \% \text{ of agreement}$$

Measuring interrater reliability during every observation period, as demonstrated in Classroom Connection 6.2, is not necessary. In fact, most teachers and parents will not be interested in collecting reliability data unless requested. If reliability data are required, a weekly reliability check (1/5 or 20% of observation periods) is usually adequate. That is, for every 5 days of data collection, there should be 1 day when an independent observation is recorded and compared with the teacher's data. For long-term interventions, every other week should be satisfactory.

Interval

Observer 1

1	2	3	4	5	6	7	8	9	10
+	+	−		+	−	+	−	+	−

Observer 2

1	2	3	4	5	6	7	8	9	10
−		−	+	+	+	+	−	−	+

Agreement between observers 1 and 2

1	2	3	4	5	6	7	8	9	10
No	No	Yes	No	No	No	Yes	No	No	No

Key: + = on-task behavior observed during interval
  − = on-task behavior not observed during interval

Summary
  Agreements = 2
  Total intervals = 10
  2/10 = 0.20 × 100 = 20% agreement

  Frequency reliability = 100%
  Agreement reliability = 20%

FIGURE 6.7   Interrater reliability (frequency and agreement) of two interval recording observations of on-task behavior

RECORDING OBSERVATIONS

Having discussed how to observe and measure behaviors, we will now review some recording methods that will simplify the observation process and facilitate the collection of reliable measurements. Methods used to record behavioral observations include permanent product recording, various data collection forms, and coding systems. In addition, several data collection aids are available for teachers to use that may increase the accuracy of data collected.

Permanent Product Recording

Permanent products are materials that are produced as a result of behavior. Teachers may then measure and evaluate the product of the behavior. For example, when a teacher

CLASSROOM CONNECTION 6.2
How Many Times Did Nick Get Out of His Seat?

Mary's seventh-grade science class included lots of hands-on experiments, and her students found her class interesting and fun. One of her students, Nick, found the class a little too interesting, and he was usually out of his seat and checking things out around the room. While Mary was pleased that Nick found her classroom exciting and was happy that he was truly interested in her science displays, she was concerned about her students' safety. Her science class contained a lot of glass containers and chemicals, and she was proud that after 4 years of teaching, not a single student had been injured in her classroom. Nick, however, was threatening her safety record. So Mary decided to have a meeting with Nick and talk to him about an intervention plan to decrease his behavior of getting out of his seat without permission. But first, she had to collect some baseline data so she could communicate to Nick the current status of his behavior, and then together they could establish some short- and long-term goals.

Mary asked her teaching aide to sit in the back of her classroom for five class periods and count how many times Nick gets out of his seat without permission per 50-minute science class. For reliability purposes, Mary decided that she would also keep track of Nick's behavior, independent of her aide, during the same five class periods. This is the aide's data for Nick's out-of-seat behavior over 5 days: 16, 14, 10, 8, and 12. This is Mary's data for the same 5 days: 12, 12, 8, 10, and 12. When they compared their data at the end of the first day, they were surprised at their low interrater reliability. But as they worked out a clearer definition of "out-of-seat behavior," their interrater reliability data improved significantly by the end of the week.

General Reflection for Classroom Connection 6.2:

What is the interrater reliability between Mary and her aide at the end of the first day of observation? What is it for the last day? Out-of-seat behavior would seem simple enough to count, but how many ways can you define "out of seat" so that another person and you may not be observing the same behavior?

gives students a paper-and-pencil math test, the test becomes a permanent product of the students' math performance. The teacher may then use the test to measure and evaluate the students' math performance. Besides academic skills, permanent product recording can be used to measure a variety of other behaviors. For example, when a teacher asks preschool students to pick up books from the floor and place them back on the shelf, a permanent product outcome would be the number of books left on the floor.

Other examples of permanent products include completed homework, artwork, writing projects, building projects, and so on. Usually, the student's performance or behavior is not measured during the completion of the product (e.g., taking the test, picking up the books). Rather, the product is measured and evaluated after it is completed. And because you don't have to observe the student during the behavior, "Teachers can use permanent product recording strategies without any major changes to their daily activities and responsibilities" (Robinson & Smith, 2005, p. 1).

Children can be taught how to observe and record data regarding their own behavior. The results of this self-monitoring may also produce permanent products, generated by the children, that teachers may use to evaluate behavior. Self-monitoring is frequently used as part of a self-management strategy to improve classroom behavior of students (see, e.g., Shapiro, DuPaul, & Bradley-Klug, 1998).

When an audio or video recorder is used during direct observation of children's behavior, the completed tape provides teachers with the ultimate permanent product of behavior. The recorded behavior can then be observed immediately or stored for future observation of specific target behaviors, which can be measured and remeasured at the teacher's convenience.

Direct observation allows teachers to measure and evaluate student performance and behavior.

Data Collection Forms

A *data collection form* is a prepared sheet of paper used to record raw data collected during behavioral observations. Sometimes referred to as *raw data sheets*, these forms are prepared to assist the observer in recording data effectively and accurately. Many examples of data collection forms are provided throughout this chapter. Note that the forms are very simple in design. Teachers are encouraged to design their own data collection forms according to their individual needs.

Figure 6.8 provides an additional sample form that teachers may use for event recording and/or duration measurement. Data collection forms should include, at a minimum, the student's name, the target behavior, the environment or situation in which the student is being observed, the name of the observer, and dates of observation. Data collection forms may also include space for observer comments.

Coding Systems

Coding systems refer to a list of codes added to a data collection form that assists teachers in efficiently recording observed behaviors. Coding systems are especially useful when many target behaviors are being observed at the same time. Under a coding system, each target behavior is given a code. Readers are encouraged to keep the coding system as simple as possible. During the observation period, the observer simply records the code corresponding to the target behavior(s) observed.

Coding systems can be used when teachers are making anecdotal observations or during interval recordings. When used during interval recordings, the observer records within each interval the code of any target behavior observed during the interval. Figure 6.9 provides an example of an interval recording form using a coding system. Teachers can calculate the percentage of intervals during which each target behavior was observed by counting the number of intervals during which any code was recorded and dividing that number by the total number of intervals.

Student's name: _____   Observer : _____
Environment: _____   Dates: from _____ to _____
Target behavior: _____
Recording code: _____

Date/Time	Frequency of Behavior	Start Time	Stop Time	Total Frequency	Total Duration

Observation comments:

FIGURE 6.8   Sample data collection form for event and/or duration recording

Another option includes having the codes prerecorded within each interval. The observer can then simply circle the appropriate code corresponding to the behavior(s) observed within each interval. There are also computer-based coding systems available (e.g. , Eco-Behavioral Assessment Software System) as well as other coding systems that have been commercially developed for use by school practitioners; however, these are usually intended for use by school psychologists in conjunction with the classroom teacher and require substantial training in their use (Volpe, DiPerna, Hintze, & Shapiro, 2005).

DISPLAYING OBSERVATIONAL DATA

Once observational data have been recorded on data collection forms, displaying the raw data on a graph provides teachers with a picture of the data. Ideally, graphs should be updated regularly as new raw data are collected. Graphs give teachers important information on behavioral trends and intervention comparisons over time that are usually difficult to decipher by looking at a list of numbers recorded on raw data sheets. Moreover, graphs provide teachers with an effective mode of communication when reporting a student's progress to other teachers. For example, during parent–teacher meetings, a simple graph reflecting a student's behavior from the beginning of the school year provides an effective way for teachers to display student progress. By using a simple graph, teachers can determine whether a student's performance is increasing, decreasing, or remaining stable.

Kerr and Nelson (1989, p. 91) outline three primary reasons for using graphs:

- To summarize data in a convenient manner for daily decision making
- To communicate program effects
- To provide feedback to teachers involved with the program

Student's name: _Jeremy, Jason, Justin_
Target behavior: _See coding system_

Coding System: T = talking appropriately to other children
                 C = working on the computer
                 D = on task at desk
                 G = playing a game with others
                 A = playing alone

Environment: _Classroom free time_   Date: _____
Start time: _____   Stop time: _____

5-minute observation period: 30-second intervals

Name		1		2		3		4		5
Jeremy										
Jason										
Justin										

Note: Next to the appropriate student's name, record the appropriate code or codes within each interval indicating which target behaviors were observed during each 30-second interval. Record a "–" if none of the target behaviors were observed.

FIGURE 6.9   Sample interval recording form using a coding system (5-minute observation period divided into ten 30-second intervals)

Graphs also provide feedback to children about their performance or progress toward a goal. Children can look at a graph and visually inspect their own progress. Moreover, many children find a graphic display of their progress especially reinforcing. The graph may become part of the treatment program as the student is visually reinforced by the accelerating trends noted on the graph. Also, children can be taught to chart their own performance data on their own graphs. The graphs can be displayed on a bulletin board at school or the refrigerator at home so the student can monitor his or her progress. Make it fun!

Line Graphs

A line graph is the most common graph used to chart a student's performance over time. The line graph, as shown in Figure 6.10, consists of a *horizontal axis* and a *vertical axis*. The horizontal axis is frequently referred to as the *abscissa* or x-*axis*. The x-axis is used to indicate the passage of time and intervention changes or phases over the duration of the intervention program. Note in Figure 6.10 that the x-axis is marked in equal intervals of time, which may represent program sessions, days, weeks, and so on. The x-axis should be clearly labeled, as is the one in Figure 6.10. In this example, the x-axis indicates

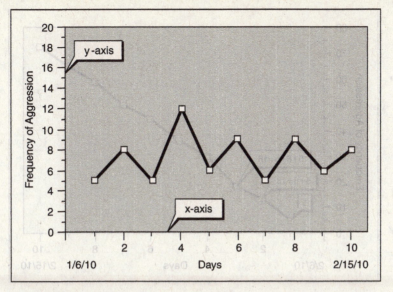

FIGURE 6.10 Example of a line graph of frequency aggression over 10 days of observation

the days on which aggression was observed and counted. Recording the dates of these observations under the *x*-axis is a good idea.

The vertical axis is frequently referred to as the *ordinate* or y-*axis*. The *y*-axis is always drawn on the left side of the *x*-axis and is used to indicate the values of a behavioral dimension (e.g., frequency, rate, duration). Thus, the *y*-axis may represent the frequency, rate, duration, latency, or percentage measurements of behavior. In our example, the *y*-axis represents the frequency of aggressive behavior. Like the *x*-axis, the *y*-axis is clearly labeled to indicate what dimension of behavior is being charted and marked at equal intervals starting at zero at the point where the *x*- and *y*-axes intersect. As you move up the *y*-axis, the values of frequency, rate, and so on, increase. As you move from left to right on the *x*-axis, time progresses.

Each data point on the graph indicates an intersection point between a value from the *y*-axis and a point in time from the *x*-axis. For example, in Figure 6.10, the first data point indicates that the student was aggressive five times on the 1st day, eight times on the 2nd day, five times on the 3rd day, and so on. When data points are charted on a graph, they may show one of four patterns or trends: accelerating, decelerating, stable, or variable. All of these data trends are reviewed, along with examples, in our later discussion on baseline and intervention measures.

Cumulative Graphs

As illustrated in Figure 6.11, teachers may display the same data charted in Figure 6.10 on a cumulative graph. In a cumulative graph, the frequency of aggression for each day is added to the previous day's data.

In our example, the student was aggressive five times on the 1st day and eight times on the 2nd day. In a typical line graph, each data point would be charted independently. In a cumulative graph, however, the first data point reflects the five aggressive acts

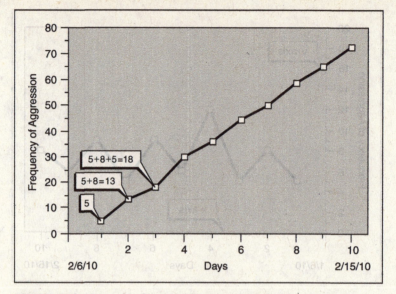

FIGURE 6.11 Example of a cumulative graph of the same data displayed in Figure 6.10

observed on the 1st day, and the second data point reflects an additional eight aggressive acts observed on the 2nd day. Thus, the second data point represents 13 aggressive acts observed over the first 2 days of observation. Each additional data point indicates the number of behaviors observed that day *plus* the number of behaviors observed in all previous days of the program.

Cumulative graphs are used when the total number of behaviors observed is required from day to day. For example, a teacher's supervision may require a daily report on the total number of target behaviors observed from a specific start date or during a specific time period. Cumulative graphs are also useful when recording skill acquisition over a specific time period. For example, a reading teacher may need to keep a cumulative record of the number of new words learned by an individual student.

As demonstrated in Figure 6.11, the cumulative graph may give the impression that the frequency of the target behavior (aggression) is increasing rapidly. A graph like this might give the wrong impression to teachers who do not understand the nature of a cumulative graph. Thus, in most cases, teachers are encouraged to use a noncumulative line graph to chart behaviors.

Bar Graphs

Another way to display raw data is with a *bar graph* or *histogram*. Like the line graph, the bar graph also has an x- and y-axis. However, instead of data points to indicate the frequency, rate, and duration of the target behavior, the bar graph uses vertical bars. Each vertical bar represents one observation period. The height of the bar corresponds with a value on the y-axis.

Figure 6.12 displays the same raw data used in the line graph shown in Figure 6.10. Since five aggressive acts were observed on the 1st day of observation, the first bar in

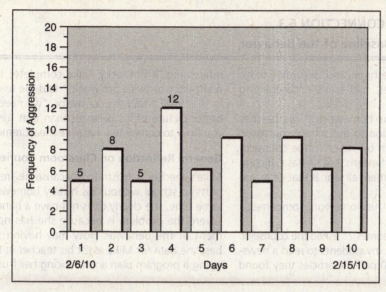

FIGURE 6.12 Example of a bar graph using the same raw data given in the line graph of Figure 6.10

Figure 6.12 is drawn to the value of 5 on the y-axis. Since eight aggressive acts were observed on the 2nd day, the second bar is drawn to the value of 8 on the *y*-axis. The corresponding frequency count of the first four bars of our example is recorded on top of each bar.

Bar graphs present an excellent opportunity for teachers to get students involved in monitoring their own behavior. While teachers can place a mark where the top of a bar should stop, children can draw in the space from zero to the line. Also, teachers can draw "empty" bars and have young children fill or color in the bars. Again, this feedback will provide children with information about their own behavior and reinforcement for increasing or decreasing behaviors.

Baseline and Intervention Measures

Baseline data refers to the measurement of a target behavior prior to the implementation of any intervention plan intended to modify the behavior. For Mike in Classroom Connection 6.3, a baseline measurement of his target behavior (completing homework) may include a count of the number of days during an observation period (e.g., 5 days) that his homework was completed (all three paragraphs). During this baseline observation period, his teacher simply observes and measures the rate of homework completion. His teacher may also choose to measure the amount of homework completed. For example, if Mike had to list 10 articles he found interesting for Monday but lists only 5 articles, his teacher would record that Mike completed 50% of his homework for Monday.

Baseline data are essential for developing realistic behavioral objectives. In our example, Mike's teacher would find it difficult to establish realistic objectives and goals for Mike without baseline data indicating his current performance levels. Baseline data provide a benchmark from which Mike's teacher can outline future performance objectives. Without baseline data, the teacher may establish objectives that are not challenging or unrealistic, given Mike's current performance.

Mike was a high school freshman and, according to his U.S. government teacher, had trouble completing homework assignments.

"He never does his homework!" his teacher yelled one day in frustration to the school counselor.

"What do you mean by 'never'?" the counselor responded. "To me, 'never' means that he has not completed a homework assignment all year. Is that what you mean to say?"

"Oh, well, he does his homework sometimes," the teacher said.

"How often is 'sometimes'?" asked the counselor.

"I don't know. I ask my students to read a newspaper each day and list 10 political articles they found

interesting. If I'm lucky, Mike completes this assignment once or twice per week," said the teacher.

"Well," said the counselor, "we need to draw a better picture of his behavior than that. Let me show you how to complete a baseline measurement."

General Reflection on Classroom Connection 6.3:

Mike's teacher is frustrated because he frequently reports to school without his history homework. At the same time, she clearly does not have a handle on how severe the problem is because she has no measurement of the behavior. How may having some solid baseline data for Mike assist his teacher in both developing a program plan and reducing her frustration?

Teachers should follow several steps when they want to obtain a baseline measure on a target behavior. These steps outline the important relationship between collecting baseline data and the establishment of behavioral objectives. Each of these steps is discussed in this chapter.

1. Identify the target behavior.
2. Define the target behavior in measurable and observable terms.
3. Observe the target behavior.
4. Collect data on the target behavior.
5. Review the data.
6. Establish behavioral objectives based on current performance measures as outlined in the baseline data.

Baseline data serve many purposes. Referring back to our example, Mike's teacher may use the baseline data on Mike's homework for the following purposes:

• To document Mike's current homework completion performance. Thus, she can communicate much more effectively with the school counselor, Mike's parents, and others about his homework.
• To help decide whether Mike's homework completion performance needs to be modified.
• To provide objective data to Mike's parents and other significant teachers about his homework completion performance in order to justify the initiation of a homework completion program.
• To serve as comparative data for future intervention program data. Once she starts her program with Mike, she will have baseline data to compare with her intervention or program data.

An important question about baseline data involves the number of observation periods necessary for a reliable baseline measurement. That is, how many observations of the target behavior are appropriate before the intervention plan can be introduced? The general

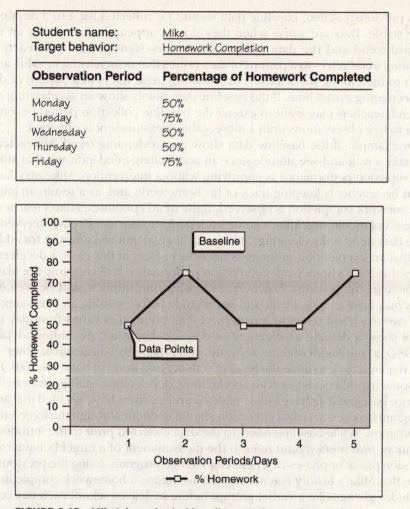

| Student's name: | Mike |
| Target behavior: | Homework Completion |

Observation Period	Percentage of Homework Completed
Monday	50%
Tuesday	75%
Wednesday	50%
Thursday	50%
Friday	75%

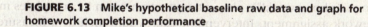

FIGURE 6.13 Mike's hypothetical baseline raw data and graph for homework completion performance

rule is that teachers should collect data points until the baseline data are stable (typically four to five). As previously stated, a *data point* refers to a point on a graph representing a single observation period. Thus, if Mike's teacher observed and measured his homework completion for 5 days, she would have five baseline data points. When these data points are transferred to a graph, a "picture" of Mike's homework completion performance can be reviewed. Figure 6.13 provides a hypothetical example of Mike's homework completion baseline data and a graph of the same data collected during the 5 days of baseline observation. Note that in this example the *y*-axis indicates the *percentage* of homework completed each day. Thus, on Monday, his teacher placed a data point at 50% indicating that Mike completed half of his homework assignment on that day. Also note that during the baseline period, his teacher observed that Mike completed at least some of his homework each day. This information provides his teacher with a more specific problem than her original complaint that Mike "never" or "sometimes" does his homework.

As previously stated, baseline data should be collected for 4 to 5 days or until the data are stable. Data are *stable* when they do not appear to have either an upward or downward trend and the data points do not vary significantly from each other. An *accelerating* trend refers to a pattern of data points that is increasing in value across time, from left to right along the *x*-axis. A *decelerating* trend refers to a pattern of data points that is decreasing across time. If the baseline data points show an accelerating or decelerating trend, teachers may want to extend the baseline collection period beyond the normal four to five observations until a more stable measurement is obtained.

For example, if the baseline data show an accelerating trend, Mike's teacher may want to take a wait-and-see attitude since an accelerating trend indicates that Mike's homework completion performance is improving without intervention. Mike may have discovered that his teacher is keeping track of his homework, and, as a result, an improvement in his homework completion is observed. If the trend continues, Mike's teacher may consider the act of monitoring Mike's homework performance an effective intervention. If the baseline data trend is decelerating, Mike's teacher may not want to wait for additional evidence that an intervention program is necessary since, in this case, a decelerating trend indicates that Mike's homework completion performance is decreasing. For inappropriate behavior (e.g., aggression), however, a decelerating trend would be welcomed, and teachers may want to take a wait-and-see attitude before starting an intervention plan.

A *variable* trend refers to a pattern of data points that varies from day to day and does not show a definite accelerating or decelerating trend. According to Tawney and Gast (1984), a "minimum of three separate, and preferably consecutive, observation periods are required to determine the level of stability and trend of data" (p. 160). Figure 6.14 shows some hypothetical data with accelerating, decelerating, stable, and variable trends.

Once baseline data have been collected and teachers have decided that an intervention program is necessary, data collection should continue through the intervention phase of the program. While baseline refers to the data collected *prior* to the introduction of an intervention, *intervention data* refer to the measurement of a target behavior *during* the intervention phase or phases of a behavior change program. Using the previous example, suppose that Mike's history teacher decides to initiate a homework completion program that includes giving Mike a verbal prompt before he leaves school each day (e.g., "Mike, don't forget to do your homework!"), plus extra attention when he completes more than 60% of his homework assignment. Intervention data would include a measurement of Mike's homework completion performance starting on the 1st day of the homework completion program and every day after until the program's behavioral criteria have been reached.

Intervention data are separated from baseline data by simply drawing a line down the graph between the two data types. Note in Figure 6.15 that the word *Baseline* is inserted on the left side of the graph. In this same manner, the word *Intervention,* or *Treatment,* should be inserted on the right side of the graph where the data points representing intervention data are graphed. For example, say that Mike's teacher decides to introduce the homework completion program (outlined earlier) for 5 consecutive school days. If the results look encouraging, Mike's teacher may decide to continue the intervention program. During the 5 days of intervention, Mike's teacher continued to observe and measure Mike's homework completion performance in the same manner that the baseline data were collected. Figure 6.15 outlines Mike's hypothetical intervention data and a graph of the five data points collected by Mike's teacher during the 5 days of intervention.

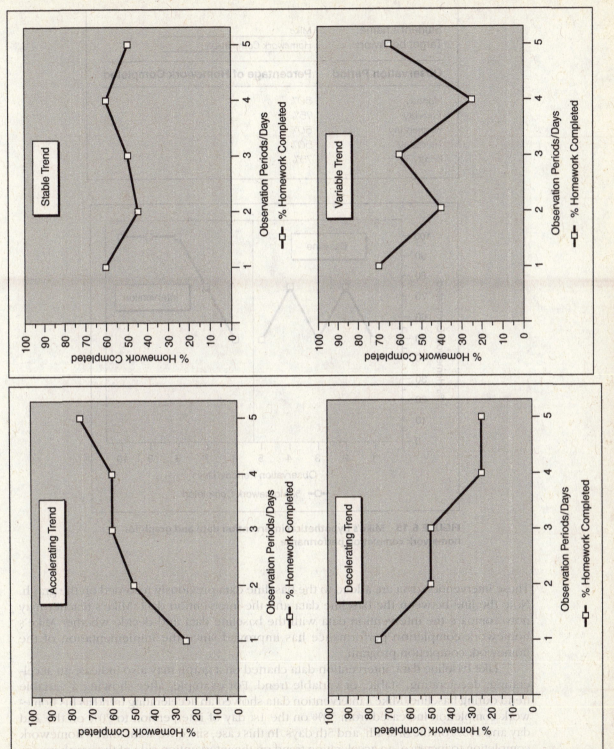

FIGURE 6.14   Examples of data showing accelerating, decelerating, stable, and variable trends

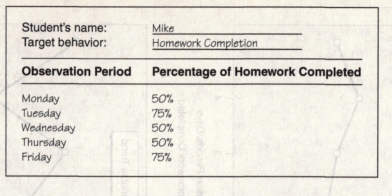

Student's name:	Mike
Target behavior:	Homework Completion

Observation Period	Percentage of Homework Completed
Monday	50%
Tuesday	75%
Wednesday	50%
Thursday	50%
Friday	75%

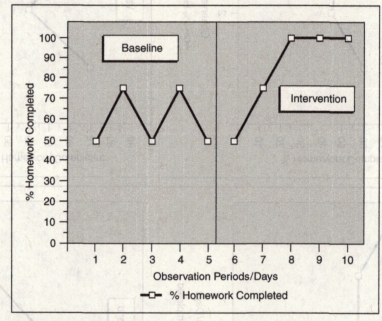

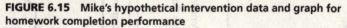

FIGURE 6.15 Mike's hypothetical intervention data and graph for homework completion performance

These intervention data are added to the baseline data previously recorded on the graph. Note the line between the baseline data and the intervention data. Mike's teacher may now compare the intervention data with the baseline data and decide whether Mike's homework completion performance has improved since the implementation of the homework completion program.

Like baseline data, intervention data charted on a graph may also indicate an accelerating, decelerating, stable, or variable trend. For example, after showing a variable trend during baseline, Mike's intervention data showed an accelerating trend as his homework completion increased from 50% on the 1st day of intervention to 70% on the 2nd day and 100% on the 3rd, 4th, and 5th days. In this case, since we want Mike's homework completion to increase, an accelerating trend on the intervention side of the graph means that Mike's history homework completion is rising and his teacher should continue the current program. If, however, the intervention data showed a decelerating, stable, or variable trend, his teacher should review and modify Mike's behavior change program.

If modifications are made to the intervention plan, a second line should be drawn down the graph (similar to the line separating baseline from the first intervention plan), separating the first and second intervention plan. The second plan may be a simple program modification or a totally new intervention. Regardless, each "new" intervention or phase of the program should be separated from each other and labeled accordingly. Teachers may then review the data collected and charted across interventions and compare the effectiveness of each. Examples of multi-intervention programs charted on a single graph are provided later in our discussion of single-subject designs.

Again, the purpose of data collection and graphing is to provide feedback about current programming so that teachers may distinguish effective from ineffective interventions. By comparing the intervention data with the baseline data, and by looking at the data trends within each intervention plan, teachers should be able to make decisions regarding the effectiveness of their interventions and make modifications accordingly. Also, the graph provides teachers with an effective manner of communicating intervention results to others.

Summary

The purposes of direct observation are to record behavioral patterns across natural settings and situations, to measure the dimensions of specific target behaviors, and to identify the variables associated with these target behaviors. Data from direct observations allow teachers to monitor and evaluate the effectiveness of behavior change programs. Before a target behavior can be observed, however, it must be identified and defined in observable and measurable terms.

After conducting an initial baseline observation to determine current performance levels of the target behavior, teachers can establish behavioral objectives, which include the desired terminal behavior and performance criteria. Once these are established, teachers must identify the dimensions of the behavior to be measured and determine how the dimensions will be measured. The five primary dimensions of behavior are frequency, duration, rate, latency, and intensity. Frequency refers to a simple count of the number of times a behavior occurs. Duration describes the time period for which a behavior continues once started. Rate refers to the frequency of a target behavior divided by the amount of observation time. Latency refers to the amount of time it takes for a student to begin a behavior once directions are provided. Last, intensity describes the force or strength of a behavior.

Measurement of behavior may include anecdotal observations, or an ABC analysis. Anecdotal observations provide teachers with a descriptive record of a behavior and related antecedents and consequences. Other measurement methods include event recording, interval recording, and time sampling.

The accuracy of behavioral observations is influenced by reactivity; observer drift; the recording procedure; the location of the observation; observer expectancy; characteristics of subjects, observers, and settings; and personal values and biases. Recommendations to reduce error in direct observations include precisely defining target behaviors, training observers, using adaptation periods for both observer and children, conducting unobtrusive observations, using permanent product recording, and observing the children frequently and systematically.

Interrater reliability refers to the accuracy of data collected across observers. Teachers will obtain satisfactory reliability measures when target behaviors are clearly defined and when all observers are adequately trained. Reliability measures may be calculated for frequency, duration, and latency measures, as well as for event, interval, and time sampling recording.

Teachers may record their observations using permanent product recording, a variety of data collection forms, and coding systems. Data collection aids include wrist counters, watches, and other homemade devices and techniques. These tools ease the task of data collection and facilitate accuracy and reliability.

Teachers are encouraged to display collected data on graphs in order to summarize data in a convenient manner, communicate program effects, and provide feedback to teachers and the student. The line graph is the most common graph, but cumulative and bar graphs are also used to display data. Graphs are used to chart both baseline and intervention data. While baseline data refer to the data collected prior to the introduction of an intervention, intervention data refer to the measurement of a target behavior during the behavior change program. A visual analysis of differences between baseline and intervention data and of the trends of the data gives teachers information regarding the effect of the intervention.

Discussion Questions

1. Discuss the importance of stating target behaviors in observable and measurable terms. Give examples of behaviors stated in observable and nonobservable ways.
2. Describe the four elements of well-stated behavioral objectives, using examples from behaviors observed in both classroom and home settings.
3. What are the dimensions of behavior? Provide examples of each as used in a classroom situation.
4. Discuss the various methods of data collection and the types of behavior and situations in which each may be used.

5. What variables may influence the accuracy of behavioral observations? What may be done to control for these influences?
6. Discuss the advantages of graphing data for teachers, parents, and students. How may this information be used during teacher–parent conferences?
7. How may students be encouraged to participate in their own data collection?

References

Alberto, P. A., & Troutman, A. C. (2009). *Applied behavior analysis for teachers* (8th ed.). Upper Saddle River, NJ: Pearson Education.

Barlow, D. H., & Hersen, M. (1984). *Single case experimental designs: Strategies for studying behavior change*. New York: Pergamon.

Bell, R. Q., & Harper, L. V. (1977). *Child effects on adults*. Hillsdale, NJ: Erlbaum.

Bijou, S. W., Peterson, R. F., & Ault, M. H. (1968). A method to integrate descriptive and experimental field studies at the level of data and empirical concepts. *Journal of Applied Behavior Analysis, 1*, 175–191.

Chafouleas, S. M., Christ, T. H., Riley-Tillman, T. C., Briesch, A. M., & Chanese, J. A. M. (2007). Generalizability and dependability of direct behavior ratings (DBRs) to assess social behavior of preschoolers. *School Psychology Review, 36*, 63–69.

Cooper, J. O., Heron, T. E., & Heward, W. L. (2007). *Applied behavior analysis* (2nd ed.). Upper Saddle River, NJ: Merrill/Pearson Education.

Foster, S. L., Bell-Dolan, D. J., & Burge, D. A. (1988). Behavioral observation. In A. S. Bellack & M. Hersen (Eds.), *Behavioral assessment: A practical handbook* (pp. 79–103). New York: Pergamon.

Green, G. (1990). Least restrictive use of reductive procedures: Guidelines and competencies. In A. C. Repp & N. N. Singh (Eds.), *Perspectives on the use of nonaversive and aversive interventions for persons with developmental disabilities* (pp. 479–493). Sycamore, IL: Sycamore.

Greene, B. F., Bailey, J. S., & Barber, F. (1981). An analysis and reduction of disruptive behavior on school buses. *Journal of Applied Behavior Analysis, 14,* 177–192.

Grossman, H. (1995). *Special education in a diverse society.* Boston: Allyn & Bacon.

Hawkins, R. P., & Dobes, R. W. (1977). Behavioral definitions in applied behavior analysis: Explicit or implicit. In B. C. Etzel, J. M. LeBlanc, & D. M. Baer (Eds.), *New directions in behavioral research: Theory, methods, and applications* (pp. 167–188). Hillsdale, NJ: Erlbaum.

Hintze, J. M. (2005). Psychometrics of direct observation. *School Psychology Review, (34)*4, 507–519.

Kazdin, A. E. (1982). *Single-case research designs: Methods for clinical and applied settings.* New York: Oxford University Press.

Kazdin, A. E. (1989). *Behavior modification in applied settings.* Pacific Grove, CA: Brooks/Cole.

Kerr, M. M., & Nelson, M. C. (1989). *Strategies for managing behavior in the classroom.* Upper Saddle River, NJ: Merrill/Pearson Education.

Koorland, M. A., Monda, L. E., & Vail, C. O. (1988). Recording behavior with ease. *Teaching Exceptional Children, 21,* 59–61.

Lennox, D. B., & Miltenberger, R. G. (1989). Conducting a functional assessment of problem behavior in applied settings. *Journal of the Association for Persons with Severe Handicaps, 14,* 304–311.

Merrell, K. W. (2001). Assessment of children's social skills: Recent developments, best practices, and new directions. *Exceptionality, 9*(1 & 2), 3–18.

Meyer, L., & Janney, R. (1989). User-friendly measures of meaningful outcomes: Evaluating behavioral interventions. *Journal of the Association for Persons with Severe Handicaps, 4,* 263–270.

Murphy, M., & Harrop, A. (1994). Observer error in the use of momentary time sampling and partial interval recording. *British Journal of Psychology, 85*(2), 169–180.

Repp, A. C., Nieminen, G. S., Olinger, E., & Brusca, R. (1988). Direct observation: Factors affecting the accuracy of observers. *Exceptional Children, 55,* 29–36.

Robinson, S. M., & Smith, S. J. (2005). *Special connections.* Unpublished manuscript, University of Kansas, Lawrence.

Shapiro, E. S., DuPaul, G. J., & Bradley-Klug, K. (1998). Self-management as a strategy to improve the classroom behavior of adolescents with ADHD. *Journal of Learning Disabilities, 31* (6), 545–556.

Snell, M. E., & Grigg, N. C. (1987). Instructional assessment and curriculum development. In M. E. Snell (Ed.), *Systematic instruction of persons with severe handicaps.* Upper Saddle River, NJ: Merrill/Pearson Education.

Tawney, J. W., & Gast, D. L. (1984). *Single subject research in special education.* Upper Saddle River, NJ: Merrill/Pearson Education.

Trudel, P., & Cote, J. (1996). Systematic observation of youth ice hockey coaches during games. *Journal of Sport Behavior, 19* (1), 50–66.

Umbreit, J., & Blair, K. S. (1997). Using structural analysis to facilitate treatment of aggression and noncompliance in a young child at risk for behavioral disorders. *Behavior Disorders, 22*(2), 75–86.

Volpe, R. J., DiPerna, J. C., Hintze, J. M., & Shapiro, E. S. (2005). Observing students in classroom settings: A review of seven coding schemes. *School Psychology Review, 34*(4), 454–474.

Wacker, D. P. (1989). Introduction to special feature on measurement issues in supported education: Why measure anything? *Journal of the Association for Persons with Severe Handicaps, 14,* 254.

Zirpoli, T. J., & Bell, R. Q. (1987). Unresponsiveness in children with severe disabilities: Potential effects on parent-child interactions. *The Exceptional Child, 34,* 31–40.

Single-Subject Designs

CHAPTER 7

Thomas J. Zirpoli

The use of single-subject designs has increased steadily since about the mid-sixties, paralleling the increased application of behavior modification techniques. Whereas previously single-subject research was generally equated with a descriptive, case-study approach, it now became associated with a more controlled, experimental approach.

—L. R. GAY (1996, PP. 374–375)

While single-subject designs are the most commonly used research design used in academic intervention studies of students with challinging behaviors (Mooney, Epstein, Reid, & Nelson, 2003), most classroom teachers do not use elaborate single-subject designs to demonstrate the effectiveness of their behavior change programs. However, as with our discussion on behavioral observation, measurement, and recording procedures in the previous chapter, we hope to demonstrate that teachers may employ these simple research designs in the classroom with little difficulty and some exciting results. We will not go into great detail about these designs. Instead, we will provide teachers with an overview of some basic single-subject designs, discuss their importance and application, and refer our readers to other sources where a more complete and detailed review of these and other single-subject designs are discussed and evaluated in far greater detail (e.g., Barlow & Hersen, 1984; Campbell, 2005; Olive & Smith, 2005; Tawney & Gast, 1984).

THE PURPOSE OF SINGLE-SUBJECT DESIGNS

When people think about research, they usually imagine large samples of "subjects" participating in one of two groups: an *experimental group* in which a "treatment" or intervention (independent variable) is presented, and a *control group* in which the intervention is not presented. These *group designs* involve many subjects, and each group's average performance (dependent variable) is usually compared in order to evaluate *experimental control*.

Under ideal circumstances, teachers may attribute the differences between the performance of the experimental and control groups to the intervention applied in the experimental group and the absence of the intervention in the control group. These attributions refer to *intervention* or *treatment effects*. By using these research designs, researchers can demonstrate the effectiveness of their interventions (e.g., teaching style, behavior change program, new curriculum) and communicate these findings to others.

The primary purpose of single-subject designs is also to demonstrate experimental control and intervention effects. However, instead of requiring work with large groups of individuals, single-subject designs allow researchers and teachers to demonstrate experimental control and intervention effects while working with "one subject or one group that is treated as a single entity" (Foster, Watson, Meeks, & Young, 2002). As Tankersley, Harjusola-Webb, and Landrum (2008, p. 84) state, "Despite its name, single-subject research designs rarely involve only one participant. Even so, the data are organized and analyzed according to a within-participant orientation that focuses on the individual. That is, each participant's behavior or performance is compared to his or her own behavior or performance across multiple conditions."

Sidman (1960), an early proponent of single-subject designs, states that group research designs, in which an average group performance is measured, do not communicate important individual performances. He points out that in many cases the performance of individual children does not resemble the group average. For example, when a teacher initiates a specific behavior reduction program (such as trying to decrease hitting) for an individual student, an average classroom performance score is unlikely to let the teacher know how effective the program is for that individual student.

Single-subject designs are ideal for teachers who wish to demonstrate a relationship between a behavior change program and behavior changes exhibited by a single child or a small group of children (Martin, 1985). For example, a classroom teacher may want to demonstrate that a behavior program developed for a small group of students within her classroom is likely to be effective with other children in the school. In this case, each data point in the single-subject design graph represents the performance of a single class or other intact group of children; the data point represents the total group score or average score. For example, in a program to increase appropriate classroom behavior, a teacher could develop a single-subject design for one student or for the whole class. When charting the frequency of appropriate behavior for one student, the data points on the graph represent the performance of the one student. When the frequency of appropriate behavior is charted for the whole class, however, the data points on the graph represent the performance of the whole group. This latter example is demonstrated in Classroom Connection 7.1.

Martin (1985) outlines the following four advantages of single-subject designs over large group research designs:

- They provide a powerful method of studying the effectiveness of an intervention or several interventions on a single subject or small group of subjects.
- The results of single-subject experimental designs are easy to interpret, usually by visually inspecting the charted data points.
- They allow teachers to decide when to initiate or modify interventions.
- The use of statistics, necessary in group research designs, is not usually needed with single-subject designs. (pp. 90–91)

CLASSROOM CONNECTION 7.1

Initiating Baseline and Intervention Conditions to Study the Effect of a New Seating Arrangement on Student Interactions

Marty, a first-grade teacher, wanted to try a new seating plan for her 28 students. Her students' desks were arranged in seven *rows* of four. After Marty implemented her new seating plan, her students' desks were arranged in seven *groups* of four, with students facing each other in small circles. Marty believed that her new seating plan would increase appropriate student interactions and decrease inappropriate interactions (e.g., touching the backs of other students, having to turn away from the teacher to ask a student in the rear a question, etc.).

Before Marty rearranged the classroom, she decided to collect baseline data on the type and number of appropriate student interactions in her classroom. She picked three target behaviors that, in her opinion, indicate appropriate student interactions:

- Asking another child for help
- Praising another child's work
- Working cooperatively on a class assignment with another child

Marty collected frequency data for each target behavior from 10 A.M. to 11 A.M. for five consecutive days. She then recorded her data on a simple line graph.

On the following Monday, Marty initiated her new seating plan. When the students arrived at school, the desks were arranged according to Marty's new plan. To measure the effect of her new seating plan, Marty continued to collect data on the same target behaviors, from 10 A.M. to 11 A.M. for 5 consecutive days. She recorded this intervention data on the same graph as her baseline data. She drew a vertical line between the five baseline and five intervention data points and recorded *Baseline* and *Intervention* on the left and right sides of the graph.

Looking at her graph, Marty noticed that the frequency of the target behaviors had increased significantly since implementing her new seating plan. Although other factors possibly may have made the difference in the students' behavior, Marty is sure that her new seating plan was the significant factor or independent variable for the change in her students' behavior.

General Reflection on Classroom Connection 7.1:

Regardless of what you think of Marty's new seating plan for her classroom, what do you think of her strategy for measuring the effectiveness of her seating plan in increasing the frequency of her three target behaviors? Do you think her measurements are valid for her purposes?

In addition to using single-subject designs for an effective measurement of behavior change, these designs are frequently employed to measure the effectiveness of various academic or instructional methods. For example, Patrick, Mozzoni, and Patrick (2000) found that single-subject designs offer an effective way to establish evidence-based practice in early intervention programs. Others have used and promoted the use of single-subject designs to work on language development for children with autism (Bellon, Ogletree, & Harn, 2000) and to measure the effectiveness of reading and math instruction for students with learning disabilities (Swanson & Sachse-Lee, 2000). Indeed, single-subject designs are an important and useful tool for special educators who work with individual students or small groups of students at a time (Tankersley, Harjusola-Webb, & Landrum, 2008). But teachers should not get the idea that single-subject designs are helpful only with students receiving specialized instruction. As we hope to demonstrate next, single-subject designs can be an effective assessment tool in general education classrooms.

Baseline and Intervention Conditions

With single-subject designs, comparisons are made between *conditions* employed during the behavior change program. A condition refers to the baseline phase and various intervention phases used to modify an individual's behavior; these are called *baseline* and *intervention conditions,* respectively.

- **Baseline condition:** In a single-subject design, the baseline condition is usually referred to as condition A. During this condition, baseline data are collected on a specific target behavior before an intervention strategy is employed.

- **Intervention condition:** This condition is usually referred to as condition B. Data collection continues throughout the intervention condition.

In Classroom Connection 7.1, Marty's students were in the baseline condition when they were in their old seating arrangement. When Marty initiated her new seating plan, the intervention condition began. Each data point on Marty's graph represents the total number of appropriate student interactions, defined by her three target behaviors, from 10 A.M. to 11 A.M. each day.

If variations to the intervention condition were employed or if new interventions were initiated, each of these would be considered a new condition (i.e., conditions C, D, E, etc.). For example, Marty's first intervention can be referred to as condition B. It was her first intervention plan initiated after baseline (condition A). If, after a few weeks, Marty decided to modify her new seating plan, the modified intervention would be called condition C. These variations to the basic baseline/intervention designs will be discussed later in this chapter.

A comparison of data across *conditions* allows teachers to determine the most effective intervention. For example, if Marty looked at her data and found that higher rates of appropriate student interactions occurred during condition B than condition C, she might decide to go back to the seating arrangement used in condition B and delete the modifications made during condition C.

TYPES OF SINGLE-SUBJECT DESIGNS

The type of single-subject design employed depends on the order in which baseline and intervention conditions are presented. In some designs, baseline is followed by several intervention phases. In other designs, the baseline period is repeated while the intervention condition is withdrawn. Teachers may also develop designs to represent intervention effects across subjects, settings, and other conditions. The designs reviewed in this chapter include the A-B, A-B-A, A-B-A-B, alternating treatments, changing criterion, and multiple-baseline designs. Each of these designs, along with examples, is discussed here.

The A-B Design

In the simplest single-subject design, the A-B design, only two conditions are used: baseline (A) and intervention (B). We have already seen examples of A-B designs in Figure 6.15, discussed in the previous chapter and in Classroom Connection 7.1. In addition to the data trends that may be identified *within* each condition of the A-B design, the most important variable within this design is the change in data recorded from the first condition (baseline) to the second condition (intervention). Small changes in the data recorded across conditions indicate a weak intervention effect. That is, regardless of the implementation of the intervention, the recorded data indicate little change in the child's behavior. A large intervention effect would be reflected by large differences observed in the data

Single-subject designs can be used when changing the behavior of one child or a small group of children.

recorded during the baseline and intervention conditions. In Classroom Connection 7.1, Marty could determine whether an intervention effect occurred by looking at the changes in data trends across the different seating plans (the original seating plan of condition A and the new seating plan of condition B).

Teachers may determine whether there is a "small" or "large" change in the data by conducting a simple visual analysis or "eyeballing" the graph for obvious differences. "A visual interpretation of graphed data is the most common form of analysis" (Odom, 1988, p. 14). For example, in Figure 7.1, two A-B designs are presented for two hypothetical programs developed to increase school attendance for two high school students. For the first student (example 1), school attendance was reinforced with special activity passes (e.g., field trips, computer time, other preferred activities). For the second student (example 2), a 1-day in-school suspension followed the student's return to school each time he skipped school. Baseline data were collected for 4 consecutive weeks followed by 7 weeks of intervention. The students' attendance percentage per week (1 day, 20%; 2 days, 40%; 3 days, 60%; 4 days, 80%; and 5 days, 100%) was graphed during baseline and intervention conditions. When looking at the differences between conditions A and B for each example, what do you conclude about the intervention effects for each attendance program? Which program would you judge as having the greater impact on school attendance?

In example 1, a visual inspection of the graph seems to reveal an intervention effect. Data collected during the intervention phase indicate that school attendance was higher during the reinforcement program compared with data gathered during the baseline condition. In example 2, an intervention effect is not apparent because significant differences are not seen between baseline and intervention data. As a result, teachers using the two attendance programs may conclude that the reinforcement program is more effective than the in-school suspension program.

Example 1:

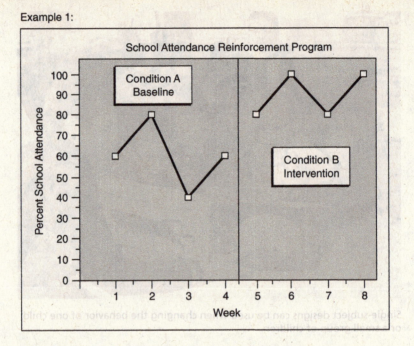

Example 2:

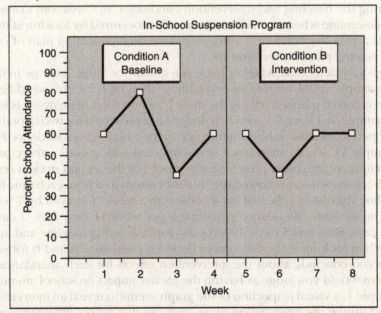

FIGURE 7.1 **A-B design demonstrating a possible intervention effect (Example 1) and no intervention effect (Example 2) on school attendance**

Although visually analyzing single-subject design data serves the needs of most educators and parents, "some authors have argued that the poor interrater reliability associated with visual analysis is a major limitation of single subject methods" (Ottenbacher & Cusick, 1991, p. 48). More formal estimates than the visual analysis of single-subject design data involve mathematical calculations to determine the stability and changes in the direction of trend lines. These methods are beyond the scope of this text. For more information on visual analysis of single-subject designs and methods that evaluate their effect size, refer to Campbell (2005) and Olive and Smith (2005).

A considerable limitation with the A-B design is that we can only *presume* that behavior changes noted during the intervention condition are a function of the intervention. Thus, we cannot be assured that the intervention program is responsible for the observed behavior changes (Foster, Watson, Meeks, & Young, 2002). Additional variables concerning teacher behavior, influences in the home, and other environmental conditions may be more responsible than the reinforcement program for behavior changes during the 4 days of intervention in our hypothetical scenario. For example, suppose the parents of the student in example 1 heard about their son's attendance problems and decided to drive their child to school each day. The change in school attendance may be more closely related to a change in parental behavior than the effects of the reinforcement program implemented by the school. Thus, the A-B design has many internal and external validity problems (Campbell & Stanley, 1966) and is considered a *quasi-experimental design* since an association between the intervention condition and behavior changes may not be made without "major reservations" (Barlow & Hersen, 1984, p. 142). For many teachers, the increase in school attendance would be accepted as a direct outcome of the reinforcement program, and the possibility that other variables are responsible for these changes would not be a primary concern. As Gay (1996) states:

> Single-subject designs are most frequently applied in clinical settings where the primary emphasis is on therapeutic impact, not contribution to a research base. However, if the development of a school-wide attendance program depended upon the results from this research, a stronger research design would be recommended. (p. 296)

Such "stronger" research designs are described in the following sections.

The A-B-A Design

An important feature of the A-B-A design is the employment of a second baseline condition after withdrawing or terminating the intervention condition. Whereas the A-B design has a baseline and intervention condition, the A-B-A design has a baseline, intervention, and second baseline condition as outlined here:

Condition A: Initial baseline

Condition B: Initial intervention

Condition A: Intervention withdrawn and baseline reintroduced

If Marty from Classroom Connection 7.1 decided that she did not like her new seating arrangement (condition B) and returned her classroom to the original seating plan (condition A), this situation would be an example of an A-B-A design. She would continue to collect data and chart the frequency of appropriate student interactions after the return to condition A. Marty could then evaluate her new seating by comparing her intervention data (condition B) with the data charted during the first and second baseline conditions.

The withdrawal of the intervention and the reintroduction of the baseline condition are referred to as a *withdrawal design* (Gay, 1996) and, sometimes, a *reversal design* (Alberto & Troutman, 1995). However, Gay (1996) argues that the A-B-A design is not a true reversal design:

> The A-B-A withdrawal designs are frequently referred to as reversal designs, which they are not, since treatment is generally withdrawn following baseline assessment, not reversed. A reversal design is but one kind of withdrawal design, representing a special kind of withdrawal. (p. 302)

In a reversal design, one intervention is withdrawn and a second intervention, opposite from the first, is implemented. This is called an *A-B-C design*. Both B and C conditions are interventions, but they are opposite to each other. For example, condition B may require a classroom teacher to reinforce *in-seat* behavior, while condition C, the reversal condition, requires the teacher to reinforce *out-of-seat* behavior. In this example, the reversal design may demonstrate the relationship between reinforcement and students' in- and out-of-seat behaviors.

The purpose of the A-B-A design is to demonstrate more clearly the relationship between student performance and an intervention. As previously stated, the change in student performance from condition A to condition B, as in the A-B design, may be coincidental. However, if student performance returns to baseline levels during the *second* baseline condition, teachers may attribute changes in student performance to the implementation and removal of the intervention. Note, however, that a return to baseline may not result in data points that mirror the first baseline condition. Some student learning during the intervention condition may be maintained in the second baseline condition.

While the A-B design tries to establish a relationship between student performance and the implementation of an intervention, the A-B-A design tries to make a relationship between student performance and the implementation *and* withdrawal of an intervention. Thus, the A-B-A design has the potential to demonstrate a more powerful intervention effect than the simpler A-B design: "Whereas the A-B design permits only tentative conclusions as to a treatment's influence, the A-B-A design allows for an analysis of the controlling effects of its introduction and subsequent removal" (Barlow & Hersen, 1984, p. 152).

Continuing with our example from Figure 7.1, suppose that after 4 weeks of the school attendance reinforcement program, the teacher decides to end the reinforcement program but continue to measure the student's attendance for another 4 weeks. In effect, the teacher is deciding to return to the baseline condition in which data on attendance are collected without an intervention program. The A-B-A design has three conditions:

Condition A: Initial baseline data are collected for 4 consecutive weeks.

Condition B: Intervention plan is employed for 4 consecutive weeks. The student is reinforced for attendance. Attendance data continue to be collected and recorded.

Condition A: Intervention plan is withdrawn, and baseline data collection condition is reintroduced for 4 consecutive weeks.

Figure 7.2 provides an example of an A-B-A design using our hypothetical data collected during all three conditions of our school attendance reinforcement program.

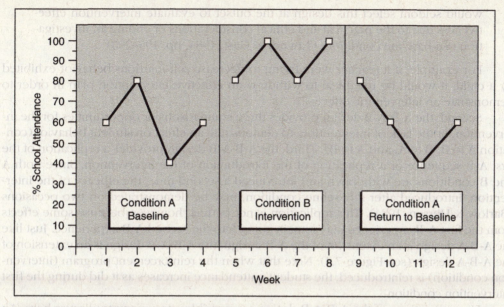

FIGURE 7.2 An A-B-A design demonstrating a change in student attendance with the implementation of the intervention (school attendance reinforcement program) and a withdrawal of the intervention

The increase in school attendance during the intervention condition and the decrease in school attendance after the intervention was withdrawn demonstrate a strong intervention effect on school attendance. Would you recommend a return to the reinforcement program? If your answer is yes, we agree. Also, a return to the intervention condition leads us to another type of single-subject design—the A-B-A-B design.

The A-B-A-B Design

In the A-B-A-B design, the intervention condition is reintroduced after the second baseline condition. The A-B-A-B design has four conditions:

Condition A: Initial baseline data are collected and recorded.

Condition B: Intervention plan is initiated. In our example, the student is reinforced for attendance according to the attendance program. Attendance data continue to be monitored and recorded throughout the intervention condition.

Condition A: Intervention plan is withdrawn and the baseline condition reintroduced.

Condition B: Baseline condition is withdrawn, and intervention plan is introduced for a second time. Student is again reinforced for attendance. Attendance data continue to be monitored and recorded.

The A-B-A-B design has several advantages over the A-B-A design. First, the A-B-A-B design ends during an intervention condition:

While the A-B-A design represents the simplest single subject research paradigm for demonstrating cause-effect relationships, . . . an applied researcher would seldom select this design at the outset to evaluate intervention effectiveness due to the practical and ethical considerations of ending an investigation in a baseline condition. (Tawney & Gast, 1984, pp. 195–200)

For example, if a teacher were trying to decrease self-injurious behavior exhibited by a child, it would be unethical to withdraw an effective intervention plan in order to demonstrate an intervention effect.

Second, the A-B-A-B design provides three comparisons or opportunities for the intervention, or the lack of intervention, to demonstrate an effect on student behavior (condition A to B, B to A, and A to B). Third, the A-B-A-B design provides a replication of the first A-B sequence or a replication of the introduction of the intervention. Since both A and B conditions are withdrawn and introduced a second time, the efficacy of the intervention, introduced after a baseline condition, may be demonstrated on two occasions (Barlow & Hersen, 1984). This replication is not perfect, however, because some effects from the first A-B experience may remain going into the second A-B experience. Just like the A-B-A design is an extension of the A-B design, the A-B-A-B design is an extension of the A-B-A design (see Figure 7.3). Note that when the reinforcement program (intervention condition) is reintroduced, the student's attendance increases as it did during the first intervention condition.

Many variations of the A-B-A-B design are possible—too many to discuss here. An example of a modified A-B-A-B design can be found in Christensen, Young, and Marchant's (2004) study of the effects of a peer-mediated program on classroom behavior and in Trolinder, Choi, and Proctor's (2004) study of the effects of directive praise on children's on-task behavior.

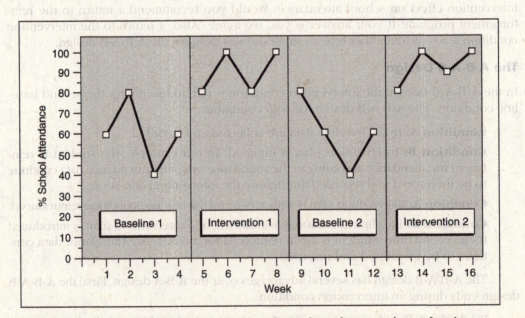

Baseline 1   Intervention 1   Baseline 2   Intervention 2

FIGURE 7.3 An A-B-A-B design demonstrating a change in student attendance after the reintroduction of the school attendance reinforcement intervention

The Alternating Treatments Design

The *alternating treatments design*—also referred to as an *alternating* or *changing conditions design, multiple-schedule design* (Hersen & Barlow, 1976), and a *multiple-element baseline design* (Ulman & Sulzer-Azaroff, 1975)—involves the relatively rapid alternating of interventions for a single subject. "Its purpose is to assess the relative effectiveness of two (or more) treatment conditions" (Gay, 1996, p. 299). This design is also an expansion of the basic A-B design. However, instead of withdrawing the intervention and reintroducing the baseline condition, the researcher introduces a second, *different* intervention strategy while continuing to monitor student performance. This second intervention, following conditions A and B, is called condition C. The number of different intervention conditions (D, E, etc.) added to the alternating treatment design depends on the number of interventions the teacher or researcher is interested in testing. Figure 7.4 provides an example of this design using two different intervention conditions (B and C) as follows:

Condition A: Baseline data are collected on target behavior.

Condition B: First intervention strategy is employed for a specific period of time.

Condition C: First intervention strategy is terminated, and a second intervention introduced for a specific period.

Frequently, each new intervention added in an alternating treatment design is a modification of the previous intervention. For example, say that a teacher wants to increase appropriate behavior during a homeroom period. The intervention in condition B may include verbal reinforcement at the end of the class period contingent on appropriate behavior. Condition C may involve using the same reinforcement program *plus* a positive note sent home. Condition D may include the reinforcement, a note home, *and* a public announcement regarding the student's outstanding behavior by the school principal.

By reviewing the data collected on student behavior during each intervention condition, teachers can compare the results of each intervention and decide which program

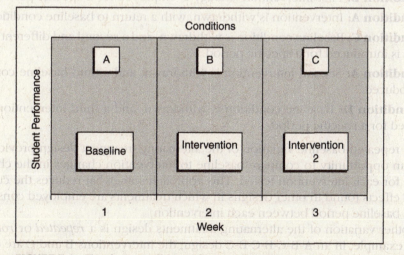

FIGURE 7.4   The three conditions of an A-B-C design

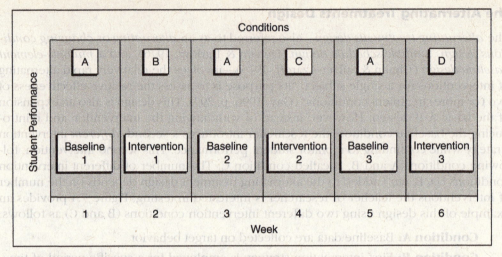

FIGURE 7.5   **An alternating treatments design with baseline condition employed between each different intervention condition**

appears to be the most effective. However, as in the basic A-B design, the alternating treatment design with a single baseline *does not* establish a cause-and-effect relationship between intervention and behavior. Data collected during each intervention may reflect cumulative intervention effects rather than the effects of any one intervention.

Another variation of the alternating research design is the *repeated-baseline alternating research design*. In this design, the teacher decides to return to the baseline condition before introducing each new intervention condition. Thus, one may have an A-B-A-C or an A-B-A-C-A-D design as described here (see also Figure 7.5):

Condition A: Baseline data are collected on target behavior.

Condition B: First intervention strategy is employed for a specific period of time.

Condition A: Intervention is withdrawn, with a return to baseline condition.

Condition C: Baseline condition is withdrawn, and a second and different intervention is introduced for a specific period.

Condition A: Second intervention is withdrawn, and a third baseline condition is introduced.

Condition D: Baseline condition is withdrawn, and a third intervention is introduced for a specific period.

The repeated-baseline variation of the alternating treatment design provides teachers with an opportunity to compare baseline to intervention changes in the child's performance for each intervention tested. This approach somewhat reduces the cumulative treatment effects found in other designs in which treatments are employed consecutively without a baseline period between each intervention.

Another variation of the alternating treatments design is a *repeated* or *rotating design*. For example, in an A-B-C-B-C-B-C design, the interventions B and C are each presented three times in a rotating fashion (see Figure 7.6).

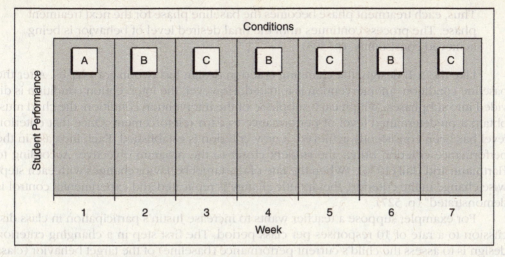

FIGURE 7.6   An A-B-C-B-C-B-C alternating treatment design

In many of the examples provided earlier, the duration of each condition is 1 week. However, as in all the designs discussed in this chapter, the actual duration of each condition may vary. For example, teachers may employ each individual intervention for 1 day or for several days. Also, the duration of each intervention does not have to be equal. For example, while the duration of condition B may be 1 day, the duration of condition C may be 1 month.

The interpretation of these varied and more complicated designs depends on the same variables described in the basic designs. Teachers need to ask the following questions regarding the data collected across conditions:

- What are the data trends within each condition?
- Regarding the direction of the data trends, how do the data trends differ from baseline to intervention conditions? A change in direction from baseline to intervention conditions may indicate an intervention effect.
- What is the difference between the mean baseline performance and the mean intervention performance? Large differences may be associated with a strong relationship between the intervention and the child's behavior.
- How rapid is the change between baseline and intervention conditions? The speed of behavior change may be related to the strength of the intervention effect.
- How do the data trends vary across different intervention conditions? Large differences may indicate different intervention effects across conditions.

The Changing Criterion Design

First described by Sidman (1960) and named by Hall (1971), the *changing criterion design* is used to increase or decrease the performance of a single behavior by gradually increasing the criterion for reinforcement across several intervals of time. Gay (1996) describes the changing criterion design as follows:

> In this design, a baseline phase is followed by successive treatment phases, each of which has a more stringent criterion for acceptable behavior level.

Thus, each treatment phase becomes the baseline phase for the next treatment phase. The process continues until the final desired level of behavior is being achieved consistently. (p. 303)

Like the A-B design, the changing criterion design has two major phases. After the baseline condition, an intervention is initiated. However, the intervention condition is divided into subphases. Within each subphase of the intervention condition, the child must obtain a predetermined level of performance to earn reinforcement. Once that criterion level has been consistently achieved, a new criterion is established. Each increase in the performance criterion brings the student closer to the program objective. According to Hartmann and Hall (1976), "When the rate of the target behavior changes with each step-wise change in the criterion, therapeutic change is replicated and experimental control is demonstrated" (p. 527).

For example, suppose a teacher wants to increase Justin's participation in class discussion to a rate of 10 responses per class period. The first step in a changing criterion design is to assess the child's current performance (baseline) of the target behavior (class discussion). Justin's teacher collected baseline data for four consecutive days and recorded a rate of zero for all 4 days. Since the teacher's goal is 10 responses per class session, the teacher must now determine

- the number of steps to be implemented between the current performance level (0) and the ultimate criterion or program objective level (10),
- the reinforcement to be provided to the child contingent on behavior that meets or exceeds the established criterion, and
- the specific reinforcement criterion for each of the steps.

Justin's teacher decides to divide her program into five steps, to use 15 minutes on the class computer as the reinforcement, and to increase the criterion by two responses per step, as follows:

Criterion for step 1: 2 responses per class

Criterion for step 2: 4 responses per class

Criterion for step 3: 6 responses per class

Criterion for step 4: 8 responses per class

Criterion for step 5: 10 responses per class

After the baseline period, the intervention condition begins. The teacher begins the intervention condition by telling Justin that he may earn 15 minutes on the computer during class free time by participating in class discussion at a rate of two times per class period. After this criterion is achieved and a stable performance is observed, Justin's teacher changes the criterion to four responses per class period. After this criterion is reached and a stable performance is noted, the next criterion level is implemented, and so on. Justin must be told that the criterion has been changed before the implementation of the next intervention subphase. Figure 7.7 provides an overview of Justin's performance (see data points) per criterion level (indicated by the vertical line per subphase). Note the rapid rate at which Justin's performance increased and the relationship between the increases in his performance and each change in the criterion for reinforcement. Justin's teacher

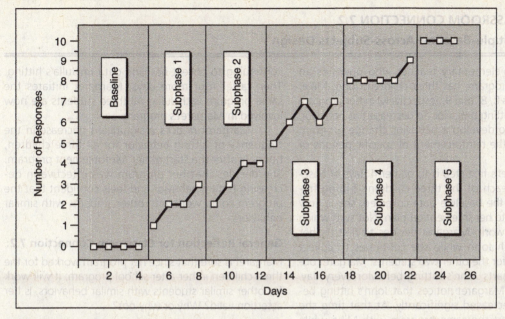

FIGURE 7.7   Changing criterion design over 26 days

has established a clear relationship between the reinforcement program and the rate of Justin's class participation.

Multiple-Baseline Designs

In many cases it may be impossible, for practical or ethical reasons, to withdraw an intervention and return to a baseline condition. For example, if an intervention involves some type of academic instruction, returning to a true baseline condition is impossible since the teacher cannot remove information learned during the intervention condition from the student's memory. In this situation, teachers may incorrectly identify the A-B design as the only alternative.

When a cause-and-effect relationship is desired and it is not possible to extend beyond the simple A-B design with a single subject, teachers should consider a multiple-baseline design. The multiple-baseline design is the most common type of single-subject design employed in published intervention studies with students with behavior challenges (Mooney, Epstein, Reid, & Nelson, 2003). It is, in fact, an extension of the A-B design, but in a different way than discussed up to this point. The multiple-baseline design retains the basic concept of the A-B design while extending these principles beyond a single subject. Instead of a sole subject providing replication of intervention effects, replication is achieved across a small sample of subjects, behaviors, or settings. This approach allows teachers to establish a cause-and-effect relationship between the intervention and behavior changes.

The three basic types of multiple-baseline designs are *across subjects, across behaviors,* and *across settings.* In each case, an A-B design is employed across three subjects (e.g., Babyak, Koorland, & Mathes, 2000; Gumpel & David, 2000), behaviors (e.g., Penno,

CLASSROOM CONNECTION 7.2
Multiple-Baseline-Across-Subjects Design

Margaret, an elementary teacher who operates an after-school program, has three children (John, Mike, and Julia, ages 8, 8, and 9, respectively) in her program who exhibit hitting behavior. To decrease this behavior, she decides to develop a behavior change program that involves the reinforcement of specific periods of no hitting.

Margaret's first step is to gather 4 days of baseline data on each of the three children's hitting frequency. With the baseline data collected, she is now ready to initiate her intervention plan. Not sure which program will work, Margaret decides to first try her plan only with John while she continues to collect baseline data for the other two students. Margaret observes and charts John's hitting behavior every day. After 4 days, Margaret notices that John's hitting behavior has decreased significantly. At that time she decides to start the same program with Mike while continuing to collect baseline data on Julia's hitting. Then, after four more days, Margaret initiates the same program with Julia. All three students are now involved in Margaret's program.

Margaret notices a significant decrease in the frequency of hitting behavior for all three children, but only after the start of her reinforcement program. She decides that her program was effective in decreasing hitting behavior and feels confident that the program could work with other students with similar behaviors.

General Reflection for Classroom Connection 7.2:

Margaret is sure that since her program worked for the three children in her after-school program, it will work for other similar students with similar behaviors. Is her assertion valid? Why or why not?

Frank, & Wacker, 2000), or settings (e.g., Fabiano & Pelham, 2003; Kennedy & Jolivette, 2008), and the intervention condition is applied to each subject, behavior, or setting at different intervals. Although not discussed here, a multiple-baseline design across treatments is another option for testing the effectivenes of various interventions (e.g., DiGennaro, Martens, & McIntyre, 2005).

THE MULTIPLE-BASELINE-ACROSS-SUBJECTS DESIGN In this design, the same intervention is employed across three children. The initiation of the intervention, however, is staggered across the three *subjects,* as demonstrated in Classroom Connection 7.2.

The data that Margaret, our teacher in Classroom Connection 7.2, collected from observing the hitting behavior of her three students are presented in Figure 7.8. As the figure shows, after a baseline condition, the same intervention condition was applied for each of the three children, but at different intervals. Four days of baseline data were collected for each of the three children. For John, the intervention was employed on the 5th day. Meanwhile, Margaret continued to collect baseline data for Mike and Julia. For Mike, the intervention was initiated on the 9th day after 8 days of baseline. Meanwhile, the intervention condition continued for John while the baseline condition continued for Julia. Finally, the intervention was applied for Julia on the 13th day. All three children were now receiving the intervention condition.

THE MULTIPLE-BASELINE-ACROSS-BEHAVIORS DESIGN In this design, the same intervention is applied to a single child across three different behaviors. As with other multiple-baseline designs, the initiation of the intervention is staggered. In this case, the start of the intervention is staggered across the three behaviors, as demonstrated in Classroom Connection 7.3.

The data charted by Gregg during his multiple-baseline-across-behaviors design are given in Figure 7.9. As this figure shows, by beginning the same program for the three

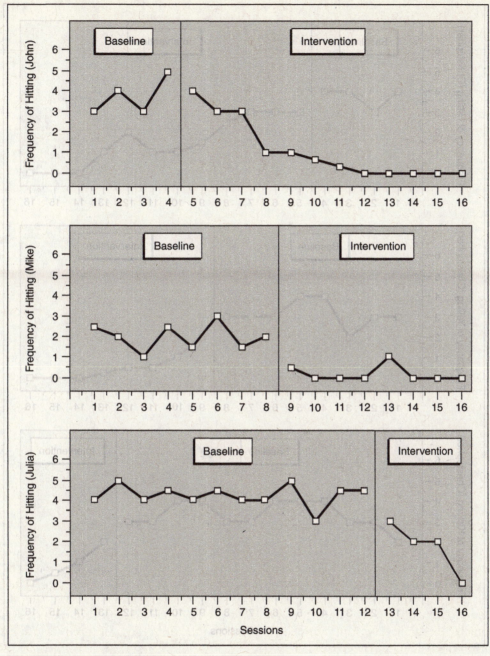

FIGURE 7.8   A multiple-baseline-across-subjects design

behaviors at different intervals, Gregg established a relationship between the initiation of his intervention and a deceleration of each of the three behaviors. In this case, as in Classroom Connection 7.3, the duration of baseline and intervention conditions was 4 days. The actual number of days for any of the conditions, however, will vary according to the child, behavior, and setting.

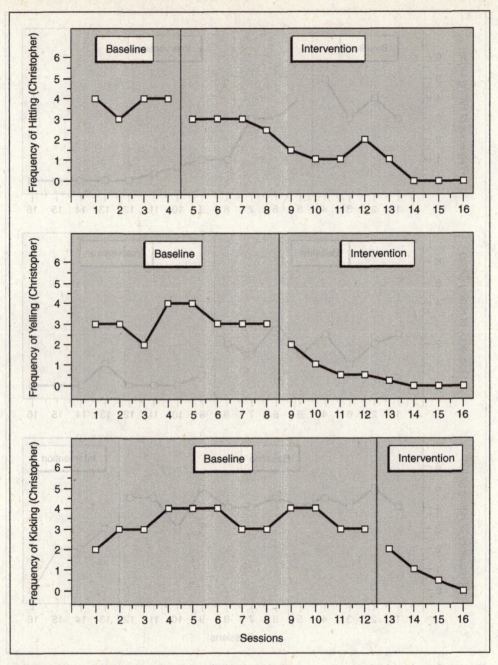

FIGURE 7.9 A multiple-baseline-across-behaviors design

behaviors at different intervals. Greg established a relationship between the initiation of his intervention and a deceleration of each of the three behaviors. In this case, as in Classroom Connection 7.3, the duration of baseline and intervention conditions was 4 days. The actual number of days for any of the conditions, however, will vary according to the child, behavior, and setting.

CLASSROOM CONNECTION 7.3
Multiple-Baseline-Across-Behaviors Design

Gregg is a middle school physical education teacher. One of his students, Christopher, is the tallest and biggest student in his third-period gym class. But Gregg notices that Christopher frequently becomes angry during physical games and activities, and will start hitting, yelling, and sometimes even kicking whoever happens to be near him at the time. The other students are afraid of Christopher because he is so much bigger than them.

After completing a functional assessment of Christopher's behaviors, Gregg observed that while Christopher enjoyed the physical activities during gym time, he had trouble keeping up with his much smaller, yet far more coordinated, classmates. In frustration, Christopher became aggressive.

Gregg decides to initiate a two-part program to decrease Christopher's inappropriate behavior. In part one of his new program, Gregg provides Christopher and his classmates with specific verbal reinforcement for appropriate interactions with classmates. He hopes that Christopher will observe the other children receiving attention for appropriate behavior and that Christopher will model his peers.

But before initiating the second part of his program, a consequence for Christopher's inappropriate behaviors, Gregg decides not to tackle all of Christopher's inappropriate behaviors at the same time. Instead, he decides to complete 4 days of baseline observation on all three behaviors, decide which one was the biggest problem, and initiate a time-out program with one behavior at a time. After collecting the baseline data, he decides to start with Christopher's hitting behavior, because it is the most severe of his challenging behaviors.

After 4 days of baseline observation and data collection, Gregg initiates the second part of his program. While verbal praise continues to be provided following appropriate interactions between students, Christopher is pulled out of any activity for 5 minutes immediately after he hits another child. Meanwhile, Gregg continues to collect baseline data for Christopher's other two behavior problems (yelling and kicking). By charting the frequency of Christopher's hitting, Gregg notices a significant decrease in Christopher's hitting frequency, yet the frequency of yelling and kicking remain the same.

After 4 more days, Gregg incorporates Christopher's yelling behavior into the time-out part of his program. Thus, hitting and yelling behavior are now followed by 5-minute periods of time-out from whatever activity Christopher is involved. Meanwhile, Gregg continues to collect baseline data for Christopher's kicking behavior.

On the 12th day of programming, Gregg includes Christopher's kicking behavior into his program. Now, all three of Christopher's inappropriate behaviors are followed by the 5-minute time-out from participation in activities. Meanwhile, and just as important, appropriate interactions continue to be verbally reinforced.

Gregg continues his program for the rest of the school year because he likes the idea of verbally reinforcing appropriate classroom behaviors. Since Christopher's aggressive behaviors only occur now and then, the occasional use of a 5-minute time-out period provides Gregg with an effective consequence for aggression. In fact, Gregg decides to use this approach as a consequence for aggression exhibited by the other students in his classroom.

General Reflection of Classroom Connection 7.3:

Gregg decides to incorporate his reinforcement and time-out program with Christopher's aggressive behaviors one at a time. Outline both the programming and design benefits of this approach. Many teachers would find it challenging to ignore Christopher's yelling and kicking while working on his more severe hitting behavior for 4 days. How would you advise these teachers so they don't invalidate the program or design aspects of Gregg's strategy?

CLASSROOM CONNECTION 7.4
Multiple-Baseline-Across-Settings Design

Brenda, a special education consultant for a large school system, has a meeting with several 10th-grade teachers about a boy named Tommy. Tommy has some attention deficits that result in a significant amount of off-task behaviors in his high school math, science, and English classes.

Baseline measures indicate that Tommy is off-task an average of 30 minutes for each of the 45-minute classes. Brenda recommends a cognitive behavior modification (see Chapter 11) program that includes

• teaching Tommy how to monitor his own on-task behavior,
• teaching Tommy how to record his own on-task behavior performance,
• teaching Tommy how to evaluate his on-task performance according to specific criteria established by his teachers, and
• developing a reinforcement menu for appropriate on-task behaviors.

Brenda suggests that the teachers use a multiple-baseline-across-settings design to evaluate the effectiveness of their program. This design is recommended since they are interested in increasing Tommy's on-task behavior in three different classes.

The program is initiated in Tommy's math class. Tommy's math teacher explains the program to him and starts the program the same day. Meanwhile, his science and English teachers continue to collect baseline data on his on-task duration data in science and English classes.

On the 5th day, Tommy's science teacher initiates the same program while his English teacher continues collecting and charting baseline data on Tommy's on-task duration in English class. Finally, on the 9th day, Tommy's English teacher tells Tommy that she too will follow the same program used in his other two classes. The on-task program is now being employed across Tommy's three classes. All three teachers communicate daily to ensure that they consistently follow the program.

General Reflection for Classroom Connection 7.4:

The multiple-baseline design across settings used to chart Tommy's on-task behaviors in multiple settings requires communication and coordination among several teachers. This is a common challenge in middle and high schools where students change classes and, as we know, behave differently in different classrooms for different teachers. What are the challenges to conducting such a study in a real school, and how would you coordinate these efforts?

THE MULTIPLE-BASELINE-ACROSS-SETTINGS DESIGN In the multiple-baseline-across-settings design, the same intervention is applied to a single child across three different settings or environments. As with other multiple-baseline designs, the initiation of the intervention is staggered. In this case, the initiation of intervention is staggered across three settings, as demonstrated in Classroom Connection 7.4.

In Classroom Connection 7.4, the same behavior change program was initiated by three different teachers across three different settings. By implementing the same on-task program across settings and at different intervals, the teachers demonstrated a relationship between Tommy's on-task behavior and their intervention plan. Data collected and charted by the three teachers are presented in Figure 7.10. Notice that Tommy's on-task behavior remains low across all three settings until the intervention plan is initiated. As the intervention is initiated per setting, Tommy's on-task behavior increases for that setting. A cause-and-effect relationship between Tommy's on-task behavior and the intervention plan is established.

In the Classroom Connections and examples provided here, the intervention condition is applied across three levels of subjects, behaviors, or settings. This approach reflects the most common application of the multiple-baseline designs. Other variations of the multiple-baseline design, however, may employ more than three levels. A minimum of two levels is required. Also, although 4 days (or sessions) per condition were used in all our

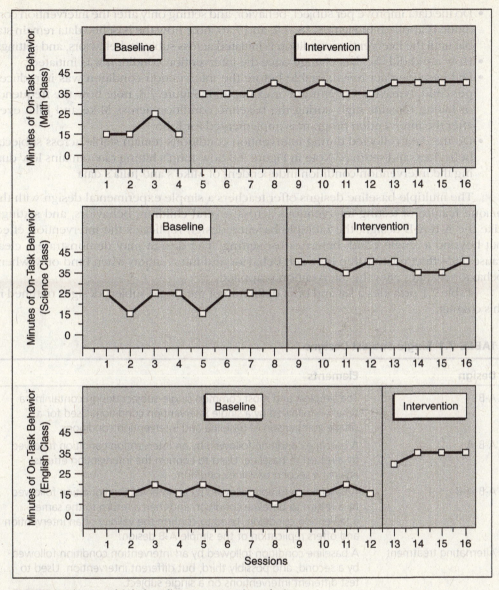

FIGURE 7.10 A multiple-baseline-across-settings design

examples, other variations of this design may include more or fewer than 4 sessions. Four, however, is usually the minimum number required if a stable data trend is to be established.

Several questions about the recorded data on a multiple-baseline design must be evaluated before a cause-and-effect relationship can be established:

- Are there significant changes from baseline to intervention conditions within each individual A-B design per subject, behavior, or setting? Note these differences in Figures 7.8, 7.9, and 7.10.
- What are the data trends or direction of data during the intervention conditions compared to the baseline conditions per subject, behavior, or setting?

- Do the data improve per subject, behavior, and setting only after the intervention condition is applied? In Figures 7.8, 7.9, and 7.10, note how the baseline data remain stable until the intervention condition is initiated across subjects, behaviors, and settings.
- How rapid did the data change once the intervention condition was initiated?
- Did baseline data remain stable before the intervention condition was introduced per child, behavior, or setting? For example, in Figure 7.8, note how the frequency of hitting remains high during the baseline condition across Mike and Julia even after the intervention program is implemented for John.
- Do the data collected during intervention conditions remain stable across subjects, behaviors, and settings? Note in Figure 7.8 how John's hitting rate remains low during the intervention condition independent of Mike's and Julia's data.

The multiple-baseline designs offer teachers a simple experimental design with the unique feature of testing interventions across several children, behaviors, and settings. Like the A-B-A-B design, the multiple-baseline design replicates the intervention effect but beyond a single child, behavior, or setting. The design may demonstrate a clear cause-and-effect relationship between behavior and intervention when (and only when) behavior changes after the intervention is applied.

Table 7.1 provides a list and brief definition of the single-subject designs outlined in this chapter.

TABLE 7.1 Single-Subject Designs

Design	Elements
A-B	The simplest and most common single-subject design containing a baseline followed by a single intervention condition. Used for a simple comparison of baseline and intervention conditions.
A-B-A	A baseline condition followed by an intervention condition followed by a return to baseline. Used to confirm the intervention effects against a second baseline condition.
A-B-A-B	A baseline condition followed by an intervention condition followed by a return to baseline condition and then a return to the same intervention condition. Used to confirm the validity of an intervention and offers replication of the simple A-B design.
Alternating treatment	A baseline condition followed by an intervention condition followed by a second, and possibly third, but different intervention. Used to test different interventions on a single subject.
Changing criterion	Used to increase or decrease student behavior by gradually increasing the criterion for reinforcement over time. Demonstrates the effectiveness of an intervention by documenting the behavior changing as a condition of the changing criterion for reinforcement.
Multiple baseline across subjects	Used to demonstrate the effectiveness of an intervention across different students exhibiting the same target behavior.
Multiple baseline across behaviors	Used to demonstrate the effectiveness of an intervention across different target behaviors.
Multiple baseline across settings	Used to demonstrate the effectiveness of an intervention to change a behavior across different settings.

Summary

The purpose of single-subject designs is to allow teachers to demonstrate experimental control and intervention effects with a single child or small group of children. Thus, these designs are ideal for classroom teachers, parents, and other teachers who want to demonstrate the effectiveness of their behavior reduction strategies.

With single-subject designs, comparisons are made between or among conditions employed during different phases of a behavior change program. Baseline and intervention conditions represent the two primary conditions employed in single-subject designs. These are labeled conditions A and B. Intervention conditions may vary and, thus, may be labeled C, D, E, and so on, to indicate a new or modified intervention plan.

Types of single-subject designs include the A-B, A-B-C, A-B-A-B, alternating treatments, changing criterion, and multiple-baseline designs. All of these designs are variations of each other and serve specific functions related to the demonstration of experimental control and intervention effects.

The A-B design is the simplest of the single-subject designs, employing a baseline and one intervention condition. When using the A-B design, we can only presume that behavior changes noted during the intervention condition are a function of the intervention. The A-B-A design employs a withdrawal of the intervention condition and a return to baseline condition. The purpose of the A-B-A design is to demonstrate more clearly the relationship between student performance and the intervention. The A-B-A-B design employs a return to condition B after a short return to baseline as in the A-B-A design. The A-B-A-B design has many advantages over the previously described designs.

The alternating treatment or changing conditions design involves alternating intervention conditions for a single subject or group of subjects. The changing criterion design is used to increase or decrease student performance by gradually increasing the criterion for reinforcement across several intervals of time. Finally, the multiple-baseline designs provide for the replication of intervention conditions across subjects, behaviors, or settings.

Discussion Questions

1. Discuss the purpose of single-subject designs and how they may be used in the classroom setting.
2. How is the effectiveness of an intervention demonstrated or not demonstrated in the A-B, A-B-A, and A-B-A-B designs?
3. Describe how the effectiveness of an intervention is demonstrated when using multiple-baseline designs. Give examples of how the multiple-baseline design may be used within a school setting across students, settings, and behaviors.
4. Why is the A-B-A-B better than the A-B?

References

Alberto, P. A., & Troutman, A. C. (1995). *Applied behavior analysis for teachers*. Upper Saddle River, NJ: Merrill/Pearson Education.

Babyak, A. E., Koorland, M., & Mathes, P. G. (2000). The effects of story mapping instruction on the reading comprehension of students with behavioral disorders. *Behavioral Disorders, 25*(3), 239–258.

Barlow, D. H., & Hersen, M. (1984). *Single case experimental designs: Strategies for studying behavior change*. New York: Pergamon.

Bellon, M. L., Ogletree, B. T., & Harn, W. E. (2000). Repeated storybook reading as a language intervention for children with autism. *Focus on Autism and Other Developmental Disabilities, 15*(1), 52–58.

Campbell, D. T., & Stanley, J. C. (1966). *Experimental and quasi-experimental designs for research*. Boston: Houghton-Mifflin.

Campbell, J. M. (2005). Statistical comparison of four effect sizes for single-subject designs. *Behavior Modification, 28*(2), 234–246.

Christensen, L., Young, K. R., & Marchant, M. (2004). The effects of a peer-mediated positive behavior support program on socially appropriate classroom behavior. *Education and Treatment of Children, 27*(3), 199–234.

DiGennaro, F. D., Martens, B. K., & McIntyre, L. L. (2005). Increasing treatment integrity through negative reinforcement: Effects on teacher and student behavior. *School Psychology Review, 34*(2), 220–231.

Fabiano, G. A., & Pelham, W. E. (2003). *Journal of Emotional and Behavioral Disorders, 11*(2), 122–128.

Foster, L. H., Watson, T. S., Meeks, C., & Young, S. J. (2002). Single-subject research design for school counselors: Becoming an applied researcher. *Professional School Counseling, 6*(2), 146–155.

Gay, L. R. (1996). *Educational research: Competencies for analysis and application*. Upper Saddle River, NJ: Merrill/Pearson Education.

Gumpel, T. P., & David, S. (2000). Exploring the efficacy of self-regulation training as a possible alternative to social skills training. *Behavioral Disorders, 25*(2), 131–141.

Hall, R. V. (1971). *Managing behavior—Behavior modification: The measure of behavior*. Lawrence, KS: H & H Enterprises.

Hartmann, D. P., & Hall, R. V. (1976). The changing criterion design. *Journal of Applied Behavior Analysis, 9*, 527–532.

Hersen, M., & Barlow, D. H. (1976). *Single-case experimental designs: Strategies for studying behavior changes*. New York: Pergamon.

Kennedy, C., & Jolivette, K. (2008). The effects of positive verbal reinforcement on the time spent outside the classroom for students with emotional and behavioral disorders in a residential setting. *Behavior Disorders, 33*(4), 211–221.

Martin, D. W. (1985). *Doing psychology experiments* (2nd ed.). Pacific Grove, CA: Brooks/Cole.

Mooney, P., Epstein, M. H., Reid, R., & Nelson, R. (2003). Status of and trends in academic intervention research for students with emotional disturbance. *Remedial and special education, 24*(5), 273–287.

Odom, S. L. (1988). Research in early childhood special education. In S. L. Odom & M. B. Karnes (Eds.), *Early intervention for infants and children with handicaps* (pp. 1–22). Baltimore: Brookes.

Olive, M. L., & Smith, B. W. (2005). Effect size calculations and single subject designs. *Educational Psychology, 25*(2), 313–333.

Ottenbacher, K. J., & Cusick, A. (1991). An empirical investigation of interrater agreement for single-subject data using graphs with and without trend lines. *Journal of the Association for Persons with Severe Handicaps, 16*, 48–55.

Patrick, P. D., Mozzoni, M., & Patrick, S. T. (2000). Evidence-based care and the single subject design. *Infants and Young Children, 13*(1), 60–73.

Penno, D. A., Frank, A. R., & Wacker, D. P. (2000). Instructional accommodations for adolescent students with severe emotional or behavioral disorders. *Behavioral Disorders, 25*(4), 325–343.

Sidman, M. (1960). *Tactics of scientific research: Evaluating experimental data in psychology*. New York: Basic Books.

Swanson, H. L., & Sachse-Lee, C. (2000). A meta-analysis of single subject design intervention research for students with LD. *Journal of Learning Disabilities, 33*(2), 114–137.

Tankersley, M., Harjusola-Webb, S., & Landrum, T. J. (2008). Using single-subject research to establish the evidence base of special education. *Intervention in School and Clinic, 44*(2), 83–90.

Tawney, J. W., & Gast, D. L. (1984). *Single subject research in special education*. Upper Saddle River, NJ: Merrill/Pearson Education.

Trolinder, D. M., Choi, H. S., & Proctor, T. B. (2004). Use of delayed praise as a directive and its effectiveness on on-task behavior. *Journal of Applied School Psychology, 20*(2), 61–83.

Ulman, J. D., & Sulzer-Azaroff, B. (1975). Multi-element baseline design in educational research. In E. Ramp & G. Semb (Eds.), *Behavior analysis: Areas of research and application* (pp. 377–391). Upper Saddle River, NJ: Prentice Hall.

Formal Behavioral Assessment

Victoria K. Russell
Towson University

Kristine J. Melloy
Cristo Rey Jesuit High School, Minneapolis

> *But I am also clear that in lecture halls, seminar rooms, field settings, labs, and even electronic classrooms—the places where most people receive most of their formal education—teachers possess the power to create conditions that can help students learn a great deal—or keep them from learning much at all. Teaching is the intentional act of creating those conditions, and good teaching requires that we understand the inner sources of both the intent and the act.*

—PALMER (1998, p. 6)

Typically when we think of behavior management, problematic behavior of students in school and other settings comes to mind. It is important for teachers and others who care for children to realize that behavior management has as much to do with promoting appropriate behavior as it does with helping students change inappropriate behavior. It is also important to realize that teachers, as well as families, peers, and environmental influences *outside* of school, have a lot to do with how students behave *in* school. It is our job to listen to what students say and watch what they do. Our students tell us, by their behavior, exactly what their strengths are and what they need. The mystery and challenge for us is to figure it all out so that we can create classrooms that are conducive to maximum opportunities for teaching and learning.

This is one of four chapters dedicated to assisting educators in completing and understanding behavioral measurement (Chapters 6 and 7) and assessment (Chapter 9) in order to (a) identify student strengths and needs related to their behavior, (b) identify environmental antecedents and consequences maintaining student behavior, (c) evaluate the relationship between classroom variables (including curriculum) and student behavior, (d) plan educational interventions directed at helping students maintain and/or change their social and academic related behaviors, (e) document baseline and intervention data via single-subject design, and (f) evaluate the effectiveness of interventions.

In this chapter, we discuss a developmental systems approach to behavioral assessment. Then, we focus on the formal assessment strategies and techniques that are used in the first two steps of a five-step model for behavioral assessment. Steps 3 through 5 are discussed in other chapters.

For steps 1 and 2, we offer an illustration of the methods applied in the case of a student named Rick. The scope of this text does not allow for an in-depth description of how to administer most of these methods. References are provided, however, to find out more specifics for each of the methods described.

A DEVELOPMENTAL SYSTEMS APPROACH TO BEHAVIORAL ASSESSMENT

Developmental-systems assessment (DSA) attempts to understand "both disturbed and nondisturbed children and their social systems, including families and peer groups" (Mash & Hunsley, 2007, p. 6). While a common set of features, or "prototypes," characterizes DSA, this approach to behavioral assessment takes into consideration influences such as the behaviors being reviewed and the characteristics of the individual child. For example, prototypes of DSA may be different depending on the child's age or whether the behaviors are internalizing or externalizing. Several prototypes appear to be common, however, to a DSA approach to behavioral assessment (Mash & Hunsley, 2007):

- Assessment should be based on "conceptualizations of personality and abnormal behavior that emphasize the child's thoughts, feelings, and behaviors as they occur in specific situations, as well as the child's more general personality traits and dispositions" (Mash & Hunsley, 2007, p. 6). Interest is on behaviors viewed as direct samples of the student's behavioral characteristics rather than as signs of underlying causes.
- Assessment is systems-oriented, with focus on the individual child and family emphasized over comparisons with a norm group. This requires description and understanding of the characteristics of the child and family; the context in which these characteristics are expressed; and the functional relationships among situations, behaviors, thoughts, and emotions.
- Assessment is primarily interested in discovering situational influences on behavior rather than historical experiences, except in cases where an earlier event (e.g., physical or sexual abuse) may help understand current behavior. Assessment, therefore, requires a wider sampling of behaviors across several environments (e.g., home, school, community environments).
- Behaviors may change as the result of the context in which they occur, or over time. As antecedent and consequent stimuli change, the behavioral response may also change or remain stable depending upon the situation. For example, a group of students who consistently follow the classroom rules when their regular teacher is present may become disruptive and noncompliant when a substitute teacher visits their classroom for the day. Likewise, a first grader who cries being dropped off at school every morning in September may exhibit more independent behaviors toward the end of the school year. Both consistency and variability of child and family behaviors must be considered against a range of influences and contexts.
- The primary purpose of assessment is to obtain information that will assist in developing effective intervention strategies. Assessment data should aid in identifying

and defining target behaviors and ideas for intervention, and conducting ongoing evaluation of the intervention effects and the achievement of treatment goals.

- During assessment a multimethod approach is employed whereby no one assessment instrument, strategy, or technique is thought to be better than another. A variety of methods are used to provide information on the student and his or her family, the contexts in which behaviors occur, and the functional relationship of the student's behavior and the situation. Furthermore, multiple informants, including the child, family, peers, and teachers, must be used to gain information across different settings and perspectives.

- Decisions about specific assessment strategies are based not only on empirical data available on student and family characteristics, but also on the literature on specific behavior disorders. The reliability and validity of assessment methods are also viewed in relation to the specific purpose for assessment.

ASSESSMENT FOR INTERVENTION PLANNING: A FIVE-STEP MODEL

With the DSA approach in mind, the first two steps of a five-step model for behavioral assessment will be described in detail. The five steps are outlined in Figure 8.1. After each step is discussed, suggestions for data collection strategies that complement that step will be provided. In addition, examples will be provided to demonstrate application of the behavioral assessment model in school settings.

Step 1: Decide Whether a Problem Exists

Teachers and others decide whether a behavior problem exists when they notice that a student demonstrates behaviors or is at risk for behaviors that potentially cause problems for themselves or others. While children may be screened in groups to determine if behaviors suggest a disability, many school systems do not implement such measures because the majority of children with emotional or behavioral disabilities self-identify (Heward, 2009). However, given that all students have potential for benefiting from behavior management, it is suggested that behavioral assessment, particularly step 1 of the process, be used in a broader, proactive sense to help teachers in their work with all students.

Characteristics of some common behavior problems are described in Chapter 14 of this text. Briefly, behavior problems are usually described in behavior categories or response classes including: on/off task, aggressiveness, disruptiveness, noncompliance, depression, and withdrawn behavior. Peers and others may describe behavior problems using comments such as "He's mean," "She is a bully," "He is shy," or "She doesn't do her work."

Step 1	Decide whether a problem exists.
Step 2	Determine whether intervention is warranted.
Step 3	Perform a functional assessment.
Step 4	Develop behavior management intervention.
Step 5	Conduct ongoing evaluation.

FIGURE 8.1   Behavioral assessment five-step model

Early identification of students who experience *externalizing* (e.g., aggressive, acting out, oppositional) and/or *internalizing* (e.g., social withdrawal, anxiousness, fears) *behavior problems* is important. Students who demonstrate externalizing behavior problems are more likely to drop out of school, become delinquent, abuse drugs, and/or have difficulties forming positive relationships (Elksnin & Elksnin, 1998; Lipsey & Derzon, 1998; Walker, Ramsey, & Gresham, 2004). Students with internalizing behavior problems are less likely to be identified for support or interventions because their behaviors do not commonly disrupt the classroom (Friend, 2008; Lane & Menzies, 2005). Early identification and intervention, however, can result in positive educational and social outcomes for most students (Friend, 2008; Morris, 2004). When most people hear the term *early intervention*, they usually think that it refers to a student's age. However, many behavior problems can develop at any age, so we encourage teachers to also think of early intervention as "early in the problem."

Because of the nature of step 1, data collection procedures are usually efficient and may be administered to large groups of students or to individuals in the quickest manner possible. Typically, teachers and others will be able to determine whether a problem exists by collecting behavioral assessment data using a variety of strategies and techniques, such as checklists and rating scales, teacher rankings, sociometric techniques, interviews, and observations.

DATA COLLECTION METHODS FOR STEP 1

Rating Scales and Teacher Ranking. Rating scales require that the person completing the instrument know the student well enough to make qualitative judgments about his or her behavior. Typically, raters are given a list of behaviors and asked to evaluate the student using a Likert-type scale to indicate the degree to which the student engages in the behavior or does not engage in the behavior (Mash & Terdal, 1997). Raters are asked to respond to each item in terms of a varied-point scale defined by labels such as "agree strongly," "agree," "undecided," "disagree," and "disagree strongly" (Melloy, 1990). A rating scale may also include self-reports by the student as part of the overall rating system. Students may be asked to respond to questions about behaviors and how the student feels he or she matches the description.

Rating scales are popular for their ease of administration and the quick assessment of student behavior that is provided. Most rating scales can be completed in about 10 to 20 minutes for an individual student. While easy to administer, rating scales offer one individual's perceptions of a behavior; a student may have different ratings for the same behavior depending on the rater (Salvia & Ysseldyke, 2007). For this reason, it is important to supplement data from rating scales with additional behavioral assessments (Gresham & Elliott, 1990; Salvia & Ysseldyke, 2007).

Teacher rankings require that the teacher rank-order the students in his or her class based on behavioral criteria established by the test author (Melloy, Davis, Wehby, Murry, & Leiber, 1998). Students ranking high on less-desirable classroom behaviors may be referred for more extensive evaluation to determine if a disability exists. As with rating scales, teacher rankings cannot be the sole means of evaluating student behavior. Different teachers establish different learning environments and behavioral expectations that must be considered when interpreting teacher ranking data (McLoughlin & Lewis, 2008).

Three instruments briefly described below highlight how rating scales and teacher rankings may be useful in gathering data during step 1. They provide a sample of available instruments that can screen both groups and individuals for behavior or emotional concerns.

Systematic Screening for Behavior Disorders (SSBD).   The Systematic Screening for Behavior Disorder (SSBD) by Walker and Severson (1999) is an assessment system that uses multiple gating procedures to identify elementary-aged students in grades 1 through 5 who demonstrate behavioral problems. During the first stage of screening, teachers are asked to rank-order every student in their class based on behavioral criteria for externalized and internalized behavior problems or disorders. Students who are ranked at the top of the list are then further assessed by a behavior rating scale in stage 2 of the assessment process. Finally, in stage 3, students who meet criteria for behavior disorders in stage 2 are observed in classroom and playground settings to determine whether their academic and social behavior deviates significantly from the behavior of their peers.

Research on the reliability and validity of the SSBD indicates that the assessment system shows promise for screening all elementary-age students for purposes of identifying those at risk of developing or maintaining behavior problems and/or disorders (Walker, Severson, & Feil, 1995). In addition, "multiple gating may help limit the number of undetected problems, as well as target time-consuming assessment methods toward the most severe problems" (Salvia & Ysseldyke, 2007, p. 519).

Child Behavior Checklist System (CBCL).   The Child Behavior Checklist System (CBCL: Achenbach, 2001) relies on multiple informant rating scales to determine emotional or behavioral problems for individuals 18 months to 30 years old. The CBCL is broken into three age levels: ages 18 months through 5 years old, ages 6 through 18 years old, and ages 18 through 30 years old. For children 18 months through 5 years old, rating scales are completed by a parent/primary caregiver and childcare provider or early childhood teacher. Both scales contain 99 items and the parent/primary caregiver form includes the Language Development Survey (LDS) to identify language delays that may be behind perceived behavior issues. The CBCL for children 6 through 18 years old has three rating scales: a parent/primary caregiver form, the Teacher Report Form (TRF), and a Youth Self-Report for individuals at least 11 years old with a fifth-grade reading level. These three rating scales may be supplemented by a Direct Observation Form for children ages 5 through 14 years old and a Semistructured Clinical Interview Form for Children and Adolescents (SCICA). The CBCL for young adults, ages 18 through 30 years old, has two rating scales: a form for parents or individuals who know the young adult well and a Young Adult Self-Report Form (YASR).

The CBCL is considered to have adequate reliability and validity for the purposes of screening (Cohen & Spenciner, 2007). A primary value of the CBCL is its measure of behavior through multiple informants and perspectives, including the child as appropriate. The CBCL considers behavior across environments, not just in academic settings. The CBCL is available in Spanish, and many of the forms have been translated into over 60 languages. Figure 8.2 and Figure 8.3 show samples of questions from a parent and teacher rating form, respectively.

Behavioral and Emotional Rating Scale, Second Edition (BERS-2).   The Behavioral and Emotional Rating Scale (BERS-2: Epstein, 2004) offers three perspectives

Below is a list of items that describe children and youth. For each item that describes your child *now or within the past 6 months,* please circle the *2* if the item is *very true or often true* of your child. Circle the *1* if the item is *somewhat or sometimes true* of your child. If the item is *not true* of your child, circle the *0.* Please answer all items as well as you can, even if some do not seem to apply to your child.

1. Acts too young for his/her age	0	1	2
2. Disobedient at school	0	1	2
3. Too shy or timid	0	1	2
4. Threatens people	0	1	2
5. Steals at home	0	1	2
6. Withdrawn, doesn't get involved with others	0	1	2
7. Not liked by other kids	0	1	2
8. Sudden changes in mood or feelings	0	1	2
9. Secretive, keeps things to self	0	1	2
10. Sleeps more than most kids during day and/or night	0	1	2

FIGURE 8.2 Sample items from a rating scale for parents

Source: From *Child Behavior Checklist for Ages 6–18* (pp. 3–4) by T. M. Achenbach, 2001. Burlington: University of Vermont. Reprinted by permission.

Below is a list of items that describe pupils. For each item that describes the pupil *now or within the past 2 months,* please circle the *2* if the item is *very true or often true* of the pupil. Circle *1* if the item is *somewhat or sometimes true* of the pupil. If the item is *not true* of the pupil, circle the *0.* Please answer all items as well as you can, even if some do not seem to apply to this pupil.

1. Argues a lot	0	1	2
2. Destroys property belonging to others	0	1	2
3. Doesn't get along with other pupils	0	1	2
4. Easily jealous	0	1	2
5. Fears going to school	0	1	2
6. Has difficulty learning	0	1	2
7. Talks out of turn	0	1	2
8. Threatens people	0	1	2
9. Overly anxious to please	0	1	2
10. Withdrawn, doesn't get involved with others	0	1	2

FIGURE 8.3 Sample items from a rating-by-others scale for teachers

Source: From *Teacher's Report Form* (pp. 3–4) by T. M. Achenbach, 2001. Burlington: University of Vermont. Reprinted by permission.

on student behavior through a Teacher Rating Scale, a Parent Rating Scale, and a Youth Rating Scale. The BERS-2 may be used for children between the ages of 5 and 18 years old. Each rating scale contains 52 items divided into 5 categories or subscales: Interpersonal Strength, Family Involvement, Intrapersonal Strength, School Functioning, and Affective Strength. In addition, the parent and youth rating scales contain questions concerning Career Strength.

The BERS-2 is a technically sound instrument that provides a snapshot of individual behavioral strengths while also supporting the screening of individuals for behavioral and emotional concerns. It is a strength-based rating scale system that works as part of a multidisciplinary assessment plan.

Sociometric Techniques.   Sociometric measures provide general information on acceptance, desirability, and social status of students through the perceptions of their peers. Sociometric strategies are useful in determining friendship (or lack of friendship) among peers (Mash & Terdal, 1997). Sociometric techniques have been most widely used to screen students who may benefit from social skills training in order to improve acceptance among peers and also offer a picture of a classroom's social structure (Downing, 2007; Sugai & Lewis, 1996). The most popular sociometric techniques are *peer nomination* and *peer rating* (McConnell & Odom, 1987).

Peer Nomination.   The peer nomination method has become the most commonly applied sociometric technique (McLoughlin & Lewis, 2008). Students are asked to select one or more classmates with whom they would and/or would not like to engage in an activity (e.g., play with, hang out with, work with). Social status scores are then derived by adding the numbers of times each student is selected by their peers across different categories. Scores derived from such measures indicate levels of popularity or acceptance.

Students complete a peer rating as part of a behavioral assessment to identify students/peers at risk for behavior problems.

Percent of student responses to positive and negative choice questions			
Childs Name	Most like to play with?	Most like to work with?	Least like to work with?
Connor	45	30	0
Elizabeth	4	5	0[a]
Ryan	90	95	0
Trevor	79	87	0
Ellie	50	45	0
Nancy	39	56	0
Heather	76	67	0
Jacob	67	85	0
Elliott	98	96	0
George	0	1	8[b]
Jennifer	0	0	50[c]
Timothy	1	3	0[a]
Cheryl	0	5	45[c]

FIGURE 8.4 Results from a peer nomination process administered in a third-grade class

[a]*Indicates students who were "amiable."*
[b]*Indicates students who were "isolated."*
[c]*Indicates students who were "rejected."*

Perry (1979) uses the two dimensions of social impact and social preference to describe social status. His classification categories include the following:

- Popular—high social impact, positive social preference
- Rejected—high social impact, negative social preference
- Isolate—low social impact, negative social preference
- Amiable—low social impact, positive social preference

Mrs. Ramirez, described in Classroom Connection 8.1, wanted to screen students who might benefit from social skills training. The results from a peer nomination in one of the third-grade classes in Mrs. Ramirez's school are depicted in Figure 8.4.

Once the results from the peer nomination are calculated, they can be graphically displayed using a sociogram. Sociograms "visually represent student relationships and social choices, based on observation or information solicited from students" (Downing, 2007, p. 27). One type of sociogram is the "target technique." The target technique allows an educator to quickly display the students in the classroom based on the categories being used to identify them. Using the Perry (1979) categories listed earlier, a bull's-eye diagram is created with four rings. Each ring coincides with one of the social preference categories starting with the popular classification at the center. Each subsequent ring out from the center corresponds to a less desired social status category. Students are plotted within the rings based on their peer nomination scores. Students placed in the outer rings of the target are those who are less accepted by their peers and who may be exhibiting

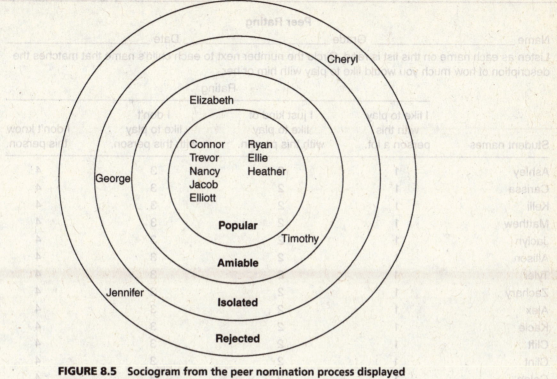

FIGURE 8.5   Sociogram from the peer nomination process displayed using the target technique

more behavior problems. A target graph using the scores from the third-grade class in Mrs. Ramirez's school is shown in Figure 8.5.

Peer Rating.   The peer rating method of sociometric assessment asks students to rank or rate their peers based on a list of behaviors or characteristics (Downing, 2007). Typically, raters are given a class roster and asked to rate each classmate according to

---

CLASSROOM CONNECTION 8.1
Using a Peer Nomination Sociometric Technique

Mrs. Ramirez, the principal of a middle school, met with the curriculum committee to discuss the need for social skills training for some of the students in grades 6 through 8. The committee decided that they would screen candidates for training using a peer nomination sociometric technique. Parents of the students were informed of this decision and were given the option for their student not to participate. Teachers in the sixth, seventh, and eighth grades were asked to develop a list of three questions to use in the peer nomination procedure.

General Reflection for Classroom Connection 8.1:

Can you assist the teachers in developing these three questions? Once the peer nominations were completed on the students, the teachers used Perry's (1979) definitions to identify each student. What are the possible labels for each student? Based on Perry's definitions, which students would be considered "at-risk" for needing social skills training?

Peer Rating

Name _____ Grade _____ Date _____

Listen as each name on this list is read. Circle the number next to each child's name that matches the description of how much you would like to play with him or her.

Rating

Student names	I like to play with this person a lot.	I just kind of like to play with this person.	I don't like to play with this person.	I don't know this person.
Ashley	1	2	3	4
Carissa	1	2	3	4
Kelli	1	2	3	4
Matthew	1	2	3	4
Jaclyn	1	2	3	4
Allison	1	2	3	4
Tyler	1	2	3	4
Zachary	1	2	3	4
Alex	1	2	3	4
Kacie	1	2	3	4
Clift	1	2	3	4
Clint	1	2	3	4
Colen	1	2	3	4
Mackenzie	1	2	3	4
Theresa	1	2	3	4

FIGURE 8.6 **Peer rating questionnaire**

Source: From *Attitudes and Behavior of Non-Disabled Elementary-Aged Children Toward Their Peers with Disabilities in Integrated Settings: An Examination of the Effects of Treatment on Quality of Attitude, Social Status and Critical Social Skills,* by K. J. Melloy, 1990, doctoral dissertation, University of Iowa, Iowa City. Reprinted by permission.

how much they like or dislike to play with or work with the student. A sample of a peer-rating instrument is presented in Figure 8.6.

Peer ratings tend to be more reliable when compared to peer nominations (McConnell & Odom, 1986). The major advantages for using the peer rating technique compared to peer nomination include (a) every student in the class is rated, (b) there are higher test-retest reliability results over time, and (c) this technique is more sensitive to subtle changes in social status depending on the criteria used (McConnell & Odom, 1986; McLoughlin & Lewis, 2008). A disadvantage of the peer rating method is that students, especially younger ones, may tend to rate most classmates in the middle of the scale or to give everyone in the class the same rating (McConnell & Odom, 1986).

Interviews with Parents, Target Students, and Others Who Know the Student. Interview data for step 1 is usually collected less formally than interview data for the other steps of behavioral assessment. For example, step 1 interviews may consist of teacher-to-teacher

Name of Student: <u>Rick</u> Age of student: <u>11</u> Grade Level: <u>5</u>

Date: <u>9/10/10</u> Name of person managing assessment: <u>M. Corn</u> Relation to student: <u>Behavior Consultant</u>

Assessment Strategy	Name of Person(s) Involved in Assessment	Summary of Results
SSBD Teacher Ranking	P. Nordness (teacher)	Rank ordered with the top three students for internalized behavior problems.
SSBD Teacher Rating	P. Nordness (teacher)	Significantly below the normative criteria for internalized behavior problems.
SSBD Academic and Playground Observations	M. Corn (Behavior Specialist)	Student observed to be on task during reading and math class; student observed to isolate himself during recess.
Sociometric Peer Nomination	P. Nordness	Student nominated by only 1 out of 25 students in the class as someone they would like to play with or work with.

FIGURE 8.7 An example of completed assessment strategies for behavioral assessment step 1: Decide whether a problem exists

discussion of a student suspected of having problem behavior. Also, teachers generally take the opportunity to discuss student behavior with parents during phone calls, email exchanges, and parent-teacher conferences. Teachers can document this data through contact logs, anecdotal reports, or email and use it in the data collection process for step 1.

Step 1 of the behavioral assessment model allows teachers and others to determine if a problem may exist related to student behavior. Behavior checklists, rating scales, teacher ranking, sociometric techniques, informal interviews, and behavioral observation anecdotal reports are assessment strategies that have been found helpful in collecting step 1 behavioral assessment data. Figure 8.7 depicts an example of the results of completed assessment strategies for step 1 for a fifth-grade child named Rick.

The results of the completed assessment strategies for step 1 for Rick indicate that he did in fact demonstrate problem behavior. His teacher and others decided that they should continue the assessment process with "Step 2: Determine Whether Intervention Is Warranted" to decide whether his problem behavior was serious enough to require the development of an individual behavior management plan. A description of step 2 in the behavioral assessment model follows.

Step 2: Determine Whether Intervention Is Warranted

After completion of step 1 of the behavioral assessment model, some students may be identified as needing further assessment of their behavior problems. In step 2 of the behavioral assessment model, the objective is to pinpoint behavior problems and to provide

Once behavioral data have been collected, a professional scores and interprets the behavior before a team meeting.

information about whether behavioral intervention is warranted. This section covers procedures that have been suggested for evaluating problem behaviors to determine whether they warrant intervention.

Behavioral assessment beyond step 1 incorporates multiple assessment methods that rely on several informants concerning the nature of the student's difficulties across multiple situations. For step 2 of the behavioral assessment model, informants may include parents, teachers, other educators, peers, and the student. Informants provide information about the target student through responses to checklists and rating scales, and they participate in direct observation sessions with the target student. The data from these sources should provide information to teachers and others to determine whether behavior management intervention is needed for prevention of more serious problems and/or intervention for current problems. The data from step 2 should also reveal student behavior strengths.

Validation of target behaviors is accomplished by interpreting the results of checklists, rating scales, and observations across persons and settings (Sugai & Lewis, 1996) and by observing peers in the same setting as the target student(s). Several examples of strategies that are appropriate for step 2 data collection methods are described next.

DATA COLLECTION METHODS FOR STEP 2

Norm-Referenced Rating Scales and Checklists. Teachers and others are often asked to provide an overall perception of a student's behavior via behavioral checklists or ratings. Behavioral ratings by others are administered as part of the total assessment process that takes place during step 2 of the behavioral assessment process. The reader should note that the rating scales used in step 2 are usually more comprehensive than those used in step 1. Step 2 checklists and rating scales are designed to get to the specific behavior(s) of concern, whereas the instruments used in step 1 are more global or general in nature. Although these instruments are useful, they should be used in combination with other methods for seeking information about the student.

Checklists and ratings scales are available for preschool-age through adolescent-age students. Included in this chapter are examples of widely used, reliable, and valid instruments for assessing a variety of behavior problems. Instruments of this type are easily administered to a variety of persons across settings, thus providing information to determine validation for intervening with a student's behavior. A sample of checklists and rating scales that have been helpful in collecting assessment information for step 2 are described briefly. The reader is encouraged to refer to the individual test manuals for specifics about administration of the instruments and other pertinent information in order to determine if a given instrument is appropriate for the assessment purposes and student.

Social Skills Rating System (SSRS). Gresham and Elliott (1990) designed the *Social Skills Rating System* (SSRS). The SSRS is available for three age levels: Preschool (ages 3 to 5 years old), Elementary (grades K–6), and Secondary (grades 7–12). Informants report on both the frequency of a described behavior and, except on the elementary scales, the perceived importance of the behavior (McLoughlin & Lewis, 2008). Three behavioral domains are measured across the different informant scales: Social Skills (parents, teacher, and student), Problem Behaviors (parents and teachers), and Academic Competence (teacher scales only). Furthermore, two behavioral domains are divided into subscales to allow measure of behavior frequency. Problem Behaviors are classified as Internalizing, Externalizing, and Hyperactivity. Social Skills subscales include Cooperation, Assertion, Responsibility, Empathy, and Self-Control. The results from the SSRs reveal social skills strengths and weaknesses (Gresham, Lane, MacMillan, & Bocian, 1999; McLoughlin & Lewis, 2008).

Walker-McConnell Scale of Social Competence and School Adjustment (WMS). Designed for use in identification of social skills deficits among students in kindergarten through 12th grade, the *Walker-McConnell Scale of Social Competence and School Adjustment* (WMS: Walker & McConnell, 1988, 1993, 1995) consists of positively worded descriptions of social skills that were designed to sample the two primary adjustment domains within school settings: adaptive behavior and social competence. The Elementary WMS (grades K–6) distributes behaviors across three subscales: Teacher Preferred Social Behavior, Peer Preferred Social Behavior, and School Adjustment. The Adolescent WMS (grades 7–12) distributes behaviors across four subscales: Self Control, Peer Relations, School Adjustment, and Empathy. The descriptions are rated by the teacher on a 5-point Likert scale ranging from "never occurs" to "frequently occurs." A limitation of the WMS during step 2 is that teachers are the only informants to complete the instrument. The comprehensive nature of step 2 assessment requires additional input from those familiar with the target student's behavior.

Conners Comprehensive Behavior Rating Scales. The *Conners Comprehensive Behavior Rating Scales* (CBRS: Conners, 2008b) uses information provided by the parents, teachers, and the student to evaluate a comprehensive range of problem behaviors. A short version (*Conners Clinical Index: Conners CI*) is available, but may only be appropriate for screening purposes (i.e., step 1 of the behavioral assessment plan).

The dimensions of student behavior that are collected from the CBRS include oppositional behavior, hyperactivity, inattention, academic difficulties, social problems, perfectionism, anxiety disorders, and violence potential, as well as an ADHD index. The parent and teachers forms are appropriate for collecting data on students ages 6 to 18 years old, whereas the student self-report form is appropriate for children ages 8 to 18 years old. The teacher, parent, and student forms all require the user to rank a student's behavior using a 4-point rating scale. For each item on a form, the user indicates whether a behavior is "not true at all" to "very much true" for the student. The CBRS is an extensive rating scale, requiring informants to respond to 179 (Self Report), 203 (Parent form), or 204 items (Teacher form). The CBRS also provides intervention suggestions for students based on the results of the checklist.

Conners (2008a) created another instrument, the *Conners 3*, which is a revision of the *Conners Rating Scales-Revised* (CRS-R: Conners, 1997). The Conners 3 has "a greater focus on ADHD and associated features" (Conners, 2008a). Like the CBRS, the Conners 3 uses multi-informants (parent, teacher, and student) to evaluate behavior for students ages 6 to 18 years old. A long (99–115 items) and short form (41–45 items) are available for the Conners 3. Two short forms are also available for screening or if time is a concern: the Conners 3 ADHD Index (Conners 3AI) and the Conners 3 Global Index (Conners 3GI). The Conners 3AI is a 10-item scale that uses items from the Conners 3 that best identify students with ADHD from those students without a diagnosis. The Conners 3GI includes 10 predictive items for general psychopathology.

Behavior Assessment System for Children, Second Edition (BASC-2). The *Behavior Assessment System for Children, Second Edition* (BASC-2: Reynolds & Kamphaus, 2005) contains forms for use by the teacher, parent, and student to gather accurate data on a student's behavior. The parent and teacher forms provide in-depth information on 10 problem and 6 adaptive behavioral dimensions. The problem behavior dimensions include aggression, anxiety, attention problems, atypicality, conduct problems, depression, hyperactivity, learning problems, somatization, and withdrawal. The adaptive behaviors measured include activities of daily living, adaptability, functional communication, leadership, social skills, and study skills. Additionally, the student self-report form also provides information on behaviors such as alcohol abuse, attitude toward parents and school, social stress, interpersonal relationships and relationships with parents, school maladjustment, self-esteem, and self-reliance. The teacher and parent forms are applicable for students 2 to 21 years old, whereas the self-report form can be completed by students beginning at age 8. The BASC-2 is unique compared with other rating scales because it is designed to measure adaptive behaviors as well as problem behaviors. Knowing both a student's strengths and behavioral challenges can lead to more valid and appropriate intervention strategies.

In sum, the BASC-2, WMS, SSRS, and CBRS rating scales provide information about behavioral strengths and deficits that students may present in the school setting. Decisions about which checklists and rating scales to use in step 2 will depend on the information needed to help determine if intervention is warranted. Since all of these instruments can be administered across persons and settings, the resulting information may be helpful in deciding the validity of intervening in a student's behavior.

Observation Data. Chapters 6 and 9 provide in-depth descriptions of behavioral assessment using naturalistic observations. Note that accurate decisions about students' behavior should not be made without collecting data through naturalistic observations (Alberto & Troutman, 1999). Although it is common for the evaluation for specific behavior problems—such as ADHD, conduct disorders, and depression—to take place in a clinical setting, it is imperative that the person conducting the assessment visit the student's school or home to observe behavior in those settings. Rating scales and checklists are based on informants' perceptions of a student's behavior; a full assessment of a student's behavior must include evaluation of the behavior as it occurs across settings (McLoughlin & Lewis, 2008).

Medical Data. Before intervention ideas are explored, mental health and medical personnel may need to examine the student to determine whether he or she has any medical problems that may be causing the behavior problems. For example, mental health professionals may assist in identifying clinical depression. Medical problems such as those associated with vision may contribute to behavioral problems. A student who experiences vision or hearing problems may not be able to access educational information as easily as his or her peers and in frustration, act out in, or withdraw from, the classroom setting. This assessment information may also be helpful in determining whether the student is eligible for special education or other helpful related services.

To rule out treatable diseases and allergies, it is necessary to include a physical examination by a physician as part of the assessment of behavioral problems. Often, parents will first report behavior problems to a physician during routine physical examinations. It is important for physicians to collaborate with behavioral experts before making recommendations about behavior intervention. Physicians can then refer parents to appropriate professionals for adequate assessment and subsequent recommendations for intervention.

In school settings, medical data for behavioral assessment also may be contributed by the school nurse. Brief medical screenings are routine in most schools throughout the United States. For example, each school year students in elementary schools are screened for vision and hearing problems. If screening information indicates a problem, it is usually suggested that the student be seen in a clinical setting for a more thorough examination and assessment.

In addition to school nurses and physicians, school psychologists, clinical psychologists, psychiatrists, and other mental health professionals can also contribute information that may be relevant to school-related behavior problems. Mental health professionals collect data using rating scales; behavioral interviews with parents, target students, and teachers and others who know the student; behavioral observations in natural and clinical settings; psychometric assessment; and laboratory measures.

Parents should share medical information with teachers that may contribute to understanding their student's behavior problems. Often, however, parents do not share their student's medical information unless they are certain the medical condition will have an impact on their student's education. When medical information is available and pertinent, it should be considered helpful in the behavioral assessment process. If this information is not relevant or not available, the behavior assessment process can be continued.

Figure 8.8 depicts an example of a format that can be used to summarize medical information that may be helpful in determining the existence of medical or psychological reasons that contribute to problem behavior.

Psychometric Assessment. An assessment team needs to obtain information about the student's academic achievement and effects of behavior problems on that achievement.

Name of Student: _____ Date: _____

Name and title of person completing review form:

Person(s) interviewed for information and relationship to student:

Source of records reviewed:

1. Identify known physical and/or mental health conditions.
   - Medical diagnosis:
   Physical health:
   Mental health:
   Does the diagnosis have known behavior features? yes no
   If yes, describe the features that the student demonstrates in the current setting:
   - Review of vision and hearing tests:

	Date of last exam, source	Nature of any problems	Accommodations required
Vision			
Hearing			

2. Complete medication summary.

Medication/ Dosage	Anticipated benefit	Behavior and other side effects	Source of information

   - Note recent change in medication:
   - Potential effect of the medication on behavior:
   - Examination of time the medication is taken and result on behavior:

3. Describe sleep cycle and diet.
   - Current sleep pattern:
   - Food allergies or restrictions:
   - Need for diet/sleep changes:

4. Describe any unusual responses or sensitivity to environmental stimuli.
   - Tactile:
   - Auditory:
   - Visual:
   - Movement:
   - Vibration:
   - Smell or taste:

5. List periodic precipitating factors.
   - Note any periodically occurring events that have led to an increase in problem behavior:

6. Does this student have an identified disability?
   - Special Education (IDEA 1997):
   - DSM IV Diagnosis:
   - Does the disability have known behavior features? yes no NA
   If "yes," describe the behavior features the student demonstrates in this setting:

FIGURE 8.8 Example of a medical review format for completing behavioral assessment model step 3

Source: Adapted from N. Kurtzman (1997). Nancy Kurtzman is an educator in the area of special education in MN. She works in public schools and as adjunct faculty at St. Mary's University. *Best practices in functional assessment.* Stillwater, MN: Stillwater Public Schools. Reprinted by permission.

When disabilities are suspected, additional information is necessary regarding intellectual functioning through psychometric assessment of *global intelligence* and *academic achievement*. A number of authors provide descriptions of assessment instruments and procedures that can be used to assess these constructs (e.g., McLoughlin & Lewis, 2008; Cohen & Spenciner, 2007). These instruments are not described in this text. This information, however, assists in making accurate decisions about the student's learning problems that may be associated with behavior problems.

Ranking Target Behaviors.   Once target behaviors have been identified based on information from steps 1 and 2, these behaviors can be ranked according to a series of questions (Wolery, Bailey, & Sugai, 1988). Responses to these questions will assist teachers and others in determining whether intervention is warranted. Often, teachers become stumped when more than one target behavior has been identified for a behavior management plan. To eliminate the guessing game that accompanies these quandaries, teachers should ask priority questions and gain the consensus of persons who have frequent contact with the target student. It is not unusual for teachers to experience a scenario similar to the one depicted in Classroom Connection 8.2.

Answering yes to questions 1 through 3 indicates that the target behavior is in need of immediate intervention development since there is potential of injury or loss of learning. If question 4 is answered yes, the behavior will probably go away as the student gets older or if other antecedents and consequences change. Any behavior that will go away on its own or with relatively simple interventions doesn't need more complicated behavior management–based intervention. If the behavior is observed to occur as often as that

---

CLASSROOM CONNECTION 8.2
Prioritizing Target Behaviors

Desmond is an eighth grader at Sunny View Middle School. Desmond's school records indicate that he is capable of doing eighth-grade work and in fact has skills in math that are more typical of a tenth-grade student. His teachers are perplexed about Desmond's behavior in school. He often looks like he is on task during independent work time but seldom hands in any of his completed assignments. Desmond rarely raises his hand in response to teacher questions, and he has little to say to his peers when they work in cooperative groups.

Lately, Desmond has been observed to demonstrate disruptive behavior during class lectures and discussions when he gets out of his seat, roams around the classroom, and at times leaves the classroom to wander in the halls. Desmond's teachers are concerned about his seemingly problematic behavior as it is resulting in poor grades and complaints from his peers. They have put their heads together and completed the assessment instruments suggested by the behavior

specialist, but they still don't know which behavior to work on first.

General Reflections for Classroom Connection 8.2:

Assist Desmond's teachers by helping them answer the following questions to prioritize target behaviors.

1. Does the behavior cause injury to the student or others?
2. Does the behavior interfere with the student's or others' learning?
3. Does the behavior present a safety risk to the student or to others?
4. Is the behavior age-appropriate or likely to be transient?
5. Does the behavior occur at frequencies similar to that of peers' behavior?
6. Is the behavior due to skill deficits in other areas?
7. Does the behavior cause others to avoid interacting with the student?

of the peers, then it probably wouldn't be valid to intervene with the behavior unless the answer to questions 1 through 3 were yes. In that case, a whole-class behavior management intervention may be appropriate. If the answer to question 6 is yes, indicating that the behavior is due to a skill deficit in some other area, then perhaps the target behavior needs to be changed. Changing the target behavior would necessitate applying the ranking questions to the new target behavior. Also, it is important to consider how changing one behavior affects the other behaviors. For example, if Desmond were taught to change his disruptive behavior to more appropriate classroom behavior through social skills training, would he then complete more of his work and hand it in? If in fact staying in his seat resulted from being taught replacement behaviors for roaming behavior, then the need to intervene with handing in assignment behavior may not be necessary. Finally, a yes for question 7 may indicate a precursor to more serious problems related to adult and peer relationships. Therefore, addressing the problem behavior now may result in preventing future problems.

A teacher's first impulse may be to count up the number of yes's and no's for each target behavior questioned, and then declare that the behavior with the most yes's is the most salient and therefore the one needing intervention first. However, to make prudent decisions about intervention priorities and whether a target behavior is worth development of an intervention, the teacher and others concerned should carefully consider the meaning of each question as it relates to the target behavior and the impact of the behavior on the target student and others.

To obtain the information they need to decide whether intervention is needed and worthwhile, teachers should (a) complete appropriate checklists and/or rating scales that provide perspectives from multiple informants; (b) conduct three to five naturalistic observations of the target student and his or her peers in a school setting in which the target behavior is demonstrated; and (c) rank the target behaviors in terms of their severity and amenity to intervention. Figure 8.9 provides an example of the results of the assessment strategies completed for Rick in step 2 of the behavioral assessment process.

After examining the assessment information, Rick's teachers decided to use the ranking questions to determine which of two target behaviors—disruptive behavior and handing in assignments—would justify intervention. Figure 8.10 provides an example of a grid format that the teachers employed to help them in their efforts.

The results shown in Figure 8.10 should help clarify for the teachers that intervention would be justified for both target behaviors. Even though it seemed that neither target behavior would cause injury, both are interfering with the target student's learning. The disruptive behavior was noted to interfere with the learning of others and to pose a safety risk to the target student and others.

Neither of the behaviors seems to be age-appropriate and they are not likely to go away without intervention. In fact, the teachers indicated in their discussion about Rick that they had tried some simple interventions that had worked in the past with other students. These interventions were not effective in helping Rick reduce his inappropriate behavior and increase appropriate behavior.

Observation and other assessment information indicated that Rick engaged in disruptive behavior more frequently than his peers and that this behavior was starting to cause problems in his relationships with adults and peers. In addition, compared with his peers, Rick was observed to hand in assignments less frequently, which was affecting his grades.

Name of Student: <u>Rick</u>

Date: <u>9/30/05</u>

Age of student: <u>11</u>

Name of person managing
assessment: <u>M. Corn</u>

Grade Level: <u>5</u>

Relation to student: <u>Behavior Specialist</u>

Assessment Strategy	Name of Person(s) Involved in Assessment	Summary of Results
Checklist: W-M Scale of Social Competence and School Adjustment	P. Nordness (Language Arts Teacher) T. Vandercook (Math and Science Teacher)	Rick's scores on the W-M indicated that he had significantly different factor scores from the norm group for the *Teacher Preferred Behavior* and *School Adjustment* dimensions. His scores on the *Peer Preferred Behavior* dimension were within normal range when compared to the norm group. These scores were consistent across two teachers.
Rating Scale: BASC-2	P. Nordness, T. Vandercook (teachers); Mrs. Rimerez (Rick's mother)	Scores on the BASC-2 were in the normal range across externalizing and internalizing dimensions. These scores were consistent across all three informants.
Naturalistic Observation: Target student and peers; classroom settings; interval recording, paper-and-pencil measure of target behaviors. Permanent product recording for the target behavior of "handing in assignments."	M. Corn (Behavior Specialist)	Observations of Rick and his peers revealed that he and his peers engaged in the target behaviors described as on/off task; participative or disruptive; and get teacher attention appropriately/not appropriately in each of the three 15-minute observations. Rick was observed to be on task at the same rate as his peers during independent-work time. However, during lecture and discussion periods, Rick was observed to be engaged in disruptive behavior at a much higher rate than his peers. This behavior resulted in peers' distraction and loss of academically engaged time for all students. A review of the teachers' assignment record books indicated that Rick handed in fewer assignments per week than his peers. His grades—in the C range—during the second and third quarter, were considerably lower than his grades—in the A range—first quarter.

FIGURE 8.9 An example of completed assessment strategies for behavioral assessment step 2: Determine whether intervention is warranted

Target Behaviors (undesired behaviors):

1. "Disruptive" is defined as getting out of seat, roaming around the room without permission and/or talking to peers while roaming.

2. "Not handing in assignments" is defined as failure to provide the teacher with a completed assignment by the due date.

	Question 1	Question 2	Question 3	Question 4	Question 5	Question 6	Question 7
Disruptive Behavior	no	yes	yes	no	no	?	yes
Assignment Behavior		yes	no	no	no	?	no

FIGURE 8.10   Example of ranking target behaviors for Rick

Source: Adapted from N. Kurtzman (1997). *Best practices in functional assessment.* Stillwater, MN: Stillwater Public Schools. Reprinted by permission.

It was not clear to the teachers whether Rick's inappropriate behavior was related to skills deficits in other areas. However, the teachers noted that Rick's behavior has changed significantly compared with his behavior in the first quarter. There did not appear to be any medical or psychological reasons that contributed to his behavior problems. Rick's teachers decided to complete a functional assessment of Rick's behavior as described in Chapter 9, to review how classroom variables may be affecting his behavior, and to continue to collect data on antecedents and consequences maintaining Rick's behavior (see Chapters 6 and 7).

Summary

The purpose of behavioral assessment is to identify student strengths and needs related to their behavior, plan educational interventions designed to assist students in changing or maintaining social and academic behavior, evaluate the effectiveness of interventions, and determine eligibility for special education services. This chapter described steps 1 and 2 of a five-step model for conducting behavioral assessment. An outline of the model was presented here, summarizing each of the first two steps for behavioral assessment and suggestions for data collection methods to gather information about students.

Step 1: Decide whether a problem exists.

Purpose: To screen for behavior problems

Data Collection Methods:

- Checklists and ratings by others
- Teacher ranking
- Self-rating
- Sociometric techniques
- Interviews with teachers, parents, others
- Behavioral observations

Step 2: Determine whether intervention is warranted.

Purpose: To identify and rank target behaviors for intervention

Data Collection Methods:

- Norm-referenced checklists and ratings scales

TABLE 8.1 Description of Indirect Assessment Instruments

Name of Instrument	Acronym	Instrument Type and Usage
Systematic Screening for Behavior Disorders (Walker & Severson, 1999)	SSBD	Multiassessment instrument (teacher rating, ranking, observation); screens for behavior problems and disorders (grades 1–5)
Social Skills Rating System (Gresham & Elliott, 1990)	SSRS	Teacher rating of individual student's social skills
Walker-McConnell Scale of Social Competence and School Adjustment (Walker & McConnell, 1988, 1993, 1995)	WMS	Teacher rating of elementary students' and adolescents' level of social competence.
Behavior Assessment System for Children, Second Edition (Reynolds & Kamphaus, 2005)	BASC-2	Teacher rating, parent rating, self-rating of student behavior; structured developmental history; and a student observation system
Behavioral and Emotional Rating Scale, Second Edition (Epstein, 2004)	BERS-2	Teacher rating, parent rating, self-rating of student behavior strengths
Child Behavior Checklist System (Achenbach, 2001)	CBCL	Teacher rating, parent rating, self-rating of student behavior; structured developmental history; and a student observation system
Conners 3 (Conners, 2008a)	Conners 3	Teacher rating, parent rating, self-rating of student behavior focused on ADHD; long and short forms
Conners Comprehensive Behavior Rating Scale (Conners, 2008b)	CBRS	Teacher rating, parent rating, self-rating of comprehensive range of behaviors; long and short forms

- Naturalistic observations
- Medical data
- Psychometric assessment
- Ranking target behavior questions

Form: *Medical Review Form*

Table 8.1 outlines the names and purposes of each assessment instrument described in this chapter.

Teachers and other educational professionals will find opportunities to maximize teaching and learning when they develop effective behavior support plans based on assessment data. The information provided in this chapter is meant to assist teachers and others in gaining knowledge about indirect behavioral assessment methods. Chapters 3 and 4 provide information about direct behavioral assessment strategies. The information in these chapters combined with the information in the chapters about intervention (i.e., Chapters 10, 11, 12, 13, and 14) and specific behavior influences (Chapters 3, 4, and 5) will contribute to this knowledge base and help teachers and others build effective interventions designed to teach and support acceptable behavior that is demonstrated by students.

Discussion Questions

1. What is behavioral assessment? List and explain the common features of behavioral assessment.
2. Choose one of the assessment instruments or techniques described in this chapter. Obtain the instrument, and study the guide for administration, scoring, and interpretation. Practice the administration of this instrument.

3. Compare the definitions of disruptive behavior given in the examples about Desmond, described in the section on step 2, and Rick. Even though these behaviors are called "disruptive behaviors," how do they differ in the way that each of the students demonstrates the behavior in the school setting?

References

Achenbach, T. M. (2001). *Child behavior checklist system.* Burlington, VT: University of Vermont.

Alberto, P. A., & Troutman, A. C. (1999). *Applied behavior analysis for teachers* (5th ed.). Upper Saddle River, NJ: Merrill/Pearson Education.

Cohen, L. G., & Spenciner, L. J. (2007). *Assessment of children and youth with special needs* (3rd ed). Boston: Pearson Education.

Conners, C. K. (1997). *Conners Rating Scales-Revised.* North Tonawanda, NY: Multi-Health Systems.

Conners, C. K. (2008a). *Conners 3.* North Tonawanda, NY: Multi-Health Systems.

Conners, C. K. (2008b). *Conners Comprehensive Behavior Rating Scale.* North Tonawanda, NY: Multi-Health Systems.

Downing, J. A. (2007). *Students with emotional and behavioral problems: Assessment, management, and intervention strategies.* Upper Saddle River, NJ: Pearson Education.

Elksnin, L. K., & Elksnin, N. (1998). Teaching social skills to students with learning and behavior problems. *Intervention in School and Clinic, 33,* 131–140.

Epstein, M. H. (2004). *Behavioral and emotional rating scale* (2nd ed.). Austin, TX: Pro-Ed.

Epstein, M. H., & Cullinan, D. (1998). *Scale for assessing emotional disturbance.* Austin, TX: Pro-Ed.

Friend, M. (2008). *Special education: Contemporary perspectives for school professionals* (2nd ed.). Boston: Pearson Education.

Gresham, F., & Elliott, S. N. (1990). *Social skills rating system.* Circle Pines, MN: American Guidance Service.

Gresham, F. M., Lane, K. L., MacMillan, D. L., & Bocian, K. M. (1999). Social and academic profiles of externalizing and internalizing groups: Risk factors for emotional and behavioral disorders. *Behavioral Disorders, 24,* 231–245.

Heward, W. L. (2009). *Exceptional children: An introduction to special education* (9th ed.). Upper Saddle River, NJ: Pearson Education.

Lane, K. L., & Menzies, H. M. (2005). Teacher-identified students with and without academic and behavioral concerns: Characteristics and responsiveness. *Behavioral Disorders, 31,* 65–83.

Lipsey, M. W., & Derzon, J. H. (1998). Predictors of violent or serious delinquency in adolescence and early adulthood: A synthesis of longitudinal research. In R. Loeber & D. P. Farrington (Eds.), *Serious and violent juvenile offenders: Risk factors and successful interventions* (pp. 6–105). Thousand Oaks, CA: Sage.

Mash, E. J., & Hunsley, J. (2007). Assessment of child and family disturbance: A developmental-systems approach. In E. J. Mash & R. A. Barkley (Eds.), *Assessment of childhood disorders* (4th ed., pp. 3–50). New York: Guilford.

Mash, E. J., & Terdal, L. G. (1997). *Behavioral assessment of childhood disorders* (3rd ed.). New York: Guilford.

McConnell, S. R., & Odom, S. L. (1986). Sociometrics: Peer referenced measures and the assessment of social competence. In P. S. Strain, M. J. Guralnick, & H. M. Walker (Eds.), *Children's social behavior, development, assessment, and modification* (pp. 215–284). New York: Academic Press.

McConnell, S. R., & Odom, S. L. (1987). Sociometric measures. In *Dictionary of behavioral assessment techniques* (pp. 432–434). Elmsburg, NY: Pergamon.

McLoughlin, J. A., & Lewis, R. B. (2008). *Assessing students with special needs* (7th ed.). Upper Saddle River, NJ: Pearson Education.

Melloy, K. J. (1990). *Attitudes and behavior of nondisabled elementary-aged children toward their peers with disabilities in integrated settings: An examination of the effects of treatment on quality of attitude, social status and critical social skills.* Unpublished doctoral dissertation, University of Iowa, Iowa City.

Melloy, K. J., Davis, C. A., Wehby, J. H., Murry, F. R., & Leiber, J. (1998). *Developing social competence in children and youth with challenging behavior.* Reston, VA: CCBD Mini Library Series, Successful Interventions for the 21st Century.

Morris, T. L. (2004). Treatment of social phobia in children and adolescents. In P. M. Barrett & T. H. Ollendick (Eds.), *Handbook of interventions that work with children and adolescents: Prevention and treatment* (pp. 171–186). London: Wiley.

Palmer, P. (1998). *The courage to teach: Exploring the inner landscape of a teacher's life.* San Francisco: Jossey-Bass.

Perry, J. C. (1979). Popular, amiable, isolated, rejected: A reconceptualization of sociometric status in preschool children. *Child Development, 50,* 1231–1234.

Reynolds, C. R., & Kamphaus, R. W. (2005). *Behavior Assessment System for Children* (2nd ed.). Circle Pines, MN: AGS.

Salvia, J., & Ysseldyke, J. E., with Bolt, S. (2007). *Assessment in special and inclusive education* (10th ed.). Boston: Houghton-Mifflin.

Sugai, G., & Lewis, T. (1996). Preferred and promising practices for social skills instruction. *Focus on Exceptional Children, 29,* 1–16.

Walker, H. M., & McConnell, S. R. (1988). *Walker-McConnell Scale of Social Competence and School Adjustment.* Austin, TX: Pro-Ed.

Walker, H. M., & McConnell, S. R. (1993). *Walker-McConnell Scale of Social Competence and School Adjustment* (rev. ed.). Austin, TX: Pro-Ed.

Walker, H. M., & McConnell, S. R. (1995). *Walker-McConnell Scale of Social Competence and School Adjustment* (rev. ed.). Austin, TX: Pro-Ed.

Walker, H. M., Ramsey, E., & Gresham, F. M. (2004). *Antisocial behavior in school: Strategies and best practices* (2nd ed.). Pacific Grove, CA: Brooks/Cole.

Walker, H. M., & Severson, H. H. (1999). *Systematic Screening for Behavior Disorders (SSBD): A multiple gating procedure* (2nd ed.). Longmont, CO: Sopris West.

Walker, H. M., Severson, H. H., & Feil, E. G. (1995). *Early Screening Project (ESP).* Longmont, CO: Sopris West.

Wolery, M., Bailey, D. B., & Sugai, G. M. (1988). *Effective teaching: Principles and procedures of applied behavior analysis with exceptional students.* Boston: Allyn & Bacon.

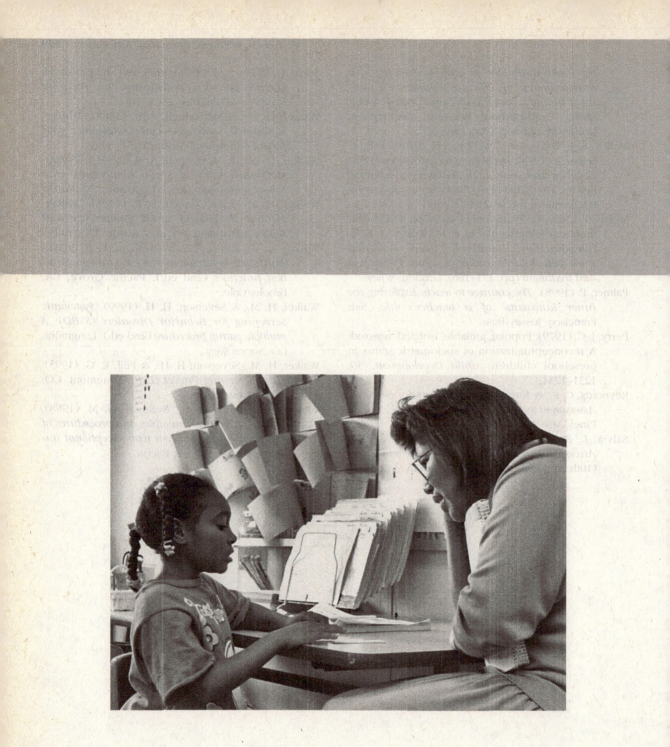

Functional and Curriculum-Based Assessment

Joel Macht and Thomas Zirpoli

If we consider problem behaviors as occurring in people, it is logical to try to change the people. If we consider problem behaviors as occurring in contexts, it becomes logical to change the context. Behavior change occurs by changing environments, not trying to change people.

—O'NEILL, HORNER, ALBIN, SPRAGUE, STOREY, AND NEWTON (1997, P. 5)

When a student's classroom behavior (a) consistently interferes with the student's own learning, (b) consistently interferes with other students' learning, or (c) consistently interferes with a teacher's ability to conduct class, some form of behavioral intervention plan (BIP) is needed (see Chapter 12). But, before developing a BIP, it is important that the function of the inappropriate behavior be explored by completing a *functional behavioral assessment* (FBA), the primary topic of this chapter. In fact, the BIP should be based upon the findings of the FBA.

The FBA is a "proactive approach to program planning and is a crucial step in providing the link to intervention based on the purpose of the student's behavior within the current environment" (Barnhill, 2005, p. 132). Understanding the function of a behavior recognizes that a student's behavior does not occur in isolation, and that the events preceding and following the behavior must be carefully analyzed. Disruptive behavior always serves some purpose for the student and an effective intervention plan can best be established only after that purpose has been determined.

Teachers should also keep in mind that (a) the student did not acquire the disruptive behavior in a day, and a resolution to the difficult behavior will also take some time; and (b) rushed decisions rarely produce effective interventions. Without a careful analysis of the conditions that appear to be associated with a student's undesired behavior, and without knowing the precise effect the environment's consequences are having on that behavior, an intervention plan could easily make matters worse both for the student and his or her teacher.

An important component of an FBA is to determine the function of a disruptive behavior. If the function of the behavior is determined to be avoidance of academic tasks, then a *curriculum-based assessment* (CBA), discussed in the second half of this chapter, will help teachers determine when the student needs additional instruction. By completing a CBA, teachers can determine whether a curriculum mismatch is contributing to a challenging classroom behavior (Macht, 1998). A curriculum mismatch can be caused by curriculum that is too difficult or too easy given the student's current performance level. Either mismatch may provide an antecedent to inappropriate classroom behavior whose function is to escape an activity or task too frustrating or boring. Thus, if a comprehensive FBA indicates that a student's behavior is related to the classroom curriculum, a CBA will assist the student's teacher in determining specific antecedents of concern.

DEFINITION AND BRIEF HISTORY OF FUNCTIONAL BEHAVIOR ASSESSMENT

A functional behavior assessment is a "collection of methods for gathering information about antecedents, behaviors, and conseqences in order to determine the reason or purpose of behavior. Once the function of a behavior is determined, this information is used to design interventions to reduce problem behaviors and to facilitate positive behaviors" (Gresham, Watson, & Skinner, 2001, p. 156). According to Gresham, et al. (2001, p. 158), the function or purpose of a target behavior usually falls into one of five categories:

- Social attention or reinforcement
- Access to something they want (an object or activity)
- Escape or avoidance of task or activity
- Escape or avoidance of other individuals
- Internal stimulation

Historically, the employment of a functional assessment of behavior can be traced back to the 1920s with the work of John Watson (1924), the 1930s with the work of Edward Thorndike (1932), and the 1940s and 1950s with the work of B. F. Skinner (1953). Later in the 1950s and early in the 1960s, two seminal works (Ayllon & Michael, 1959; Michael & Meyerson, 1962) were published in the first of a series of three books on human behavior (Ulrich, Stachnik, & Mabry, 1966) that introduced a perspective on applied behavior analysis that was the precursor to functional assessment.

Determining the function of a challenging behavior was a response developed out of frustration for many who understood that viewing challenging student behavior in isolation from the events of the student's classroom environment resulted in wasted time and resources employing standardized assessments and ineffective interventions. The 1997 reauthorization of the Individuals with Disabilities Act (IDEA) first required "a functional behavioral assessment and a behavioral intervention plan be developed for each child whose behaviors have resulted in a change in placement or in suspension or removal to an alternative placement" (Murdick, Gartin, & Stockall, 2003, p. 25). This requirement was reinforced in the 2004 reauthorization of the IDEA.

Today, all teachers, regardless of educational setting, are encouraged to complete functional analyses of student behavior to assess antecedent factors (e.g., task difficulty) and contextual factors (e.g., classroom seating arrangement). As Scott and colleagues (2004) state, "Unquestionably, FBA must become an integral part of an overall systemic approach to academic and behavioral management that is proactive in nature and implemented with young children, so that minor problem behaviors are addressed before they develop into severe challenges" (p. 194).

While the IDEA requires the completion of an FBA, "it does not specify the procedures associated with one" (Watson et al., 2001, p. 153). However, we hope the following section provides teachers with the basic strategies they need to complete an FBA and, thus, develop more effective interventions for their students. We recognize the limitations and constraints of this one chapter and hope teachers will read other sources that will assist them in completing a comprehensive FBA. For example, Sulzer-Azaroff and Mayer (1991) have written an essential strategies book describing the essence of functional assessment and applied behavior analysis. O'Neill and his colleagues (1997) have fashioned a comprehensive and highly pragmatic handbook of functional assessment, including exercises that are ideal for the student beginning or refining his or her studies in the area. Lastly, Scott and his colleagues (2004) review an FBA's "significant promise as a procedure to be used proactively with students with behavioral challenges who are educated in part, or wholly, in general education classrooms" (p. 189). Some suggestions from these and other resources are provided below.

COMPONENTS OF A FUNCTIONAL BEHAVIOR ASSESSMENT

A thorough functional assessment of a student's behavior will yield the following valuable information and strategies for each will be discussed below:

- A description of the student's target behaviors;
- the frequency, duration and intensity of the student's target behaviors;
- the discovery of the setting events, in and out of school, that trigger the occurrence of the student's undesired behavior;
- the identification of the consequences used by teachers and school officials that may be maintaining the problem behaviors; and
- strategies for identifying appropriate replacement behaviors which may be reinforced and maintained through a BIP.

Gresham et al. (2001, p. 156) outline three methods of a comprehensive FBA:

- *Indirect methods* employ the collection of information about the target behavior using interviews, formal and informal, of people who live and work with the student, a review of student records about his or her behavior, and the use of preformatted checklists and behavior rating scales that the teacher completes about the student.
- *Direct methods* employ systematic observation of the behavior in the natural setting to include an A-B-C analysis or a permanent product (e.g., recordings, pictures, hard copies of academic work) of the behavior.
- *Experimental analysis* methods employ systematic observation of the behavior in laboratory or controlled environments sometimes used to test or validate the function of the behavior.

Murdick and colleagues (2003) state that for most classroom teachers, the direct observation method of FBA is the "most familiar to teachers and, thus easiest for them to implement" (p. 25). More than likely, classroom teachers will leave the experimental analysis to professional researchers or school consultants (see Scott et al., 2004).

A Basic Understanding of Behavior

A significant aspect of functional assessment is the understanding that a student's behavior never occurs in isolation. If a teacher holds the philosophy that a student's inappropriate behavior is solely the result of a student's disability or personality trait or other internal variable, a FBA will seem to be a waste of time and resources. A more accurate and functional philosophy is to view a student's behavior within the larger environmental context in which it occurs. Without viewing behavior in its context, it is easy to think that the student owns the behavior (i.e., has a behavioral disorder) and that the teacher's actions are unimportant. That bias tends toward identifying a disability within the student instead of a deficiency in the student's environment. Doing so may well produce very ineffective interventions as the function of the behavior is neither understood nor addressed.

Identify the Target Behavior

The initial component of functional assessment sets the rhythm for the subsequent steps. You need to define precisely what the student is doing (i.e., the target behavior). The target behavior must be directly observable and measurable so that when the frequency, duration and/or intensity of the behavior are measured during baseline and intervention, a reliable measurement may be recorded. Thus, think verbs, not adjectives or adverbs. "Aggression" becomes hitting, punching or pushing; "Off-task" becomes leaving the work area or laying head on desk (Blakeley-Smith, Carr, Cale, & Owen-DeSchryver, 2009). These operational behaviors provide the opportunity for measurement so that progress, or the lack of, may be documented and the BIP modified accordingly. A more complete review of identifying target behaviors is provided in Chapter 6.

Observe and Collect Baseline Data on the Target Behavior

Once the target behavior is identified, the frequency, duration, and/or duration of the behavior must be collected. This will provide the teacher with (a) information on the severity of the problem (Is it really a problem?), and (b) data to compare the intervention data with once the BIP is implemented. Data collection is a must in order to determine the effectiveness of the intervention and determine the need for any modifications to the BIP. A comprehensive overview of data collection and evaluation methods is provided in Chapters 6 and 7.

Identify the Setting Events or Antecedents of the Target Behavior

After you've defined the student's target behaviors and collected data on those behaviors, the teacher needs to determine when those behaviors are most (and least) likely to occur. As the name implies, *setting events* (or antecedents) do not cause the problem behavior to occur, rather they set the stage for the behaviors. A red traffic light is a familiar example. The traffic light sets the stage for you to brake your car; it doesn't guarantee you will do so, of course. You can predict with a good deal of certainty that in the presence of a red traffic light, most people, most often, will depress the brake pedal. Notice the term *predict*. It plays a very important role in functional assessment. Classroom Connection 9.1, what is the antecedent to Daniel's target behavior?

An important component to the FBA is collecting information about a student's target behavior by interviewing teachers, parents, and other individuals who come in

CLASSROOM CONNECTION 9.1
Making Matters Worse

Daniel had worn out his welcome after only the first 3 weeks in his new high school. When Mr. Thompson requested that his freshman American literature class open their books to an assigned page, Daniel would slam his book against his desk and sit back in his chair, his arms folded belligerently. When Mr. Thompson repeated his request, his frustrated voice aimed at the student, Daniel would remain defiant and tell his teacher that the work was "stupid and boring." Mr. Thompson frequently provided the student one more opportunity to get to work before sending him to the school's study center, which was euphemistically called a cool-down room. Had anyone looked closely at the room, they would have discovered it had become a cool gathering spot for several veteran students who had learned they could meet and enjoy each other's company in the loosely monitored time-out room. The same students, of course, had also discovered how to avoid classroom work, hardly the intent of the school's

hardworking teachers. While Daniel's absence provided Mr. Thompson with a respite from his challenging behavior, the teacher's poorly fashioned behavioral program guaranteed Daniel's future disruptiveness.

General Reflection for Classroom Connection 9.1:

Mr. Thompson would have employed an entirely different behavioral approach to Daniel's disruptiveness had he a better understanding of FBA and the antecedents and consequences that were maintaining Daniel's behavior. What might a functional assessment of Daniel's noncompliance reveal? Later in the week when Mr. Thompson requested that his students get ready for a movie related to a current reading assignment, young Daniel turned rapidly compliant. He even chided his friends to listen to the teacher. Why do you think Daniel's behavior changed so suddenly? What recommendations would you provide for Mr. Thompson in dealing with Daniel's behavior?

contact with the student. Barnhill (2005) and Miltenberger (2001) developed lists of interview questions to facilitate the disclosure of possible setting events once the target behavior is identified. They include:

- When does the target behavior usually occur?
- Where does the target behavior usually occur?
- Who is present when the target behavior occurs?

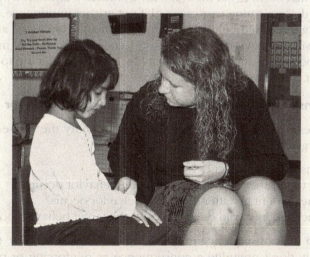

Teachers have to think about why students behave or the function of their behavior before they can change the behavior.

- What activities or events precede the target behavior?
- What do people say or do immediately prior to the target behavior?
- Does the child demonstrate any other behaviors prior to the target behavior?
- When, where, with whom, and in what condition is the target behavior least likely to occur?

PROXIMATE SETTING EVENTS   Setting events can occur in close proximity to a student's disruptive behavior. Often these events occur inside the classroom. *Proximate setting events* can include the time of the day, the day of the week, a classroom's activities or their cancellation, and the adult in front of the room (e.g., a substitute teacher). Questions that may help identify immediate antecedent or proximate setting events include the following:

- What academic or nonacademic activities during a school day seem strongly associated with a student's problem behavior?
- What changes in routines seem to set the stage for the problem behaviors?
- What times of the day seem to increase the likelihood of the problem behaviors?
- Does the disruptive behavior occur more often during particular classrooms or classroom assignments or in the presence of particular teachers?

DISTANT SETTING EVENTS   *Distant setting events* occur well before school begins, usually at home, but occasionally in transit to school. They can be related to physical or emotional conflicts that upset the child and influence his or her behavior long before reaching school. Parental notification may help school personnel deal with an unsettled student the moment he or she arrives at school. Concerns include illness, arguments with siblings and parents, as well as unexpected changes in routines. Interviewing parents about the student's target behavior may yield important information about a student's classroom behavior. Many behaviors, for example, are learned at home and then exhibited at school to serve a similar function.

WHERE IS THE BEHAVIOR LEAST LIKELY TO OCCUR?   While determining the proximate and distant events that seem to set the stage for a student's undesired behavior is necessary, an additional determination carries equal if not greater importance. When observing a student exhibiting undesired behaviors, identify as many conditions as possible where the student's undesired behaviors are *least likely* to occur. If a student misbehaves in Mr. Smith's class but cooperates and participates in Ms. Jones's class, a trip to Ms. Jones's class might reveal for Mr. Smith what he needs to do.

Identify the Consequences Maintaining the Target Behavior

The following types of question may help teachers identify the consequences that are maintaining the target behavior:

- What happens after the target behavior occurs?
- What do you (and others) do when the target behavior occurs?
- What does the student get after the target behavior occurs?
- What does the student avoid during or after the target behavior occurs?

When determining the consequence maintaining the target behavior, teachers need to be careful that they don't prejudge a consequence as reinforcing or punishing for the student. For example, a teacher might be surprised to learn that sending a student to a time-out chair is actually reinforcing and maintaining disruptive classroom behavior during a reading activity. But if the student is embarrassed to demonstrate his poor reading skills, avoiding the activity by sitting in the time-out chair serves an important function for the student (avoidance of reading in front of his peers). In Chapter 10, we will discuss the role of reinforcement in maintaining behavior. A teacher's goal, of course, is to maintain appropriate behavior. But a FBA frequently demonstrates that what the teacher perceives as a negative response (frown, yelling, time-out) may provide to the student just what he wanted (attention from the teacher or avoidance of a difficult task). The interview questions outlined above will frequently reveal the consequences that are serving to maintain and reinforce the target behavior. And who should be asked these questions? Anyone who observes the student's target behaviors may provide important clues. In Classroom Connection 9.1, what consequences are maintaining Daniel's target behavior?

Identify the Function or Purpose of the Target Behavior

Once you have determined the target behaviors and have documented, when possible, the antecedents or setting events that predict when those behaviors are most and least likely to occur, and you have identified the consequences that seem to be maintaining the target behavior, you need to turn your attention to two questions: "What purpose does the disruptive behavior serve?" and "What is the student gaining or avoiding from the undesired behavior?"

The philosophy on which functional assessment is based holds that a student's behavior occurs because the behavior produces something the student finds of value (e.g., attention or activity) or because the behavior enables the student to avoid (or be removed from) something the student finds unpleasant or frustrating (a math worksheet). For example, Boyajian, DuPaul, Handler, Eckert, and McGoey (2001) completed a functional analysis of three preschoolers, ages 4 and 5 years, exhibiting frequent aggressive behavior. All three boys were considered "at risk" for ADHD. But the results of the functional analysis "indicated that the aggressive behavior was maintained" by reinforcement contingencies (p. 278), not a medical disorder. And, as stated by Scott and Kamps (2007, p. 151), "Intervention is not based on behavior—it is based on the function of that behavior."

In a second example of how behavior may serve a function, Kearney (2004) and Kearney and Albano (2004) looked at the functional profiles of students who do their best to avoid attending school. Kearney (2004, p. 276) found that students avoid school for one or more of the following "functional conditions":

- To avoid school-based stimuli that provoke anxiety and depression
- To escape aversive school-based social situations
- To pursue attention from significant others (e.g., parents)
- To pursue tangible reinforcers outside school

INTERVIEW THE STUDENT   In addition to interviews with teachers and other individuals working with the student, O'Neill and his colleagues (1997) discuss the advantages for interviewing students directly about their own disruptive behaviors. Asking students why they are misbehaving may provide teachers with some very interesting information, particularly if they have a positive relationship with and trust the questioner. A few carefully crafted questions might help the student divulge what payoffs he or she receives for the undesired actions. For example, "Jon, what do you gain from that behavior?" or "Jon, do you like the way your teacher or peers respond to that behavior?"

Hoff, Ervin, and Friman (2005, p. 45) used a combination of student interviews, teacher interviews, and direct observations "to generate hypotheses regarding the association between classroom environmental conditions and the occurrence of disruptive behavior" by a 12-year-old boy diagnosed with ADHD/ODD within a general education classroom. Their interviews with the student and the teacher tried to identify "the situations and conditions when disruptive behavior was more likely to occur and less likely to occur" (p. 49).

While there are more formal and structured questionnaires published to assist teachers in identifying antecedents and consequences of target behaviors (see Cunningham & O'Neill, 2007), these are not necessary, and we advise teachers to use the more simple questions and guidelines provided in this chapter.

Identify Replacement Behaviors

In addition to identifying target behaviors that you want to change, it is also necessary to determine what target behavior(s) you prefer the student to exhibit in place of the targeted challenging behavior(s). These are called *replacement behaviors*. For example, if a student is yelling out answers in a classroom, the teacher may want to teach the student to raise his hand and wait to be recognized. Raising his hand and waiting to be called needs to be taught and reinforced as a substitute or replacement behavior for the target behavior of yelling out. This strategy then becomes an important component of the student's BIP (to teach and reinforce hand-raising behavior). In a second example, if you have determined that a student is receiving a significant amount of attention for a target behavior (falling out of his seat), you need to (a) remove the attention for the target behavior and (b) determine an appropriate replacement behavior (staying in seat) that serves the same function for the student (attention) and is more socially appropriate and less disruptive for the classroom. To identify replacement behaviors, the teacher needs to ask, "What other, more appropriate behavior can the student exhibit in my classroom to receive attention so that he does not have to engage in the target behavior to receive attention?" And if the function of the behavior is to avoid an academic task or other nonpreferred activity, the teacher needs to ask, "How can I make the activity more reinforcing or less stressful for the student so that he does not need to engage in the target behavior to avoid the activity?" For example, the teacher may write a behavior plan that provides the student with opportunities to select items from a reinforcement menu (see Reinforcement Menu in Chapter 10) when he participates in the activity in increasing durations without disruptive behaviors (see Shaping in Chapter 10).

As outlined in Chapter 10, once a replacement behavior is identified, a reinforcement program should be incorporated to reinforce and maintain this new replacement behavior. This strategy becomes part of the student's BIP.

Park (2007) proposes the acronym "ERASE" to describe all the components of a comprehensive FBA as follows:

E = Explain: What is the target behavior, and what happens before and after the behavior?

R = Reason: What is the student getting or avoiding by this behavior?

A = Appropriate: What do you want the student to do instead of the target behavior?

S = Support: Support and reinforce the replacement behavior identified above.

E = Evaluate: Define criterion for success and monitor student progress.

CURRICULUM-BASED ASSESSMENT

As we have reviewed above in discussions about FBA, looking at a behavior's payoff and purpose, rather than its deviation from what is perceived as normal or expected, might suggest that something in the classroom environment needs evaluating. This evaluation includes two major components about the classroom environment that are related to student behavior: the general antecedents and consequences to behavior, the topic of discussion thus far in this chapter, and the classroom curriculum or content of the academic material that the teacher is trying to teach. In a sense, the first component deals with the environmental issues related to how the material is presented (classroom rules, where students sit, how teacher and students interact, etc.). The second component deals with the actual content or material taught in the classroom (a specific level of math, science, etc.). As stated by Scott and Kamps (2007, p. 151), "Because students spend the vast majority of their day in the classroom and the focus of the classroom is academics, it seems grossly inappropriate to ignore the relationship between academic and social behavior."

An FBA must consider the curriculum content in relation to the student's present performance level (PPL). As stated in the introduction of this chapter, a curriculum mismatch may serve as an antecedent to inappropriate behavior when the function of the challenging behavior is to escape an activity that is too difficult or boring. Making sure that there is an appropriate match between the classroom curriculum and each student's academic readiness is an important part of teaching and managing a classroom. If the teacher's curriculum is the same for all students, success will elude both teacher and students, and some students' behavior is likely to become an issue of concern.

CBA: DEFINITION AND BRIEF HISTORY

Curriculum-based assessment (CBA) is a strategy for determining the instructional needs of students in an effort to match the students' needs and abilities with the classroom curriculum. The primary goal of CBA is to eliminate curriculum mismatches between students' skills and teachers' classroom assignments and expectations in order to increase student performance and a reduction in challenging student behavior within the classroom.

Shapiro and Derr (1990) succinctly characterized CBA as a method teachers can use to determine the instructional needs of their students and the strategies to more expeditiously modify their curriculum when it doesn't accomplish what was intended. For example, in Classroom Connection 9.2, small modifications allowed Sara to be less anxious about a writing assignment and remain in class without exhibiting inappropriate behaviors. A CBA will frequently pinpoint to teachers (a) the specific area where a student is having difficulty and (b) the antecedent of disruptive behavior.

Variations within the CBA model have been clearly described in the professional literature. Shapiro and Derr (1990) have offered in some detail the distinctions attributed to CBA by many of its proponents (Blankenship, 1985; Deno, 1985; Gickling & Havertape, 1981; Idol, Nevin, & Paolucci-Whitcomb, 1986, 1999; Shapiro & Lentz, 1985, 1986.) Additionally, several authors (Choate, Enright, Miller, Poteet, & Rakes, 1992; Howell, Fox, & Morehead, 1993; King-Sears, 1994; Shinn, 1989) have discussed

- the different theoretical underpinnings of CBA;
- the multiple advantages of CBA over traditional standardized assessment tools (see also Witt, Elliot, Daly, Gresham, & Kramer, 1998); and
- the myriad benefits of CBA when used in classrooms with diverse students.

CLASSROOM CONNECTION 9.2
Eye of the Beholder

When it was time for a hated creative writing assignment, fourth-grade Sara could say, "Forget it" quicker than her teacher, Melissa, could hand her students a blank sheet of paper. Sara would frequently take the handout from the teacher, transform it into a snowball shape, and leave her desk to wonder the room as if a visitor. Cornered, coaxed, and often cajoled, she'd turn defiant in words and expression. "I won't," she'd say, inviting the inevitable trip to the school's resource room where Jane, the resource teacher, would work with Sara and help her with the assignment. Asked to intervene, the school's behavioral psychologist, Jason, met several times, separately, with Melissa, Jane, and Sara. During one of his interviews Jason asked Melissa to collect baseline data on Sara's behavior for a couple of weeks along with an ABC analysis (see Chapter 6) of her behavior. He also asked Melissa to allow him to visit her classroom during the next creative writing assignment so he could observe Sara's behavior within the context of the classroom environment. Also, during one of his meetings with Sara, Jason conducted a CBA of Sara's basic writing skills. Then, Jason held a meeting with Melissa to share his observations. "The writing instructions cue her," Jason explained, "A blank page triggers her refusal, which allows her to (a) escape the assignment and (b) spend individual time with Jane. Both are reinforcing and maintaining her refusal behavior." Jason told Melissa that based upon his observations of Sara's writing that Sara could write fairly well. He advised Melissa that Sara might be more cooperative if she were provided more structure in the writing assignment and less of a blank page which seems to serve as an antecedent to her target behavior. "When I asked her to write about a red dog with white spots who's hungry, and drew borders around the space within which I asked Sara to write, thereby providing a more manageable cue than the full blank page, she did very well," Jason told Melissa. Jason instructed Melissa to ask Sara to outline the amount of space on a page she wants for her writing, and to give her specific instructions on what to write. Jason explained that each time Melissa has a writing assignment, Sara could be asked to write a little more than the last time, and that she should earn reinforcement for a successful assignment. Jason also suggested that, for a while at least, Sara be allowed to visit Jane, the resource teacher, as part of her reinforcement program. Over time, Jason thought, the extra instructions could be faded as Melissa became more confident in her writing skills and the ability to face a blank page.

General Reflection for Classroom Connection 9.2:

Define Sara's target behavior? What were the antecedents and consequences for Sara's target behavior? What role did Melissa and Jane play in Sara's behavior? What advice would you give Melissa on slowing fading out the writing prompts when giving her a writing assignment? If Sara displayed the refusal behavior in the future, would you send her to Jane's resource room? What would you do instead?

Despite the seemingly large number of differences within the CBA model, the fact remains that most researchers and practitioners see a consistent overlap in the model's value, mechanics, and application (Shinn, 1989).

CBA: Appropriate for All Students

Curriculum-based assessment is appropriate for *all* students, not only for students who are receiving special services or who have Individual Education Plans (IEPs). According to Macht (1998), CBA can prevent the unnecessary labeling of many students, and he wonders how many students currently labeled "learning disabled" or "emotionally disturbed" have suffered from an undiscovered curriculum mismatch beginning as early as kindergarten. When teachers are assessing student performance, CBA requires them to focus on what students can do rather than describe what they can't do. Thus, the phrase "the student can't read" gives way to what the student *does* read. An effective teacher then builds on what students can do.

A "No Fault" Approach

If a student fails to make progress within a teacher's curriculum, it is assumed that the teacher's instructional strategies were unsuccessful and in need of modification. This holds true even for those students assigned to special education. The blaming game (e.g., poor teacher, disinterested parent, disordered brain, or inadequate nervous system) serves little practical purpose.

No one individual (or one variable) ever owns a student's particular learning problem. Moreover, teachers are rarely able to effect a change in variables outside their classroom. The significant variable that demands most of our attention is the teacher's strategy within the classroom. Regardless of a student's predicted innate strength or observed academic weaknesses, a teacher's flexible, efficient, and effective classroom strategy is the tool that will yield success.

Diverse Students and the Need for a Broad-Based Curriculum

Few classroom teachers today may claim not to have a highly diverse student presenting highly diverse entering skills and curriculum pacing needs. You will therefore need to have at your disposal a broad-based curriculum to be used within your classroom so that all of your students can benefit from their time with you.

It is worth repeating that is highly unlikely that every student in your classroom will be ready for the same degree of work, either its academic content or the pacing (speed) with which the content is presented. The attitude, voiced by a disgruntled teacher, "I was hired to teach third grade; if one of my students is not ready for third grade, that's not my problem," is counterproductive and far from the best practice. There will be a student in third grade whose skills are closer to first or fourth grade; there will be a student in tenth grade whose entering skills are more in line with seventh grade. The deviation is the teacher's challenge. How the teacher deals with this challenge will greatly affect student performance and classroom behavior.

CURRICULUM PROBES: THE PRIMARY TOOL FOR CBA

Curriculum probes are the primary tool for the CBA model and are used to assess a student's current skill level. Probes are most often teacher-made, functional, criterion-referenced tests (CRTs) that the teacher builds directly from his or her own curriculum (e.g., math problems, spelling words, reading passages, and writing assignments).

Probes can contain relatively few questions or exercises, or their numbers can be expansive. A piece of paper containing a few strategically chosen math problems is a probe. Having a student decode a line or two from a paragraph probes decoding proficiency. Having a student tell you about the location or setting of a story is a probe. Asking the same student a few comprehension questions, calling for literal or inferential interpretations, is also a probe. Every time you request a student to write a sentence or two, you have conducted a writing probe.

Probes communicate to you what your students can do and at what point on a sequential curriculum to begin your lessons. By comparing the results of the probes you used on Monday with the same probes administered on the following Tuesday or Wednesday, you will know whether your teaching strategies have been successful. You will also know whether you can proceed or whether you have to practice further. This strategy is likely to play a significant role in the behavior of students.

Developing Probes

To build your own probes, consider the following sequence:

1. Thoroughly analyze the curriculum you are going to use with your students.
2. Build questions and problems from that curriculum, making sure that your questions and problems sample a wide area (perhaps three full grade levels) of possible entering skills.
3. Order your questions and problems by difficulty. Remember, easy is only easy for a student if the student knows the answer. Develop multiple forms with similar items also listed in order of increasing difficulty.
4. Administer the items.
5. Score the items correct or incorrect, with descriptions of errors in the latter case.
6. Using folders for each student, describe approximate entering skills.
7. Develop simple graphs with which to record student performance (see Chapter 6).

Examples of Probes

The following probe descriptions are presented to provide a structure from which to build your own probes. Consider your own curriculum and goals and preferences when developing your probes. Keep in mind that probes are intended to help you better understand the types of academic experiences your students bring with them into your class.

WRITING PROBES   Writing probes are the easiest, for they require only that a teacher obtain a sample of a student's writing. Usually, the sample is taken under two circumstances:

- The teacher provides the student with a concrete topic and asks the student to write about that topic.
- The teacher provides no identifiable structure; rather, the student is asked to write about any topic of choice.

Writing probes should always have a time limit—one that fits your teaching schedule. Evaluating the probe follows from your particular interests at the moment. Content, punctuation, use of phonics, creativity, spelling, syntax, plot development, and logical flow represent only a few issues that may pique your curiosity. Writing probes can be administered in groups, as well as on an individual basis. In addition to giving you a picture of progress, your writing probes will be used to determine the types of exercises or assignments you will choose to use with a particular student.

MATH PROBES   When developing math probes, as with any probe, you will need to decide what specific skill you wish to assess. Assuming interest in calculation skills is priority for the moment, your math probes will contain a wide range of problems requiring different types of solutions (e.g., recognition of numbers; which is correct: $3 > 2$ or $2 > 3$; $23 + 45 =$; $327 - 186 =$; $54 \times 30 =$; $144 \div 6 =$; $\frac{1}{2} \times 3\frac{1}{6} =$; etc.).

When developing math probes, you want to present problems well below and above your students' *expected PPLs*. Determine the degree of difficulty the student has mastered and the level that begins to produce reliable errors. More than likely, colleagues already have printed math exercises that can be used as probes for your students. Placing those probes in a folder in a central location within the school would make their access easy.

You can probe mathematical concepts that go far beyond typical calculations. A problem (which will serve as a probe) such as the following, administered to your entire class, can provide you with a great deal of valuable information regarding your students' readiness to move from concrete calculations to abstract thinking, to understanding of concepts, to application, integration, and generalization:

> *Billy ate 1/4 of a candy bar; Mary ate another 1/4 of the same candy bar; and Ms. Smith ate 1/2 of the same candy bar. Questions: (a) How much of the candy bar has been eaten? (b) How much more candy did Ms. Smith have than Billy?*

READING PROBES   Reading probes present the greatest challenge, and you would be well advised to consult with your school's reading specialists. While reading probes can be conducted in groups, individual probing provides the most valuable information.

Sitting across from a student, determining the level at which reading occurs comfortably and fluidly, having the opportunity to do an immediate miscue or error analysis, and being able to gauge a student's literal or inferential comprehension skills with the material at hand often comprise, again, the most fruitful way of measuring some of a student's reading proficiency.

For group probes, develop multiple, brief paragraphs (three to five sentences or more), ranging from beginning levels to complex reading materials. These paragraphs can be presented to a group of students who are requested first to read each paragraph, beginning at a difficulty level determined by you, and then to answer two or three questions regarding the reading materials. The students should continue this brief reading-and-answering assignment until the materials end, or until they are no longer able to decode the paragraphs with ease. With younger students in a group, asking them to circle selected sight words, or to circle a picture that begins with a "p" sound, can also serve as a probe to determine roughly what entering or readiness skills the students possess.

Who Administers Probes?

You and your colleagues will decide who will be responsible for administering subject area probes. Ideally, classroom teachers will do the majority of the probing since they have the most up-to-date, accurate knowledge of their students' academic successes and difficulties. When necessary, you should request assistance with probing from members of your school's resource team. Your school may decide that various members of a resource team will assume responsibility for probing all the students.

When Are Probes Administered?

For very important reasons, CBA probes are administered before, during, and after instruction. Probes administered *before* instruction will provide you with data allowing you to make good decisions concerning your students' placement into curriculum materials, thereby reducing, if not eliminating, curriculum mismatches and associated behavior problems. Your initial probe will tell you what materials and exercises your students have mastered.

Probes administered *during* instruction offer you data indicating how your students are doing with your current instruction, thereby providing you with a data-level basis upon which to adjust your instructional strategies. These "on-the-spot" probes reduce the probability that you will continue to use teaching methods that are proving ineffective for various students.

Probes administered immediately *after* instruction and periodically throughout the year will help you know what your students have learned. The posttest probe can be identical to the original probe, or it can contain a slight modification. Probes administered throughout the school year provide useful information on your students' long-term retention abilities and will assist you when communicating student progress to parents and school officials.

Where Are Probes Administered?

The ultimate goal of those proponents of CBA is to have all general classroom teachers administer probes in their classrooms daily, perhaps hourly. With practice, this goal is achievable. If you are new to the CBA model, you might consider seeking assistance from members of your school team, from a special education teacher in particular, to help you design and administer the probes in your classroom. You can try the process with one or two students and expand coverage as your confidence increases.

Schools often provide laboratory or study space within the building where students from various classes, struggling with specific components of their studies, meet to receive assistance from a professional assigned by the school's administration. A resource room, a quiet hallway, and a corner of the school's library are possible locations for such brief gatherings where probing present performance levels, errors, and measuring effectiveness of teacher strategies occur. Other points to consider include the following:

- *Assess frequently.*   If you want to know how a student is doing on a certain skill or academic behavior, administer brief probes frequently. Such repeated assessment will quickly alert you to the fact that you need to modify your instruction.
- *Vary assessment.*   Use a variety of student responses to probe a student's accuracy and understanding. Include written and oral answers, fill-in-the-blank answers, multiple-choice answers, finding-error answers, as well as identification of correct and incorrect answers, correct and incorrect spellings and grammar, and the like.
- *Check generalization* of acquired skills by using assessments outside the classroom.
- *Prioritize.*   Assess the most important and most critical academic behaviors most often. Decide which academic behaviors are most in need of change and then gather as much data about those behaviors as possible.
- *Keep good data.*   Have growth-over-time charts and hard copies of students' work to share with teachers and parents, both informally and during meetings pertaining to a student's academic achievement. Help everyone concentrate on what the student is doing correctly.

Recording Progress: Growth-Over-Time Charts

CBA probes yield data points that can be recorded on students' growth-over-time charts (review single-subject design information in Chapter 7). Plot whatever skill you were working on: the number of addition problems correctly solved, the number of words correctly read, the number of correctly used noun-verb agreements, and so on. The ascending or descending direction of the plotted data lines will tell you whether your instructional strategies are working (see Figure 6.14 in Chapter 6).

A flat data line is most often an indication that your instructional strategy needs to be modified. This is an extremely important point, particularly when you are working with a student who is suspected of having learning problems. Without exception, learning problems are only solved with good strategies. If a student is making no (or minimal) progress in any of the subject areas, you must reevaluate your strategies. Once again, seek advice from your school's assistance team to gain fresh ideas as to how to help a student over an academic hurdle.

Two important notes about probes: Probes are not to be used to determine grades, and they are not to be used to compare the performances of students. Instead, probes are used to determine what experiences and instructional strategies individual students need. Probes help teachers modify and improve their curriculum.

ERROR ANALYSIS

Probes lend themselves to immediate (and very easy) analysis of a student's errors. Asking one of your students to share how he or she arrived at an answer may provide you with just what you need to develop all sorts of innovative ways of helping the student work through the presenting hurdles. Questions for students may include the following:

"How did you arrive at your answer?"

"What were you thinking about when completing the problem?"

"What steps did you use to answer the question?"

These types of questions can illuminate what skills and concepts a student presently possesses and which ones he or she has yet to acquire. In Classroom Connection 9.3, a few questions from the teacher not only would have revealed why Kim answered her quiz question incorrectly, but would have provided Kim with a great learning opportunity at the same time.

The Value of Student Errors

Students' errors provide teachers with a window into their thoughts and problem-solving skills. They present golden opportunities for teaching and golden opportunities for learning. Remember these points about student errors:

- Students must feel comfortable making errors and admitting to teachers the areas of confusion and difficulty.
- Students must know that, within a teacher's classroom, student errors are not only acceptable but welcomed and encouraged.
- Students need to know that all their answers, even those that are incorrect, are nevertheless very valuable.

Many students believe that errors are bad (they've learned this lesson through lower grades and deprecating marks and notations on assignments), and they are often reluctant to even try to answer a difficult question if they think there is a chance they will make a mistake. You must, therefore, prepare your students to accept that errors are important,

CLASSROOM CONNECTION 9.3
Student Errors Lead to New Student Experiences

Third grader Kim received her spelling paper back from her teacher. She was upset by the dramatic sad face in the upper right-hand corner, the large "–2" slashed in red ink underneath the face's down-turned lips, and the two "X's" the teacher had marked across sentences 9 and 10. The students were handed their papers without further comment.

At dinner that evening, Kim's mother sensed her daughter's uncharacteristic gloom and gently pressed her for an explanation. Reluctantly, Kim left the table and returned with the crumpled paper she had extricated from her backpack. Her mother promptly shared it with her husband. "I will help you with this after dinner," Kim's father told her.

The assignment consisted of 10 words and 10 sentences, each sentence with a blank to be filled in by one of the words at the top of the page. For several of the young students, Kim including, a few of the words were new. The ninth sentence read; "The fisherman used the _____ to help him catch fish." Kim had two remaining words from which to choose: *bait* and *zebra*. Having not a clue of the meaning of *bait*, she chose *zebra*, explaining to her father that the zebra went with the fisherman to the river's edge and the zebra, like the Alaskan bears she had seen on television, helped the fisherman grab the fish as they swam close by—a good answer her father thought.

Had the teacher used her exercise as a probe, rather than as a vehicle to grade, Kim and several others in the class who also struggled with the word *bait* would have been the winners. The teacher could have used the students' errors in any number of productive ways: (a) to learn which words were unfamiliar, (b) to ask other students who had experience with fishing for assistance, (c) to show pictures of different fish and explain how the smaller ones were bait for the larger ones, (d) to discuss the differences between a bear's claws and a zebra's hoofs, or (e) to present any number of other educational opportunities.

Choosing instead to return the papers to the students with the telling marks, the teacher lost a perfect opportunity to help her students and herself.

General Reflection for Classroom Connection 9.3:

Clearly there is a place for both probes and tests in education. How may they be used as both an opportunity to teach and to evaluate student progress? When is it appropriate to probe, and when is it appropriate to test?

and you must prepare them to share with you when they do not understand all or part of an assignment or its instruction.

You'll need a means to keep track of your students' errors. As demonstrated in Classroom Connection 9.4, take notice of reliable, consistent errors. An occasional academic error can be overlooked. A consistent error, or an error with a distinct, repeated pattern, must be recorded and explored. You can use a notebook that you either carry with you or keep close by to record student errors. The notebook should contain each student's name along with sufficient room to describe the student's responses. Your students should see you recording errors. Explain the purpose behind your actions, and assure them that you are keeping a record of the errors so you can develop different strategies. Do not be surprised if the question of grades comes up!

Error analysis is a simple process that will help you identify which components of an assignment are creating difficulty for one of your students. Again, asking the simple question "How did you arrive at your answer?" will provide you with enormous insights and ideas for new approaches to use with the student.

Remember these three important points regarding student errors:

• The vast majority of student errors are conceptual in nature. The student is missing an important component or two or an entire conceptualization of the present problem,

CLASSROOM CONNECTION 9.4
You Don't Know How to Do These?

Jack loved math. He loved numbers. And he loved putting them together and coming up with all sorts of answers. Unfortunately, his answers were not always correct. Having noticed consistent errors with regrouping, Jack's teacher built a quick probe as a prelude to error analysis. She presented him with the following items:

9	14	24	16	24	34
+7	+3	+11	+8	+27	+18

After looking over the problems, the student gave his teacher a full-toothed smile and asked, "You don't know how to do these?" She smiled and asked him to help her out. He did, more than he could have imagined.

9	14	24	16	24	34
+7	+3	+11	+8	+27	+18
16	17	35	114	411	412

The teacher watched Jack work over the problems and immediately noticed that he had added from left to right, the "10s" first, opening the door for the "1s" to step out rather prominently. It was quite apparent that the full concept of addition had eluded him. When he was finished, and satisfied, she asked him to tell her how he had arrived at his answers. With an incredulous look, he explained, "You add the top numbers and the bottom numbers. It's simple," he said, pointing to the last problem. "Three plus 1 is 4; 4 plus 8 is 12." He smiled and let his eyes say, "Obvious, don't you think?"

General Reflection for Classroom Connection 9.4:
How did using a math probe help Jack's teacher understand his thinking process when confronted with an addition problem? What other math probes could be employed to determine Jack's understanding of other basic math concepts?

and unless the confusion or absence of knowledge is rectified, the problems will persist and begin to affect material built upon what is missing.

- It is tempting to conclude that a student's absence of correct work (or any work!) is a motivational problem. Although such a cause is possible, motivational problems are less common than expected. More often, they appear as an issue when in fact a student is experiencing consistent conceptual difficulties. Motivation should never be the first explanation used to account for a student's poor academic work. A strategically asked question of a student might reveal the real problem: A conceptual component is missing.

- Do not help a student with an erroneous answer without first running an error analysis. Avoid the "Let me show you how to do that" knee-jerk reaction when a student makes an error. Helping the student before you have discovered the confusion or deficiency may not assist the student beyond getting an answer correct.

CBA AND CLASSROOM BEHAVIOR

The primary purpose of discussing CBA in this chapter and text is to understand the relationship between the classroom curriculum and student behavior. In this text, you are presented with technical skills to measure and chart behavior. However, to simply measure the dimension of a target behavior without looking at the behavior in light of the student's environment, including the student's current relationship with the classroom curriculum, is inviting a misunderstanding of the real problem.

Educators are encouraged to seek answers to the following questions when faced with a student's challenging behavior:

- Could the student's misbehavior be a result of a curriculum that is too easy or too difficult?
- Could the student's misbehavior be a result of the student's inability to understand an academic concept being taught?
- Could the student's misbehavior be a result of any other classroom factor over which the teacher has direct control and thus can modify?
- Could the student's misbehavior be related to an identified learning disability that is not being addressed with appropriate classroom accommodations/modifications as outlined in the student's Individual Education Plan (IEP)?

Behavior Problems as a Sign of Academic Problems

Unfortunately, not too many psychologists would consider the classroom curriculum as an antecedent to a problem behavior. Instead, many would focus on identifying the student's "disability" (e.g., ADD/ADHD).

It is hardly a coincidence that many students who present behavior and attention problems while in class are the same students experiencing difficulty with their academically related assignments. Researchers have known of this relationship for a long time. For example, Center, Dietz, and Kaufman (1982) have documented that a mismatch between academic materials that the student could not successfully complete usually resulted in higher levels of disruptive classroom behavior. It is also not surprising to discover that for many students, their disruptive behavior is very situation specific, occurring most often when required to participate in nonpreferred tasks rather than preferred ones.

Controlling Instructional Difficulty

A significant amount of research has been done on the behavior of students with a history of challenging behaviors while involved in preferred versus nonpreferred tasks (Foster-Johnson, Ferro, & Dunlap, 1994). The variable of choice, that is, letting students choose their tasks, has also been extensively investigated (Dunlap et al., 1994). While letting students choose their tasks has been shown to increase desirable student behavior, Cole, Davenport, and Bambara (1997) have demonstrated that it is the participation in a preferred activity, not the variable of choice, that seems to have the biggest effect on student behavior.

Students prefer activities that they can complete successfully. These tasks are more reinforcing than tasks that produce consistent errors and, as was the instance with Mrs. Case's student, John, accompany frustration and embarrassment. When a student says, "I love reading," chances are the student is successful at reading. Students generally choose activities they prefer, they prefer activities where success is likely, and their behaviors are more socially acceptable under such conditions.

Realistically, public school teachers can rarely have students choose to spend their entire school day with favorite activities within a curriculum. But teachers can make accommodations to the required curriculum in order to assist students in being more successful and lowering their errors and frustration.

For students to have success with their academic requirements, materials must be presented at an instructional level rather than a frustration level. A teacher's instructional demands, therefore, must be tied to each student's academic entering skill and not to group goals or curriculum goals that are unrelated to what the teacher is doing within his or her classroom. Instructional demands must be based on students' PPL data. A student whose reading skills are comfortably positioned in third-grade texts will experience difficulty if a teacher's instructional demands require the same student to read and comprehend material designed for students at the sixth- or seventh-grade level.

Curriculum-based assessment can help teachers eliminate many of the educational factors responsible for students' undesirable classroom behavior. As a result, CBA has become one of the strongest tools in many teachers' behavior management portfolios.

CBA AND EXCEPTIONAL STUDENTS

The term *exceptional* has been purposely chosen to represent all students who, in any number of ways, deviate from the norms of the general education population. These students may struggle with their work or may excel far beyond predictions. They may have physical and motor issues that interfere with traditional schooling, and they may have cognitive challenges that demand gentle, incremental learning, with constant repetition.

Curriculum-based assessment is as critical for students with IEPs as those without. At the same time special education labels, including *learning disabilities, intellectually disabled, attention deficit disorder*, and the myriad of others that have been generated over the past century, provide us with little in the way of academic information. Despite the grouping of same-labeled students in all exceptionality textbooks, students labeled in any manner are unique and, from a functional perspective, are not part of any group with shared academic or social/behavioral characteristics. Two students, both labeled with cerebral palsy, are likely to differ to the same degree that any two 10-year-olds will differ. Being told that you have a student labeled *learning disabled* coming into your classroom provides you with nothing on which to develop curriculum or strategies. The same can be said for any student labeled in any fashion.

To know what an exceptional student can do academically, and thus develop a good fit between the student's entering skills and your curriculum, you must put aside labels, age, assigned grade level, IQ scores, and professional statements that have foretold what the student will not be able to accomplish. Instead, we should follow the same systematic approach we have been discussing in this chapter:

1. Reexamine your classroom curriculum and consider what student skills are essential to that curriculum.
2. List those skills in logical order. Write an objective for each skill on the list. Ask, "What do I want the student to do?"
3. Prepare items (probes) from your classroom curriculum to assess each listed objective. The items should span from easy to difficult questions. Reduce the number of items to make the probe administratively manageable. Sequence the items in random order or present items beginning with the most simple and progressing to the most difficult, stopping when the student no longer answers correctly.
4. Determine the modality a student will use to express his or her knowledge (oral, ASL, computer based, written, pointing, etc.).

5. Determine the student's entering skills or present performance level with respect to those skills you have selected from your curriculum.

6. Determine at what point within your curriculum the student begins exhibiting reliable academic errors.

7. Determine through error analysis the conceptual base for the student's errors.

8. Build academic assignments and exercises to help the student move beyond the errors that are inhibiting the student's progress.

9. Develop and implement new strategies to assist the student with the new curriculum.

10. Identify errors the student is making with the new curriculum.

11. Select valid indicators of a student's progress (what specific skill—described precisely— you want him or her to learn); develop growth-over-time graphs and monitor slope of curve.

12. Reevaluate your curriculum strategies and make alterations if they are warranted.

13. Repeat item 5 from this list and proceed with a continuous loop between items 5 and 8.

Summary

A *functional behavioral assessment* is a general term used to determine possible consequences within the environment that might be maintaining the very behavior a teacher wishes to eliminate. Several steps are outlined to guide teachers through the important elements of a functional assessment within the classroom environment:

1. Identify what the student is doing that you perceive as undesired and interfering.

2. Determine what active behavior you wish the student to do instead of what not to do. Remember, telling a student not to fight doesn't tell him or her what you would prefer.

3. Determine the conditions and circumstances when both the desired and undesired behaviors are most and least likely to occur.

4. Determine how the environment (you and the other students) is responding to both the desired and undesired behaviors.

5. Determine what you need to do to provide desired payoffs to the desired behaviors.

6. As O'Neill and his colleagues (1997, p. 5) suggest, always ask yourself the following question: "What desired behavior on the part of the student could produce the same consequences that appear to be maintaining the undesired behavior?"

Teachers must consider the importance of the classroom curriculum when assessing the function of a student's challenging behavior. Prior to present performance level (PPL) testing, remind students that they will not be criticized or punished for errors; rather, their errors will tell you where to start the next lesson.

Observe a student's performance on academic assignments to obtain ideas where to begin PPL or entering skill assessment. Administer probes to identify roughly where within curriculum a student succeeds at or near 100%.

During PPL assessment, push the student beyond the point at which he or she makes no errors. A student's errorless performance does not translate to his or her PPL. Push the student beyond achieved success until reliable errors are observed. Watch carefully to determine the general areas that are creating difficulty. Note errors. By looking at the level of academic difficulty where the student's success is probable and then noting where his or her errors are likely, you will know roughly where to begin your lessons.

Avoid the temptation to tell the student what he or she did right or wrong. Do not show the student how to correct errors. You will need an error analysis to know the type of error the student is making.

Carefully analyze the student's responses to your materials. Look for areas of mastery and frequent errors. Look for patterns of errors and initiate error analysis. Based on the student's errors, determine what exercises and practice materials the student needs to move beyond the present error level. Remember, instructional pacing accommodations may be necessary.

Once practice materials and exercises have been chosen, select suitable instructional strategies. Schedule individual and group instructional periods throughout the day. Consider grouping students for brief periods during the day using PPLs and error analyses as the basis for the groupings. Consider cross-grade groupings with fellow teachers. Cross-grade groupings are based on PPLs and error analyses.

Keep track of the student's progress and yield to results. Develop new strategies if the present ones are not working, as indicated by your data.

CBA defines success for each student as growth beyond the student's present performance level. Success is not defined as the attainment of a particular goal or objective used for an entire class of students. It is not defined as being the best in class or scoring high on a standardized test. Success is growth and improvement, measured on an individualized basis.

Used correctly, CBA guarantees all students a measure of sought-after academic success. Since you will have determined through your probes the entering skills for each of your students, you will know each student's individual instructional levels. Do your best to ensure a good curriculum fit between your assignments and your students' varying instructional levels, and you will help your students attain the growth we all want for them.

Discussion Questions

1. Read the following three paragraphs and see whether you can identify the antecedents or setting events, target behavior, and consequences of each:
   a. When Miguel is part of a large group and is getting little attention from his teacher, he is most likely to yell an obscenity in order to have his teacher remind him that obscenities are not nice.
   b. When Tanya has difficulty with her reading assignment, she closes her book and puts her head on her desk in order to avoid having to complete her work. Seeing Tanya with her head down, the teacher chooses not to call on her.
   c. When Paul is with Mr. Lee in language arts, he is always ready with an answer to a comprehension question and always willing to read a passage from an assigned chapter. Mr. Lee calls on Paul often.

2. Discuss the differences between a functional assessment of a student's challenging behavior and a standardized behavioral assessment. What may be the useful outcomes of each for the classroom teacher?

3. What does the statement "Behaviors never occur in isolation" mean?

4. What kind of information may be collected about a student's environment when completing a functional assessment of a target behavior?

5. Discuss how the data collection tools outlined and described in Chapter 3 may be used to help teachers complete a functional analysis.

6. Based on your previous observations of student behavior, discuss examples where a student exhibited undesirable behavior that served a functional purpose for the student. How were these situations resolved?

7. Are there examples in your school where undesirable behavior has a payoff for students? How can this be resolved?

8. What are the advantages of curriculum-based assessment compared with standardized assessment? Consider the following variables: (a) quality of information provided to the teacher, (b) quality of information provided for direct instructional use, (c) student feedback, and (d) parent–teacher communication.

9. For the classroom teacher, what are the benefits of a curriculum-based assessment in regard to the evaluation of student academic performance?

10. What is the difference between a "probe" (as discussed in this chapter) and a typical classroom "test"?

References

Ayllon, T., & Michael, J. (1959). The psychiatric nurse as a behavior engineer. *Journal of Experimental Analysis of Behavior, 2,* 323–334.

Barnhill, G. P. (2005). Functional behavioral assessment in schools. *Intervention in School and Clinic, 40*(3), 131–143.

Blakeley-Smith, A., Carr, E. G., Cale, S. I., & Owen-DeSchryver, J. S. (2009). Environmental fit: A model for assessing and treating problem behavior associated with curricular difficulties in children with autism spectrum disorders. *Focus on Autism and Other Developmental Disorders, 24*(3), 131–145.

Blankenship, C. S. (1985). Using curriculum-based assessment data to make instructional decisions. *Exceptional Children, 52,* 233–238.

Boyajian, A. E., DuPaul, G. J., Handler, M. W., Eckert, T. L., & McGoey, K. E. (2001). The use of classroom based brief functional analyses with preschools at-risk for Attention Deficit Hyperactivity Disorder. *School Psychology Review, 30*(2), 278–294.

Center, D. B., Dietz, S. M., & Kaufman, M. E. (1982). Student ability, task difficulty and inappropriate classroom behavior. *Behavior Modification, 6,* 355–375.

Choate, J. S., Enright, B. E., Miller, L. J., Poteet, J. A., & Rakes, T. A. (1992). *Curriculum-based assessment and programming.* Boston: Allyn & Bacon.

Cole, C. L., Davenport, T. A., & Bambara, L. M. (1997). Effects of choice and task preference on the work performance of students with behavior problems. *Behavior Disorders, 22,* 65–74.

Cunningham, E. M., & O'Neill, R. E. (2007). Agreement of functional behavioral assessment and analysis methods with students with EBD. *Behavioral Disorders, 32*(3), 211–221.

Deno, S. (1985). Curriculum-based measurement: The emerging alternative. *Exceptional Children, 52,* 219–232.

Dunlap, G., dePerczel, M., Clark, S., Wilson, D., Wright, S., White, R., & Gomez, A. (1994). Choice making to promote adaptive behavior for students with emotional and behavioral challenges. *Journal of Applied Behavior Analysis, 27,* 505–518.

Foster-Johnson, L., Ferro, J., & Dunlap, G. (1994). Preferred curricular activities and reduced behaviors in students with intellectual disabilities. *Journal of Applied Behavior Analysis, 27,* 493–504.

Gickling, E. E., & Havertape, J. F. (1981). Curriculum-based assessment. In J. A. Tucker (Ed.), *Non-test-based assessment.* Minneapolis: University of Minnesota.

Gresham, F. M., Watson, T. S., & Skinner, C. H. (2001). Functional behavioral assessments: Principles, procedures, and future directions. *School Psychology Review, 30*(2), 156–172.

Hoff, K. E., Ervin, R. A., & Friman, P. C. (2005). Refining functional behavioral assessment: Analyzing the separate and combined effects of hypothesized controlling variables during ongoing classroom routines. *School Psychology Review, 34*(1), 45–57.

Howell, K. W., Fox, S. L., & Morehead, M. K. (1993). *Curriculum-based evaluation: Teaching and decision making.* Pacific Grove, CA: Brooks/Cole.

Idol, L., Nevin, A., & Paolucci-Whitcomb, P. (1986). *Models of curriculum-based assessment.* Rockville, MD: Aspen.

Idol, L., Nevin, A., & Paolucci-Whitcomb, P. (1999). *Models of curriculum-based assessment: A blueprint for learning.* Austin, TX: Pro-Ed.

Kearney, C. A. (2004). The functional assessment of school refusal behavior. *Behavior Analysis Today, 5*(3), 275–283.

Kearney, C. A., & Albano, A. M. (2004). The functional profiles of school refusal behavior: Diagnostic aspects. *Behavior Modification, 28,* 147–161.

King-Sears, M. E. (1994). *Curriculum-based assessment in special education.* San Diego, CA: Singular.

Macht, J. E. (1998). *Special education's failed system: A question of eligibility.* Westport, CT: Bergin & Garvey.

Michael, J., & Meyerson, L. (1962). A behavioral approach to human control. *Harvard Educational Review, 32,* 382–402.

Miltenberger, R. G. (2001). *Behavior modification: Principles and procedures*. Belmont, CA: Wadsworth.

Murdick, N. L., Gartin, B. C., & Stockall, N. (2003). Step by step: How to meet the functional assessment of behavior requirements of IDEA. *Beyond Behavior, 12*(2), 25–30.

O'Neill, R. E., Horner, R. H., Albin, R. W., Sprague, J. R., Storey, K., & Newton, J. S. (1997). *Functional assessment and program development for problem behavior: A practical handbook* (2nd ed.). Pacific Grove, CA: Brooks/Cole.

Park, K. L. (2007). Facilitating effective team-based functional behavior assessment in typical school settings. *Beyond Behavior,* Fall, 21–31.

Scott, T. M., Bucalos, A., Liaupsin, C., Nelson, C. M., Jolivette, K., & DeShea, L. (2004). Using functional behavior assessment in general education settings: Making a case for effectiveness and efficiency. *Behavioral Disorders, 29*(2), 189–201.

Scott, T. M., & Kamps, D. M. (2007). The future of functional behavioral assessment in school settings. *Behavioral disorders, 32*(3), 146–157.

Shapiro, E. S., & Derr, T. F. (1990). Curriculum-based assessment. *The handbook of school psychology* (2nd ed., pp. 365–387). New York: Wiley.

Shapiro, E. S., & Lentz, F. E. (1985). Assessing academic behavior: A behavioral approach. *School Psychology Review, 14,* 325–338.

Shapiro, E. S., & Lentz, F. E. (1986). Behavioral assessment of academic behavior. In T. R. Kratochwill (Ed.), *Advances in school psychology* (Vol. 5, pp. 87–139). Hillsdale, NJ: Erlbaum.

Shinn, M. (1989). *Curriculum-based measurement: Assessing special children*. New York: Guilford.

Skinner, B. F. (1953). *Science and human behavior*. New York: MacMillan.

Sulzer-Azaroff, B., & Mayer, G. R. (1991). *Behavior analysis for lasting change*. Fort Worth, TX: Harcourt Brace College.

Thorndike, E. L. (1932). *The fundamentals of learning*. New York: Teachers College Press.

Ulrich, R., Stachnik, T., & Mabry, J. (1966). *Control of human behavior*. Glenview, IL: Scott, Foresman.

Watson, J. (1924). *Behaviorism*. New York: Norton.

Watson, T. S., Gresham, F. M., & Skinner, C. H. (2001). Introduction to the mini-series: Issues and procedures for implementing functional behavior assessments in schools. *School Psychology Review, 30*(2), 153–155.

Witt, J. C., Elliot, S. N., Daly, E. J., III, Gresham, F. M., & Kramer, J. J. (1998). *Assessment of at-risk and special needs children*. Boston: McGraw-Hill.

STRATEGIES FOR INCREASING POSITIVE BEHAVIORAL SUPPORTS

Positive Behavioral Supports: Reinforcement Strategies

CHAPTER 10

Thomas J. Zirpoli

The teacher must plan for a learning environment that supports the development of skills that promote successful academic and social interaction in the classroom. In short positive behavioral support is a method of considering how the environment might make success more likely for all students.

—STROUT (2005, P. 3)

*P*ositive behavioral support (PBS) refers to the use of positive reinforcement strategies as the principal method of changing behavior. Safran and Oswald (2003) state, "Interventions within the PBS umbrella are built on the foundations of applied behavior analysis (ABA) and repackaged in a more positive, collaborative, and holistic framework" and thus are "more acceptable to practitioners in educational settings" (p. 361).

All students exhibit at least some appropriate behaviors throughout each day. Too often, however, teachers ignore students when they behave appropriately and are doing what they were asked to do. Research has demonstrated that when students are reinforced for appropriate behaviors, they will exhibit such behavior more frequently (Skinner, 1938, 1969; Tankersley, 1995) and engage in challenging behavior less frequently (Beare, Severson, & Brandt, 2004). Even teacher behavior has been shown to be malleable to reinforcement strategies (DiGennaro, Martens, & McIntyre, 2005). In spite of this evidence, Beaman and Wheldall (2000) found that "there is little evidence to suggest that teachers universally, systematically deploy contingent praise as positive reinforcement" and that "praise for appropriate classroom social behavior is only rarely observed" (p. 431). Unfortunately, it is easier for teachers to focus on inappropriate behavior, and students soon learn to behave poorly in order to gain attention (Bandura, 1973; Beaman & Wheldall, 2000; Maag, 2001).

Positive behavioral supports developed through the implementation of simple reinforcement strategies, employed at the classroom level by classroom teachers, can have a significant influence on the social climate of an entire school (Willert & Willert, 2000). They also can make teaching classroom social skills fun for both teachers and students (Babyak, Luze, & Kamps, 2000).

REINFORCEMENT

Definition

Reinforcement is any stimulus that maintains or increases the behavior exhibited immediately prior to the presentation of the stimulus. However, a stimulus takes on the value of a reinforcer only if it has been demonstrated that the behavior it followed was maintained (at the current rate, duration, or intensity) or increased (from the current rate, duration, or intensity). If the rate, duration, or intensity of the behavior is not maintained or increased after a stimulus, then that stimulus cannot be considered a reinforcer.

For example, when a classroom teacher provides her students with social praise following appropriate behavior in the cafeteria, the social praise (a potentially reinforcing stimulus) may be defined as an effective reinforcer if the praise maintains or increases the students' appropriate cafeteria behavior in the future. However, if the teacher notes that appropriate cafeteria behaviors have not been maintained or improved, then the teacher's social praise cannot be considered a reinforcer in that case. The teacher may need to consider another, more powerful reinforcer or a variation to her social praise. In summary, teachers cannot assume that an item, activity, or other stimulus will be reinforcing to a student; this can only be determined by testing the effect of the potential reinforcer on the student's behavior, as discussed later in this chapter.

It is also important to note that a stimulus may act as a reinforcer for one behavior but not for a second behavior, even if the same student is exhibiting both behaviors. For example, while a young student may maintain appropriate classroom behavior in response to social praise, other, more powerful reinforcers, such as positive notes home or a token economy program, may be necessary to maintain acceptable academic performance. Also, items and activities considered reinforcing for one student may not be so for another student, even if the students are the same age or in the same grade.

Types of Reinforcers

The list of potential reinforcers for students is limited only by a teacher's imagination. Reinforcers may be verbal statements, foods and drinks, objects, time to participate in preferred activities, and so on. Teachers should not limit their understanding of reinforcers to giving candy. In fact, young children will quickly become satiated when food, especially candy, is used as a reinforcer. *Satiation* refers to a condition in which a current reinforcer loses its reinforcement value. That is, the reinforcer is no longer maintaining the target behavior. For example, when food is used as a reinforcer, a child may become too full to want additional reinforcers. Thus, teachers are encouraged to consider other types of reinforcers before edibles: More attention should be given to the use of praise (Lampi, Fenty, & Beaunae, 2005; McVey, 2001), reinforcing activities, and other social opportunities students enjoy. These types of reinforcers may serve both as reinforcers and learning opportunities for students of all ages.

In a study of specific reinforcers used in schools, Gottfredson and Gottfredson (2001) found that 96% of schools used informal recognition; 95%, formal recognition (certificates, etc.); 87%, jobs or privileges; 84%, activities; 82%, social rewards; 81%, material rewards; 61%, token reinforcers; and 8%, money.

Reinforcement may be positive or negative. Both positive *reinforcement* and *negative reinforcement* increase behavior. The word *positive* refers to the *presentation* of a stimulus following a behavior, not the nature of the stimulus itself. In turn, the word *negative* refers to the *removal* of a stimulus; it does not describe the quality of the stimulus. Also, as discussed later, reinforcers may be *primary* or *secondary*. Both primary and secondary reinforcement increase or maintain target behaviors.

POSITIVE REINFORCEMENT   *Positive reinforcement* is the contingent *provision* of a stimulus (e.g., a treat, an object, or an activity) following a target behavior, which results in an increase or a maintenance of the frequency, duration, and/or intensity of the target behavior (Skinner, 1938, 1969). For example, letting a student spend extra time playing with the classroom computer (stimulus) after the student completes specific classroom tasks (response) may be considered positive reinforcement *if* the future rate of the target behavior (completing specific classroom tasks) is increased or maintained. Positive reinforcement is recommended as the intervention of first choice when trying to teach new behaviors, increase appropriate behaviors, or decrease inappropriate behavior. Many researchers have used the simple provision of positive reinforcement in the form of verbal praise to help teachers increase academic performance and decrease the frequency of disruptive classroom behavior (Gresham, Ramsey, & Walker, 2003; Kennedy & Jolivette, 2008).

NEGATIVE REINFORCEMENT   *Negative reinforcement* is the contingent *removal* of a stimulus following a target behavior, which results in an increase or a maintenance of the frequency, duration, and/or intensity of the target behavior (Pfiffner & O'Leary, 1987). Usually, the removed stimulus is an aversive stimulus. Negative reinforcement is *not* punishment; again, the effect of negative reinforcement is an *increase* in the target behavior, not a *decrease*, which would be the effect of a punishing stimulus. Unfortunately, negative reinforcement plays an important role in reinforcing many problematic behaviors, from food refusal (Kitfield & Masalsky, 2000; Levin & Carr, 2001) to self-injurious behaviors (Iwata et al., 1994). According to Cipani and Spooner (1997, p. 339), "Addressing all problem behaviors as if they are a function of positive reinforcement omits a vast array of behavioral strategies that can potentially control behavior that is maintained by negative reinforcement" (p. 339).

Two variations of negative reinforcement can be used. In the first variation, the student performs the target behavior to escape an *ongoing* aversive stimulus (Iwata, 1987). For example, when a teacher tells a student he must remain in the time-out corner until he no longer exhibits tantrum behavior, that teacher is using negative reinforcement. The purpose here is to teach the student to perform a target behavior (nontantrum behavior) in order to have the aversive stimulus (remaining in the time-out corner) removed. In a second variation, the student performs the target behavior in order to avoid a *potential* or *likely* aversive stimulus. For example, when a student performs a target behavior (studying a history lesson) in order to avoid a threatened, aversive stimulus (receiving a failing grade), then the target behavior is maintained by negative reinforcement.

Negative reinforcement is quite different from positive reinforcement, with numerous disadvantages. It involves removing an aversive event contingent on a specific target behavior. Thus, the students focus their attention on avoiding the aversive event.

Another significant disadvantage of negative reinforcement in applied settings is the escape and avoidance behavior produced when students are trying to behave appropriately in order to avoid an aversive stimulus. For example, consider the differences between two classrooms. In classroom A, the students behave appropriately because their teacher recognizes their good behavior and the students enjoy his or her attention (positive reinforcement). The students in classroom A are likely to enjoy school and have a healthy attitude about learning. In contrast, the students in classroom B behave appropriately only to avoid their teacher's aversive behavior (negative reinforcement). The students in classroom B probably do not like going to school and are not motivated, except by fear and anxiety, to do well. Some of the students may try to avoid or escape this situation by skipping school or dropping out of school altogether. These side effects represent the primary reasons why negative reinforcement is not recommended as a preferred intervention.

The relationships among the type of reinforcement, stimulus, and outcome for target behavior are as follows:

Reinforcement	Stimulus	Target Behavior
Positive	Presented	Increases
Negative	Removed	Increases

PRIMARY REINFORCERS   *Primary reinforcers* are stimuli that are naturally reinforcing to individuals—food, liquids, and warmth, for example. In other words, they are unlearned or unconditioned. Individuals do not have to be taught that eating tasty food or drinking refreshing drinks will make them feel good (naturally reinforcing).

SECONDARY REINFORCERS   *Secondary reinforcers* are stimuli that are *not* naturally reinforcing. Their value to the individual has been learned or conditioned through an association, or a *pairing*, with primary reinforcers. For example, when a preschool teacher pairs giving verbal praise (a potential secondary reinforcer) with delivering a glass of juice (a primary reinforcer) to a young child, the verbal praise takes on some of the reinforcement value associated with the glass of juice. The purpose here is to *fade out*, or decrease, the use of juice as a reinforcer and *fade in*, or increase, the value of verbal praise. If successful, verbal praise will become a secondary reinforcer capable of maintaining or increasing the target behavior.

SOCIALLY VALID REINFORCERS   A reinforcer is considered *socially valid* when its provision is congruent with the norms of the student's social setting. The variables that determine what is socially valid include culture, setting, age of the student, the specific situation, and the relationship between the teacher and the student. For example, patting a child on the buttocks may be a socially acceptable form of reinforcement among football players on the playing field (setting); in a different setting (a classroom), this same form of reinforcement is not socially acceptable. And teachers should not forget the power of peers in both social skills training and reinforcement (e.g., Blake, Wang, Cartledge, & Gardner, 2000). Thus, considering all these variables is important when selecting reinforcers and developing a reinforcement menu.

As stated, a reinforcer is considered socially valid when it is consistent with the norms of the student's social setting. Sometimes, however, effective reinforcement means using reinforcers, at least temporarily, that may not be consistent with the "typical" social behavior of a setting. For example, giving students points for completing classroom tasks may not be a natural consequence or socially congruent with the "real" world. Used temporarily, however, as an initial step to manage behavior and with the objective of eventually fading the point system to a more natural or typical social reinforcement (verbal praise), the use of extrinsic reinforcement is clearly a worthy investment.

EXTRINSIC VERSUS INTRINSIC REINFORCEMENT Extrinsic rewards are observable (e.g., giving a child extra time on the classroom computer following the completing of 30 minutes of on-task reading). Intrinsic rewards are internal motivators (e.g., a child reads a book because the activity itself is enjoyable; an extrinsic or external reinforcement is not necessary for the child to complete the task).

An ongoing debate regarding the use of extrinsic reinforcement is the effect these reinforcers have on a student's intrinsic motivation to complete a task or behave a certain way. Other concerns include speculation that extrinsic reinforcers decrease students' creativity, self-esteem, competence, and impede a student's learning. However, a review of the literature on the effects of extrinsic reinforcement by Akin-Little, Eckert, Lovett, and Little (2004, p. 344) concludes that "little detrimental effect is found with the use of external reinforcement" and that receiving extrinsic reinforcement does not harm a student's intrinsic motivation (Cameron, 2001).

Identify High-Preferenced Reinforcers

High-preferenced activities (e.g., a computer game, free time, recess) frequently serve as excellent secondary reinforcers. Premack (1959) promotes the idea of using high-preferenced activities as reinforcement for the completion of low-preferenced activities. Keyes (1994) demonstrated the *Premack principle* when he reinforced fourth and fifth graders with increasing amounts of time on the classroom computer as they completed increasingly higher levels of academic tasks.

Research has demonstrated that high-preference items and activities serve as the most effective reinforcers in behavior management programs, even if the activity is socially restricted (Boyd, Alter, & Conroy, 2005). And researchers have found several ways to identify high-preference reinforcers. Using the most functional approach, teachers can simply observe and record what students do during both instructional and free-time activities to see what they like (What toys they play with most, etc.)

A more systematic method of developing a list of effective reinforcers is through trial and error or *preference assessment*. A systematic assessment, conducted by direct observation, of different reinforcers for both their preference and influence on behavior is likely to produce the most potent list of reinforcers. For example, Galensky, Miltenberger, Stricker, and Garlinghouse (2001) demonstrated what they called a *stimulus preference assessment*, also called a *choice assessment*, with three children in order to determine preferred foods over nonpreferred foods to be used as part of a reinforcement program. They simply presented food items two at a time and asked the children, separately, to select their preference from the two choices. Each of six food items was presented five times, each time with a different alternative. Preference was determined by the number of times each food item was chosen across the five trials. This same process may also be used to identify high-preference stimuli among toys, activities, and so on. The reinforcement value of these high-preference stimuli is then evaluated. In other words, while the item or activity may be preferred over other tested items, the real test of any stimuli is determining if the item or activity increases the behavior it is meant to reinforce. This second phase is referred to as *reinforcer assessments*.

A systematic trial-and-error assessment of potential reinforcers tends to produce a more accurate list of effective reinforcers than teacher predictions. Surveying students' preferences also yielded effective reinforcers (Northrup, 2000; Payne, Mancil, & Landers, 2005).

The following list provides some suggestions for reinforcers:

Tangible	Social	Activities
Stars	Verbal recognition	Choice time
Rubber stamps	Verbal praise	Lunch with teacher
Check marks	Student of the day	Read a story
Points	First in line	Pass out materials
Toys	Leader of the day	Feed class pet
Edibles	Phone call home	Use computer
Magazines	Note home	Run errands
Puzzles	Activity leader	Listen to tape

ESTABLISHING AN EFFECTIVE REINFORCEMENT PROGRAM

Implementing a reinforcement system does not have to be a significant change to an already established classroom program. Classroom reinforcement strategies may include simple changes in activity schedules or a simple commitment on the part of teachers to increase their attention to appropriate behaviors. Teachers should review the schedule of typical activities in which students participate within the educational setting and ask the following questions:

- How may some of these activities, which are known reinforcers to the students, be used to reinforce appropriate behaviors?
- How may some students, as a result of appropriate behaviors, have greater access to preferred activities within the educational setting?
- How may students' schedules be manipulated so that less desirable tasks and activities are followed by more desirable activities?

As mentioned at the beginning of the chapter, teachers may easily fall into the habit of ignoring appropriate behaviors and instead may focus on inappropriate behaviors. Developing a reinforcement program may help busy teachers ensure that they will pay attention to appropriate behaviors.

Reinforcement is most effective in maintaining or increasing a target behavior when it is individualized for a particular student and when it is presented contingent on the target behavior (Keyes, 1994). Other factors associated with the effective use of reinforcement include these:

- *Immediacy of the reinforcement.* As the interval between the behavior and reinforcement increases, the relative effectiveness of the reinforcer decreases. At least initially, an effective reinforcement program provides reinforcement immediately after the target behavior. Later, the latency between the behavior and reinforcement may be increased.

Allowing extra time on the computer and other desired classroom activities may serve as effective and functional reinforcers.

- *Behavior-specific praise.*   When presenting verbal praise, be specific in what behavior you are reinforcing (Fullerton, Conroy, Correa, 2009; Stormont & Reinke, 2009). For example, "John, thank you for raising your hand" when giving John verbal praise for raising his hand.
- *Combining verbal praise with the reinforcement.*   When presenting the reinforcer, remind the student of the behavior that entitled him or her to the reinforcer so that an association is built between the appropriate behavior and reinforcer. Also, the learned association between the reinforcer and verbal praise will increase the reinforcement properties of verbal praise.
- *Schedule of reinforcement.*   During the initial phase of the reinforcement schedule, reinforce the student after every occurrence of the target behavior. This also develops a link between the appropriate behavior you want to increase and reinforcement. Later in the program, continuous schedules of reinforcement should be faded to intermittent schedules. These schedules are discussed later in this chapter.
- *Type of reinforcement.*   Some reinforcers will be more effective than others depending on the student's individual preferences. By asking the student and testing

different potential reinforcers, teachers can generate a *reinforcement menu* (a list of potential reinforcers from which a student may select a single reinforcer).

- ***Quality and quantity of reinforcement.***   The quality of a reinforcer refers to its freshness and the immediacy of its effect on behavior. Teachers need to determine the right quantity of reinforcers to deliver—just enough to make the program interesting yet not too much so that the student becomes satiated.
- ***Who provides the reinforcement.***   Reinforcers are more effective when they are given by significant others or by people the student likes or admires. When provided by people the student does not like or trust, they may lose some or all of their reinforcing properties.
- ***Consistency.***   The reinforcement program should be followed consistently. Moreover, all other teachers who come in contact with the student should understand and implement the program consistently.

When developing an effective reinforcement program, teachers need to balance spontaneity and structure. That is, although the program must be planned and systematically applied, teachers also need to be spontaneous in delivering reinforcers. We will outline some important elements in developing an effective reinforcement program in the following sections.

Establishing Clear and Consistent Expectations

Teachers need to be clear and direct in identifying behaviors which are and are not acceptable within the different school environments (Hardman & Smith, 1999). These are sometimes referred to as "Precorrective Statements" or "descriptions of behavior expectations for different settings that are specific and proactive" (Stormont & Reinke, 2009, p. 26). Clear instructions outline behavioral expectations in *specific* and *observable* terms. For example, the rule "Respect others" does have an appealing sound and is certainly a worthy goal for all individuals. However, the rule fails to outline the specific behaviors that demonstrate respect for others and the precise behaviors that violate this rule. Teachers need to be more detailed, such as "Never hit other children," "Say 'excuse me' before interrupting others," "Ask permission before taking things that don't belong to you," "Say 'please' and 'thank you,'" and so on. These examples are specific and observable.

Rules and expectations for behavior should be stated in positive terms whenever possible. Instead of saying, "Don't take things without permission," say, "Ask permission before taking things." Small differences such as this make significant differences in the student's environment by creating a positive, affirming atmosphere. When most rules state what students *cannot* do, then the focus of adult attention will likely be on the punishment of inappropriate behaviors, not the establishment of positive behavioral supports. When the rules state what students *can* do, then teachers will tend to focus on the reinforcement of appropriate behaviors. Rules concerning some inappropriate behaviors, however, such as hitting, need to be stated directly. As a guideline, plan to state at least three appropriate-behavior rules for every inappropriate-behavior rule.

Rules and behavioral expectations are taught through direct instruction. In addition, rules are more likely to be followed if expectations are "consistently taught, encouraged and reinforced on a daily basis. When teachers are inconsistent, it portrays to students that the rules are not always applicable or in force, setting the occasion for students to test the applicability of rules" (Strout, 2005, p. 7).

Teachers Must Set the Example

Once rules and expectations are established, teachers need to be consistent in following them, acting themselves as models of appropriate behavior. If teachers ask students to say "please" and "thank you," then the teachers should use "please" and "thank you" when talking to the students. If the rule says "No yelling," then teachers should set the example. Similarly, if parents spank children, they should not be surprised if their children are aggressive and attempt also to solve their problems by hitting. Remember, children learn from watching others, especially significant others such as parents and teachers.

The Delivery of Reinforcers

After you have established your rules and expectations, discussed them with the students, and outlined a reinforcement menu, the next step is to develop a reinforcement delivery program. Reinforcers are most effective in increasing behaviors when they are delivered

- immediately after the behavior you intend to increase,
- when they are fresh (the child is not satiated with the reinforcer), and
- by significant adults whom the student admires.

The methods of delivering reinforcers to students are as endless as the selection of reinforcers. Again, teachers are encouraged to use their imaginations. The important guidelines here are for teachers to be *consistent* and to *make it fun*. If the reinforcement program is developed for an entire classroom, teachers may want to establish a token economy reinforcement program as described later in this chapter. When this program is targeted to change a specific behavior for one child, then the following steps will be helpful.

First, as previously stated, try to describe the target behavior in positive terms. For example, if Robert will not sit in his chair for longer than a few seconds at a time, state the target behavior in terms of *increasing* Robert's in-seat behavior. In this way, teachers will more likely focus on reinforcing the appropriate behavior (Robert's in-seat behavior) instead of the inappropriate behavior (Robert's out-of-seat behavior).

Second, collect baseline data on how often the student currently stays in his seat. Baseline data, as outlined in Chapter 6, measure a student's behavior before the introduction of a behavior change program. This involves measuring, for 30 to 60 minutes per day, for about 4 days, the number of seconds or minutes (duration) the student is currently staying in his seat. Calculate the average duration (total duration of sitting divided by number of observation periods), and this average will serve as the baseline for the student's sitting behavior. An example of baseline data would be to determine, through direct observation, that Robert currently averages 90 seconds of in-seat behavior per 30 minutes of classroom observation.

Third, the teacher should establish an appropriate *program goal*. That is, given the student's age and program needs, how many minutes is it reasonable to expect him or her to sit? Consistent with the earlier example, say the program goal is to teach Robert to stay in his seat for 15 consecutive minutes. Baseline data, the program goal, and the overall behavior change program should be shared with Robert. His teacher should explain to him why his in-seat behavior needs to increase and how he will be reinforced for longer periods of in-seat behavior.

Fourth, given the gap between the baseline data or current level of performance (90 seconds of in-seat behavior) and the program goal (15 minutes of in-seat behavior), the teacher should determine a *reinforcement schedule* to reinforce behaviors (i.e., longer periods of sitting) that will bring the student closer to the program goal. Given our example, phase 1 of the reinforcement schedule may include reinforcing Robert each time he stays in his seat for two consecutive minutes. Phase 2 may include reinforcing him each time he stays in his seat for three consecutive minutes. Phase 3 may include reinforcing him for five consecutive minutes of in-seat behavior, and so on. The last phase of the reinforcement schedule would include reinforcing Robert for 15 consecutive minutes, the program goal.

The speed of progression from one phase to the next will depend on the child's progress for each phase. A *performance criterion* for moving from one phase of the reinforcement schedule to the next should be established. For example, the criterion for moving from phase 1 to phase 2 may state that "Robert must meet the objective of phase 1, staying in his seat for two consecutive minutes, for two consecutive observation periods." When this criterion is reached, the reinforcement schedule changes as outlined in phase 2.

Several other reinforcement schedule variations are available. Understanding these different reinforcement delivery schedules will help caregivers develop effective and individualized reinforcement delivery plans.

Preventing Reinforcement Satiation

Giving students a variety of reinforcement choices (reinforcement menu) is important because a single reinforcer may quickly lose its appeal. Students may become satiated when the same reinforcement is used too frequently. Moreover, what may be reinforcing one day may not be reinforcing another day, even with the same student. Having a variety of reinforcers to select from allows teachers to keep the reinforcement program fresh and exciting for teachers and students (Egel, 1981).

Too often, teachers blame a reinforcement program for "not working" instead of evaluating the effectiveness of the selected reinforcers. Egel (1981) found that when the same reinforcer was presented, correct responses and on-task behavior declined over time. Varying the reinforcers, however, produced significantly improved and consistent responding. Egel's study "provides further documentation of the importance of providing variation within the teaching situation" (p. 345).

Teachers may prevent reinforcement satiation by

- varying the reinforcer or using a different reinforcer for each target behavior,
- monitoring the amount of reinforcement delivered and using only enough to maintain the target behavior,
- avoiding edible reinforcers (if you must use them, do so minimally and offer a variety),
- moving from a constant to an intermittent schedule of reinforcement as soon as possible, and
- shifting from primary to secondary reinforcers as soon as possible.

SCHEDULES OF REINFORCEMENT

A *reinforcement schedule* refers to the frequency or timing of the delivery of reinforcement following a specific target behavior or general appropriate behavior. The specific schedule of reinforcement delivery has been found to have significant effects on the target behavior. For example, Cuvo, Lerch, Leurquin, Gaffaney, and Poppen (1998) found that while young children tended to maximize reinforcement and minimize work when given a choice, they switched to the greater work choice when reinforcement on the easier choice was thinned. Thus, they were willing to engage in a greater workload associated with a richer reinforcement schedule.

A reinforcer may be delivered on a *continuous* or *intermittent* schedule. When a student is reinforced each and every time the target behavior is exhibited, a continuous schedule of reinforcement is being employed. Although not always the case, the initiation of a continuous reinforcement program is usually best until an association between the target behavior and reinforcement is established. For example, Newman and Buffington (1995) found that a continuous schedule was more effective in teaching students to follow instructions. A continuous schedule is recommended for working with young children or teaching a new behavior. As discussed earlier, this schedule should then be faded to an intermittent or more natural socially acceptable schedule.

When a student is reinforced after some occurrences, but not each and every one of the specific target behaviors, an intermittent schedule of reinforcement is being employed. An intermittent schedule is used after the student has learned that there is an association between the target behavior and the reinforcer, and the teacher wants to fade (sometimes referred to as *thinning*) to a more natural reinforcement schedule. We will outline variations of the continuous and intermittent schedules of reinforcement.

Ratio Reinforcement Schedules

A ratio reinforcement schedule consists of reinforcing a person contingent on an established *number of occurrences* of the target behavior. Although the specific number of occurrences may be fixed or variable, a ratio schedule is always based on the number of behavior occurrences exhibited. For example, reinforcing a student after a specific number of tasks is completed means that a ratio schedule of reinforcement is being employed.

FIXED RATIO SCHEDULES   Reinforcing a student each and every time the target behavior occurs is called a *fixed ratio of one* (FR1) schedule of reinforcement (also called a *continuous schedule of reinforcement*). If, however, a teacher reinforces a student every second time the target behavior is exhibited, then this would be considered *a fixed ratio of two*, or FR2, schedule of reinforcement. Reinforcing a child every third time the target behavior is exhibited would be an example of a *fixed ratio of three* (FR3), and so on. An advantage of fixed ratio schedules is that they provide a systematic schedule of reinforcement; caregivers know exactly when to reinforce the target behavior based on a fixed number of behaviors.

VARIABLE RATIO SCHEDULES   When a student is reinforced following a variable ratio schedule, reinforcement is delivered following an *average* number of behavior occurrences. For example, when a student is reinforced on an average of every third time she says "please," the schedule would be considered a *variable ratio of three*, or VR3. Variable ratio schedules of reinforcement are not recommended because the delivery of reinforcers for appropriate behavior may become less systematic and consistent. Some teachers may find it difficult to monitor the delivery of reinforcement based on an average number of behaviors. Because a fixed ratio schedule is easier to monitor, it will probably result in a more consistent application of the reinforcement program.

Interval Reinforcement Schedules

An interval schedule of reinforcement provides reinforcement after an established *interval of time* has elapsed, contingent on a target behavior occurring during the interval. Although the specific interval or length of time between reinforcers may be fixed or variable, an interval schedule is always based on the passage of time. Delivering reinforcement following a specific period of time is best for behaviors that can be measured in terms of duration. In-seat and on-task behaviors, for example, can be measured by duration as well as frequency. Thus, when trying to decrease a student's out-of-seat behavior, teachers will find that reinforcing periods of in-seat behavior with an interval reinforcement schedule, as demonstrated in Classroom Connection 10.1, is more functional and effective than with a ratio schedule. In another example, Conyers, Miltenberger, Romaniuk, Kopp, and Himle (2003) used tokens to reinforce intervals of appropriate behavior to effectively reduce disruptive behavior within a preschool program.

CLASSROOM CONNECTION 10.1
Example of Using an Interval Schedule of Reinforcement

Ann, a middle school teacher, has a student named Paul who frequently gets out of his seat and walks around the classroom during a 30-minute study hall period, from 2:30 to 3:00 each school day. This behavior is disruptive to the other students trying to study or get a head start on homework assignments before going home. After collecting some baseline data, Ann discoverers that Paul averages about 5 consecutive minutes of sitting at his desk before getting out of his seat. She decides that since Paul is already on a token economy program (discussed later in this chapter), she will reinforce Paul's in-seat behavior on an interval schedule of reinforcement. Her goal is to teach Paul to remain seated (except when he receives permission to get out of his seat) for 15 consecutive minutes.

Ann has a meeting with Paul and tells him that he could earn an extra token whenever he stays in his seat for 5 consecutive minutes. In this new program, she explains, time in-seat will start at 2:30 (the beginning of study hall), and Paul will have opportunities to earn an extra token at 2:35, 2:40, 2:45, 2:50, 2:55, and 3:00. She explains to Paul that during this first phase of the program, he could earn a total of six extra tokens per day. Ann will use the classroom clock to keep track of the time. Ann starts the program and reinforces Paul with a token at the end of each 5-minute interval if he remains seated during the previous 5-minute interval.

After the first week of programming, Ann tells Paul that he is doing very well and that he now needs to remain seated for 10 consecutive minutes to earn extra tokens. However, Ann also raises the number of tokens Paul can earn from one to three. During this second phase, Paul is told that he can now earn a total of nine extra tokens (three at 2:40, 2:50, and 3:00).

After another week on phase 2, Ann has another meeting with Paul and tells him that he now has to remain seated for 15 consecutive minutes to receive extra tokens. She also raises the number of extra tokens Paul can earn to six, giving Paul two opportunities to receive reinforcement at 2:45 and 3:00. Paul does very well with this program and frequently earns the full 12 extra tokens during the 30-minute study hall period. Throughout this program, Ann makes it a point to pair the provision of tokens to Paul with social praise.

General Reflection for Classroom Connection 10.1:

A frequent mistake teachers make in setting up reinforcement programs is setting the bar too high for the student to earn reinforcement, especially at the start of the program. As a result, the student never really builds the connection between appropriate behavior and the reinforcement. In the first phase of Ann's program for Paul, Paul had to sit in his seat initially for only 5 minutes to earn a token. Why do you think she picked this time interval as a starting point for Paul's program?

Two primary applications exist for interval reinforcement schedules. In the first application, the student is reinforced after a specific interval of time contingent on the appropriate behavior. For example, when trying to increase in-seat behavior, Ann reinforced Paul after a set interval of time. During the first week of Ann's reinforcement program, Paul was reinforced after 5 consecutive minutes of in-seat behavior. At the end of each time interval, Ann had to decide whether Paul earned the promised reinforcement (extra tokens). If Paul did not remain seated during the previous interval, reinforcement was not provided.

In a second application, teachers could decide to begin a new time interval every time the targeted inappropriate behavior (e.g., getting out of seat) is exhibited. In Classroom Connection 10.1, if Ann wanted to use this second application, she would reset the interval each time Paul got out of his seat. For example, if Paul got out of his seat at 2:31 and returned to his seat at 2:32, his next reinforcement opportunity would be 5 minutes later at 2:37. A new 5-minute interval would begin once Paul returned to his seat.

FIXED INTERVAL SCHEDULES   When a student is reinforced following a specific interval of time (e.g., for every 10 consecutive minutes of appropriate behavior), a *fixed interval of 10 schedule*, or FI10, of reinforcement has been applied. Reinforcement for every 5 consecutive minutes of appropriate behavior is a *fixed interval of 5*, or FI5, and so on. As with fixed ratio schedules, fixed interval schedules provide teachers and parents with a systematic reinforcement schedule; they know exactly when to reinforce the target behavior. In Classroom Connection 10.1, Paul was reinforced on a fixed interval of 5 minutes of in-seat behavior during phase 1, a fixed interval of 10 minutes during phase 2, and a fixed interval of 15 minutes during the last phase of his in-seat behavior program.

VARIABLE INTERVAL SCHEDULES   When a student is reinforced following a variable interval schedule, reinforcement is delivered following an *average* interval of time. For example, reinforcing a student for staying on task for an average of every 10 minutes would be considered a *variable interval of 10*, or VI10. As with variable ratio schedules, variable interval schedules of reinforcement are not recommended at the beginning of a behavior change program when consistency is especially important. Again, some teachers may find it difficult to monitor the delivery based on an average interval of time and to maintain a consistent program of reinforcement delivery. Once a new behavior has been established, however, more intermittent reinforcement schedules, interval and ratio, are very effective (Baer, Blount, Detrich, & Stokes, 1984). A summary of reinforcement schedules is provided in Table 10.1.

TABLE 10.1 Summary of Reinforcement Schedules

	Fixed	Variable
Ratio	Reinforcement is delivered contingent on a *fixed* number of occurrences of the target behavior.	Reinforcement is delivered contingent on an *average* number of occurrences of the target behavior.
Interval	Reinforcement is delivered after a *fixed* interval of time has elapsed, contingent on the occurrence of target behavior during the interval.	Reinforcement is delivered after an *average* interval of time has elapsed, contingent on the occurrence of a target behavior during the interval.

SHAPING AND CHAINING NEW BEHAVIORS

Shaping Behaviors

Shaping refers to the reinforcement of *successive approximations* of a terminal behavior. Generally, shaping is used to teach *new* behaviors and skills—behaviors that are not already part of the student's repertoire. A successive approximation to a terminal behavior may be any intermediate behavior that, when combined with other intermediate behaviors, forms the topography of the terminal behavior. Within each step or successive approximation, responses that meet the criteria for that step are reinforced, while other responses are not (see the differential reinforcement discussion in Chapter 12). As the student moves from one step to the next, the criterion for reinforcement changes as expectations increase. Each step in the shaping process brings the student's behavior closer to the terminal behavior. Classroom Connection 10.2 demonstrates how shaping was used to teach a student how to walk independently from her classroom to a resource room.

In Classroom Connection 10.2, each of the three steps has two substeps: walking with, then without, supervision. Each of the steps and substeps is a successive approximation to the new terminal behavior of walking independently from point A to point D without supervision. The appropriate performance of successive approximations of the terminal behavior was reinforced to shape Aldy's behavior according to the topography of the terminal behavior.

The process of shaping includes several steps:

1. Determine the terminal behavior or behavioral goal.
2. Determine the successive approximations or steps necessary to complete the terminal behavior.
3. Identify a "starting point," or behavior that the student currently performs that approximates either the terminal behavior or the first step to the terminal behavior (Aldy already walks to the restroom, point B, with the rest of her class).
4. Reinforce closer approximations of the terminal behavior until the behavioral criterion for each successive approximation, or step, has been achieved (reinforce improvement, not perfection) (Panyon, 1980).
5. Move from one step to the next until the terminal behavior has been learned/shaped (withhold reinforcement for behaviors that are not clear steps toward the terminal behavior) (Panyon, 1980).

Shaping is generally thought of as a method of teaching *new* behaviors or skills. But it may be used to *modify* the rate, duration, or intensity of current behaviors. Thus, while the basic topography of the behavior remains the same, the dimensions of the topography are gradually modified. Examples of this second application of shaping include increasing motor activities, in-seat behavior, the number of correct responses per specific time interval, and so on.

Shaping may also be used to *decrease* the rate, duration, or intensity of current behaviors. Again, the student is not learning a new response (the purest application of shaping); the student is learning a new topography of a current response. For example, by reinforcing small decreases in the volume of a student's talking within a classroom setting, shaping may be used to modify a current behavior (talking too loud) to a more socially acceptable level of performance.

CLASSROOM CONNECTION 10.2
The Use of Shaping to Teach Independent Travel from Classroom to Resource Room

Aldy, a first grader, was a new student at Luke Elementary. Born and raised in Indonesia, she was attending school in America for the first time. Because of her poor English language skills, Aldy was scheduled to attend an ESL (English as a second language) class every day in the school's resource room. Unfortunately, Luke Elementary is a large school, and the resource room is a significant distance from Aldy's classroom. Aldy, not used to large school buildings, was very anxious about getting lost. Her teacher, Maria, decided to use shaping to teach her how to walk from Aldy's classroom (point A) to the resource room (point D) independently.

Marie noted that on the way to the resource room, Aldy would have to pass the restrooms (point B) and the school cafeteria (point C). To teach Aldy how to walk independently from point A to point D, Marie first showed her how to walk from point A to B with supervision, then without supervision. Correct performance of this behavior was practiced and reinforced for 5 days (the time it took for Aldy to learn

how to walk independently from the classroom to the restrooms).

In a second step, Marie showed Aldy how to walk from point A to point C with supervision, then without supervision. In this second step, the criterion for reinforcement was changed. Aldy was now required to walk all the way to point C without supervision, not just point B. This was also practiced until Aldy could independently walk from the classroom to the cafeteria. Correct responses were reinforced.

In the last step, Marie showed Aldy how to walk from point A to point D with supervision, then without supervision. Within 3 weeks, Aldy learned to independently walk from her classroom to the resource room.

General Reflection for Classroom Connection 10.2:

Can you think of other behaviors in school, in addition to teaching a student how to walk from point A to point B, where shaping would be an appropriate strategy? How would you employ a shaping strategy in decreasing various inappropriate classroom behaviors?

One of the primary advantages of shaping is the emphasis on reinforcing appropriate behaviors (successive approximations) as a strategy for teaching new or modified behaviors. Also, the process involved in shaping new behaviors forces teachers to evaluate the student's current performance (baseline), to review the topography of the terminal behavior, and to establish a systematic program for the delivery of reinforcement.

Chaining Behaviors

Chaining refers to the performance of a series or sequence of behaviors rather than just one independent behavior. For example, if a classroom teacher wants students to walk into the classroom, hang up their coats, put their lunch boxes into their lockers, and sit at their desks, these four behaviors may be taught separately or together as one *behavior chain*. Each of the four behaviors serves as a link in the behavior chain. Each link serves as a *discriminative stimulus* S[D] for the performance of the next link or response and as a conditioned reinforcer for the previous link:

Step One: Walking into their classroom.

Step Two: Hanging up their coats.

Step Three: Putting their lunch boxes into their lockers.

Step Four: Sitting at their desks.

In our example, walking into the classroom serves as the S^D for the students to hang up their coats. Hanging up their coats serves as the S^D for putting their lunch boxes in their lockers, and putting their lunch boxes away serves as the S^D for sitting at their desks.

The development of a behavior chain, or any chain of skills, is called a *task analysis*. In the previous example, the four behavior links make up a task analysis of the teacher's expectations for her students when they walk into the classroom. Later we provide a task analysis for washing hands. Notice how much more detail is provided in the washing hands task analysis compared with the first example (teacher's expectations). The amount of detail contained in the behavior chain must depend on the complexity of the behavior and the characteristics of the child. More difficult tasks and behaviors may require a more detailed task analysis.

In the initial stages of teaching a behavior chain, teachers should reinforce the student for correctly completing each behavior *and* for completing each behavior in the correct sequence. After the student has learned the appropriate sequence of behaviors, reinforcement may be faded from after the performance of each link to after the performance of the whole chain of behaviors. In addition, this behavior chain can be linked to other behavior chains and serve as the S^D for a second chain. For example, the completion of the behavior chain for coming into the classroom may serve as the S^D for the beginning of another behavior chain (e.g., stop talking, establish eye contact with the teacher, and wait for directions). There are two primary variations to teaching behavior chains: forward chaining and backward chaining.

FORWARD CHAINING   *Forward chaining* refers to the teaching of each behavior link, starting with the first link and moving "down" to the next link in the chain, until all the behaviors in the chain have been learned and can be performed in the appropriate sequence. A basic decision to be made in using forward chaining is whether to use serial training, concurrent task training, or total task training.

In *serial training*, behaviors are taught in order, one at a time, to a set of criteria before the next behavior is added and taught. For example, when teaching students the sequence of behaviors for coming into the classroom, step 1 (walking into the classroom) would be taught to a specific performance criterion before step 2 (hanging up their coats) is taught.

In *concurrent task training*, two or more behaviors in the behavior chain are taught at the same time (Snell & Zirpoli, 1987). Thus, steps 1 and 2 of the behavior chain would be taught concurrently. Research has found that concurrent training may be more effective than serial training (Waldo, Guess, & Flanagan, 1982), as well as more interesting and motivating to both the student and teacher. It also may be more readily integrated into the daily routine because training is conducted within the context of other tasks (Dunlap & Koegel, 1980).

Total task training refers to teaching all steps in the behavior chain simultaneously. Total task training is actually an extension of concurrent training, has the same advantages of concurrent training, and is considered the most effective method for less difficult behavior chains (Johnson & Cuvo, 1981; Spooner & Spooner, 1984).

BACKWARD CHAINING   *Backward chaining* refers to teaching each behavior link in a behavior chain, starting with the *last* link and moving "up" the behavior chain, until all the behaviors in the chain have been learned and can be performed in the appropriate sequence. For example, if a preschool teacher were teaching a young child a simple behavior chain for washing hands, as outlined in the following list, the teacher would physically assist the child through all the steps in the chain until the last step (step 10—hang up the towel). At that point, the teacher begins instruction on step 10. This sequence continues until the child can complete step 10 independently. After the criterion for step 10 is achieved, the teacher begins instruction on the second-to-last step (step 9—dry your hands with the towel) in the sequence. At this point, the teacher would assist the child through all of the preceding steps (1–8), provide instruction for step 9, and let the child complete the last step independently. Each preceding step becomes the S^D for the next step in the behavior chain and serves as the conditioned reinforcer for the previous step. For example, step 9 becomes the S^D for step 10 and the conditioned reinforcer for step 8.

Stimulus: Teacher states that it is time to eat lunch.

Step One:	Turn on the water.
Step Two:	Wet your hands.
Step Three:	Pick up the soap.
Step Four:	Rub soap on your other hand.
Step Five:	Put the soap down.
Step Six:	Rub your hands together.
Step Seven:	Rinse your hands.
Step Eight:	Turn off the water.
Step Nine:	Dry your hands with the towel.
Step Ten:	Hang up the towel.

Research on which method is better, forward or backward chaining, is mixed. Spooner and Spooner (1984) remind us that "different learners do better with different procedures" (p. 123). In general, forward chaining is recommended because it presents a more natural teaching sequence than backward chaining and allows more effective use of concurrent and total task training. When making these programming decisions (i.e., forward or backward chaining and serial, concurrent, or total task training), teachers should consider the difficulty level of the behavior chain and the child's intellectual ability.

TOKEN ECONOMY REINFORCEMENT PROGRAMS

A *token economy* program is a symbolic reinforcement system (Kazdin, 1977; Kazdin & Bootzin, 1972). It is called an economy system because it is based on a monetary system, with money as the most common form of tokens. Just as one who has a job receives money for the completion of specific tasks, which can then be exchanged for food, housing, and other material objects, the same principle applies in a token economy reinforcement program. Students receive tokens for specific appropriate behaviors, which they may exchange for objects or activities that have been identified as reinforcing. After the students have learned to associate the tokens with the purchase of reinforcers, the tokens become valuable and desirable.

Gottfredson and Gottfredson (2001, p. 330) found that 61% of schools reported using some sort of token reinforcers such as "coupons, tokens, or scrip that can be redeemed for backup reinforcers." However, Safran and Oswald (2003) note that in one schoolwide token economy program, 72% of the tokens were given by only 25% of the teachers, suggesting that we still have a long way to go in convincing teachers of the power of positive reinforcement.

Token economy reinforcement programs have been used successfully with many different ages and populations, including preschoolers (Conyers et al., 2003); students with hearing impairments (Buisson, Murdock, Reynolds, & Cronin, 1995) and learning disabilities (Higgins, Williams & McLaughlin, 2001); persons with mental illnesses (Corrigan, 1995); and students with various behavioral challenges (Lucker & Molloy, 1995) and disabilities (Musser, Bray, Kehle, & Jenson, 2001).

Token economy programs offer several advantages, especially for classroom teachers or day care providers who work with large groups of students:

- Tokens can be distributed to small or large groups of students with minimum effort (Lloyd, Eberhardt, & Drake, 1996).
- Tokens allow teachers to delay the provision of reinforcers during busy periods of the day.
- Tokens let teachers offer a single reinforcer (the token) to many students who may have different reinforcer preferences. The students learn, however, that accumulating tokens throughout the day will allow them to purchase the reinforcer of their preference at a later time.
- Because the provision of tokens is followed by students choosing from a variety of reinforcers, tokens are seldom subject to satiation.
- Tokens can be given to students without interrupting teaching and other activities (Lloyd et al., 1996).
- While using tokens to improve classroom behavior, teachers can also teach students economic concepts such as price, savings inflation, rent, and so on (Hail, 2000).

Characteristics of Tokens

Tokens may be tally marks or points recorded on the board or check marks recorded on a piece of paper at the student's seat. Tokens may also be plastic chips, points, happy faces, stickers, stars, pennies, pieces of colored paper, pieces of cloth, ribbons, marbles, or any small, attractive object. Tokens should be something that the students can see, touch, and count. With the exception of tally and check marks, tokens should not be so large or small that young children are unable to handle, store, and save them for later purchases. Also, teachers want to be sure that tokens cannot be obtained from other sources via counterfeiting or stealing.

Most important, students must understand that they can exchange the tokens for various reinforcers and how many tokens they will need to purchase each reinforcer. Initially, teachers may need to guide young children through the exchange system to demonstrate how the program works.

Establishing a Token Economy Program

Several important steps are necessary to establish a token economy reinforcement program. Each of these steps is described in Classroom Connection 10.3.

For a token economy to be most effective in increasing appropriate behavior, a student should never experience a zero token balance by the exchange period. Teachers

CLASSROOM CONNECTION 10.3
Example of a Token Economy Program

Marge, a fifth-grade teacher, has a class of 30 students. Several of her students demonstrate challenging behaviors such as noncompliance, running around the classroom, hitting, interrupting others, yelling, and so on. Marge is thinking about starting individual behavior reduction programs for each of her "problem students," but decides instead to initiate a classroomwide token economy program. In this way, she thinks that she can focus her attention and energy on reinforcing students for appropriate behaviors and thus indirectly decrease most of the inappropriate classroom behaviors at the same time.

Marge's first step is to identify the target behaviors she wants to increase. She tries to think of appropriate behaviors that are incompatible with many of the challenging behaviors her students are exhibiting. She develops a list of five target behaviors that will be reinforced within her token economy program:

- Following the teacher's directions
- Walking in the classroom
- Keeping hands to self
- Raising hand to be recognized before speaking out
- Talking in a quiet voice

Marge's second step is to *identify the medium of exchange*, or what will serve as tokens for her program. She decides to use colored strips of construction paper (1 inch wide and 5 inches long).

Her third step is to *identify reinforcers the students will be able to purchase with the tokens they earn*. To develop this list, Marge wisely decides to talk with her students about her plan and asks them for reinforcement suggestions. Her students are very helpful and have many ideas for reinforcers. Several of their ideas, however, are not acceptable, which Marge communicates to the students. She also includes many activities as reinforcers. With her students' help, Marge develops a list of 15 reinforcers for the reinforcement menu: getting 5 minutes' extra time on the computer, having 5 minutes' extra free time, being first in line for 1 day, being the class leader for 1 day, receiving a pad of stationery paper (several were donated), receiving one baseball card (donated), receiving a new ballpoint pen (donated), picking a game during gym class, bringing a positive note home, serving on a panel of judges for the next class competition, having an extra show-and-tell session, picking your own seat assignment for 1 day, taking an extra trip to the water fountain, picking and reading a story to the class, and taking an extra trip to the library.

Marge writes the five target behaviors and the reinforcement menu on two big sheets of cardboard. Each list is hung on the front classroom wall for everyone to see.

Having decided that a student will earn one token each time she observes him or her exhibiting any of the target behaviors, Marge next *identifies the price or number of tokens necessary to purchase each reinforcer on the reinforcement menu*. To do this, she follows these simple guidelines:

- The greater the supply of an item listed on the reinforcement menu, the lower the price, or the fewer number of tokens necessary to purchase that reinforcer. For example, Marge had hundreds of baseball cards, so these could be purchased for only one token.
- The lower the supply of the item, the higher the price. Marge had only 10 stationery pads, for instance, so she decided that these could be purchased for 10 tokens.
- The greater the demand for an item, the higher the price. Many students, for example, wanted to buy extra time on the class computer. The cost, Marge decided, would be 10 tokens.
- The lower the demand for an item, the lower the price. For example, the students were not very interested in picking and reading a story to the class. Because this was an activity Marge wanted to promote, she charged only one token for it.
- The greater time required (for an activity), the higher the price. Because extra free time removed the students from 5 minutes of academic time, Marge required 15 tokens for this item on the reinforcement menu.
- The less time required, the lower the price. For example, it took little time to write a positive note home, and, besides, Marge viewed this as an effective strategy for promoting positive teacher–parent relationships. Thus, the positive note home cost only one token.

(continued)

CLASSROOM CONNECTION 10.3 (*Continued*)
Example of a Token Economy Program

Marge's next step is to *pick a time when the students will have the opportunity to exchange their tokens for reinforcers.* She decides that the classroom exchange period will be every Friday, after lunch. Marge explains to the students that they do not have to exchange their tokens; they can save them if they want. She also tells her students that she will modify the price of each reinforcer after each exchange period, based on supply and demand, but that price changes will not be made between exchange periods.

General Reflection for Classroom Connection 10.3:

Marge asked her students for suggestions about what items and activities should be included on her reinforcement menu. What do you think of this strategy? How can Marge get students' input in identifying target behaviors, how many tokens students can earn, how much reinforcement items will cost, and other aspects of the token economy program? How is this helpful to her program?

should make an effort to identify at least one appropriate behavior, in even the most challenging student, to enable that student to participate in the token economy program. Finally, students should have the opportunity to purchase something small, even if they have earned only one token. In Marge's program in Classroom Connection 10.3, several items could be purchased for one token. An effective token economy program includes several characteristics:

- Tokens should be something students can see, touch, and count.
- Tokens should not be so small or large that young children cannot store them, handle them, and count them. Tally marks or checks may be effective with some, especially older, students.
- Students must be able to exchange the tokens for actual reinforcers.
- Students should not be able to obtain tokens from sources other than their teacher. If stealing is a potential problem, the teacher may choose to store the tokens.
- Students must understand that they can exchange the tokens they earn for various reinforcers. To learn how the system works, some students, especially young children, may have to be "walked" through the exchange process immediately after earning tokens.
- Teachers must respect the differences in their students' spending habits. Some students will prefer to save their tokens; some will prefer to spend all their tokens at each exchange.
- Each student should have the opportunity to earn at least one token per exchange period. Also, no maximum should be placed on the number of tokens a student may earn.
- Students who earn only a few tokens, or even just one, should have the opportunity to exchange their tokens for small reinforcers.

CONTINGENCY CONTRACTING

Contingency contracting involves the establishment of a written behavioral contract between a student and teacher regarding the performance of specific target behaviors and the exchange of specific consequences. Used with individual students or a group of students, written contracts are an easy way to develop positive behavioral supports within the classroom environment.

Contracts provide a means for teachers and students to place in writing behavioral expectations, reinforcers, and other consequences.

Contracts are useful tools that may be employed in a variety of settings to teach a variety of skills. Contingency contracting has been successfully used to improve school attendance (Din, Isack, & Rietveld, 2003) and general classroom behavior (Roberts, White, & McLaughlin, 1997), improve on-task behavior (Allen, Howard, Sweeney, & McLaughlin, 1993; miller & Kelley, 1994), increase homework performance (Miller & Kelley, 1994), increase homework accuracy (Miller & Kelley, 1994), reduce disruptive behaviors (Wilkinson, 2003), and modify personal hygiene and grooming behaviors (Allen & Kramer, 1990).

DeRisi and Butz (1975, p. 7) outline several steps in establishing a behavioral contract, which have been modified and expanded on here:

- Select the target behavior(s) you want to increase. Limit the number of target behaviors to two or three.
- Describe the target behavior(s) in observable and measurable terms so that the student's progress may be effectively monitored.
- Identify motivating reinforcers.
- Establish general guidelines and timelines of the contract—who will do what and what will be the consequences.
- Write the contract so that all individuals involved can understand it; use age-appropriate wording.
- Require the individuals involved to sign the contract indicating their understanding and agreement to its terms.
- Consistently reinforce the performance of the target behavior in accordance with the terms of the contract.
- Monitor and collect data on the performance of target behavior(s).
- Discuss and rewrite the contract when data do not show an improvement in the performance of the target behavior. All individuals involved should sign any contract modifications.

Advantages of Contracts

Contracts have many advantages when used to modify behavior. Behavioral contracts encourage teachers to communicate their expectations clearly and provide students with a good understanding of the rewards and consequences available for their behavior. Teachers are encouraged to use their imagination in developing behavioral contracts and to make them positive tools for changing behavior. Other advantages of contingency contracts are as follows:

- They are easy to use in natural environments and do not restrict the student's participation in normal educational activities (Kerr & Nelson, 1989).
- The teacher's focus is on giving positive reinforcement for appropriate behaviors agreed on in the contract.
- The behavioral expectations of both student and teacher are outlined in writing.
- Reinforcement is presented in a systematic manner.
- Consequences for the performance or nonperformance of the target behavior are specific and clearly understood by the student and teacher.
- Contracts may be modified and rewritten as necessary to meet current needs.
- Contracts may be employed with an individual student, with a group of students, or for an entire classroom.

Examples of simple behavioral contracts that may be used in educational settings are provided in Figures 10.1, 10.2, 10.3, and 10.4.

Contract

I _____
Student's name here

will _____

_____

_____

I _____
Teacher's name here

will _____

_____

_____

_____   _____
Student's signature   Teacher's signature

_____
Date

FIGURE 10.1 Sample contract between a student and teacher

Contract

Contract between _____ and _____
If I do _____

Then I can _____

_____

_____   _____
Student's signature   Teacher's signature

_____
Date

FIGURE 10.2   Sample contract between a student and teacher

Contract

This is an agreement between _____
                                                      Student's name

and _____ .
                    Teacher's name

This contract begins on _____ and ends on _____

The terms of this contract are as follows:
Student will _____

_____

_____

Teacher will _____

_____

If student completes his/her part of the agreement, teacher will
provide student with reinforcement as outlined in the teacher part
of the agreement above. If student does not complete his/her part
of the agreement, teacher will withhold reinforcement.

_____   _____
Student's signature   Teacher's signature

_____
Date

FIGURE 10.3   Sample contract between a student and teacher

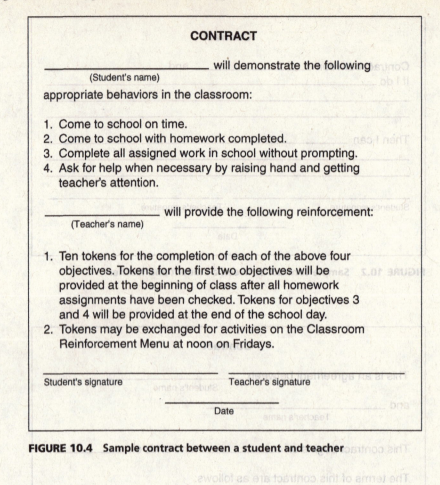

CONTRACT

_____ will demonstrate the following
(Student's name)

appropriate behaviors in the classroom:

1. Come to school on time.
2. Come to school with homework completed.
3. Complete all assigned work in school without prompting.
4. Ask for help when necessary by raising hand and getting teacher's attention.

_____ will provide the following reinforcement:
(Teacher's name)

1. Ten tokens for the completion of each of the above four objectives. Tokens for the first two objectives will be provided at the beginning of class after all homework assignments have been checked. Tokens for objectives 3 and 4 will be provided at the end of the school day.
2. Tokens may be exchanged for activities on the Classroom Reinforcement Menu at noon on Fridays.

_____   _____
Student's signature   Teacher's signature

_____
Date

FIGURE 10.4   Sample contract between a student and teacher

GENERALIZATION

Generalization refers to the degree to which a behavior change transfers to other settings, situations, or behaviors in addition to the setting, situation, or target behavior involved in the behavior change program. Haring (1988) refers to generalization as "appropriate responding in untrained situations" (p. 5). The two primary types of generalization are _stimulus generalization_ and _response generalization_.

Stimulus Generalization

Stimulus generalization describes the degree of behavior change in settings or situations other than the training setting, even when no training occurred in the new setting (Carr, Robinson, Taylor, & Carlson, 1990). If, during science class, for example, the teacher reinforces a student for reading directions on written assignments before asking questions, and then, in math class, the student begins to read directions before asking questions, the new behavior (reading directions before asking questions) has generalized from the science to the math class.

Response Generalization

Response generalization refers to the degree to which a behavior change program influences other behaviors in addition to the target behavior (Carr et al., 1990). For example, if a teacher develops a reinforcement program to increase a student's use of "please," and the student also exhibits an increase in the use of "thank you," then the behavior change program shows a response generalization. In a second example, if a teacher develops a behavior change program to decrease physical aggression (the target behavior), and the student also demonstrates a decrease in verbal aggression (not the target behavior), then the behavior change program shows a response generalization.

In these cases, response generalization is credited with changing behaviors other than the target behavior in the same direction (increasing or decreasing a response) as the target behavior. Response generalization may, however, change behaviors in the opposite direction of the target behavior. For example, a program resulting in a *decrease* in self-injurious behavior may also result in an *increase* in other prosocial behaviors. Also, an *increase* in on-task behaviors may result in a *decrease* of disruptive behaviors. Although the evidence tends to suggest that these behavior changes result from response generalization (Kazdin, 1989), few would disagree that they may also represent some spread of treatment effects.

Promoting Generalization of Behavior Change

Haring (1988) states that "generalization is, perhaps, the most important phase of learning" (p. 5). In most cases, however, generalization does not occur spontaneously. To ensure that new behaviors are used in natural settings, generalization must be integrated into the acquisition phase of teaching (Snell & Zirpoli, 1987). Several methods are used to accomplish this objective.

TEACHING IN NATURAL SETTINGS   The term *natural setting* refers to the setting in which a behavior is most likely to occur or should occur (Gaylord-Ross & Holvoet, 1985). For example, if a preschool teacher wants to establish a reinforcement program to increase "sharing" behavior, the best place to teach this behavior is within the environments where students are expected to share. Pulling students out of the classroom for individualized training by a behavior therapist, for example, is usually not recommended. Behaviors that are learned in the pull-out environment are unlikely to generalize automatically to the classroom or other functional environments. The behavior therapist, teacher, and parents must collaborate to integrate skill acquisition and generalization successfully into the student's natural environments (e.g., classroom, playground, home).

SELECTING NATURAL ANTECEDENTS FOR STIMULUS CONTROL   *Natural antecedents* are events or situations that should act as natural prompts or cues for a specific target behavior (Ford & Mirenda, 1984; Snell & Zirpoli, 1987). For example, several situations occur within a classroom setting in which students are expected to stop talking and listen (e.g., when the teacher is talking, reading to the class, or giving instructions). Teaching students to stop talking and listen, following these naturally occurring situations, is another example of integrating skill acquisition and generalization. The most effective way for teachers to identify the natural antecedents or stimuli for behaviors is through direct observation of students within the natural environment of the classroom.

At times artificial stimuli (prompts and cues) are necessary to teach appropriate behaviors or to increase the opportunity for reinforcing a target behavior. For many students, the use of artificial prompts is a necessary, important element during the initial stages of behavior acquisition. Using a tone sound from a tape recorder during the initial stages of a self-instruction program to teach in-seat behavior is an example of an artificial prompt. These artificial prompts clearly have a useful place in behavior management. It is also important, however, to pair artificial prompts with natural stimuli and to fade them as soon as possible (Wolery & Gast, 1984).

SELECTING NATURAL CONSEQUENCES AS REINFORCERS   In addition to teaching within natural settings and associating appropriate behaviors with natural antecedents and stimuli, teachers should employ natural consequences for behaviors (Snell & Zirpoli, 1987). Thus, although a token economy program—or any other program using artificial reinforcers— may be appropriate and necessary for many students, one of the goals of reinforcement programs should be to fade artificial reinforcers (e.g., from tokens to praise) and schedules (e.g., from continuous to intermittent) and to teach students to respond to natural rein-forcers. Natural classroom reinforcers include receiving positive statements made by the teacher or other students, having completed artwork or other assignments hung on the classroom bulletin board, and getting a good grade on an assignment. Such reinforcement may not be possible in all cases, however, and the long-term use of artificial reinforcers (e.g., tokens, extra attention) may be necessary to maintain appropriate behavior with some students. In addition to selecting natural reinforcers, Gregory, Kehle, and McLoughlin (1997) found that teaching students self-management techniques also promoted generaliza-tion and maintenance of appropriate behavior in regular education settings.

REINFORCING GENERALIZATION   As with other behaviors discussed in this chapter, the generalization of learned behaviors for one stimulus, setting, or situation is likely to in-crease when generalization is systematically reinforced. Generalization may be increased by reinforcing the child for exhibiting target behaviors outside the training setting or situa-tion or, more directly, by training *for* generalization. In a procedure referred to as *sequential modification* (Stokes & Baer, 1977), a skill or behavior is taught in one setting or situation; then additional settings or situations are systematically added to the training program until generalization is achieved in all targeted settings or situations. For example, a behavior change program may begin and continue within a specific classroom setting until the target behavior is achieved. Then teachers gradually expand the program to other settings within the school until complete generalization (within the school) is achieved.

MAINTENANCE

Maintenance refers to the degree to which a behavior change is maintained over time after a behavior change program has been completed. For example, in-seat behavior is considered maintained when a teacher terminates the behavior change program used to increase in-seat behavior in the first place, and in-seat behavior remains at an acceptable level. If, at the end of the behavior change program, the duration of in-seat behavior decreases to an unacceptable level, then the behavior change was not maintained, and the program may have to be reinstated.

Promoting the Maintenance of Behavior Change

The methods for promoting maintenance are similar to those used to promote generaliza-tion. When training is conducted within natural settings, using natural antecedents and consequences, behavior changes are likely to be maintained after artificial stimuli and consequences (and other training conditions) are faded.

The following methods are likely to promote the generalization and maintenance of learned behaviors:

- ***Teach within settings where the behavior is likely to occur and within multiple settings; avoid artificial training areas or pull-out training.*** Teaching a student appropriate classroom behaviors within a resource room (artificial environment) is unlikely to generalize to the regular classroom or to be maintained after the student leaves the resource room unless the same behaviors are taught and reinforced in the regular classroom.
- ***Implement the behavior change program with a variety of teachers across multiple settings.*** All teachers who have contact with a student should consistently follow the behavior change program.
- ***Identify common elements between the teaching environment and other environments in which you want the behavior to be generalized.*** This tip is especially important when students change classes throughout the school day. Collaboration, cooperation, and consistency are important elements for effective behavioral generalization and maintenance across school personnel and environments.
- ***Gradually shift from artificial stimulus controls to natural stimulus controls that occur in the student's natural environment.*** Be flexible, however, to the student's individual needs.
- ***Shift from continuous to intermittent schedules of reinforcement as soon as possible.*** These decisions should be based on the student's progress as outlined in your program data.
- ***Pair artificial reinforcers (e.g., tokens) with natural reinforcers and consequences (social praise) provided within the natural environment.***
- ***Phase out artificial reinforcers that are unlikely to be provided in the natural environment.***
- ***Introduce delays in the provision of reinforcement that would be likely to occur in the natural environment.*** For example, while initially students may exchange tokens at the end of each day, weekly exchange intervals will teach students to plan and save for future consequences. Again, teachers must, however, be sensitive to what works for their students and be flexible enough to modify the behavior change plan as necessary.
- ***Reinforce generalization and maintenance.*** Don't forget to tell your students when you notice the generalization of skills across different environments, and verbally reinforce them when appropriate behaviors are maintained after the "official" program is completed.

Summary

Reinforcement increases the probability that a behavior will reoccur, or at least be maintained, at the current rate, duration, or intensity. Reinforcing appropriate behavior is the most effective method of increasing appropriate and decreasing inappropriate behaviors.

Reinforcers may be tangible, social, or physical (activities). Primary reinforcers are naturally reinforcing, whereas secondary reinforcers are learned or conditioned through their association with primary reinforcers. Teachers must be sure that reinforcers are socially valid and age-appropriate.

It is important that teachers identify effective reinforcers through preference and reinforcement assessments. High-preference reinforcers have been found to be more effective than low-preference reinforcers in behavior change programs.

A *reinforcement menu* is a list of potential reinforcers that may be used for an individual student or a group of students to reinforce appropriate behavior. By having a variety of reinforcers to select from, students will not become satiated with a single reinforcer.

Factors associated with effective reinforcement programs include the immediacy of presentation; consistency; pairing with verbal praise; schedule of presentation; and the type, quality, quantity, and presenter of the reinforcement to the student. Teachers are encouraged to establish clear rules and guidelines, model the target behavior, and consistently reinforce behaviors targeted for increase.

Reinforcement may be delivered on a continuous or an intermittent schedule. A *continuous schedule* involves the delivery of reinforcement each and every time the target behavior is observed. When an *intermittent schedule* is employed, a student is reinforced after some, but not all, occurrences of the target behavior. Reinforcement may also be delivered on a fixed ratio, variable ratio, fixed interval, and variable interval schedule.

Shaping refers to the reinforcement of successive approximations of a terminal behavior. It is generally used to teach new behaviors and skills. *Chaining* is the performance of a series or sequence of behaviors rather than of one behavior independently. Chaining may be presented in a forward or backward sequence.

A *token economy reinforcement* program is a symbolic reinforcement system. Students are presented with tokens for objects or activities that are reinforcing. Tokens, which may take many forms, allow teachers to delay giving reinforcers during busy periods of the day and are effective with individuals or large groups of students. Establishing a token economy program includes identifying the target behavior, medium of exchange, price of each item on the reinforcement menu, and time when the students will exchange their tokens for reinforcers.

Contingency contracting involves the development of a written agreement between a student and teacher(s) regarding the performance of target behaviors and the exchange of specific consequences. Contracts are highly recommended because they are easy to use in natural environments, do not restrict the student's participation in educational activities, focus on the reinforcement of appropriate behaviors, outline behavioral expectations in writing, may be used with individuals or groups of students, and may be modified to meet the needs of different students and situations.

Generalization refers to the degree to which a behavior change transfers to other settings, situations, or behaviors beyond the training environment. There are two types of generalization, stimulus and response. *Stimulus generalization* describes the degree of behavior change from training to other settings. *Response generalization* refers to the degree to which a behavior change program generalizes to other behaviors.

Maintenance is the degree to which a behavior change is maintained over time after the completion of a behavior change program. Teachers may promote generalization and maintenance by teaching in natural environments, selecting natural antecedents for stimulus control, selecting natural consequences as reinforcers, shifting from continuous to intermittent schedules of reinforcement, introducing delays in reinforcement similar to the natural environment, and reinforcing generalization.

Discussion Questions

1. What are the different types of reinforcement teachers may use in various environments (school, home, etc.) to increase appropriate behavior?
2. Describe the factors associated with the effective use of reinforcement.
3. List the different types of reinforcement schedules, and give examples of the use of each reinforcement schedule within a classroom environment.
4. Discuss the process of shaping new behaviors. Give an example of shaping a series of behaviors within a classroom setting.
5. What are the important elements of an effective contingency contracting program? Give examples of when contracts might be effective within the classroom settings.
6. What do we mean when we talk about program generalization and maintenance? How can they both be facilitated during and after a behavior management program?

References

Akin-Little, K. A., Eckert, T. L., Lovett, B. J., & Little, S. G. (2004). Extrinsic reinforcement in the classroom: Bribery or best practice. *School Psychology Review, 33*(3), 344–362.

Allen, L. J., Howard, V. F., Sweeney, W. J., & McLaughlin, T. F. (1993). Use of contingency contracting to increase on-task behavior with primary students. *Psychological Reports, 72,* 905–906.

Allen, S., & Kramer, J. (1990). Modification of personal hygiene and grooming behaviors with contingency contracting: A brief review and case study. *Psychology in the Schools, 27,* 244–251.

Babyak, A. E., Luze, G. J., & Kamps, D. M. (2000). The good student game: Behavior management for diverse classrooms. *Intervention in School and Clinic, 35*(4), 216–224.

Baer, R. A., Blount, R. L., Detrich, R., & Stokes, T. F. (1984). Using intermittent reinforcement to program maintenance of verbal/nonverbal correspondence. *Journal of Applied Behavior Analysis, 20,* 179–184.

Bandura, A. (1973). *Aggression: A social learning analysis.* Upper Saddle River, NJ: Prentice Hall.

Beaman, R., & Wheldall, K. (2000). Teachers' use of approval and disapproval in the classroom. *Educational Psychology, 20*(4), 431–447.

Beare, P. L., Severson, S., & Brandt, P. (2004). The use of a positive procedure to increase engagement on-task and decrease challenging behavior. *Behavior Modification, 28*(1), 28.

Blake, C., Wang, W., Cartledge, G., & Gardner, R. (2000). Middle school students with serious emotional disturbances serve as social skills trainers and reinforcers for peers with SED. *Behavioral Disorders, 25*(4), 280–298.

Boyd, B. A., Alter, P. J., & Conroy, M. A. (2005). Using their restricted interests: A novel strategy for increasing the social behaviors of children with autism. *Beyond Behavior, 14*(3), 3–9.

Buisson, G. J., Murdock, J. Y., Reynolds, K. E., & Cronin, M. E. (1995). Effects of tokens on response latency of students with hearing impairments in a resource room. *Education and Treatment of Children, 18*(4), 408–421.

Cameron, J. (2001). Negative effects of reward on intrinsic motivation—a limited phenomenon. *Review of Educational Research, 71,* 29–42.

Carr, E. G., Robinson, S., Taylor, J. C., & Carlson, J. I. (1990). *Positive approaches to the treatment of severe behavior problems in persons with developmental disabilities: A review and analysis of reinforcement and stimulus-based procedures* (Monograph No. 4). Chicago: Association for Persons with Severe Handicaps.

Cipani, E., & Spooner, F. (1997). Treating problem behavior maintained by negative reinforcement. *Research in Developmental Disabilities, 18*(5), 329–342.

Conyers, C., Miltenberger, R., Romaniuk, C., Kopp, B., & Himle, M. (2003). Evaluation of DRO schedules to reduce disruptive behavior in a preschool classroom. *Child and Family Behavior Therapy, 25*(3), 106.

Corrigan, P. W. (1995). Use of a token economy with seriously mentally ill patients: Criticisms and misconceptions. *Psychiatric Services, 46*(12), 1258–1262.

Cuvo, A. J., Lerch, L. J., Leurquin, D. A., Gaffaney, T. J., & Poppen, R. L. (1998). Response allocation to concurrent fixed-ratio reinforcement schedules with work requirements by adults with mental retardation and typical preschool children. *Journal of Applied Behavior Analysis, 31*, 43–63.

DeRisi, W. J., & Butz, G. (1975). *Writing behavioral contracts*. Champaign, IL: Research Press.

DiGennaro, F. D., Martens, B. K., & McIntyre, L. L. (2005). Increasing treatment integrity through negative reinforcement: Effects on teacher and student behavior. *School Psychology Review, 34*(2), 220–231.

Din, F. S., Isack, L. R., & Rietveld, J. (February 26, 2003). *Effects of contingency contracting on decreasing student tardiness*. Paper presented at the 26th Annual Conference of the Eastern Educational Research Association, Hilton Head Island, SC.

Dunlap, G., & Koegel, R. K. (1980). Motivating autistic children through stimulus variation. *Journal of Applied Behavior Analysis, 13*, 619–627.

Egel, A. L. (1981). Reinforcer variation: Implications for motivating developmentally disabled children. *Journal of Applied Behavior Analysis, 14*, 345–350.

Ford, A., & Mirenda, P. (1984). Community instruction: A natural cues and correction decision model. *Journal of the Association for Persons with Severe Handicaps, 9*, 79–87.

Fullerton, E. K., Conroy, M. A., & Correa, V. I. (2009). Early childhood teachers' use of specific praise statements with young children at risk for behavioral disorders. *Behavioral Disorders, 34*(3), 118–135.

Galensky, T. L., Miltenberger, R. G., Stricker, J. M., & Garlinghouse, M. A. (2001). Functional assessment and treatment of mealtime behavior problems. *Journal of Positive Behavior Interventions, 3*(4), 211–224.

Gaylord-Ross, R. J., & Holvoet, J. F. (1985). *Strategies for educating students with severe handicaps*. Boston: Little, Brown.

Gottfredson, G. D., & Gottfredson, D. C. (2001). What schools do to prevent problem behavior and promote safe environments. *Journal of Educational & Psychological Consultation, 12*(4), 313–344.

Gregory, K. M., Kehle, T. J., & McLoughlin, C. S. (1997). Generalization and maintenance of treatment gains using self-management procedures with behaviorally disordered adolescents. *Psychological Reports, 80*, 683–690.

Gresham, R. M., Ramsey, E., & Walker, H. M. (2003). Sometimes, practice makes perfect: Overcoming the automaticity of challenging behavior by linking intervention to thoughts, feelings, and actions. *Education and Treatment of Children, 27*, 476–489.

Hail, J. M. (2000). Take a break: A token economy in the fifth grade. *Social Education, 64*(4), 5–7.

Hardman, E., & Smith, S. W. (1999). Promoting positive interactions in the classroom. *Intervention in School and Clinic, 34*(3), 178–180.

Haring, N. G. (1988). *Generalization for students with severe handicaps: Strategies and solutions*. Seattle: University of Washington Press.

Higgins, J. W., Williams, R. L., & McLaughlin, T. F. (2001). The effects of a token economy employing instructional consequences for a third-grade student with learning disabilities: A data-based case study. *Education and Treatment of Children, 24*(1), 99–107.

Iwata, B. A. (1987). Negative reinforcement in applied behavior analysis: An emerging technology. *Journal of Applied Behavior Analysis, 20*, 361–378.

Iwata, B. A., Pace, G. M., Dorsey, M. F., Zarcone, J. R., Vollmer, T. R., Smith, R. G., et al. (1994). The functions of self-injurious behavior: An experimental-epidemiological analysis. *Journal of Applied Behavior Analysis, 27*, 215–240.

Johnson, B. F., & Cuvo, A. J. (1981). Teaching mentally retarded adults to cook. *Behavior Modification, 5*, 187–202.

Kazdin, A. E. (1977). *The token economy: A review and evaluation*. New York: Plenum.

Kazdin, A. E. (1989). *Behavior modification in applied settings*. Pacific Grove, CA: Brooks/Cole.

Kazdin, A. E., & Bootzin, R. R. (1972). The token economy: An evaluative review. *Journal of Applied Behavior Analysis, 5*, 343–372.

Kennedy, C., & Jolivette, K. (2008). The effects of positive verbal reinforcement on the time spent outside the classroom for students with emotional and behavioral disorders in a residential setting. *Behavior Disorders, 33*(4), 211–221.

Kerr, M. M., & Nelson, C. M. (1989). *Strategies for managing behavior problems in the classroom*. Upper Saddle River, NJ: Merrill/Pearson Education.

Keyes, G. (1994). Motivating reluctant learners. *Teaching Exceptional Children, 27*, 20–23.

Kitfield, E. B., & Masalsky, C. J. (2000). Negative reinforcement based treatment to increase food intake. *Behavior Modification, 24*(4), 600–609.

Lampi, A. R., Fenty, N. S., & Beaunae, C. (2005). Making the three Ps easier: Praise, proximity, and precorrection. *Beyond Behavior, 15*(1), 8–12.

Levin, L., & Carr, E. G. (2001). Food selectivity and problem behavior in children with developmental disabilities: Analysis & intervention. *Behavior Modification, 25*(3), 443–471.

Lloyd, J. W., Eberhardt, M. J., & Drake, G. P. (1996). Group versus individual reinforcement contingencies within the context of group study conditions. *Journal of Applied Behavioral Analysis, 29*(2), 189–200.

Lucker, J. R., & Molloy, A. T. (1995). Resources for working with children with attention-deficit-hyperactive-disorder (ADHD). *Elementary School Guidance & Counseling, 29*, 260–266.

Maag, J. W. (2001). Rewarded by punishment: Reflections on the disuse of positive reinforcement in education. *Exceptional Children, 67*(2), 173–186.

McVey, M. D. (2001). Teacher praise: Maximizing the motivational impact. *Journal of Early Education and Family Review, 8*(4), 29–34.

Miller, D. L., & Kelley, M. L. (1994). The use of goal setting and contingency contracting for improving children's homework performance. *Journal of Applied Behavior Analysis, 27*, 73–84.

Musser, E. H., Bray, M. A., Kehle, T. J., & Jenson, W. R. (2001). Reducing disruptive behaviors in students with serious emotional disturbance. *School Psychology Review, 30*(2), 294–305.

Newman, B., & Buffington, D. M. (1995). The effects of schedules of reinforcement on instruction following. *Psychological Record, 45*(3), 4663–4677.

Northrup, J. (2000). Further evaluation of the accuracy of reinforcer surveys: A systematic replication. *Journal of Applied Behavior Analysis, 33*(3), 335–339.

Panyon, M. V. (1980). *How to use shaping*. Austin, TX: Pro-Ed.

Payne, L. D., Mancil, G. R., & Landers, E. (2005). Consequence-based behavioral interventions for classroom teachers. *Beyond Behavior, 15*(1), 13–20.

Pfiffner, L. J., & O'Leary, S. G. (1987). The efficacy of all positive management as a function of the prior use of negative consequences. *Journal of Applied Behavior Analysis, 20*, 265–271.

Premack, D. (1959). Toward empirical behavior laws: I. Positive reinforcement. *Psychological Review, 66*, 219–233.

Roberts, M., White, R., & McLaughlin, T. F. (1997). Useful classroom accommodations for teaching children with ADD and ADHD. *Journal of Special Education, 21*(2), 71–84.

Safran, S. P., & Oswald, K. (2003). Positive behavior supports: Can schools reshape disciplinary practices? *Exceptional Children, 69*(3), 361–373.

Skinner, B. F. (1938). *The behavior of organisms*. New York: Appleton-Century-Crofts.

Skinner, B. F. (1969). *Contingencies of reinforcement: A theoretical analysis*. New York: Appleton-Century-Crofts.

Snell, M. E., & Zirpoli, T. J. (1987). Intervention strategies. In M. E. Snell (Ed.), *Systematic instruction of persons with severe handicaps*. Upper Saddle River, NJ: Merrill/Pearson Education.

Spooner, S. B., & Spooner, D. (1984). A review of chaining techniques: Implications for future research and practice. *Education and Training of the Mentally Retarded, 10*, 114–124.

Stokes, T. F., & Baer, D. B. (1977). An implicit technology of generalization. *Journal of Applied Behavior Analysis, 10*, 349–367.

Stormont, M., & Reinke, W. (2009). The importance of pre-corrective statements and behavior-specific praise and strategies to increase their use. *Beyond Behavior, 18*(3), 26–32.

Strout, M. (2005). Positive behavioral support at the classroom level. *Beyond Behavior, 14*, 13–18.

Tankersley, M. (1995). A group-oriented contingency management program. *Preventing School Failure, 40*(1), 19–23.

Waldo, L., Guess, D., & Flanagan, B. (1982). Effects of concurrent and serial training on receptive labeling by severely retarded individuals. *Journal of the Association for the Severely Handicapped, 6*, 56–65.

Wilkinson, L. A. (2003). Using behavioral consultation to reduce challenging behavior in the classroom. *Preventing School Failure, 47*(3), 100–105.

Willert, J., & Willert, R. (2000). An ignored antidote to school violence: Classrooms that reinforce positive social habits. *American Secondary Education, 29*(1), 27–33.

Wolery, M., & Gast, D. L. (1984). Effective and efficient procedures for the transfer of stimulus control. *Topics in Early Childhood Special Education, 4*, 52–77.

Cognitive Behavior Modification

CHAPTER 11

Mitchell L. Yell
University of South Carolina

Todd Busch
Minnesota State University, Mankato

Erik Drasgow
University of South Carolina

> *Cognitive-behavioral modification refers to a collection of techniques and strategies that are used to alter behavior by teaching individuals to actively participate in understanding and modifying their own thoughts and behaviors.*
>
> —MAYER, LOCHMAN, AND VAN ACKER (2005, P. 197)

ognitive behavior modification (CBM) is not a specific type of intervention. Rather, it is a term that refers to a number of different but related interventions. Problem solving, anger control, self-instruction, alternate response, self-control, self-management, self-monitoring, self-evaluation, and self-reinforcement training are all interventions that are included under the rubric of CBM.

This chapter begins by examining the conceptual basis, purpose, advantages, and origin of CBM. Next, we review specific interventions. Our review of each intervention begins with a definition, is followed by a summary of relevant research, and ends with guidelines for using the intervention.

WHAT IS COGNITIVE BEHAVIOR MODIFICATION?

All CBM interventions share three basic assumptions (Hughes, 1988):

- Behavior is mediated by cognitive events (e.g., thoughts, beliefs).
- A change in cognitive mediating events results in a change of behavior.
- All persons are active participants in their learning.

CBM is based on the reciprocal relationship between one's thoughts and behaviors. Thus, the intent of these interventions is to modify thoughts and beliefs to change behavior. The major goal of CBM, therefore, is to teach students to manage their own behavior through cognitive self-regulation.

CBM interventions have been used with a wide variety of students and behaviors. Table 11.1 lists examples of the application of CBM to diverse populations and behaviors.

Proponents of CBM believe that sole reliance on externally controlled behavioral interventions makes a student overly dependent on a teacher. But if a teacher uses the techniques and procedures

TABLE 11.1 Selected Studies and Reviews Using Cognitive Behavioral Interventions

Subjects or Behaviors	Studies and Reviews
Students with autism	Koegel and Koegel (1990)
Students with behavior disorders	Carr and Punzo (1993)
	Clark and McKenzie (1989)
	Dunlap, Clarke, Jackson, Wright, Ramos, and Brinson (1995)
	Kern, Dunlap, Childs, and Clarke (1994)
	Kern, Wacker, Mace, Falk, Dunlap, and Kromrey (1995)
	Levendoski and Cartledge (2000)
	McLaughlin, Krappman, and Welsh (1985)
	Rhode, Morgan, and Young (1983)
	Smith, Young, West, Morgan, and Rhode (1988)
Students with learning disabilities	Lloyd, Hallahan, Kosiewicz, and Kneedler (1982)
	Lloyd, Bateman, Landrum, and Hallahan (1989)
	Rooney, Polloway, and Hallahan (1985)
Students with mental retardation	Osborne, Kosiewicz, Crumley, and Lee (1987)
Students with severe and multiple disabilities	Shapiro, Browder, and D'Huyvetter (1984)
Students with visual disabilities	Storey and Gaylord-Ross (1987)
Students without disabilities	Olympia, Sheridan, Jenson, and Andrews, (1994)
Students with attention deficit hyperactivity disorder (ADHD) or attention deficit disorder (ADD)	Barkley, Copeland, and Sivage (1980)
	Kendall and Finch (1979)
Aggressive behavior	Christie, Hiss, and Lozanoff (1984)
	Smith, Lochman, and Daunic (2005)
Anger	Christie, Hiss, and Lozanoff (1984)
Noncompliance	O'Brien, Riner, and Budd (1983)
Social skills	Kilburtz, Miller, and Morrow (1985)
Depression	Reynolds and Coats (1986)
	Maag and Swearer (2005)
Academic deficits	Burkell, Schneider, and Pressley (1990)
	Harris (1986)
	Harris and Graham (1992)
	Levendoski and Cartledge (2000)
	Symons, McGoldrick, Snyder, and Pressley (1990)
Anxiety and phobic disorder	King, Heyne, and Ollendick (2005)
Attributions	Tollefson, Tracy, Johnson, and Chatman (1986)
Problem solving	Smith and Daunic (2006)

of CBM to teach a student self-management, the student then becomes less dependent on the teacher and on external control. Several researchers have discussed the advantages of teaching students to manage their behavior (e.g., Alberto & Troutman, 1999; Cooper, Heron, & Heward, 1987; Maag & Swearer, 2005; Mayer, Lochman, & Van Acker, 2005; Schloss & Smith, 1998; Shapiro & Cole, 1984; Smith, Lochman, & Daunic, 2005; Smith & Daunic, 2006). These advantages include the following:

- Self-management represents a proactive rather than reactive approach to behavior management. Teaching students to control their behavior will *prevent* behavior problems from occurring.
- Students with self-management skills can learn and behave more appropriately without the constant supervision of the teacher.
- Self-management may enhance the generalization of behavior change. When behaviors are under external control by the teacher, the behaviors may not occur in situations and settings where the teacher is absent. When students manage their own behaviors, however, these behaviors are more likely to endure and to carry over to different situations and settings.
- Behavioral improvements established through self-management procedures may be more resistant to extinction than behavioral improvements established through external control procedures. When behavioral improvements are established through external control procedures, these improvements may disappear when the external reinforcers are removed. However, some researchers have suggested that this is less of a problem when behaviors are improved through self-management and reinforcement may be internal.

THE ORIGINS OF COGNITIVE BEHAVIOR MODIFICATION

CBM represents a synthesis of cognitive psychology and behavior modification (Mayer, Lochman, & Van Acker, 2005). Kendall and Hollon (1979) describe it as "a joining of forces rather than a break for independence" (p. 6). According to Kendall and Hollon:

> The cognitive-behavioral approach ... is a purposeful combination of the performance-oriented and methodologically rigorous behavioral techniques with the treatment and evaluation of cognitive-mediational phenomena. Thus internal as well as environmental variables are targets for treatment and are scientifically evaluated as contributors to behavior change. (p. 3)

Although scholars have identified additional forces that contributed to the development of CBM, the primary forces were behavioral psychology and cognitive psychology. We will briefly summarize the forces that led to the development of CBM intervention.

Trends in Behavioral Psychology

The traditional behavioral approach has modified behavior by altering environmental events (i.e., antecedents and consequences). The environment is altered through the application of the principles of behavior. Behavioral principles include reinforcement, punishment, and extinction. These principles are used to establish behaviors, increase or maintain behaviors, or reduce or eliminate behaviors.

The 1970s were a time of growing dissatisfaction with behaviorism. Kazdin (1982) argued that conceptual stagnation was occurring within behaviorism. Little in the way of new theory was developed, and the applied research seemed merely to catalog the same behavioral interventions with new populations, problems, or settings. Another source of dissatisfaction was that behavior management procedures were not fostering changes that were durable or that generalized to other settings, across behaviors, or across subjects (Meichenbaum, 1980).

The conceptual stagnation and the growing dissatisfaction with the behavioral model may have helped to foster the shift toward more cognitively oriented interventions (Kazdin, 1982). The shifting view acknowledged that behavior modification should involve cognitive processes and that cognitions are involved in the learning process (Craighead, 1982).

In 1978, Bandura advanced his concepts of reciprocal determinism by suggesting that environmental, cognitive, and behavioral variables interact with each other. Moreover, he highlighted the importance of observation in learning and the influence that a person's beliefs in his or her capabilities has on behavior (Bandura, 1977). His work served as the basis of social learning theory, which was the foundation of what was to become the cognitive-behavioral model (Meyers, Cohen, & Schlester, 1989).

Research on self-control and self-regulation was also an important contribution to the movement toward CBM (Harris, 1982). Homme (1965) stated that cognition was subject to the same laws as other behavior and that changing these cognitions could change behavior. Kanfer and Karoly (1972) developed a model of self-regulation that included self-monitoring, self-evaluation, and self-reinforcement. According to Kanfer and Karoly, self-regulation occurred when a student observed his or her performance, compared it with some criterion, and reinforced him- or herself. These and other events within the behavioral field began to acknowledge the interaction between cognitive and environmental events in human behavior.

Trends in Cognitive Psychology

Cognitive psychologists believe that behavior is influenced by what we think (i.e., cognitions). Cognitive psychologists believe the main determinants of human behavior are within the individual. Thus, interventions are aimed at directly altering thoughts, perceptions, beliefs, and attributions. An important influence on cognitive behavior modification was the development of cognitive therapy.

According to Craighead (1982), Ellis and Beck began the development of cognitive interventions. Beck (1976) believed that many problems were due to misinterpretations, and identifying faulty perceptions and teaching people more accurate ones could help those who had problems. Individuals progressed through four stages in Beck's cognitive therapy. First, the individual had to become aware of his or her thoughts; second, the individual had to recognize that the thoughts were inaccurate; third, the individual had to substitute accurate judgments for inaccurate ones; and, finally, he or she needed feedback as to the correctness of the changes.

Similarly, Ellis believed that it is an individual's inaccurate perceptions of events that cause disturbances. To modify these inaccurate perceptions, Ellis (1973) developed rational emotive therapy (RET). In RET, individuals are taught that it is not what happens to them that makes them upset and causes them to behave counterproductively. Rather, it is what they *think* about what happens to them that causes them to be upset.

The theories of Beck and Ellis share two primary assumptions. First, dysfunctional behavior is the result of inappropriate cognitive processes (what individuals thought about events). Second, intervention must modify these inappropriate cognitions (Craighead, 1982).

Theories concerning the relationship between private speech and behavior have also influenced the development of CBM. *Private speech* refers to overt or covert speech that is directed at oneself. Theories about the role of private speech have their roots in the work of Vygotsky and Luria. Vygotsky (1962) proposed that the internalization of a verbal system was a crucial step in a child's control over his or her behavior. Vygotsky's student Luria (1961) proposed a normal developmental sequence by which the child came to regulate his or her behavior. In this developmental sequence, the child's behavior was first controlled by verbalizations of adults. The next stage involved the child controlling his or her own behavior through overt verbalizations. Finally, by the age of 5 or 6, the child's behavior was controlled by his or her own covert verbalizations.

Jenson (1971) referred to verbal control of behavior as "verbal mediation." He defined verbal mediation as "talking to oneself in relevant ways when confronted with something to be learned, a problem to be solved, or a concept to be attained" (p. 101). This developmental sequence generally results in the verbal mediation ability becoming automatic. These theories led to the development of interventions that attempted to modify behaviors through self-statements.

THE PROCEDURES OF COGNITIVE BEHAVIOR MODIFICATION

All CBM interventions share the common element of stressing procedures that teach students to manage their own behaviors. That is, teachers use behavioral principles with their students (e.g., reinforcement) to teach them cognitive strategies. The strategies use some form of self-instruction or verbal mediation to control behavior. CBM procedures are varied and concentrate on difference types of verbal mediation. For example, some CBM procedures teach monitoring and evaluate their behavior, whereas others teach students to respond to provocation by following certain cognitive steps. We now examine the different interventions that fall under the rubric of CBM.

Self-Management Training

Self-management is a cognitive-behavioral intervention. As such, the goal of a self-management intervention is to teach the student to manage his or her behavior. The primary advantage of self-management training allows teachers to teach students techniques that will make them less dependent on the teacher's environmental manipulations. In this section, we will discuss three procedures often used in self-management training: self-monitoring, self-evaluation, and self-reinforcement. Although each of these procedures is often discussed separately, in reality they are often combined and taught as self-management packages.

SELF-MONITORING When using self-monitoring or self-recording procedures, students record the frequency of a particular behavior or behaviors. Self-monitoring has been used to improve student's behavior (DiGangi & Maag, 1992; Polsgrove & Smith, 2004) and academic achievement (Webber, Scheuermann, McCall, & Coleman, 1993). Reid (1996) reviewed the research on self-monitoring and found that these procedures had been proven to be effective with diverse populations and behaviors. Moreover, Reid found that these procedures could easily be used in classroom settings.

There are two aspects to self-monitoring. First, a student must be aware of the behavior that he or she is counting. Second, the student must record what he or she has done. For example, students may count the number of times they raise their hand to

Self-monitoring teaches students how to measure and evaluate their own behavior.

volunteer in class or talk out in class without permission by observing the behavior and then marking the occurrences on a piece of paper.

Just the act of having a student collect self-monitoring data may often result in increases in desired behavior. This may be because self-monitoring procedures force the student to monitor his or her behavior. Baer (1984) states that a reason for behavioral improvement is that self-monitoring provides cues that increase the student's awareness of potential consequences for a particular behavior. Polsgrove and Smith (2004) note that self-monitoring may result in a student recognizing a discrepancy between external criteria and his or her performance, thus leading to behavioral change.

Researchers have also found that behavior often improves simply because the student is collecting the behavioral data. Broden, Hall, and Mitts (1971) investigated the effects of self-monitoring on two disruptive students. They found that the act of recording their disruptive behaviors dramatically decreased these behaviors. This has been termed a *reactive effect*. This means that the behavior may change in the desired direction simply as a function of self-monitoring (Alberto & Troutman, 1999).

Accuracy in Self-Monitoring.   Teachers may be concerned with students' accuracy in self-monitoring. In a number of investigations, students have accurately recorded their behaviors; in other investigations, however, they have not been accurate. An important question is whether accuracy is a significant variable during self-monitoring. O'Leary and Dubay (1979) demonstrated that the accuracy of a student's self-collected data did not necessarily correlate with the student's behavior or academic performance. That is, when trying to increase appropriate behaviors, the act of self-monitoring alone may be more important than the accuracy of the student's data.

Reinforcement for Accurate Self-Monitoring.   If a student is to be reinforced on the basis of self-monitoring data, some researchers believe that contingencies regarding the accuracy of the data should apply. Otherwise, students may rate their behavior as appropriate to receive reinforcement even when inappropriate (Gross & Wojnilower, 1984). Thus, they may be reinforced for inaccurate self-monitoring. When accuracy is a concern, matching procedures may be employed to check the student's data. With matching procedures, a student's data are matched with the recorded data of independent observers. The student is reinforced when his or her self-monitoring data closely match the data collected by the independent observer. For example, a student could be reinforced when his or her self-monitoring data matched the data recorded by teachers. The teacher could tell the student that he or she would give the student bonus points if the self-monitoring data were within one point of the teacher's recording. In addition to reinforcing the student for matching, the student should also be reinforced for appropriate behavior exhibited during the self-monitoring program.

In a review of the self-monitoring research, Webber et al. (1993) conclude that self-monitoring could be successfully used with special-education students of various ages in various settings to increase attention to task, positive classroom behaviors, and some social skills. Self-monitoring was also successful in decreasing inappropriate classroom behaviors. Additional benefits of self-monitoring included enhancing the likelihood of generalization and the ease of teaching the procedures to students.

Teaching Students to Self-Monitor.   To teach self-monitoring, the teacher must train the student to collect data on his or her behavior. First, the student must be aware of the particular behavior that will be counted. To assist the student to identify the behavior of concern, the teacher must have a precise, operational definition. Second, the student must be taught how to record occurrences or nonoccurrences of the behavior. The collected data provide the child and the teacher with feedback regarding the frequency of the behavior. Teachers may find it useful to teach students how to chart and graph the behavior they count. Students will often find this very motivating (Workman, 1998).

Students will usually have to be taught self-monitoring by teachers. Programs to teach students to use self-monitoring strategies should include the components listed in Table 11.2.

TABLE 11.2 Teaching Self-Monitoring

Teaching Steps	Description
1. Select a target behavior	Choose a behavior that interferes with teaching, the student's education, or the education of others.
2. Operationally define the target behavior	Precisely define the target behavior so both the student and the teacher agree when it occurs.
3. Monitor the target behavior	Set up a monitoring system to ensure accuracy (e.g., random student–teacher matches).
4. Evaluate progress	The student and the teacher should have frequent evaluation meetings so that the teacher can provide feedback and monitor progress.
5. Fade self-monitoring	When the student's behavior approaches desired levels, the self-monitoring procedure should be faded (e.g., increasing the intervals between self-monitoring periods, using self-monitoring less frequently).

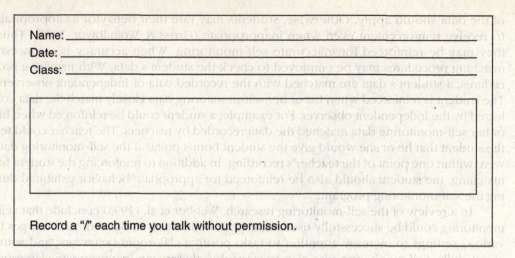

Name: _____

Date: _____

Class: _____

Record a "/" each time you talk without permission.

FIGURE 11.1   Example of a self-monitoring form using event sampling

Self-monitoring systems can be used with event recording procedures and time sampling procedures. In event recording, the student counts the number of times a particular behavior occurs. An example of event recording would be if the teacher taught a student to record the number of times he or she raised a hand to ask a question or make a comment during class. Figure 11.1 depicts a self-monitoring form using event recording.

In time sampling recording, a student might count the number of occurrences of a particular behavior within a specified period of time. For example, a student may mark whether he or she is seated when an audible beep on a tape is heard. This is a more sophisticated type of recording procedure. In addition to requiring that a student observe his or behavior accurately, the teacher must provide a tape with an audible tone. The tone serves as a cue for the student to record if the behavior occurred. Figure 11.2 is an

Name: _____

Date: _____

Environment: _____

Start time: _____ Stop time: _____

Intervals (forty 1-minute intervals)

Every time you hear the beep, record a "+" if you were paying attention or a "–" if you were not paying attention.

FIGURE 11.2   Example of a self-monitoring form using time sampling

CLASSROOM CONNECTION 11.1
A Classroom Example of Self-Monitoring

Nick, a second-grade student, blurted out answers in class without first raising his hand. He realized that his behavior was disruptive to the class but did not seem to be able to control it. Nick's teacher, Miss Quam, had put Nick on a behavior management system in which he was rewarded with a point every time he raised his hand for permission to speak. The system seemed to work, but Miss Quam wanted Nick to be able to control the behavior himself rather than having it controlled by an external management system. She decided to implement a self-monitoring system with reinforcement.

Miss Quam had a conference with Nick to explain the disruption caused by his blurting out answers in class. She explained that they would be working together to help Nick control this behavior. They talked about the fact that the class would not be disrupted if Nick raised his hand when he knew an answer. Together they practiced the desired behavior. Miss Quam also told Nick that he would be monitoring his own behavior. She explained to Nick that when he became aware of the correct behavior it would be easier for him to do it.

Nick was given a chart to record his hand-raising behavior. Every time he would raise his hand to get permission to answer a question, he was to put a slash mark on the chart. Miss Quam also marked each occasion of Nick raising his hand on a chart at her desk. At the end of each period, Nick and Miss Quam would compare charts. They would count the number of matching slashes, and Nick would receive that number of points. Verbal praise would also be given. Together

they practiced marking the chart. When Miss Quam was satisfied that Nick understood the procedure, she told him that they would start doing it in class the next day. On Fridays they would review the charts for every day of the week to see whether the procedure was helping.

The procedure was in place for 2 weeks and was very successful. Nick was raising his hand for permission to speak and very seldom blurted out an answer. During the evaluation meetings, he expressed a great deal of satisfaction with his newfound control. At this point Miss Quam decided to start fading the procedure. First she withdrew the point reinforcers. The next Monday, Nick was told he only had to do the procedure twice a day rather than for each academic period. By Thursday, he was told he had only to count once a day. A week later, Nick was only recording his behavior on Mondays and Fridays. The hand-raising behavior continued at a high rate, so Miss Quam told Nick they would only do the procedure once in a while. After stopping the program, Miss Quam noted that Nick still raised his hand for permission to talk and seldom blurted out in class.

General Reflection for Classroom Connection 11.1:

What are the reinforcement properties of Nick's self-monitoring program? How and why do you think the element of being in control of your own data collection affects Nick's behavior? Do you think Nick's data will be accurate, and do you think that makes a difference? Can you think of examples of adults monitoring their behavior in an effort to control their behavior?

example of self-monitoring using time sampling. A classroom example of self-monitoring is presented in Classroom Connection 11.1.

SELF-EVALUATION   In self-evaluation, or self-assessment, the student compares his or her behavior against a preset standard to determine whether the performance meets a particular criterion (Cole, 1987). Maag (1989) refers to self-evaluation as self-monitoring followed by a covert evaluation of the behavior.

Research has indicated that self-evaluation can be a useful intervention. For example, Smith, Young, West, Morgan, and Rhode (1988) trained four boys with behavior disorders in a self-evaluation procedure. The target behaviors were off-task and disruptive behaviors. The training was conducted in three phases. In the first phase the boys were taught classroom rules. Behavior was rated on a 5-point scale in accordance with how closely they followed the rules. The boys rated their behavior on an evaluation card every 10 minutes. Each student was asked to record a "5" or "excellent" if he followed classroom rules and worked on assigned tasks for the entire interval; "4" or "very good" if he followed classroom rules and worked for the entire interval with the exception of one minor infraction; "3" or "average" if he followed the rules and worked without any serious offenses except for receiving two reminders to get to work; "2" or "below average" if he followed rules and worked for approximately half of the interval; "1" if he followed the rules and worked for half the interval but had to be separated from the group; and "0" or "unacceptable" if he did not follow classroom rules nor do any work during the interval. The students were told to rank their behavior on the scale and that their teachers would do the same. The teacher would mark each boy's card to indicate her rating at the end of a certain period of time. The two scales would be compared, and the students would receive points for matching or nearly matching the teacher. Points could be exchanged for tangible reinforcers.

In the second phase, the students continued to evaluate their behavior, but they only matched evaluations with the teacher every 15 minutes. During the third phase, students continued to evaluate themselves on the scale; however, they only matched evaluations with the teacher once every 30 minutes. Phase 3 was not as effective in reducing inappropriate behaviors as phases 1 and 2. Results indicated that the self-evaluation procedures paired with teacher matching were effective in reducing off-task and disruptive behavior in the special-education classroom. The authors concluded that self-evaluation paired with teacher matching was an effective intervention and that the procedures were effective even though the behaviors were not first brought under control by an external behavior management procedure. Data collected in regular classrooms did not show *treatment generalization.* According to the authors, this was anticipated because regular classroom teachers were unwilling or unable to implement the procedure. They suggest that peers in the regular classroom might be used in the program to match evaluations, thereby freeing the teachers from this responsibility.

Similarly, Nelson, Smith, and Colvin (1995) reported the results of an investigation of a self-evaluation procedure on the recess behavior of students with behavior problems. In the investigation, the authors also describe the effects of using peers to enhance the generalizability of the procedure. Target students were taught the guidelines for appropriate recess behavior using direct instruction and role-playing. Next the students were taught to rate their actual recess behavior against the recess guidelines using a 4-point scale with 3 as excellent and 0 as unacceptable. Students rated their behavior on point cards twice during the morning recess period. A peer matched to the target student also rated his or her behavior. Following recess, points were totaled and exchanged for backup reinforcers. Results indicated that the self-evaluation procedure produced clear improvements in the recess behaviors of the target students (e.g., positive social behavior toward peers, isolation, positive social behavior toward adults, appropriate equipment use, and game playing). The authors also report that the improved recess behaviors generalized to the afternoon recess period.

Teaching Students to Self-Evaluate.   Teaching students to use self-evaluation requires a criterion or goal by which the student can compare his or her performance. Additionally, teaching students to self-evaluate must begin with teaching the student to self-monitor. This is because self-monitoring is a prerequisite for self-evaluation; the student needs data

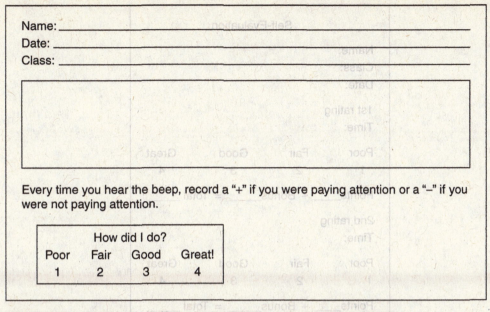

Name: _____

Date: _____

Class: _____

Every time you hear the beep, record a "+" if you were paying attention or a "–" if you were not paying attention.

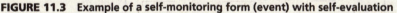

How did I do?			
Poor	Fair	Good	Great!
1	2	3	4

FIGURE 11.3   Example of a self-monitoring form (event) with self-evaluation

to compare his or her performance against. Once data exist, the student will have information on which the performance can be evaluated. The end result of self-evaluation is that the student decides whether his or her behavior has reached the desired level.

Perhaps the simplest method of self-evaluation is to include a rating scale at the bottom of a self-monitoring sheet. The student first monitors and records the target behavior and then evaluates his or her behavior against a preset standard. For example, if the student is monitoring talkouts during a 1-hour class period, after the monitoring is completed the student tallies the data and compares it with a criterion level. The student then evaluates the behavior monitored against a rating scale. A rating scale may have a range from 1 to 4 with a definition for each point on the scale (e.g., 4 = excellent, 3 = good, 2 = fair, and 1 = poor). An example of a self-monitoring sheet with an evaluation scale is depicted in Figure 11.3.

Figure 11.4 is an example of a self-evaluation rating scale that requires students to make evaluative judgments on their behavior following longer periods of time and without a formal self-monitoring system.

When using self-evaluation training to teach students to evaluate their own behavior, the following guidelines will be helpful:

First, students must be able to accurately monitor their own behavior. To do a self-evaluation procedure students must be adept at monitoring behaviors, then they may (a) compare the behaviors they monitored with a preset criterion and (b) evaluate their performance.

Second, the teacher and student should set a daily goal. This goal will then serve as a criterion by which the student can self-evaluate. The goal describes the level of performance toward which the student should work.

Third, the student should receive feedback from the teacher. If the student reaches the goal, he or she should receive systematic reinforcement. If the teacher is concerned

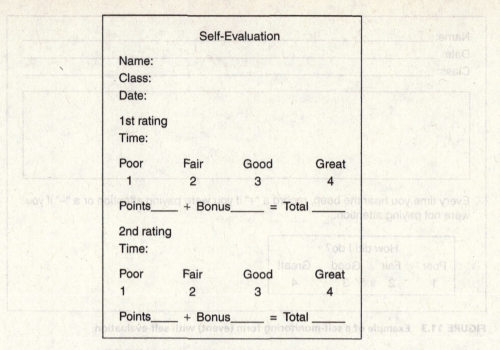

```
                    Self-Evaluation

        Name:

        Class:

        Date:

        1st rating
        Time:

        Poor         Fair         Good         Great
          1            2            3            4

        Points_____ + Bonus_____ = Total _____

        2nd rating
        Time:

        Poor         Fair         Good         Great
          1            2            3            4

        Points_____ + Bonus_____ = Total _____
```

FIGURE 11.4   Example of a self-evaluation form

about accuracy in ratings, he or she may want to include a matching procedure for additional reinforcement.

Finally, teachers should systematically fade their presence in the process. If self-evaluation training is to be effective, the student must be able to self-evaluate independently of the teacher.

SELF-REINFORCEMENT   In traditional behavior modification programs, the practitioner specifies the target behavior and delivers the reinforcers for performance of the behaviors. In many self-management packages, the student chooses a reinforcer and delivers the reinforcer following appropriate behavior. This is referred to as *self-reinforcement*. Research on the use of self-reinforcement is unclear. Some researchers have demonstrated that self-determined reinforcers can be as effective as or even more effective than teacher-controlled reinforcers (Hayes, Rosenfarb, Wulfert, Munt, Korn, & Zettle, 1985), while others contend that there is little empirical evidence to support the efficacy of self-reinforcement (Maag, 1989).

Self-reinforcement, like reinforcement delivered by teachers, must be delivered in a systematic and consistent manner. Research has indicated that initially reinforcement should be teacher managed and delivered. As the child progresses, teacher involvement should be decreased and the student's involvement increased. Wolery, Bailey, and Sugai (1988) offer the following guidelines for self-reinforcement:

- The student should be fluent at accurate self-monitoring.
- The student should be involved in setting the criteria for receiving reinforcement and selecting reinforcers.

- Teachers should provide reinforcement for target behaviors displayed by the student, accurate matches between teacher and student data, and accurate determination by the student of whether the criteria for reinforcement were met.
- Matching requirements and teacher evaluation should be faded over time.
- Opportunities for the students to evaluate their performance, determine criteria for reinforcement, select reinforcers, and administer reinforcement should be systematically increased.
- Naturally occurring reinforcers should be used throughout the process.

Other factors that contribute to the maintenance of desired behavior are continuous teacher praise, peer reinforcement for appropriate behavior, and accurate self-evaluation (Drabman, Spitalnik, & O'Leary, 1973).

While most self-management packages include self-reinforcement, some have investigated the effectiveness of self-punishment. In self-punishment, the student is taught to punish rather than reinforce his or her own behaviors. In several investigations (Humphrey, Karoly, & Kirschenbaum, 1978; Kaufman & O'Leary, 1972), the self-punishment procedure used was response cost in conjunction with a token economy. Humphrey et al. (1978) compared self-punishment with self-reinforcement. Their study took place in a chaotic elementary classroom. A self-reinforcement system and a self-punishment system were compared. The students in the self-reinforcement condition reinforced themselves with tokens for accurate performance on reading assignments. The students in the self-punishment condition began each morning with tokens and removed them for inaccurate work or failure to complete work on time. The researchers found that under both conditions the rate of attempted reading assignments was accelerated and accuracy was maintained. The self-reinforcement condition, however, produced slightly better results.

Teaching Students to Use Self-Reinforcement.   When teaching students to use self-reinforcement, three important factors must be addressed. First, students must be able to monitor their behavior and evaluate their behavior. They must be able to evaluate their performance, and the evaluation must be positive, before they can self-reinforce. Second, the teacher and students must decide whether the self-reinforcement will be external (e.g., tokens, tangibles, preferred activities) or internal (self-praise). Finally, the teacher and students should set a criterion level before the student can self-reinforce. Teachers should adhere to the principle of shaping successive approximations when having students use self-reinforcement (see Chapter 5).

APPLICATION   According to Sugai and Lewis (1990), when teaching self-management skills to students, certain conditions must be maintained. During the preintervention phase of training, the student should be involved. Together, the teacher and student should develop the goals of the self-management program as well as the criteria and contingencies necessary to meet the goals. The recording instrument must be developed at this time and should be simple and easy to use. The student must be trained in the use of the recording procedure, including direct instruction and numerous opportunities for practice. Prior to implementing the procedure, the student must be as fluent as possible in self-monitoring. If a self-reinforcement component will be used, the teacher should involve the student in selecting reinforcers. The student must then be trained in the use of the self-reinforcement procedure.

TABLE 11.3 Guidelines for Increasing the Effectiveness of Self-Management Training

- The behavior to be self-managed should first be brought under external control so the student associates the appropriate behavior with reinforcement.
- Behavioral contracts for self-management can be used initially to provide structure.
- The student must have numerous opportunities to practice self-management with immediate feedback given.
- The student must be motivated to participate; this can be encouraged by involving the student in the procedure from the initial stages.
- To involve the student in the process and to increase motivation, teachers should record and post the student's behavioral performance.
- The teacher should periodically monitor the procedure and provide "booster" sessions if necessary.

During the intervention phase of the procedure, a matching strategy is suggested. During this phase, the student is reinforced for appropriate behavior and accurate self-monitoring. Prompts should be provided to cue the student when to self-monitor and record (e.g., beeps on a recorder). The matching procedure, as well as the actual self-monitoring procedure, should be faded when the behavioral criteria are reached. Following the fading of the intervention, teachers should continue to collect data to ensure that behaviors continue at appropriate levels in all settings. If the target behaviors fall below criteria, the procedure may have to be reimplemented. Guidelines for increasing the effectiveness of self-management are included in Table 11.3.

SELF-INSTRUCTIONAL TRAINING

Definition

In self-instructional training, students are taught a generic set of statements that they say to themselves when confronted with various situations. For example, when doing a mathematics assignment requiring long division, the student may be taught a self-instructional strategy to solve long division problems. Similarly, when confronted with a situation that may lead to anger, the student may be taught a self-instructional strategy to keep him- or herself calm. Self-instruction is the use of personal verbal prompts. Teachers who train students in self-instruction teach them to guide their behavior using these prompts.

Research Basis

Luria's (1961) developmental theory serves as the basis of self-instructional training. Although most students follow a normal developmental sequence in which they acquire self-regulation, for some children this does not occur or only partially occurs. These students are deficient in the ability to use internal speech to control behavior. Similarly, students who have not developed mediational skills will have difficulties in solving problems.

Research on Self-Instructional Training and Problem Behavior

Meichenbaum and Goodman (1971) investigated hyperactive and impulsive students. They found that many of the students in their studies had deficiencies in internal speech and verbal mediation abilities. Because of their verbal mediation problems, these students did not use self-talk to control their behavior. In a series of investigations, Meichenbaum and his colleagues (Meichenbaum, 1977; Meichenbaum & Asarnow, 1979; Meichenbaum & Goodman, 1971) used Luria's developmental sequence to teach them to use self-instructions to control their behavior. In other words, the students were taught to talk to themselves as a method to learn to control their impulsive behaviors.

Meichenbaum and Goodman taught the impulsive students to ask themselves a series of questions when confronted with tasks that would typically lead to impulsive behavior. The students were taught to say four types of statements or questions:

- *Problem definition:* For example, "What do I need to do?"
- *Attention focusing and response guidance:* For example, "What should I do to solve this problem?
- *Self-reinforcement:* For example, "I did a good job."
- *Self-evaluative*, coping skills, and error correction: For example, "I didn't do so well, but that's OK, I can start over again."

Meichenbaum and Goodman's study proved to be very successful. Based on their work with impulsive students, the researchers developed the generic self-instructional training protocol, provided in Table 11.4.

Self-instructional training has also been used with aggressive children. Aggressive children tend to react to problem situations with anger, not taking time to "stop and think" or consider alternatives in responding to provocative situations.

Camp, Blom, Herbert, and Van Doornick (1977) conducted some of the earliest studies examining the use of self-instruction training with aggressive children. The primary purpose of these researchers' studies was to teach aggressive children to engage in coping self-instructions when responding to provocations. *Coping* refers to the child's ability to deal with perceived aversive events in a constructive rather than negative manner (e.g., walking away from a perceived insult rather than starting a fight). Camp and her colleagues developed the *Think Aloud* program to teach aggressive

TABLE 11.4 Steps in Teaching Students to Use Self-Instructions

Step 1: Cognitive modeling	The teacher models task performance while using self-instructions. This stage requires the teacher to model aloud. The student observes in this stage.
Step 2: Overt external guidance	The student performs the same task under the teacher's direction. The teacher says the self- instructions aloud while the student performs the task.
Step 3: Overt self-instructions	The student performs the same task, while saying the self-instructions aloud. The teacher observes and provides feedback.
Step 4: Faded self-instructions	The student performs the task while whispering the instructions to him- or herself. The teacher observes and provides feedback.
Step 5: Covert self-instructions	The student performs the task using covert self-instructions.

boys to use coping self-instructions. The self-instructional training methods were very similar to those developed by Meichenbaum and Goodman. The Think Aloud program attempted to train the aggressive boys in using self-instructions in a problem-solving sequence. The children were taught a generic format of instructional prompts to (a) identify a problem, (b) generate a solution, (c) monitor their use of the solution, and (d) evaluate their performance. The instructional prompts were questions the children would use when confronted with a provocative situation. The questions the children asked themselves were (a) "What is my problem?" (b) "What is my plan?" (c) "Am I using my plan?" and (d) "How did I do?" The researchers' goal was to teach these aggressive children to talk to themselves when confronted with situations that would often lead to aggression. The procedures were very successful in achieving the desired results.

Research on Self-Instructional Training and Academic Problems

Interventions using self-instructional procedures were originally devised for the purpose of altering behavior problems in children. However, these procedures have also been extended to academic interventions, particularly in the area of academic strategy training (Lloyd, 1980). Self-instructional procedures, when applied to academic performance, are designed to help learners improve their academic problem-solving behaviors.

It has been theorized that many behavior problems actually stem from learning problems. Torgeson (1982) has stated that learning problems in children might be due to a failure to apply basic abilities efficiently by using effective task strategies. Students who manifest these failures have been referred to as *inactive learners* (Torgeson, 1982). To remediate these inefficient learning strategies, teachers should assess the cognitive task strategies needed for competence in a particular area. For example, if a student is being taught long division, the teacher should teach the student the steps necessary to complete a long division problem. If these steps are then taught to students, and they use them appropriately, they will become more active, self-regulating learners.

In designing CBM strategies, researchers conduct a cognitive task analysis of the processes involved and determine what processes are used by academically successful students. Researchers then develop a training procedure that will enhance the use of these processes (Wong, 1989). The purpose of these training procedures is to help learners improve their academic performance by using cognitive mediation strategies.

The basic procedures in many of these interventions are similar. The teacher models the processes while using self-instructions; students then follow the examples, first overtly and then covertly (Meichenbaum, 1977). According to Meichenbaum, the teacher modeling provides a window on the thinking processes. Eventually, by learning the strategies through modeling and self-instructions, the students take over their own learning.

A few examples will illustrate this process. Rinehart, Stahl, and Erickson (1986) taught summarization to grade school students using modeling and self-instructional training. The students were taught to produce summaries of reading material that included main and supporting ideas. The researchers found that the students trained in the procedure, when compared with students not trained, improved their recall of main ideas.

The teachers in this study used the self-instruction developed by Meichenbaum and Goodman (1971) to teach their students the verbal prompts that they should use when summarizing materials. This process entails three steps:

Step One: The teachers explained the purpose of summarization to the students.

Step Two: The teachers modeled writing summaries of sample paragraphs. They used overt self-instructions while producing the summaries. The students did similar self-instructing. The teachers would model monitoring of the summaries using the following instructions: "Have I found the overall idea that the paragraph or group of paragraphs is about? Have I found the most important information that tells more about the overall idea? Have I used information that is not directly about the overall idea? Have I used any information more than once?" Students then completed summaries while the teachers provided feedback.

Step Three: When the students became proficient in summarizing short paragraphs using this strategy, the teachers extended the summarization procedure to longer paragraphs.

Graham and Harris (1985) report another example of using a self-instructional program to teach writing skills to students with learning disabilities. These researchers developed an instructional program based in part on Meichenbaum's (1977) self-instructional training. In teaching the writing program to students, the researchers assessed the student's level of performance, described the learning strategy, and modeled the strategy using self-instructions (see Table 11.5).

After modeling the story, the teacher and student discussed the importance of using self-instructions. The student was asked to identify the self-instructions and to write examples of self-instructions in his or her own words. The self-control strategy training resulted in increases in student performance above baseline levels. The authors conclude that self-control strategy training improved and maintained composition skills among children with learning disabilities.

When using self-instructional training to teach academics, teachers do not need to adhere precisely to any formula. Instead, teachers should follow the general procedural outline outlined by Meichenbaum and Goodman to teach the strategy. Whether teaching a child to do long division or to do a household chore, the teacher or parent can use cognitive behavior modification by modeling the task and self-instructing while modeling. Through self-instructions the child is taught to do a kind of thinking they could not, or

---

TABLE 11.5 Self-Instructions

Problem definition: What is it I have to do? I have to write a good story. Good stories make sense and use many action words.

Planning: Look at the picture and write down good action words. Think of a good story. Write my story—make good sense and use good action words.

Self-evaluation: Read my story and ask, "Did I write a good story? Did I use action words?" Fix my story—can I use more good action words?

Self-reinforcement: That was a great story.

would not, otherwise do (Meichenbaum & Asarnow, 1979). The child's internal dialogue is used to facilitate performance.

Application

Teachers should use the following guidelines based on Meichenbaum and Goodman's (1971) work when using cognitive behavior modification to teach students skills or strategies. First, the teacher should determine what it is the student needs to know and what is the current level of performance. Second, the teacher must describe the strategy to be taught and model it to the student while using self-instructions. Third, the student should practice the strategy using self-instructions under the teacher's guidance. The self-instructions are spoken aloud. It is important at this stage that the student has as many opportunities to practice as possible. Fourth, when the student can successfully perform the strategy under controlled practice conditions using overt self-instructions, he or she is allowed to practice independently using covert self-instructions. Students should be encouraged to monitor their use of strategies and to continue to use them. Explaining that the skills that are being taught will help decrease problem behaviors or increase performance in academic subjects can increase student motivation.

For example, if the teacher had determined that the child could not do long division, he or she would decide on a strategy for teaching the skill to the student. If the teacher decided to use the divide, multiply, subtract, bring down, check model (Burkell, Schneider, & Pressley, 1990) to teach the student, he or she would explain the model and how it is used. The teacher would then model the strategy using self-instructions ("First I divide"; "The next step is to multiply"; etc.) while doing a long division problem to successful completion. The next step would involve having the student practice long division problems while the teacher gives the self-instructions. The student would then practice long division using self-instructions (still under the teacher's guidance) until he or she has mastered the strategy. When the teacher is satisfied that the student has mastered the self-instructional procedure, the student should independently practice the skill using the self-instructional strategy covertly. Evaluation of the success of the cognitive behavior procedures must take place during training and on completion of training.

Whatever the purpose and content of training, the methods of training will be similar. Whatever the type of self-instructional training, five basic components should be included for teaching both behavior and academic strategies (see Table 11.6).

When using self-instructional training to teach students to be more reflective and deliberate in their responses to problems, teachers will find the following guidelines helpful.

TABLE 11.6 Generic Self-Instruction Protocol

1. *Problem definition instructions:* The student first learns to define the problem.
2. *Problem approach instructions:* The student verbalizes potential strategies to solve the problem.
3. *Attention-focusing instructions:* The student focuses his or her attention on the problem by asking whether he or she is using the strategy.
4. *Coping statement instructions:* If a mistake is made, the student uses statements to cope with the error and to encourage another try.
5. *Self-reinforcement instructions:* The student reinforces him- or herself for doing a good job.

First, it is important that teachers model the self-instruction process. Teachers should perform the task and verbally self-instruct while the student is observing. It is important in modeling that teachers use the same self-instructional process as the student will be using.

Second, teachers must consider the student's ability. It has been shown that if students need practice prior to performing a task or if they are unable to perform a task, self-instructions can actually interfere with their performance. Self-instructions will not enable students to perform tasks that are not in their repertoires. Similarly, they must be capable of understanding the statements to be used.

Third, teachers should systematically fade their presence in the process. If self-instructional training is to be effective, the student must be able to self-instruct independently of the teacher.

Fourth, teachers must systematically reinforce the student's accurate use of self-instructions and demonstrations of target behaviors.

PROBLEM-SOLVING TRAINING

Definition

Children are faced with conflicts, choices, and problems daily. Successful problem solving is necessary for effective coping and independence. The ability to confront and solve these problems successfully is an important factor in social and emotional adjustment. The inability to solve problems in an effective manner can lead to future social and emotional difficulties. Researchers have attempted to remediate difficulties in problem solving through formal training. The training represents a form of self-instruction to teach procedures for systematically approaching, evaluating, and solving interpersonal problems (Braswell & Kendall, 1988). Training in problem solving has been effective in reducing behavior problems and aggression, controlling impulsivity, and increasing appropriate social interaction (Harris, 1982).

Theoretical Foundation and Research Base

Goldstein (1999) states that problem solving typically involves a stepwise sequence of problem definition, identification of alternative solutions, choice of an optimal solution, implementation of the solution, and evaluation of the solution's effectiveness. D'Zurilla and Goldfried (1971) present five steps that could be used to teach problem-solving ability:

1. *Orientation to the problem:* Help the student learn to recognize problems and to realize that one can deal with problems in appropriate ways.
2. *Definition of the problem:* Clearly define the problem and any factors related to it.
3. *Generation of alternatives:* The teacher and student think of as many solutions to the problem as possible.
4. *Decision making.* The teacher and student consider all alternatives generated in the previous step and devise a plan for implementing the chosen alternative.
5. *Verification.* Implement the plan and monitor the results. If the problem is not solved, the teacher and student should start over at step 1.

The seminal work in problem solving was done by Spivak, Shure, and colleagues in the mid- to late 1970s. The training program developed by Spivak and Shure (1974) is

TABLE 11.7 Guidelines for Teaching Problem Solving

1. *Alternative solution thinking:* The ability to generate different options or potential solutions to a problem was central to effective problem solving.
2. *Consequential thinking:* The ability to consider consequences that a behavior might lead to; this goes beyond the consideration of alternatives to the consideration of the consequences of potential solutions.
3. *Causal thinking:* The ability to relate one event to another over time with regard to why a particular event happened or will happen.
4. *Interpersonal sensitivity:* The ability to perceive that an interpersonal problem exists.
5. *Means–ends thinking:* The step-by-step planning done in order to reach a given goal. Means–ends thinking involves insight, forethought, and the ability to consider alternative goals.
6. *Perspective taking:* The ability of the individual to recognize and take into account the fact that different people have different motives and may take different actions.

called *interpersonal cognitive problem solving* (ICPS). The program is designed to teach children *how* to think, not *what* to think (Goldstein, 1999). Spivak and Shure believe that many teachers do not effectively teach problem solving. For example, in dealing with a young child who hits another child, teachers might typically respond with one of the following actions: They may (a) demand that the behavior stop ("Stop because I said so"), (b) explain why an action is inappropriate ("You might hurt your classmate"), (c) help the student understand the effect of the situation ("You hurt your classmate"), and (d) isolate the student ("Stay in the hallway until you're ready to behave appropriately"). These responses have serious limitations if the teacher's goal is to help the student develop effective ways of handling personal and interpersonal problems because the teacher does the thinking for the student.

In ICPS, children are taught a problem-solving process rather than solutions to problems. The core of the program is the six specific problem-solving skills listed in Table 11.7.

Siegel and Spivak (1973) also developed an ICPS training program for older adolescents and adults. It is designed to teach basic problem-solving skills. The program teaches four problem-solving steps: (a) recognition of the problem, (b) definition of the problem, (c) alternative ways of solving the problem, and (d) deciding which solution is the best way to solve the problem.

Goldstein (1999), drawing on the work done by Spivak and Shure, developed a problem-solving training program as part of the Prepare Curriculum. The Prepare Curriculum is a series of courses designed to teach adolescents and younger children prosocial competencies. It is specifically designed for youngsters demonstrating prosocial deficiencies that fall toward either end of a continuum defined at one extreme by chronic aggressiveness, antisocial behavior, and juvenile delinquency and at the other extreme by chronic withdrawal, asocial behavior, and social isolation. The problem-solving course is taught to groups of students over an 8-week period. Group structure is provided by a set of rules and procedures explained at the beginning of a session. During each session, a poster that shows the problem-solving process being covered during that session is displayed.

The program also uses a "problem log" that students fill out. The logs are to be an accurate record of any problems that students encounter. The purpose of the problem log is to help students determine what their problem situations are and to assist them to

Problem Diary

What was the problem? Describe the problem.

What did you do to stop the problem?

Did your choice solve the problem?

How would you rate your solution (circle one)?

Poor   Fair   Good   Great

How will you handle this problem if it happens again?

FIGURE 11.5   Problem diary

begin thinking about ways of handling the problems. An example of a problem diary similar to Goldstein's problem log is provided in Figure 11.5.

Problem logs are also used in role-plays. Skills taught in the program include the following:

- *Stop and think.*   Students in the program are taught that when a problem is encountered, they must stop and think, or they might decide too quickly. They are to use this time to think of alternate ways to handle the problem.
- *Problem identification.*   Once the students realize a problem exists and have stopped to think, they have to state the problem clearly and specifically.
- *Gathering information from their own perspective.*   Students have to decide how they see a problem and gather information about the problem before acting. If all the information is not available, trainees are taught to ask for it.
- *Gathering information from other's perspectives.*   Students learn the necessity of looking at situations from other people's points of view.
- *Alternatives.*   Students are taught that to make a good choice in any situation requires more than one way of acting.
- *Evaluating consequences and outcomes.*   Once trainees are taught to consider a number of alternatives, they are told they must consider the consequences of each. Once a decision is made it must be evaluated.

In a review of research on interpersonal problem-solving training, Coleman, Wheeler, and Webber (1993) found that although researchers were generally successful in demonstrating cognitive gains as a result of the training, they were far less successful in demonstrating generalization. The authors stated that the generalization problems called into question the basic premise of problem-solving training, which is that students will rely on the trained skills in real-life situations. Based on their review, the authors offer these recommendations for teachers in using problem-solving training: (a) try to individualize training by including only those students who demonstrate problem-solving deficits; (b) assess the quality and quantity of alternative solutions that students generate as a result of the training; (c) pair problem-solving training with social skills training and other behavioral interventions to remediate problem-solving deficits; and (d) evaluate the success of the program by choosing appropriate outcome measures such as problem-solving tasks, behavior ratings, and behavior observations.

Application

The work of D'Zurilla and Goldfried (1971), Spivak and Shure (1974), and Goldstein (1999) present useful models teachers can use to teach problem solving to students. The following guidelines based on the work of these researchers should be followed when using cognitive behavior modification to teach children problem-solving skills.

First, the teacher should direct instruction to teach the fundamental concepts of problem solving. We cannot assume the students will pick up these important skills by merely observing others. Important concepts should be presented using lecture, discussion, examples, and nonexamples. When appropriate, role-playing situations involving problem solving should be part of instruction. Additionally, students should be reinforced for appropriate participation in classroom activities.

Second, whenever possible, problem situations should be taken from students' real-life experiences, so that the instruction is much more likely to be socially valid. This means that the situations will be more meaningful for the students because they are congruent with the students' social setting and age. The use of a problem diary can be used as a springboard to class discussions (see Figure 11.5). Having students brainstorm during group discussions can also be used to generate lists of potential problems.

Third, problem-solving training should include the following components: (a) recognizing the problem, (b) defining the problem and the goal, (c) generating alternative solutions, (d) evaluating the solutions, and (e) making a plan to solve the problem. This can be done individually or during group discussions. Also discuss the relevance of problem solving for students' lives.

Fourth, provide your students with numerous opportunities to practice problem solving. This should be done in and outside the classroom (e.g., home setting).

Finally, be a model of effective problem solving. When a problem arises, deal with it in an effective manner, and share your methods of arriving at a solution with the students. Additionally, if you observe students using effective problem-solving strategies outside the classroom, reinforce them.

ANGER CONTROL TRAINING

Definition

In anger control training, children are taught to inhibit or control anger and aggressive behavior through self-instructions. Three well-known anger training procedures are those developed by Novaco (1975), Feindler and her colleagues (Feindler & Fremouw, 1983; Feindler, Marriott, & Iwata, 1984), Goldstein and Glick (1987), and Goldstein (1999).

These programs train children to respond to internal or external provocations with anger control procedures rather than anger and aggression.

Theoretical Foundation and Research Base

Novaco (1979) defined anger arousal as an affective stress reaction.

> Anger arousal is a response to perceived environmental demands—most commonly, aversive psychosocial events. Anger arousal results from particular appraisal of aversive events. External circumstances provoke anger only as mediated by their meaning to the individual. (pp. 252–253)

Novaco noted the importance of the individual's appraisal of events. Because he believed that anger is created, influenced, and maintained by self-statements, he designed a program based on Meichenbaum's self-instructional training. The purpose of the training is to develop an individual's ability to respond appropriately to stressful events. The goals of the program are to (a) prevent maladaptive anger from occurring, (b) enable the individual to regulate arousal when provocation occurred, and (c) provide the person with the skills to manage the provocation.

Anger control intervention consists of three stages: cognitive preparation, skill acquisition, and application training. In the cognitive preparation phase, trainees are educated about anger arousal and its determinants, the identification of circumstances that trigger anger, the positive and negative functions of anger, and anger control techniques as coping strategies. In the skill acquisition phase, trainees learn cognitive and behavioral coping skills. They are taught to recognize anger and to use alternative coping strategies. The self-instructional element of training is emphasized in this phase. In the final phase, application training, the trainees practice the skills taught through role-playing and homework assignments.

The self-instructional component of this intervention consists of self-statements in the four stages of the provocation sequence: (a) preparation for provocation, (b) impact and confrontation, (c) coping with arousal, and (d) reflecting on the provocation. Examples of self-instructions are listed in Table 11.8.

In the late 1970s and early 1980s, Feindler and her colleagues (Feindler & Fremouw, 1983; Feindler, Marriott, & Iwata, 1984) researched and refined the techniques of anger control training. In a series of investigations, support was provided for the cognitive preparation and skill acquisition phases and self-instructional training developed by Novaco (1979). The investigations refined the three processes of Novaco's training (i.e., cognitive preparation, skill acquisition, and application training) to include five sequences to be taught to students:

1. *Cues:*   The physical signals of anger arousal
2. *Triggers:*   The events and internal appraisals of those events that serve as provocations
3. *Reminders:*   Novaco's self-instructional statements that were used to reduce anger arousal
4. *Reducers:*   Techniques such as deep breathing and pleasant imagery that could be used along with reminders to reduce anger arousal
5. *Self-evaluation:*   The opportunity to self-reinforce or self-correct

---

TABLE 11.8 Self-Instructions for an Anger Control Training Program

---

Preparing for provocation

This could be a rough situation, but I know how to handle it. I can work out a plan to deal with this problem.

Easy does it, stick to the issues and don't take it personally.

There won't be any need for an argument. I know what to do.

Impact and confrontation

As long as I keep my cool, I'm in control of the situation.

I don't need to prove myself.

Don't make more out of this than you have to.

There is no point in getting mad. Think of what you have to do.

Look for positives, and don't jump to conclusions.

Coping with arousal

My muscles are getting tight. Relax and slow things down.

Time to take a deep breath.

He probably wants me to get angry, but I'm going to deal with it constructively.

Subsequent reflection—Conflict unresolved

Forget about the aggravation. Thinking about it only makes you upset. Try to shake it off.

Remember relaxation. It's a lot better than anger.

Don't take it personally. It's probably not as serious as I think.

Subsequent reflection—Conflict resolved

I handled that one pretty well. That's doing a good job.

I could have gotten more upset than it was worth.

My pride can get me into trouble, but I'm doing better at this all the time.

I actually got through that without getting angry.

Goldstein and Glick (1987) added to the work of Meichenbaum, Novaco, and Feindler in developing another form of *anger control training*. The goals were to teach children and adolescents to understand what caused them to become angry and aggressive and to master anger reduction techniques. According to Goldstein (1999):

> Many youngsters believe that in many situations they have no choice: The only way for them to respond is with aggression. Although they may perceive situations in this way, it is the goal of Anger Control Training to give them the skills necessary to make a choice. By learning what causes them to be angry and by learning to use a series of anger reduction techniques, participating trainees will become more able to stop their almost "automatic" aggressive responses long enough to consider constructive alternatives. (p. 256)

Anger control training consists of modeling, role-playing, and performance feedback. Group leaders describe and model the anger control techniques and conflict situations in which they may be used. In role-playing, the students take part in role-plays in which they practice the just-modeled techniques. Role-plays are of actual provocative encounters provided by the students. Each role-playing session is followed by a brief

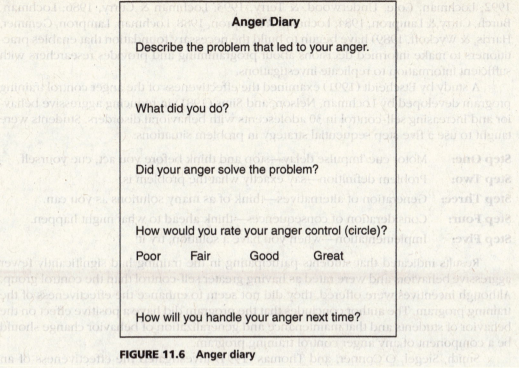

Anger Diary

Describe the problem that led to your anger.

What did you do?

Did your anger solve the problem?

How would you rate your anger control (circle)?

Poor   Fair   Good   Great

How will you handle your anger next time?

FIGURE 11.6   Anger diary

performance feedback period during which the group leaders point out to the students involved in the role-playing how well they used the technique. Group leaders also provide reinforcement following role-plays.

A unique aspect of the program used in the role-plays is the "hassle log." The hassle log is a structured questionnaire that students fill out on actual provocative encounters. They have to answer questions concerning where they were when the hassle occurred, what happened, who else was involved, what they did, how they handled themselves, and how angry they were. The log is constructed so that even young children can fill it out; written responses are not required, and children simply check off options on the form. The trainees complete a form for each provocative encounter, whether they handle it in an appropriate manner or not. The advantage of the hassle log is that it provides accurate pictures of actual provocative encounters that occur, it helps trainees learn about what makes them angry and how they handle themselves, and it provides role-playing material. An example of a similar anger diary is shown in Figure 11.6.

During the 10-week training period, the group leaders also teach (a) the ABCs of aggressive behavior (A—What led up to the behavior? B—What did you do? C—What were the consequences?); (b) how to identify cues and triggers; (c) the use of reminders and anger reducers; (d) the importance of thinking ahead (the consequences of anger); and (e) the nature of the angry behavior cycle (identifying anger-provoking behavior and changing it).

It is difficult to draw reliable conclusions about the effectiveness of interventions designed to modify behavioral responses to anger without repeating techniques used in previous investigations. Lochman and his colleagues (see, e.g., Lochman, 1985; Lochman,

1992; Lochman, Coie, Underwood, & Terry, 1993; Lochman & Curry, 1986; Lochman, Burch, Curry,& Lampron, 1984; Lochman & Lampron, 1988; Lochman, Lampron, Gemmer, Harris, & Wyckoff, 1989) have begun to build the necessary foundation that enables practitioners to make informed decisions about programming and provides researchers with sufficient information to replicate investigations.

A study by Etscheidt (1991) examined the effectiveness of the anger control training program developed by Lochman, Nelson, and Sims (1981) in reducing aggressive behavior and increasing self-control in 30 adolescents with behavioral disorders. Students were taught to use a five-step sequential strategy in problem situations:

Step One: Motor cue/impulse delay—stop and think before you act, cue yourself.

Step Two: Problem definition—say exactly what the problem is.

Step Three: Generation of alternatives—think of as many solutions as you can.

Step Four: Consideration of consequences—think ahead to what might happen.

Step Five: Implementation—when you have a solution, try it!

Results indicated that students participating in the training had significantly fewer aggressive behaviors and were rated as having greater self-control than the control group. Although incentives were offered, they did not seem to enhance the effectiveness of the training program. The author concludes that the program did have a positive effect on the behavior of students and that maintenance and generalization of behavior change should be a component of any anger control training program.

Smith, Siegel, O'Conner, and Thomas (1994) investigated the effectiveness of an anger control training program in reducing the angry and aggressive behaviors of students with behavior problems. Students were taught a cognitive behavior strategy called ZIPPER. ZIPPER is a mnemonic for zip your mouth, identify the problem, pause, put yourself in charge, explore choices, and reset. The strategy was directly taught to students, modeled, role-played, and rehearsed. Additionally, the instructors gained the students' commitment to using the strategy outside the training. Results indicated that the students were able to learn the strategy and that the intervention resulted in a decreased level of the targeted behaviors. Data on maintenance indicated that the students were able to maintain the decreased levels of anger and aggression over time. The students enjoyed learning the strategy, and the teacher and paraprofessional in the classroom were very satisfied with the procedure. There was also some indication of generalization: a lunchroom monitor noted that the trained students seemed less angry and aggressive and were able to get along with other students.

Application

Students with problem behavior often have difficulty controlling their anger. Teaching students to control anger will be extremely valuable to their long-term adjustment. The work of Novaco (1979), Feindler et al. (1984), and Goldstein (1999) present important models teachers can use to teach anger control to students. The following guidelines based on the work of these researchers should be followed when using cognitive behavior modification to teach students anger control skills.

First, the teacher should direct instruction to teach the fundamental concepts of anger control. Important concepts in controlling anger should be presented using lecture, discussion, and role-playing situations. Additionally, students should be reinforced for appropriate participation in classroom activities.

Second, whenever possible, real-life situations involving anger should be taken from students' experiences. In this way the instruction is much more likely to be socially valid. This means that the situations will be more meaningful for the students because they are congruent with their social setting and age. The use of an anger diary can be used to generate individual or class discussions (see Figure 11.6).

Third, anger control training should include the following components: (a) recognizing anger (e.g., cues and triggers), (b) coping with anger (e.g., using reminders and reducers), (c) generating alternative solutions to anger, and (d) self-evaluation. This can be done individually or during group discussions. Also discuss the relevance of anger control for students' lives.

Fourth, provide your students with numerous opportunities to discuss anger control. Because anger control should be practiced in the school and home setting, students' parents should be aware of and participate in their child's anger control program. Finally, be a model of effective anger control. When a problem arises that could lead to an angry confrontation, manage the situation in an effective manner. Moreover, share your methods of arriving at a solution with the students. Additionally, if you observe students using effective anger control strategies outside of the classroom, reinforce them.

ALTERNATE RESPONSE TRAINING

Definition

In alternate response training, a student is taught an alternative or competing response that interferes with opportunities for an undesirable response to be emitted (Wolery et al., 1988). If an alternative response already exists in the student's repertoire, it can be strengthened as he or she learns to use the alternative behavior. In using alternate response training, a student must first be taught to self-monitor.

Relaxation training procedures designed to relieve stress and calm students have been investigated by researchers as an alternative response procedure. A widely used relaxation training procedure is progressive muscle relaxation (Maag, 1989). The training involves having students tense and relax muscles while focusing on the relaxation of particular parts of the body. Eventually the student focuses on relaxing the entire body. Muscle relaxation is a form of alternate response training that has been used to decrease disruptions and aggression and increase social skills and academic performance.

Theoretical Foundation and Research Base

Robin, Schneider, and Dolnick (1976) developed an alternate response intervention called the *turtle technique*. The turtle technique was developed to teach aggressive students to manage their aggressive impulses. The procedure consists of teaching the students to pull their arms and legs close to their bodies, put their heads on their desks, and imagine that they are turtles withdrawing into their shells. The students were taught to do this when they perceived that a provocative situation was about to occur, they felt frustrated or angry, or a teacher or classmate called out "turtle." They were also taught a muscle relaxation procedure. Once they mastered this technique, they were taught to relax while doing the turtle. Eventually, the students learn to relax and imagine withdrawing from the situation rather than actually going into the turtle position. Robin et al. (1976) found that students who had been taught the procedure behaved less aggressively. Morgan and Jenson (1988) state that the turtle technique and other similar approaches are worthy of consideration in selecting interventions.

Knapczyk (1988) reduced aggressive behaviors by students in regular and special class settings by using alternative social response training. Participants in the study were two male junior high school students in special-education programs. Both had been referred because of aggressive behavior. The treatment involved training the students in social skills that could be used as alternatives to the aggressive behavior. The students learned alternate responses through modeling and rehearsal. Videotapes were prepared and shown to the students that provided examples of events that often led to aggressive behavior. The tapes had two male students (of high social status in the school) demonstrating alternative responses to the aggression. One of the actors played the part of the participant. In response to a particular event the student actor would first simulate aggressive behaviors. The student would then demonstrate an acceptable alternative response rather than the aggressive response. The other student actor represented the reactions of peers. The teacher and participant viewed the videotapes together. Following a discussion, the participant was asked to demonstrate the appropriate behavior and provide additional alternatives. Results indicated that the treatments reduced the level of aggressive behaviors and led to an increase in peer-initiated interactions.

Application

When teaching students to use alternate responses to anger or other maladaptive behaviors, three important factors must be addressed. First, the student must be able to monitor his or her behavior. Specifically, the student must be able to recognize when the behavior that the teacher hopes to eliminate is occurring. For example, students must be able to recognize when they are becoming angry (e.g., stomach muscles tighten, fists clench). Teaching self-monitoring, therefore, is an essential prerequisite to alternate response training. Second, after the student has become adept at self-monitoring, the student is taught a specific technique that will compete with the maladaptive behavior. For example, Robin et al. (1976) taught students that when they were getting angry to imagine they were turtles pulling into their shells so that they could not be bothered. It is important that this technique is taught directly to students, that the teacher models the specific technique, and that students are given many opportunities to practice the procedure. When the technique is used appropriately, the teacher must reinforce the student. A classroom example of alternative response training is presented in Classroom Connection 11.2.

ATTRIBUTION RETRAINING

Definition

The cognitive behavior procedure of attribution retraining is based on attribution theory. Attribution theory posits that individuals seek causes for events in their environment and that these perceived causes influence subsequent behavior (Palmer & Stowe, 1989). Performance attributions can be influenced by a student's current performance, his or her history of performance, and the performance of others. A number of researchers

CLASSROOM CONNECTION 11.2
Alternate Response Training

Jerry is a fourth-grade student in a self-contained classroom for children with learning disabilities. He also has problems controlling his temper. His temper tantrums frequently follow requests to do academic work. The special-education teacher had implemented a point system with a response-cost component in an attempt to reduce the tantrums. The program had succeeded in reducing the tantrums but did not eliminate them. Because the tantrums were so disruptive to the class and Jerry became so upset following them, the teacher referred the problem to Mr. Cleveland, the school behavior specialist.

Mr. Cleveland observed Jerry at various times during the next week. He was present during two of Jerry's tantrums. He observed that prior to a tantrum, Jerry grew tense, grimaced, and frequently chewed on his fingernails. This behavior would escalate into tantrums in which Jerry would swear, throw books, damage objects, and so forth.

In a conversation with the special-education teacher and Mr. Cleveland, Jerry expressed frustration with his tantrums. He said he didn't like to "blow up" but couldn't help it. He also said that the tantrums made it hard for him to learn, that kids were afraid of him, and that his parents were upset about Jerry's violent temper. Jerry also said he wanted to be able to control his behavior.

Because Jerry was motivated to change his behavior and the tantrum behavior had been controlled with external management procedures, Mr. Cleveland felt that a cognitive behavior intervention may be effective. He chose to try a form of alternate response training with Jerry.

Jerry was first taught to recognize when a tantrum was about to occur by becoming aware of the tension in his body and his angry feelings. The next step was to teach him an alternate response to the tension and anger. Together Jerry and Mr. Cleveland decided on a technique using deep breathing, self-instruction, and visualization. When Jerry felt angry and tense, he was to fold his arms on his desk, put his head on his arms, breathe deeply 10 times, and say to himself, "Stop and think." While saying this silently, he was to think of a red stop sign with the words *stop and think* on it. Jerry was also told to go through this procedure when the teacher told him to stop and think. If Jerry performed the procedure correctly and didn't have a tantrum, he received social praise from the teacher. Following the procedure, the teacher was to reissue the original request if it was an academic or behavioral direction.

Within a few weeks of using the procedure, Jerry's temper tantrums were significantly reduced. The instances of the teacher having to remind Jerry to stop and think also were almost entirely eliminated. Jerry felt more in control of his behavior.

General Reflection for Classroom Connection 11.2:

In this example, Jerry is in the fourth grade. Do you think this alternate response training would work with younger students? How about older students? Think about how Jerry's original point system developed by his teacher might be integrated into the new program developed by the behavior specialist.

have examined the consequences of repeated failure on a student's attributions and the subsequent effects on his or her motivation and achievement (Palmer & Stowe, 1989). Attribution theorists believe that students with positive attributions impute successes to their effort and ability and failure to a lack of effort. When they experience repeated failure, however, they may impute failure to their lack of ability and success to good luck. As a result of these attributions, students become less likely to attempt or persist at accomplishing tasks. This lower level of persistence and effort can lead to additional failures.

Theoretical Foundations and Research Base

Attribution retraining attempts to replace negative attributions with positive attributions and thereby increase task persistence. The positive attributions are effort-oriented statements concerning their successes and failures (Maag, 1989). Dweck (1975) investigated attributional retraining with students who had difficulty solving math problems. The children were taught to make an effort-oriented statement, such as "Failure makes you try harder," when working on math problems. Results indicated that the students persisted longer on the problems. Borkowski, Weyhing, and Turner (1986) believed that attributions can also influence a student's use of learning strategies. Schunk (1983) indicated that attribution retraining may not work when a student has a specific skill deficit. However, attribution retraining is more likely to be successful when the student is not using the skills that he or she possesses.

Application

Attribution retraining usually consists of two phases (Licht & Kistner, 1986). In the first phase, the student is set up to experience some degree of failure. The failure is not severe and might consist of a few problems among a set that are too difficult for the student. In the second phase, the student is taught to make statements that attribute the failures to insufficient effort.

According to Licht and Kistner (1986), the following points are of crucial importance when teaching attributional statements. The teacher must convey to the students that increased effort leads to success rather than simply that they are not trying hard enough. It is also important that the student in attribution retraining does experience some success. Having students make self-statements like "increased effort will lead to increased success" will be more readily accepted when the student experiences some success. If he or she does experience success, this will validate the self-statements. Attribution retraining is likely to be successful if the student believes that the use of the strategy will contribute to future success.

Concerns have been raised about having students attribute their failures to lack of effort because this might convey to them that they are lazy. Anderson and Jennings (1980) suggest that students be taught to attribute their difficulties to ineffective task strategies. This would lead to less blame on the student's part. Licht and Kistner (1986) have suggested that attribution retraining be coupled with problem solving and strategy training. It might be advisable for the teacher to teach attributional statements and strategies as an integrated approach.

DEVELOPMENT AND GENERALIZATION OF CBM PROGRAMS

Developing cognitive behavior programs requires more than choosing a strategy and following a program of implementation. Harris (1982) outlines a three-stage process for constructing and implementing cognitive behavior interventions.

The first stage is *task analysis*. In this stage, the teacher must determine the cognitions and strategies necessary for successful performance in whatever is being taught. In determining the necessary strategies, the teacher might perform the task him- or herself and note the strategies used or observe those who do well on a task to determine necessary strategies. According to Meichenbaum (1976), determination of strategies involved in a task, the production of appropriate strategies, and the application and monitoring of these strategies are important considerations.

The second stage is *learner analysis*. In analyzing the learner, the teacher must consider a variety of characteristics (e.g., age, cognitive capabilities, language development, learning ability, initial knowledge state). These characteristics will influence the development of the training procedure. It is very important that the cognitive behavior training procedures and requirements be matched to the learner's characteristics if the training is to be successful.

The third stage is *development* and *implementation*. The teacher must establish the goals of training. The next step is to select the cognitive behavior procedures that are appropriate given the results of the task and learner analysis. In designing the intervention, the teacher must tailor the learning activities to the desired goals (Brown, Campione, & Day, 1981). After developing the cognitive behavior procedure, the teacher initiates training.

Previous chapters have documented powerful behavioral strategies that have been used successfully by teachers to modify behaviors in students. The effects of behavioral change programs, however, often are not generalized to other settings or maintained in treatment settings when the intervention procedures are withdrawn (Kerr & Nelson, 2006). Morgan and Jenson (1988) refer to self-management strategies as being among the more promising strategies to facilitate generalization. When behaviors are under external control by the teacher, the behaviors might not be controlled in situations and settings in which the teacher is not able to apply the external control procedures. When students are able to manage their behaviors, these behaviors will be more likely to last and to carry over to different situations and settings, even without external control by teachers. However, in a review of self-management strategies, Nelson, Smith, Young, and Dodd (1991) found that treatment effects of self-management procedures do not automatically generalize. They suggest that treatment effects will generalize if generalization is systematically programmed.

Kaplan (1995) offers several suggestions that teachers may use to encourage children to use CBM strategies outside the training environment. The following is a list of some of the suggestions:

- *Model the strategies.* The teacher should model the strategies taught when appropriate. Students should be able to observe the strategies in action. Teachers should share how they are using the strategies to help modify their behavior.
- *Teach the strategies to mastery.* The teacher should teach the skills and subskills in the CBM strategy taught to mastery. Periodic assessments may be necessary to determine whether a student has achieved mastery. When mastery is achieved, a student is much more likely to use the strategy. According to Kaplan (1995), a student has achieved mastery of a strategy when he or she is both fast and accurate in its use.
- *Reinforce appropriate use of strategies.* Whenever the teacher observes a student using a CBM strategy outside the training context, it is important that the teacher reinforce him or her. Teachers should also encourage the student's peers to reinforce appropriate behavior.
- *Program for generalization by giving homework assignments.* Give homework assignments that will require the CBM strategies to be used in environments outside the training context.
- *Discuss the relevance of each strategy when it is taught.* Students must be taught how the particular strategy is relevant to them and their situations. An effective way to do this is for the teacher to discuss the relevance of the strategy prior to training.

Summary

In this chapter, we have examined a number of interventions that fall under the general category of cognitive behavior modification. The review was not exhaustive but meant only to give the reader a flavor of the number of different strategies available for affecting the teacher's desired outcomes. Cognitive behavior strategies have been used to modify behavior, facilitate academic performance, train problem-solving ability, and foster self-control. The major aim of CBM is to teach students to be their own agents of change, in control of their behavior and learning.

Discussion Questions

1. What is cognitive behavior modification? List and explain the three basic assumptions and goals of CBM.
2. Discuss some advantages of teaching students to manage their own behavior using CBM.
3. Discuss problem solving and anger control training.
4. Discuss the three components of self-management training: self-monitoring, self-evaluation, and self-reinforcement.
5. List and explain guidelines for increasing the effectiveness of self-monitoring strategies.
6. Discuss procedures for encouraging the generalization of CBM strategies.

References

Alberto, P. A., & Troutman, C. A. (1999). *Applied behavior analysis for teachers* (5th ed.). Upper Saddle River, NJ: Merrill/Pearson Education.

Anderson, C. A., & Jennings, D. L. (1980). When experiences of failure promote expectations of success: The impact of attributing failure to ineffective strategies. *Journal of Personality, 48,* 393–407.

Baer, D. M. (1984). Does research on self-control need more control? *Analysis and Intervention in Developmental Disabilities, 4,* 211–284.

Bandura, A. (1977). *Social learning theory.* Upper Saddle River, NJ: Prentice-Hall.

Barkley, R., Copeland, A., & Sivage, C. (1980). A self-control classroom for hyperactive children. *Journal of Autism and Developmental Disorders, 10,* 75–89.

Beck, A. T. (1976). *Cognitive therapy and emotional disorders.* New York: International Universities Press.

Borkowski, J. G., Weyhing, R. S., & Turner, L. A. (1986). Attributional retraining and the teaching of strategies. *Exceptional Children, 53,* 130–137.

Braswell, L., & Kendall, P. C. (1988). Cognitive-behavioral methods with children. In K. S. Dobson (Ed.), *Handbook of cognitive-behavioral therapies* (pp. 167–213). New York: Guilford.

Broden, M., Hall, R. V., & Mitts, B. (1971). The effect of self-recording of the classroom behavior of two eighth grade students. *Journal of Applied Behavior Analysis, 4,* 191–199.

Brown, A. L., Campione, J. C., & Day, J. D. (1981). Learning to learn: On training students to learn from text. *Educational Researcher, 10,* 14–21.

Burkell, J., Schneider, B., & Pressley, M. (1990). Mathematics. In M. P. Pressley & Associates (Eds.), *Cognitive strategy instruction that really improves children's academic performance* (pp. 147–177). Cambridge, MA: Brookline Books.

Camp, B., Blom, G., Herbert, F., & Van Doornick, W. (1977). "Think aloud": A program for developing self-control in young aggressive boys. *Journal of Abnormal Child Psychology, 5,* 157–169.

Carr, S. C., & Puzo, R. P. (1993). The effects of self-monitoring of academic accuracy and productivity on the performance of students with behavioral disorders. *Behavioral Disorders, 18*(4), 241–250.

Christie, D. J., Hiss, M., & Lozanoff, B. (1984). Modification of inattentive classroom behavior: Hyperactive children's use of self-recording with teacher guidance. *Behavior Modification, 8,* 391–406.

Clark, L. A., & McKenzie, H. S. (1989). Effects of self-evaluation training on seriously emotionally disturbed children on the generalization of their classroom rule following and work behaviors across settings and teachers. *Behavioral Disorders, 14,* 89–98.

Cole, C. L. (1987). Self-management. In C. R. Reynolds & L. Mann (Eds.), *Encyclopedia of special education* (pp. 1404–1405). New York: Wiley.

Coleman, M., Wheeler, L., & Webber, J. (1993). Research on interpersonal problem-solving training: A review. *Remedial and Special Education 14,* 25–37.

Cooper, J. O., Heron, T. E., & Heward, W. L. (1987). *Applied behavior analysis.* New York: Merrill/Macmillan.

Craighead, W. F. (1982). A brief clinical history of cognitive-behavior therapy with children. *School Psychology Review, 11,* 5–13.

DiGangi, S. A., & Maag, J. W. (1992). A component analysis of self-management training with behaviorally disordered youth. *Behavioral Disorders, 17,* 281–290.

Drabman, R. S., Spitalnik, R., & O'Leary, K. D. (1973). Teaching self-control to disruptive children. *Journal of Abnormal Psychology, 82,* 10–16.

Dunlap, G., Clarke, S., Jackson, M., Wright, S., Ramos, E., & Brinson, J. (1995). Self-monitoring of classroom behaviors with students exhibiting emotional and behavioral challenges. *School Psychology Quarterly, 10,* 165–177.

Dweck, C. S. (1975). The role of expectations and attributions in the alleviation of learned helplessness. *Journal of Personality and Social Psychology, 31,* 674–685.

D'Zurilla, T. J., & Goldfried, M. R. (1971). Problem solving and behavior modification. *Journal of Abnormal Psychology, 78,* 107–126.

Ellis, A. (1973). Rational-emotive therapy. In R. Corsini (Ed.), *Current psychotherapies.* Itasca, IL: Peacock.

Etscheidt, S. (1991). Reducing aggressive behavior and improving self-control: A cognitive-behavioral training program for behaviorally disordered adolescents. *Behavioral Disorders, 16,* 107–115.

Feindler, E. L., & Fremouw, W. J. (1983). Stress inoculation training for adolescent anger problems. In D. Meichenbaum & M. E. Jaremko (Eds.), *Stress reduction and prevention.* New York: Plenum.

Feindler, E. L., Marriott, S. A., & Iwata, M. (1984). Group anger control training for junior high school delinquents. *Cognitive Therapy and Research, 8,* 299–311.

Goldstein, A. P. (1999). *The prepare curriculum: Teaching prosocial competencies (rev. ed.).* Champaign, IL: Research Press.

Goldstein, A. P., & Glick, B. (1987). *Aggression replacement training: A comprehensive intervention for aggressive youth.* Champaign, IL: Research Press.

Graham, S., & Harris, K. H. (1985). Improving learning disabled students' composition skills: Self-control strategy training. *Learning Disability Quarterly, 8,* 27–36.

Gross, A. M., & Wojnilower, D. A. (1984). Self-directed behavior change in children: Is it self-directed? *Behavior Therapy, 15,* 501–514.

Harris, K. R. (1982). Cognitive-behavior modification: Application with exceptional students. *Focus on Exceptional Children, 15,* 1–16.

Harris, K. R. (1986). Self-monitoring of attentional behavior versus self-monitoring of productivity: Effects on on-task behavior and academic response rate among learning disabled children. *Journal of Applied Behavior Analysis, 19,* 417–423.

Harris, K. R., & Graham, S. (1992). *Helping young writers master the craft: Strategy instruction and self-regulation in the writing process.* Cambridge, MA: Brookline Books.

Hayes, S. C., Rosenfarb, I., Wulfert, E., Munt, E. D., Korn, Z., & Zettle, R. D. (1985). Self-reinforcement effects: An artifact of social standard setting? *Journal of Applied Behavior Analysis, 18,* 201–214.

Homme, L. E. (1965). Perspectives in Psychology: XXIV. Control of coverants, the operants of the mind. *Psychological Record, 15,* 501–511.

Hughes, J. N. (1988). cognitive behavior therapy. In L. Mann & C. Reynolds (Eds.), *The encyclopedia of special education* (pp. 354–355). New York: Wiley.

Humphrey, L. L., Karoly, P., & Kirschenbaum, D. S. (1978). Self-management in the classroom: Self-imposed response cost versus self-reward. *Behavior Therapy, 9,* 592–601.

Jenson, A. (1971). The role of verbal mediation in mental development. *Journal of Genetic Psychology, 118,* 39–70.

Kanfer, F. H., & Karoly, P. (1972). Self-control: A behavioristic excursion into the lion's den. *Behavior Therapy, 3,* 398–416.

Kaplan, J. S. (1995). *Beyond behavior modification: A cognitive-behavioral approach to behavior management in the schools* (3rd ed.). Austin, TX: Pro-Ed.

Kaufman, S. K., & O'Leary, K. D. (1972). Reward, cost, and self-evaluation procedures for disruptive adolescents in a psychiatric hospital school. *Journal of Applied Behavior Analysis, 5*, 293–309.

Kazdin, A. E. (1982). Current developments and research issues in cognitive-behavioral interventions: A commentary. *School Psychology Review, 11*, 75–82.

Kendall, P. C., & Hollon, S. D. (1979). *Cognitive-behavioral interventions: Therapy, research and procedures*. New York: Academic Press.

Kern, L., Dunlap, G., Childs, K. E., & Clarke, S. (1994). Use of a classwide self-monitoring program to improve the behavior of students with emotional and behavioral disorders. *Education and Treatment of Children, 17*(3), 445–458.

Kern, L., Wacker, D. P., Mace, F. C., Falk, G. D., Dunlap, G., & Kromrey, J. D. (1995). Improving the peer interactions of students with emotional and behavioral disorders through self-evaluation procedures: A component analysis and group application. *Journal of Applied Behavior Analysis, 28*, 47–59.

Kendall, P. C., & Finch, A. J. (1979). Developing non-impulsive behavior in children's cognitive behavioral strategies on self-control. In P. C. Kendall & S. D. Hollan (Eds.), *Cognitive-behavioral interventions: Therapy, research and procedures*. New York: Academic Press.

Kerr, M. M., & Nelson, C. M. (2006). *Strategies for managing behavior problems in the classroom* (6th ed.). Upper Saddle River, NJ: Merrill/Pearson Education.

Kilburtz, C. S., Miller, S. R., & Morrow, L. W. (1985). Structured learning using self-monitoring to promote maintenance and generalization of social skills across settings for a behaviorally disordered adolescent. *Behavioral Disorders, 11*, 147–55.

King, N. J., Heyne, D., & Ollendick, T. (2005). Cognitive-behavioral treatments for anxiety and phobic disorders in children and adolescents: A review. *Behavioral Disorders, 30*, 241–257.

Koegel, R. L., & Koegel, L. K. (1990). Extending reductions in stereotypic behavior of students with autism through a self-management package. *Journal of Applied Behavior Analysis, 23*, 119–127.

Knapczyk, D. R. (1988). Reducing aggressive behaviors in special and regular class settings by training alternative social responses. *Behavioral Disorders, 14*, 27–39.

Levendoski, L. S., & Cartledge, G. (2000). Self-monitoring for elementary children with serious emotional disturbance: Classroom applications for increased academic responding. *Behavioral Disorders, 25*, 211–234.

Licht, B. G., & Kistner, J. A. (1986). Motivational problems of learning disabled children: Individual differences and their implications for treatment. In J. K. Torgeson & B. Y. L. Wong (Eds.), *Psychological and educational perspectives on learning disabilities* (pp. 225–249). New York: Academic Press.

Lloyd, J. W. (1980). Academic instruction and cognitive behavior modification: The need for attack strategy training. *Exceptional Education Quarterly, 8*, 53–63.

Lloyd, J. W., Bateman, D. F., Landrum, T. J., & Hallahan, D. P. (1989). Self-recording of attention versus productivity. *Journal of Applied Behavior Analysis, 22*, 315–323.

Lloyd, J. W., Hallahan, D. P., Kosiewicz, M. M., & Kneedler, R. D. (1982). Reactive effects of self-assessment and self-recording on attention to task and academic productivity. *Learning Disability Quarterly, 5*, 216–227.

Lochman, J. E. (1985). Effects of different treatment lengths in cognitive behavioral interventions with aggressive boys. *Child Psychiatry and Human Development, 16*, 45–56.

Lochman, J. E. (1992). Cognitive behavioral intervention with aggressive boys: Three-year follow-up and preventative effects. *Journal of Consulting and Clinical Psychology, 60*, 426–432.

Lochman, J. E., Coie, J. D., Underwood, M. K., & Terry, R. (1993). Effectiveness of a social relations intervention program for aggressive and nonaggressive, rejected children. *Journal of Consulting and Clinical Psychiatry, 61*, 1053–1058.

Lochman, J. E., Burch, P. R., Curry, J. F., & Lampron, L. B. (1984). Treatment and generalization effects of cognitive-behavioral and goal-setting interventions with aggressive boys. *Journal of Consulting and Clinical Psychology, 52*, 915–916.

Lochman, J. E., & Curry, J. F. (1986). Effects of social problem-solving and self-instruction training with aggressive boys. *Journal of Clinical Child Psychology, 15*, 159–164.

Lochman, J. E., & Lampron, L. B. (1988). Cognitive behavioral interventions for aggressive boys: Seven months follow-up effects. *Journal of Child and Adolescent Psychotherapy, 5*, 15–23.

Lochman, J. E., Lampron, L. B., Gemmer, T. C., Harris, R., & Wyckoff, G. M. (1989). Teacher consultation and cognitive-behavioral interventions with aggressive boys. *Psychology in the Schools, 26*, 179–188.

Lochman, J. E., Nelson, W. M., & Sims, J. (1981). A cognitive-behavioral program for use with aggressive children. *Journal of Clinical Child Psychology, 19*, 146–148.

Luria, A. (1961). *The role of speech in the regulation of normal and abnormal behaviors*. New York: Basic Books.

Maag, J. W. (1989). Use of cognitive mediation strategies for social skills training: Theoretical and conceptual issues. In R. B. Rutherford, Jr., & S. A. DiGangi (Eds.), *Severe behavior disorders of children and youth* (Vol. 12, pp. 87–100). Reston, VA: Council for Children with Behavioral Disorders.

Maag, J. W., & Swearer, S. M. (2005). Cognitive-behavioral interventions for depression: Review and implications for school personnel. *Behavioral Disorders, 30*, 259–276.

Mayer, M., Lochman, J. E., & Van Acker, R. (2005). Introduction to the special issue: Cognitive-behavioral interventions with students with EBD. *Behavioral Disorders, 30*, 197–212.

McLaughlin, T. F., Krappman, V. F., & Welsh, J. M. (1985). The effects of self-recording for on-task behavior of behaviorally disordered special education students. *Remedial and Special Education, 6*, 42–45.

Meichenbaum, D. (1976). Cognitive factors as determinants of learning disabilities: A cognitive functional approach. In R. M. Knights & D. J. Baker (Eds.), *The neuropsychology of learning disorders: Theoretical approaches*. Baltimore, MD: University Park Press.

Meichenbaum, D. (1977). *Cognitive behavior modification: An integrative approach*. New York: Plenum.

Meichenbaum, D. (1980). Cognitive behavior modification with exceptional students: A promise yet unfulfilled. *Exceptional Education Quarterly, 8*, 83–88.

Meichenbaum, D., & Asarnow, J. (1979). Cognitive-behavioral modification and metacognitive development: Implications for the classroom. In P. C. Kendall and S. D. Hollon (Eds.), *Cognitive-behavioral interventions: Theory, research, and procedures* (pp. 11–35). New York: Academic Press.

Meichenbaum, D., & Goodman, T. J. (1971). Training impulsive children to talk to themselves: A means of developing self control. *Journal of Abnormal Psychology, 77*, 115–126.

Meyers, A. W., Cohen, R., & Schlester, R. (1989). A cognitive-behavioral approach to education: Adopting a broad-based perspective. In J. N. Hughes & R. J. Hall (Eds.), *Cognitive behavioral psychology in the schools: A comprehensive handbook* (pp. 62–84). New York: Guilford.

Morgan, D. P., & Jenson, W. R. (1988). *Teaching behaviorally disordered students: Preferred practices*. Upper Saddle River, NJ: Merrill/Pearson Education.

Nelson, J. R., Smith, D. J., & Colvin, G. (1995). The effects of a peer-mediated self-evaluation procedure on the recess behavior of students with behavior problems. *Remedial and Special Education, 16*, 117–126.

Nelson, J. R., Smith, D. J., Young, R. K., & Dodd, J. (1991). A review of self-management outcome research conducted with students who exhibit behavioral disorders. *Behavior Disorders, 13*, 169–180.

Novaco, R. W. (1979). *Anger control: The development and evaluation of an experimental treatment*. Lexington, MA: Lexington.

O'Brien, T. P., Riner, L. S., & Budd, K. S. (1983). The effects of a child's self-evaluation program on compliance with parental instructions in the home. *Journal of Applied Behavior Analysis, 16*, 69–79.

O'Leary, S. D., & Dubay, D. R. (1979). Application of self-control procedures by children: A review. *Journal of Applied Behavior Analysis, 2*, 449–465.

Olympia, D. E., Sheridan, S. M., Jenson, W. R., & Andrews, D. (1994, Spring). Using student-managed interventions to increase homework completion and accuracy. *Journal of Applied Behavior Analysis, 27*, 85–99.

Osborne, S. S., Kociewicz, M. M., Crumley, E. B., & Lee, C. (1987, Winter). Distractible students use self-monitoring. *Teaching Exceptional Children*, 66–69.

Palmer, D. J., & Stowe, M. L. (1989). Attributions. In C. R. Reynolds & L. Mann (Eds.), *Encyclopedia of special education* (pp. 151–152). New York: Wiley.

Polsgrove, L., & Smith, S. W. (2004). Informed practice in teaching self-control to children with emotional and behavioral disorders. In R. B. Rutherford, M. M. Quinn, & S. R. Mathur (Eds.), *Handbook of research in emotional and behavioral disorders* (pp. 399–425). New York: Guilford.

Reid, R. (1996). Research in self-monitoring: The present, the prospects, the pitfalls. *Journal of Learning Disabilities, 29*, 317–331.

Reynolds, W. M., & Coats, K. L. (1986). A comparison of cognitive-behavioral therapy and relaxation training for the treatment of depression in adolescents. *Journal of Consulting and Clinical Psychology, 54*, 653–660.

Rhode, G., Morgan, D. P., & Young, R. (1983). Generalization and maintenance of treatment gains of behaviorally handicapped students from resource rooms to regular classrooms using self-evaluation procedures. *Journal of Applied Behavior Analysis, 16,* 171–188.

Rinehart, S. D., Stahl, S. A., & Erickson, L. G. (1986). Some effects of summarization training on reading and studying. *Reading Research Quarterly, 21,* 422–438.

Robin, A., Schneider, M., & Dolnick, M. (1976). The turtle technique: An extended case study of self-control in the classroom. *Psychology in the Schools, 12,* 120–128.

Rooney, K. J., Polloway, E. A., & Hallahan, D. P. (1985). The use of self-monitoring procedures with low IQ learning disabled students. *Journal of Learning Disabilities, 18,* 384–389.

Schloss, P., & Smith, M. A. (1998). *Applied behavior analysis in the classroom* (2nd ed.). Boston: Allyn & Bacon.

Schunk, P. H. (1983). Ability versus effort attributional feedback: Differential effects on self-efficacy and achievement. *Journal of Educational Psychology, 75,* 848–856.

Shapiro, E. S., Browder, D. M., & D'Huyvetter, K. K. (1984). Increasing academic productivity of severely multihandicapped children with self-management: Idiosyncratic effects. *Analysis and Intervention in Developmental Disabilities, 4,* 171–178.

Shapiro, E. S., & Cole, C. L. (1994). *Behavior change in the classroom: Self-management interventions.* New York: Guilford.

Siegel, J. M., & Spivak, G. (1973). *Problem-solving therapy* (Research report 23). Philadelphia: Hahnemann Medical College.

Smith, D. J., Young, K. R., West, R. P., Morgan R. P., & Rhode, G. (1988). Reducing the disruptive behavior of junior high school students: A classroom self-management procedure. *Behavioral Disorders, 13,* 231–239.

Smith, S. W., & Daunic, A. P. (2006). *Managing difficult behavior through problem solving instruction: Strategies for the elementary classroom.* Boston, MA: Pearson/Merrill Education.

Smith, S. W., Lochman, J. E., & Daunic, A. P. (2005). Managing aggression using cognitive-behavioral interventions: State of the practice and future directions. *Behavioral Disorders, 30,* 227–240.

Smith, S. W., Siegel, E. M., O'Conner, A. M., & Thomas, S. B. (1994). Effects of cognitive-behavioral training on angry behavior and aggression of three elementary-aged students. *Behavioral Disorders, 19,* 126–135.

Spivak, G., & Shure, M. B. (1974). *Social adjustment of young children.* San Francisco: Jossey-Bass.

Storey, K., & Gaylord-Ross, R. (1987). Increasing positive social interactions by handicapped individuals during a recreational activity using a multicomponent treatment package. *Research in Developmental Disabilities, 8,* 627–649.

Sugai, G. M., & Lewis, T. (1990). Using self-management strategies in classes for students with behavioral disorders. Paper presented at the annual conference of Teacher Educators of Children with Behavioral Disorders, Tempe, AZ.

Symons, S., McGoldrick, Snyder, T., & Pressley, M. (1990). Why be optimistic about cognitive strategy instruction? In C. B. McCormick, G. E. Miller, & M. Pressley (Eds.), *Cognitive strategy research: From basic research to educational applications* (pp. 24–48). New York: Springer–Verlag.

Tollefson, N., Tracy, D. B., Johnsen, E. P., & Chatman, J. (1986). Teaching learning disabled children goal implementation skills. *Psychology in the Schools, 8,* 194–204.

Torgeson, J. K. (1982). The learning disabled child as an inactive learner: Educational implications. *Topics in Learning and Learning Disabilities, 2,* 45–52.

Vygotsky, L. (1962). *Thought and language.* New York: Wiley.

Webber, J., Scheuermann, B., McCall, C., & Coleman, M. (1993). Research on self-monitoring as a behavior management technique in special education classrooms: A descriptive review. *Remedial and Special Education, 14,* 38–56.

Wolery, M., Bailey, D. B., & Sugai G. M. (1988). *Effective teaching: Principles and procedures of applied behavior analysis with exceptional students.* Boston: Allyn & Bacon.

Wong, B. Y. L. (1989). On cognitive training: A thought or two. In J. N. Hughes & R. J. Hall (Eds.), *Cognitive behavioral psychology in the schools: A comprehensive handbook* (pp. 209–219). New York: Guilford.

Workman, E. A. (1998). *Teaching behavioral self-control to students* (2nd ed.). Austin, TX: Pro-Ed.

STRATEGIES FOR DECREASING BEHAVIOR

Schoolwide Strategies for Positive Behavior Supports

CHAPTER 12

Thomas Zirpoli

Schools are complex environments where the collective skills, knowledge, and practices of a culture are taught, shaped, encouraged, and transmitted. Teachers are challenged to provide effective and explicit instruction that maximizes students' acquisition of concepts, skills, and information, and students are challenged to remain attentive, responsive, and engaged to benefit from these instructional opportunities.

—SUGAI (2009, P. 1)

It is no coincidence that chapters regarding reinforcement and cognitive behavior modification were placed in this text before our discussion of general strategies for building school-wide positive behavior supports (SWPBS) and strategies for decreasing inappropriate behavior. Understanding how to use reinforcement in all its forms is critical to promoting schoolwide culture that discourages and prevents inappropriate behaviors. Indeed, reinforcement strategies must be the intervention of first choice when teachers need to change a student's behavior, and these positive behavior supports must be the primary element of any behavior intervention plan (BIP). The focus on building a culture of positive reinforcement dramatically changes the quality of any environment where individuals live and work (Turnbull & Smith-Bird, 2005), as well as the quality and inclusiveness of educational settings (Wheeler & Richey, 2005).

In this chapter, we will discuss a three-tier intervention strategy for behavior management to encourage appropriate behavior and decrease inappropriate behavior, with the focus on school and classroomwide programs and interventions (Tier 1 interventions). Then, in Chapter 13 we will focus on small-group (Tier 2) and individual strategies (Tier 3) for students who need an individualized BIP. Of course, classroom strategies employed by teachers overlap those included in all three tiers. As described by McIntosh, Campbell, Carter, and Dickey (2009, p. 82), teachers provide a "continuum of intervention through multiple tiers of intensity." For example, a classroom teacher will implement school and classroomwide policies and strategies with all the students in the classroom, while conducting small-group and individualized interventions as needed for some students within her room, and while running individualized behavior intervention plans for others.

Lastly, before we begin our discussion of schoolwide strategies for positive behavior supports, teachers are reminded that inappropriate behaviors must be viewed in light of function (see Chapter 9), the social and cultural context in which the behavior is exhibited (see Chapter 3), and the impact on the individual's educational development (see Chapter 2).

THE THREE-TIER MODEL AND BEHAVIOR MANAGEMENT

The three-tier model of intervention is most frequently associated with response to intervention strategies that are usually applied to various levels of academic instruction, especially in the area of reading, and more specifically as it applies to the assessment and instruction for students with learning disabilities. According to the National Center for Learning Disabilities (2009, p. 1), response to intervention or RTI is:

> *a multi-tiered, collaborative approach to providing academic and behavioral supports to struggling learners at increasing levels of intensity. The goal of RTI is to ensure that all children have access to high-quality instruction and learning opportunities and that struggling learners are identified, supported, and served early and effectively. RTI can be used for making decisions about general, compensatory, and special education, resulting in a well-integrated and seamless system of instruction and intervention directed by student outcome data and matched to student needs.*

However, the philosophy of RTI has more recently been applied as a model for the assessment and intervention of students with challenging behaviors and more specifically to the application of SWPBS (Sandomierski, Kincaid, & Algozzine, 2009).

Sugai (2009) refers to the three-tier RTI model as a continuum of evidence-based interventions with tier one providing a core curriculum for all students, tier two providing a modification of the core curriculum for small groups of students not demonstrating progress within tier one, and tier three providing a more individualized and intensive intervention for students not demonstrating progress to the tier two program. Another way to view the three-tier model is to think of tier one as a model of *primary prevention* strategies for all students, tier two as a model for *secondary prevention* for students at risk for problem behaviors or who do not respond to the universal interventions, and tier three for *tertiary prevention* that involves individualized interventions and supports, based upon a functional behavioral assessment (see Chapter 8) (Horner, Sugai, Smolkowski, Eber, Nakasato, Todd, & Esperanza, 2009; McIntosh, et al., 2009; Sugai, 2007; Walker, Horner, Sugai, Bullis, Sprague, Bricker et al., 1996). Stewart, Benner, Martella, and Marchand-Martella (2007) conducted a review of three-tier models for behavior management and identified positive effects on overall school environment for teachers and students. Some of these findings included reductions in the overall level of problem behaviors; a decrease in the number of suspensions, expulsions, and emergency removals; a decrease in the number of office referrals resulting in more instructional contact with students; and an increase in student social skills.

SCHOOLWIDE POSITIVE BEHAVIOR SUPPORTS

An example of the three-tier RTI model for behavior management is School-Wide Positive Behavior Support (SWPBS: McIntosh et al., 2009). Within the SWPBS model, educators are encouraged to develop effective schoolwide or universal policies, strategies, and interventions that encourage and reinforce students to perform at their optimal level (tier one), with the option of small-.group (tier two) and individualized interventions (tier three) as necessary based upon student progress and the results of ongoing student monitoring. Within this model, effective behavior management strategies include the following elements according to McIntosh et al. (2009, p. 82):

- Continuously monitoring and screening students at each level to identify those in need of additional supports.
- Implementing evidence-based strategies and interventions with fidelity.
- Providing a continuum of intervention strategies through multiple tiers of intensity so that the needs of all students can be served.
- Examining student progress data to help make programming decisions and decisions regarding special education eligibility.

Within the SWPBS three-tier model, tier one is the application of general schoolwide policies and procedures that provide students with age-appropriate structure, routines, and supports for the development and reinforcement of appropriate behavior. This general application teaches and encourages prosocial behaviors which, in turn, decrease the likelihood of students engaging in inappropriate behavior (Nelson, Hurley, Synhorst, Epstein, Stage, & Buckley, 2009; Sugai, 2007). In this three-tier pyramid of interventions, Sugai referred to tier-one interventions as *universal interventions* (Sugai, 2001).

Teacher praise for on-task student behavior often results in increased on-task behavior.

According to Horner et al. (2009, p. 134), SWPBS "is a systems approach to establishing both the overall social culture and intensive behavior supports needed to achieve academic and social success for all students." As stated earlier, tier one is the primary prevention tier of SWPBS and "involves defining, teaching, monitoring, and rewarding a small set of behavioral expectations for all students across non-classroom and classroom settings."

It must be emphasized that tier-one strategies set the stage for all behavior in the school building, for students and teachers, and that the culture of the school is established at this level, starting with the leadership provided by building administrators. As stated by Bambara et al. (2009, p. 167), "the importance of establishing a school culture in which all members of a school community share a common understanding and appreciation" for a SWPBS system is the most important variable determining the success of a SWPBS system. The three biggest barriers to establishing a receptive school culture: (a) a lack of understanding of PBS, (b) conflicting beliefs and school practices, and (c) misperceptions of PBS and effective behavior management practices (Bambara et al., 2009, p. 167).

Within the SWPBS three-tier system, tier-one interventions:

- encourage the development of schoolwide rules and procedures that are communicated to teachers, students and parents and that are part of the school's mission, curriculum, and culture (see Kostewicz, 2008);
- encourage administrators, teachers, and support staff to use positive behavioral supports to reinforce the students who are following the school's rules, and this is demonstrated in how administrators, teachers, and support staff communicate and interact with students on a daily basis;
- do not tolerate unprofessional and inappropriate behavior on the part of administrators, teachers, and support staff, such as yelling at students, demeaning students, or embarrassing students. These types of interactions are not part of the school's culture and violate the philosophy of the RTI model of prevention and research-based intervention;
- encourage the development and reinforcement of prosocial behaviors in all students in all activities throughout the school building and grounds, including classrooms, bathrooms, hallways, playgrounds, buses, hallways, cafeteria, and sports fields;
- encourage the use of data collection and record keeping (see Chapters 6, 7, & 8) that alert educators to students who need additional and focused behavioral and social support than that which is provided within the tier-one or tier-two levels of intervention; and
- continue to monitor classroom environments to ensure that a student's poor response to tier-one intervention is not due to a poorly managed classroom or a mismatch between the student's academic ability and the core curriculum (see Chapter 9).

The best SWPBS program will fail if classroom teachers do not understand how to apply basic reinforcement strategies (see Chapter 10), or if a teacher lacks the necessary skills and tools to manage classroom behavior. Most educators have observed that a challenging student can be more or less challenging depending upon the classroom and teacher involved. Thus, as stated above, we must be sure that students are referred for additional supports based upon student need, not due to poor teaching and classroom management.

Obviously, a significant component of the RTI and SWPBS models is professional development. Bambara et al. (2009) reported that the lack of professional development of school personnel was one of the most reported barriers to sustaining PBS systems in their schools.

TABLE 12.1 Response to Intervention (RTI) and Behavior Management: A Three-Tier Approach

Tier 1: Schoolwide strategies or universal interventions developed and applied by school building administrators, teachers, and staff, with the purpose of developing a positive school culture focused on reinforcing appropriate behavior, discouraging inappropriate behavior (primary prevention), and intervening when necessary following the observation of inappropriate behavior. General and ongoing monitoring of student behavior is necessary to identify students who are struggling socially and need more intensive interventions in either smaller groups or with a more individualized approach including a behavior intervention plan. Tier-one strategies are typically successful with 80% to 90% of students.

Tier 2: Small-group strategies and interventions developed and applied within classroom or other specific settings by classroom teachers or other specialists for students who are not responsive to tier-one schoolwide strategies and need additional supports to avoid more serious problem behaviors (secondary prevention). Specific data collection on targeted behaviors (see Chapter 6) is ongoing so that educators may assess when these more intensive interventions are no longer necessary or may identify students who need more individualized interventions and supports. Tier-two interventions may be necessary for 5% to 15% of students.

Tier 3: Individual student strategies and interventions developed and applied by classroom teachers, aides, and parents, with the purpose of providing individualized intensive intervention strategies to increase a student's appropriate behavior while decreasing his inappropriate behavior (tertiary prevention). These strategies and interventions are usually outlined in an individual Behavior Intervention Plan or BIP. Individual monitoring and data collection on targeted behaviors are necessary to document student progress and the effectiveness of the BIP. Tier-three interventions may be necessary for 1% to 5% of students.

Horner et al. (2009, p. 134) state that implementing a comprehensive three-tier intervention model "involves a 2- to 3-year process of professional development and systems change."

The intervention model presented in RTI and SWPBS is "best represented as a blended integration that has relevance and application across the range of teaching and learning environments that exist in schools and communities" (Sugai, 2009, p. 3). Thus, classroom teachers implement all three tiers of the SWPBS model within their classrooms concurrently. Movement from tier to tier should not be considered an automatic road map to special-education placement or services, but may provide a structure for the assessment, identification, and monitoring of students with special needs. Hopefully, the use of SWPBS will decrease the number of students with challenging behaviors who are referred for special education, labeled, and/or placed on medications.

Table 12.1 provides an overview of the three-tier SWPBS model.

Guidelines for Tier One SWPBS

While there has certainly been significant media coverage of inappropriate student behavior, including criminal behavior, in our nation's public schools, the facts about crime and violence in our schools may not be congruent with the media coverage or the public's perception. Over 70% of high school students in the Horatio Alger Association (2005) study reported that their schools are dealing with behavior problems effectively. National data on violence and criminal behavior in schools support this observation. The U.S.

Department of Justice (2005) found that violent crime in U.S. schools has declined dramatically since 1994. Juvenile homicides in schools are down, but the proportion of students who reported being threatened or injured with a weapon at school has remained stable since 1993 (National Center for Education Statistics, 2007). The only behavior that has shown an increase over the past decade is bullying (see Chapter 14). However, this may reflect a recent focus on bullying behavior by the media and an increase in reporting.

School districts around our nation are under intense political pressure to improve school safety for all students, and this pressure has led many schools to consider school-wide programs such as SWPBS (Bradshaw, Debnam, Koth, & Leaf, 2009). Shukla-Mehta and Albin (2003) identify several universal guidelines (tier-one supports) to help schools establish a SWPBS plan for all students across all settings:

- Establish school rules that are consistently enforced throughout the building.
- Communicate school rules to staff, students, and parents frequently.
- Teach students socially appropriate behavior to replace problem behavior.
- Establish consistent consequences for following and breaking school rules.
- Treat minor infractions flexibly, but make consequences for serious offenses nonnegotiable.
- Use social reinforcement to increase appropriate behavior.
- Establish student-organized conflict-resolution and peer mediation programs.
- Offer students opportunities to display responsible behavior.
- Divide large schools into schools-within-schools by floor or section.
- Promote and reinforce academic performance for all students.
- Promote and reinforce school-related extracurricular activities for students.
- Have the principal be a highly visible model of the above.

COMMUNICATING HIGH STANDARDS AND EXPECTATIONS Schoolwide standards must be established by school administrators and communicated to all employees who will have contact with students. Professional development may be necessary to ensure that the policies and standards of the school are understood by everyone. Then, monitoring by school administrators is necessary to ensure a fair and consistent implementation of the school's standards and related policies and procedures.

The Horatio Alger Association (2005) published its annual report on our nation's youth and found that 88 percent of high school students reported that they wanted to be challenged more in school (academically and socially) and that if their teachers would raise standards, they would be willing to work harder. Seventy-two percent of the students in this same study reported that they would work harder to meet higher academic standards. At the elementary level, Figlio and Lucas (2003) found that third, fourth, and fifth graders responded positively to higher grading standards set by their teachers.

School standards should not only be high, but clearly communicated to teachers, employees, students, and parents. Nelson and Colvin (1996) found that among elementary students, setting clear standards had a positive effect on students' social behavior in common areas of the school. Indeed, one of the assumptions of the SWPBS model is clear and effective communication between teachers and students. When standards are not clear or not communicated effectively, students become confused and consequences among teachers and other school employees become inconsistent. This leads to a breakdown in both the standards and student behavior. For example, when one teacher is enforcing a higher standard of the high school dress code than another teacher, the standard is not followed and students are likely to ignore the rules.

Importantly, within a SWPBS model, there is an ongoing monitoring program in place to encourage and reinforcement students who meet or exceed the school's standards (Horner et al., 2009). These programs not only encourage and reinforce appropriate behavior for all the students in the school, but they reinforce the standards established by the school. Thus, if students who follow the rules are reinforced, other students learn that the rules are considered important.

SCHOOL ORGANIZATION   Organizing schools, especially large schools, into smaller units or groups (by grades and teams) may promote appropriate student behavior. For example, at Westminster Middle School in Maryland, each of the three floors of the school contains a single grade (sixth, seventh, and eighth), and each grade is broken up into two teams, one on each side of the school. While the school is large, a team of teachers spends their entire day working with one small team of students. According to Gottfredson and Gottfredson (2001, p. 318), because teachers have contact with a smaller number of students, they are more easily "recognized and controlled," and students become more attached to a smaller group of teachers.

BLOCK SCHEDULING   *Block scheduling* is defined as organizing the school day into larger blocks of time (more than 60 minutes) instead of the traditional school schedule of six to eight classes per day (45 to 55 minutes per class) (Black, 1998). The main case for block scheduling is that longer class periods will allow teachers to cover subject matter in greater depth and that fewer course periods will significantly decrease transition periods throughout the school day.

There are various models of block scheduling. The most common and successful form is the 4×4, where students take four courses (90 minutes in length) during each of two semesters per academic year. One advantage to block scheduling is that students do indeed spend more time focused on academic work within the classroom and less time changing classes and socializing with others in the hallways. Teachers can spend more time on a topic before students have to run to their next class. When compared with schools using the standard five- to seven-class daily schedule, some schools using the block schedule reported fewer discipline problems and improved class attendance, but results on academic achievement are mixed (Arnold, 2002; Mattox, Hancock, & Queen, 2005). Some studies also found that block scheduling reduced both teacher and student stress since both had fewer classes to juggle at a time (Nichols, 2000; Peterson, Schmidt, Flottmeyer, & Weincke, 2000).

SCHOOL UNIFORMS   About one in four schools have some form of student uniform requirement as part of their schoolwide strategies to promote appropriate student behavior (Gottfredson & Gottfredson, 2001). While research linking uniforms directly to better academic performance is inconclusive, Walker (2007, p. 1) states that uniforms are linked to "fewer discipline problems/referrals and violence as well as higher attendance rates." For example, schools in Long Beach, California, became the first to require public school students to wear uniforms and report a significant decrease in assaults, thefts, vandalism, and weapon and drug violations (Ritter, 1998). Warren, Edmonson, Griggs, Lassen, McCart, Turnbull, and Sailor (2003) found that students not in uniform within a uniform-required school were more noncompliant and/or disruptive during class. They also found that dealing with students out of uniform led to additional power struggles with teachers and an increase in disciplinary referrals. Walker (2007) lists the following advantages for school uniforms:

- Increases students' attention in class
- Reduces the wearing of gang attire and colors
- Makes identification of outsiders within the school building easier
- Levels the socioeconomic playing field
- Provides a sense of community
- Builds school pride

PEER MEDIATION   While the terms *conflict resolution* and *peer mediation* are frequently used interchangeably, peer mediation is really a part of an overall schoolwide conflict- resolution program. *Peer mediation* is a process by which students volunteer to receive training on how to mediate conflicts between their peers and help their peers find a fair solution to their conflict. Gottfredson and Gottfredson (2001) found that "40% of schools have programs involving youth in regulating student conduct (e.g., student courts or peer mediation programs)" (p. 326). Two primary goals of peer mediation are (a) to offer students an opportunity to discuss their feelings and conflicts openly with peers and (b) to provide schools a process to deescalate disputes before students resort to more violent solutions.

Ryan, Pierce, and Mooney (2008) describe eight types of peer-mediated interventions:

1. *Classwide peer tutoring.* All students participate in tutoring dyads with participants serving as tutor or tutee.
2. *Cooperative learning.* Small teams of students with different abilities help each other understand the academic material presented within a classroom.
3. *Cross-age tutoring.* Older students tutor younger students.
4. *Peer tutoring.* Students who need assistance are paired with other students.
5. *Peer-assisted learning strategies.* Teachers pair students who need help with other students, but pairs change depending upon the topic and all students have the opportunity to serve as tutor and tutee.
6. *Peer assessment.* Peers are used to assess the performance of other students.
7. *Peer modeling.* Students model appropriate behavior for other students to emulate.
8. *Peer reinforcement.* Peers reinforce each other for appropriate behavior.

Conboy (1994), who coordinated a peer mediation program at a high school in Minneapolis, cites four main outcomes of peer mediation:

- Peer mediation offers school officials and other educators a positive alternative to manage conflict.
- Peer mediation helps prevent conflicts from escalating.
- Peer mediation helps create a more positive school climate for educators and students by helping resolve disputes.
- Peer mediation teaches and empowers students to think of alternative ways to solve their own conflicts with peers.

Peer mediation starts with the recruitment of students who are willing to be trained as peer mediators. Students are usually selected by teachers because of their potential to be good listeners and problem solvers. After they are trained, school officials contact peer mediators when a third party is needed to mediate a dispute or conflict.

Carruthers, Sweeney, Kmitta, and Harris (1996) found that students who serve as mediators benefit from their training and experiences, and they maintain their conflict-resolution skills after school. Also, mediators report improved attitudes toward school, improved academic performance, and a more positive attitude toward dealing with conflict in their own lives. And with students helping resolve conflict, teachers report less stress in the classroom, more time for academics, and a greater capacity for students to solve their own disputes (Lane & McWhirter, 1992).

Conboy (1994) recommends the following steps during the dispute resolution:

- All parties are asked by the peer mediator to make a pledge that they will listen to the other person's point of view and honestly try to solve their dispute without name-calling or other put-downs.
- The peer mediator helps the conflicting parties define the problem, what happened, and how they felt.
- The mediator repeats what was said in order to ensure that everyone understands what was said and how everyone feels.
- The mediator asks both parties to brainstorm solutions to their conflict that would be fair to both sides.
- The agreement to the conflict is developed into a written contract and signed by all parties to the conflict.

Some student mediation programs are available statewide. For example, the Massachusetts Office of Attorney General (2005) started the Student Conflict Resolution Expert (SCORE) program in 1989 to promote and train thousands of student mediators across schools in that state. From 1989 to 2004, 60,000 students in Massachusetts participated in the SCORE program involving 25,000 conflicts, and student mediators helped 97% of them reach a resolution. One-third of the mediations resulted from students referring themselves or other students; another third, a referral by school administrators; and the rest, other sources. More than 60% of the disputes mediated in the SCORE program involve rumors, physical fights, or threats. Interestingly, 66% of the students participating in the mediation program were female.

Research on the effectiveness of peer mediation is impressive. Decreases in physical violence and increases in cooperation among students have been reported (Johnson & Johnson, 1996). Thompson (1996) found that conflict resolution provides students with alternatives to conflict, involves students in school decisions, increases student self-regulation, and heightens student responsibility for their behavior.

TEACH SOCIAL SKILLS   One of the most important responsibilities of schools is to teach students to be socially competent. According to Rutherford, Chipman, Digangi, and Anderson (1992), social skills are specific, identifiable, learned behaviors performed effectively that produce positive consequences in social situations. Social skills are primarily acquired through learning, and teachers can teach social competence in many ways. The most obvious way, however, is through modeling, as demonstrated by Mr. Jones in Classroom Connection 12.1, where a principal shows how to embed social skills training into a middle school awards ceremony.

CLASSROOM CONNECTION 12.1
Teaching Social Skills to Middle School Students During an Awards Ceremony

Mr. Jones is principal of the local middle school. At the end of each semester, he schedules an awards ceremony where students who have made the honor roll are recognized and presented with a certificate. Parents and other family members are invited to the ceremony to share in the celebration of their children. At the start of each awards ceremony, Mr. Jones talks to the students and tells them how they will line up to receive their certificates, how they are to greet him with a handshake, how they are to accept the certificate with a "thank you," and how they should walk back to their chairs. Then, as each student walks up to the front of the room, Mr. Jones makes sure they follow his directions. Each student not only learns how to greet, shake hands, and say, "thank you," but also observes their peers demonstrating the same behaviors. For Mr. Jones, all school assemblies are opportunities to teach his students appropriate social skills.

General Reflection for Classroom Connection 12.1:

In looking at Mr. Jones' method of teaching social skills at every opportunity in his middle school, what other opportunities could he use to teach other social skills throughout the school day and throughout the school year during other schoolwide activities? How could Mr. Jones enroll or include assistance from parents in this effort?

As Gaustad (1992) explains, many students simply don't have appropriate social skills because no one ever taught them how to behave appropriately in different social situations. Thus, ensuring that students learn appropriate social skills, in the classroom and on the athletic field, must be an important component and goal of a schoolwide PBS program. Meadan and Monda-Amaya (2008) emphasize the role and importance of teachers in setting the tone and building the structure for appropriate social interactions within schools and classrooms. The elements of this structure include creating an accepting classroom environment (e.g., establishing clear and positive classroom rules and expectations), creating a voice for each student in the classroom (e.g., promoting individual talents and interests), and creating opportunities for social interaction (e.g., using cooperative learning and peer tutoring). Fenty, Miller, and Lampi (2008) made the following suggestions on how to embed social skills instruction into the daily classroom routine:

- Engage in daily morning meeting activities to build community and communication within the classroom.
- Take advantage of teachable moments to teach social skills, such as when students are lining up to go to lunch.
- Teach social skills as you would other academics by using effective instructional strategies.
- Connect social skills training to academic lessons such as taking turns reading and waiting your turn.
- Use role-play to teach social skills and have students discuss each other's performance.
- Provide and demonstrate examples of both good and poor examples.

In addition to these universal strategies to promote social competence in schools and classrooms, direct instruction with small groups (tier two) or individuals (tier three) is frequently necessary when school- or classroomwide strategies are not enough. When tier-three interventions are necessary, a variety of social skills curricula are available, as well as other methods to teach social skills to individual students. Some of these methods will be discussed in Chapter 13.

IMPLEMENTATION OF SWPBS

There are several steps a school must take in order to implement a SWPBS plan. The list below is based upon the phases and steps outlined in the Implementation Phases Inventory (IPI) (Bradshaw, Debnam, Koth, & Leaf, 2009), which is discussed in the next section on assessing the fidelity of SWPBS. The steps are divided into four phases of implementation.

Phase One: Preparation for SWPBS

1. Secure school district support by identifying a point of contact and securing time for coaching, training, and release time for meetings and planning.
2. Secure school administrators support by securing (a) their participation in the process, (b) funding, (c) time on meeting agendas, and (d) agreement on integrating SWPBS with other school initiatives.
3. Secure staff support and investment in the philosophy and process of SWPBS.
4. Identify SWPBS team members as outlined in previous sections.
5. Secure training for the SWPBS team.
6. Identify a school SWPBS coach. This will likely be someone from the outside, perhaps from the district level or from a local university.
7. Secure training for the SWPBS coach if an internal person is selected.
8. Hold at least two meetings of the SWPBS team prior to the beginning of school to develop or update the action plan for SWPBS launch and implementation.
9. Secure training for at least one member of the SWPBS team in functional behavioral assessment so that person can train other members of the team and school personnel.
10. Identify three to five schoolwide behavioral expectations.

Phase Two: Initiation of SWPBS

1. Schedule monthly SWPBS team meetings.
2. Secure SWPBS coach attendance at all SWPBS team meetings.
3. Schedule monthly trainings by SWPBS coach.
4. Develop teaching plans for schoolwide behavioral expectations.
5. Develop a system to reinforce students for following school policies (see Chapter 10).
6. Develop a system to collect discipline data (see Chapters 6 and 7).
7. Post student behavioral expectations throughout the school, in classrooms and in nonclassroom settings.
8. Train new and returning school personnel at the start of each year.
9. Develop a strategy for collecting positive student behavior.
10. Develop an effective relationship between the coach and the school.
11. Develop a system for identifying students in tier one and tier two who need additional supports and more intensive interventions.
12. Decide which behavior problems are to be handled in the classroom vs. those to be handled by the school administration.
13. Share the SWPBS plan with parents at conferences and in newsletters.

Phase Three: Implementation of SWPBS

1. Teach students about schoolwide behavior expectations throughout the school year. Integrate expectations into the core curriculum.
2. Reinforce positive student behaviors consistently.
3. Complete office referral forms as necessary.
4. Gather and enter discipline data into a database.
5. Provide the SWPBS coach with monthly reports and data.
6. Coordinate SWPBS strategies and language with other schoolwide efforts.
7. Implement procedures for handling inappropriate student behavior consistently.
8. Summarize and report to staff discipline data.
9. Make decisions about SWPBS using discipline data.
10. Have the SWPBS team make decisions on SWPBS implementation based upon discipline data.
11. Ensure students in need of additional supports receive the interventions they require.

Phase Four: Maintenance of SWPBS

1. Use data to make decisions regarding additional training.
2. Provide staff with necessary professional development.
3. Use data to update and modify SWPBS action plan.
4. Develop a set of materials and tools to sustain SWPBS.
5. Establish links with the community to provide incentives for students and staff.
6. Sustain staff and student morale.
7. Involve parents in SWPBS activities.
8. Develop a plan to train new SWPBS team members.
9. Develop a plan to assist and advise teachers about handling challenging situations.
10. Develop a system to assess the effectiveness of tier-two and tier-three interventions.
    Used by permission.

Obstacles to Schoolwide Programs

The implementation of a SWPBS is, at best, challenging because it involves major changes throughout the school system and, to be successful, requires full cooperation from everyone who has contact with students. In listing possible reasons for poor outcomes in one state school system trying to implement a new three-tier model, Johns (personal communication, 6.12.09) listed the following possible obstacles and concerns:

- Some school personnel see the three-tier model as simply a new method of identifying students with disabilities, not a school improvement program.
- New models of intervention are unlikely to be successful when they are mandated by school districts without buy-in by school administrators and teachers at the school building level.
- Schools may try to do too much, too soon, without adequate preparation or professional development.
- Resources necessary to make significant changes within a school or school system are not provided and, thus, the model is never fully implemented and tested.
- Schools may disagree on what the three-tier model is and what it requires.

- Squandered resources on computer programming, books, and consultants, and diverting classroom teachers away from classroom activities proven increase academic achievement.
- More research needs to be conducted before educators know that the three-tier model is an effective intervention model for entire school districts.

SWPBS TEAMS

Within educational settings, the establishment of SWPBS teams or advisory committees is strongly recommended. These committees were once called by other names such as the "behavior management committee" or the "human rights committee." Regardless of their name, these committees serve to review general behavior management policies throughout the school and specific behavior intervention plans for individual students. Bambara, Nonnemacher, and Kern (2009) discuss a two-team approach: One to review universal strategies and policies schoolwide, and the other to review specific behavior intervention plans for individual students.

The SWPBS Team

The SWPBS team has the responsibility of looking at the overall picture of school policies and procedures regarding student behavior and the management of student behavior. The purpose of the team is to develop schoolwide policies and procedures to ensure that students are learning appropriate social skills, that programs are in place to encourage and reinforce students for following school policies and demonstrating appropriate social behaviors, that general student behavior is monitored and measured so that the team can assess the effectiveness of SWPBS systems, and that procedures are in place to effectively support students who need additional supports and intervention, either in small-group training sessions (e.g., social skills training) or individually through a behavior intervention plan.

Membership on the School-Wide PBS team should include the principal, vice principal for student affairs, and an array of general education, special-education, and resouce teachers who have an interest in SWPBS and have some expertise in SWPBS. For high schools, schoolwide teams may need to include more members, as the number of staff and faculty is greater than that of elementary or middle schools. In addition, since high school students play a more active role in their school organization, high school students may be represented on their SWPBS team (Flannery, Sugai, & Anderson, 2009).

As stated by Horner et al. (2009, p. 134), schoolwide behavioral expectations are defined, taught, and rewarded within a management system that also includes a continuum of consequences for behavioral error and continuous collection and use of data for decision making. The team should meet monthly to review this schoolwide student data (office referrals, suspensions, school fights, etc.), consider input from teachers who are implementing the SWPBS program and from parents and students affected by the plan, and make adjustments to the plan as needed.

The Individual Student PBS Team

While the SWPBS team monitors the overall SWPBS system, the Individual Student PBS (ISPBS) team reviews and monitors individual student behavior intervention plans and

Establishing rules, reinforcing appropriate behavior, and having consistent consequences for inappropriate behavior make up the most effective intervention plan.

the data collected related to each specific plan. The ISPBS will specify the target behaviors to be monitored and the type of student data to be collected.

Membership on this team will vary by student. If the student has an IEP, the IEP team may also serve as the student's ISPBS team, but not necessarily. Certainly some members of the IEP team may also be members of the student's ISPBS team. But the ISPBS team may include other educators, such as the school psychologists or behavior support specialists who have the expertise to advise the team regarding the student's behavior, the interpretation of the student's data, and recommendations for the student's BIP. The ISPBS team may then share these recommendations with the IEP team and then the BIP may become part of the IEP.

ASSESSING SWPBS FIDELITY

There are several instruments available to assess the implementation of SWPBS in schools, and three of them are described below.

Schoolwide Evaluation Tool (SET)

Developed by Sugai, Lewis-Palmer, Todd, & Horner (2001), the *Schoolwide Evaluation Tool* (SET) is designed to assess the degree to which schools are implementing SWPBS to include the following seven features of SWPBS as outlined by Bradshaw, Debnam, Koth, and Leaf (2009, p. 146). These features are: expectations defined, behavioral expectations taught, system for rewarding behavioral expectations, system for responding to behavioral violations, monitoring and evaluation, management, and district-level support. Data are collected through multiple sources, including a review of discipline records, policies and procedures, student handbooks, observations of visual displays in hallways and classroom, and interviews with staff (a minimum of 10) and students (a minimum of 15). This tool is completed by a trained external observer who has completed a 2-day SET assessor training. Administration of SET takes about 4 hours with another hour to score. Scores range from 0% to 100% on seven subscale scores and an overall SET score.

Team Implementation Checklist (TIC)

Developed by Sugai, Todd, & Horner (2001), the *Team Implementation Checklist* (TIC) is designed to help SWPBS teams monitor their own progress in the implementation of SWPBS. The team collectively completes the TIC checklist on a monthly or quarterly basis. School-Wide PBS benchmarks are evaluated, and it takes about 10 minutes to complete (Bradshaw et al., 2009). Unlike the SET, completed by an independent assessor, the TIC represents the perceptions of the SWPBS team. Questions on the TIC survey ask the team to assess 17 start-up activities and 6 ongoing activities as "Achieved," "In Progress," or "Not Started." A third section of the TIC allows the team to assess their action plan for SWPBS activities including "Who" and "When" inquires.

Implementation Phases Inventory (IPI)

Developed by the Positive Behavior Intervention Supports Maryland Statewide Initiative, the *Implementation Phases Inventory* (IPI) documents "a school's specific phase or stage" of SWPBS implementation (Bradshaw, Barrett, & Bloom, 2004, p. 147). The IPI is also used as a guide to the steps necessary for schools to implement SWPBS. The survey includes 44 questions about the school's SWPBS activities divided into four phases. These phases include: preparation (10 subscale questions), initiation (13 subscales), implementation (11 subscales), and maintenance (10 subscales). Items listed under each phase are evaluated as "Not in place," "Partial," or "Full Implementation." The IPI can be completed in about 10 minutes and scored in 5 minutes, and schools are encouraged to complete the IPI twice per year.

SWPBS FOR CLASSROOM TEACHERS

Thus far, our focus has been on schoolwide strategies for PBS. Now we would like to focus on classroomwide issues related more directly to the day-to-day interaction that teachers have with their students. Of course, all of these strategies throughout this chapter and Chapter 13 overlap and are applicable to all education settings.

Classroom Organization

The physical organization of classrooms is also an important consideration for supporting appropriate behavior. The level of organization within a classroom setting will depend upon the age of the students. For example, a seating chart is highly recommended for preschool, elementary, and middle school students, but may be optional for high school students. For preschool and elementary students, having bins or folders for student assignments is highly recommended. For high school students, Murphy and Korinek (2009, p. 301) studied "a card system combining elements of self-management and teacher monitoring to increase the frequency and duration" of appropriate student behavior. Simple 3 by 5 inch, color-coded cards were used to facilitate communication between teachers and students regarding behavior. This simple classroom management system (a) provided structure and support for student learning, (b) offered students "an explicit, yet unobtrusive means to guide students' behavior," (c) provided teachers a means to monitor student behavior and provide feedback, (d) provided students with ongoing feedback on performance and assignments, and (e) allowed teachers to tailor the program to individual student needs within a classroomwide program without singling out students with greater needs.

Regardless of the age of students, teachers must remember that they are the model for how students organize their work. If a teacher has a disorganized classroom, this will not be an appropriate model for students. Specific strategies for organizing class work, homework, and classroom materials are essential. Teachers may even have to help students organize their backpacks. Teachers must take a leading role in helping students learn how to organize their schoolwork. Modeling these strategies is the first step in this process. Then, teachers must show their students how to organize, provide appropriate materials for organization, and lastly, monitor student organization.

Trussell (2008) recommended these universal guidelines on classroom organization:

- Display individual student and group work. This creates a positive learning environment, reinforces students' efforts, and provides models of good performance for other students.
- Limit classroom barriers so students and teachers may move about the room. Consider cluster arrangements of desks to open up walkways within the classroom.
- Consider the placement of frequently used materials and equipment such as pencil sharpener, wastebasket, computers, posted rules, and daily schedules.
- Post classroom rules where they will be visible.
- Post a daily schedule and limit downtime.
- Tell students what to do with finished assignments (in school assignments and homework).
- Teach procedures for students to appropriately solicit assistance from teachers.
- Teach procedures for students to respond to teacher questions.
- Teach procedures for students to access the restroom and for reentering the classroom.
- Teach procedures for taking attendance, lunch count, and so on.
- Maintain a ratio of 4 to 1 positive to negative feedback to students.

Focus on Prevention

It is always best, of course, to prevent behavior problems in the classroom if possible. In a classic study still applicable for teachers today, Long and Newman (1976) discuss three categories of ecological manipulation that can be incorporated into classroom management strategies to prevent challenging behaviors: classroom environment, classroom activities, and teacher behavior. By monitoring and modifying the classroom environment, classroom activities, and their own behavior, teachers may facilitate acceptable student behavior and prevent unacceptable behavior. Here are some basic behavior management strategies for classroom teachers:

- *Classroom rules: Inform students of what is expected of them.*   Teachers are encouraged to develop classroom rules and to review the rules frequently with students. Rules may even be posted to serve as a reminder for teachers and students. Rules should be limited, stated positively, and age-appropriate (Gable, Hester, Rock, & Hughes, 2009; Kostewicz, 2008).
- *Establish a positive learning climate.*   Teachers establish a positive learning climate by reinforcing students for following the classroom rules and demonstrating other appropriate behaviors, by interacting with the students in a consistent manner, and by being flexible enough to accommodate the individual needs of all the classroom students. In addition, teachers need to make learning a fun experience so that students will want to come to school and will arrive motivated to learn.
- *Provide meaningful learning experiences.*   Relating academic lessons and tasks to the daily lives of students will increase student interest and provide for effective generalization of skills.
- *Avoid threats.*   When rules are clearly stated and understood, threats are unnecessary. Instead of threats, teachers should remind students of the classroom rules and other behavioral expectations and consistently provide consequences for both appropriate and inappropriate behaviors.
- *Demonstrate fairness.*   Teachers are more likely to interact with all students equally and consistently when classroom rules are clearly stated and understood.
- *Build and exhibit self-confidence.*   Students who feel good about themselves and their schoolwork are likely to interact with others appropriately. Teachers have many opportunities to model self-confidence (e.g., "I know I can do this") and encourage student self-confidence throughout the day.
- *Recognize positive student attributes.*   All students have positive attributes that may be recognized to build self-esteem and self-confidence. Also, teachers should recognize, be sensitive to, and celebrate individual student differences.
- *Use positive modeling.*   Students are likely to model the behavior of teachers and other significant adults. This provides teachers with many opportunities to teach students how to deal appropriately with anger, mistakes, and everyday frustrations.
- *Pay attention to the physical arrangement of the classroom.*   The classroom should allow for a smooth flow of student traffic and visual monitoring of student behavior. An organized teacher and classroom environment may encourage students to be better organized.
- *Limit downtime.*   The more time students spend in downtime, the more opportunities are available for inappropriate behaviors. Both teacher and students should be prepared for the day. The time a teacher spends preparing for class will be time saved when students are busy and challenged (and not engaged in inappropriate behavior).

When challenging behaviors are observed in the classroom or anywhere on school property, the general strategies listed below will assist teachers and other school employees in responding appropriately.

Interrupt the Behavior Chain

LaVigna and Willis (1991) and Carter and Grunsell (2001) discuss several strategies related to *interrupting the behavior chain* of inappropriate behavior. These methods are helpful in preventing and deescalating inappropriate behaviors. Suggestions for interrupting the behavior chain include proximity control, humor, instructional control, problem-solving facilitation, and stimulus change.

MAINTAIN PROXIMITY CONTROL   *Proximity control* is a method of anticipating a student's potential response to an event or a situation and interrupting the usual sequence of behaviors by positioning one's body a certain way, remaining calm, and facilitating communication. For example, a classroom teacher may notice that the students are beginning to talk too loudly during a community library visit; and, anticipating that the students will become louder, the teacher breaks the behavioral chain by reminding the students to talk quietly. By anticipating a potential problem, the teacher is able to position herself among the students, calmly communicate her expectations, and prevent a potential situation in which she might have had to yell above the students' noise for them to have heard her instructions.

INJECT HUMOR INTO THE SITUATION   Injecting *humor* into a situation may also interrupt a behavior chain. Humor will often reduce the tension of an explosive situation. A teacher might respond to a student who is ready to lose control by telling the student a story about a similar situation occurring in the past ("Did I ever tell you that that happened to me once?").

MAINTAIN INSTRUCTIONAL CONTROL   *Instructional control* or providing instructions on expected behaviors is also useful in interrupting a behavior chain. For example, after a classroom schedule is abruptly changed and the students begin to respond in frustration, the teacher provides clear instructions about what they will do next and what the expectations are for student behavior.

FACILITATE PROBLEM SOLVING   *Problem-solving facilitation* involves offering positive alternatives to inappropriate behavior. For example, a teacher may suggest to a student, "Let's sit and talk about what you can do about this," after observing that the student is ready to behave inappropriately in response to a frustrating experience. Problem-solving skills are also facilitated when teachers talk to students about alternatives to the inappropriate behaviors students observe in their everyday environment (e.g., students fighting on the playground, world events students hear on the news). These kinds of problem-solving discussions are easily integrated into both academic and social activities.

CONSIDER A STIMULUS CHANGE   *Stimulus change* refers to a range of teacher behaviors that prevent challenging behaviors by modifying environmental stimuli that might precipitate challenging behavior. Stimulus change may include removing objects, relocating people, removing unnecessary demands and requests, changing the location or timing of events, and making other rearrangements of environmental stimuli. For example, teachers frequently modify seating arrangements in response to disruptive interactions among students. A greater effort to anticipate and prevent inappropriate behaviors through environmental modifications, rather than direct behavior modification, is encouraged. Environmental changes may be temporary while teachers gradually reintroduce the stimulus that elicited the behavior. For example, a toy that students have fought over may be temporarily removed and gradually reintroduced in a more controlled manner.

Remember the Fair Pair Rule

The *fair pair rule*, a term coined by White and Haring (1976), states that when a teacher targets a behavior for elimination, "an alternative behavior is selected to replace the challenging behavior" (Wacker, Berg, & Northrup, 1991, p. 11). For example, when Susan wants to eliminate calling out behavior in her classroom, she decides to reinforce her students for raising their hands and waiting to be called upon before speaking. Preferably, the behavior targeted for increase (raising hand) is an appropriate substitute for, serves the same function for the student, or at least incompatible with, the challenging behavior targeted for elimination (calling out).

Be Consistent

When students are provided with rules and behavioral guidelines, teachers must be consistent about enforcement and reinforcement (Gable, Hester, Rock, & Hughes, 2009). For example, if the rule states that Robert must sit in the corner for 2 minutes when he hits other students, teachers must implement the consequence each time the rule is broken. A verbal warning may follow mild inappropriate behaviors, such as an occasional rude comment or noncompliance, as long as this is stated in the rules. Severe inappropriate behaviors, however, such as hitting or other acts of aggression, should not be followed with a warning.

Consistency teaches students that there is a relationship between following the rules and reinforcement. Consistency also teaches that there are consequences when the classroom rules are not followed. When teachers are not consistent, students tend to become confused about the rules and teacher expectations. For example, if a teacher is inconsistent with the enforcement of a classroom rule (e.g., "Students must receive permission from the teacher before leaving the class"), some students may think that the rule is not very important or that it is not important *always* to obey the rule. Some students may generalize this attitude to other classroom rules. Thus, teachers should not establish rules they are unable or unwilling to enforce consistently as demonstrated in Classroom Connection 12.2.

Avoid Reinforcing Inappropriate Behavior

Teachers must be careful that students do not get more attention following inappropriate behaviors than they would following appropriate behaviors. Inappropriate behavior should be calmly followed with the provision of a specific consequence as outlined in the

CLASSROOM CONNECTION 12.2
Consistency and Compliance to School- and Classwide Rules

Ms. Hawkins is a fifth-grade teacher in a local elementary school. She has a group of students who liked to see how far they could stretch her classroom rules before Ms. Hawkins applied a consequence. They soon learned that as far as Ms. Hawkins was concerned, rules were not made for stretching.

One of Ms. Hawkins' classroom rules is that students may not talk to other students while she is speaking. Ms. Hawkins is sensitive to the social needs of her young fifth graders and gives them ample time to socialize with each other. But, she also believes that listening when an adult is speaking is an important social skill for her students to learn. Thus, she consistently requires her students to stop talking and listen when she speaks. She is consistent about this rule. When she is finished speaking, she ends with a statement of verbal praise for her students' listening and attention skills. When one of her students breaks the rule, she consistently corrects the student and calmly applies an appropriate consequence (e.g., loss of a classroom privilege for that day). Over time, her students have learned to comply to this rule. When she calls for their attention, her students stop talking to each other and give her their attention.

After the winter break, Ms. Hawkins agreed to work with Lisa, a student teacher from a nearby college, during the spring semester. Ms. Hawkins has told Lisa about her classroom rules, plus they are posted on the classroom wall, but the intern is not consistent about following through. For example, when Lisa speaks to the class, she does not wait for the students to give her their attention and she does not consistently apply consequences when students talk to each other while she is talking to them. When the students get really loud and out of control, Lisa will finally punish a few students and they will become quiet for a few minutes. Then, a couple of the students will start talking. Instead of following through on the stated classroom rules and consequences, Lisa ignores them until their behavior gets totally out of control again.

During a meeting with Ms. Hawkins, Lisa wonders out loud why she can't demand the attention of her student like Ms. Hawkins. She thinks it is because of her young age or because the students don't perceive her as a "real" teacher.

General Reflection for Classroom Connection 12.2:

In looking at this situation, what advice would you give Lisa if you were in Ms. Hawkins' shoes? What other examples can you think of as a teacher where consistency is the key to success within a classroom or school building? What role, if any, would the SWPBS team play with student teachers like Lisa?

behavior change program. It is important that "the challenging behavior never results in the desired consequence" (Wacker et al., 1991, p. 11).

Teachers should avoid long lectures and excessive one-to-one interaction with students after inappropriate behavior. This type of attention may be reinforcing to some students, especially when done in the other students' presence. For example, a high school student may enjoy a teacher reprimand conducted in full view of classmates if he perceives the incident as a way of increasing his status among his peers. The teacher can deliver the same comments, quietly at the student's desk, without drawing a significant amount of attention to the student's inappropriate behavior. This approach may be called a "soft" reprimand.

Limit Consequences for Inappropriate Behavior

The consequences a student experiences for acting inappropriately should be short and to the point. Whether we are talking about time-out or the removal of a toy or other preferred object, a short period of time is usually as effective as longer intervals. Taking a toy away from a child for an hour or, at most, for the day following an inappropriate behavior is long enough. Consequences for inappropriate behavior should seldom be carried over into the next day. Indeed, the next day will provide teachers with new opportunities to identify and reinforce appropriate behavior. In behavior management, longer (e.g., longer time-out periods, longer periods of restriction or "grounding,") does not necessarily mean better. For example, if a student breaks a rule in school and the consequence is the removal of recess, the removal of one recess period should be sufficient if the student considers recess reinforcing.

Deal with Inappropriate Behavior Immediately

When teachers send students to the principal's office for inappropriate behavior or when a mother says, "Wait 'til your dad comes home," the stated consequence for the inappropriate behavior will probably not be immediately or consistently applied. In addition, children of these caregivers will learn that it is not necessary to behave appropriately in the absence of the threatened adult (e.g., the principal or dad). By teaching the child that the first caregiver either will not or cannot deal with the inappropriate behavior, the caregiver is, in effect, teaching the child that it is safe to behave inappropriately with that caregiver.

Stop Shouting

Shouting at students is not an effective method of controlling challenging student behavior and certainly does not build a system of positive behavior supports. A teacher who is shouting at her students is probably frustrated because she feels that her students are not listening to her. But her frustration and shouting are more likely due to her own inconsistent use of consequences resulting in students who have learned to be noncompliant. But her students have learned that it is not necessary to listen to her, at least most of the time. Consistently enforcing the classroom rules, in a calm voice, is always more effective than shouting at your students.

Putting It All Together

Zirpoli (2003) outlined the following universal strategies for classroom teachers:

- Provide appropriate supervision inside and outside of the school building, especially during student arrival and dismissal times, during class changes, and where students congregate (lunchroom, gym, etc.).
- Provide appropriate structure and routines within the school, classrooms, and other school environments so that students understand what is expected of them from arrival on school grounds to dismissal.
- Model the appropriate behavior they wish to observe from their students.
- Reinforce appropriate behavior observed from students and build a culture of positive behavior supports that encourage and promote appropriate social skills.
- Provide predictable and consistent discipline in order to promote compliance with school policies and fairness across students.
- Avoid looking for biological causes of inappropriate behavior. Look within the school and classroom environment for antecedents to inappropriate behavior before looking for a medical problem within the student.

- Be a teacher, not a friend, when providing guidance to students.
- Let students know that you like them, and that you are interested in them and the activities in which they participate in and out of school.
- Have fun! Effective administrators and teachers enjoy their work, enjoy interacting with students, and know how to enjoy and have fun with their students while maintaining a professional working relationship with them.

Summary

The purpose of this chapter is to discuss school-wide and classwide positive behavior supports that promote, encourage, and reinforce appropriate social behavior in all students. A three-tier model, based upon the response to intervention (RTI) model, is presented as a strategy to manage behavior. Tier one incorporates universal behavior management designs throughout the school. Tier-two strategies are employed when more intensive, small-group interventions are necessary for some students. Tier-three interventions (outlined more in Chapter 13) are necessary for some students who need individualized behavior intervention plans (BIPs). Guidelines for establishing schoolwide positive behavior supports (SWPBS) include communicating high standards and expectations, looking at how schools and classrooms are organized, considering school uniforms, establishing a peer mediation system, and teaching social skills.

The implementation of a schoolwide PBS system includes four stages: preparation, initiation, implementation, and maintenance. Obstacles to schoolwide programs are also outlined. School-Wide PBS teams have the responsibility to monitor school policies and procedures, as well as outcome data so that adjustments to the SWPBS program may be implemented as needed. Individual student PBS teams monitor the development of individual student BIPs and data collected once the plans are in place. Data are then used to measure the effectiveness of the BIP and determine what modifications need to be made. Membership on the schoolwide PBS will usually remain stable while membership on the individual student PBS team will vary by student.

There are several instruments available to assess the implementation of SWPBS in schools. Three discussed in this chapter include the School-Wide Evaluation Tool (SET), the Team Implementation Checklist (TIC), and the Implementation Phases Inventory (IPI).

Classwide PBS strategies include focusing on prevention, methods to interrupt the behavior chain, remembering to replace an inappropriate behavior with a functional behavior, being consistent, avoiding reinforcing inappropriate behavior, limiting consequences for inappropriate behavior, dealing with inappropriate behavior immediately, monitoring your voice while speaking to students, and a summary of recommendations provided by the author (Zirpoli, 2003) and Trussell (2008).

Discussion Questions

1. In looking at the schoolwide strategies presented in this chapter, how would you evaluate your school in terms of schoolwide positive behavior supports? What recommendations would you make to your building administrators?

2. In looking at the behavior management strategies employed in the classrooms within your school, what do you see as other strategies for positive behavior supports not mentioned in this text, and what recommendations would you make to your fellow teachers?

3. All schools have their own culture and changing the culture of a school building is challenging and takes time. Who is responsible for the culture of your school, and what role do building administrators, staff, and teachers play in the maintenance of this culture, especially in relationship to how employees interact with students?

4. Do you think the employment of SWPBS will increase or decrease the referral for formal testing rate in your school? What impact, of any, will SWPBS have on the number of students in your school receiving special-education services?

References

Arnold, D. (2002). Block schedule and traditional schedule achievement: A comparison. *National Association of Secondary School Principals, NASSP Bulletin, 86*, 42–53.

Bambara, L. M., Nonnemacher, S., & Kern, L. (2009). Sustaining school-based individualized positive behavior support. *Journal of Positive Behavior Interventions, 11*(3), 161–176.

Black, S. (1998). Learning on the Block. *American School Board Journal, 185*(1), 32–33.

Bradshaw, C. P., Barrett, S., & Bloom, J. (2004). The *Implementation Phases Inventory*. Baltimore: PBIS Maryland. Available from http://www.pbismaryland.org/forms.htm.

Bradshaw, C. P., Debnam, K., Koth, C. W., & Leaf, P. (2009). Preliminary validation of the *Implementation Phases Inventory* for assessing fidelity of school wide positive behavior supports. *Journal of Positive Behavior Interventions, 11*(3), 145–160.

Carruthers, W. L., Sweeney, B., Kmitta, D., & Harris, G. (1996). Conflict resolution: An examination of the research literature. *The School Counselor, 44*, 5–17.

Carter, M., & Grunsell, J. (2001). The behavior chain interruption strategy: A review of research and discussion of future directions. *Journal of the Association for Persons with Severe Handicaps, 26*(1), 37–49.

Conboy, S. M. (1994). *Peer mediation and anger control: Two ways to resolve conflict*. St. Paul, MN: University of St. Thomas.

Fenty, N. S., Miller, M. A., & Lampi, A. (2008). Embed social skills instruction in inclusive settings. *Intervention in School and Clinic, 43*, 186–192.

Figlio, D. N., & Lucas, M. E. (2003). Do high grading standards affect student performance. *Journal of Public Economics, 88*(9), 1815–1834.

Flannery, K. B., Sugai, G., & Anderson, C. M. (2009). School-wide positive behavior support in high school. *Journal of Positive Behavior Intervention, 11*(3), 177–185.

Gable, R. A., Hester, P. H., Rock, M. L., & Hughes, K. G. (2009). Back to basics: Rules, praise, ignoring, and reprimands revisited. *Intervention in School and Clinic, 44*, 195–205

Gaustad, J. (1992). *School discipline*. Eugene, OR: ERIC Clearinghouse on Educational Management (ED350727).

Gottfredson, G. D., & Gottfredson, D. C. (2001). What schools do to prevent problem behavior and promote safe environments. *Journal of Educational and Psychological Consultation, 12*(4), 313–344.

Horatio Alger Association. (2005). *The state of our nation's youth*. Alexandria, VA: Author.

Horner, R. H., Sugai, G., Smolkowski, K., Eber, L., Nakasato, J., Todd, A. W., & Esperanza, J. (2009). A randomized, wait-list controlled effectiveness trail assessing school-wide positive behavior support in elementary schools. *Journal of Positive Behavior Interventions, 11*(3), 133–144.

Johnson, R. T., & Johnson, D. W. (1996). Conflict resolution and peer mediation programs in elementary and secondary schools: A review of the research. *Review of Educational Research, 66*, 459–473.

Kostewicz, D. E. (2008). Creating classroom rules for students with emotional and behavioral disorders: A decision-making guide. *Beyond Behavior, 17*(3), 14–21.

Lane, P., & McWhirter, J. J. (1992). A peer mediation model: Conflict resolution for elementary and secondary school children. *Elementary School Guidance and Counseling, 27*, 15–21.

LaVigna, G. W., & Willis, T. J. (1991, February). *Non-aversive behavior modification*. Workshop presented by the Institute for Applied Behavior Analysis, Minneapolis, MN.

Long, N. J., & Newman, R. G. (1976). Managing surface behavior of children in school. In N. J. Long, W. C. Morse, & R. G. Newman (Eds.), *Conflict in the classroom: The education of the emotionally disturbed children* (3rd ed., pp. 308–317). Belmont, CA: Wadsworth.

Mattox, K., Hancock, D., & Queen, J. (2005). The effect of block scheduling on middle school students' mathematics achievement. *National Association of Secondary School Principals, NASSP Bulletin, 82,* 56–65.

McIntosh, K., Campbell, A. L., Carter, D. R., & Dickey, C. R. (2009). Differential effects of a tier two behavior intervention based on function of problem behavior. *Journal of Positive Behavior Interventions, 11*(2), 82–93.

Meadan, H., & Monda-Amaya, L. (2008). Collaboration to promote social competence for students with mild disabilities in the general classroom: A structure for providing social support. *Intervention in School and Clinic, 43,* 158–167.

Murphy, S. A., & Korinek, L. (2009). It's in the cards: A class-wide management system to promote student success. *Intervention in School and Clinic, 44,* 300–306

National Center for Education Statistics. (2007). *Indicators of school crime and safety.* Washington, DC: U.S. Department of Education.

National Center for Learning Disability. (2009). *Definition of RTI.* Washington, DC: Author.

Nelson, R. J., Colvin, G., & Smith, D. J. (1996). The effects of setting clear standards on students' social behavior in common areas of school. *Journal of At Risk Issues, 3*(1), 10–18.

Nelson, R. J., Hurley, K. D., Synhorst, L., Epstein, M. H., Stage, S., & Buckley, J. (2009). The child outcomes of a behavior model. *Exceptional Children, 76*(1), 7–30.

Nichols, J. D. (2000, April). *The impact of block scheduling on various indicators of school success.* Paper presented at the Annual Meeting of the American Educational Research Association, New Orleans, LA.

Peterson, D. W., Schmidt, C., Flottmeyer, E., & Weincke, S. (2000, November). *Block scheduling: Successful strategies for middle schools.* Paper presented at the National Middle School Association Conference, St. Louis, MO.

Ritter, J. (1998, October 29). School uniforms changing culture of classroom. *USA Today.*

Ryan, J. B., Pierce, C. D., & Mooney, P. (2008). Evidence-based teaching strategies for students with EBD. *Beyond Behavior, 17*(3), 22–29.

Sandomierski, T., Kincaid, D., & Algozzine, B. (2009). *Response to intervention and positive behavior supports: Brothers from different mothers or sisters from different misters?* New York: National Center for Learning Disabilities.

Shukla-Mehta, S., & Albin, R. W. (2003). Twelve practical strategies to prevent behavioral escalation in classroom settings. *Preventing school failure, 47*(4), 156–161.

Stewart, R. M., Benner, G. J., Martella, R. C., & Marchand-Martella, N. E. (2007). Three-tier models of reading and behavior: A research review. *Journal of Positive Behavior Intervention, 9,* 239–253.

Sugai, G. (2001). School climate and discipline: School-wide positive behavior support. Keynote presentation to the National Summit on Shared Implementation of IDEA. Washington, DC.

Sugai, G. (2007, December). *Responsiveness-to-intervention: Lessons learned and to be learned.* Keynote presentation at and paper for the RTI Summit, U.S. Department of Education, Washington, DC.

Sugai, G. (2009). *School-wide positive behavior support and response to intervention.* Washington, DC: Office of Special Education Programs, U.S. Department of Education.

Sugai, G., & Lewis, J. (1996). Preferred and promising practices for social skills instruction. *Focus on Exceptional Children, 29*(4), 1–16.

Sugai, G., Lewis-Palmer, T., Todd, A., & Horner, R. H. (2001). *School-wide evaluation tool.* Eugene: University of Oregon.

Sugai, G., Todd, A. W., & Horner, R. H. (2001). *Team implementation checklist* (Version 2.2). Eugene: University of Oregon.

Thompson, S. M. (1996). Peer mediation: A peaceful solution. *The School Counselor, 44,* 151–154.

Trussell, R. P. (2008). Classroom universals to prevent problem behaviors. *Intervention in School and Clinic, 43,* 179–185.

Turnbull, A. P., & Smith-Bird, E. (2005). Linking positive behavior support to family quality of life outcomes. *Journal of Positive Behavior Interventions, 7*(3), 174–180.

U.S. Department of Justice. (2005). *National Crime Victimization Survey.* Washington, DC: Author.

Wacker, D., Berg, W., & Northrup, J. (1991). Breaking the cycle of challenging behaviors: Early treatment key to success. *Impact, 4,* 10–11.

Walker, H. M., Horner, R. H., Sugai, G., Bullis, M., Sprague, J. R., Bricker, D. et al. (1996). Integrated approaches to preventing antisocial behavior patterns among school-aged children and youth. *Journal of Emotional and Behavioral Disorders, 4,* 194–209.

Walker, K. (2007). *The principals' partnership: Research brief on school uniforms.* Omaha, NE: Union Pacific Foundation.

Warren, J. S., Edmonson, H. M., Griggs, P., Lassen, S. R., McCart, A., Turnbull, A., & Sailor, W. (2003). *Journal of Positive Behavior Interventions, 5,* 80–91.

Wheeler, J. J., & Richey, D. D. (2005). *Behavior management: Principles and practices of positive behavior supports.* Upper Saddle River, NJ: Merrill/Pearson Education.

White, O. R., & Haring, N. G. (1976). *Exceptional teaching.* Upper Saddle River, NJ: Merrill/Pearson Education.

Zirpoli, T. J. (2003). *Cures for parental wimp syndrome: Lessons on becoming a stronger parent.* Westminster, MD: Zirpoli Publishing and Consulting.

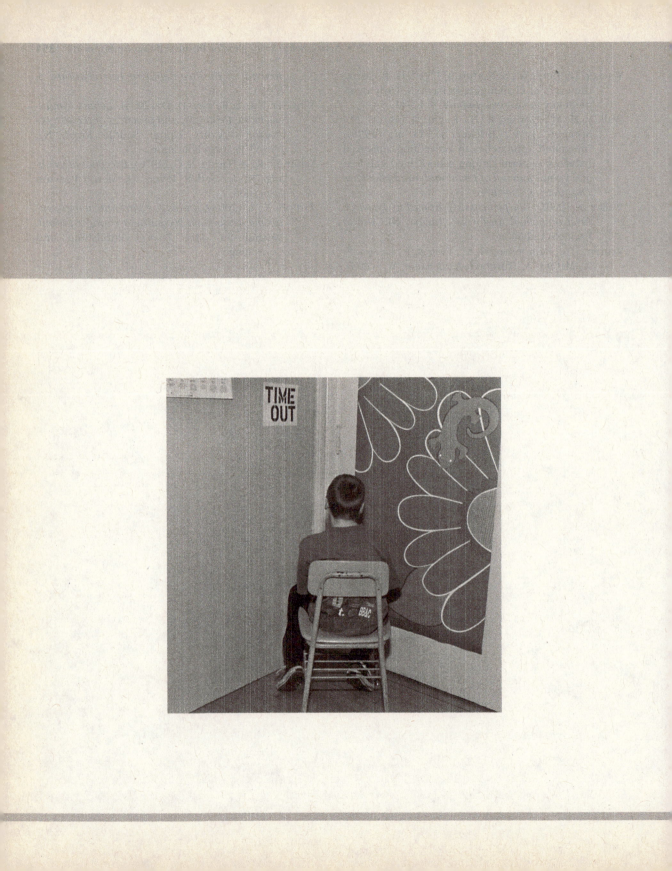

CHAPTER 13

Individual Strategies for Positive Behavior Supports

Thomas J. Zirpoli

Effective behavioral interventions employ strategies and procedures that prevent behavior problems as compared to those that rely on aversive consequences to punish or otherwise deter problem behaviors.

—GRESHAM (2004, P. 326)

In the previous chapter we discussed school- and classwide strategies to build a culture of positive behavioral supports within the school building and the classroom. These universal policies and procedures will encourage and promote appropriate social skills in students, and a large majority of students will be successful with these tier-one supports. Sugai and Horner (2007) found that at least 80% of students will respond positively to the school- and classwide prevention strategies found in tier-one interventions, that about 15% of students will demonstrate at-risk behavior and require specialized small-group interventions, and that another 5% of students will need specialized and individualized intervention in the form of a behavior intervention plan (BIP).

In this chapter, we will outline strategies appropriate for teachers writing behavior intervention plans (BIP) and other general forms of interventions as teachers interact with students on a day-to-day basis, especially students needing more intensive, tier-three supports. We begin with an outline of the components of a BIP. Then we provide a through discussion of differential reinforcement strategies because we want to encourage the use of positive behavior supports for both increasing appropriate behaviors and decreasing antisocial behaviors. Finally, we provide a summary of specific strategies used to reduce inappropriate behaviors that may be included within a BIP.

BEHAVIORAL INTERVENTION PLANS

The IDEA Act of 2004 requires that after a functional behavioral assessment identifies a target behavior in need of modification, a Behavioral Intervention Plan (BIP) must be developed to guide the classroom teacher in decreasing or eliminating the challenging behavior. The BIP needs to be individualized to the needs of the specific student; but other than that, the law does not specify the contents of a BIP. Etscheidt (2006, p. 225) reviewed administrative decisions and case law decisions and provided the following five "themes" related to an appropriate BIP:

1. A BIP must be developed if a student's behavior is interfering with his or her learning. Etscheidt (2006) found that when schools failed to provide students with a BIP when necessary, hearing officers and the courts were likely to determine that the student's IEP is inappropriate and that funding for private school placement was appropriate.

2. The development of a student's BIP must be based upon assessment data. Hearing officers and courts have determined that BIPs must be based upon "recent, meaningful assessments" that are "properly conducted and interpreted," and that include a functional based assessment (FBA: see Chapter 9) "to ascertain the variables associated with each of the student's problem behaviors" (p. 229).

3. Like the IEP, the BIP must be individualized to meet the needs of the student. Tier-one schoolwide PBS programs or even tier-two programs specifically written for small groups of students with common academic needs or behavior challenges are not considered individualized. The BIP must reflect the individual assessment data from the student. Group counseling, for example, does not meet the standard that requires a BIP to be "individually tailored and student-specific" (p. 230).

4. The BIP must include reinforcement strategies and other positive behavior supports. These strategies and supports must be spelled out and specific. A simple list of goals and objectives is not appropriate. While the inclusion of consequences for inappropriate behavior is appropriate, a BIP that is punitive in nature, without the use of reinforcement and other positive behavior supports is insufficient.

5. The BIP must be implemented with fidelity and data collected to monitor its effectiveness. Collecting data is also not sufficient if the student's team does not use the data to make programming decisions. For example, if data suggest that the BIP is ineffective, the BIP needs to be modified. In addition, schools need to monitor the implementation of a BIP. If the BIP is not implemented with fidelity, professional development and training are necessary to ensure that everyone who has contact with the student knows how to respond to his or her behavior and is familiar with the general strategies of the BIP. For example, if a student's target behavior is supposed to be ignored as part of an overall plan outlined in the BIP, but several people in the school are not aware of this and provide the student with attention when they observe the behavior, then in this case the BIP is not being implemented with fidelity and this may be considered by a hearing officer or court as a violation of the student's right to an appropriate education.

In this text, we recommend that the BIP contain, at a minimum, the following information: student's name, target behavior, baseline data, program goal or terminal behavior, reinforcement menu, reinforcement schedule, performance criteria, differential reinforcement strategies, and consequences following the target behavior. Two examples of a BIP are found in Figures 13.1 and 13.2.

When teachers develop a BIP for a student needing intensive, individualized intervention, they are encouraged to incorporate the strategies of differential reinforcement described below.

Student's name: *John (15 years old)*

Target behavior: *Cursing during gym period*

Baseline data: *John was observed for 5 consecutive days during gym class (50 minutes each). John cursed an average of five times during each 50-minute gym class (range = 4–6).*

Program goal: *John will reduce his cursing rate to zero per 50-minute gym class for 10 consecutive days.*

Reinforcement menu: *John may pick one item from the reinforcement menu below per reinforcement opportunity.*

- *Ten minutes of playing with a video game of his choice during study hall*
- *Ten minutes of listening to music using his iPod during study hall*
- *Ten minutes of computer time during study hall*
- *Choice of one item under $1.00 at the school store*

Reinforcement schedule:

Phase 1: *John may select one reinforcer from the R-menu when his cursing rate is less than five per 50-minute gym class.*

Phase 2: *John may select one reinforcer when his cursing rate is less than three per 50-minute gum class.*

Phase 3: *John may select two reinforcers when his cursing rate is less than two per 50-minute gym class.*

Phase 4. *John may select two reinforcers when his cursing rate is zero per 50-minute gym class.*

Performance criteria for phase change: *John will move to each new phase of this BIP after achieving the current phase objective for three consecutive gym periods. For example, after John has achieved the objective for phase 1, reducing the rate of cursing to less than five for three consecutive gym periods, he is moved to phase 2 and told of the changes and higher expectations necessary to pick from the R-menu. At each phase change, John and his gym teacher review the R-menu to see if it needs to be modified.*

Differential Reinforcement for Alternative Behaviors (DRA): *Throughout the gym period when John is observed using appropriate words to communicate with other students, John's gym teacher will provide John with verbal praise for using appropriate words ("John, thank you for using appropriate words" or "John, I like the way you are using appropriate words with your friends.")*

Consequences for the target behavior: *When John does curse in his gym class, the teacher will use extinction and ignore the behavior. At the end of the 50-minute gym class, John will be told if he did or did not meet the criteria of his current program phase. If he did meet the criteria, he will be verbally reinforced (Good job, John!) and asked to select the appropriate number of items from the R-menu. If he does not meet the criteria, he will be told, "John, you did not earn a reinforcer today. Try again next time." Do not give John any additional attention for not achieving his daily objective.*

FIGURE 13.1 **Behavior Intervention Plan using differential reinforcement of lower rates of inappropriate behavior (DRL) and alternative behaviors (DRA) to reduce cursing behavior during gym period**

Student's name: *Julia (6 years old)*

Target behavior: *Taking items from other students*

Baseline data: *A 4-day baseline measure was taken by Julia's teacher, from 9:00 am until 3 pm, on the number of items taken from other students (without their permission). Over the 4-day period, Julia was caught taking item from classmates an average of 12 times during the 6-hour school day.*

Program goal: *Julia will take zero (0) items from other students without their permission during the entire 6-hour school day for 10 consecutive days.*

Reinforcement menu: *Julia may select from the following reinforcement menu items:*

- *One special pencil picked from the teacher's supply*
- *One extra cracker during snack time*
- *One sticker from the teacher's supply*
- *Five minutes on the computer*
- *Five minutes listening to music using headphones*

Reinforcement schedule:

Phase 1: *Julia may select one reinforcer when the frequency of taking items from other students is reduced to under 10 times per 6-hour school day.*

Phase 2: *Julia may select one reinforcer when the frequency of taking items from other students is reduced to under 8 times per 6-hour school day.*

Phase 3: *Julia may select one reinforcer when the frequency of taking items from other students is reduced to under 6 times per 6-hour school day.*

Phase 4: *Julia may select one reinforcer when the frequency of taking items from other students is reduced to under 4 times per 6-hour school day.*

Phase 5: *Julia may select one reinforcer when the frequency of taking items from other students is reduced to 2 times or fewer per 6-hour school day.*

Phase 6: *Julia may select two reinforcers from the R-menu when the frequency of taking items from other students is reduced to zero times per 6-hour school day.*

Performance criteria for phase change: *Julia will move to each new phase of her BIP after achieving the current phase objective for three consecutive days. For example, after Julia has achieved the objective for phase 1, not taking items from other students without permission for three consecutive days, she will be moved to phase 2 and will be told of the changes in expectations to earn reinforcements.*

Differential Reinforcement for Other Behaviors (DRO): *Throughout the day, at least once per hour, Julia's teacher will provide Julia with verbal praise for not having items in her possession that do not belong to her. This will continue through phase 6 of this program plan.*

Consequences for the target behavior: *When Julia is observed with an item that does not belong to her, she will be asked, "Who does that item belong?" After the teacher determines where the item came from, the teacher will bring Julia to the item's owner and say, "Julia, please return the item." At the end of each day, Julia's teacher will report on her progress and either provide Julia with an opportunity to select an item or items from the reinforcement menu (if Julia met the criteria of her current phase), or tell Julia, "Julia, you did not meet your criteria for the day. Try again tomorrow."*

FIGURE 13.2   Behavior Intervention Plan using differential reinforcement of lower rates of behavior (DRL) and other behaviors (DRO) to reduce taking items from other students behavior

DIFFERENTIAL REINFORCEMENT STRATEGIES

Differential reinforcement refers to two primary applications of reinforcement to maintain or increase the occurrence of appropriate behavior. First, a behavior may be reinforced only when it is exhibited following an appropriate *discriminative stimulus* (SD). For example, talking in class may be appropriate in some situations but inappropriate in others. By reinforcing talking only when it follows certain antecedents (e.g., when the teacher asks a question) and not reinforcing talking at other times, teachers can apply differential reinforcement to talking behavior.

A second application of differential reinforcement refers to the reinforcement of one target behavior while other behaviors are ignored. Thus, as the reinforced behavior increases, it becomes differentiated from other behaviors, related or unrelated, that are likely to decrease in the absence of reinforcement. When reinforcing behaviors that are incompatible with, or provide an alternative to, inappropriate behaviors, teachers are using differential reinforcement to increase appropriate behaviors.

Generally, differential reinforcement increases the rate, duration, or intensity of behaviors that students already have in their repertoire but do not perform at acceptable levels. For example, a student may know how to raise his hand to get a teacher's attention, but instead, he frequently calls out the teacher's name in the middle of an assignment, interrupting the other students. When the teacher responds to the student after he raises his hand instead of his using calling-out behavior, the student learns which behavior is effective in getting the teacher's attention. In a second example, clinicians can use differential reinforcement to increase the rate of eating behavior for children exhibiting food refusal by ignoring food-refusal behavior and replacing it with attention for eating (see McCartney, Anderson, & English, 2005).

The focus of any behavior program should be reinforcement of appropriate behaviors.

The use of differential reinforcement as part of a behavior change strategy was identified as the most acceptable strategy by both applied behavior analysis (ABA) and positive behavior supports (PBS) experts (Brown, Michaels, Oliva, & Woolf, 2008). Because the focus of differential reinforcement is the use of positive reinforcement, these strategies should be part of most positive behavior support plans and the heart of most behavior intervention strategies. Again, when developing a BIP, the teacher needs to ask (a) How can I reinforce the student when he does not exhibit the challenging behavior? and (b) What alternative behaviors can I reinforce that will replace the challenging behavior? Variations of these two strategies using differential reinforcement are discussed next.

Differential Reinforcement of Other Behaviors

Differential reinforcement of other behaviors (DRO), first described and used by Reynolds (1961), refers to the delivery of reinforcement after the child *has not exhibited* a target behavior during a predetermined interval of time, regardless of other behaviors occurring during the interval. For example, Ramasamy, Taylor, and Ziegler (1996) eliminated out-of-seat behavior of a 14-year-old boy by providing an edible reinforcer or free time contingent on his staying in his seat. During the first phase of intervention, the boy was reinforced every 15 minutes for staying in his seat. In the second phase, he was reinforced every 30 minutes. In the third phase, he was reinforced every 45 minutes, and in the last phase, he was reinforced every hour.

A DRO schedule may also be used for providing reinforcement contingent on the absence of several inappropriate behaviors during a specific interval. For example, if a student screams and occasionally kicks others, reinforcement may be provided contingent on the absence of both screaming and kicking or contingent on the absence of only screaming or only kicking. Because the DRO procedure entails reinforcing the *omission* of specified inappropriate behaviors, the term *differential reinforcement of the omission* of behavior is sometimes used (Deitz & Repp, 1983).

The primary purpose of this procedure is to target the reduction of a *specific* inappropriate behavior in a student who has perhaps several less severe inappropriate behaviors, which are put on hold. Prioritizing inappropriate behaviors and targeting the reduction of one behavior at a time may be an acceptable solution for teachers working with students who have many behavior problems and have not responded to strategies for school- and claswide positive behavior supports.

FIXED- OR WHOLE-INTERVAL DRO　A DRO schedule has several different applications. In the first application, the DRO schedule is fixed (e.g., every 10 minutes or every 30 minutes). If the inappropriate behavior does not occur during the predetermined fixed interval, the student is reinforced. If the inappropriate behavior does take place at any time during the interval, the student is not reinforced at the end of the interval; a new interval begins only at the end of the preceding interval. For example, a student who frequently fights with other students may be placed on a DRO with a fixed interval of 30 minutes beginning at 9:00 A.M. and ending at 3:00 P.M. At 9:30 and each 30-minute interval thereafter, teachers would determine whether the student exhibited fighting behavior. If fighting behavior did not occur, the student would qualify for a reinforcer. If fighting behavior showed up at any time during the 30-minute period, the student would not qualify for a reinforcer. With this DRO 30-minute fixed schedule, the student could earn up to 12 reinforcers.

Providing reinforcement when a targeted behavior has not been exhibited for an entire predetermined interval has also been referred to as *whole-interval DRO* (Repp, Barton, & Brulle, 1983).

Repp, Felce, and Barton (1991) note that DRO is more effective when the interval between reinforcement is initially small than when it is large. In fact, they have found that a shorter DRO is about twice as effective as a longer DRO. They also state that the specific DRO interval should be related to the rate of behavior during baseline or the number of inappropriate behaviors divided into the duration of the class period. For example, if the average number of target behaviors were 10 within a 60-minute class period, then the DRO interval should be 6 minutes.

MOMENTARY DRO   A second variation, labeled *momentary DRO* (Repp et al., 1983), also uses a fixed, predetermined interval during which the occurrence of a target behavior is monitored. However, the student is reinforced only if the target behavior is not being emitted at the specific moment of observation—the end of each interval. For example, if a teacher were using a momentary DRO-5 (minutes), the student would be observed every 5 minutes. If, at that moment, the target behavior is not occurring—even if it had occurred at another moment during the interval—the student would be reinforced. If, at that moment, the target behavior is occurring, the student would not earn reinforcement, regardless of the student's behavior during the rest of the interval. The student's next opportunity for earning a reinforcer would be at the end of the next interval (5 minutes).

In a comparison of whole-interval DRO and momentary DRO, Repp et al. (1983) found the whole-interval DRO to be more effective, especially in the initial stages of programming. They suggest that momentary DRO may be used as part of a maintenance program. But in a multiple baseline design, Miller and Jones (1997) found that momentary DRO was more effective than whole-interval DRO in reducing stereotyped behavior in one subject and as effective with a second. They suggested that momentary DRO was easier to use and required less vigilance in applied settings.

DRO-RESET INTERVAL   In a third variation of DRO, described by Donnellan, LaVigna, Negri-Shoultz, and Fassbender (1988) as a *DRO-reset* interval, the interval of time is reset, or starts over, each time the targeted inappropriate behavior occurs. Using the previous example, if the student fought with another student at 9:15, the 30-minute interval would immediately be reset at 9:15 and end at 9:45 instead of 9:30. On the DRO-reset schedule, the student is reinforced for every 30 minutes during which no fighting occurs. The clock is always reset after each fight. With the DRO-fixed interval, the student who has a fight at 9:15 would not have another opportunity for reinforcement until 10:00 (45 minutes after his last fight), the end of the next interval.

DRO-INCREASING INTERVAL OR DRO-FADING SCHEDULE   In a fourth variation of the DRO schedule, the expected interval of appropriate behavior increases over time in relation to the student's progress. Research has demonstrated that DRO schedules are more effective when the interval is short at the start of the program and gradually increases than when the interval is initially long (Repp et al., 1991; Repp & Slack, 1977). This variation of DRO may be referred to as a *DRO-increasing interval* schedule or a *DRO-fading* schedule. The purpose of this variation is to fade or decrease the provision of reinforcement gradually from a frequent-opportunity schedule to a less-frequent-opportunity schedule. Using this procedure, the student is reinforced for the absence of a targeted inappropriate behavior for a specific interval (e.g., 30 minutes). However, after a predetermined number of successful intervals (e.g., three 30-minute intervals), the duration of the interval increases (e.g., from 30 to 45 minutes). Now the student must not exhibit the inappropriate behavior for a longer interval to qualify for reinforcement. If the inappropriate behavior does occur, the length of the interval stays the same. In effect, fading the reinforcement delivery schedule is determined by the student's progress. As the student progresses to longer intervals of appropriate behavior, teachers may wish to increase the quantity or quality of reinforcement. Otherwise, the student may feel penalized for making progress (i.e., getting reinforced less often for behaving appropriately for longer periods of time). The four variations of DRO are outlined as follows:

Variation	Reinforcement (R+) Delivery
Whole-interval	R+ is delivered if target behavior does not happen at any time during interval.
Momentary	R+ is delivered if target behavior is not occurring at the moment of observation at the end of interval.
Reset-interval	R+ is delivered if target behavior is not demonstrated for a full interval period of time; clock is reset after each target behavior.
Increasing-interval	R+ is delivered if target behavior is not exhibited at any time during interval. Duration of interval gradually increases as student makes progress.

Fading reinforcement schedules are an important element in any reinforcement program. Busy teachers are not likely to reinforce target behaviors consistently every 10, 15, or 30 minutes for extended periods. Also, the student needs to learn to behave appropriately in response to a more natural, intermittent schedule of reinforcement. On the other hand, it is important for teachers to understand that all students have different needs and that some students will continue to need more support than others.

LaVigna and Donnellan (1986) give three cautions concerning the use of DRO. First, because reinforcement is provided as a result of the *nonoccurrence* of a targeted inappropriate behavior, a specific appropriate behavior is not reinforced. Other types of differential reinforcement programs may be more effective for teachers increasing specific appropriate behaviors. Second, providing reinforcement contingent on a targeted inappropriate behavior not occurring may lead to the inadvertent reinforcement of other inappropriate behavior as well as appropriate behaviors. Finally, under a DRO-reset schedule, the student may learn to exhibit the inappropriate behavior *immediately* after the timer is set and, after the timer is reset, still receive reinforcement at the end of the new interval. In effect, the student still receives a reinforcer at the end of each interval, even if the inappropriate behavior occurred. Changing to a DRO-fixed schedule and not resetting the interval after each inappropriate behavior may eliminate this concern. Then, the student would not receive a reinforcer at the end of the interval because the inappropriate behavior had been exhibited at the beginning of the interval. A new interval would begin only at the end of the previously scheduled interval.

Differential Reinforcement of Alternative Behaviors

Differential reinforcement of alternative behaviors (DRA) refers to reinforcement of a more appropriate *form* of a targeted inappropriate behavior. Unlike DRO, DRA is more specific about the targeted behaviors to be reinforced. For example, when a teacher reinforces a student for politely *asking* for a treat instead of *demanding* a treat, the teacher is reinforcing an alternative, socially appropriate form of a behavior that has the same intent—to get a treat. Piazza, Moes, and Fisher (1996) used DRA to reduce destructive behaviors of an 11-year-old boy. The intervention included differential reinforcement of compliance to staff requests. Following compliance with a specific number of instructions, the boy was allowed free time and social interaction. Over time, the number of demands the boy was required to complete per session was increased. The boy's compliance increased, and his destructive behavior decreased.

The DRA procedure has several advantages. First, it emphasizes the reinforcement of specific appropriate behaviors. Unlike the DRO procedure, in which the teacher must monitor the occurrence or absence of inappropriate behaviors, the DRA procedure forces teachers to focus on the occurrence of appropriate behaviors. Second, the DRA procedure encourages teachers to review alternative behaviors that may be taught (if not already in the student's repertoire) or increased (if already in the student's repertoire). Too frequently, teachers are eager to punish inappropriate behaviors without considering alternative behaviors they could reinforce. Again, focusing on reinforcement instead of punishment will have a significant, positive influence on the student's home and classroom environment. Third, the DRA procedure has a double effect on the student's behavior. Not only does appropriate behavior increase when reinforced, but the targeted inappropriate behavior is likely to decrease (Vollmer, Roane, Ringdahl, & Marcus, 1999). In contrast, when punishment of inappropriate behavior is used alone, decreases in inappropriate behaviors are unlikely to occur in conjunction with increases in appropriate behaviors. Finally, the DRA procedure is easy to teach and use.

Implementing a DRA procedure can vary in several ways. Appropriate alternative behaviors may be reinforced based on a ratio schedule (number of appropriate behaviors) or an interval schedule (duration of appropriate behaviors). In addition, these ratio and interval schedules of reinforcement may be fixed or variable.

Differential Reinforcement of Incompatible Behaviors

Differential reinforcement of incompatible behaviors (DRI) refers to the reinforcement of behaviors that are topographically incompatible with targeted inappropriate behaviors. *Topographically incompatible* means that it is physically impossible for the incompatible and the target behaviors to occur at the same time. This procedure is also referred to as *differential reinforcement of competing behaviors* (DRC) (Donnellan et al., 1988). Reinforcement of incompatible or competing behaviors is even more specific than DRO or DRA as to what types of behaviors are targeted. For example, keeping your hands in your lap is incompatible with hitting others, and on-task behavior is incompatible with off-task behavior. Thus, when a teacher reinforces hands-in-lap behavior, hitting-others behavior is likely to decrease; and the reinforcement of on-task behavior is likely to reduce off-task behavior.

Of course, not all inappropriate behaviors have topographically incompatible behaviors that would be appropriate or functional to reinforce. For example, although sitting

TABLE 13.1 DRO, DRA, and DRI Examples

Target Behavior	Behavior Reinforced per Program		
	DRO	DRA	DRI
Out of seat	Absence of	Asking permission	In seat
Off task	Absence of	————	On task
Hitting	Absence of	Cooperation/talking	Hands in lap
Self-stimulation	Absence of	Playing with toys	Keeping still
Noncompliance	Absence of	————	Compliance
Temper tantrum	Absence of	Taking/asking	————
Talking out	Absence of	Raising hand	Being quiet
Throwing objects	Absence of	Playing basketball	Writing
Hands in mouth	Absence of	Brushing teeth	Hands in lap
Running	Absence of	Walking	Standing still
Foul language	Absence of	Appropriate language	Being quiet

still (the absence of movement or behavior) is incompatible with overactivity, self-stimulation, and a variety of behaviors identified as inappropriate in certain settings, reinforcing students for not moving is not recommended. Instead, teachers should identify alternative, functional behaviors to increase using a DRA or DRO procedure. Table 13.1 lists examples of differential reinforcement programs.

Differential Reinforcement of Lower Rates of Behavior

Differential reinforcement of lower rates of behavior (DRL), first described by Skinner (1938), refers to the reinforcement of small *decreases* in the rate of a target behavior compared to the baseline rate of that behavior. Unlike the DRA, DRI, and DRO procedures, DRL is especially useful when trying to decrease the frequency of a behavior that occurs often. With a DRA or DRI approach, few appropriate behaviors may occur during the high rate of inappropriate behavior, which thus leaves few opportunities to reinforce alternative (DRA) or incompatible (DRI) behaviors. In addition, when there is a high rate of inappropriate behavior, reinforcement delivered under a DRA or DRI schedule may inadvertently become associated with the inappropriate behavior. A DRO procedure may also be problematic when an inappropriate behavior occurs at a high rate. Since this procedure calls for providing reinforcement contingent on the absence of the targeted inappropriate behavior for a specific interval, the student may never qualify for a reinforcer.

A DRL procedure may also be recommended for a behavior considered appropriate and functional except for a high rate of occurrence. Asking to use the bathroom is an appropriate behavior; however, when it occurs frequently throughout the school day, it may disrupt the classroom and have an adverse effect on the student's academic performance. In this case, the classroom teacher would be interested in decreasing the rate of the behavior to an acceptable level rather than trying to eliminate the behavior.

The use of DRL may take one of two forms. In the first form, reinforcement is provided contingent on a target behavior as long as a predetermined interval of time has passed since the target behavior last occurred (Skinner, 1938). For instance, the teacher would determine that a student could leave the classroom for the bathroom if a certain length of time had passed since the student's previous request. The objective with this form of DRL is to increase the intervals between target behaviors from the current baseline interval to a more socially acceptable level.

In a second form of DRL, reinforcement is provided contingent on a lower rate of the target behavior within a specific interval of time (Dietz & Repp, 1983). In keeping with our example, teachers may decide to monitor the average hourly rate of the target behavior (asking to use the bathroom) and then reinforce the student each hour, contingent on a lower hourly rate of the target behavior. For example, the student may be reinforced for making two or fewer requests to use the bathroom per hour. As the student progresses in reducing the rate of the target behavior, reinforcement becomes contingent on a new criterion (an even lower hourly rate of the target behavior) until an acceptable level is achieved.

An important element in both DRL and differential reinforcement of higher rates of behavior is the completion of a baseline measurement of the target behavior. Before new criteria or objectives are set for reduced rates of behavior, an accurate baseline measurement is a must. Baseline data will reveal a benchmark for expected behavior or behavior change. For example, if teachers did not know the hourly baseline rate (how often the student asked to use the bathroom), they would not know whether the behavior had decreased during intervention or whether the decrease was significant enough for the student to earn a reinforcer. If teachers know that the baseline rate of the target behavior was 10 requests per hour, however, then they know that the first step in their DRL program should be to reinforce the student contingent on an hourly rate of fewer than 10 requests (e.g., eight or fewer per hour). After the student has consistently (for 3 or 4 consecutive hours) stayed below the baseline rate, a new and lower rate (e.g., six per hour) is established. Now, to earn a reinforcer, the student must exhibit the target behavior fewer than six times per hour. Additional reductions in the criteria for reinforcement should be made as the student progresses. Figure 13.1 outlines a sample BIP using a combination of DRL and DRA schedule of reinforcement, paired with a reinforcement menu, to decrease cursing behavior. Figure 13.2 outlines a sample BIP for a 6-year-old student using a combination of DRL and DRO to reduce taking items from other students, paired with a reinforcement menu.

Differential Reinforcement of Higher Rates of Behavior

Differential reinforcement of higher rates of behavior (DRH: also called a *changing criterion design*) refers to the reinforcement of *increases* in the rate of a target behavior compared to the baseline rate of that behavior. DRH is typically used to increase behaviors that are already in the student's repertoire but do not occur frequently or consistently enough. A student may know how to say "please" and "thank you" but may use the two terms infrequently. Reinforcing the student for using these expressions more often is likely to increase the use of the behaviors that already exist in the student's repertoire.

The application of DRH is similar to the application of DRL, except that the purpose of DRH is to *increase* the rate of a target behavior within a specific interval of time. As with DRL, teachers must first complete a baseline observation of the target behavior to establish a current rate. Then, they should reinforce increases in the rate, above baseline, until the rate of the target behavior occurs at an acceptable level.

SPECIFIC BEHAVIOR REDUCTION STRATEGIES FOR BEHAVIOR INTERVENTION PLANS (BIP)

The discussion of behavior reduction strategies assumes that behavior is influenced by the environment. It is important to understand that the teacher's behavior within the classroom and the parents' behavior in the home are significant variables in the teaching of appropriate behavior and the modification of inappropriate behavior. If teachers and parents are not willing to evaluate their own behavior as a contributing factor to both appropriate and inappropriate behavior in their children, there is little hope of helping the student. Many parents suffer from Parental Wimp Syndrome (Zirpoli, 2003), which is associated with a general lack of supervision, expectations, rules, and consistent consequences. Unless these parents are willing to learn how to become stronger parents, their children will remain at risk for failure, regardless of interventions provided by the student's school. However, challenges within students' home environment should not discourage teachers from teaching prosocial behaviors to students at school. Students are capable of learning to behave differently in different environments.

A number of behavior reduction strategies are available to teachers and other educators to decrease inappropriate behavior within the classroom or with individual students. While some strategies are recommended, others are advised only with modifications. These recommendations will be communicated within the discussion of each procedure. Some common strategies used to reduce inappropriate behavior that are recommended for possible inclusion in behavior intervention plans (BIP) include *social skills instruction, extinction, time-out, response cost, restitution, positive practice, overcorrection, and the use of medications.*. Interestingly, some of these methods, still strongly supported by applied behavior analysis (ABA) experts, are losing favor with those advocating for more positive behavior supports (PBS: Brown, et al., 2008).

Individual Social Skills Instruction

In Chapter 12 we discussed school- and classwide strategies to teach, model, and promote appropriate social skills for students. When schoolwide or classroom-based social skills instruction is not enough, however, direct instruction with small groups or individual students may be necessary (Walker, Colvin, & Ramsey, 1995). But first, teachers need to decide why a student is struggling socially. Gresham, Cook, Crews, and Kern (2004) identify three types of social skills deficits:

1. Social skills deficits related to *acquisition:* The student does not know these skills and/or the student does not understand the appropriate situation in which to use those skills. Appropriate interventions for acquisition deficits include modeling, coaching, and direct instruction (see Boutot, 2009, and Simpson, 2005, for examples).
2. Social skills deficits related to *performance:* The student is not performing these skills "at an acceptable level in a given situation" (p. 164) even though the student is capable of performing the skills. Appropriate interventions for performance deficits include prompting, shaping, and positive reinforcement (see Chapters 1 and 10).
3. Social skills deficits related to *fluency:* The student does not perform these skills "due to a lack of exposure to sufficient models of social behavior" (p. 164). Interventions for fluency deficits include all of the above.

There are a variety of formal social skills curriculum available for small groups and individual students, and Melloy (2001) provides a comprehensive outline of these. While these methods may take on several forms, they should all employ positive reinforcement and the use of differential reinforcement strategies discussed in the previous section (see Kennedy & Jolivette, 2008, for example). As outlined in Chapter 10, reinforcement may be used to teach and support new behaviors in many ways. For social skills instruction, positive reinforcement may be as simple as the use of verbal praise (see Kennedy & Jolivette, 2008) when social competency is demonstrated or the employment of a behavior intervention plan (BIP), including the use of a reinforcement menu where a student can select the reinforcement of choice after a standard of behavior, outlined in the student BIP, is demonstrated. Reinforcement may also be delivered using a token economy program where each targeted social skill demonstrated by the student earns a token. The student then has the opportunity to buy items from a reinforcement menu at the end of the day or end of the week using his or her tokens. The major components of a reinforcement program to teach a social skill include:

1. A targeted social skill you want the student to learn or demonstrate at a higher frequency (e.g., John will raise his hand to be recognized instead of yelling out and disrupting the classroom discussion in order to obtain his teacher's attention)
2. The development of a reinforcement menu for the student to select from (this list is developed with John)
3. A schedule of reinforcement that should be determined. (For example, how often will John be allowed to select a item from the menu? How many demonstrations of the target behavior (raising his hand without yelling out when he wants his teacher's attention) will John need to demonstrate before he earns a reinforcer? At the start of the program, John should be on a continuous schedule of reinforcement. For a complete discussion of reinforcement schedules and how to fade from a continuous to an intermittent schedule of reinforcement, see Chapter 10.)

As stated above, while some students simply have not learned to be socially competent, Kennedy and Jolivette (2008) state that other students with poor social skills may have learned and developed patterns of antisocial behavior, such as aggressive, disruptive, and defiant behaviors, as a way of gaining attention or escaping academic environments in which they are unsuccessful. For these students, strategies have been studied to reduce inappropriate social interactions. Two of these strategies are presented below.

SOCIAL STORIES A *social story* can be written, in picture form or in video form, to remind students how to respond to different situations that have previously been the antecedent of inappropriate social behavior. "The primary purpose of social story is to provide descriptive information concerning a social concept or situation, such as the people involved, the sequence of events, and the thoughts and feelings of others" (Sansosti and Powell-Smith, 2008, p. 163). Social stories may be written, pictorial, recorded for video, or a combination of the above. Scattone, Tingstrom, and Wilczynski (2006) found that social stories were helpful in reducing inappropriate social behavior, if not promoting appropriate social behavior. Thiemann and Goldstein (2001) successfully used social stories with peer partnering for practice and video feedback with five students with autism and social deficits twice per week to increase targeted social communication skills with peers. Sansosti and Powell-Smith (2008) used computer- presented social stories using Microsoft

PowerPoint and video models constructed using a digital camcorder to demonstrate targeted social skills to students with Asperger's syndrome. As in the previous study, peer models were used in the video presentations to demonstrate targeted behavior.

SOCIAL SCRIPTS   *Social scripts* provide information, instructions, and a visual reminder to students on how to respond in situations that have previously served as an antecedent to inappropriate behavior. Boutot (2009) provides the example of a student who speaks out in class whenever he has something to say. In this case, a social script strategy called "I Will" cards are developed to remind the student of what he should do. In this case, the card would say, "When I have something to say in class, I will raise my hand." Thus, when the student starts to speak without raising his hand, the teacher refers him to his "I Will" card for directions. In addition, the student reviews his cards at least daily. Social scripts like the "I Will" cards are based on cognitive behavior therapy interventions "such as self-instruction, self-monitoring, and self-reinforcement" (Boutot, 2009, p. 278). While useful for all students who need tier-three interventions for behavior management, social scripts are especially helpful for students with autism spectrum disorders (Sansosti and Powell-Smith, 2006). The use of social scripts requires very little professional development and few materials. Teachers may be very creative with social script cards, making them colorful and including lots of pictures for visual prompts. They may be used in small groups or with individual students.

Extinction

When students engage in inappropriate behaviors to elicit teacher or peer attention, extinction is sometimes the best strategy. *Extinction* is a procedure that gradually reduces the frequency and/or intensity of a target behavior by withholding reinforcement from the previously reinforced behavior. It requires teachers to ignore behavior that, under normal circumstances, would typically lead to attention, a form of reinforcement. By withholding this reinforcement, "extinction can be used to eliminate the connection between the behavior and the positive consequences that follow it" (Kazdin, 1989, p. 174). Gilliam (1989) states that "to discontinue the effect the behavior has on the environment (extinction)" is one of "the most fundamental" ways to eliminate behavior (p. 5).

Extinction is only effective in reducing behaviors that are motivated by attention or some other form of reinforcement. For example, in what may be the first published article regarding the withholding of reinforcement to reduce an inappropriate behavior, Williams (1959) outlines an extinction program to eliminate temper tantrums in a 21-month-old boy. The boy had been sick for the first 18 months of life and had learned to associate crying behavior with parental attention. Although he had recovered, he still used the crying behavior as a way to gain significant amounts of parental attention and to avoid going to bed at night. By ignoring this behavior, the parents helped gradually eliminate the child's crying at bedtime.

Extinction will not be effective for behaviors that are intrinsically reinforcing. "We should only ignore the behaviors motivated by our attention" (Barbetta, Norona, & Bicard, 2005, p. 16). Examples of behaviors that are intrinsically reinforcing include thumb sucking, daydreaming, and self-stimulatory behaviors. Also, extinction should not be used for physical aggression, even if attention seems to be the motivating factor. Also, some behaviors, such as severe self-injury or those that may hurt others, may require a more direct intervention approach than extinction.

Consistent with the theme of this text, Shukla-Mehta and Albin (2003) recommend using extinction with differential reinforcement strategies, discussed earlier in this chapter, to teach and reinforce appropriate alternatives to inappropriate behaviors. For example, Galensky, Miltenberger, Stricker, and Garlinghouse (2001) used the combination of extinction and reinforcement of appropriate eating behaviors as part of an overall behavior intervention plan to reduce mealtime behavior problems in young children with developmental disabilities.

EXTINCTION AND CONSISTENCY   Consistency is the most important factor related to the efficacy of extinction. For extinction to be effective in reducing a target behavior, teachers must be willing to ignore the behavior each and every time the behavior is observed. Teachers must alert other teachers and caregivers about the extinction program so that everyone who has contact with the student consistently withholds reinforcement following the target behavior. Accidental reinforcement must be prevented.

Teachers must determine whether the student's primary source of reinforcement is from teachers or peers. If the primary source of reinforcement is from the student's peers, teachers may not be in a position to control the delivery of reinforcement, and extinction is unlikely to be an effective procedure in reducing the target behavior. For example, if a student exhibits disruptive behavior within an educational setting in order to gain recognition from friends, an extinction program initiated by the teacher without the cooperation of the student's friends is unlikely to be effective.

As with other behavior reduction procedures, extinction should not be used in isolation and must be paired with the reinforcement of appropriate behaviors. When the inappropriate behavior is consistently ignored, it will be extinguished over a period of time. Like Leon in Classroom Connection 13.1, the student will learn that inappropriate behaviors are ignored and that only appropriate behaviors will yield the desired attention or reinforcement.

CLASSROOM CONNECTION 13.1
Using Extinction in the Classroom

Ann has a class of 12th graders who are fairly bright. One day she notices that one of her students, Leon, is acting very silly, which is disruptive to the other students. She also notices that the other students are giving him a lot of attention for his silly behavior. After class, several of her students talk to her about Leon's behavior and how disruptive it is to them. She advises them that Leon is probably seeking their attention and that if they would ignore him, Leon will eventually stop. She also warns them that once they start extinction, Leon's behavior will become more disruptive before it gets better. Sure enough, during the next few days, as the students do a good job ignoring him, Leon, thinking he needs to try harder to get their attention, becomes even more disruptive than ever. After several days, however, Leon realizes that the other students no longer find his silly behavior funny, and he settles down. Ann is sure to call on him and draw attention to Leon when he is acting appropriately. She wants to ensure that Leon learns that he can receive her attention, and the attention of his peers, following appropriate, not inappropriate, behavior.

General Reflection for Classroom Connection 13.1:

Ann had to gain the cooperation of Leon's classmates in order to decrease his disruptive behavior. As long as they found his behavior funny and he found their attention reinforcing, there was really little Ann could do. What do you think of this analysis? Also, what are the challenges of gaining student cooperation in situations like this at the elementary, middle, and high school levels?

OTHER FACTORS AFFECTING EXTINCTION   Kazdin (1989) cites several factors that may influence a behavior's resistance to extinction:

- The schedule of reinforcement that previously maintained the behavior (continuously reinforced behaviors decrease more rapidly than intermittently reinforced behaviors).
- The amount or strength of reinforcement that previously maintained the behavior (the greater the amount or strength of reinforcement associated with the behavior, the more resistance to extinction).
- The length of time the reinforcement was previously associated with the target behavior (the longer the association between the reinforcement and the behavior, the more resistance to extinction).
- The frequency of extinction used in the past to disassociate the reinforcement and the behavior (the greater the number, the more rapid the extinction).

EXTINCTION BURST   Extinction is an effective procedure for reducing inappropriate attention-getting behavior in children. However, one aspect of the procedure may make extinction very difficult for some teachers to use. Often a student has learned that demands will eventually be met if he or she is persistent and engages in the inappropriate behavior until teachers "give in" or "give up."

What happens when a teacher decides to ignore behavior that has previously been reinforced? The student is likely to repeat the behavior with greater frequency and intensity in hopes that the teacher will eventually give in (again). This is called an *extinction burst.* An extinction burst is a temporary increase in the frequency or intensity of a target behavior immediately after the introduction of extinction. For example, when a teacher decides to ignore a student's talking-out behavior, which previously resulted in getting the teacher's attention, the student's behavior may initially increase. By being consistent and reinforcing the student for appropriate methods of getting the teacher's attention (raising hand), the student's talking-out behavior will decrease.

Unfortunately, many teachers do not know about extinction bursts and, at this point, incorrectly judge the extinction program as ineffective. On the contrary, the extinction burst demonstrates that the teacher has identified at least some of the primary reinforcements maintaining the target behavior, that these reinforcers have been effectively withheld, and that the extinction procedure is having an impact on the student's behavior. With a little persistence and patience on the part of the teacher, once the extinction burst period is over, the student's behavior will improve. Teachers must decide *before* using extinction whether they will be able to ignore the inappropriate behavior through the extinction burst phase. If this is not possible, then another procedure is recommended.

SPONTANEOUS RECOVERY   *Spontaneous recovery* refers to the temporary recurrence of a target behavior during extinction even though the behavior has not been reinforced. The frequency or intensity of the behavior is usually not significant during spontaneous recovery. The biggest danger during this time is that the behavior will receive significant teacher attention or other forms of reinforcement. This, of course, will increase the likelihood of the behavior's recurring in the future. However, if teachers are consistent with the extinction procedure, the behavior is less likely to recur. Figure 13.3 demonstrates an example of both an extinction burst and spontaneous recovery during an extinction program used to reduce the frequency of a student's tattling behavior.

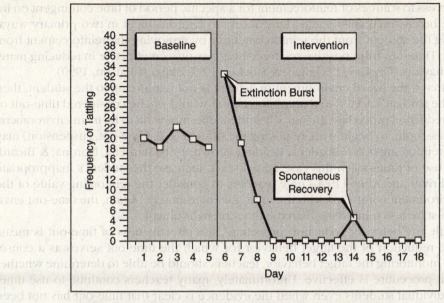

FIGURE 13.3   Demonstration of extinction burst and spontaneous recovery during extinction program for reduction of tattling behavior

ADVANTAGES OF EXTINCTION   Extinction has many advantages over other behavior reduction procedures, especially those considered "intrusive" or "aversive." First, extinction may be effective in reducing inappropriate behavior without the use of any physical or verbal consequences (e.g., repeatedly telling the student, "No!") that may decrease the student's self-esteem or establish a "battle" between the teacher and the student. Second, because extinction does not involve the use of any aversive punishments, negative side effects from these procedures are avoided. Third, although the effects of extinction may be gradual, the duration of effects is usually long lasting. Finally, the reinforcement of appropriate behaviors, while ignoring the inappropriate target behavior, is a critical element of extinction. Next to positive reinforcement, this point makes extinction, in our opinion, a procedure of first choice when teachers are trying to reduce minor inappropriate behaviors.

POTENTIAL SIDE EFFECTS AND DISADVANTAGES OF EXTINCTION   Except for the temporary increase in the target behavior that occurs during the extinction burst, the extinction procedure has only minor potential side effects. For example, the student may become frustrated when teachers no longer provide attention that has come to be expected following a target behavior. This may lead to a significant extinction burst and the demonstration of other inappropriate behaviors (e.g., aggression) as well. As long as teachers provide reinforcement for other appropriate behaviors and are consistent with the extinction procedure, these side effects should be only temporary setbacks.

Time-Out from Positive Reinforcement

Time-out from reinforcement is another effective method used when working with a student in need of individualized attention and intervention. Time-out entails removing a student's access to sources of reinforcement for a specific period of time contingent on inappropriate behavior. Teachers may deny access to reinforcement in two primary ways: by removing the student from the reinforcement or by removing the reinforcement from the student. Time-out from positive reinforcement has proven effective in reducing many kinds of behaviors (Onslow, Packman, & Stocker, 1997; Skiba & Raison, 1990).

Note that if the initial environment or activity is *not* reinforcing to the student, then removing the student's access to that reinforcement would *not* be considered time-out or a behavior reduction procedure. In fact, if a student does not want to be in an environment, such as a classroom, to begin with, removing the student (e.g., time-out, suspension) may actually be reinforcing (Costenbader & Reading-Brown, 1995; Barbetta, Norona, & Bicard, 2005). The use of time-out in this case may, in fact, increase the student's inappropriate behavior. Shriver and Allen (1996) urge teachers to consider the reinforcing value of the time-in environment compared with the time-out environment. Again, the time-out environment must be less reinforcing than the time-in environment.

As with any behavior reduction procedure, the effectiveness of time-out is measured by the reduction of the target behavior for which the time-out serves as a consequence. By monitoring the target behavior, teachers should be able to determine whether the time-out procedure is effective. Unfortunately, many teachers continue to use time-out with individual students even when the evidence is clear that time-out has not been an effective behavior reduction procedure for those students. Because some types of time-out involve removing a challenging student from the environment, some teachers use time-out as a method of taking a temporary "break" from the student. This, however, is not time-out from positive reinforcement and is unlikely to serve as an effective behavior reduction procedure. In fact, the temporary "break" from the student may be negatively reinforcing for teachers, and, despite a lack of effectiveness, they continue to use the procedure.

One of the primary issues regarding time-out is the length of the time-out period. Two- to 8-minute time-out periods are suggested for young children contingent on inappropriate behavior. Time-out periods should be given in increments of 1 minute per year of age (e.g., 2 years = 2 minutes of time-out) for children 10 years old and younger. Longer periods are not more effective and may even lead to an increase in inappropriate behavior (Harris, 1985). Teachers should use an alarm clock, a timer, or other method to act as a cue to end the time-out period and to ensure that the student does not spend more time in time-out than scheduled. Several types of time-out procedures are available. There are also some terminology issues concerning other procedures incorrectly identified under the heading of "time-out." These will be discussed next.

NONEXCLUSION TIME-OUT   *Nonexclusion time-out* is discussed in several texts and articles as a procedure in which the student is *not* removed from the reinforcing environment, but in some way or another, attention and other forms of reinforcement are taken from the student (Alberto & Troutman, 2006; Cooper, Heron, & Heward, 1987; Kazdin, 1989). At first reading, some readers may be confused by the similarity of nonexclusion time-out and extinction. While extinction involves withholding reinforcement previously associated with a target behavior, nonexclusion time-out refers to the temporary removal of *all* reinforcement for a short period. For example, as a result of an extinction program, Julia is ignored by her teacher when she speaks in class without first raising her hand. While Julia was previously able to receive her teacher's attention in this manner, her teacher now calls on Julia only when she raises her hand. If the same teacher were using a nonexclusion time-out procedure, the teacher would remove all attention and other reinforcement from Julia for a specific period of time (e.g., 2 minutes) each time Julia speaks in class without first seeking recognition by raising her hand. With extinction, a specific reinforcement (teacher's attention) previously associated with the target behavior (speaking out) is withheld. With nonexclusion time-out, all attention and reinforcement are removed for a limited period contingent on the target behavior.

Several variations of nonexclusion time-out are possible. The three most common variations are planned ignoring, removal of a specific reinforcer, and the time-out ribbon.

Planned Ignoring.   *Planned ignoring* refers to the removal of any social attention for a short period of time contingent on the occurrence of an inappropriate behavior. For example, when working with a student or a group of students, a teacher may look away from the student/students for 30 seconds contingent on inappropriate behavior. This procedure was used successfully as part of a behavior intervention plan to reduce inappropriate behavior in a 9-year-old boy diagnosed with attention-deficit/hyperactive disorder, anxiety, and a speech and language impairment (Stahr, Cusing, Lane, and Fox, 2006).

Removal of Specific Reinforcers.   *Removal of specific reinforcers* refers to taking away such reinforcers as food, toys, or materials for a short time contingent on the occurrence of an inappropriate behavior. For example, a parent may remove a child's food for 60 seconds contingent on inappropriate behavior during mealtime, or a teacher may remove a toy from a student for 2 minutes after the student throws the toy at another student.

The Time-Out Ribbon.   The *time-out ribbon* refers to a procedure first used by Foxx and Shapiro (1978) in which all the students in a classroom were given a ribbon to wear. In addition, the students received edibles and praise for appropriate behavior and for wearing their ribbon. When targeted inappropriate behavior occurred, a teacher removed the ribbon and attention from the student for 3 minutes or until the inappropriate behavior was terminated. Inappropriate behavior decreased from 42% during baseline to 6% during the time-out ribbon program.

The time-out ribbon procedure has been effective with both groups and individuals. For example, McKeegan, Estill, and Campbell (1984) used the time-out ribbon procedure to eliminate stereotypic behavior of a single student. The student learned that, contingent on stereotypic behavior, the ribbon, along with any associated attention or reinforcement, was removed. Yeager and McLaughlin (1994) effectively used a time-out ribbon program to significantly increase compliance within a classroom. Salend and Gordon (1987) used one large ribbon for a whole group of students and demonstrated the effectiveness of an interdependent, group-oriented time-out ribbon procedure. While the class had possession of the ribbon (on display in front of the class), a token system was employed in which the group received one token for every 2 minutes they refrained from inappropriate verbalization. However, when a group member engaged in inappropriate verbalization, the ribbon was removed for 1 minute. The students could not earn tokens during this 1-minute period. Inappropriate verbalizations were significantly reduced.

Teachers may employ many variations to the time-out ribbon. For example, Fee, Matson, and Manikam (1990) used a wristband covered with smiling-face stickers, instead of a ribbon, with preschool students. The wristband was removed for three consecutive minutes contingent on targeted inappropriate behaviors.

An effective teacher knows which behaviors to ignore, which behaviors to reinforce, and which behaviors to punish.

EXCLUSION TIME-OUT *Exclusion time-out* refers to the *physical removal* of a student from a reinforcing environment or activity for a specific period of time. In our opinion, exclusion time-out is the only "true" time-out procedure since, by definition, time-out is the removal of the student from reinforcement. Within exclusion time-out, there are three widely accepted subtypes or levels of time-out.

Contingent Observation Time-Out. A *contingent observation time-out* is a type of exclusion time-out that involves removing the student from a reinforcing activity (e.g., story time, game) to the "sideline" contingent on the target behavior (Porterfield, Herbert-Jackson, & Risley, 1976). Rather than being isolated, the student is allowed to remain on the periphery of the group and observe the other students participating in the activity and behaving appropriately (Skiba & Raison, 1990). After a short time, the student is allowed to return to the group. For example, when a hockey player commits a foul, she must sit on the sideline for a specific time period. The hockey player may observe other members of the team play, but she may not rejoin the activity until the time-out period is over. White and Bailey (1990) used a contingent observation time-out procedure called "sit and watch" to decrease disruptive behaviors (noncompliance, aggression, and throwing objects) with elementary students during physical education classes. An example of contingent observation time-out is presented in Classroom Connection 13.2.

Isolation Time-Out. *Isolation time-out* is a procedure that requires the teacher to remove the student totally from the reinforcing activity contingent on the target behavior. This procedure is one step beyond contingent observation, and the student is *turned away* from the reinforcing activity. An isolation time-out area may be a designated corner or other isolated space in the environment. The students need to know beforehand that they are placed or sent to this area as a result of their inappropriate behavior.

This technique is especially effective in decreasing physically aggressive behavior in young children. When the student exhibits the target behavior (e.g., hitting others), he or

CLASSROOM CONNECTION 13.2
The Use of Contingent Observation Time-Out to Decrease Aggressive Behavior in a Third-Grade Classroom

Susan is a third-grade teacher in a large school with a diverse population of students. Her most common complaint about her students is the frequency of aggressive play she observes throughout the day. Some examples of aggressive play observed by Susan include children pushing each other, pretending to shoot each other with make-believe guns, verbal aggression ("I'm going to kick you!"), and other acts of violence against classmates. Susan decides to have a talk with her students one morning and tells them that, from now on, any acts of aggression observed in the classroom will result in the student being placed in a time-out corner for 5 minutes. Susan gives her students examples of the types of aggression she is talking about and shows them where the time-out corner will be.

Soon after her talk, Susan observes one of her students, Michael, hitting another student for getting in his way. She immediately directs Michael to the time-out corner and tells him that he must stay there for 5 minutes for hitting. Michael tries to explain his behavior and talk his way out of his consequence, but Susan ignores him and sets the timer for 5 minutes. During the 5 minutes, Susan goes about her work with the other students. When the timer rings, she directs Michael to return to his activity.

For this new program to work, Susan knows that she must be very consistent. After several days, her children learn that Susan will be consistent, that there is no benefit of testing her resolve, and that their teacher means it when she says she will not tolerate any more aggressive behavior. Susan also verbally praises her students for their improved classroom behavior, and they talk about how the class is both safer and more fun for all of them. Susan understands, however, that the continued success of her program depends upon the consistent implementation of her time-out program throughout the school year.

General Reflection for Classroom Connection 13.2:

What do you think would have happened after Susan's talk with her class if she did not place Michael in time-out? What do you think would happen to the class's frequency of aggressive behavior if Susan were to slack off and not enforce her no-aggression rule after a couple of weeks? How would that affect Susan's other tasks in running her classroom? How may Susan involve parents in her efforts to decrease aggression in the classroom?

she is immediately removed from the activity and placed in the time-out area for a predetermined period. For young students, teachers should gently but firmly take the student to the predetermined area, then briefly tell the student why he or she is being placed in time-out, and how long he or she must remain there (e.g., "You may come out of time-out when the timer goes off"). Older students may simply be instructed, "You [committed the target behavior]. Go to time-out." Other general guidelines for using isolation time-out include these:

- The time-out area should be set up so that the teacher can clearly observe the student but the student cannot participate in the activity from which he or she was just removed. Isolation time-out may include placing the student behind a partition within the environment or other open space next to the environment. School hallways are usually not good time-out areas since the classroom teacher may not be able to monitor the student during the time-out period.

- The isolation time-out area may contain a chair for the student to sit on so that expectations for what the student will do while in the time-out area are clear (i.e., sit on the chair).

- The teacher should set a timer for the amount of time the student is to spend sitting in the time-out area. Using a timer clearly delineates to the student how long he or she must stay in time-out and also eliminates the possibility that the teacher will lose track of how long the student has been in time-out. Again, it is important to note that longer time-out periods do not mean that the student will be less inclined to engage in the inappropriate behavior in the future. Time-out periods longer than 10 minutes are unlikely to be any more effective than 2-minute periods. Remember, consistency is more important than duration.

- An important factor regarding the effectiveness of time-out is the reinforcement value of the environment from which the student has been removed. Students should not be allowed to interact with others, including the teacher, while in the time-out area. Remember, the purpose of time-out is to remove the student from reinforcement.

- If the student refuses to remain in the time-out area, the teacher should return him or her to the area and tell the student that he or she may not return to the group until the time in time-out is completed. If this does not work, the student may be given a choice between sitting in the time-out area or being completely removed from the environment. This step may be enough of a deterrent that the student will choose to stay in the less restrictive area. Also, other backup consequences may be employed to reinforce appropriate time-out behavior.

- Keep in mind that the student will want to return to the activity if he or she has learned that reinforcement may be earned through appropriate behavior.

Seclusion Time-Out.   *Seclusion time-out* involves the complete removal of the student to a separate, usually closed, room or cubicle (i.e., time-out room) "outside the individual's normal educational or treatment environment that is devoid of positive reinforcers and in which the individual can be safely placed for a temporary period of time" (Cooper et al., 1987, p. 445). An example of seclusion time-out is sending a student to a time-out room within the educational setting. Small areas (e.g., closets) that are too confining and poorly ventilated or lit are *not* recommended and may be considered abusive.

Personal observations indicate that the use of seclusion time-out has been and continues to be misused and abused in many educational settings. First, students are being removed from environments or activities they do not find reinforcing. Thus, teachers may be negatively reinforcing inappropriate behavior. Second, students are frequently sent to seclusion time-out for periods of time that are too long and serve only to provide teachers with a break from the student. Lastly, in many cases time-out continues to be used despite data indicating its ineffectiveness with specific students. Teachers must use their data to make informed decisions about the effectiveness of interventions.

ADVANTAGES OF TIME-OUT   Time-out from positive reinforcement has several advantages:

- It is easy to integrate a time-out procedure with a positive reinforcement program to increase appropriate behaviors.

- Effects from time-out procedures are usually rapid, and the duration of effects is usually long lasting.

- The nonexclusion time-out process may be employed without removing the student from the educational environment.

- Nonexclusion time-out involves little or no physical contact with the student following inappropriate behavior.
- Time-out gives teachers an alternative to more intrusive behavior reduction strategies.
- Time-out provides students with the opportunity to regain control of their own behavior (Taylor, 1997).

POTENTIAL SIDE EFFECTS AND DISADVANTAGES OF TIME-OUT   A primary concern about the use of time-out is the removal of students from the instructional setting, which may affect the student's academic performance. Skiba and Raison (1990) examined the relationship between time-out usage with elementary students and academic achievement. They found that "considerably less instructional time was lost to time-out than to other sources of classroom absence, such as suspension or truancy" (p. 36). The amount of time-out usage was stated as "low to moderate for the majority of students," or an average of seven time-out periods (74 minutes) per month per student. When time-out usage is high, teachers should begin to question not only the impact on educational performance but also the effectiveness of the time-out procedure for the individual students (Costenbader & Reading-Brown, 1995). In addition, some courts and the U.S. Office of Civil Rights have ruled that excessive and prolonged use of time-out, especially if it interferes with the student's appropriate education, may be a violation of Section 504 and the IDEA (Yell, 2006).

Response Cost

Response cost is the systematic removal of reinforcers, sometimes in the form of tokens, points, money, or check marks, contingent on inappropriate behavior. Often used in conjunction with a token economy program (described in Chapter 10), this intervention requires systematically removing tokens as a consequence of inappropriate behavior (Walker, 1983). The number of tokens lost per inappropriate behavior is predetermined and usually depends on the severity of the behavior.

The response cost system should be explained to the student prior to implementation. Moreover, it is wise to list and post both the behaviors that will result in a removal of reinforcers and the number of reinforcers that will be lost per inappropriate behavior. A response cost program should always be employed in conjunction with a token economy program. Thus, along with a list of inappropriate behaviors that will lead to the removal of reinforcers, a list of appropriate behaviors that will warrant the earning of additional reinforcers should also be posted. Research has repeatedly indicated that the combination of response cost with other reinforcement programs is more effective than response cost alone (Phillips, Phillips, Fixsen, & Wolf, 1971; Walker, 1983; Walker, Hops, & Fiegenbaum, 1976).

Teachers should be sure that a student does not have all reinforcers removed or "go in the hole." For example, a student on a response cost program should not owe teachers 10 tokens at the end of the day. By reinforcing appropriate behavior more frequently than removing tokens for inappropriate behavior, the student will not have a deficit of tokens. Teachers should reinforce appropriate behavior two to four times for every response to inappropriate behavior. In this way, the primary focus of the educational setting will be on reinforcing appropriate behaviors rather than punishing inappropriate behaviors.

TABLE 13.2 Comparison of Extinction, Time-out, and Response Cost Procedures

Procedure	Definition	Example
Extinction	Removal of attention and other reinforcement previously associated with a target behavior	Teacher ignores student during tantrum behavior
Time-out	Removal of all reinforcement for a short, specific time period contingent on a target behavior	Teacher removes student from activity contingent on hitting other
Response cost	Removal of a predetermined number of reinforcers (tokens, points, check marks) contingent on a target behavior	Teacher removes one token from student contingent on off-task behavior

Table 13.2 provides a comparison of response cost with extinction and time-out. While all three involve the removal of reinforcement, response cost removes a specific reinforcement in increments. Also, the amount of the reinforcement removed is directly proportional to the frequency of inappropriate behavior.

As Pazulinec, Meyerrose, and Sajwaj (1983) explain:

> In both extinction and timeout procedures, the reinforcing consequence following a response is withheld. In contrast, response cost involves the removal of a positive stimulus contingent upon the occurrence of an undesirable behavior. In timeout the individual is restricted from receiving reinforcement or from participating in ongoing setting activities, whereas the response cost condition imposes no restrictions. (p. 71)

Pazulinec et al. (1983) outline several variations to response cost. In the first variation, a student is noncontingently provided with reinforcers at the beginning of a specific period of time (e.g., day, class period). Then, the student must give back reinforcers contingent on the occurrence of specific target behaviors. This variation may also be used with a group of students. For example, a classroom teacher may give the students 10 points and state that if the class still has 5 points by the end of the day, the students will receive a special reinforcement. Points would be removed throughout the day contingent on inappropriate target behaviors. This first variation is not recommended for several reasons:

- By providing the students with reinforcers noncontingently, this approach does not allow for teaching appropriate behaviors through the contingent presentation of reinforcers.
- A program that removes tokens, without a procedure to earn tokens, increases the chance that students will develop a negative balance. Moreover, after a teacher has taken away all of a student's tokens, what will he or she do following the next inappropriate behavior?
- This variation provides attention only for inappropriate behaviors.

In a second variation of response cost, students earn reinforcers throughout the response cost program. Thus, unlike the first variation, students are not provided with

CLASSROOM CONNECTION 13.3
Example of a Token Economy Classroom Program

Marie is a first-grade teacher in a classroom of 24 students. As part of her classroom behavior management program, Marie divides her students into groups of four. She varies group membership throughout the school year in an effort to find the best student combination per group. The desks of the four students are placed in a circle. For each group, Marie places a clear plastic jar on one of the group members' desks. Contingent on appropriate behavior demonstrated by either an individual member of a group or a whole group, Marie drops a token into the jar. Because the jars are made of clear plastic, the students can see the tokens accumulate in their group jars. Marie tries to maintain a high rate of giving tokens to make the program fun. However, when students within a group are observed to be off task or not following her directions, Marie quietly removes a

token from that group's plastic jar. She doesn't have to say anything or interrupt her teaching because the students know why she took a token from them. That is, they were either not paying attention or were off task. A special pencil is provided to each member of the group who ends the day with the most tokens. Marie provides a couple of extra privileges to the group who ends the week with the most tokens.

General Reflection for Classroom Connection 13.3:

What would be the advantages and disadvantages of modifying Marie's program so that it would not include response cost procedures following inappropriate behavior? Given the emphasis today on positive behavioral supports, do you think response cost programs are still appropriate?

"free" reinforcers, which may be taken away contingent on inappropriate behavior. Rather, reinforcers must be earned contingent on appropriate behavior and, at the same time, reinforcers may be taken away contingent on inappropriate behavior. This second variation may be considered a combination token economy and response cost program, and it may also be employed with a group or classroom of students. Walker (1983, p. 48) reports that the two variations of response cost described so far are "equally effective" in school settings.

In a third variation, teachers may divide their students into smaller groups and give each group opportunities to earn reinforcers and, contingent on inappropriate behavior, lose reinforcers. Special reinforcers may be provided to the group of students who ended the day with the most tokens or points. For example, many classroom teachers have activities (e.g., a companion reading program) throughout the day when students are divided into several small groups. These group periods provide teachers with opportunities to use a group token economy and response cost program to manage classroom behavior. Each group could earn or lose tokens contingent on behavior. At the end of the lesson, the group with the most tokens could earn a special reinforcer (e.g., extra time on the computer). An example of a combination token economy and response cost classroom program is provided in Classroom Connection 13.3.

ADVANTAGES OF RESPONSE COST   Using response cost programs to modify behavior offers many advantages. However, the advantages listed here assume the use of response cost in conjunction with a positive reinforcement program:

- Response cost programs are easily integrated with token economy or other positive reinforcement programs.
- Response cost programs are easily implemented within classroom settings.

- Response cost programs may be employed with very young or older students (Reynolds & Kelley, 1997).
- Response cost programs may be directed at specific target behaviors that need modification.
- Response cost programs allow an immediate consequence to inappropriate behavior without disruption of the classroom routine.

POTENTIAL SIDE EFFECTS AND DISADVANTAGES OF RESPONSE COST   Because the major element of response cost is the removal of reinforcers as a consequence of inappropriate behavior, teachers may direct too much attention toward inappropriate behavior rather than appropriate behavior. Used alone, this method is not consistent with the model of positive behavior support as it does not focus teachers' attention on reinforcing appropriate behavior.

A second disadvantage of response cost programs is the potential for some students to lose all reinforcers and then "give up." Both of these disadvantages may be avoided when opportunities to earn tokens are also available whenever a response cost program is employed.

Restitution, Restitution Overcorrection, and Positive Practice

The terms *restitution, overcorrection*, and *positive practice* are frequently used in the literature to describe procedures designed to decrease inappropriate behavior (Alberto & Troutman, 2006; Cooper et al., 1987). In this chapter, the terms are presented separately in order to clarify their definitions and expand on their practical applications with some applications recommended and some not.

RESTITUTION   *Restitution*, also known as *simple correction*, refers to a procedure that requires an individual to return the environment to its state prior to a behavior that changed the environment (Azrin & Besalel, 1980). The classic example is asking a student who spills a glass of milk to clean up the spill. Whether the child spilled the milk deliberately or accidentally, restitution teaches students to be responsible for their behavior and is recommended as part of a SWPBS program. Restitution should not be employed punitively but rather in a matter-of-fact way, especially if the behavior was an accident. Other examples of restitution are provided in Table 13.3

RESTITUTION OVERCORRECTION   Foxx and Azrin (1973) define *restitution overcorrection* as a step beyond simple correction of the environment. Contingent on inappropriate behavior, the student is required not only to perform restitution but to "restore the situation to a state vastly improved from that which existed before the disruption" (Foxx & Azrin, 1973, p. 2). Restitution overcorrection should not be used as a consequence of unintentional spills or other accidents. Rather, restitution overcorrection is intended to serve as a "punishing" consequence for deliberate inappropriate behaviors causing property damage. For example, if a high school student wrote on the classroom wall with a marker, restitution overcorrection would require him to clean the damaged wall (restitution) and the other three walls (overcorrection) of the classroom. When damage is purposeful, restitution overcorrection is recommended. Table 13.3 provides additional examples of restitution overcorrection.

TABLE 13.3 Examples of Restitution and Restitution Overcorrection

If the Child	Restitution Only Ask Child to	Restitution Overcorrection Ask Child to
Damages family car	Pay for repair	Pay for new car
Throws things	Pick up the items thrown and return to appropriate storage place	Pick up all items in environment and return to appropriate place.
Makes a mess during play or other activities	Clean play area to condition prior to activity	Clean play area and beyond
Writes on the wall	Wash the writing from the wall	Wash the entire wall
Drops food on the floor during lunch	Sweep up food after lunch	Sweep entire floor
Damages school materials	Repair or replace materials	Repair or replace materials plus repair other damaged materials
Damages school property	Repair property to condition prior to behavior	Repair damaged property and perform additional service to school property
Throws litter on the playground	Pick up the litter thrown on the playground	Pick up all litter on the playground and around the school

POSITIVE PRACTICE   *Positive practice* is practicing an appropriate behavior as a consequence for inappropriate behavior. The behavior practiced is the correct, or positive, behavior the student should have exhibited instead of the observed inappropriate behavior. "It means stopping all activities, whenever an error occurs, and then carefully performing the correct behavior several times" (Azrin, Besalel, Hall, & Hall, 1981). For example, when a student throws a piece of paper across the classroom toward a wastepaper basket, the teacher may ask the student to pick up the paper, walk to the wastepaper basket, place the paper into the basket, and return to his seat. On the completion of this appropriate behavior, the teacher should reinforce the student ("Thank you") for performing the behavior correctly.

Positive practice is not meant to be a positive consequence for inappropriate behavior. Forcing the student to practice the correct response is intended to be a punitive procedure—a strategy to decrease the chance that the student will exhibit the behavior again. Foxx and Azrin (1972) and Foxx and Bechtel (1983) warn that the use of reinforcement for correct responses during positive practice may encourage the student to behave inappropriately (in order to have additional opportunities for positive practice and reinforcement). Foxx and Bechtel (1983) recommend that the term *positive practice* be discontinued since the word *positive* gives the wrong impression about the procedure. Lenz, Singh, and Hewett (1991) suggest that the term *directed rehearsal* be used "instead of the generic term *overcorrection*" (p. 71).

Positive Practice Overcorrection.   Many texts do not distinguish between positive practice and positive practice overcorrection, but a distinction is made here because of the nonpunitive use of positive practice described in the previous section. Although

TABLE 13.4 Punitiveness of Different Variations of Positive Practice with and Without the Use of Positive Reinforcement

	With Reinforcement	Without Reinforcement
Positive practice	Not punitive and recommended	Punitive and not recommended
Positive practice overcorrection	Punitive and not recommended	Most punitive and not recommended

positive practice may be completed with a nonpunitive, educational intent, positive practice overcorrection is clearly intended as a punishing consequence for inappropriate behavior. With overcorrection, the student is required to perform the correct or appropriate behavior repeatedly. The operative word here is *repeatedly*. Using our previous example, the student may be required to repeat the steps of putting the paper in the wastepaper basket 10 times. The student is not repeatedly reinforced for correct responses during the positive practice overcorrection procedure. Variations of positive practice are outlined in Table 13.4.

Medications

Throughout this text, teachers have been encouraged to review and evaluate their own behavior and the student's overall environment before trying to change a student's behavior. The same approach should be followed before a teacher recommends that a student be placed on medication to change behavior. Teachers are also advised to question professionals who are quick to prescribe medications before environmental variables have been thoroughly evaluated and proven behavior management techniques, including a BIP, have been explored.

The use of medications to control inappropriate behavior has received a significant amount of public attention focused on the use of methylphenidate and other stimulants used to control the behavior of children labeled hyperactive or having an attention-deficit disorder (ADD) or attention-deficit hyperactivity disorder (ADHD). Clearly, medication can be helpful for some children (Jensen et al., 2005). It is also clear, however, that medications are overprescribed and that many children are taking medication when less intrusive behavior management interventions would prove effective (Reid, Trout, & Schartz, 2005). Berry (1998) of Duke University Medical Center, in a report issued by the National Institute of Health over 10 years ago, stated that mind-altering medications are prescribed too often to children and criticized the lack of studies on their long-term effects. Since the publication of that report, the use of medications in children for behavior management purposes, especially the use of stimulants for ADD/ADHD, has increased. About 8 percent of all school-aged children have been diagnosed with ADD/ADHD and more than half of these children are treated with medication (Visser & Lesesne, 2007).

While sometimes necessary, medicating a student does not change the antecedents and consequences within the student's environment—an environment that may be reinforcing inappropriate behaviors or that seldom teaches and reinforces appropriate behaviors.

In this case, the effects of medication may only mask the real problems, which remain unsolved. Researchers have consistently shown that medication treatment combined with behavior management interventions result in more positive outcomes than medication treatment alone (Forness, Freeman, & Paparella, 2006).

Schoenfeld and Konopasek (2007) provide a summary and description of the different categories of medications commonly used with school-aged children. These categories are: Stimulants, antidepressants, mood stabilizers, antianxiety, antipsychotics, and anticonvulsants. Stimulants are mainly used to treat ADD/ADHD and help children feel more alert by increasing neuron-to-neuron communication within the brain. Stimulants are the most common form of psychiatric medication used in schools today and have been shown to have a therapeutic effect in 70 to 80 percent of children diagnosed with ADD/ADHD. Stimulants take effect quickly with some remaining effective for up to 12 hours. The other medications listed below may take days or weeks to take affect. Common stimulants include Adderall, Dexedrine, Cylert, Concerta, Daytrana, Focalin, Metadate, and Ritalin.

Antidepressants are used to treat anxiety disorders, depression, obsessive-compulsive disorder (OCD), and Tourette's syndrome. Common antidepressants include Paxil, Prozac, Zoloft, Elavil, and Effexor. Mood Stabilizers are used to treat bipolar disorder. Common mood stabilizers include Tegretol, Depakote, and Symbyax. Antianxiety medications are used to treat anxiety disorders and, sometimes, epilepsy. Common antianxiety medications include Ativan, Klonopin, Valium, and Xanax. Antipsychotics are used to treat bipolar disorder, schizophrenia, Tourette's syndrome, and other conditions causing hallucinations, delusions, or detachment from reality. Common antipsychotic medications include Abilify, Haldol, Navane, Risperdal, and Zyprexa. Lastly, anticonvulsants are sometimes used to treat bipolar disorder, but more commonly, of course, to treat epilepsy by suppressing abnormal neuron activity in the brain. Common anticonvulsant medications include Depakote, Trileptal, and Neurontin.

Teachers should be aware of the types of medications students are taking, understand their potential side effects, and be responsible for monitoring the student's targeted behaviors so that those responsible for medication and dose changes can make informed decisions.

Summary

The IDEA Act of 2004 requires that a Behavioral Intervention Plan (BIP) be developed for students when it becomes necessary to decrease or eliminate challenging behavior that interferes with academic progress. At a minimum, we recommend that the BIP contain the following information: student's name, target behavior, baseline data, program goal or terminal behavior, reinforcement menu, reinforcement schedule, performance criteria, differential reinforcement strategies, and consequences following the target behavior.

Differential reinforcement of behavior refers to the reinforcement of behavior following an appropriate discriminative stimulus, or the reinforcement of a target behavior while other behaviors are ignored. Differential reinforcement schedules include the differential reinforcement of other behaviors, differential reinforcement of alternative behaviors, differential reinforcement of incompatible behaviors, and differential reinforcement of lower and higher rates of behaviors.

A number of behavior reduction strategies are available to teachers. These include extinction, time-out, response cost, restitution, positive practice, and overcorrection.

Extinction is the withholding of reinforcement from a previously reinforced behavior. Time-out refers to taking away an individual's access to sources of reinforcement for a specific period of time. Response cost is the systematic removal of reinforcers, such as tokens and points, contingent on inappropriate behavior. Note that all of these interventions should be used in conjunction with the positive reinforcement of appropriate behaviors.

Restitution is the act of returning the environment to the condition prior to inappropriate behavior. Restitution overcorrection, a step beyond simple restitution, refers to vastly improving the environment contingent on inappropriate behavior. The nonpunitive use of restitution is supported as an acceptable part of a PBS program.

Positive practice refers to the required practice of appropriate behaviors contingent on inappropriate behavior. Positive practice overcorrection is the punitive, repeated practice of appropriate behavior. Although not part of the historic or technical definition of positive practice or overcorrection, reinforcing correct performance of behaviors during and outside of practice procedures is recommended.

Medications are frequently employed to modify children's behavior. The most common medications used include stimulants to control aggressive and disruptive behaviors, antidepressants, and antipsychotics to treat children with severe behavior disorders. Teachers are encouraged to become knowledgeable about the associated side effects of any medications prescribed to their students. Medications should not serve as a treatment of first choice or a quick fix to behavior challenges that may be remedied by modifying the environment or using basic behavior management strategies.

References

Alberto, P. A., & Troutman, A. C. (2006). *Applied behavior analysis for teachers*. Upper Saddle River, NJ: Merrill/Pearson Education.

Azrin, N. H., & Besalel, V. A. (1980). *How to use overcorrection*. Austin, TX: Pro-Ed.

Azrin, N. H., Besalel, V. A., Hall, R. V., & Hall, M. C. (1981). *How to use positive practice*. Austin, TX: Pro-Ed.

Baker, J. N. (1987, January). Paddling: Still a sore point. *Newsweek*, p. 62.

Barbetta, P. M., Norona, K. L., & Bicard, D. F. (2005). Classroom behavior management: A dozen common mistakes and what to do instead. *Preventing School Failure, 49*(3), 11–19.

Berry, D. A. (November, 1998). *Report on ADHD*. Washington, DC: National Institute of Health.

Boutot, E. A. (2009). Using "I Will" cards and social coaches to improve social behaviors of students with Asperger Syndrome. *Intervention in School and Clinic, 44*, 276–281.

Brown, F., Michaels, C. A., Oliva, C. M., & Woolf, S. B. (2008). Personal paradigm shifts among ABA and PBS experts: Comparisons in treatment acceptability. *Journal of Positive Behavior Intervention, 10*(4), 212–227.

Cooper, J. O., Heron, T. E., & Heward, W. L. (1987). *Applied behavior analysis*. Upper Saddle River, NJ: Merrill/Pearson Education.

Costenbader, V., & Reading-Brown, M. (1995). Isolation timeout used with students with emotional disturbance. *Exceptional Children, 61*(4), 353–363.

Dietz, S. M., & Repp, A. C. (1983). Reducing behavior through reinforcement. *Exceptional Education Quarterly, 3*, 34–46.

Donnellan, A. M., LaVigna, G. W., Negri-Shoultz, N., & Fassbender, L. L. (1988). *Progress without punishment: Effective approaches for learners with behavior problems*. New York: Teachers College Press.

Etscheidt, S. (2006). Behavioral Intervention Plans: Pedagogical and legal analysis of issues. *Behavioral Disorders, 31*(2), 223–243.

Fee, V. E., Matson, J. L., & Manikam, R. (1990). A control group outcome study of a non-exclusionary time-out package to improve social skills with preschoolers. *Exceptionality, 1*, 107–121.

Forness, S. R., Freeman, S. F. N., & Paparella, T. (2006). Recent randomized clinical trials comparing behavioral interventions and psychopharmacologic treatments for students with EBD. *Behavioral Disorders, 31*, 284–296.

Foxx, R. M., & Azrin, N. H. (1972). Restitution: A method of eliminating aggressive-disruptive behaviors of retarded and brain damaged patients. *Behavior Research and Therapy, 10*, 15–27.

Foxx, R. M., & Azrin, N. H. (1973). The elimination of autistic self-stimulatory behavior by overcorrection. *Journal of Applied Behavior Analysis, 6*, 1–14.

Foxx, R. M., & Bechtel, D. R. (1983). Overcorrection: A review and analysis. In S. Axelrod & J. Apsche (Eds.), *The effects of punishment on human behavior* (pp. 133–220). New York: Academic Press.

Foxx, R. M., & Shapiro, S. T. (1978). The time-out ribbon: A non-exclusionary time-out procedure. *Journal of Applied Behavior Analysis, 11*, 125–136.

Galensky, T. L., Miltenberger, R. G., Stricker, J. M., & Garlinghouse, M. A. (2001). Functional assessment and treatment of mealtime behavior problems. *Journal of Positive Behavior Interventions, 3*(4), 211–224.

Gilliam, J. E. (1989). Positive reinforcement and behavioral deficits of children with autism: C. B. Ferster's thoughts versus current practice. *Focus on Autistic Behavior, 4*, 1–16.

Gresham, F. M. (2004). Current status and future directions of school-based behavioral interventions. *School Psychology Review, 33*(3), 326–343.

Gresham, F. M., Cook, C. R., Crews, S. D., & Kerns, L. (2004). Social skills training for children and youth with emotional and behavioral disorders: Validity considerations and future directions. *Behavior Disorders, 30*, 32-46.

Harris, K. R. (1985). Definitional, parametric, and procedural considerations in time-out interventions and research. *Exceptional Children, 51*, 279–288.

Jensen, P. S., and 14 others. (2005). Cost-effectiveness of ADHD treatments: Findings from the Multimodal Treatment Study of Children with ADHD. *American Journal of Psychiatry, 162*(9), 1628–1636.

Kazdin, A. E. (1989). *Behavior modification in applied settings*. Pacific Grove, CA: Brooks/Cole.

Kennedy, C., & Jolivette, K. (2008). The effects of positive verbal reinforcement on the time spent outside the classroom for students with emotional and behavioral disorders in a residential setting. *Behavioral Disorders, 33*(4), 211–221.

LaVigna, G. W., & Donnellan, A. M. (1986). *Alternatives to punishment: Solving behavior problems with non-aversive strategies*. New York: Irvington.

LaVigna, G. W., & Willis, T. J. (1991, February). *Non-aversive behavior modification*. Workshop presented by the Institute for Applied Behavior Analysis, Minneapolis, MN.

Lenz, M., Singh, N. N., & Hewett, A. E. (1991). Overcorrection as an academic remediation procedure. *Behavior Modification, 15*, 64–73.

McCartney, E. J., Anderson, C. M., & English, C. L. (2005). Effect of brief clinic-based training on the ability of caregivers to implement escape extinction. *Journal of Positive Behavior Interventions, 7*(1), 18–32.

McKeegan, G., Estill, K., & Campbell, B. (1984). Use of nonseclusionary time-out for the elimination of stereotypic behavior. *Journal of Behavior Therapy and Experimental Psychiatry, 15*, 261–264.

Melloy, K. J. (2001). Development of social competence. In T. Zirpoli and K. Melloy (Eds). *Behavior management: Applications for teachers* (3rd ed., pp. 248–280). Upper Sadddle River, NJ: Merrill/Pearson Education.

Miller, B. Y., & Jones, R. S. (1997). Reducing stereotyped behaviour: A comparison of two methods of programming differential reinforcement. *British Journal of Clinical Psychology, 36*, 297–302.

National Committee to Prevent Child Abuse. (1995). *Seven good reasons to stop spanking*. Washington, DC: Author.

Onslow, M., Packman, A., & Stocker, S. (1997). Control of children's stuttering with response-contingent timeout. *Journal of Speech, Language, and Hearing Research, 40*, 121–131.

Pazulinec, R., Meyerrose, M., & Sajwaj, T. (1983). Punishment via response cost. In S. Axelrod & J. Apsche (Eds.), *The effects of punishment on human behavior* (pp. 71–86). New York: Academic Press.

Phillips, E. L., Phillips, E. A., Fixsen, D. L., & Wolf, M. (1971). Achievement place: Modification of behaviors of pre-delinquent boys within a token economy. *Journal of Applied Behavior Analysis, 4*, 45–59.

Piazza, C. C., Moes, D. R., & Fisher, W. W. (1996). Differential reinforcement of alternative behavior and demand fading in the treatment of escape-maintained destructive behavior. *Journal of Applied Behavior Analysis, 29*, 569–572.

Porterfield, J. K., Herbert-Jackson, E., & Risley, T. R. (1976). Contingent observation: An effective and acceptable procedure for reducing disruptive behavior of young children in a group setting. *Journal of Applied Behavior Analysis, 9*, 55–64.

Ramasamy, R., Taylor, R. L., & Ziegler, E. W. (1996). Eliminating inappropriate classroom behavior using a DRO schedule. *Psychological Reports, 78*, 753–754.

Reid, R. T., Trout, A. L., & Schartz, M. (2005). Self-regulation interventions for children with attention deficit hyperactivity disorder. *Council for Exceptional Children, 71*(4), 361–377.

Repp, A. C., Barton, L. E., & Brulle, A. R. (1983). A comparison of two procedures for programming the differential reinforcement of other behaviors. *Journal of Applied Behavior Analysis, 16*, 435–445.

Repp, A. C., Felce, D., & Barton, L. E. (1991). The effects of initial interval size of the efficacy of DRO schedules of reinforcement. *Exceptional Children, 57*, 417–425.

Repp, A. C., & Slack, D. J. (1977). Reducing responding of retarded persons by DRO schedules following a history of low-rate responding: A comparison of ascending interval sizes. *Psychological Record, 27*, 581–588.

Reynolds, G. S. (1961). Behavioral contrast. *Journal of the Experimental Analysis of Behavior, 4*, 57–71.

Reynolds, L. K., & Kelley, M. L. (1997). The efficacy of a response cost–based treatment package for managing aggressive behavior in preschoolers. *Behavior Modification, 21*(2), 216–230.

Salend, S., & Gordon, B. (1987). A group-oriented time-out ribbon procedure. *Behavioral Disorders, 12*, 131–137.

Sansosti, F. J., & Powell-Smith, K. A. (2006). Using social stories to improve the social behavior of children with Asperger Syndrome. *Journal of Positive Behavior Intervention, 8*, 43–57.

Sansosti, F. J., & Powell-Smith, K. A. (2008). Using computer-presented social stories and video models to increase the social communication skills of children with high-functioning Autism Spectrum disorders. *Journal of Positive Behavior Interventions, 10*, 162–178.

Scattone, D., Tingstrom, D. H., & Wilczynski, S. M. (2006). Increasing appropriate social interactions of children with autism spectrum disorders using social stories. *Focus on Autism and Other Developmental Disabilities, 21*(4), 211–222.

Schoenfeld, N. A., & Konopasek, D. (2007). Medicine in the classroom: A review of psychiatric medications for students with emotional or behavioral disorders. *Beyond Behavior, 17*(1), 14–20.

Shriver, M. D., & Allen, K. D. (1996). The time-out grid: A guide to effective discipline. *School Psychology Quarterly, 11*(1), 67–74.

Shukla-Mehta, S., & Albin, R. W. (2003). Twelve practical strategies to prevent behavioral escalation in classroom settings. *Preventing school failure, 47*(4), 156–161.

Skiba, R., & Raison, J. (1990). Relationship between the use of timeout and academic achievement. *Exceptional Children, 57*, 36–46.

Skinner, B. F. (1938). *The behavior of organisms*. New York: Appleton-Century-Crofts.

Stahr, B., Cushing, D., Lane, K., & Fox, J. (2006). Efficacy of a function-based intervention in decreasing off-task behavior exhibited by a student with ADHD. *Journal of Positive Behavior Interventions, 8*, 201–211.

Sugai, G., & Horner, R. (2007). *SW-PBS & RTI: Lessons being learned*. Washington, DC: Office of Special Education Programs Center on PBIS, Department of Education.

Taylor, J. (1997). When timeout works some of the time. *School Psychology, 12*, 4–22.

Thiemann, K. S., & Goldstein, H. (2001). Social stories, written text cues, and video feedback: Effects on social communication of children with autism. *Journal of Behavior Analysis, 34*(4), 425–446.

Visser, S. N., & Lesesne, C. A. (2007). National estimates and factors associated with medication treatment for childhood attention-deficit/hyperactivity disorder. *Pediatrics, 119*, 99–106.

Vollmer, T. R., Roane, H. S., Ringdahl, J. E., & Marcus, B. A. (1999). Evaluating treatment challenges with differential reinforcement of alternative behavior. *Journal of Applied Behavior Analysis, 32*, 9–23.

Walker, H. M. (1983, February). Application of response cost in school settings: Outcomes, issues and recommendations. *Exceptional Education Quarterly*, pp. 47–55.

Walker, H. M., Colvin, G., & Ramsey, E. (1995). *Antisocial behavior in school: Strategies and best practices*. Albany, NY: Brooks/Cole Publishing.

Walker, H. M., Hops, H., & Fiegenbaum, E. (1976). Deviant classroom behavior as a function of combinations of social and token reinforcement and cost contingency. *Behavior Therapy, 7*, 76–88.

White, A. G., & Bailey, J. S. (1990). Reducing disruptive behaviors of elementary physical education students with sit and watch. *Journal of Applied Behavior Analysis, 23*, 353–359.

Williams, C. D. (1959). The elimination of tantrum behavior by extinction procedures. *Journal of Abnormal and Social Psychology, 59*, 266–272.

Yeager, C., & McLaughlin, T. F. (1994). Use of time-out ribbon with and without consequences as procedures to improve a child's compliance. *Perceptual and Motor Skills, 79*(2), 945–946.

Yell, M. L. (2006). *The law and special education*. Upper Saddle River, NJ: Merrill/Pearson Education.

Zirpoli, T. J. (2003). *Cures for parental wimp syndrome: Lessons on becoming a stronger parent*. Westminster, MD: Zirpoli Publishing and Consulting.

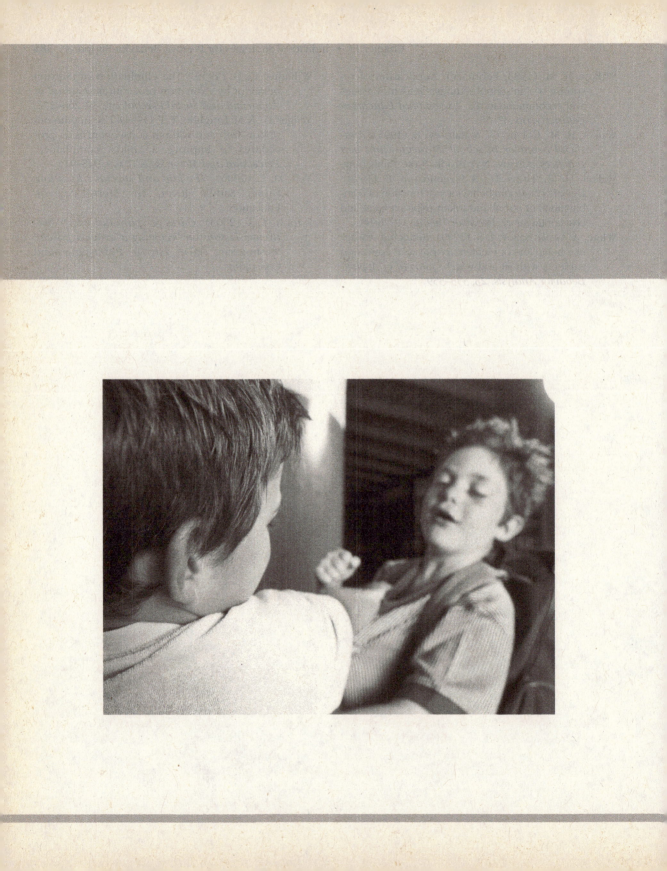

Strategies for Specific Behavior Challenges

CHAPTER 14

Thomas J. Zirpoli and Kristine J. Melloy

You can't make anyone do anything.

—JOHNSON, AGELSON, MACIERZ, MINNICK, AND MERRELL (1995)

If there is one thing we have tried to communicate in this text, it is that for teachers to effectively manage the behavior of their students, they must manage their own behavior and the classroom environment. Indeed, as Johnson et al. (1995) state, you can't make anyone do anything. But, by managing your behavior, as well as the antecedents and consequences within your classroom, you can have a significant impact on your students' behavior.

In this chapter, we discuss specific challenging behaviors that are commonly seen in school settings, typical antecedents and consequences that maintain these behaviors, and effective interventions. These behaviors include behaviors related to conduct (disruptive and oppositional defiant behaviors, noncompliance, aggression, bullying, and temper tantrums), attention and activity (inattentive, hyperactivity, impulsivity, and stereotypy), and mood (separation anxiety and depression).

Before each of these challenging behaviors is discussed, it is important to note that the majority of students who demonstrate challenging behaviors engage in more than one of these behaviors at the same time. One of the problems teachers experience in completing functional behavioral assessments is related to identifying a target behavior when more than one behavior is demonstrated. However, when we realize that many behaviors are related, it becomes easier to figure out the most salient behavior, the behavior to work on first. For example, a student who is considered disruptive in a classroom may also be described as someone who does not follow teacher directions (i.e., noncompliant behavior) and as a student who trips his classmates when they walk by his desk (i.e., aggressive behavior). In this case, the disruptive behavior looks like noncompliance and aggressive behavior.

When we identify challenging behavior, we need to make sure that we describe exactly what the student does, for example, when he or she is being disruptive. This description will be helpful in identifying the most salient target behavior and thereby will assist in determining an effective intervention. Ask yourself, of the three challenging behaviors described in the previous example, which one seems to be the most serious? If you said tripping classmates, give yourself a pat on the back. Hurting others or causing potential danger to others is often the most salient behavior and the type of behavior that warrants immediate intervention. Fortunately, once we intervene with one behavior, other related behaviors may change without direct intervention (McMahon, Wacker, Sasso, & Melloy, 1994). In our example, the student who learns a replacement behavior for getting his peers' attention by tripping them will probably be less likely to disrupt the class. Perhaps the student will learn that he can get the teacher's attention more appropriately when he engages in compliant, rather than noncompliant, behavior.

Students who exhibit one or more of these challenging behaviors do not typically demonstrate these behaviors at a level that would warrant a disability label. On the contrary, intervention in the form of behavior management for challenging behaviors would assist most students, like Brian in Classroom Connection 14.1, in modifying their behavior before the problem becomes so serious that more intensive intervention (e.g., medication or special education) would be necessary. We hope to provide educators an overview of these challenging behaviors and urge them to consult other sources for more in-depth information (e.g., Hennggeler, Schoenwald, Borduin, Rowland, & Cunningham, 1998; Kauffman & Landrum, 2009; Mash & Barkley, 1998; Sarason & Sarason, 2005; Zionts, 1996).

CLASSROOM CONNECTION 14.1
Brian: A Student to Think About

It was a new year at Westminster High School, and Brian was a student in Ms. Romano's freshman Spanish class. Ms. Romano noticed on the first 2 days of class that Brian was frequently inattentive, noncompliant to her directions, and disruptive to the class. For example, when Ms. Romano introduced her students to the language lab on the second day of class, Brian refused to follow her directions and said that he didn't feel like working. Instead, Brian sat in his desk with his legs stretched out and his arms crossed, and he made several inappropriate comments about how much he hated Spanish. Since all the students were wearing headphones listening to a Spanish tape, however, they did not hear Brian's comments. On the third day of class, Brian's comments were loud and disruptive, especially when Ms. Romano was speaking to the students in Spanish. Ms. Romano ignored Brian's inappropriate behavior but decided to keep him after class for a meeting. Brian told Ms. Romano that he didn't want to take Spanish, but his counselor had told him that he had to take a language course to graduate high school. Ms. Romano told him that if his behavior didn't improve, he would fail the class, which would also keep him from graduating. So, Brian promised that he would try to follow her directions, increase his participation, and decrease his disruptive behavior.

Brian was better for a couple of days; however, his behavior quickly began to deteriorate. Frustrated, Ms. Romano began documenting Brian's behavior by writing anecdotal reports of his daily behavior. She presented her daily reports to the teacher assistance team and hopes they will help her develop a behavioral intervention plan for Brian.

General Reflection for Classroom Connection 14.1:

Since you chair the teacher assistance team, think about the following four questions about Brian's behavior and potential intervention plans as you read through this chapter: (a) How would you describe Brian's behavior in behavioral terms? (b) Based on the brief description provided in Classroom Connection 14.1, what do you think may be the function of Brian's behavior? (c) What alternative behaviors would you suggest Ms. Romano reinforce in order to reduce his disruptive behaviors, and how? and (d) What suggestions would you provide Ms. Romano when developing an intervention plan for Brian's disruptive and noncompliant behavior?

BEHAVIORS RELATED TO CONDUCT

Disruptive Behavior and Oppositional Defiant Disorders

The function of disruptive behavior typically includes gaining positive or negative attention, escaping from work, and self-gratification. Oppositional defiant behaviors (ODD) involve "a recurrent pattern of negativistic, defiant, disobedient, and hostile behavior toward authority figures that persists for 6 months" (American Psychiatric Association, 2000, p. 40). Taylor, Burns, Rusby, and Foster (2006) listed the following behaviors associated with ODD: Argues, loses temper, refuses to obey rules or cooperate with peers, annoys on purpose, blames others for mistakes, becomes easily annoyed, appears angry, and attempts to get even. They also make the point that oppositional behavior towards adults or authority figures and oppositional behavior towards peers are two distinct constructs.

Educators frequently use the terms *oppositional defiant disorder* and *conduct disorder* to describe (and label) students who are disruptive in the classroom (Ronen, 2005). Disruptive behavior covers a wide range of behaviors demonstrated in school and other settings. Teachers and peers commonly describe students who engage in disruptive behaviors ranging from those demonstrated by the "class clown" to aggressive and violent behavior. Common sense tells us that the intervention used to decrease inappropriate clowning behavior will be quite different from an intervention designed to prevent or decrease aggressive behavior. However, the effect of the consequences will be the same: If the behavior is reinforced, it will increase or be maintained; if the behavior is consistently punished, the behavior will decrease.

Several examples of disruptive behaviors and definitions written in observable, measurable terms follow:

- *Off-task talking:* The student speaks out without permission or interrupts others who are talking.
- *Getting out of seat:* The student lifts his or her buttocks off the chair and walks around the classroom without permission. He or she may stop to chat with peers or may just continue to walk around with no purpose related to an academic task.
- *Making noises:* The student creates sounds, either verbally or physically, that are clearly not related to the task (e.g., tapping a pencil repeatedly, tipping the chair back until it falls over).
- *Playing with objects:* The student engages in play with things, such as pens, pencils, or small toys, that may be related or unrelated to the task. To constitute an inappropriate behavior, the play must not be part of the task and clearly not appropriate for the time.
- *Throwing objects:* The student projects things, such as pencils, paper airplanes, or furniture, into the air or across the floor when this behavior is not related to an educational task.
- *Climbing:* The student ascends to the top of furniture or other objects/persons in the room for no reason related to a classroom task.

Often these behaviors are more annoying than anything and can be effectively managed using the behavior management interventions described next.

COMMON CAUSES AND ANTECEDENTS OF DISRUPTIVE AND OPPOSITIONAL DEFIANT BEHAVIOR

Deficits in Learned Behavior.   One cause of disruptive behavior appears to be the mismanagement of inappropriate behavior early in the student's education. Beard and Sugai (2004, p. 396) found a "developmental course" of "minor offenses" in the student's early years that develop into "major offenses" in later years because effective early intervention programs and appropriate consequences were not employed. Ostrander (2004) talks about the development of disruptive or oppositional behaviors, starting out as temper tantrums, yelling, and whining in young children and, without appropriate intervention, developing into aggression, stealing, and vandalism during adolescence.

Kazdin and Whitley (2006) observed that many children who demonstrate disruptive and oppositional behaviors were associated with dysfunctional parenting and families in conflict. Sutherland (2000) reports that students who are disruptive receive low rates of reinforcement for appropriate behavior; the ratio of reprimands to praise statements these students receive is greater than 2:1. Again, these are related to poor parenting skills and families in conflict.

Unfortunately, students who are described as class clowns often say and do funny things, but usually at an inappropriate time. When the student is laughed at, this reaction serves to reinforce and maintain the behavior. Rather than develop interventions that squelch the student's sense of humor, it would be better to teach him or her to manifest the behavior at appropriate times (e.g., during recess), in an appropriate manner (e.g., not meant to hurt others' feelings), and in appropriate places (e.g., on the playground).

Deficits in School Readiness Skills.   Students who lack competence in school readiness skills (e.g., asking permission, sitting and listening, following directions, playing with other studentsi) are often a challenge to teachers, especially preschool and kindergarten teachers (McGinnis & Goldstein, 1997). Students, especially boys, who don't learn how to pay attention and how to control impulsiveness at an early age are at risk for later conduct disorders (Snyder, Prichard, Schrepferman, & Patrick, 2004).

It is imperative for teachers of young students to understand that school readiness skills are learned behaviors. If these behaviors are are not learned at home, then they must be taught at school. When these students are taught these skills, become competent in them, and are reinforced for demonstrating these prosocial behaviors, their disruptive behavior decreases significantly (Melloy, Davis, Wehby, Murry, & Lieber, 1998). Jumping to the conclusion that a young student has a disability because he has not yet learned these basic skills is inappropriate and will not help the student learn the appropriate school-readiness behaviors he will need to be a successful student.

Deficits in Curriculum and Teaching Strategies.   Daniels (1998) suggests that inappropriate curriculum or teaching strategies, individual learning styles, and student disability could contribute to student misbehavior. Students often experience feelings of frustration related to the classroom curriculum and the strategies teachers use for instruction. For example, a middle school student who is a poor reader is likely to struggle through classes that require a significant amount of reading (e.g., social studies and science). As stated in Chapter 9, a student's frustration with difficult curriculum may lead to misbehavior. Also, curriculum that is not interesting or seems irrelevant to the student's life experience can create situations that result in disruptive behavior. Disregard for individual learning style and poor instructional delivery also serve as antecedents for disruptive behavior. For example, a student who has trouble taking notes may have difficulties in a class where the teacher uses overheads instead of handouts. Teachers who present appropriate curriculum in a style that addresses individual student strengths and needs are likely to experience more appropriate classroom behavior among their students.

INTERVENTIONS FOR DISRUPTIVE AND OPPOSITIONAL DEFIANT BEHAVIOR

Functional Assessment. A common function for disruptive behavior is getting others' attention (i.e., peers and teachers). Thus, if teachers want to teach and reinforce acceptable replacement behaviors for disruptive behavior, a classroom plan to increase on-task behaviors, follow directions, cooperate with others, participate in class, raise hand to ask or answer a question, use a quiet voice, keep hands to self, and stay in seat is recommended.

Tyson (2005, p. 159) states that a growing population of disruptive children from poor backgrounds need to learn, at an early age, how to interact with others, establish moral standards, assume responsibility, and "attain the capacity for emotional regulation." Students must learn that engaging in prosocial behavior can achieve the same outcome or function as disruptive behavior and that they are considered more favorably by their peers and teachers when they engage in these behaviors. The following section describes several effective interventions for disruptive behavior.

Early Intervention. There is no doubt that early intervention of inappropriate behavior will prevent the challenging and antisocial behavior from growing out of control as the student grows older. As Snyder et al. (2004) state, young children's difficult behavior "appears to negatively affect social experiences and status with peers in a manner that increases risk for early and persisting conduct problems" (p. 579). Research also shows that students with poor social skills (inattentive, hyperactive, aggressive, or depressive behaviors) tend to group with other students with poor social skills (Mariano & Harton, 2005). Thus, it is important for teachers to teach young children appropriate social skills so that they are not alienated from healthy peers who model appropriate social skills.

Avoid Pitfalls. Teachers tend to provide students with more attention following misbehavior than appropriate behavior. To avoid this pitfall, teachers are encouraged to develop a comprehensive classroom management plan that promotes positive social behavior and discourages disruptive behavior through positive reinforcement strategies (e.g., Francois, Harlacher, & Smith, 1999). Also, Fields (2004, p. 108) reminds teachers not to engage in a "power struggle" with a disruptive, noncompliant student, but to control emotions, defuse or de-escalate exchanges with the student, and reconnect after the student has calmed down. Fields refers to this strategy as "defensive management" with the purpose of helping teachers "avoid unproductive conflict" with students (p. 103).

Teaching Self-Discipline Skills. Several authors report that teaching students self-discipline and the skills to make good choices resulted in decreased disruptive behavior and increased self-management (Hoff & DuPaul, 1998; Schmid, 1998; Shapiro, DuPaul, & Bradley-Klug, 1998). For example, Hoff and DuPaul found that three elementary-aged students were able to learn self-management strategies and consequently decreased their disruptive behavior. Schmid (1998) taught students a three-step self-discipline procedure that resulted in improved self-management and less disruptive behavior. The three-step strategy involved teaching the students to:

1. say "Stop, I don't like that!";
2. try to ignore the objectionable behavior; and
3. report to a responsible adult if steps 1 and 2 didn't work.

Sukhodolsky, Golub, Stone, and Orban (2005) employed anger control and problem-solving training techniques that involved modeling, behavioral rehearsal, and corrective feedback to reduce disruptive behavior in boys (mean age of 9.6 years).

These strategies are excellent examples of placing the focus on students managing their own behavior rather than relying heavily on others for behavior management.

Schoolwide and Classroom Rules.   A number of authors discuss the effectiveness of interventions based on behavioral, cognitive, psychoeducational, and social learning theories in teaching, promoting, and supporting replacement behavior for disruptive behavior in students and adolescents. Nelson, Martella, and Galand (1998) describe the effects of establishing, teaching, and reinforcing schoolwide rules and routines on the disruptive behavior of elementary school students. A 4-year study revealed that students who were taught and expected to follow school rules and routines were more likely to demonstrate prosocial behavior in the school setting. In addition, the authors found that providing a plan for a systematic teacher response to disruptive behavior resulted in fewer formal office referrals for disciplinary action. Malone, Bonitz, and Rickett (1998) confirm these research findings with their study on teacher perceptions of disruptive behavior. The teachers in the study believed that having classroom rules and expecting students to follow them was the best way for disciplining students.

One of the most common interventions for disruptive behavior is in-school or out-of-school suspension (Gottfredson & Gottfredson, 2001). However, the effects of this type of intervention have repeatedly been proven to have little or no effect on students' disruptive behavior. Stage (1997) completed a study on the effects of in-school suspension on the disruptive behavior of 36 twelve to seventeen-year-old students with emotional behavioral disorders. The results of this study revealed that students' disruptive behavior did not decrease as a result of in-school suspension. A number of alternative interventions to in-school suspension are available that are more effective in decreasing disruptive behavior by teaching, reinforcing, and increasing appropriate replacement behaviors, such as staying on task, asking permission, and getting others' attention through appropriate social interactions. When punishment procedures are needed in addition to positive behavioral supports, interventions such as participation in academic activities after school or attending school on Saturdays, in place of suspension, are suggested so students are not reinforced for inappropriate behavior by earning less time in school.

Noncompliant Behavior

Compliance is generally described as obedience to adult directives and prohibitions, cooperation with requests and suggestions, and/or the willingness to accept suggestions in a teaching situation (Rocissano, Slade, & Lynch, 1987).

Noncompliance, then, is defined as oppositonal or resistant behavior, such as disobedience to directives, uncooperativeness with requests and suggestions, and unwillingness to accept suggestions. One facet of compliance/noncompliance is the issue of teaching students how to become independent and make appropriate choices regarding their own behavior—characteristics that are admired in U.S. society. Regardless, noncompliant behavior becomes challenging when a student is frequently defiant and this behavior is expressed in an unpleasant, negative manner.

Skiba, Peterson, and Williams (1997) report that the primary reasons students are referred to the principal's office for discipline are related to noncompliant and disrespectful behavior. Indeed, teachers report that a major challenge and frustration in the classroom is with students who seem to know what they are supposed to do but won't perform the appropriate behavior on cue (Maag, 1997).

Kuczynski, Kochanska, Radke-Yarrow, and Girnius-Brown (1987) describe four categories of noncompliance in a study with young students and their mothers. A student was described as engaging in *passive noncompliance* when she did not overtly refuse or defy the request but instead went on about her business as if she had not been addressed. A student who overtly refused requests with angry, defiant, or negative facial, body, and/or verbal expressions was described as behaving with *direct defiance*. Students who replied "No" or "I don't want to" with no apparent negative verbal or body language were described as engaging in *simple refusal* behavior. Finally, *negotiation behavior* was defined as attempts by the student to convince the parent to issue a new directive through bargaining. A case example, in which Beth's teacher asks her to put her science project away and get ready for math, shows each of these types of noncompliance.

- *Passive noncompliance:* Beth continues working on her science project.
- *Direct defiance:* Beth throws her pencil to the floor, yells at her teacher that she isn't finished with her project, and looks away from her teacher.
- *Simple refusal:* Beth tells her teacher that she is not going to stop work on her science project. Beth is smiling and doesn't raise her voice.
- *Negotiation:* Beth asks her teacher if she can work on her science project for 10 more minutes before doing math. When her teacher says "No," Beth asks for 5 minutes, then 3 minutes, and so on.

COMMON CAUSES AND ANTECEDENTS OF NONCOMPLIANT BEHAVIOR

Teacher–Student Interactions. The reader is reminded of the opening statement for this chapter: "You can't make anyone do anything." Unfortunately, students are considered oppositional and noncompliant when they resist our efforts to make them do things. Think about how often you have experienced the following scenario:

The students in Ms. Nice's class are exuberantly working on a group project for which there is a high amount of interest and activity. However, all good things must come to an end, and Ms. Nice announces that in a few minutes it will be time to change to another class. In an effort to be polite to her students, Ms. Nice approaches each small group to warn them of the impending transition and ask them if they would like to put their materials away and get ready for the next class. Ms. Nice is surprised when students in several groups tell her, "No, I don't want to stop what I'm doing," and then continue with their project.

Why is Ms. Nice surprised? She did give the impression that the students had a choice about continuing or stopping the project when she asked them rather than told them what was expected. If you expect students to do something, tell them what it is you want and then reinforce the students for being compliant. Also, if the student does not follow your directions, you must have an intervention plan that is employed fairly and consistently.

Wachs, Gurkas, and Kontos (2004) discuss the predictors of noncompliance in early childhood classroom settings and note that "child compliance was predicted by child temperament, caregiver behaviors, daycare quality, and level of daycare chaos" (p. 439). Classroom teachers control three out of four of these variables.

Teachers may also promote noncompliant behavior by their own, sometimes stubborn, refusal to change their behavior to better meet the needs of their students. Teachers and others who personalize behaviors demonstrated by their students will set themselves up for resistance. Consider the following scenario:

A group of high school students had finished using their calculators for a math assignment and the teacher walked around the room to collect them. One student looked the teacher in the eye and then held onto his calculator when she reached for it. Rather than struggling with the student, who obviously wanted to battle her for the calculator, the teacher walked on and ignored his comment about taking his calculator by force. In less than a minute, the student raised his hand, asked the teacher to come to his desk when she acknowledged him, and gave her the calculator with no further problem.

In minimizing the amount of attention given to the student for noncompliant behavior, the teacher was able to promote compliant behavior with very little effort on her part.

Parent–Child Interactions.　Holden and West (1989) also offer information on parent factors that contribute to compliant and noncompliant behavior. They observed the interactional styles of mothers and their children and the consequences of those styles within a play setting. The mothers were given directions to be either "directors" or "forbidders" in separate trials in which the mother and child were placed in a setting with toys that were either out of bounds or in bounds. In the proactive trial, mothers were instructed to direct their child's attention to objects, suggest activities, or play games. In the reactive trial, mothers were not allowed to direct their child in play and were instructed to interact with their child only when he or she needed to be prohibited from playing with a toy that was out of bounds.

The authors reported that children were more likely to comply with requests and suggestions for play in the proactive trial than in the reactive trial. This research has important implications related to the causes of noncompliance in students. It provides confirmatory data for the idea that attending to the student for appropriate behavior (i.e., compliance) will prevent the need for the student to engage in inappropriate behavior (i.e., noncompliance) in order to get the attention of the adult. These findings also offer important information related to the function of compliant versus noncompliant behavior since getting others' attention has been found to be a typical outcome of compliance and noncompliance.

Wicks-Nelson and Israel (1991) suggest that adults sometimes teach children to be noncompliant when they are not consistent in follow-up on commands. In fact, they found that when adults are inconsistent, children demonstrate a higher incidence of noncompliance. In other words, teachers sometimes teach their students that it is not necessary to comply since there is not a consequence for noncompliance. The opposite effect was experienced when adults positively reinforce students for compliance and have a consistent consequence for noncompliance.

Zirpoli (2003) also warns preschool and kindergarten teachers that if their young students have not learned to be compliant to parent requests at home, this skill will have to be taught at school. Also, just because a student learns that compliance is not necessary in one environment (e.g., home or another classroom), this does not mean the student cannot learn to be compliant in your classroom. Students learn to behave differently within different environments depending on expectations within that environment.

INTERVENTIONS FOR NONCOMPLIANT BEHAVIOR

Functional Assessment.   Functional assessments frequently identify the function of noncompliance to be a student's desire to maintain power or control over a situation or to escape a task. For example, José became very resistive when he was given a writing assignment. Assessment revealed that, although José had good ideas for writing and was able to physically produce written work, he had quite a bit of trouble with spelling. Rather than risk being embarrassed by misspelling words, José sat back at his desk and refused to write. Teaching José to ask for assistance in spelling and providing him with a word list for each writing assignment resulted in completion of writing assignments. A curriculum-based assessment of José's current writing and spelling skills compared with classroom curriculum expectations may have alerted his teachers to this mismatch and the potential for challenging behavior during this assignment.

Teach Compliance.   Simply put, if teachers want their students to be compliant, they need to teach them to be compliant. In communicating to their students, teachers need to mean what they say and say what they mean. In other words, when you tell your students to do something, you must follow through with a "Thank you" if the students comply or a consequence if the students do not comply. Compliance is a skill. It must be taught, and it must be reinforced.

Again, many students report to school without learning at home to follow directions from their parents. Thus, they are not in the habit of following directions from adults. But students can quickly learn that, at least in school, they need to be compliant, regardless of poor parenting at home.

Pfiffner and O'Leary (1987) investigated the effects of an all-positive behavior management program on the noncompliant behavior of 8 first through third graders. Prior to the study, these students had no experience with negative consequences for their inappropriate behavior, which was operationally defined as off-task and academic inaccuracy. Using an alternating treatment design, the authors applied interventions within three conditions (Pfiffner & O'Leary, 1987, p. 266):

- *Regular positives alone condition:*   Students earned positive consequences for on-task behavior in the form of social praise, bonus work, and public posting of completed work.
- *Enhanced positives alone condition:*   The teachers increased the frequency and quality of positive consequences (described previously).
- *Enhanced positives and negatives condition:*   The teachers administered positive consequences for appropriate behavior and reprimands for off-task behavior.

The results of this study indicated that students in the third condition improved their on-task behavior significantly when they were positively reinforced for appropriate behavior and received negative consequences for inappropriate behavior. The all-positive behavior management conditions were not as effective in changing the behavior of these students. These findings are critical because, in many education settings, *discipline* and *punishment* seem to be dirty words. This is especially the case in pre-K and elementary-level classrooms, where many teachers have been encouraged to rely solely on positive reinforcement and redirection as their only consequence. While positive consequences are strongly encouraged throughout this text, Pfiffner and O'Leary (1987) offer empirical evidence that at times it is more effective to use reinforcement and punishment procedures together versus reinforcement alone. This approach has again been confirmed by Mandal (2002), who used praise for compliance and time-out for noncompliance as an effective training package for decreasing noncompliance.

Oliver and Skinner (2002) employed a strategy called *behavior momentum* to increase compliant behavior with elementary students. With this technique, the teacher makes a series of high-probability compliance requests—requests that the teacher is sure the student will follow—that are reinforced and followed with a request that has been previously followed with noncompliance. This strategy provides compliance practice for the student, demonstrates to the student the positive outcomes of following directions (reinforcement), and pairs high-compliance requests with low-compliance requests.

Schoolwide and Classroom Rules.   Although suspension is a punishment procedure frequently used in schools as a consequence for noncompliant behavior, Costenbader and Markson (1998) found that suspension's effect on noncompliant behavior is similar to those reported by Stage (1997) for disruptive behavior. These authors quoted 32% of the students surveyed as saying that suspension was not effective in changing their behavior. And since escape is sometimes a function of noncompliant behavior, suspending students may actually reinforce, rather than punish, noncompliance.

To ensure compliant behavior, teachers and administrators must consistently apply schoolwide and classroom rules. For example, if the school's dress code is not consistently enforced across all teachers and staff, expect students to be noncompliant and violate the dress code.

Aggressive Behavior

Aggression is classified by Kauffman and Landrum (2009, p. 276) as an overt conduct disorder "characterized by acting out toward others verbally or physically." It is the most serious of inappropriate behaviors and has the most serious consequences for both the student and those in his or her environment. Wood, Cowan, and Baker (2002, p. 72), for example, found that "approximately half of the variance in sociometric and teacher ratings of peer rejection was accounted for by aggression and social withdrawal for boys and girls."

The function of aggression includes gaining power and control, affiliation, escape, gaining attention, and self-gratification. While severe violent behavior may include physical and sexual assault, and even homicide, common aggressive behaviors displayed in school settings "include hitting, pushing, isolating a peer on purpose, and name-calling" (Horne, Stoddard, & Bell, 2007, p. 262).

In this chapter, aggressive behaviors refer to those behaviors—verbal, nonverbal, or physical—that injure another indirectly or directly and/or result in extraneous gains for the aggressor (see Table 14.1). These behaviors are typically described in terms such as those that appear frequently in the literature (Hunt, 1993; Sasso, Melloy, & Kavale, 1990).

TABLE 14.1 Examples of Target Behaviors for Physical and Verbal Aggression

Examples of Physical Aggression

- *Kicking:* A student uses his or her foot/feet to make contact with another's body in a manner that inflicts discomfort, pain, and/or injury.
- *Hitting:* A student uses his or her hand(s) (i.e., open or in a fist) to strike another person's body with the intention of inflicting discomfort, pain, and/or injury.
- *Spitting:* A student projects saliva onto another person, which causes the other person's body parts or clothing to become wet. (Note that sometimes students may pretend to spit on another. Even though no saliva is actually projected, the behavior is considered aggressive because it may result in the same effect—degradation and discomfort on the part of the other person.)
- *Biting:* The student's teeth make contact with another's skin and cause discomfort, pain, and/or injury.
- *Grabbing/holding:* A student forcibly takes another person with his or her hand(s) and then inhibits the movement of the other in a manner that results in discomfort, pain, and/or injury.
- *Fighting:* Two or more students are engaged in hitting, kicking, grabbing, and/or holding behavior, which may result in one or more students falling to the ground or being shoved against a structure (e.g., wall, door, ledge, cupboard). This behavior results in discomfort, pain, and/or injury to the aggressor and aggressee.
- *Throwing:* A student directs materials (e.g., book, pencil, objects, furniture, papers) toward a person by sending the object through the air with a motion of the hand or arm. This is considered aggressive behavior (a) if the prerequisite body language is present and (b) whether or not the object actually strikes the targeted person causing pain or injury—the intention is enough to consider the behavior to be aggressive.

Examples of Verbal Aggression

- *Bossy behavior:* The student commands others in a demanding tone.
- *Teasing others:* The student makes fun of another person(s) by verbally expressing words that result in emotional discomfort, pain, and/or injury of the other person. The other person demonstrates his or her feelings of hurt by crying, running away, verbal aggression, and/or pretending to ignore the aggressor.
- *Tattling:* The student repeatedly reports on trivial behaviors of others that are not endangering others to an adult who is in authority (e.g., teacher, paraprofessional). An example would be a student who reports to the teacher that "Billy is pulling Kate's hair" in an exaggerated tone of voice.
- *Nonconstructively criticizing the work of others:* The student puts down the work of others using condescending terms (e.g., "That's a stupid idea"), which results in the other person expressing hurt feelings or anger.
- *Picking on others:* The student says things to another person that emphasize a perceived fault of the other (e.g., "Hey, Angela, look at Mario. He can't even do these baby math problems!"), which results in the person feeling humiliation, hurt, and/or anger. Behaviors of the person being picked on that demonstrate these feelings include a dejected look, verbal retorts, and/or anger outbursts.
- *Making sarcastic remarks:* The student uses phrases to comment on another's appearance, performance, and so on, that are derogatory in nature and result in emotional discomfort and/or pain in the person to whom the remarks were directed. The remarks are generally made in a sarcastic tone of voice (e.g., words exaggerated, nasty tone). An example of a sarcastic remark is "Don't count on Barbara to show up. She always has more important things to do," which is voiced in a nasty tone of voice. Sarcastic remarks can also be made in a pleasant tone of voice, but the result is that the other person is hurt or humiliated by the remark (e.g., a teacher remarks, "Wow, isn't it nice that Lori could join us again?" after a student returns from time-out for behaving aggressively). Hurt and humiliation are demonstrated by behaviors such as putting one's head down, getting a red face, or crying.

The student's body language for all of these aggressive behaviors is a stance that clearly communicates anger, rage, frustration, humiliation, and/or other feelings that motivate aggressive behavior.

In instances where verbal aggression is manifested, students will not always demonstrate the body language described (e.g., tattling), but the intent of the behavior is still clearly to hurt another person or to gain something for the aggressor. It is also important to keep in mind that even playful hits, kicks, and punches and sarcastic statements are forms of aggressive behavior. Educators and others should encourage students and reinforce them for using alternative behaviors to express affection and liking for others.

Hunt (1993, pp. 16–18) describes five patterns of aggressive behavior: overaroused aggression, impulsive aggression, affective aggression, predatory aggression, and instrumental aggression.

- *Overaroused aggression:* Students engage in behavior that is characterized by high levels of activity that result in frequent accidents and aggressive incidents. Students who push and shove their peers often provoke or initiate an aggressive response from their peers. Unlike motivation for other types of aggressive behavior, students who demonstrate overaroused aggression rarely select their victims.
- *Impulsive aggression:* Students are generally quiet and passive in their demeanor but seemingly have a low tolerance for frustration. When frustrated, the student may burst into a flurry of activity and violence that can be uncharacteristically destructive.
- *Affective aggression:* Students demonstrate rageful aggression. Their behavior is described as appearing to be chronically angry, resentful, and hostile.
- *Predatory aggression:* Students seem to be seeking revenge. Individuals who demonstrate predatory aggression are described as persons who wait for a chance to get back at another person in a hurtful, harmful manner.
- *Instrumental aggression:* Students act as the intimidating bully. Students who engage in instrumental aggression demonstrate behaviors that allow them to get their own way through intimidation of others.

COMMON CAUSES AND ANTECEDENTS OF AGGRESSIVE BEHAVIOR

Developmental. According to a number of researchers, aggression is an externalizing antisocial behavior frequently associated with family conflict, poor family conflict resolution strategies, and poor parenting (Brubacher, Fondacaro, Brank, Brown, & Miller, 2009; Hollenstein, Granic, Stoolmiller, & Snyder, 2004; Patterson, 1992). Brubacher and colleagues outline the development of aggression, especially bullying behavior (see next section) through "the intergenerational perpetuation of aggressive behavior" (p. 15). Included in their list of family characteristics associated with aggression is a lack of warmth and emotional support from adults within the home, poor overall parenting skills, inconsistent discipline, a reliance on corporal punishment when discipline is employed, exposure to domestic and other forms of violence in the home (see modeling issues in next section), high levels of family conflict, and poor resolution strategies for these conflicts which serve as a poor model for the student when confronted with conflict at school. Aggressive students are frequently impulsive, have difficulty following rules, lack a sense of empathy towards other students, and have poor problem-solving and overall social skills (Brubacher et al., 2009).

Low levels of parental supervision and the use of inconsistent, harsh parental discipline result in the student being "trained" to engage in aggressive behavior such as hitting. Aggression may become functional in the sense that the student may be allowed to escape from tasks when he or she acts aggressively. For example, a student may be sent to her room after hitting her brother while they do dishes. Also, aggressive behaviors may be positively reinforced through laughter, attention, and approval, which results in maintenance of the behaviors.

Students in these situations do not learn socially appropriate responses to others. Because aggressive behaviors are usually learned in early childhood, these students become rejected by peers early in their school years because they do not demonstrate the social skills that allow them to be socially competent. This is in contrast to the idea that students become aggressive after they are rejected by their peers.

In addition to their rejection by peers, aggression is also associated with academic failure (Patterson, DeBaryshe, & Ramsey, 1989). Patterson et al. (1989) and Wood et al. (2002) report that students who engage in aggressive behaviors spend less time on academic tasks and have more difficulty with classroom survival skills (e.g., staying in seat, answering questions, cooperating with others in group activities, following directions). These behaviors are associated with a higher incidence of academic failure. Once students have learned aggressive behavior and experienced peer rejection and academic failure, they are at a higher risk for developing delinquent behavior (Patterson et al., 1989). These students have a tendency to become involved with deviant peer groups who also engage in aggressive behaviors (e.g., fighting, property destruction, gang activities). The members of the groups positively reinforce each other for engaging in antisocial behaviors, thus increasing the probability of their repeated occurrence. Unfortunately, long-term outcomes for students who seemingly follow this developmental sequence of aggressive behavior are not generally desirable. Students who engage in antisocial behavior throughout childhood and adolescence are at an extremely high risk for becoming school dropouts, having difficulty maintaining employment, committing crimes, and having marital difficulties.

Modeled Aggressive Behavior. On any given day, students are faced with many instances that result in feelings of anger, frustration, and/or humiliation. These feelings often result in students reacting aggressively. In addition to the developmental model outlined in the previous section, the most commonly accepted cause for aggressive behavior is that these behaviors are learned through modeling (e.g., Bandura, 1973; Kronenberger et al., 2005; Wicks-Nelson & Israel, 1991; Widom, 1989). For example, students observe aggressive behavior models when adults, especially parents, engage in verbally abusive or physical punishment of students. When students grow up in violent homes and neighborhoods, violence is the model they observe and learn in response to problems and conflicts at school (Rudo, Powell, & Dunlap, 1998).

Students cannot be expected to expand their repertoire of responses to anger if they see only a limited number of inappropriate responses modeled. Thus, it is important for teachers to model appropriate alternatives to aggressive behavior by remaining calm in anger-inducing situations, talking out the problem, or walking away from the problem until they feel calm enough to discuss the situation. This alternative to aggression may be the only appropriate model for some students to observe. In addition, through the use of role-playing, these responses can be modeled and practiced in a formal social skills training.

Media Influence.   The media also offer plenty of aggressive models for students through TV programs geared to the interest of young persons (Hughes, 1996; Lieberman, cited in Walker, Colvin, & Ramsey, 1995). Lieberman suggests that students who are exposed to media violence become desensitized to aggressive and violent behavior. This factor has led to increased levels of violent and aggressive behavior among youth (Walker et al., 1995). Widom (1989) reviewed the literature on the relationship of TV violence to aggressive behavior in students and concluded that television violence was clearly related to aggressive behavior. One has to watch only a few minutes of professional wrestling on TV, a popular show for young boys, to understand the problem. Unfortunately, many parents, especially fathers, don't realize the negative influence these shows have on their sons' behavior at home and school. But teachers see the effects every day.

Many studies have focused on the relationship between television and video game violence and subsequent manifestation of aggressive behavior in students (Friedrich-Cofer & Huston, 1986; Kronenberger et al., 2005). A review of longitudinal studies revealed that viewing TV violence at one age correlated with aggressive behaviors demonstrated at a later age. "Of a large number of parent, family, and socioeconomic variables measured at age 8, television was the single best predictor of aggression in 18-year-olds" (Friedrich-Cofer & Huston, 1986, p. 367). Students who are exposed to high levels of media violence become desensitized to aggression and violence. Interestingly, Wied, Goudena, and Matthys (2005) found that 8- to 12-year-old boys referred for disruptive behaviors were found to show less empathy to sad situations than an age-matched control group. Aggression observed in film and computer games may desensitize students to the consequences of their own aggression. These findings present serious implications for our society in the face of the expanding and increasingly violent movies and games available to students through cable and Internet sources.

Social Skills Deficits.   Some have proposed that students act aggressively because they lack alternative skills that would allow them to choose a socially acceptable behavior to deal with a provocative situation in an assertive rather than aggressive manner (Dubow, Huesmann, & Eron, 1987; Hollinger, 1987). Dubow and others (1987) report the need for students to develop social competence before they experience a history of reinforcement for solving problems with aggressive behavior. Aggressive students often have a limited repertoire of social problem-solving behaviors. Often, due to environmental interactions and opportunities for modeling, aggressive behaviors are manifested as the only choice for situations that require problem-solving skills.

Neel, Jenkins, and Meadows (1990) found results that conflict with those of researchers who report that aggressive behavior was caused by deficits in social skills. In their study of 19 preschoolers, ages 3 to 4, Neel and his colleagues found that students who were aggressive demonstrated similar usage of social skills compared with their nonaggressive peers. They conclude that students who were aggressive used a number of social problem-solving strategies just as their nonaggressive counterparts did. The difference was that students who were aggressive used more intrusive types of strategies (e.g., barging into a game) compared with the more socially acceptable strategies used by their nonaggressive peers (e.g., asking for information and questioning before joining the group). A number of authors have suggested this in previous research (e.g., Melloy, 1990). The findings of Neel and others suggest that the development of social competence in students who are aggressive should concentrate on strategy content rather than on the number of strategies within the student's repertoire.

Melloy (1990) describes several types of peer acceptance of students who demonstrate aggressive behavior. Some students who are aggressive are accepted as leaders by their peers because their peers are afraid to reject them. Other students who are aggressive are often rejected by their peers. A common scene on a playground is for a group of students to terminate their play and move to another area when an aggressive peer tries to join the group.

In the long run, a history of rejection by one's peers can lead to a dependence on less desirable peers and membership in deviant subcultures, which often leads to social maladjustment (Center, 1990; Weinberg & Weinberg, 1990). Students in these subcultures are frequently reinforced for engaging in aggressive behaviors.

INTERVENTIONS FOR AGGRESSION

Functional Assessment.   Sasso and his colleagues (1990) have demonstrated that social skills training could assist elementary and junior high students in acquiring, maintaining, and generalizing social skills as alternatives to aggression. The authors report on a study that took place over an entire school year with three aggressive students, ages 8, 10, and 13, receiving special-education services. The subjects were part of a larger class of eight students in a large, midwestern elementary and junior high school. The students were all integrated into regular classes for at least one class period per day. Students were taught social skills using the structured learning approach and the curriculum from *Skillstreaming the Elementary School Student* (McGinnis & Goldstein, 1984). Pertinent to the Sasso et al. study was the training of replacement behaviors for aggression that serve the same function of the inappropriate behavior. These alternative behaviors included accepting consequences, dealing with accusations, negotiating, responding to teasing, asking permission, and staying out of fights.

Following intervention, all of the students in the study reduced levels of aggressive behavior in comparison to baseline levels and generalized these more appropriate behaviors to their regular classroom and other school settings. Use of social skills training along with positive reinforcement for appropriate behaviors are among the current promising practices in teaching students alternative behaviors to aggression.

Using cognitive behavior management (CBM) strategies (see Chapter 11), students are taught to use techniques such as self-talk and self-instruction to deal with stressful situations. Etscheidt (1991) used CBM with 30 adolescents, ages 13 to 18, who demonstrated aggressive behavior. The purpose of the study was (a) to determine the effectiveness of cognitive behavior management on the reduction of aggressive behavior and increases in prosocial behavior, and (b) to determine whether the addition of positive consequences would increase the effectiveness of cognitive training.

One group of students was exposed to cognitive training from the *Anger Control Program Model* (Lochman, Nelson, & Sims, cited in Etscheidt, 1991). The intent of the program was to assist students "in modifying their aggressive behaviors by altering their cognitive processing of events and response alternatives" (Etscheidt, 1991, p. 110). During training, students in group 1 participated in 12 lessons with these goals:

- Self-awareness
- Exploration of reactions to peer influences

- Identification of problem situations
- Generation of alternative solutions to problems
- Evaluation of solutions
- Recognition of physiological awareness of anger arousal
- Integration of physiological awareness
- Self-talk and social problem-solving techniques to reduce aggressive behavior

The students were also taught to use the following five strategies in problem situations:

1. *Motor Cue/Impulse Delay:*   Stop and think before you act; cue yourself.
2. *Problem Definition:*   Say how you feel and exactly what the problem is.
3. *Generation of Alternatives:*   Think of as many solutions as you can.
4. *Consideration of Consequences:*   Think ahead to what might happen next.
5. *Implementation:*   When you have a really good solution, try it! (Etscheidt, 1991, p. 111)

The students in group 2 received cognitive training and were positively reinforced for use of the skills taught. A control group received no cognitive training or positive consequences for use of the training strategy.

The results of the study indicate a significant decrease in aggressive behavior and a significant increase in self-control behavior in group 1 and group 2 students compared with the control group. No significant differences between groups 1 and 2 were noted. The author attributes this to the fact that, prior to cognitive training, a behavior management program existed in the students' classroom. Adding additional positive consequences may not have been as effective because of this factor.

Students were found to be more responsive to behavior change when they were reinforced for acceptable behavior than when they were merely punished upon engaging in unacceptable behavior (Meadows, Melloy, & Yell, 1996). Building relationships with students and providing meaningful curriculum in a positive classroom climate were also effective in reducing aggressive behavior and increasing acceptable school behavior (Abrams & Segal, 1998). Goal setting, behavioral contracts, and token economies were other behaviorally based interventions that teachers used effectively in promoting and supporting acceptable replacement behavior for aggression (Ruth, 1996). Behavior reduction strategies including suspension and exclusionary time-out were not effective in assisting students (especially older students) to change aggressive behavior to prosocial behavior (Costenbader & Markson, 1998; Maag, 1996).

Schoolwide and Classroom Rules.   Principals and teachers must make it clear that there is a zero-tolerance rule for aggression on school grounds. All aggression exhibited on school grounds must be consistently followed with a specific consequence, such as participation in a school service project, contacting parents, and so on. This agreement should be shared with all students and their families and, again, to be effective, it must be dealt with consistently and openly so that all students receive the message that aggression will not be tolerated.

Bullying Behavior

According to the National Center for Educational Statistics (2007), 21% of elementary schools, 43% of middle schools, and 22% of high schools reported problems with bullying

Supervision is critical to any antibullying program.

behavior in 2005–2006. Horne, Stoddard, and Bell (2007) report that bullying peaks in sixth grade and then declines through the high school years. Bullying is defined as one or more students seeking to have power over another student through the use of ongoing verbal, physical, or emotional harassment, intimidation, or isolation. Bullying is clearly a form of aggression. A bully intends to hurt, threaten, or frighten his or her victim. Bullying may involve *direct* (physical or verbal) or *indirect* (psychological) attacks on a student. Direct bullying may involve hitting, name-calling, teasing, tripping, threatening, or taking or destroying a student's belongings. Indirect forms of bullying may involve spreading rumors or gossip about a student in order to isolate the victim from his or her peer group. According to Carran and Kellner (2009), the most common forms of bullying behavior reported by victims were: name calling, rumors spread about them, being excluded from social groups, inappropriate sexual comments made to them, and various types of physical aggression.

   Bullying has become a widespread topic of conversation in and out of schools. Although some people still have the impression that bullying is just "kids being kids" or a rite of passage, many educators are not taking the subject lightly. Technology has increased the forms of bullying. Today, bullying behavior can be observed in person or over the Internet. For example, a bully can spread rumors about another student by way of e-mails, instant messaging, or even blogs. Cell phones provide another common resource for bullies.

COMMON CAUSES AND ANTECEDENTS OF BULLYING BEHAVIOR   The development of bullying behavior is very similar to the development of aggression (see Brubacher et al., 2009, above). Bullies come in all shapes and sizes and genders. Some bullies in schools are popular and some are disliked. However, bullies typically

- have average or above-average self-esteem,
- find satisfaction from causing harm to others,

- seek attention or acceptance from peers,
- seek to make themselves look tough and in charge,
- have little empathy toward their victims or others,
- seek to dominate other people or situations, and
- are described as hot-tempered and impulsive.

Bullying may be common among students who come from abusive homes or where physical punishment is frequently employed. For example, in our Classroom Connection 14.2, Steve receives little parental supervision or attention from his father, and shows little empathy for Sam. Students frequently model behavior observed within their home environment, including abusive behavior exhibited by parents to each other or toward others.

CLASSROOM CONNECTION 14.2
Dealing with a Bully

By Teresa Sturm

Sam, a middle school student, has been the victim of bullying behavior by his classmate, Steve. The incidents have occurred sporadically throughout the year, escalating from verbal to physical attacks. Eventually, Sam reported the incidents to his teacher, Ms. Johnson, who in turn reported the events to the principal, Ms. Smith. After several warnings to Steve, Ms. Smith felt confident that she had made a significant impression on Steve that his bullying behavior would not be tolerated. However, soon after his meeting with Ms. Smith, Steve approached Sam in the cafeteria and started pushing him in retaliation for "tattling." Steve's behavior was observed by another teacher and after reporting to the principal's office, Steve was suspended from school for 5 days.

During Steve's suspension, Ms. Smith started to investigate a process called community conference. Not knowing what else to do, she contacted a community conference facilitator and they scheduled a meeting with everyone involved, including both boys' parents. During the conference, Steve was asked to explain his behavior to the group. He stated that he wanted people to like him and to think he was cool. He said that some of the kids laughed at him and called him "four eyes" and "loser." He also said that by bullying Sam, he earned some respect among his peers. He said that he was mad at Sam for "telling on me," and that he wanted to get back at Sam for "tattling" and for getting him suspended from school.

Now it was Sam's turn. Sam told the group about how Steve's behavior impacted his life on a daily basis in school and at home. Sam was afraid every minute of the day because he was afraid of running into Steve. His grades were going down and he no longer had any enthusiasm to participate in school activities because he was afraid Steve would also be involved. Sam's mother also had the opportunity to tell Steve how his behavior had caused her to worry about her son's safety and that Sam was becoming a different person because of the bullying.

Steve's mother talked about problems at home between her and her husband, leading to a separation and the absence of a father figure at home for Steve. The group expressed support for Steve and his mom, but Ms. Smith told them that, regardless of what was happening at home, bullying at her school would not be tolerated.

As the conference came to an end, an agreement was reached outlining ways in which the relationship between Steve and Sam could be repaired. The boys agreed to try and put the past behind them, to start saying positive things to each other, and—to remember that—they shook hands. Sam accepted Steve's apology, and the two boys returned to school the next day.

General Reflection for Classroom Connection 14.2:

What specific positive behavioral support systems could be initiated to reinforce appropriate behavior and the absence of bullying behavior for Steve? What specific consequences should also be in place if Steve starts bullying behavior again? How should his classroom teacher and school principal monitor his behavior? What would be the benefits of a follow-up community conference?

Like Steve, bullies frequently plan out their attacks. They often choose isolated locations or playgrounds, hallways, restrooms, or school buses where there may be limited adult supervision of their behavior. Bullies are usually very self-centered in that they are concerned with only their own needs and pleasures. They frequently do not accept responsibility for their behavior or the consequences of their bullying (Coloroso, 2003). Victims of bullying are frequently considered passive or submissive around peers. They may be highly cautious and sensitive at a young age and may have difficulty asserting themselves with peers.

INTERVENTIONS FOR BULLYING BEHAVIOR   A review of intervention research for bullying behavior by Merrell and Isava (2008, p. 26) found "meaningful and clinically important positive effects for about one-third of the variables." Perhaps this poor assessment of bullying programs is the result of early experimentation with a variety of strategies and that, over the long-term, the more successful strategies will surface. Meanwhile, prevention is the best intervention for bullying behavior, and the universal strategies of schoolwide PBS (see Chapter 12) are the best strategies to prevent bullying behavior from becoming a major issue within school settings. By implementing a schoolwide PBS program, school administrators and teachers develop a culture that is incongruent with bullying behavior and a zero-tolerance for such behavior. Prevention begins with educating everyone in the school about bullying, providing appropriate supervision in and outside of the school building, having clear and consistent rules about bullying behaviors, and providing support for the victims of bullying (Dake, Price, Telljohann, & Funk, 2003; Frey, Hirschstein, Edstrom, & Snell, 2009).

Also, bullying must not be treated as an ordinary conflict between two students. While conflict between two students involves a disagreement between two equals, bullying is "an imbalance of power between perpetrator and victim" (see Crothers & Kolbert, 2008, p. 133). Whereas most conflicts between students may be resolved without outside intervention, outside intervention is usually necessary to decrease bullying incidents. In addition, research has shown that those who demonstrate bullying behavior in middle and high school are likely to be at risk for antisocial behavior as adults. Sixty percent of individuals identified as bullies in grades 6 through 9 were arrested at least once by the age of 30 (Ma, 2002; Quinn et al., 2003). Thus, effective intervention for bullying behavior has both short-term consequences for the school and long-term consequences for society.

As previously stated, the first step to decreasing bullying behavior in schools is to have a firm policy of zero tolerance for bullying behavior. Surveys show that over 60% of victims told someone that they were being bullied and the person told is frequently a teacher or other adult at school (Carran & Kellner, 2009). Students need to know that these reports will be followed by action and that adults at school will communicate that bullying behavior is not acceptable and will have consequences. Parents must also receive this message from school administrators, especially the parents of bullies.

Supervision is also critical to any antibullying program. Since bullies seek and plan opportunities to bully within schools where there is limited adult supervision, increased adult supervision in hallways, bathrooms, and playgrounds is critical.

Schoolwide programs that increase and build supportive relationships among students have also been developed. For example, the Olweus Bullying Prevention Program

(Olweus, 2005)—which involves school administrators, teachers, parents, and students—recommends the following measures:

- The formation of a bullying prevention or intervention committee within each school
- The study of the extent of bullying in their school through an anonymous student questionnaire
- Staff training on bullying identification and remediation
- The adoption of schoolwide rules against bullying, and increased adult supervision of students throughout the school day and in all locations
- The development of consequences for students' bullying behavior
- Teaching students about empathy toward others
- Intervention for students who bully and who are bullied
- The involvement of parents
- The intervention and reporting of bullying behavior by bystanders who observe the behavior

Another program, referred to as community conferencing (Chisholm, 2007), calls for a formal process that brings everyone involved and affected by the bullying behavior together to address and change the behavior. This process is employed in Classroom Connection 14.2. For a more complete listing of school-based antibullying programs, see Horne, Stoddard, and Bell (2007).

Temper Tantrum Behavior

Temper tantrums have been defined as noxious behavior demonstrated by students when their demands are not met or when they are tired (Sasso et al., 1990). Blechman (1985) defines temper tantrums as taking place "when a student, who has not been mistreated, is out-of-control for at least 1 minute, screaming, crying, throwing things, or hitting" (p. 89). Tantrum behavior is characterized by a variety of acting-out behaviors including crying, stamping, throwing self, screaming, kicking, clinging, jumping up and down, shouting, pounding, and other annoying behaviors.

Temper tantrums are among the most common challenging behaviors of young students (Blechman, 1985), and they need to be eliminated before developing into more serious oppositional behaviors (Ostrander, 2004). Although tantrum behavior is exhibited by persons of all ages, it is usually affiliated with toddlers and young students and is frequently associated in the literature with aggressive and noncompliant behavior (e.g., Kuczynski et al., 1987; McMahon & Wells, 1989; Sasso et al., 1990).

COMMON CAUSES AND ANTECEDENTS OF TANTRUM BEHAVIOR   Students have temper tantrums for one primary reason: The behavior works! Temper tantrum behavior can be traced directly to an adult's pattern of giving in to the student's wishes as soon as he or she begins to tantrum. The most common function of tantrum behavior is to gain attention or demand something. For example, when Tyler wants to go to the grocery store with his mother, tantrum behavior is used to get what he wants. Tyler's mother does not like the tantrum behavior, so she lets Tyler accompany her to the store. Then, Tyler promptly stops his tantrum, gets his coat, and smilingly goes to the store with his mother. By giving in to Tyler's behavior, his mother is reinforcing his behavior. In the future, Tyler will be more

CLASSROOM CONNECTION 14.3
Learning That Tantrums Don't Work

A preschool teacher named Susan told the story of a 4-year-old boy named Michael who one day refused to put his coat on before going outside for recess. The school was located in Minnesota, and it was a very cold September day. Susan told Michael that he would stay inside the classroom with the teacher's aide until he put on his coat. She then took the rest of the class outside. Michael immediately fell to the floor and had a temper tantrum that lasted most of the 20-minute recess period. At the end of the day, when Michael's mother came to bring him home, Susan told her what had happened during recess. Michael's mother stated that she and her husband usually let Michael decide when to wear a coat. "In my classroom," replied Susan, "I make those decisions, and if Michael wants to go outside for recess when it is cold, he will wear his coat."

The next day after lunch, Susan asked the kids to get their coats so they could play outside for recess. All her students, including Michael, put on their coats and lined up by the door to go outside. Susan never had to argue with Michael again about wearing his coat.

General Reflection for Classroom Connection 14.3:

Do you think that Michael has temper tantrums at home? Based on Michael's behavior and his mother's response, how would you predict his parents respond to his tantrums? What would have happened if Susan allowed Michael to go outside without a coat? How would you evaluate Susan's response to Michael's mother? Do you think Michael will repeat this behavior in Susan's class?

likely to engage in tantrum behavior when he is told "No" as a result of the positive consequences he experienced for his tantrum behavior. In Classroom Connection 14.3, we see the real-life example of a preschool student who had to learn that temper tantrums did not work with his teacher.

INTERVENTIONS FOR TANTRUM BEHAVIOR   If students have temper tantrums because they know tantrum behavior will get them what they want, then the best intervention to prevent tantrum behavior is to teach students that this behavior no longer works. Tantrum behavior can be significantly decreased through the use of extinction. When reinforcement for tantrum behavior is withdrawn, and the student's behavior is ignored, the tantrum behavior will probably be greatly reduced or eliminated.

It is also important for teachers of young children to follow routines (e.g., "First we put on our coat; then we go outside") so that students learn what the rules are and what is expected of them. Warnings and transition periods for young children are also recommended (e.g., "Children, in 5 minutes you will have to put away your toys and prepare for story time").

Lastly, it is difficult for young children to function when they are tired or overwhelmed with stimuli. The preschool curriculum must be developmentally appropriate for the age of the students. Structure, order, and routine are important elements for teachers when working with young children.

BEHAVIORS RELATED TO ATTENTION AND ACTIVITY

A review of the literature reveals an association among the problems of inattention, hyperactivity, and impulsivity. Some refer to attention-deficit hyperactivity disorder (ADHD) as "a disorder of inattention, impulsivity, and hyperactivity" (Biederman & Faraone,

2005). Regardless of what these three behaviors are called, teachers frequently see all three exhibited by the same students who are struggling in school both academically and socially (Spira & Fischel, 2005).

In this section, we will look at each of these behaviors separately, as well as stereotypic behaviors sometimes observed in populations of students with disabilities.

Inattentive Behavior

Attention has been defined as the ability to remain oriented to a task for the length of time required to complete the task, or for an amount of time that seems socially acceptable (Kounin, 1970; Ruff, Lawson, Parrinello, & Weissberg, 1990). McGee, Williams, and Silva (1985) identify three behavioral dimensions associated with attention: "planning, organization, and execution of tasks or activities" (pp. 487–488). Poor planning in children with attention deficits was also linked to poor performance on cognitive tasks (Papadopoulos, Panayiotou, Spanoudis, & Natsopoulos, 2005).

Parents and teachers often describe these students as having trouble starting and/or finishing things and being easily distracted. These students may become off task at even the slightest noise (e.g., someone's pencil dropping on the floor) or change in the environment (e.g., someone coming to the door of the classroom to talk to the teacher). These students often have trouble getting back on task once they have been distracted. As a result, they may have difficulty completing academic tasks, possibly resulting in poor academic achievement.

Students who have attention problems are also described as poor listeners. For example, 15-year-old Matthew rarely uses any body language (e.g., eye contact) to indicate that he is listening to another person. At school, the students have been instructed to look at a person who is talking (e.g., a peer giving a speech in front of the class). During these situations, Matthew is often observed to stare out the window. In his home, where he is expected to stand or sit in close proximity to the person speaking but not to make eye contact, Matthew often looks away while someone talks to him. He reports that he can concentrate better on what is being said when he is not distracted by looking at people and noticing something about what they are wearing or their hairstyle.

Inattention is a problem that often exists with other behavioral deficits such as impulsivity and hyperactivity. Its existence as an independent construct has been debated (Kauffman & Landrum, 2009). Regardless of its definition, inattention is a common challenge for teachers of students of all ages.

COMMON CAUSES AND ANTECEDENTS OF INATTENTIVE BEHAVIOR

Genetics.   Many researchers state that attention deficits and related behaviors are genetic (Johnson, McGue, & Iacono, 2005). For example, Selikowitz (2004) states that ADHD is primarily a genetic disorder related to the function of neurotransmitters in the brain that cause a student to have an attention disability. Many researchers question this simplistic explanation considering the complexity of all behavior and the interaction of genetics and environmental influences, especially given other independent variables such as the quality of the child's environment and parental influences. But even if attention deficits had a genetic etiology, this explanation does not help teachers develop intervention strategies and suggests that there is nothing a teacher can do to improve the student's behavior. We believe that most experienced teachers would reject this proposition based on their own experiences in changing behavior.

Learning to Be Attentive.   Teachers frequently talk about students who don't sit and listen. These students have not learned how to sit and listen, typically taught at home, starting at a young age, when parents have their children sit and listen to them read a story. But many students do not have this early childhood experience and come to school without these important school readiness skills. These students must be taught these skills at school, hopefully at the preschool or kindergarten level. Thus, students should not be evaluated for having an attention deficit disorder before the teacher is sure that the student simply has a school readiness deficit.

Ruff and Lawson (1990) investigated the development of attention in 67 preschoolers ages 1 through 5. Their studies were conducted using observations of free play as the measure of focused attention. They found that as students grew older, their attention became more focused when they were presented with a variety of activities that involved complex problem-solving aspects. This suggests a learning mechanism for attentive behaviors.

INTERVENTIONS FOR INATTENTIVE BEHAVIOR

Teach Attentive Behavior.   For young students, school readiness, including attention skills, must be taught. Practice sitting and listening and the reinforcement of on-task behavior for increasing intervals of time as an effective way to teach young children how to be attentive. This training should start at home, of course. But for many students these skills are not learned at home and must be taught at the preschool and kindergarten setting.

DuPaul, Stoner, Tilly, & Putnam (1991) offer some guidelines for developing behavior change interventions to assist students to increase attention skills:

- A functional assessment should be used to assess problem behaviors.
- The students should receive more frequent and specific feedback for attentive behavior.
- Both positive and negative consequences should be incorporated into behavior management programs.
- Tasks should be broken down into specific instructions and delivered to the student a few steps at a time.
- The focus of behavior change programs should be based on "concrete results of appropriate behavior rather than on specific task-related behaviors" (p. 690).
- Preferred activities should be used as reinforcers, rather than tangible rewards such as candy.
- Priming students with discussion of privileges that can be earned prior to the assignment of academic tasks will increase task completion (p. 691).

Teach Self-Instruction and Monitoring Skills.   Self-instruction and self-monitoring strategies have been effective in increasing attentive behavior (Lloyd, Bateman, Landrum, & Hallahan, 1989; Vanderbilt, 2005). During a self-instruction program, students receive a prompt (usually a recorded tone) throughout class. Each time they hear the prompt, the students would ask themselves whether they were paying attention and completing their task. Davis and Hajicek (1985) employed self-instructional verbalizations that had a student remind him- or herself to "Pay attention" or "Do your work" after a recorded tone was sounded every 60 seconds. This strategy helped the students significantly improve their attending and accuracy rate on academic tasks.

Self-instruction usually includes a self-monitoring procedure, in which a student records on paper if he or she was (+) or was not (−) paying attention or completing his or her work at set intervals. Vanderbilt (2005) recommends that once the teacher and student decide how frequently the student will record his or her behavior, the student needs to practice self-monitoring so the teacher can "lead the student step-by-step through the self-monitoring process and discuss any possible questions and points of confusion" (p. 22).

Lloyd and his colleagues (1989) assisted five upper elementary students in changing their attending behavior through self-monitoring and recording. Using self-monitoring, the students's arithmetic productivity and attention to task improved significantly. Self-monitoring provides students with the opportunity for direct feedback as they review their own recorded data with or without the teacher.

Self-instruction and self-monitoring provide examples of educational interventions that increase and modify task and setting antecedents that have been found to improve attentional performance in students, even those labeled ADHD (Zentall, 2005).

Hyperactive Behavior

According to Taylor, Burns, Rusby, and Foster (2006), *hyperactivity* refers to behaviors that include fidgeting, out-of-seat behavior, running about, limited ability to play quietly, talking too much, excessive physical activity, blurting out answers, limited ability to wait turn, and interrupting behavior. While most of these behaviors are expected of young students in many environmental contexts, these same behaviors, in excess, may prove troublesome within the home, school, and community environments. In severe cases, childhood hyperactivity has been found to be a risk indicator for the development of antisocial behaviors in adulthood (Freidenfelt & Klinteberg, 2007).

Hyperactivity is one of the most overused terms in education. Controversy has arisen over whether or not hyperactivity exists as an independent behavioral construct. It is often associated with inattention, impulsivity, and conduct disorders (Gaynor, 1990; Gresham, Lane, & Beebe-Frankenberger, 2005; Kauffman & Landrum, 2009; Kohn, 1989; Shaw, Lacourse, & Nagin, 2005). Taylor et al. (2006) found hyperactivity to be distinct from ODD. Like inattention, the function of hyperactivity seems to be to gain attention, to escape from tasks, or to provide self-gratification.

Interestingly, symptoms of many students labeled hyperactive often seem to disappear when the student is engaged in something he or she enjoys such as playing video games, watching TV, or engaging in free play. This should tell us much about the etiology of the behavior. If it were biological, hyperactivity would be either constant or random. But if the behavior follows environmental antecedents, the etiology is environmental, not biological, and medication will not solve the fundamental problem.

COMMON CAUSES AND ANTECEDENTS OF HYPERACTIVE BEHAVIOR

Multiple Factors.   There is not one cause of hyperactivity, though a number of theories have been suggested. Brain damage, biological factors, food additives, difficult temperament, and psychoanalytic factors have all been proposed as explanations for hyperactivity without sufficient scientific research to conclude that any one of them alone or in combination is a cause for hyperactivity (Kauffman & Landrum, 2009).

Other explanations for hyperactive behavior revolve around theories of modeling, imitation, and environmental interaction (Campbell & Werry, 1986; David & Wintrob, 1989; Kauffman & Landrum, 2009; Kohn, 1989). Clearly, the most plausible explanation for hyperactive behavior is that it is caused by a combination of factors, including learned behavior.

There is significant overlap of antecedents and risk factors for disruptive behavior, hyperactivity, attention problems, impulsivity, conduct problems, and most other challenging behaviors (Shaw et al., 2005). Gresham and colleagues (2005) found that by grade 6, students showing hyperactivity, impulsivity, and inattention are at greater risk for academic failure. Bussing, Zima, and Belin (1998) found that students in grades 2 and 4 who demonstrated hyperactivity, inattention, and impulsivity also received special-education services for learning disabilities and emotional/behavioral disorders. This suggests a link between these behaviors, including the possibility that the causative factors of each behavior is shared. It may also be the case that students who have not learned to pay attention and other school readiness skills at home do poorly at school and thus are more likely to be labeled learning disabled by educators. That brings us to environmental factors.

Environmental Factors. Kohn (1989) states that hyperactive behavior is caused by environmental factors such as classroom dynamics and/or family dynamics. He states that students demonstrate hyperactive behavior in classrooms where the work is not stimulating and where the pace of instruction is not conducive to the student's ability. Kohn also suggests that hyperactive behavior may be the result of academic failure, rather than the cause of that failure.

Kohn further reports that some "family patterns often accompany hyperactivity" (p. 94). These patterns are described in terms of mental health issues among family members, a heavy emphasis on punitive and authoritative approaches to behavior management, and marital problems between the student's parents. Harden (1997) suggests that students who demonstrate hyperactivity when in a boring, nonstimulating situation can be helped to engage in more appropriate behavior with interventions such as restricting television watching and establishing family routines (e.g., mealtimes and bedtime).

Parent–Student Interactions. David and Wintrob (1989) studied the role of mother–child communication patterns in the development of hyperactive/conduct-disturbed behavior. The authors conducted research with 30 boys, who had been diagnosed as hyperactive/conduct disordered, and their mothers. Mothers and their sons were given pictures to discuss while their interactions were videotaped. Examples of the exchanges that were taped included an interaction about a picture that could have been described as a type of flying animal. The following interaction was considered to demonstrate a negative communication pattern between a mother and her son:

SON: That's a bat.

MOTHER: Don't be stupid! That's not a bat; that's a butterfly.

In comparison, this interaction was considered to be a positive interaction between the mother and her son:

SON: That is a bat.

MOTHER: Very good! That's what it looks like.

David and Wintrob (1989) found that mothers' communication with sons labeled hyperactive was socially inappropriate in comparison with the communication patterns of mothers and their sons without hyperactivity. They state that even though their study was conducted with mothers and sons, there is a possibility that others who communicate with students may influence students' behavior (e.g., fathers, siblings, teachers). They point out that "in most instances the primary caretaker will be most influential in this regard" (p. 390).

INTERVENTIONS FOR HYPERACTIVITY   A number of effective strategies are available for decreasing hyperactivity, but few studies are available in current literature that focus solely on hyperactivity. Most of the research focuses on hyperactivity combined with inattention and impulsivity as constructs of attention deficits. This section describes the literature that is available on behavioral interventions that were effective in decreasing hyperactive behavior. The most popular of these interventions include consistent reinforcement consequences, social skills training, and cognitive behavior management.

Teach Appropriate Social Skills.   Students who are hyperactive will respond best in settings where the rules for behavior have been clearly established. In addition, the rules must be consistently enforced, and students should be reinforced for following the rules. Students with hyperactivity are most successful in structured classroom settings where the rules are obvious and consistently enforced (Gordon, 1991; Schaub, 1990).

Students with hyperactivity also respond well in educational programs that include positive reinforcement. Students who are positively reinforced using praise and tokens for appropriate behavior (e.g., staying in seat, asking permission, following rules) are more likely to engage in behaviors incompatible with hyperactivity (DuPaul & Eckert, 1997; Melloy, 1990). Paniagua, Morrison, and Black (1990) report on the effective use of positive reinforcement to reduce the hyperactive behavior of a 7-year-old boy. They found that offering a toy as positive reinforcement for promising to inhibit behavior and actual inhibition of the behavior was effective in reducing hyperactive behavior.

Students labeled hyperactive often receive low social status ratings from their peers and deviant scores on teacher ratings of behavior (McConnell & Odom, 1986). These students benefit from training in social skills using a structured learning approach (McGinnis & Goldstein, 1997). Social skills that are incompatible with hyperactive behavior include staying in seat, completing tasks, joining in a group, and offering help to others. Modeling, role-playing, receiving feedback, and generalization training in these skills can reduce hyperactive behavior in students.

Mathes and Bender (1997) report that self-monitoring of behavior and psychostimulant medication were helpful to three boys, ages 8 through 11 years, in improving their on-task behavior. Other studies have also reported on the effectiveness of self-regulation or self-management interventions in helping students increase attention and academic productivity and reduce hyperactivity (e.g., Barry & Haraway, 2005; Reid, Trout, and Schartz, 2005).

Impulsive Behavior

Campbell and Werry (1986) define impulsivity as "erratic and poorly controlled behavior" (p. 120). Teachers who refer to a student as being impulsive usually conjure up images of students who rarely stop to think before they act, who attempt tasks before they fully understand the directions, who often demonstrate remorse when their actions have led to errors or mishaps, who call out frequently in class (usually with the wrong answer), and who have difficulty organizing their materials.

Kauffman & Landrum (2009) state that while impulsive behavior may be normal in young students, as students grow older, most learn alternative responses. Olson, Bates, and Bayles (1990, p. 318) point out that 2-year-old students will begin to "inhibit prohibited actions owing to remembered information," but state that "self-regulation does not develop until the 3rd or 4th year of life."

Students who manifest impulsive behavior often get into trouble in social situations such as games and play activities (Melloy, 1990). Because they demonstrate poor impulse control, these students are apt to take their turn before its time, or to respond incorrectly to game stimuli (e.g., questions). Some students who have poor impulse control may respond to teasing, for example, by hitting the person who teases them. They are often sorry for their actions and can discuss what they should have done had they taken time to think about their action. Unfortunately, impulsivity places students at higher risk for smoking (Kollins, McClernon, & Fuemmeler, 2005), illegal drug use (Semple, Zians, Grant, & Patterson, 2005), eating disorders (Peake, Limbert, & Whitehead, 2005), and suicide (Swann, Dougherty, Pazzaglia, Pham, Steinberg, & Moeller, 2005).

D'Acremont and Van der Linden (2005) identify four dimensions of impulsivity:

- *Urgency:*   Student is in a hurry.
- *Lack of premeditation:*   Student acts before he thinks or plans.
- *Lack of perseverance:*   Student gives up on a task.
- *Sensation seeking:*   Student seeking fun without thinking of consequences.

They also found that among impulsive children, boys had higher scores for sensation seeking and girls for urgency. Assessment of impulsivity usually involves the use of behavioral checklists, behavior ratings, mazes, match-to-sample tasks, and behavioral observations (Olson et al., 1990; Shafrir & Pascual-Leone, 1990; Vitiello, Stoff, Atkins, & Mahoney, 1990).

Students who manifest impulsive behavior will benefit from social skills training.

COMMON CAUSES AND ANTECEDENTS OF IMPULSIVE BEHAVIOR

Multiple Factors.   As is the case for so many attention and activity behaviors, no one actually knows what causes impulsivity (Campbell & Werry, 1986; Kauffman & Landrum, 2009). Impulsivity is most likely related to the same multiple factors discussed in the prior sections on attentiveness and hyperactivity, including childhood temperament, family environment, gender, and parental characteristics (Leve, Kim, & Pears, 2005).

Failure to Self-Monitor.   Shafrir and Pascual-Leone (1990) conducted a study with 378 students between 9 and 12 years of age to determine the effect of attention to errors on academic tasks and the relationship to reflective/impulsive behavior. Shafrir and Pascual-Leone administered a number of measures, including mazes and match-to-sample tasks, to determine response behavior, and tests of academic achievement to evaluate arithmetic abilities. They report that students who completed tasks quickly and accurately tended to take time to check their answers. If an error occurred, they took time to correct the error and used the information learned in correction of the error to assist them in completing the rest of the task. This resulted in fewer errors overall and completion of the task in a more timely fashion. They call these students *postfailure reflective* (p. 385).

In comparison, students who are referred to as *postfailure impulsive* (Shafrir & Pascual-Leone, 1990, p. 385) were found to complete tasks slowly and inaccurately. These students plodded through the task without checking answers for correctness. They simply went on to the next problem with no reference to previously completed tasks. Shafrir and Pascual-Leone conclude that the lack of postfailure reflection by this group led to more errors because they did not learn from their previous errors. The implications of the results of this study are that students possess some type of "reflection/impulsivity cognitive style" (p. 386), which was first proposed by Kagan (see Kagan, Pearson, & Welch, 1966). Also, students who appear to be taking their time (slow thinkers) in actuality make more errors than the students who complete the tasks quickly (reflective thinkers).

Parent–Child Interactions.   Olson and his colleagues (1990) attempted to assess parent–child interactions through behavioral observation to determine if parental interaction style was a predictor of impulsive behavior. According to Olson et al., the purpose of their study was to "identify the relative contributions of different parent–student interaction antecedents to students's later self-regulatory abilities" (p. 320). This longitudinal study involved 79 mother–child dyads. Their findings indicate that "responsive, sensitive, and cognitively enriching mother–child interactions are important precursors of childhood impulse control" (p. 332). Children, especially boys, were more likely to develop impulsivity if their mothers manifested punitive and inconsistent behavior management styles.

INTERVENTIONS FOR IMPULSIVE BEHAVIOR

Teach Waiting and Self-Control Skills.   Impulsivity may be decreased by teaching students appropriate waiting behaviors, and by a reinforcement plan for appropriate responding behavior. For example, after an assignment has been given, a teacher may teach a student to place her hands on her desk, establish eye contact with the teacher, and listen for directions. The teacher should praise the student for demonstrating these waiting behaviors.

Students who manifest impulsive behavior will benefit from training in social skills such as self-control. At the same time, students may be taught relaxation techniques.

Reinforcement will increase the possibility that a student will demonstrate behaviors that are alternatives to impulsivity. The student just described learned social skills through direct instruction and reinforcement for use of the skills to replace impulsive behavior. Schaub (1990) also found that, for intervention, targeting behaviors that were positive and incompatible with undesirable behaviors was effective with students who demonstrated impulsive behavior. Bornas, Servera, and Llabres (1997) suggest that teachers use computer software to assist students in preventing impulsivity. The authors describe several software products that are effective in preventing impulsivity through instruction in problem solving and self-regulation.

Give Smaller and Shorter Tasks One at a Time.   A student who hurries through an assignment without stopping to read the directions or to check for errors could be given smaller amounts of a task to accomplish at one time, rather than the whole task at once. This would give the student a smaller chunk of the problem to deal with and more opportunities for reinforcement since the student would be more likely to solve the problem correctly.

Sometimes, a student considered impulsive can handle solving only one problem at a time. In this case, the student should be allowed to solve the problem and receive feedback immediately. As the student becomes more confident and is able to pace him- or herself more efficiently, then he or she may be able to handle larger and larger portions of projects and assignments.

Stereotypical Behavior

Students who exhibit *stereotypic behavior* typically engage in repetitious, invariant responses that occur at an excessively high rate and do not appear to have any adaptive function (Baumeister, 1978). Like temper tantrums, however, stereotypic behaviors seem to serve the function of getting the attention of others. In fact, individuals who engage in stereotypic behavior provided the earliest clues to understanding the functions of behavior including attention, escape, tangible reinforcement, and sensory reinforcement (Durand & Carr, 1985).

Stereotypic behavior is observed among a relatively small population, especially among individuals with developmental disabilities. Specific responses vary from student to student and include self-stimulatory behavior and self-injurious behavior. The major implication for students is that these behaviors often interfere with the student's educational and social inclusion.

SELF-STIMULATORY BEHAVIOR   *Self-stimulatory behaviors* (SSBs) are stereotypic behaviors that are repetitive and frequent but do not cause physical injury to the student exhibiting them. These behaviors often include "body rocking, hand flapping, eye rubbing, lip licking, or repeating the same vocalization over and over" (Kauffman & Landrum, 2009, p. 403). Self-stimulatory behaviors are not always intrusive behaviors for the student or others around them, but they may become self-injurious and may interfere with the student's educational program.

Common Causes and Antecedents of Self-Stimulatory Behavior.   Self-stimulatory behavior is learned behavior that is maintained by reinforcement in the form of sensory feedback (Iwata, Vollmer, & Zarcone, 1990; Rapp, Miltenberger, Galensky, Ellingson, & Long, 1999). Considerable controversy surrounds the operant learning theory as a cause for SSB

(Lovaas, Newsom, & Hickman, 1987). Lewis, Baumeister, and Mailman (1987) argue that Lovaas and his colleagues' theory of SSB as a learned behavior is flawed and needs to take into account biological factors.

Students who engage in severe stereotypic behavior are frequently autistic or severely developmentally disabled. A number of these students are successful in inclusive classroom settings because they respond to interventions designed to assist them in adopting more appropriate behavior for those settings. For example, when the function of SSB is used by students to communicate their wants, needs, and desires, it may be possible to teach them other ways to communicate (sign language, pictures cards, etc.). Also, through social skills instruction and reinforcement for engaging in prosocial behavior, stereotypic behavior may be decreased or eliminated. Interventions that are effective in bringing about these changes are described next.

SELF-INJURIOUS BEHAVIOR *Self-injurious behaviors* (SIBs) inflict harm on the person exhibiting them. Ross, Heath, and Toste (2009, p. 83) define self-injury as, "The deliberate, self-inflicted destruction of body tissue without suicidal intent and for purposes not socially sanctioned." These behaviors may include eye poking, scratching, cutting, slapping, hair pulling, head-banging, or any other behavior where an individual purposefully inflicts harm to self.

These behaviors are frequently associated with students who are diagnosed as having autism and developmental disabilities. As Conroy, Asmus, Sellers, and Ladwig (2005) point out, many of these students may be found in general education settings. Self-injurious behaviors are frequently associated with 2% to 3% of nondisabled adolescents, especially females, who engage in cutting behavior, skin scratching, and hair pulling (Kauffman & Landrum, 2009). And between 24% and 44% of females with eating disorders (anorexia and bulimia) exhibit some form of self-injurious behavior (see Ross, Heath, & Toste, 2009).

Common Causes and Antecedents of Self-Injurious Behavior. Bellfiore and Dattilio (1990) propose three explanations for the "onset, maintenance, and continuance of self-injury" (p. 29):

- SIB is learned behavior that is maintained by operant contingencies of either the "positive reinforcement paradigm" (p. 24) or the "negative reinforcement paradigm" (p. 25).
- SIB is elicited as an attempt to increase or decrease sensory stimulation or arousal.
- SIB is related to genetic anomalies or biochemical imbalances, such as Lesch-Nyhan syndrome or Cornelia de Lang syndrome.

Durand and Carr (1985) outline four functions of SIB:

- *Social attention.* SIB appears to be shaped and maintained by attention from others as a consequence.
- *Tangible consequences.* Some students exhibit SIB in order to gain access to tangible rewards such as playing with a desired toy.
- *Escape from aversive situations.* Students who engage in SIB in order to remove themselves from an unpleasant task (e.g., an academic task) are said to be motivated by escape.
- *Sensory stimulation.* This manifests in the form of auditory, visual, or tactile stimulation, which is reinforcing to the student.

INTERVENTIONS FOR STEREOTYPIC BEHAVIOR   Of all the challenging behaviors described in this chapter, stereotypic behavior has been described more often in the literature as being responsive to behavioral interventions (e.g., Conroy et al., 2005; Crnic & Reid, 1989; Day, Horner, & O'Neill, 1994; Northup et al., 1994; Zarcone, Iwata, Smith, Mazaleski, & Lerman, 1994). Social skills training and functional communication training are recommended by Durand and Carr (1985) and Hastings and Noone (2005) to teach skills that replace the social and/or communication function of the self-injurious behavior. For example, Durand and Carr suggest that if the SIB is maintained by social attention, the teacher should teach the student appropriate attention-seeking behavior. Students have been taught to ask whether they are doing good work, and other appropriate phrases, for gaining teacher attention. Students who are nonverbal have been taught to use sign language or point to a picture card that is an alternative to verbal communication.

This appropriate communication behavior must then be maintained through positive reinforcement (e.g., Day et al., 1994; Northup et al., 1994). For example, Northup and his colleagues (1994) provided teacher training and support for using functional analysis to determine antecedents and maintaining factors for SIB in five students ages 5 to 11 years who had severe disabilities. Following training, they were able to identify positive or negative reinforcers and/or punishers that appeared to maintain the students's behavior (e.g., access to music, escape from a task). The teachers were also trained to provide intervention that would assist students in increasing appropriate behaviors and decreasing SIB (e.g., activate a microswitch to get the teacher's attention vs. handmouthing). These strategies were effective in increasing appropriate communication skills and decreasing SIB in all five students.

Before teachers decide to reduce a student's SSB directly, a functional assessment of the SSB will likely lead to the conclusion that environmental antecedents and consequences should be the focus of an intervention plan (Conroy, Asmus, Sellers, & Ladwig, 2005). Increasing environmental stimulation by providing a greater array of stimulating activities and materials is likely to prove effective in reducing these behaviors, especially if their function is self-stimulation. Also, students who engage in SSB may be redirected to other incompatible behaviors with verbal and physical prompts. These appropriate behaviors should then be reinforced. Remember, the reinforcement must be stronger than the self-stimulation the student is providing himself. For a more extensive review of SSB and SIB, as well as related interventions, readers are referred to Repp and Singh (1990).

BEHAVIORS RELATED TO SEPARATION ANXIETY AND DEPRESSION

Separation Anxiety

Wood (2006, p. 345) defines *anxiety* as "a negative mood state that occurs in anticipation of a perceived threat" and that negatively impacts school performance and social functioning. While students in school may be anxious about many things, separation anxiety is common with young children. Babies younger than 6 months old usually adjust well to being away from their parents. However, around 4 to 7 months old, babies develop *object permanence* and begin to understand that people and objects exist even when they are out of sight. Thus, when a parent leaves their child's sight, the child understands that the parent went somewhere else. Since they don't yet understand that the parent will return at some point, the child may become anxious. This is called *separation anxiety*.

Many young students entering preschool, kindergarten, and even elementary school, suffer from separation anxiety. It is a difficult time for both students and parents and presents a challenging time for teachers.

COMMON CAUSES AND ANTECEDENTS OF SEPARATION ANXIETY Separation anxiety usually peaks between 8 and 12 months when toddlers become agitated and upset whenever their parents leave them (Harkness, 2005). Harkness (2005) states that separation anxiety can show itself anytime between 8 months and 3 years of age, and it can be triggered by a new child care situation, a move to a new home, or tension within the home.

Some children never experience separation anxiety, but for many children, being taken to a new educational setting (e.g., preschool or kindergarten) may be the trigger for their first real sensation of being separated from their parents. The degree of anxiety felt by the young child depends on many factors. Some children are more dependent on their parents and have had few experiences being separated from them. Some children have learned that being separated from their parents is not a permanent situation. Thus, the child's previous experiences play a significant role in how a child will deal with separation from his parents.

In rare cases, separation anxiety can last for many years and may be a sign of other problems at home. In other cases, when separation anxiety appears out of the blue, after months of attending school without any problems, the child may be telling his parents and teachers that there is a problem at school and this should be investigated.

INTERVENTIONS FOR SEPARATION ANXIETY Time and experience are, for most cases, the best cure for separation anxiety. Once the student learns that his parents always return, he will begin to feel less anxious when his parents leave. In addition, how parents respond to a student who is anxious has a significant impact on the student's behavior. If parents look and act anxious, the student will think that his anxiety is justified. After all, the student may be thinking, "If Mom and Dad are anxious about me being at preschool, this can't be good and I better be anxious, too." However, if Mom and Dad communicate confidence and assurance, the student will understand that the new situation is not a dangerous place.

Reinforcement rules also influence the student's behavior. As Harkness (2005) states, if a parent comes running back to the classroom every time her child cries, the student will soon learn to use crying behavior to manipulate his parent's behavior. If the student learns that by being anxious the parent will stay around longer, the student will learn to use this behavior to prevent his parent from leaving the classroom.

While parents may feel guilty about leaving a crying child, the best advice for parents is to have a set good-bye routine and leave. Teachers should help determine the place and time for the routine. For example, some schools have a rule that parents must say good-bye to their children within the school foyer. Parents are not allowed to walk their child down the hallway and into their classroom. At the end of the school foyer and before the school hallway, a sign reads "Hugging Zone." The hugging zone is where parents say good-bye to the children, give them a hug, tell them that Dad or Mom will pick them up after school, and leave. By providing parents and children with a place and routine, teachers can help parents learn how to help their children overcome separation anxiety.

Once the parent has left, Harkness (2005) recommends that teachers try to distract crying students with activities, songs, or any activity that will redirect the student's attention. It is important for the teacher to have a set morning routine to help students become adjusted and comfortable within their new environment. Again, consistency is critical.

Depression

Some may question the inclusion of a discussion of depression in this chapter. But depression is briefly mentioned here because its symptoms are frequently disruptive to classroom instruction. Depression is a growing diagnosis among schoolchildren, especially adolescents, and its implications place students at risk for many of the externalizing behaviors discussed in this chapter (Kauffman & Landrum, 2009).

Kazdin (1990) points out that there is a difference between depressed mood, which commonly occurs in everyday life, and depression as a disability. Teachers can play a significant role in identifying depression in students and are frequently the first professionals to notice a problem (Maag & Forness, 1991).

There is no test for depression, but some behaviors serve as warning signs that a student may need support in dealing with depression. The American Psychiatric Association (2000) lists the following behaviors that are typically linked to depression in children and adolescents:

- Sadness and/or irritability
- Poor appetite or overeating
- Insomnia or hypersomnia
- Low energy or fatigue
- Feelings of worthlessness or hopelessness
- Poor concentration and difficulty in making decisions
- Thoughts or talk of suicide

Depression is included in a category called *mood disorders* by the American Psychiatric Association (2000). Depression, obviously, refers to a significantly depressed mood. *Dysthymia* refers to a less severe type of depression that is not disabling. But mood disorders also include significantly elevated moods or euphoria known as *mania,* and a third condition called *bipolar disorder* for individuals who experience "rapidly alternating moods" from one mood (depression) to the other (manic) (American Psychiatric Association, 2000, p. 333). Individuals now labeled bipolar were once considered *manic-depressive* and may show these behaviors:

- Abrupt, rapid mood swings
- Periods of extreme hyperactivity
- Prolonged, explosive temper tantrums or rages
- Exaggerated ideas about self or abilities

Factors that may place students at risk for depression include a family history of mental health disabilities, abuse within the family (physical, emotional, or sexual), and parental divorce.

There is a lot of confusion and overlap when it comes to students with mental health disabilities. Depression, for example, may overlap with conduct disorders, attention deficits, impulsivity, and aggressive and other inappropriate behaviors. Many of these students today are lumped together into the attention-deficit disorder category, which seems to have become a catchall for students who exhibit any misbehavior (see Maag & Forness, 1991; Reynolds, 1991).

COMMON CAUSES AND ANTECEDENTS OF DEPRESSION   Sarason and Sarason (2005) identify five risk factors for depression:

- *Heredity:*   Twin studies demonstrate the strong association between depression and biological closeness.
- *Age:*   The risk for the first onset of depression is highest for women between the ages of 20 and 29; the risk for the first onset of depression for men is between the ages of 40 and 49.
- *Gender:*   Women are twice as likely to suffer from depression as men.
- *Negative life events:*   Examples include divorce or the death of a family member. Depression among divorced men and women is significantly higher than among married men and women.
- *Lack of social support:*   This includes from spouse, family, and/or good friends, when needed.

Kauffman and Landrum (2009) and others outline two primary causes of depression: *endogenous* (genetic or biological etiology) and *reactive* or *situational* (a response to environmental events).

INTERVENTIONS FOR DEPRESSION   Treatment methods for depression have centered around psychotherapy or counseling and medication with antidepressant drugs. Usually a combination of therapy and medication is recommended as most effective in working with students who have emotional or behavioral disorders (Forness, 2005). Recently, however, some antidepressant drugs have been linked to suicide among children and young adults. Thus, interventions such as counseling (cognitive and behavioral therapy), social skills training, cognitive restructuring (learning new thinking patterns), and even advice on nutrition, exercise, and sleep may be the best first steps before prescribing powerful antidepressant drugs to children.

It is not the purpose of this text to provide an extensive review of interventions for mental health disabilities. Readers are recommended to seek other sources for a more complete discussion of mental health issues of children and adolescents (see, e.g., Kauffman & Landrum, 2009; Jensen, 2005; Sarason & Sarason, 2005).

Summary

Throughout this chapter, we have attempted to give you a brief overview of common challenging behaviors that teachers and others are confronted with in the school and other settings. Typical challenging behaviors demonstrated by students include disruptiveness, oppositional defiant behaviors, noncompliance, agressiveness, bullying, temper tantrums, inattention, hyperactivity, and impulsivity. In addition to these externalizing behaviors, teachers may also observe separation anxiety, depression, and stereotypy. For each of these challenging behaviors, we provided a brief discussion on (a) typical observable, measurable behaviors; (b) common causes and antecedent stimuli; and (c) ideas for interventions to teach, promote, and support acceptable behaviors.

It is suggested that effective interventions be designed based on data from functional assessment since all behavior has a purpose. Once the function of behavior has been determined, teachers and parents will find their work to develop an effective intervention simplified.

In addition, because all students are observed to engage in some level of prosocial behavior, we promote the reinforcement of prosocial behaviors as a means to replace and eliminate inappropriate behaviors. We hoped to provide teachers with ideas for helping their students learn how to manage their own behavior and consequently experience academic and social success.

Discussion Questions

Read the following paragraph; then consider the questions that follow.

Carla, a 13-year-old seventh grader, is repeatedly truant from school. When asked what she does when she does not attend school, Carla replies that she has a tough time getting out of bed in the morning. She figures that since she will be late for her first class and will get a tardy slip, she may as well just blow off the entire school day. Her teachers and counselors have tried to talk to her about this, maintaining that it is in fact better to be late for the first hour than to miss the whole day. Her homeroom teacher has even tried to help Carla by calling her in the morning to get her out of bed. Carla answers the *phone, says "Thanks for calling," adds that she will get up, and then goes back to sleep. Punishing Carla with detention and failing grades has not been effective in helping her change her behavior.*

1. What do you suppose is the main behavior problem demonstrated by Carla? Which category of behavior problem does this behavior fall under?
2. If you were to conduct a functional assessment of Carla's behavior, what might the hypothesis statement look like?
3. Develop a list of possible interventions that you would predict to be effective in helping Carla develop replacement behaviors for her truant behavior.

References

Abrams, B. J., & Segal, A. (1998). How to prevent aggressive behavior. *Teaching Exceptional Students, 30,* 10–15.

American Psychiatric Association. (2000). *Diagnostic and statistical manual of mental disorders— text revision* (DSM-IV-TV, 4th ed.). Washington, DC: Author.

Bandura, A. (1973). *Aggression: A social learning analysis.* Upper Saddle River, NJ: Prentice Hall.

Barry, L. M., & Haraway, D. L. (2005). Self-management and ADHD: A literature review. *Behavior Analysis Today, 6*(1), 48–64.

Baumeister, A. A. (1978). Origins and control of stereotyped movements. In C. E. Meyers (Ed.), *Quality of life in severely and profoundly mentally retarded people* (pp. 353–384). Washington, DC: American Association on Mental Deficiency.

Beard, K. Y., & Sugai, G. (2004). First steps to success: An early intervention for elementary children at risk for antisocial behavior. *Behavioral Disorders, 29*(4), 396–409.

Bellfiore, P. J., & Dattilio, F. M. (1990). The behavior of self-injury: A brief review and analysis. *Behavioral Disorders, 16*(1), 23–31.

Biederman, J., & Faraone, S. (2005). Attention-deficit hyperactivity disorder. *Lancet, 366*(9481), 237–248.

Blechman, E. A. (1985). *Solving student behavior problems at home and at school.* Champaign, IL: Research Press.

Bornas, X., Servera, M., & Llabres, J. (1997). Preventing impulsivity in the classroom: How computers can help teachers. *Computers in the Schools, 13,* 27–40.

Brubacher, M. R., Fondacaro, M. R., Brank, E. M., Brown, V. E., & Miller, S. A. (2009). Procedural justice in resolving family disputes: Implications for childhood bullying. *Psychology, Public Policy, and Law, 15*(3), 149–167.

Bussing, R., Zima, B., & Belin, T. (1998). Students who qualify for LD and SED programs: Do they differ in level of ADHD symptoms and comorbid psychiatric conditions? *Behavioral Disorders, 23,* 85–97.

Campbell, S. B., & Werry, J. S. (1986). Attention deficit disorder (hyperactivity). In H. C. Quay & J. S. Werry (Eds.), *Psychopathological disorders of childhood* (3rd ed., pp. 111–155). New York: Wiley.

Carran, D. T., & Kellner, M. H. (2009). Characteristics of bullies and victims among students with emotional disturbance attending approved private special education schools. *Behavioral Disorders, 34*(3), 151–163.

Center, D. B. (1990). Social maladjustment: An interpretation. *Behavioral Disorders, 15*(3), 141–148.

Chisholm, J. T. (2007). *Community Conferencing Program.* Milwaukee, WI: Milwaukee County District Attorney's Office.

Coloroso, B. (2003). *The bully, the bullied and the bystander.* New York: Harper Resources.

Conroy, M. A., Asmus, J. M., Sellers, J. A., & Ladwig, C. N. (2005). The use of an antecedent-based intervention to decrease stereotypic behavior in a general education classroom: A case study. *Focus on Autism and Other Developmental Disabilities, 20*(4), 223–230.

Costenbader, V., & Markson, S. (1998). School suspension: A study with secondary school students. *Journal of School Psychology, 36,* 59–82.

Crnic, K. A., & Reid, M. (1989). Mental retardation. In E. J. Mash & R. A. Barkley (Eds.), *Treatment of childhood disorders* (pp. 247–285). New York: Guilford.

Crothers, L. M., & Kolbert, J. B. (2008). Tackling a problematic behavior management issue: Teachers' intervention in childhood bullying problems. *Intervention in School and Clinic, 43*(3), 132–139.

D'Acremont, M., & Van der Linden, M. (2005). Adolescent impulsivity: Findings from a community sample. *Journal of Youth and Adolescence, 34*(5), 427–435.

Dake, J. A., Price, J. H., Telljohann, S. K., & Funk, J. B. (2003). Teacher perceptions and practices regarding school bullying prevention. *Journal of School Health, 73,* 347–355.

Daniels, V. I. (1998). How to manage disruptive behavior in inclusive classrooms. *Teaching Exceptional Students, 30,* 26–31.

David, O. J., & Wintrob, H. L. (1989). Communication disturbances and hyperactive/conduct disordered behavior. *Psychiatry, 52,* 379–392.

Davis, R. W., & Hajicek, J. O. (1985). Effects of self-instructional training and strategy training on a mathematics task with severely behaviorally disordered students. *Behavioral Disorders, 10,* 275–282.

Day, H. M., Horner, R. H., & O'Neill, R. E. (1994). Multiple functions of problem behaviors: Assessment and intervention. *Journal of Applied Behavior Analysis, 27,* 279–289.

Dubow, E. F., Huesmann, R., & Eron, L. D. (1987). Mitigating aggression and promoting prosocial behavior in aggressive elementary schoolboys. *Behavioral Research Therapy, 25*(6), 527–531.

DuPaul, G. J., & Eckert, T. L. (1997). The effects of school-based interventions for attention deficit hyperactivity disorder: A meta-analysis. *School Psychology Review, 26,* 5–27.

DuPaul, G. J., Stoner, G., Tilly, W. D., III, & Putnam, D., Jr., (1991). Interventions for attention problems. In G. Stoner, M. R. Shinn, & H. M. Walker (Eds.), *Interventions for achievement and behavior problems* (pp. 665–713). Silver Spring, MD: National Association of School Psychologists.

Durand, V. M., & Carr, E. G. (1985). Self-injurious behavior: Motivating conditions and guidelines for treatment. *School Psychology Review, 14*(2), 171–176.

Etscheidt, S. (1991). Reducing aggressive behavior and improving self-control: A cognitive-behavioral training program for behaviorally disordered adolescents. *Behavioral Disorders, 16*(2), 107–115.

Fields, B. (2004). Breaking the cycle of office referrals and suspensions: Defensive management. *Educational Psychology, 20*(2), 103–115.

Forness, S. R. (2005). The pursuit of evidence-based practice in special education for children with emotional or behavioral disorders. *Behavioral Disorders, 30*(4), 311–330.

Francois, R., Harlacher, G., & Smith, B. (1999). *Improving student behavior in the classroom by using assertive discipline strategies.* Masters

Action Research Report, St. Xavier University, Chicago (ED431550).

Freidenfelt, J., & Klinteberg, B. (2007). Exploring adult personality and psychopathy tendencies in former childhood hyperactive delinquent males. *Journal of Individuals Differences, 28*(1), 27–36.

Frey, K. S., Hirschstein, M. K., Edstrom, L. V., & Snell, J. L. (2009). Observed reductions in school bullying, non-bullying aggression, and destructive bystander behavior: A longitudinal evaluation. *Journal of Educational Psychology, 101*(2), 466–481.

Friedrich-Cofer, L., & Huston, A. C. (1986). Television violence and aggression: The debate continues. *Psychological Bulletin, 100*(3), 364–371.

Gaynor, J. (1990). Attention deficit hyperactivity disorder may be etched in sand. *Beyond Behavior, 2*(1), 17–18.

Gordon, M. (1991). *ADHD/hyperactivity: A consumer's guide for parents and teachers*. DeWitt, NY: GSI Publications.

Gottfredson, G. D., & Gottfredson, D. C. (2001). What schools do to prevent problem behavior and promote safe environments. *Journal of Educational and Psychological Consultation, 12*(4), 313–344.

Gresham, F. M., Lane, K. L., & Beebe-Frankenberger, M. (2005). Predictors of hyperactivity, impulsivity, inattention and conduct problems: A comparative follow-back investigation. *Psychology in the Schools, 42*(7), 721–736.

Harden, G. D. (1997). Is it going to be boring? *Principal, 76,* 43–44.

Harkness, M. J. (2005). *Kids' health for parents*. Jacksonville, FL: Nemours Foundation.

Hastings, R. P., & Noone, S. J. (2005). Self-injurious behavior and functional analysis: Ethics and evidence. *Education and Training in Developmental Disabilities, 40*(4), 335–342.

Henggeler, S. W., Schoenwald, S. K., Borduin, C. M., Rowland, M. D., & Cunningham, P. B. (1998). *Multisystemic treatment of antisocial behavior in students and adolescents*. New York: Guilford.

Hoff, K. E., & DuPaul, G. J. (1998). Reducing disruptive behavior in general education classrooms: The use of self-management strategies. *School Psychology Review, 27,* 290–303.

Holden, G. W., & West, M. J. (1989). Proximate regulation by mothers: A demonstration of how differing styles affect young students's behavior. *Student Development, 60,* 64–69.

Hollenstein, T., Granic, I., Stoolmiller, M., & Snyder, J. (2004). Child impulsiveness. *Journal of Abnormal Child Psychology, 32*(6), 595–618.

Hollinger, J. D. (1987). Social skills for behaviorally disordered students as preparation for mainstreaming: Theory, practice and new directions. *Remedial and Special Education, 8,* 17–27.

Horne, A. M., Stoddard, J. L., & Bell, C. D. (2007). Group approaches to reducing aggression and bullying in school. *Group dynamics: Theory, research, and practice, 11*(4), 262–271.

Hughes, J. N. (1996). Television violence: Implications for violence prevention. *School Psychology Review, 25,* 134–151.

Hunt, R. D. (1993). Neurobiological patterns of aggression. *Journal of Emotional and Behavioral Problems, 27,* 14–19.

Iwata, B. A., Vollmer, T. R., & Zarcone, J. H. (1990). The experimental (functional) analysis of behavior disorders: Methodology, applications, and limitations. In A. C. Repp & N. N. Singh (Eds.), *Perspectives on the use of nonaversive and aversive interventions for persons with developmental disabilities* (pp. 301–330). Sycamore, IL: Sycamore.

Jensen, M. M. (2005). *Introduction to emotional and behavioral disorders*. Upper Saddle River, NJ: Merrill/Pearson Education.

Johnson, S., Agelson, L., Macierz, T., Minnick, M., & Merrell, T. (1995, March/April). *Leadership training institute: Interventions for youth with emotional/behavioral disorders who engage in violent and aggressive behavior*. University of St. Thomas, St. Paul, MN.

Johnson, W., McGue, M., & Iacono, W. G. (2005). Disruptive behavior and school grades: Genetic and environmental relations in 11-year-olds. *Journal of Educational Psychology, 97*(3), 391–405.

Kagan, J., Pearson, L., & Welch, L. (1966). Conceptual impulsivity & inductive reasoning. *Child Development, 37*(3), 583–594.

Kauffman, J. M., & Landrum, T. J. (2009). *Characteristics of emotional and behavioral disorders of children and youth* (8th ed.). Upper Saddle River, NJ: Merrill/Pearson Education.

Kazdin, A. E. (1990). Childhood depression. *Journal of Child Psychology & Psychiatry, 31,* 121–160.

Kazdin, A. E., & Whitley, M. K. (2006). Comorbidity, case complexity, and effects of evidence-based treatment for children referred for disruptive behavior. *Journal of Consulting and Clinical Psychology, 74*(3), 455–467.

Kohn, A. (1989, November). Suffer the restless students. *Atlantic Monthly,* 90–97.

Kollins, S. H., McClernon, F. J., & Fuemmeler, B. F. (2005). Association between smoking and attention-deficit hyperactivity disorder symptoms in a population-based sample of young adults. *Archives of General Psychiatry, 62*(10), 1142–1147.

Kounin, J. (1970). *Discipline and group management in classrooms.* New York: Holt, Rinehart, & Winston.

Kronenberger, W. G., Mathews, V. P., Dunn, D. W., Yang, W., Wood, E. A., Giaugue, A. L., Larsen, J. J., Rembusch, M. E., Lowe, M. J., & Tie-Qiang, L. (2005). Media violence exposure and executive functioning in aggressive and control adolescents. *Journal of Clinical Psychology, 61*(6), 725–737.

Kuczynski, L., Kochanska, G., Radke-Yarrow, M., & Girnius-Brown, O. (1987). A developmental interpretation of young students's noncompliance. *Developmental Psychology, 23*(6), 779–806.

Leve, L. D., Kim, H. K., Pears, K. C. (2005). Childhood temperament and family environment as predictors of internalizing and externalizing trajectories from ages 5 to 17. *Journal of Abnormal Child Psychology, 33*(5), 505–520.

Lewis, M. H., Baumeister, A. A., & Mailman, R. B. (1987). A neurobiological alternative to the perceptual reinforcement hypothesis of stereotyped behavior: A commentary on self-stimulatory behavior and perceptual reinforcement. *Journal of Applied Behavior Analysis, 20,* 253–258.

Lloyd, J. W., Bateman, D. F., Landrum, T. J., & Hallahan, D. P. (1989). Self-recording of attention versus productivity. *Journal of Applied Behavior Analysis, 22,* 315–323.

Lovaas, I., Newsom, C., & Hickman, C. (1987). Self-stimulatory behavior and perceptual reinforcement. *Journal of Applied Behavior Analysis, 20,* 45–68.

Ma, X. (2002). Bullying in middle school: Individual and school characteristics of victims and offenders. *School Effectiveness and School Improvement, 13,* 63–89.

Maag, J. W. (1996). *Parenting without punishment: Making problem behavior work for you.* Philadelphia: Charles.

Maag, J. W. (1997). Managing resistance: Looking beyond the student and into the mirror. In P. Zionts (Ed.), *Inclusion strategies for students with learning and behavior problems, perspectives, experiences, and best practices.* Austin, TX: Pro–Ed.

Maag, J. W., & Forness, S. R. (1991). Depression in children and adolescents: Identification, assessment, and treatment. *Behavior Disorders, 20,* 5–23.

Malone, B. G., Bonitz, D. A., & Rickett, M. (1998). Teacher perceptions of disruptive behavior: Maintaining instructional focus. *Educational Horizons, 76,* 189–194.

Mandal, R. L. (2002). Evaluation of a compliance training package from a single component to successive components. *Dissertation Abstracts International: Section B: The Sciences & Engineering, 62*(7), 33–69.

Mariano, K. A., & Harton, H. C. (2005). Similarities in aggression, inattention, hyperactivity, depression, and anxiety in middle childhood friendships. *Journal of Social & Clinical Psychology, 24*(4), 471–496.

Mash, E. J., & Barkley, R. A. (1998). *Treatment of childhood disorders* (2nd ed.). New York: Guilford.

Mathes, M. Y., & Bender, W. N. (1997). The effects of self-monitoring on students with attention-deficit hyperactivity disorder who are receiving pharmacological interventions. *Remedial and Special Education, 18,* 121–128.

McConnell, S. R., & Odom, S. L. (1986). Sociometrics: Peer-referenced measures and the assessment of social competence. In P. S. Strain, M. J. Guralnick, & H. M. Walker (Eds.), *Students's social behavior: Development, assessment, and modification* (pp. 215–284). Orlando, FL: Academic Press.

McGee, R., Williams, S., & Silva, P. A. (1985). Factor structure and correlates of ratings of inattention, hyperactivity, and antisocial behavior in a large sample of 9-year-old students for the general population. *Journal of Consulting and Clinical Psychology, 53*(4), 480–490.

McGinnis, E., & Goldstein, A. (1984). *Skillstreaming the elementary school student.* Champaign, IL: Research Press.

McGinnis, E., & Goldstein, A. (1997). *Skillstreaming the elementary school student* (Rev. ed.). Champaign, IL: Research Press.

McMahon, C. M., Wacker, D. P., Sasso, G. M., & Melloy, K. J. (1994). Evaluation of the multiple effects of a social skill intervention. *Behavioral Disorders, 20,* 35–50.

McMahon, R. J., & Wells, K. C. (1989). Conduct disorders. In E. J. Mash & R. A. Barkley (Eds.), *Treatment of childhood disorders* (pp. 73–132). New York: Guilford.

Meadows, N. B., Melloy, K. J., & Yell, M. L. (1996). Behavior management as a curriculum for students with emotional and behavioral disorders. *Preventing School Failure, 40,* 124–129.

Melloy, K. J. (1990). *Attitudes and behavior of non-disabled elementary-aged students toward their peers with disabilities in integrated settings: An examination of the effects of treatment on quality of attitude, social status and critical social skills.* Unpublished doctoral dissertation, University of Iowa, Iowa City.

Melloy, K. J., Davis, C. A., Wehby, J. H., Murry, F. R., & Lieber, J. (1998). Developing social competence in students and youth with challenging behaviors. L. M. Bullock & R. A. Gable (Eds.), *The second CCBD mini-library series: Successful interventions for the 21st century.* Reston, VA: The Council for Students with Behavioral Disorders.

Merrell, K. W., & Isava, D. M. (2008). How effective are school bullying intervention programs? A meta-analysis of intervention research. *School Psychology Quarterly, 23*(1), 26–42.

National Center for Educational Statistics. (2007). *Indicators of school crime and safety.* Washington, DC: Author.

Neel, R. S., Jenkins, Z. N., & Meadows, N. (1990). Social problem-solving behaviors and aggression in young students: A descriptive observational study. *Behavioral Disorders, 16*(1), 39–51.

Nelson, J. R., Martella, R., & Galand, B. (1998). The effects of teaching school expectations and establishing a consistent consequence on formal office disciplinary actions. *Journal of Emotional and Behavioral Disorders, 6,* 153–161.

Northup, J., Wacker, D. P., Berg, W. K., Kelly, L., Sasso, G. M., & DeRaad, A. (1994). The treatment of severe behavior problems in school settings using a technical assistance model. *Journal of Applied Behavior Analysis, 27,* 33–47.

Oliver, R., & Skinner, C. H. (2002). Applying behavior momentum theory to increase compliance: Why Mrs. H. revved up the elementary students with the Hokey-Pokey. *Journal of Applied School Psychology, 19*(1), 75–94.

Olson, S. L., Bates, J. E., & Bayles, K. (1990). Early antecedents of childhood impulsivity: The role of parent–student interaction, cognitive competence, and temperament. *Journal of Abnormal Student Psychology, 18*(3), 317–334.

Olweus, D. (2005). A useful evaluation design, and effects of the Olweus Bullying Prevention Program. *Psychology, Crime & Law, 11*(4), 389–402.

Ostrander, R. (2004). Oppositional defiant disorder and conduct disorder. In F. M. Kline & L. B. Silver (Eds.), *Educator's quick guide to mental health issues in the classroom.* Baltimore: Brookes.

Paniagua, F. A., Morrison, P. B., & Black, S. A. (1990). Management of a hyperactive–conduct disordered student through correspondence training: A preliminary study. *Journal of Behavior Therapy and Experimental Psychiatry, 21*(1), 63–68.

Papadopoulos, T. C., Panayiotou, G., Spanoudis, G., & Natsopoulos, D. (2005). Evidence of poor planning in children with attention deficits. *Journal of Abnormal Child Psychology, 33*(5), 611–623.

Patterson, G. R. (1992). Developmental changes in antisocial behavior. In R. D. Peters, R. J. McMahon, & V. L. Quinsey (Eds.), *Aggression and violence throughout the life span* (pp. 52–82). Newbury Park, CA: Sage.

Patterson, G. R., DeBaryshe, B. D., & Ramsey, E. (1989). A developmental perspective on antisocial behavior. *American Psychologist, 44,* 329–335.

Peake, K. J., Limbert, C., & Whitehead, L. (2005). Gone, but not forgotten: An examination of the factors associated with dropping out from treatment of eating disorders. *European Eating Disorders Review, 13*(5), 330–337.

Pfiffner, L. J., & O'Leary, S. G. (1987). The efficacy of all-positive management as a function of the prior use of negative consequences. *Journal of Applied Behavior Analysis, 20,* 265–271.

Quinn, K. B., Barone, B., Kearns, J., Stackhouse, S. A., & Zimmerman, M. E. (2003). Using a novel unit to help understand and prevent bullying in schools. *Journal of Adolescent and Adult Literacy, 46,* 582–591.

Rapp, J. T., Miltenberger, R. G., Galensky, T. L., Elllingson, S. A., & Long, E. S. (1999). A functional analysis of hair pulling. *Journal of Applied Behavior Analysis, 32,* 329–337.

Reid, R., Trout, A. L., & Schartz, M. (2005). Self-regulation interventions for children with attention deficit/hyperactivity disorder. *Exceptional Children, 71*(4), 361–377.

Repp, A. C., & Singh, N. N. (1990). *Perspectives on the use of nonaversive and aversive interventions for persons with developmental disabilities*. Sycamore, IL: Sycamore.

Reynolds, W. M. (1991). Psychological interventions for depression in children and adolescents. In G. Stoner, M. R. Shinn, & H. M. Walker (Eds.), *Interventions for achievement and behavior problems* (pp. 649–683). Silver Spring, MD: National Association of School Psychologists.

Rocissano, L., Slade, A., & Lynch, V. (1987). Dyadic synchrony and toddler compliance. *Developmental Psychology, 23*(5), 698–704.

Ronen, T. (2005). Students' evidence-based practice intervention for children with oppositional defiant disorder. *Research on Social Work Practice, 15*(3), 165–179.

Ross, S., Heath, N. L., & Toste, J. R. (2009). Non-suicidal self-injury and eating pathology in high school students. *American Journal of Orthopsychiatry, 79*(1), 83–92.

Rudo, Z. H., Powell, D. S., & Dunlap, G. (1998). The effects of violence in the home on students's emotional, behavioral, and social functioning: A review of the literature. *Journal of Emotional and Behavioral Disorders, 6*, 94–113.

Ruff, H. A., & Lawson, K. R. (1990). Development of sustained, focused attention in young students during free play. *Developmental Psychology, 26*(1), 85–93.

Ruff, H. A., Lawson, K. R., Parrinello, R., & Weissberg, R. (1990). Long term stability of individual differences in sustained attention in the early years. *Student Development, 61*, 60–75.

Ruth, W. J. (1996). Goal setting and behavior contracting for students with emotional and behavioral difficulties: Analysis of daily, weekly, and total goal attainment. *Psychology in the Schools, 33*, 153–158.

Sarason, I. G., & Sarason, B. R. (2005). *Abnormal psychology: The problem of maladaptive behavior*. Upper Saddle River, NJ: Pearson.

Sasso, G. M., Melloy, K. J., & Kavale, K. A. (1990). Generalization, maintenance, and behavioral covariation associated with social skills training through structured learning. *Behavioral Disorders, 16*(1), 9–22.

Schaub, J. M. (1990, March). *ADHD: Practical intervention strategies for the classroom*. Presentation to the East Metro Special Education Cooperative, Edina, MN.

Schmid, R. (1998). Three steps to self-discipline. *Teaching Exceptional Students, 30*, 36–39.

Selikowitz, M. (2004). *ADHD: The facts*. Oxford, New York: Oxford University Press.

Semple, S. J., Zians, J., Grant, I., & Patterson, T. L. (2005). Impulsivity and methamphetamine use. *Journal of Substance Abuse Treatment, 29*(2), 85–93.

Shafrir, U., & Pascual-Leone, J. (1990). Postfailure reflectivity/impulsivity and spontaneous attention to errors. *Journal of Educational Psychology, 82*(2), 378–387.

Shapiro, E. S., DuPaul, G. J., & Bradley-Klug, K. L. (1998). Self-management as a strategy to improve the classroom behavior of adolescents with ADHD. *Journal of Learning Disabilities, 31*(6), 545–556.

Shaw, D. S., Lacourse, E., & Nagin, D. S. (2005). Developmental trajectories of conduct problems and hyperactivity from ages 2 to 10. *Journal of Child Psychology & Psychiatry & Disciplines, 46*(9), 931–942.

Skiba, R. J., Peterson, R. L., & Williams, I. (1997). Office referrals and suspension: Disciplinary intervention in middle schools. *Education and Treatment of Students, 20*, 295–315.

Snyder, J., Prichard, J., Schrepferman, L., & Patrick, M. R. (2004). Child impulsiveness, inattention, and early peer experiences, and the development of early onset conduct problems. *Journal of Abnormal Child Psychology, 32*(6), 579–595.

Spira, E. G., & Fischel, J. E. (2005). The impact of preschool inattention, hyperactivity, and impulsivity on social and academic development: A review. *Journal of Child Psychology & Psychiatry & Allied Disciplines, 46*(7), 755–773.

Stage, S. A. (1997). A preliminary investigation of the relationship between in-school suspension and the disruptive classroom behavior of students with behavioral disorders. *Behavioral Disorders, 23*, 57–76.

Sukhodolsky, D. G., Golub, A., Stone, E. C., & Orban, L. (2005). Dismantling anger control training for children: A randomized pilot study of social problem-solving versus social skills training components. *Behavior Therapy, 36*(1), 15–23.

Sutherland, K. S. (2000). Promoting positive interactions between teachers and students with emotional/behavioral disorders. *Preventing School Failure, 44*, 110–115.

Swann, A. C., Dougherty, D. M., Pazzaglia, P. J., Pham, M., Steinberg, J. L., & Moeller, F. G. (2005). Increased impulsivity associated with severity of suicide attempt history in patients with bipolar disorder. *American Journal of Psychiatry, 162*(9), 1680–1687.

Taylor, T. K., Burns, G. L., Rusby, J. C., & Foster, E. M. (2006). Oppositional defiant disorder toward adults and oppositional defiant disorder towards peers: Initial evidence for two separate constructs. *Psychological Assessment, 18*(4), 439–443.

Tyson, P. (2005). Affects, agency, and self-regulation: Complexity theory in the treatment of children with anxiety and disruptive behavior disorders. *Journal of the American Psychoanalytic Association, 53*(1), 159–187.

Vanderbilt, A. A. (2005). Designed for teachers: How to implement self-monitoring in the classroom. *Beyond Behavior, 15*(1), 21–24.

Vitiello, B., Stoff, D., Atkins, M., & Mahoney, A. (1990). Soft neurological signs and impulsivity in students. *Developmental and Behavioral Pediatrics, 11*(3), 112–115.

Wachs, T. D., Gurkas, P., & Kontos, S. (2004). Predictors of preschool children's compliance behavior in early childhood classroom settings. *Journal of Applied Developmental Psychology, 25*(4), 439–457.

Walker, H. M., Colvin, G., & Ramsey, E. (1995). *Antisocial behavior in school: Strategies and best practices.* Pacific Grove, CA: Brooks/Cole.

Weinberg, L. A., & Weinberg, C. (1990). Seriously emotionally disturbed or socially maladjusted? A critique of interpretations. *Behavioral Disorders, 15*(3), 149–158.

Wicks-Nelson, R., & Israel, A. C. (1991). *Behavior disorders of childhood* (2nd ed.). Upper Saddle River, NJ: Merrill/Pearson Education.

Widom, C. S. (1989). Does violence beget violence? A critical examination of the literature. *Psychological Bulletin, 106*(1), 3–28.

Wied, M., Goudena, P. P., & Matthys, W. (2005). Empathy in boys with disruptive behavior disorders. *Journal of Child Psychology & Psychiatry & Allied Disciplines, 46*(8), 867–880.

Wood, J. (2006). Effect of anxiety reduction on children's school performance and social adjustment. *Developmental Psychology, 42*(2), 345–349.

Wood, J. J., Cowan, P. A., & Baker, B. L. (2002). Behavior problems and peer rejection in preschool boys and girls. *Journal of Genetic Psychology, 163*(1), 72–88.

Zarcone, J. R., Iwata, B. A., Smith, R. G., Mazaleski, J. L., & Lerman, D. C. (1994). Reemergence and extinction of self-injurious escape behavior during stimulus fading. *Journal of Applied Behavior Analysis, 27,* 307–316.

Zentall, S. (2005). Theory and evidence based strategies for children with attention problems. *Psychology in the Schools, 42*(8), 821–836.

Zionts, P. (1996). *Teaching disturbed and disturbing students* (2nd ed.). Austin, TX: Pro-Ed.

Zirpoli, T. J. (2003). *Cures for parental wimp syndrome: Lessons on becoming a stronger parent.* Westminster, MD: Zirpoli Publishing and Consulting.

NAME INDEX

SUBJECT INDEX